# Europe

## Europa | Evropa | Európa |

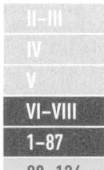

GW00418714

A map of North Atlantic and Western Europe showing UNESCO World Heritage Sites.

GRØ

Grønlands-havet

Spitsberg...

Jan Mayen (N)

Irminger Hav

Norwegian Sea

**35**

IS — Pingvellir, Surtsey

Vegaøyan

Føroyar (DK)

**8** — Røros, Geirangerfjorden, Urnes (Stavkirke), Bergen

Shetland (GB)

A T L A N T I C

Heart of Neolithic Orkney
St. Kilda

**33**

N — Tanumshede

**16** — Varberg, Jelling, Helsingør

GB — Edinburgh, New Lanark, Hadrian's Wall, Durham, Fountains Abbey, Liverpool, Saltaire, Derwent, Caernarfon, Pont cysyllte, Ironbridge, Blaenavon, Bath, Blenheim Palace, London, Stonehenge, Canterbury, Dorset

North Sea

DK — Roskilde

Giant's Causeway

IR — Boyne Valley, Skellig Michael

**35**

West Devon Mining landscape

O C E A N

N.P. Schlesw.-Holst. Wattenmeer
N.P. Nieders. Wattenmeer
Waddenzee
Lübeck, Wismar, Bremen

**26**

NL — Beemster, Amsterdam, Woudagemaal, Schokland, Windmolen, Utrecht

D — Hildesheim, Potsdam, Alfeld, Wittenberg, Essen, Goslar, Dessau, Köln, Quedlinburg, Wartburg, Eisleben, Weimar, Messel, Bamberg, Lorsch, Speyer, Würzburg, Limes, Regensburg, Maulbronn, Strasbourg, Wieskirche

B — Bruxelles, Antwerpen, Béguinages, Tournai, Spiennes, Canal Aachen Rheintal, Brühl, Belforts, Trier

L — Luxembourg, Völklingen, Nancy

Saint-Vaast-la-Hougue
Le Havre
Brugge

**40**

le Mont Saint-Michel, Amiens, Versailles, Reims, Paris, Provins, Chartres, Val de Loire, Fontainebleau

**41** **42**

St-Savin, Bourges, Vézelay, Fontenay, Besançon, La Chaux-de-Fonds, Reichenau, Salines

CH — Lavaux, Bern, Sardona, Albulabahn, Müstair, Jungfrau, Bellinzona, Monte S. Giorgio, Prehist. Pile Dwellings

St. Gallen, Salzburg

A — Dolomiti, Inc. Rupestri, Aquiléia

CZ — Praha, Zd'ár n..., Holašovice, Český Krumlov

F — Lyon, Albi, Can. du Midi, Orange, Pont du Gard, Avignon, Arles

Santiago de Compostela
A Coruña, Lugo, Oviedo
Camino de Santiago
Las Médulas

**54**

Blaye, Saint-Emilion, Bordeaux, Routes de Santiago d. C., Puente de Vizcaya, Cuevas de Altamira, Atapuérca, Mont Perdu / Mte. Perdido, Grotte de Lascaux, Cévennes

E — Guimarães, Alto Douro, Vale do Côa, Burgos, San Millán, Salamanca, Segovia, Ávila, El Escorial, Alcalá de Henares, Toledo, Aranjuez, Cuenca, Mérida, Guadalupe, Baeza, Córdoba, Sevilla, Úbeda, Granada, P. N. Côto de Doñana

**55** **56**

I — Crespi d'Adda, Vicenza, Sacro Monte, Milano, Verona, Venézia, Padova, Torino, Génova, Modena, Mantova, Ferrara, Ravenna, Cinque Terre, Firenze, Pisa, Siena, S. Gimignano, Val d'Orcia, Pienza, Cervéteri, Assisi, Urbino, C. del Vaticano, Tivoli, Clitunno, Roma, Caserta, Nápoli, Costiera Amalfitana, Paestum

HR — Poreč

RSM — San Marino

**58**

Mosteiro de Batalha, Alcobaça, Tomar
Sintra

**68**

Lisboa, Cáceres

P — Évora

AND — Vall de Boi, Madriu-Perafita-Claror Valley, Carcassonne, Mont-Louis, Poblet, Barcelona, Tárraco, Arte rupestre, València, Serra de Tramuntana, Elx, Ibiza

MC — La Scandola

V

**69** **70**

**71** **72** — Isole Eólie, Barúmini, Agrigento, Villa del Casale, Val di Noto, Malta

Mediterranean Sea

Titwan (Tetouan)
Al Jazá'ir
Tunis
Sousse

El-Jadida
Volubilis
Fâz (Fès')
Miknas (Meknès)

**80**

**81**

Marrakush

MA

DZ

TN

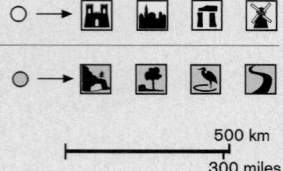

| | ☎ | 💶 | 🚓 | ✚ | SOS | 🦺 | 🍷‰ | 🚗 | 🚙 | 🛫 | ↱ |
|---|---|---|---|---|---|---|---|---|---|---|---|
| A | +43 | EUR | 133 | 144 | 112 | ✓ | 0,5‰ | ✗ | ✓ | ✓ | 120 ÖAMTC |
| AL | +355 | ALL | 129 | 126 | ✗ | ✗ | 0,0‰ | ✗ | ✗ | ✗ | 6 84 00 12 22 ACA |
| AND | +376 | EUR | 110 | 116 | 112 | ✓ | 0,5‰ | ✗ | ✓ | ✗ | 8 03 400 ACA |
| B | +32 | EUR | 101 | 112 | 112 | ✓ | 0,5‰ | ✗ | ✓ | ✗ | (070) 34 47 77 TCB |
| BG | +359 | BGN | 166 | 150 | 112 | ✓ | 0,5‰ | ✓❄ | ✓ | ✓ | (02) 91146 UAB |
| BIH | +387 | BAM | 122 | 124 | 112 | ✓ | 0,3‰ | ✓ | ✓ | ✗ | 033 1282 BIHAMK |
| BY | +375 | BYR | 02 | 03 | ✗ | ✗ | 0,0‰ | ✓ | ✓ | ✓ | 116 BKA |
| CH | +41 | CHF | 117 | 144 | 112 | ✗ | 0,5‰ | ✗ | ✓ | ✓ | 03 18 50 53 11 TCS |
| CY | +357 | EUR | 112/199 | 112/199 | 112 | ✓ | 0,5‰ | ✗ | ✓ | ✗ | (02) 22 31 31 31 CAA |
| CZ | +420 | CZK | 158 | 155 | 112 | ✓ | 0,0‰ | ✓ | ✓ | ✓ | 1230 ÚAMK |
| D | +49 | EUR | 110 | 112 | 112 | ✓ | 0,5‰ | ✗ | ✓ | ✗ | (01802) 22 22 22 ADAC |
| DK | +45 | DKK | 112 | 112 | 112 | ✗ | 0,5‰ | ✓ | ✓ | ✗ | 93 17 08 FDM |
| E | +34 | EUR | 112 | 112 | 112 | ✓ | 0,5‰ | ✗ | ✓ | ✓ | 915 94 33 47 RACE |
| EST | +372 | EEK | 110 | 112 | 112 | ✗ | 0,0‰ | ✓ | ✓ | ✗ | 6979 188 EAK |
| F | +33 | EUR | 17 | 15 | 112 | ✓ | 0,5‰ | ✗ | ✓ | ✓ | 08 00 08 92 22 AIT |
| FIN | +358 | EUR | 112 | 112 | 112 | ✓ | 0,5‰ | ✓ | ✓ | ✗ | 200 80 80 AL |
| FL | +423 | CHF | 117 | 144 | 112 | ✓ | 0,8‰ | ✗ | ✓ | ✗ | 031850 53 11 TCS |
| GB | +44 | GBP | 999 | 999 | 112 | ✓ | 0,8‰ | ✗ | ✗ | ✗ | (0800) 88 77 66 AA |
| GR | +30 | EUR | 100 | 166 | 112 | ✓ | 0,5‰ | ✗ | ✓ | ✓ | 10 400 ELPA |
| H | +36 | HUF | 107 | 104 | 112 | ✓ | 0,0‰ | ✓ | ✓ | ✓ | 188 MAK |
| HR | +385 | HRK | 92 | 94 | 112 | ✓ | 0,5‰ | ✓❄ | ✓ | ✓ | 987 HAK |
| I | +39 | EUR | 112 | 118 | 112 | ✓ | 0,5‰ | ✓ | ✓ | ✓ | 800 116 200 ACI |
| IRL | +353 | EUR | 999 | 999 | 112 | ✗ | 0,8‰ | ✗ | ✓ | ✗ | 1800 66 77 88 AA |
| IS | +354 | ISK | 112 | 112 | 112 | ✓ | 0,5‰ | ✓ | ✓ | ✗ | 5 11 21 12 FIB |
| L | +352 | EUR | 113 | 112 | 112 | ✓ | 0,5‰ | ✗ | ✓ | ✗ | 26 000 ACL |
| LT | +370 | LTL | 112 | 112 | 112 | ✓ | 0,4‰ | ✓ | ✓ | ✗ | 880 00 00 00 LAS |
| LV | +371 | LVL | 02 | 03 | 112 | ✓ | 0,5‰ | ✓ | ✓ | ✗ | 1888 LAMB |
| M | +356 | EUR | 191 | 196 | 112 | ✓ | 0,8‰ | ✗ | ✓ | ✗ | 21 24 22 22 RMF |
| MC | +377 | EUR | 17 | 15 | 112 | ✓ | 0,5‰ | ✗ | ✓ | ✗ | 08 00 08 92 22 AIT |
| MD | +373 | MDL | 902 | 903 | ✗ | ✓ | 0,0‰ | ✗ | ✗ | ✗ | 22 29 27 03 ACM |
| MK | +389 | MKD | 192 | 194 | ✗ | ✓ | 0,5‰ | ✓ | ✓ | ✓ | 23 18 11 96 AMSM |
| MNE | +382 | EUR | 92 | 94 | ✗ | ✓ | 0,5‰ | ✓ | ✓ | ✓ | 19 807 AMSCG |
| N | +47 | NOK | 112 | 113 | 112 | ✓ | 0,2‰ | ✓ | ✓ | ✗ⅼ | 08505 NAF |
| NL | +31 | EUR | 112 | 112 | 112 | ✓ | 0,5‰ | ✗ | ✓ | ✗ | (088) 269 28 88 ANWB |
| P | +351 | EUR | 112 | 112 | 112 | ✓ | 0,5‰ | ✗ | ✓ | ✓ | (021) 942 9103 ACP |
| PL | +48 | PLN | 997 | 999 | 112 | ✓ | 0,2‰ | ✓ | ✓ | ✓ | (022) 532 84 33 PZM |
| RKS | +381 | EUR | 92 | 961 | 112 | ✗ | 0,5‰ | ✓ | ✓ | ✗ | 01 34 40 677 HAK |
| RO | +40 | RON | 995 | 112 | 112 | ✗ | 0,0‰ | ✓ | ✓ | ✓ | (021) 222 22 222 ACR |
| RSM | +378 | EUR | 112 | 118 | 112 | ✓ | 0,5‰ | ✓ | ✓ | ✗ | 800 116 200 ACI |
| RUS | +7 | RUB | 02 | 03 | 112 | ✗ | 0,0‰ | ✓ | ✓ | ✗ | 495 747 66 66 RAS |
| S | +46 | SEK | 112 | 112 | 112 | ✓ | 0,2‰ | ✓ | ✗ | ✗ | 771 91 11 11 M |
| SK | +421 | EUR | 158 | 112 | 112 | ✓ | 0,0‰ | ✓ | ✓ | ✓ | 18124 SATC |
| SLO | +386 | EUR | 113 | 112 | 112 | ✓ | 0,5‰ | ✓ | ✓ | ✓ | 1987 AMZS |
| SRB | +381 | RSD | 92 | 94 | ✗ | ✓ | 0,3‰ | ✓ | ✓ | ✓ | 987 AMSS |
| TR | +90 | TRY | 155 | 112 | 112 | ✗ | 0,5‰ | ✗ | ✓ | ✓ | (0212) 28 28 140 TTOK |
| UA | +380 | UAH | 02 | 03 | ✗ | ✓ | 0,0‰ | ✗ | ✗ | ✗ | (032) 2976 550 112UA |
| V | +39 | EUR | 112 | 118 | 112 | ✓ | 0,5‰ | ✓ | ✓ | ✗ | 800 116 200 ACI |

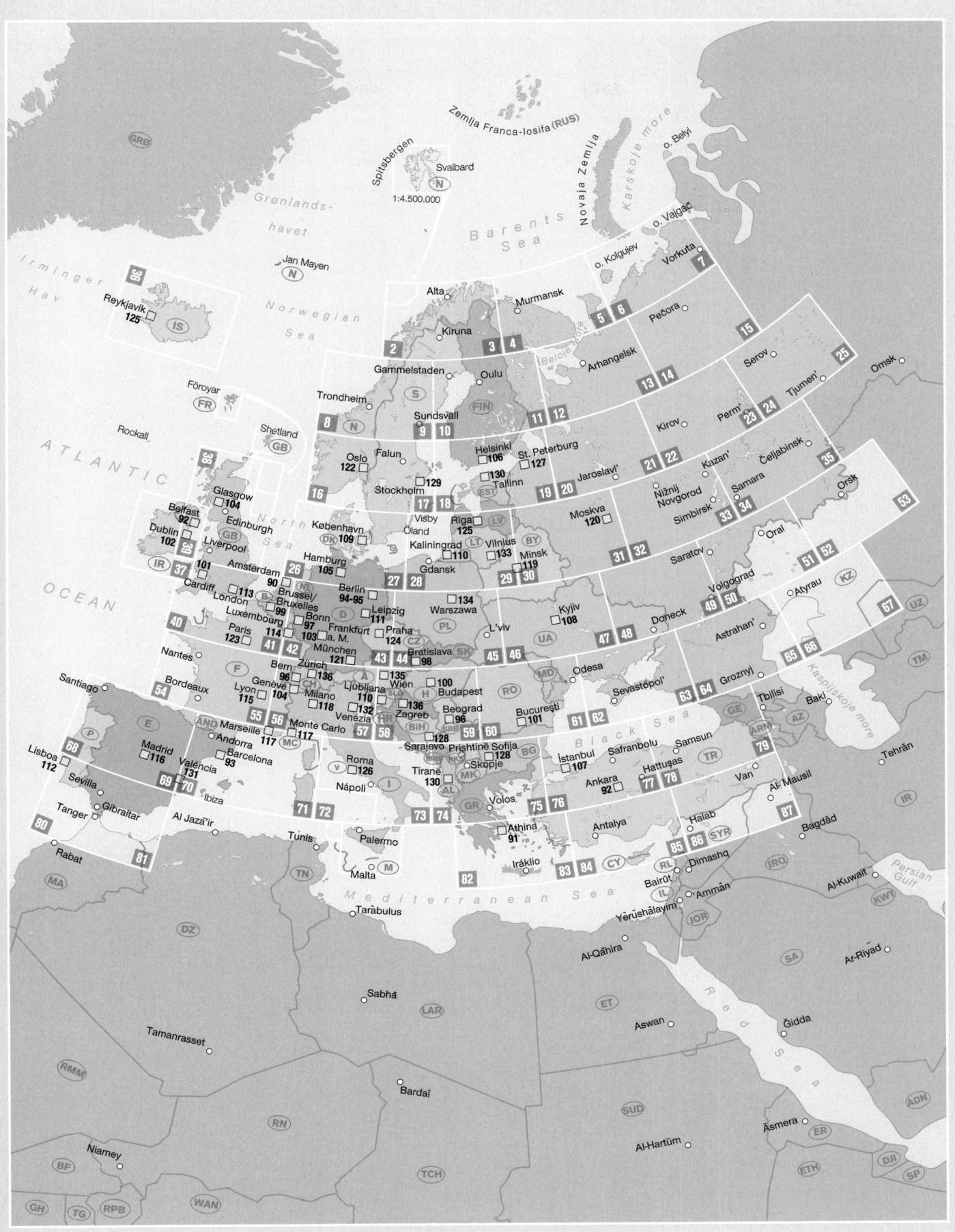

# Legend | Légende | Zeichenerklärung | Legenda
## 1 : 2 000 000

| GB | D |
|---|---|
| F | NL |

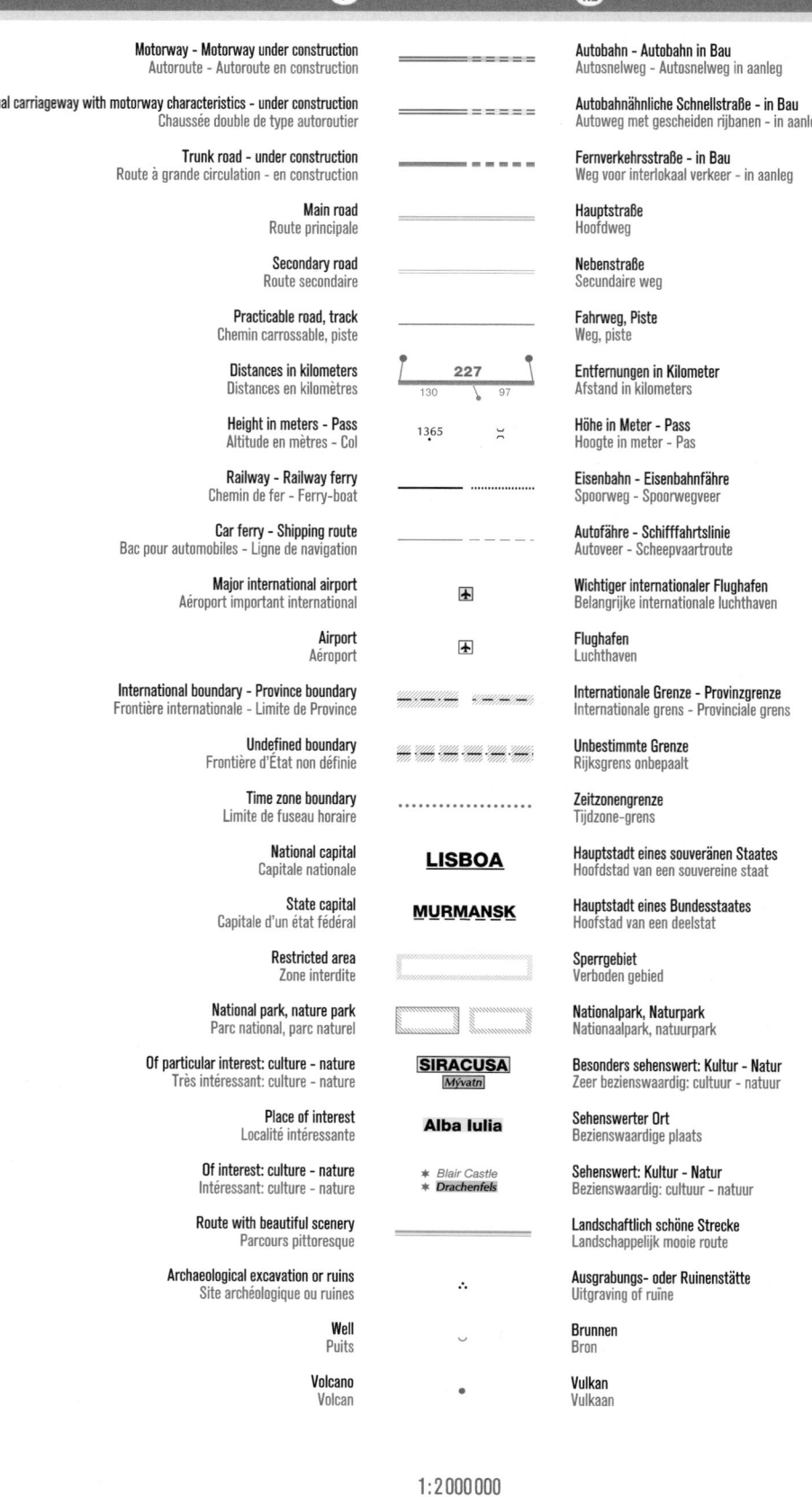

| | | |
|---|---|---|
| **Motorway - Motorway under construction**<br>Autoroute - Autoroute en construction | | **Autobahn - Autobahn in Bau**<br>Autosnelweg - Autosnelweg in aanleg |
| **Dual carriageway with motorway characteristics - under construction**<br>Chaussée double de type autoroutier | | **Autobahnähnliche Schnellstraße - in Bau**<br>Autoweg met gescheiden rijbanen - in aanleg |
| **Trunk road - under construction**<br>Route à grande circulation - en construction | | **Fernverkehrsstraße - in Bau**<br>Weg voor interlokaal verkeer - in aanleg |
| **Main road**<br>Route principale | | **Hauptstraße**<br>Hoofdweg |
| **Secondary road**<br>Route secondaire | | **Nebenstraße**<br>Secundaire weg |
| **Practicable road, track**<br>Chemin carrossable, piste | | **Fahrweg, Piste**<br>Weg, piste |
| **Distances in kilometers**<br>Distances en kilomètres | 227<br>130    97 | **Entfernungen in Kilometer**<br>Afstand in kilometers |
| **Height in meters - Pass**<br>Altitude en mètres - Col | 1365 | **Höhe in Meter - Pass**<br>Hoogte in meter - Pas |
| **Railway - Railway ferry**<br>Chemin de fer - Ferry-boat | | **Eisenbahn - Eisenbahnfähre**<br>Spoorweg - Spoorwegveer |
| **Car ferry - Shipping route**<br>Bac pour automobiles - Ligne de navigation | | **Autofähre - Schifffahrtslinie**<br>Autoveer - Scheepvaartroute |
| **Major international airport**<br>Aéroport important international | ✈ | **Wichtiger internationaler Flughafen**<br>Belangrijke internationale luchthaven |
| **Airport**<br>Aéroport | ✈ | **Flughafen**<br>Luchthaven |
| **International boundary - Province boundary**<br>Frontière internationale - Limite de Province | | **Internationale Grenze - Provinzgrenze**<br>Internationale grens - Provinciale grens |
| **Undefined boundary**<br>Frontière d'État non définie | | **Unbestimmte Grenze**<br>Rijksgrens onbepaalt |
| **Time zone boundary**<br>Limite de fuseau horaire | | **Zeitzonengrenze**<br>Tijdzone-grens |
| **National capital**<br>Capitale nationale | **LISBOA** | **Hauptstadt eines souveränen Staates**<br>Hoofdstad van een soevereine staat |
| **State capital**<br>Capitale d'un état fédéral | **MURMANSK** | **Hauptstadt eines Bundesstaates**<br>Hoofdstad van een deelstat |
| **Restricted area**<br>Zone interdite | | **Sperrgebiet**<br>Verboden gebied |
| **National park, nature park**<br>Parc national, parc naturel | | **Nationalpark, Naturpark**<br>Nationaalpark, natuurpark |
| **Of particular interest: culture - nature**<br>Très intéressant: culture - nature | **SIRACUSA**<br>*Mývatn* | **Besonders sehenswert: Kultur - Natur**<br>Zeer bezienswaardig: cultuur - natuur |
| **Place of interest**<br>Localité intéressante | **Alba Iulia** | **Sehenswerter Ort**<br>Bezienswaardige plaats |
| **Of interest: culture - nature**<br>Intéressant: culture - nature | ✳ *Blair Castle*<br>✳ *Drachenfels* | **Sehenswert: Kultur - Natur**<br>Bezienswaardig: cultuur - natuur |
| **Route with beautiful scenery**<br>Parcours pittoresque | | **Landschaftlich schöne Strecke**<br>Landschappelijk mooie route |
| **Archaeological excavation or ruins**<br>Site archéologique ou ruines | ∴ | **Ausgrabungs- oder Ruinenstätte**<br>Uitgraving of ruine |
| **Well**<br>Puits | ◡ | **Brunnen**<br>Bron |
| **Volcano**<br>Volcan | ● | **Vulkan**<br>Vulkaan |

## 1 : 2 000 000

| 0 | 20 | 40 | 60 | 80 | 100 km |
|---|---|---|---|---|---|

| 0 | 10 | 20 | 30 | 40 | 50 | 60 miles |
|---|---|---|---|---|---|---|

| I / E | | DK / S |
|---|---|---|
| Autostrada - Autostrada in costruzione<br>Autopista - Autopista en construcción | | Motorvej - Motorvej under bygning<br>Motorväg - Motorväg under byggnad |
| Doppia carreggiata di tipo autostradale - in costruzione<br>Autovía - en construcción | | Motortrafikvej med to vejbaner - under bygning<br>Motortrafikled - under byggnad |
| Strada di grande communicazione - in costruzione<br>Ruta de larga distancia - en construcción | | Fjerntrafikvej - under bygning<br>Fjärrtrafikväg - under byggnad |
| Strada principale<br>Carretera principal | | Hovedvej<br>Huvudled |
| Strada secondaria<br>Carretera secundaria | | Bivej<br>Sidoväg |
| Strada carrozzabile, pista<br>Camino vecinal, pista | | Mindre vej, bane<br>Körväg, vildmarksled |
| Distanze in chilometri<br>Distancias en kilómetros | 227   130   97 | Afstænder i kilometer<br>Avstånd i kilometer |
| Altitudine in metri - Passo<br>Altura en metros - Puerto de montaña | 1365 | Højde i meter - Pas<br>Höjd i meter - Pass |
| Ferrovia - Traghetto ferroviario<br>Ferrocarril - Transbordador para ferrocarriles | | Jernbanelinie - Jernbanefærge<br>Järnväg - Tågfärja |
| Traghetto auto - Linea maríttima<br>Ferry - Ruta marítima | | Bilfærge - Skibsrute<br>Bilfärja - Sjöfartslinje |
| Aeroporto internazionale di particolare importanza<br>Aeropuerto importante internacional | ✈ | Vigtig international lufthavn<br>Viktig internationell trafikflygplats |
| Aeroporto<br>Aeropuerto | ✈ | Lufthavn<br>Trafikflygplats |
| Confine internazionale - Confine di Provincia<br>Frontera internacional - Frontera provincial | | International grænse - Provinsgrænse<br>Internationell gräns - Provinsgräns |
| Confine di Stato indefinito<br>Frontera indeterminada | | Ubestemt grænse<br>Osäker gräns |
| Limite fuso orario<br>Límite del huso horario | | Tidszonegrænse<br>Tidszongräns |
| Capitale di stato sovrano<br>Capital de un estado soberano | **LISBOA** | Suværæn stats hovedstad<br>Huvudstad i suverän stat |
| Capitale dello stato federale<br>Capital de estado | **MURMANSK** | Forbundsstatsgrænse<br>Delstatsgräns |
| Zona vietata<br>Zona prohibida | | Afspærret omrade<br>Spärrzon |
| Parco nazionale, parco naturale<br>Parque nacional, parque natural | | Nationalpark, naturpark<br>Nationalpark, naturpark |
| Molto interessante: cultura - natura<br>De interés especial: cultura - natura | **SIRACUSA**<br>*Mývatn* | Særlig seværdig: kultur - natur<br>Särskilt sevärd: kultur - natur |
| Località interessante<br>Población de interés | **Alba Iulia** | Seværdig by<br>Sevärd ort |
| Interessante: cultura - natura<br>De interés: cultura - natura | ✳ *Blair Castle*<br>✳ ***Drachenfels*** | Seværdig: kultur - natur<br>Sevärd: kultur - natur |
| Percorso pittoresco<br>Ruta pintoresca | | Landskabelig smuk vejstrækning<br>Naturskön sträcka |
| Scavo o rovine<br>Escavación o ruinas historicas | ∴ | Udgravnings- eller ruinsted<br>Utgrävnings- eller ruinplats |
| Pozzo<br>Fuente | ⌣ | Brønd<br>Brunn |
| Vulcano<br>Volcán | ● | Vulkan<br>Vulkan |

1 : 2 000 000

| 0 | 20 | 40 | 60 | 80 | 100 km |
|---|---|---|---|---|---|

| 0 | 10 | 20 | 30 | 40 | 50 | 60 miles |
|---|---|---|---|---|---|---|

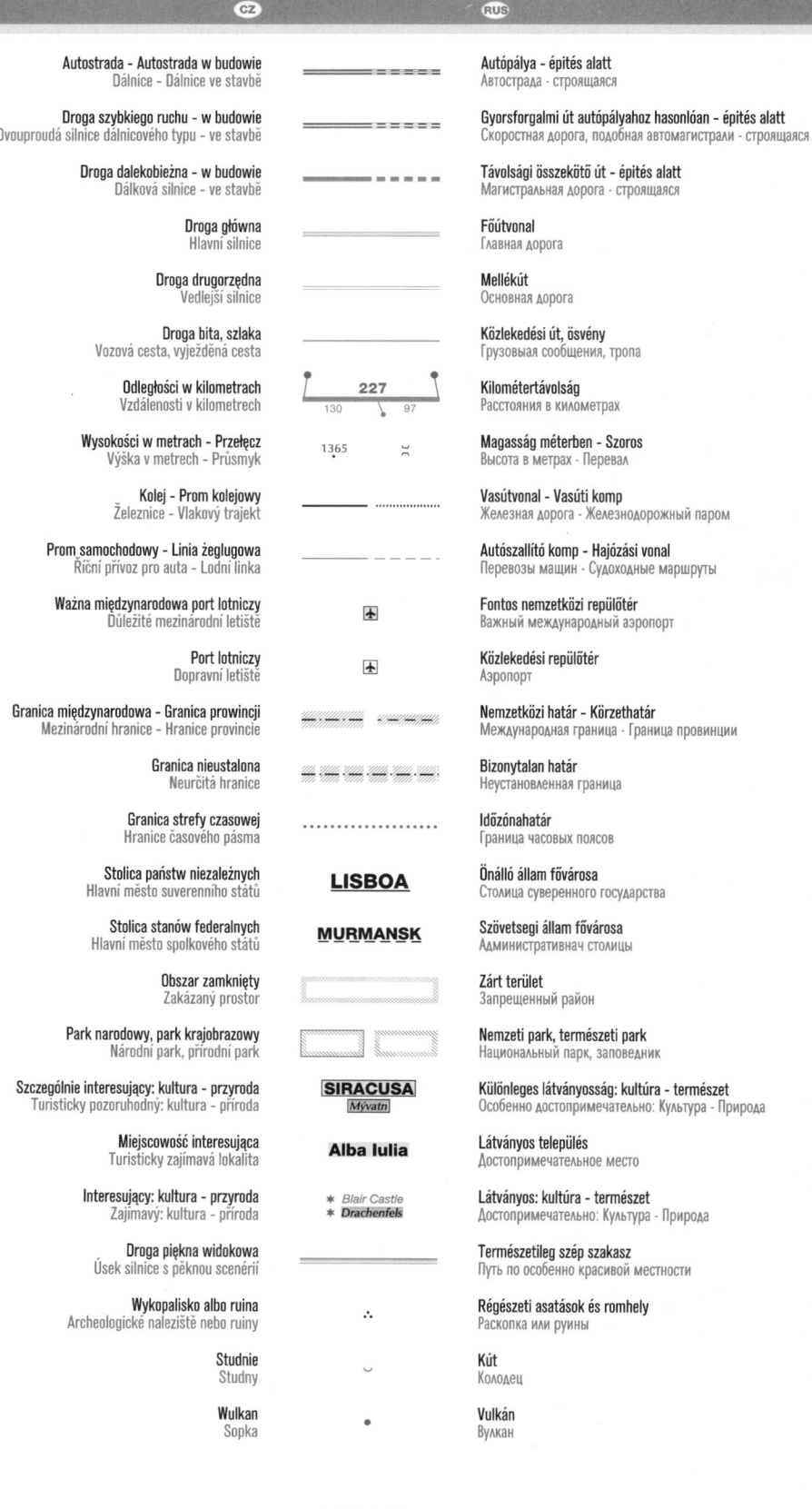

| PL CZ | | H RUS |
|---|---|---|
| **Autostrada - Autostrada w budowie**<br>Dálnice - Dálnice ve stavbě | | **Autópálya - épités alatt**<br>Автострада - строящаяся |
| **Droga szybkiego ruchu - w budowie**<br>Dvouproudá silnice dálnicového typu - ve stavbě | | **Gyorsforgalmi út autópályahoz hasonlóan - épités alatt**<br>Скоростная дорога, подобная автомагистрали - строящаяся |
| **Droga dalekobieżna - w budowie**<br>Dálková silnice - ve stavbě | | **Távolsági összekötő út - épités alatt**<br>Магистральная дорога - строящаяся |
| **Droga główna**<br>Hlavní silnice | | **Főútvonal**<br>Главная дорога |
| **Droga drugorzędna**<br>Vedlejší silnice | | **Mellékút**<br>Основная дорога |
| **Droga bita, szlaka**<br>Vozová cesta, vyježděná cesta | | **Közlekedési út, ösvény**<br>Грузовые сообщения, тропа |
| **Odległości w kilometrach**<br>Vzdálenosti v kilometrech | 227   130   97 | **Kilométertávolság**<br>Расстояния в километрах |
| **Wysokości w metrach - Przełęcz**<br>Výška v metrech - Průsmyk | 1365 | **Magasság méterben - Szoros**<br>Высота в метрах - Перевал |
| **Kolej - Prom kolejowy**<br>Železnice - Vlakový trajekt | | **Vasútvonal - Vasúti komp**<br>Железная дорога - Железнодорожный паром |
| **Prom samochodowy - Linia żeglugowa**<br>Říční přívoz pro auta - Lodní linka | | **Autószallító komp - Hajózási vonal**<br>Перевозы мащин - Судоходные маршруты |
| **Ważna międzynarodowa port lotniczy**<br>Důležité mezinárodní letiště | ✈ | **Fontos nemzetközi repülőtér**<br>Важный международный аэропорт |
| **Port lotniczy**<br>Dopravní letiště | ✈ | **Közlekedési repülőtér**<br>Аэропорт |
| **Granica międzynarodowa - Granica prowincji**<br>Mezinárodní hranice - Hranice provincie | | **Nemzetközi határ - Körzethatár**<br>Международная граница - Граница провинции |
| **Granica nieustalona**<br>Neurčitá hranice | | **Bizonytalan határ**<br>Неустановленная граница |
| **Granica strefy czasowej**<br>Hranice časového pásma | | **Időzónahatár**<br>Граница часовых поясов |
| **Stolica państw niezależnych**<br>Hlavní město suverenního státu | **LISBOA** | **Önálló állam fővárosa**<br>Столица суверенного государства |
| **Stolica stanów federalnych**<br>Hlavní město spolkového státu | **MURMANSK** | **Szövetségi állam fővárosa**<br>Административнач столицы |
| **Obszar zamknięty**<br>Zakázaný prostor | | **Zárt terület**<br>Запрещенный район |
| **Park narodowy, park krajobrazowy**<br>Národní park, přírodní park | | **Nemzeti park, természeti park**<br>Национальный парк, заповедник |
| **Szczególnie interesujący: kultura - przyroda**<br>Turisticky pozoruhodný: kultura - příroda | **SIRACUSA**<br>*Mývatn* | **Különleges látványosság: kultúra - természet**<br>Особенно достопримечательно: Культура - Природа |
| **Miejscowość interesująca**<br>Turisticky zajímavá lokalita | **Alba Iulia** | **Látványos település**<br>Достопримечательное место |
| **Interesujący: kultura - przyroda**<br>Zajimavý: kultura - příroda | ✶ *Blair Castle*<br>✶ *Drachenfels* | **Látványos: kultúra - természet**<br>Достопримечательно: Культура - Природа |
| **Droga piękna widokowa**<br>Úsek silnice s pěknou scenérií | | **Természetileg szép szakasz**<br>Путь по особенно красивой местности |
| **Wykopalisko albo ruina**<br>Archeologické naleziště nebo ruiny | ∴ | **Régészeti asatások és romhely**<br>Раскопка или руины |
| **Studnie**<br>Studny | ⌣ | **Kút**<br>Колодец |
| **Wulkan**<br>Sopka | • | **Vulkán**<br>Вулкан |

## 1 : 2 000 000

| 0 | 20 | 40 | 60 | 80 | 100 km |
|---|---|---|---|---|---|

| 0 | 10 | 20 | 30 | 40 | 50 | 60 miles |
|---|---|---|---|---|---|---|

1:2 000 000 / 1cm = 20 km

Photo: Satellitenaufnahme, Europa (getty images/GSO Images)

Bi  Bk  Ca

20

Bb  Bc  Bd  Be  Bf

21

22

**Svalbard (Nor.)**

Danskøya
Albert I Land  1131
Reinsdyr  96
Haakon VII  614
Land
Andrée  1468
Land
Ny Ålesund  145.1
Grampianfjellet  1064
Prins Karls  Oscar II
Forland  Land
Forland  nasjonalpark
Daudmannsodden  997
Lågneset  Isfjord Radio
Barentsburg  Grumantbyen  Longyearbyen
Nordenskiöld  Gustav V  1235
Land  714
Van Mijenfjorden  Heer
Wedel  1217  Land
Jarlsberg  Nathorst Land
Land  1035
Torell  nasjonalpark
Land  676
Øyrlandsodden  Sørkapp  Land
Sørkappøya

Phippsøya
Sjuøyane
Verlegen-  Nordkapp  Parryøya
huken  Kapp  Martensøya
Spotoppen  Kjeldsen
Gustav  Prins  Kapp
V Land  Oscars  Laura
Land  Foynøya
Nordaust-Svalbard  nat-res  Storøya
Wahlenbergfj.  340
Gustav  Adolf
Von  Land
Otterøyane  764
Wilhelmøya  Kvitøya
(Nor.)  410
Nat-res
Erik Eriksenstretet
Nordaust-Svalbard
nat-res  Abeløya
Svenskøya  230  320
Kongsøya
Kong Karls Land
Edgeøya  nat-res
Edge-  jøkulen
Tjuvfjorden  461
Stonepynten
395
Halvmåneøya
Tusen-  øyane

Olgastretet

Storfjorden

# Norwegian Sea

Andenes
Bleik
Nordmela  82
Andøya
Risøyhamn  Åse
Myre
Langøya  821
Straumsjøen  820
Steine  Guvåg
Stokmarknes  Sortland
Hadseløya  Sigerfjord
Melbu  Møysalen  Gulles-
Fiskebøl  1262  fjordbotn
E10
Austvågøy  1084
Trolltindan
205  Svolvær
Vestvågøy  Kabelvåg
Leknes  815  Henningsvær
Flakstadøya  842
Flakstad
Ballstad  Stamsund
Moskenesøya  E10
1034  Reine
Sørvågen
Moskenstraumen
Værøy  Sørland
Røst  Røst
Røsthavet

Helligvær
Landegode  834
Bliksvær  Løding
Bodø  63
Sandhornøy  17
Fugløya  Leikanger
Inndyr  812
Bejarn  813
Ørnes  Høgtind
Åmøya  1404
Vågaholmen
Nesøya  Kilvik
Jektvika  Reppen
Kilboghamn  Svartisen  1599
Lovund  Lunderøy  nasjonal-  park
Tomma  1294  Høgtuvbreen  Grønlin-
Rølvsøy  17  grotten
12  Mo i Rana
Nesna  Hemnes
808  34

Arctic Circle
Irgenfjorden

Vesterålen

Grytøya
Åse
Sjurvik  Bjarkøy  Grøtavær
Bjarkøy
Stonglandet
Dyrøya  166
Løksa  18
Andørja  848
Sjøvegan
Rolla  1276  Setermoen
Ibestad  Myrlandshaug
Sørrollnes  825  Grovfjord
1306  Fossbakken
Steinsland  1458
83  Rivtin  Øvre Dividal
Ramnes  Bogen  nasjonalpark
Tjeldøya  Bjerkvik  1633
Narvik  18
Lødingen  E10  Vadvetjåkka
Kjeldebotn  n.p.
21  Björkliden
Skårberget  Ballangen  Beisfjord  Abisko
1003  1744  Skjomen  1901
Ulvsvåg  Storstein-  Abisko
81  fjellet  nat. p.
Kjøpsvik  1503  Katterjåkk
Giccecokka  Kåtotjåkka
1520  1991
Hamarøy  Sitas-  Torneträsk
Finnøya  jaure
Hellemobotn
835  Kebnekaise
263  V. Ritjemjåkk  2111
E06  Nordfold  1845  Kebne-
1482  Akkavare  kaisefjällst.
Mørsvikbotn  Singistugorna
Gaskačokka  Nikkaluokta
1513  Kisurisstugan
Padjelanta  Stora Sjöfallets
Tårnvik  national-  n.p.
975  Rågo  Vaisaluokta-  Vietas
Røsvik  Vastenjaure  stugan  2015
Festvåg  park  Padjelanta
826  Stortoppen  Saltoluokta-
Straumen  Aitihaure  2089  fjällst.
Fauske  national-  Sareks  Ruokto
830  Staloluokta-  Sitojaure-
Skierstad  stugorna  nationalpark  stugorna
Monus  park  2002  2008
Rognan  Pårtefjällen  Stora
67  Sulitjelma  Kvikkjokk
Vesterli  1907  Pieskehaure-
Saltdalen  stugan  Tjåkta-
Storjord  Pieskehaure  Riepenjåkka  Saggat
Bjerndalsokka  Tarrajåkkå  Tjåmotis
Ølsjfjellet  1587  Mavas-
1751  jaure  1464  Randijaur
Saltfjellet  1627  Bartur-  Kårats
Stødi  Kaisetjåkkå  Karatj
Svartisdalen  te
95  Fierras
E06  1605  Sådva  Riebnes
Nasarfjället  jaure  Vuonatj-
245  viken
121  Ballasviken  Stenudden
Pieljekaise  931
Toftlia  nationalpark  Lövnäs
Adolfsström  1138
Svaipavalle  Jäkkvik

SVERIGE

NORGE
Umeå
0  10  20  30  40  50 km
0  10  20  30 miles

9  Arvidsjaur  Arvidsjaur  Luleå

Nordkvaløy
Rebbenesøy  Helgøy  Fugløya
Måsvik  Mikkelvik  Vanna  959
Arnøy
Komagvik  Vannareid  Årviksand
Ringvassøy  Reinøy  Laukslatta
Skulgam  863  Hessfjord  Kågen
Tromvik  Store  Finnkroken  Russelv  Hamn-
Blåmannen  Olderdvik  eidet
1044  Nordneidet  Uløya
Kvaløy  Kvaløysletta  1596  866
Sandneshamn  Djupvik  Sørkjosen
Tromsø  91  E06
Fjordgård  Bākke-  862  Jøvik  Svensby  Olderdalen
Berg  jord  Fagernes  Skibotn  m
864  Vikran  E06  Jiekkevarrebreen  Kåfjord-
Grylefjord  957  65  1833  botn  E08
Kaldfarnes  86  68  Gibostad  858  Kantornes  868
Senja  Lunneborg  Oteren
86  Finnsnes  Seljelvnes  44  1360  G
Silsand  Sørreisa  Moen  Otertind  Rognli
Ånderdalen  Brøstadbotn  Maselvfossen  87
nasjonalpark  84  Andselv  Övergård
Dyrøya  Bardu  Tverrelvmo  Paltsan
elva  Björkås  1444
Setermoen  1713  Kumma-
Innset  vuopio  R
Övre Dividal  O  Alte-  1120
nasjonalpark  vatnet  Kiepanjaure  Råstojaure
1633  Leina-  vatnet  Kåtojaure
N  Björkliden  341  Pulsujärvi
O  Tornetrāsk  Laimoluokta
R  Rautas-  Tjålme  836
järvi  Kätotjåkka  Vittangivaara
B  200  Rensjön  Kurravaara
O  Tornetrāsk  Kiruna  Jukkasjärvi
R  Kiirunavaara  Holmajärvi
D  Kaalasjärvi  1001  Kalixfors
L  Lietekkåbbå  Kaitumälven  Kaitum
A  Satihaure  Fjällåsen  819
N  Saltoluokta-  Killinge  Puoltikasvaara
D  Ruokto  Harrå  Tjautjas
Lulevatten  819
Malmberget  Koskull-
Porjus  820  Gällivare  Dundret
709  Muddus
SVE  nationalpark
103  E45  Leip
Jokkmokk  542
97
Vuollerim  Murjek

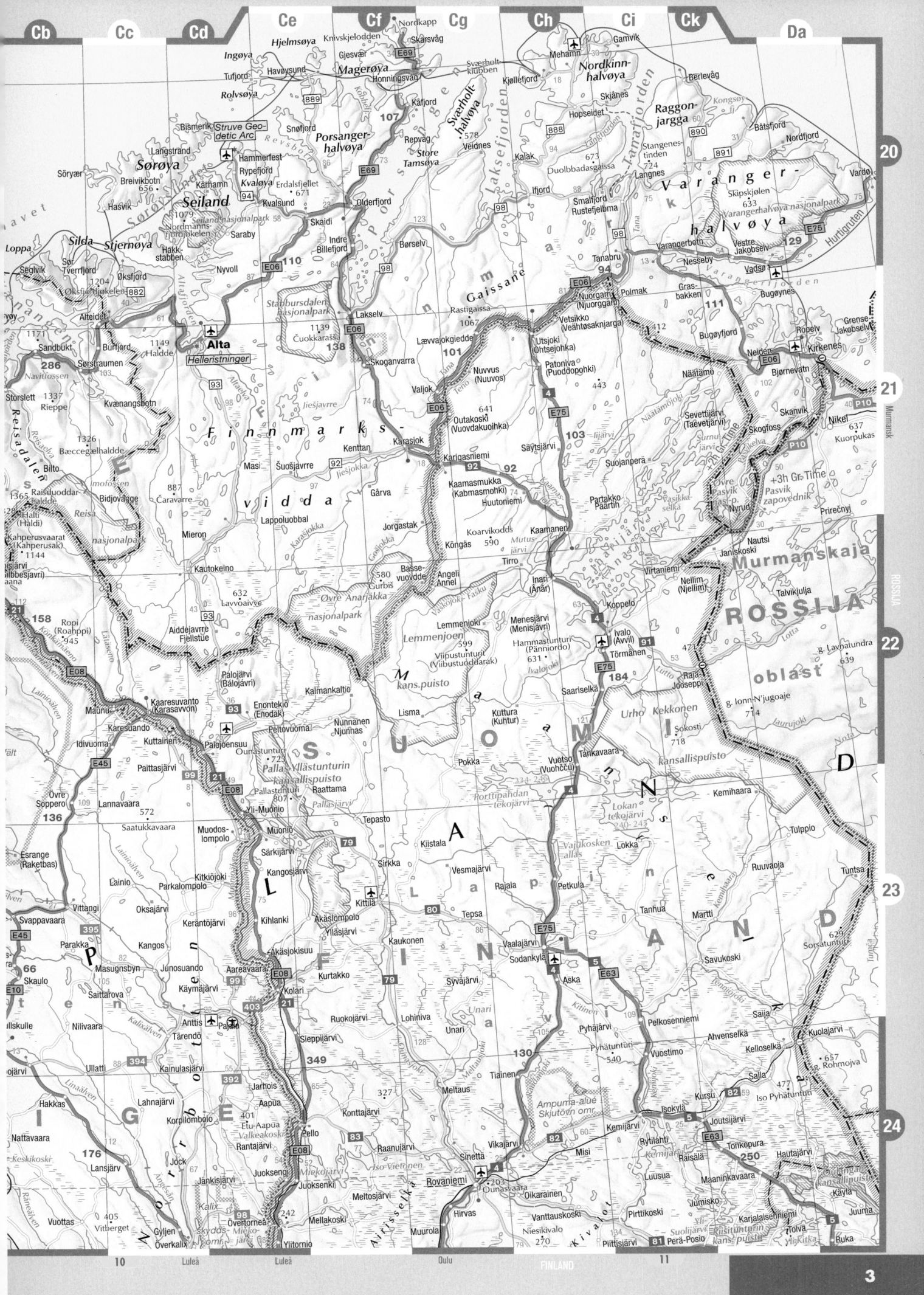

20
21
22
23
24

3

Lagernoe
(Novaja Zemlja)

e       n       t       s

e       a

m. Kanin Nos
Kanin Nos

K   a   n   i   n
204
g. Korytova
242
g. Mohovaja

m. Lajdennyj
o. Korga
o-va Kambaľnickie
Koški

K   a   m   e   n'
225
m. Mikulkin

Rybnaja

Mesna

o. Nokuev
Varzino
•283

Syjatonosskij
zaliv
m. Svjatoj Nos
p-ov Svjatoj Nos

Gremiha
Lyjjok
Iokanga

Šojnskaja guba
Šojna
Šojna

Kija

Neneckij

m. Zapadnyj
Ludovatyj Nos

Čёšskaja
guba

e
g

o   r   e

m
o
r
e

K   a   n   i   n   s   k   i   j       b   e   r   e   g

Lumbovskij zaliv
o. Lumbovskij
303
Lumbovka
Lumbovka
Lumbovka

Vyhča

oz.
Šuč'e

Čёša

avtonomnyj

efurta
296

Kačkovka
Kačkovskij zaliv
Losinga

Lebjaž'a

J
g. Manjuk
342
Kolmak

A

Orlovskij zaliv
m. Orlovskij

m. Konušin
Čiža

Čiža

P   -   o   v

K   a   n   i   n

Aŕeŕjok

Kanevka

por.
Kolmackij
Ponoj

Jažma

k   a   n   i   n   s   k   a   j   a       t   u   n   d   r   a
Perepusk
Vižas
Vižas
Oma
Oma

p
o
v

302

Purnač

Ponoj
Ponoj

o. Gorjainov

m. Mihailovskij

Nes'

T   e   r   s   k   i   j       b   e   r   e   g

Pjalka

oz.
Bab'e

o. Moržovec

Arctic Circle
Mezenskaja
M   e   z   e   n   s   k   a   j   a

Niž. Mgla

91

okrug

oz. Vižas

Verh.-
Ondom-
ozero

Pjalica
Pjalica

Sosnovka

o. Sosnovec

Arhangels'k

m. Voronov

m. Abramov

Kojda

Niža

b   e   l

g   u   b   a

Kojda

Niža

Majda

Kon   š   nskij   bereg

Sёmža

147

Pulonga
Pulonga

Arhangelskaja oblasť

Sёmža

20

21

22

23

24

20

21

22

23

24

*B a r e n t s*

*S e a*

*P e č o r s k o*

m. Kostin Nos
192
p-ov Mučnoj
Krasino
m. Sal

*o. Kolguev*
Pesčanka  Pesčanoe
Gubistaja
g. Paarkov
Sarlopy
166
Bugrino

kosa Vost. Tonkie (Ploskie) Koški
kosa Zap. Tonkie (Ploskie) Koški

p-ov Russkij
Zavorot
m. Russkij
Zavorot
Hodovariha
Kuzneckaja guba
o. Dolgij

m. Lajdennyj
o. Korga
o-va Kambaľnickie
Koški

*p-ov Kanin*

Rybnaja

m. Mikulkin

225

*P o m o r s k i j   p r o l i v*

*o. Sengejskij*
Sengejskij  proliv
Sengejskij

Tobseda
oz.
Pesčanoe
Kolokolkova
guba
Neruta
138
Korovinskaja
guba
Pečorskaja guba
Nosovaja
Jušino

*T  i  m  a  n  s  k  i  j*
g. Tenja Seda
182
Sengajha
Veľt
*z  e  m  e  ľ  s  k  a  j  a*   *t  u  n  d  r  a*
*Neneckaja grjada*
R

m. Sv. Nos
Gornostaľja
guba

*M  a  l  o*
Andeg
Pečora
oz. Golodnaja
Guba

Čёšskaja guba

Indiskaja
guba
m. Barmin Nos
Indiga
Vyučeskij
Indiga
Čеrnaja
Indigskie
ozёra
Kuja
Nar'jan-Mar
Kamenka
Oksino
Pylemec
Labožskoe

Velikaja
Velikaja
Šojma
oz.
Urdjužskoe
31

m. Suvojnyj Nos
g. Pron'kina
256
*Č  a  i  c  y  n  s  k  i  j   k  a  m  e  n'*
Volonga
Volonga
g. Kovriga
303
Kotkino
Toŝviska

*T  i  m  a  n  s  k  i  j   k  a  m  e  n'*
*K  o  s  m  i  n  s  k  i  j   k  a  m  e  n'*
*k  r  j  a  ž*
Beluš'e
226
Sula
Sula
Bol. Jangыta
Leždug
Ērmica
Ŝapkina
Egorovo
Snopa
Nižnjaja Peša
Bol. Pula
Novyj Bor

Verhnjaja Peša
Kosma
Bezhošcica
Snopa
Oma
Arctic Circle
Volokovaja
Volok
*v  o  z  v  y  š  e  n  n  o  s  t'*
Tobыš
Tobыš
Myla
Sozva
Medvežka
Jurjaga
Nalim-Ju

Tarasovo
oz. Vars
oz.
Kosminskoe
*T  o  b  ы  š  s  k  a  j  a*
Krestovka
Okunev Nos
167

0  10  20  30  40  50 km

0  10  20  30 miles

ROSSIJA

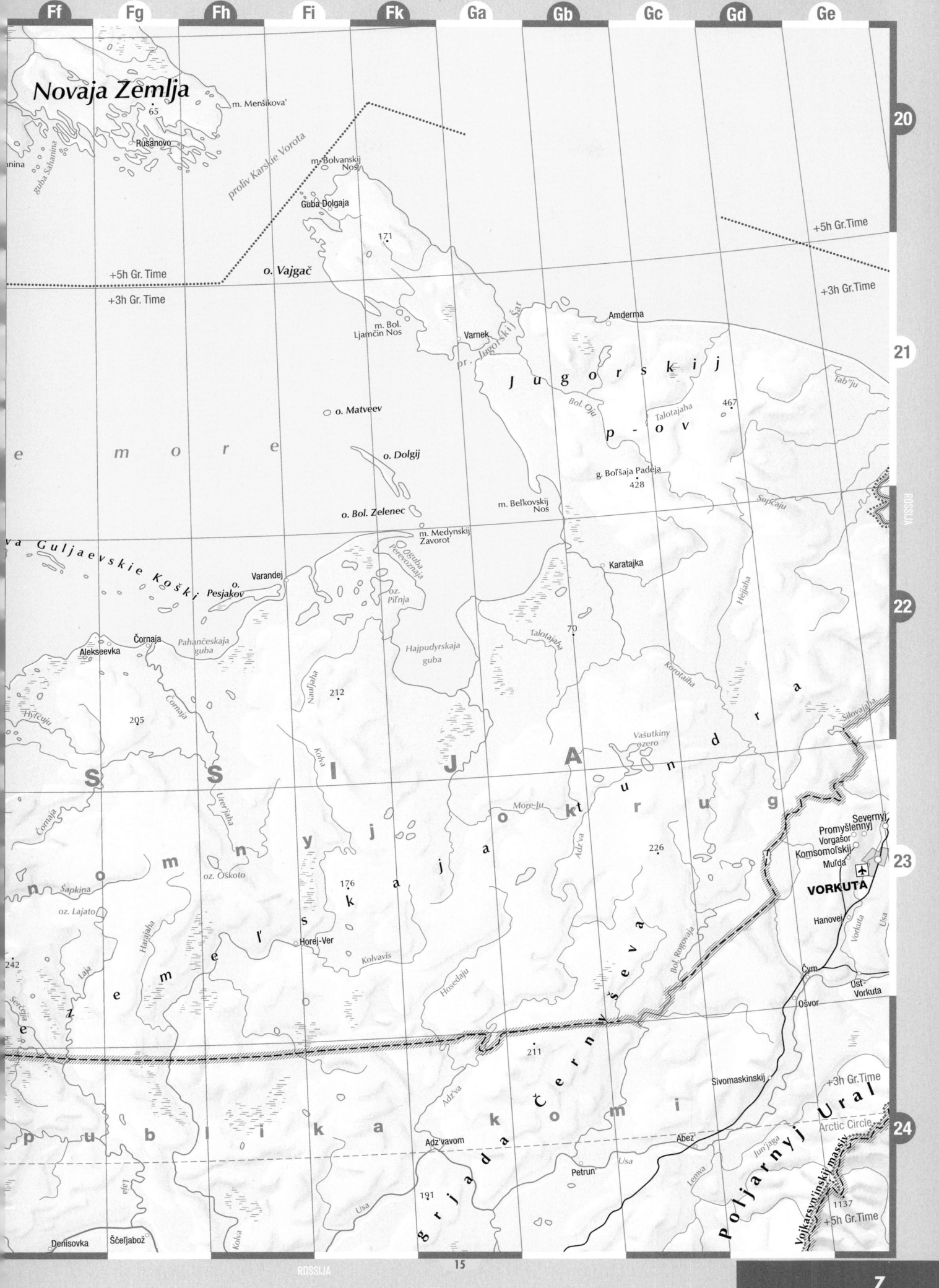

*Novaja Zemlja*

guba Sahanina

·65

Rusanovo

m. Menšikova'

m. Bolvanskij Nos

proliv Karskie Vorota

Guba Dolgaja

·171

o. Vajgač

+5h Gr. Time

+3h Gr. Time

m. Bol. Ljamčin Nos

Varnek

pr. Jugorskij Šar

Amderma

+5h Gr.Time

+3h Gr.Time

J u g o r s k i j

o. Matveev

Bol. Oju

Talotajaha

·467

Tab"ju

p - o v

o. Dolgij

g. Boľšaja Padeja
·428

Sopčaju

o. Bol. Zelenec

m. Beľkovskij Nos

m. Medynskij Zavorot

guba Perevoznaja

Karatajka

Heijaha

va G u l j a e v s k i e   K o š k i

Varandej

oz. Piľnja

o. Pesjakov

Čornaja

Pahančeskaja guba

Hajpudyrskaja guba

Talotajaha

·70

Talotajaha

Korotaiha

Alekseevka

Naulijaha

·212

Silovajaha

Hylčuju

·205

Čornaja

Vašutkiny ozero

S   S   I   J   A

Kolka

More-Ju

Adz"va

·226

n           o      m            n    y        j

Šapkina

oz. Oškoto

k         a        j             a            k   t         r     u       g

Severnyj
Promyšlennyj
Vorgašor
Komsomoľskij
Muľda

oz. Lajato

·176

Ureijaha

s

č   e   r   n   y   š   e   v   a

✈

VORKUTA

Haratajha

ľ

Horej-Ver

Bol. Rogovaja

Hanovej

Vorkuta

Usa

e           m

Kolvavis

Čym

·242

Laja

Serkola

Hosedaju

Ust-Vorkuta

Ošvor

·211

Laja

Usa

Sivomaskinskij

+3h Gr.Time

P o l j a r n y j   U r a l

g   r   i   a   d   a

k   o   m   i

Arctic Circle

Abez'

·24

p       u        b       l       i       k       a

Adz"vavom

Usa

Jun"jaga

Lemva

Vojkarsyninskij massiv

Petrun'

·191

Denisovka

Ščeľjabož

Kolva

Usa

·1137

+5h Gr.Time

ROSSIJA

20  21  22  23  24

## ATLANTIC OCEAN

## Norwegian Sea

Vega
Gladstad
791
Brønnøy

Leka
Solsem
Vikna
Rørvik
Kolvereid
77
Valøya
776
Jøa
Brekksillan
Foldefjorden
Otter øya
769
Sør-
Flatanger
766
Namsos
Jøssund
Bangsund
Sjøåsen
Solem
Sundet
715
Finnvollheia
33
Snåsavat
123
Harsvik
540
676
Afjord
Sprova
Malm
Sunnan
Lysøysund
Follafoss
Steinkjer
Botngard
715 516
Fosna
Verdalsøra
Brekstad
710 37
Husbysjøen
720 755
Ytterøy
Vuku
72
Leksvik
Skogn
Levanger
Rissa
601
E06 0
Morkabygd
Kjøl
Frøya
Hellesvik
Flatval
Feren
Titran
Frøyfjorden
Fillan
Fjellværøya
710
Vannvikan
Trondheimsfj.
Frosta
Su
Veidholmen
Kvenvær
Sandstad
Skatval
Stjørdalshalsen
Forsnes
369
38
Selbekken
714
54
Flornes
E14
Merå
Hopen
713
Dyrnes
Smøla
Storoddan
TRONDHEIM
Malvik
Hommelvik
68
Kopperå
669
Kyrksæterøra
Heimdal
Klæbu
35
680
59
Orkanger
Elistranda
Melhus
Stordal
Aure
833
Fannrem
E39
Reinsfjell
11
Tømmervåg
149
Ruten
Løkken
933
Selbu
100
Leira
1020
924
48
705
Fongen
1132
Kristiansund
Engian
700
Meldal
96
Støren
Storerikvollen
70
Tustna
63
Halsa
65
Rindal
Nesjøen
Storbakken
65
54
Surna
1219
Soknedal
Lauvun
Østby
Hustadvika
Averøya
Tingvoll
670
Singsås
30
1322
Averøya
16
Skei-Surnadalsøra
46
Berkåk
90
Ålen
1322
Bud
Nordmøre
64
1020
20
670
Todal
1667
Rennebu
Enodden
Elnesvågen
E39
Kleive
820
Snøta
12
Trøndelag
1264
Gossa
66
Eidsvåg
Innset
Eorolshogna
1332
Nordøyane
Hjellset
198
1332
Glåmos
Brekker
Midsund
Molde
Sunndalsøra
92
Brekker
Austnes
Vestnes
Møre
Isfjorden
70
Oppdal
3
74
Røros
156
Roald
Brattvåg
9
Andalsnes
E06
(600)
Alnes
6 E136
64
Grøa
621
1229
Os
1199
Sjøholt
233
NORGE
104
Høggia
og
Tresfjord
1633
Femu
Sørøyane
Langevåg
650
69 1795
Romsdal
Orkla
40
Sandøy
Kvalsvik
Sykkylven
Stordal
Trolltindane
1950
Snøhetta
E06
Narbuvoll
Ulsteinvik
104
Vartdal
1739
Marstein
180
Dovrefjell
1025
26
Fosnavåg
1307
Liabygd
63
Bjorli
n.p.
Tynset
1591
Sandøy
Larsnes
Slogen
Eidsdal
E136
1660
Holøydal
Stadlandet
Sæbø
1597
Pyttegga
Lora
Hjerkinn
Tron
1604
Leikanger
Fiskå
Volda
556
1984
Lesjaskog
Lesja
Alvdal
Nord-
Selje
113
Eide
49
Storhø
Hedmark
Vågsøy
Ørsta
Systre
7 (624)
Reinheimen nasjonalpark
Dombås
Folldal
27
Sunnmøre
63
1926
1833
(820)
1827
Store
Måløy
E39
Geirangerfjorden
715
Tverrfjell
Dovre
Sølnkletten
Barkald
Bremanger-
Stårheim
Nordfjorden
Grodås
Dalsnibba
Norberg
Oppland
Rondane
52
polten
614
Nordfjordeid
66
Pollfoss
1833
Vågåmo
47
n.p.
Øvre
Bremanger-
landet
15
57
60
39
Oppstryn
Ottadalen
227
2178
58
Rondane
Rendal
Kalvåg
Alfotbreen
Sandane
2083
Øiden
Garmo
15
Atnbrua
219
1755
Flora
Svelgen
1632
Utvik (630)
Lom 29
Otta
30
Sølen
217
Sogn og
Hyen
Bøverdal
Jotunheimen
Bjølstad
Norddal
615
68
Jostedalsbreen
Breheimen
n.p.
Otnes
E39
5
69 Eikefjord
Fjordane
E39 102
n.p. Jostedalen
Jotunheimen
Glittertinden
n.p.
Galdhøpiggen
2470
2470

24
25
26
27
28
29

Gulf of

Bothnia

0 10 20 30 40 50 km
0 10 20 30 miles

Murmansk

24

M18  Pežostrov  Keret'
Louhi  Sonostrov
Ambarnyj  Gridino
Engozero  m. Tolstik
Unduksa  Kalga
330  o-va
Ivanovy Ludy
o. Olenij
oz. Keret'
Verh. Kumozero  55  94
Engr ozero

Kaškarancy  Kandalakša
Kuzomen'  Kandalakšskaja
guba
Varzuga
Niž. Ondomozero  Verh. Ondomozero
Čavan'ga  Streľna  Capoma  Pjalica
Tetrino  Streľna  Pulonga
Terskij  bereg
m. Incy

25

E105  Niž. Kumozero
Levickoe  oz. Pon'goma
Sombozero  54
Komsomoľskij
A135  Juma
Kuzema  Von'ga
g. Pon'goma
Sig  Von'ga
60

Beloe  more
Incy
Tova  oz. Tova
Niž. Zolotica  Verh. Zolotica
g. Erga 210  216
m. Kerec
Kozly

26

Panozero
oz. Leževo  171
oz. Muezero
Novoe  Mašozero
Bérezova  oz. Tungudskoe
Avneporog
Kem'
Kem'
oz. Ležero  76
Šuerečkoe
g. Šuerečkaja
Šuj-ostrov
Bol. Žužmuj
Mal. Žužmuj
Belomorsk
Sorokskaja guba
Sosnovec
Lehta  Pušnoj  207
Letnerečenskij

o. Černecki
Soloveckie o-va
o. Soloveckie
Soloveckie  80
o. Boľšaja Muksalma
o. Anzerskij
o. Žižginskij
Letnij Navolok
Uhtnavolok
m. Orlovskij
Letnjaja Zol.  113
Lopšen'ga
m. Krasnogorskij Rog
Pušlahta
Mjandozero  202
Onežskij p-ov
Pertominsk
Sjus'ma
Leto  bereg  70
Patrakeevka
o. Mudjugskij
Podborka
Išm

SEVERODVINSK
Nenoksa  Solza
ARHANGEĽSK
Vas'kovo  M18
Novodvinsk
Volost'
Bruselica
Tundra
Una
Ljamca
Purnema  m. Glubokij
Kjanda
Tamica
Pokrovskoe

Tunguskaja
vozvyšennost'
Respublika
A134  210
Vača  82
Ondozero  151
Voldozero  160
Rigozero  27
Šalgovaara  264
Popov Porog
Padany  120
Evgora  243
Segozero
Kar. Maseľga
Maseľga

Ider
Sum-o.
Virma
Sumskij Posad
Kockoma
Nadvojcy
Vorenža
Polga
Segeža
260
Vyg-ozero  80
o. Sigovec
Valdaj
Vorožgora
Kolijgora
por. Mednik  243
Ogorelyši

Mjagostrov  114
Koležma
Kondostrov
Hedostrov
Virandozero
Njuhča
Malen'ga
Unežma  72
Kuša
Maložujka
Nimen'ga
g. Šapočka  320
Poморский  berег
Onežskaja guba
Onežskij  bereg
guba Nimen'ga
Vorzogory
Ponga
Usť-Koža
Anciferovskij Bor
Kovkula
Priluki
Pošad
202
g. Šiverka  271
Ulitino
Jarnema
Savinskij

Onega
Porog  56
Glazaniha
Mudjuga
Kodino
Letneozerskij
Verhovskij  151  77
Emca

Arhangeľsk
porogi
200
Švakino  Samoded
Obozerskij  67
Malinovka  78
R  O

Karelija
oz. Semčezero  63
Justozero  64
170
E105
oz. Sunda ozero
Girvas
Sopoha
vdp. Kivač
Guba Spasskaja
Kondopoga
Kiži Pogost
Kulmuksa

Medvežegorsk
Pinduši  52
Lobskoe
Proletarka
P17
Šun'ga  Kažma
Tolvuja
Kedrozero  202
Velikaja Guba
Tambicy
Bojaščina
Kurgenicy

oz. Verh. Volozero
Tihvin Bor
Sergievo
Ogorelyši
Vodlozerskij nacionaľnyj park
P5
Pjaľma
Tambicy
Peščanoe
Kuganavolok
oz. Vodlozero
oz. Raznozero
Niž. Usť'e
Poča
Kenozerskij nac.-park
oz. Kenozero

242
oz. Monastyrskoe
200
280
Fedovo  93  78
Kokovka
Šalakuša
Mirnyj
Plesetck
Denislav'e  197
Oksovskij
Stupinskaja
oz. Undozero

Čaľna
Šuja
Jalguba
Matrosy  52
Prjaža  311
Derevjanka
P19
Derevjannoe

PETROZAVODSK
E105
Onežskoe  ozero
Vytegra
Šaľskij
Pudož  P2  50
Krivcy
P5  74
Oktjabr'skaja
Kubovo
Steševskaja
Vodla
Usť'-Reka
Ileksinskaja
Usačevskaja

Pogost
Selehovskaja
Pogost
Rjapusovskij Pogost
Most
Lema
Konevo
P1
Zaozernyj  80

ROSSIJA
S.-Peterburg
Murmansk

0  10  20  30  40  50 km
0  10  20  30 miles

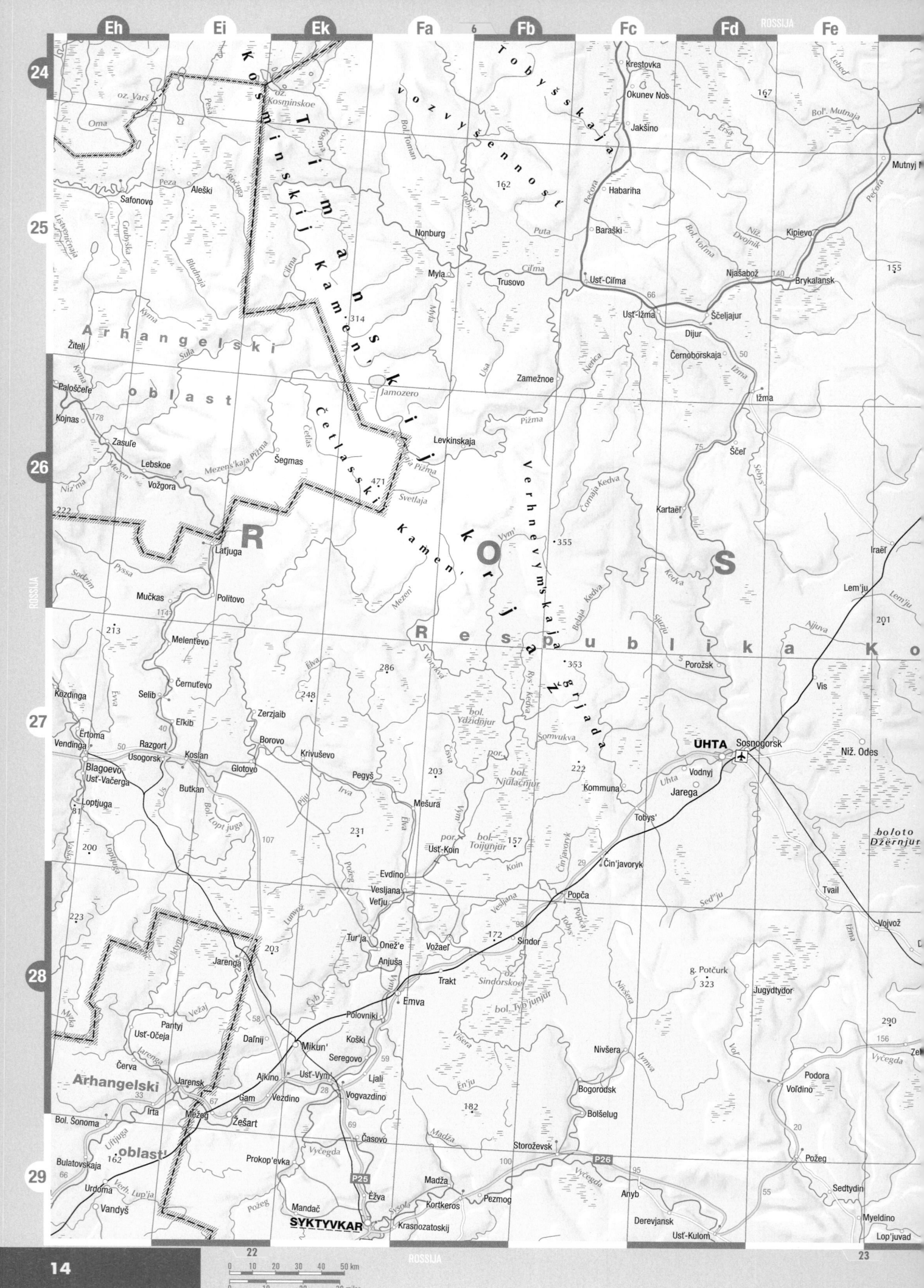

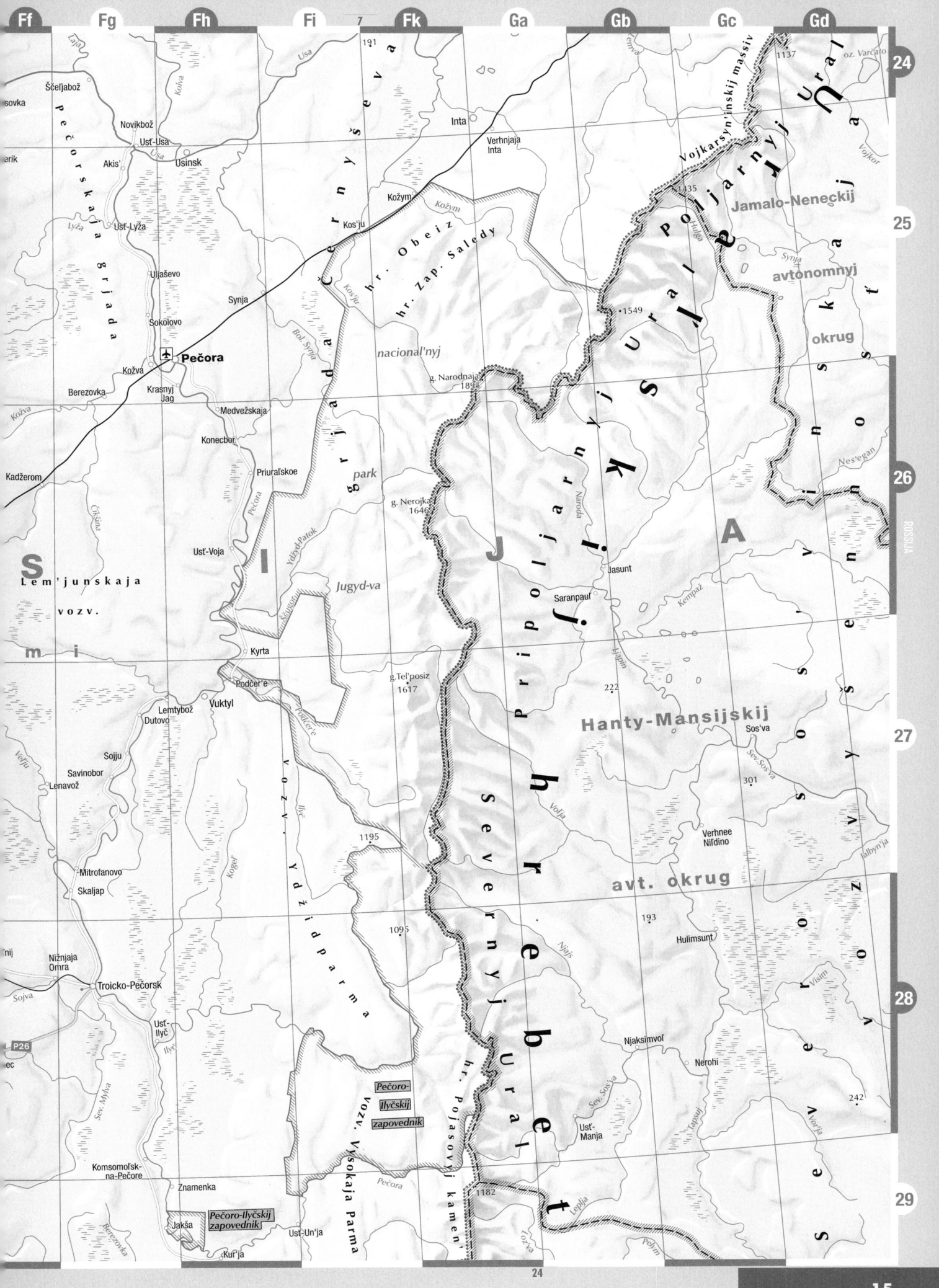

191

24

Laja

Ščeľjabož

-osovka

Pečorskaja grjada

Novikbož

Kolva

Usť-Usa

Akis'

Usinsk

Usa

Usa

Lyža

Usť-Lyža

Uljaševo

Synja

Sokolovo

Berik

Kožva

Pečora

Krasnyj Jag

Berezovka

Medvežskaja

Kadžerom

Čikšina

Kožva

Konecbor

Priuraľskoe

Usť-Voja

Pečora

Bol. Synja

Č e r n y š e v a   g r j a d a

Inta

Verhnjaja Inta

Kožym

Kožym

Kos'ju

Kos'ju

hr. Obeiz

hr. Zap. Saledy

nacional'nyj

park

g. Narodnaja
1894

g. Nerojka
1646

Jugyd-va

Ylyzd-Patok

P r i p o l j a r n y j   U r a l

Vojkarsynĭnskij massiv

1137

1435

•1549

Narodainka

oz. Varčato

Ural

Vojkar

Jamalo-Neneckij

avtonomnyj

okrug

Synja

Nes'egan

R O S S I J A

J A

Jasunt

Saranpauľ

S

Lem'junskaja

vozv.

mi

Kyrta

Podčer'e

Vuktyl

Lemtyböž

Dutovo

Sojju

Savinobor

Lenavož

Mitrofanovo

Skaljap

'nij

Nižnjaja
Omra

Troicko-Pečorsk

Sojva

Sev. Mylva

Usť-
Ilyč

P26

ec

Komsomoľsk-
na-Pečore

Znamenka

Berezovka

Jakša

Kur'ja

Usť-Un'ja

Pečoro-
Ilyčskij
zapovednik

Pečoro-Ilyčskij
zapovednik

Vysokaja Parma Parma

Ilyč

vozv.

Ydzid parma

Kogel

Podčer'e

Eganga

vozv.

1195

1095

1182

Pečora

Tošva

Leplja

Lapsuj

Njaksimvoľ

Usť-
Manja

Nerohi

Hulimsunt

Verhnee
Niľdino

Sos'va

Njajs

volja

Sev. Sos'va

Sev. Sos'va

301

193

222

Kempaž

Ljapin

Narod

J

V y s e r o s s   v s y š s s e r o s s e r o š s o v   v o s e r v

Ural

p o l j a r n y j   p r i o l d h r e b   S e v e r n y j   U r a l

hr. Pojasovyj kamen'

Severnyj hrebet

S e v e r n y j   h r e b e t

Hanty-Mansijskij

avt. okrug

Visim

242

25

26

27

28

29

24

29

Norddal

Sogn

Floro

Svanøy

Sula

Ytre Sula

Sandøy

156

One

BERGEN

Store Sotra

32

STAVANGER

33

North Sea

DANMARK

0 10 20 30 40 50 km

0 10 20 30 miles

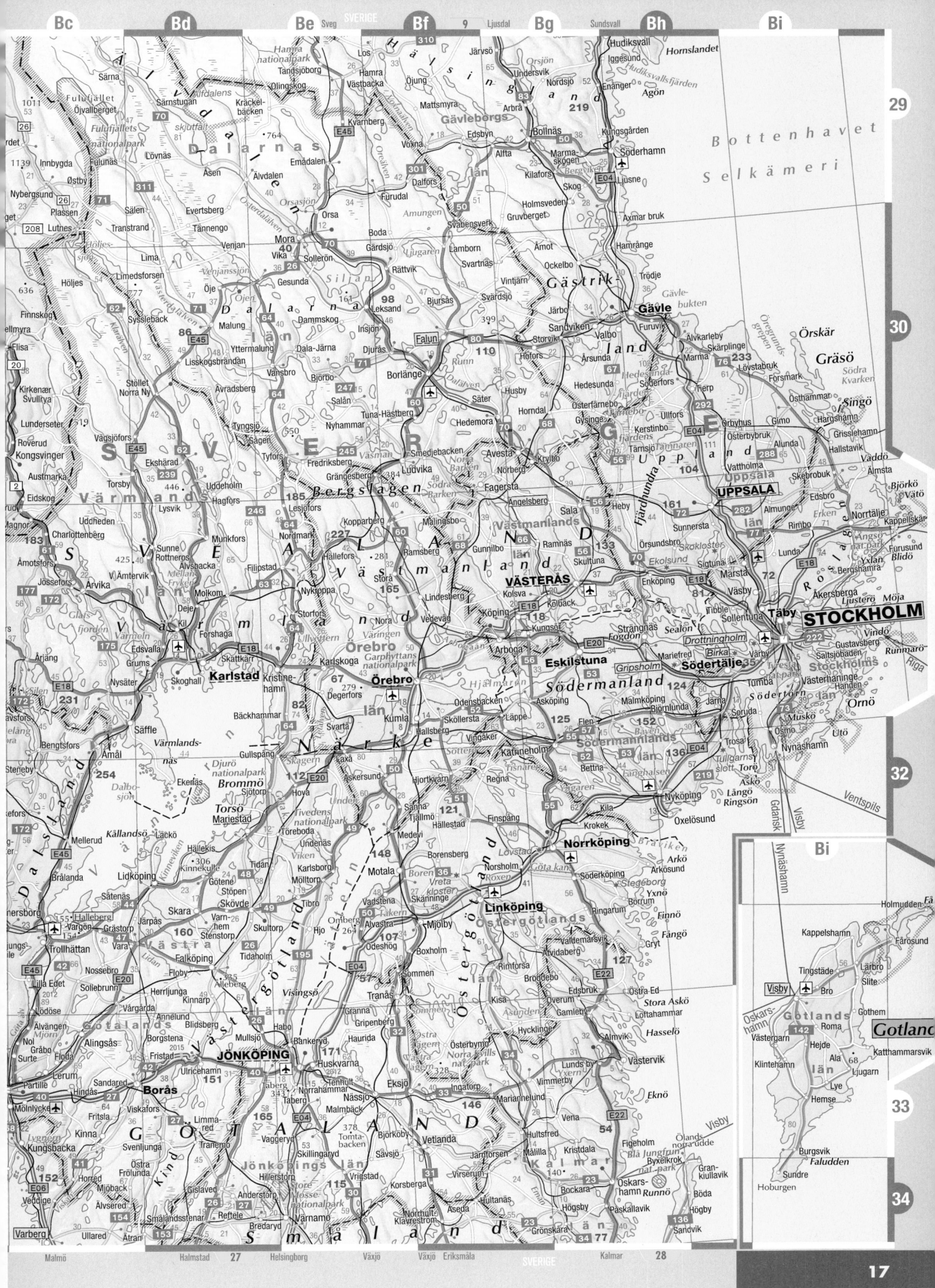

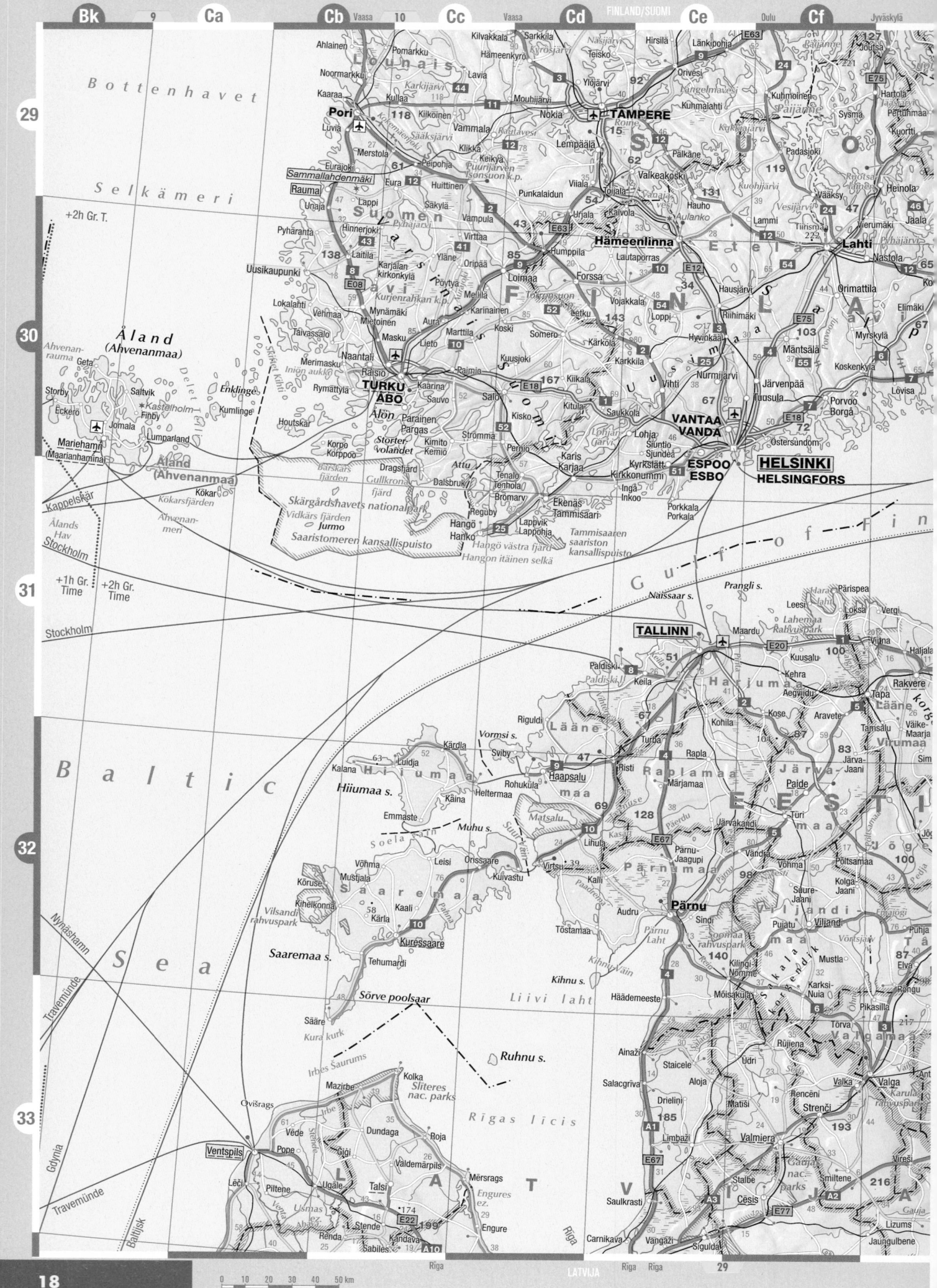

Bottenhavet

Selkämeri

+2h Gr. T.

29

Ahlainen
Pomarkku
Kilvakkala
Sarkkila
Nässjärvi
Hirsilä
Länkipohja
E63
127
Joutsa
Noormarkku
Löunais-
Hämeenkyrö
Kyrösjärvi
Teisko
221
Bak...
Kullaa
Lavia
Mouhijärvi
3
Ylöjärvi
92
Orivesi
Kuhmoinen
24
Hartola
Pertumaa
Kaaraa
Karkijärvi
118
44
Nokia
TAMPERE
Pälkäne
Padasjoki
Kuortti
Pori
118
Kilköinen
11
15
Roine
12
Kykkusjärvi
Päijänne
Sysmä
Luvia
Vammala
Lempäälä
62
119
Merstola
Klikka
Keikyä
78
Valkeakoski
Hauho
Aulanko
Lammi
Tiirismaa
Heinola
Eurajoki
Peipohja
Puurijärven
Viiala
222
12
50
Lahti
46
Sammallahdenmäki
Eura
12
Huittinen
Toijala
131
39
24
47
Jaala
Rauma
Säkylä
Punkalaidun
54
Hämeenlinna
12
65
Unaja
47
Lappi
Vampula
2
Urjala
E63
Hausjärvi
44
Orimattila
Pyhäranta
43
Virttaa
50
Humppila
Lautaporras
10
Riihimäki
103
Elimäki
Hinnerjoki
41
Yläne
85
Loimaa
Forssa
143
54
Loppi
25
Mäntsälä
67
138
Laitila
Oripää
52
Hyvinkää
55
Koskenkylä
8
Karjalan
kirkonkylä
Pöytyä
Melillä
Vojakkala
34
17
Nurmijärvi
4
7
Uusikaupunki
E08
Kurjenrahkan k.p.
Aura
Karinainen
Somero
Kärkölä
Karkkila
Järvenpää
Lövisa
Lokalahti
59
Mynämäki
Masku
Marttila
Koski
Kuusjoki
Vihti
38
67
50
Tuusula
22
Porvoo
Vehmaa
Mietoinen
10
Lieto
Kiikala
Saukkola
Borgå
Täivassalo
Raisio
Kaarina
Salo
167
1
Lohja
E18
Merimasku
Naantali
Sauvo
Kisko
Kitula
69
Siuntio
VANTAA
Östersundom
Rymättylä
TURKU
Paraine
52
Pernio
Karjaa
Sjundeå
VANDA
Houtskär
ÅBO
Ålön
Pargas
Strömma
Karis
Kirkkonummi
51
ESPOO
Iniön
Kimito
Tenala
Kyrkslätt
ESBO
HELSINKI
Korpo
Kemiö
Attu
Tenhola
Ekenäs
Inkoo
Porkkala
HELSINGFORS
Korppoo
Storter-
Dragsfjärd
Brömarv
Tammisaari
Inga
Porkala
volandet
Dalsbruk
Barskärs
Gullkrona
Reguby
fjärden
Vidkärs fjärden
fjärd
Jurmo
Lappvik
Skärgårdshavets nationalpark
Hangö
25
Lappohja
Tammisaaren
Saaristomeren kansallispuisto
Hanko
saariston
Hangö västra fjärd
kansallispuisto
Hangon itäinen selkä

Åland
(Ahvenanmaa)
Ahvenan-
rauma
Geta
Storby
Saltvik
Eckerö
Kastelholm
Finby
Jomala
Lumparland
Mariehamn
(Maarianhamina)
Åland
(Ahvenanmaa)
Ahvenan-
meri
Kappelskär
Ålands
Hav
Stockholm
Ålands
Meri

30

31

+1h Gr.
Time
+2h Gr.
Time

Stockholm

Gulf of Fin

Prangli s.
Pärispea
Naissaar s.
Leesi
Loksa
Vergi
Harak...
Lahemaa
TALLINN
Maardu
Rahvuspark
E20
Kuusalu
100
Viinistu
Paldiski
51
8
Keila
Kehra
16
Haljala
Paldiski lj.
26
Harjuma
41
Aegviidu
Tapa
Rakvere
Riguldi
67
Kose
Kohila
Aravete
5
Lääne
Tamsalu
Kärdla
Vormsi s.
18
Turba
Rapla
4
87
83
Väike-
52
Luidja
Sviby
47
9
Risti
Raplamaa
46
Järva-
Maarja
63
Haapsalu
4
Rapla
Jaani
Sim
Kalana
Hiiumaa
Rohuküla
Märjamaa
128
38
Järvakandi
Paide
Kaina
Heltermaa
69
Türi
23
Hiiumaa s.
maa
10
Lihula
E67
Pärnu-
Jaagupi
Vändra
17
Põltsamaa
100
Emmaste
Muhu s.
24
Kasa
Päerdu
80
98
Soela
Virtsu
39
Suure-
Jaani
Kolga-
Jaani
43
Võhma
Leisi
Orissaare
Kalli
Pärnumaa
Mustla
Vôhma
Kuivastu
Pärnu
Viljandi
Kõruse
58
Kärla
10
Audru
Sindi
140
Pujatu
Viljandi
Võrtsjärv
76
Kihelkonna
Kaali
Sakala
Pühajärvi
Vilsandi
Saaremaa
Mõisaküla
korgendik
87
rahvuspark
Kuressaare
Tõstamaa
Pärnu
Kilingi-
Elva
Tehumardi
Laht
Nõmme
4
Rõngu
Saaremaa s.
30
Karksi-
Nuia
Pikasilla
Sõrve poolsaar
Liivi laht
Häädemeeste
28
Törva
Valga...
3
217
Sääre
Kihnu s.
Rüjiena
Valga
Kura kurk
Irbes Šaurums
Ruhnu s.
Ainaži
Karula
Kolka
Staicele
Udri
rahvuspark
Mazirbe
Sliteres
Salacgriva
Aloja
Rencēni
Strenči
Drielini
Matiši
nac. parks
Ovišrags
Rigas līcis
A1
185
Kolka
Limbaži
Valmiera
193
Vēde
Irbe
Dundaga
Roja
Stalbe
Vangaži
Gauja
Pope
L
Piltene
35
nac.
Smiltene
Leči
Ugale
A
Valdemārpils
26
Mērsrags
parks
Cēsis
E77
Ventspils
Gigi
Talsi
29
T
Saulkrasti
A2
216
Usmas
174
V
Engures
Stende
E22
199
Kandava
ez.
A
Sabiles
A10
Engure
Carnikava
Vangaži
Siguldā
Lizums

32

33

Baltic

Sea

Nynäshamn

Travemünde

Gdynia

Baltijsk

Riga   Rīga   Rīga   29

LATVIJA

0   10   20   30   40   50 km
0   10   20   30 miles

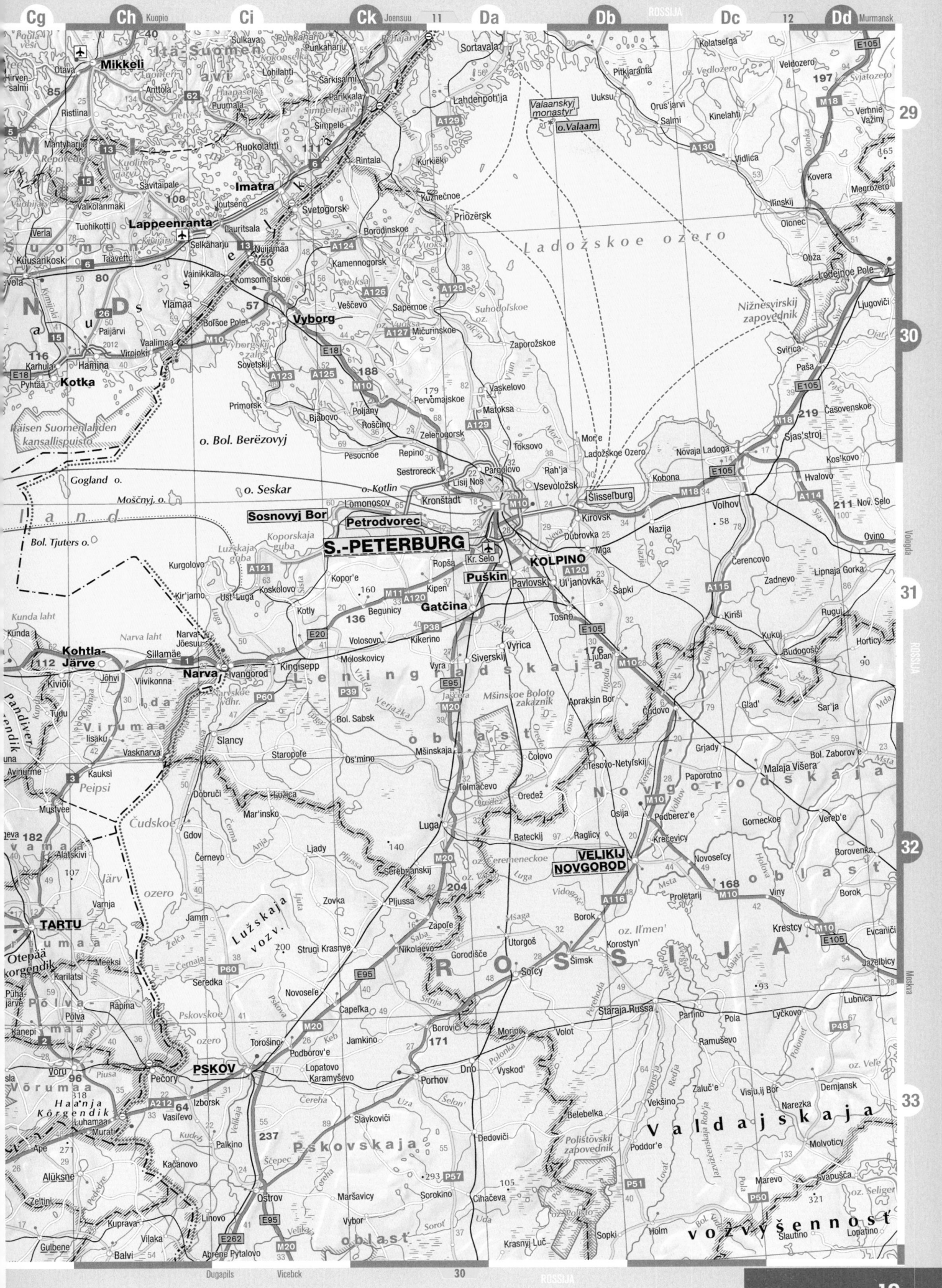

29
30
31
32
33

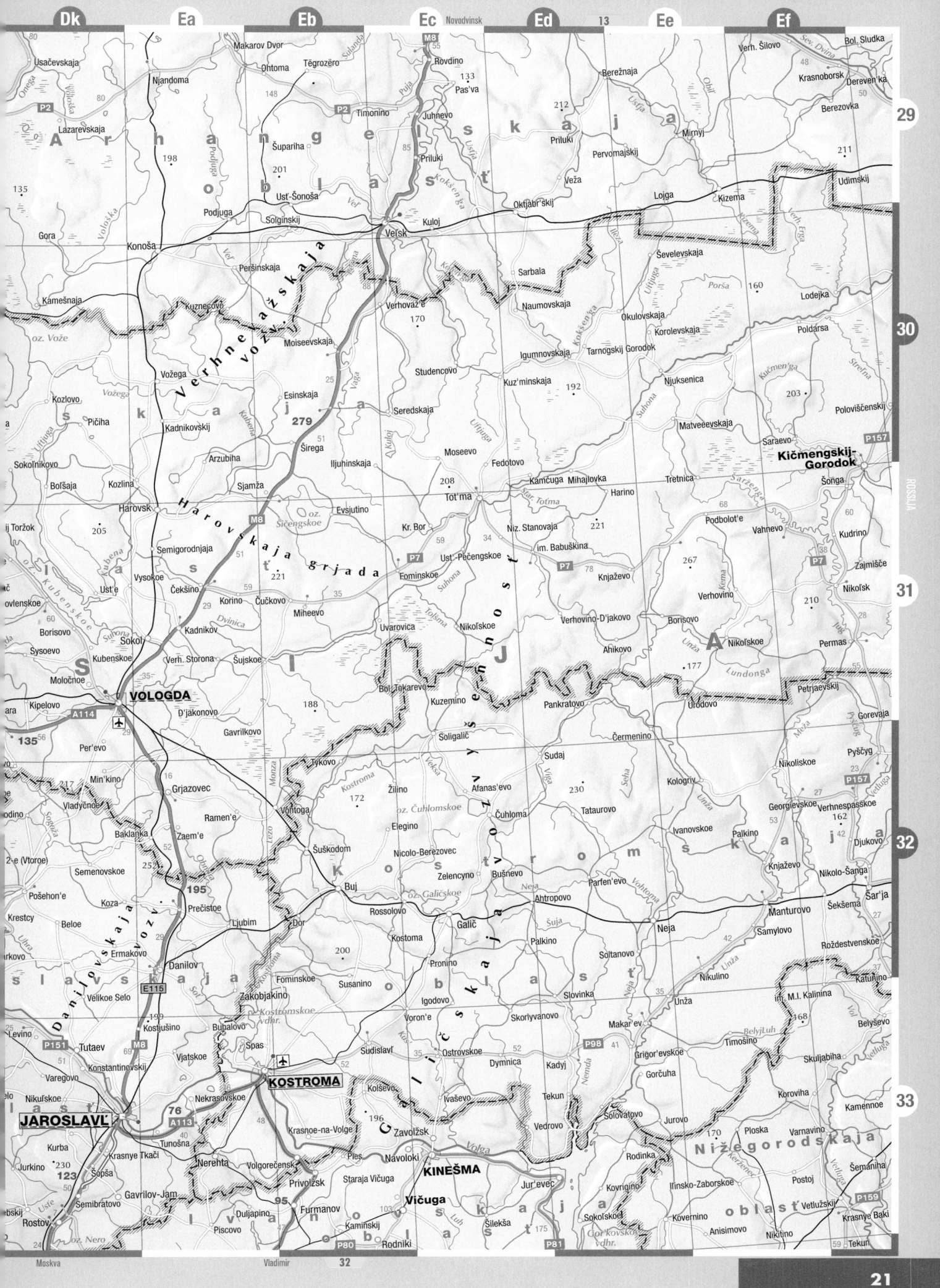

Novodvinsk

**Arhangel'skaja oblast'**

Usačevskaja
80
Omega
P2
Lazarevskaja
135
Gora
Kamešnaja
oz. Vože
Kozlovo
Sokol'nikovo
Bol'šaja
Pičiha
ij Toržok
205
Ust'e
Harovsk
Semigorodnjaja
Vysokoe
Čekšino
Kadnikovskij
Arzubiha
Sjamža
Evsjutino

Makarov Dvor
Njandoma
198
Ohtoma
Tëgrzëro
148
Šupariha
201
Podjuga
Solginskij
Konoša
Peršinskaja
Kuznecovo
Moiseevskaja
Vožega
Vožega
Esinskaja
279
Širega
51
Iljuhinskaja
Kadnikovskij
221
Korino
Čučkovo
Miheevo

M8
55
Rovdino
Juhnevo
133
Pas'va
Priluki
85
Kuloj
Vel'sk
Verhovaž'e
170
Studencovo
Seredskaja
Moseevo
208
Tot'ma
Kr. Bor
P7
Ust'-Pečengskoe
Fominskoe
35
Uvarovica
Nikol'skoe

Timonino
P2
Priluki
Veža
Oktjabr'skij
Naumovskaja
Igumnovskaja
Kuz'minskaja
Fedotovo
Kamčuga Mihajlovka
59
34
Niz. Stanovaja
im. Babuškina
Knjaževo
Verhovino-D'jakovo
Ahikovo
Bol. Tokarevo
Kuzemino

Berežnaja
Pervomajskij
Sarbala
Ševelevskaja
Tarnogskij Gorodok
192
Njuksenica
Matveeevskaja
Harino
221
78
P7
267
Verhovino
Borisovo
A Nikol'skoe
177

212
Mirnyj
Porša
160
Okulovskaja
Korolevskaja
Saraevo
68
Podbolot'e
Vahnevo
Lundonga
Uródovo

Verh. Šilovo
48
Krasnoborsk
Lojga
Kizema
Udimskij
211
Lodejka
Poldarsa
203
Polovščenskij
**Kičmengskij-Gorodok**
Šonga
60
Kudrino
P7
38
Zajmišče
Nikol'sk
210
Permas
55
Petriaevskij
Gorevaja

Sev. Dvina
Bol. Sludka
Derevén'ka
50
Berezovka
29
30
RUSSIJA
P157
31

M8
Harovskaja grjada
S
VOLOGDA
A114
Kadnikov
Verh. Storona
Šujskoe
188
Kipelovo
135
56
Per'evo
29
217
Min'kino
16
Vladyčnoe
Baklanka
52
Semenovskoe
25
Pošehon'e
Koza
Krestcy
Beloe
Ermakovo
Danilov
E115
Velikoe Selo
199
Kostjušino
P151
Tutaev
69
M8
Konstantinovskij
Varegovo
Nikul'skoe
Levino
Kurba
Jurkino
230
Šopša
50
Rostov
24
oz. Nero
Semibratovo

Soligalič
Tykovo
Žilino
172
Vohtoga
Ramen'e
Zaem'e
195
Prečistoe
Ljubim
Dor
200
Fominskoe
Zakobjakino
Bunalovo
Spas
Vjatskoe
Sudaj
Afanas'evo
Čuhloma
oz. Čuhlomskoe
Elegino
Nicolo-Berezovec
Zelencyno
Bušnevo
Buj
Rossolovo
Galič
oz. Galičskoe
Kostoma
Pronino
Susanino
Igodovo
Voron'e
Sudislavl
123
Tunošna
Krasny Tkači
Nerehta
Volgorečensk
Privolzsk
95
Duljapino
Piscovo
Kamiński
P80
Rodniki

**KOSTROMA**
A113
76
40
Nekrasovskoe
48
Krasnoe-na-Volge
196
Zavolzsk
Ples
Navoloki
Staraja Vičuga
Kolševo
Ivaševo
**KINEŠMA**
**Vičuga**
Šilekša
103
175

Čermenino
230
Sudaj
Viga
Seha
Kologriv
Tataurovo
Ivanovskoe
Palkino
Parfen'evo
Ahtropovo
Palkino
Šuja
Neja
Soltanovo
Skorlyvanovo
35
Ostrovskoe
Dymnica
Kadyj
Tekun
Vedrovo
Solovatovo
Jurovo
Jur'evec
Kovrigino
Rodinka
 Il'insko-Zaborskoe
Sokol'skoe
Gor'kovskoj vdhr.
Kovernino
Anisimovo

Nikoliskoe
Pyščyg
P157
27
Georgievskoe
Verhnespasskoe
162
53
42
Djukovo
Knjaževo
Nikolo-Šanga
Manturovo
Šeksema
27
Neja
42
Samylovo
Roždestvenskoe
Nikulino
Unža
im. M.I. Kalinina
168
Belyševo
Makar'ev
P98
41
Timošino
Grigor'evskoe
Gorčuha
Korovina
Kamennoe
Skuljabiha
Ploska
Varnavino
170
**Nižegorodskaja**
Postoj
Šemanīha
P159
**oblast'**
Vetlužskij
59
Tekun

s l a v s k a j a    o b l a s t'
**JAROSLAVL'**

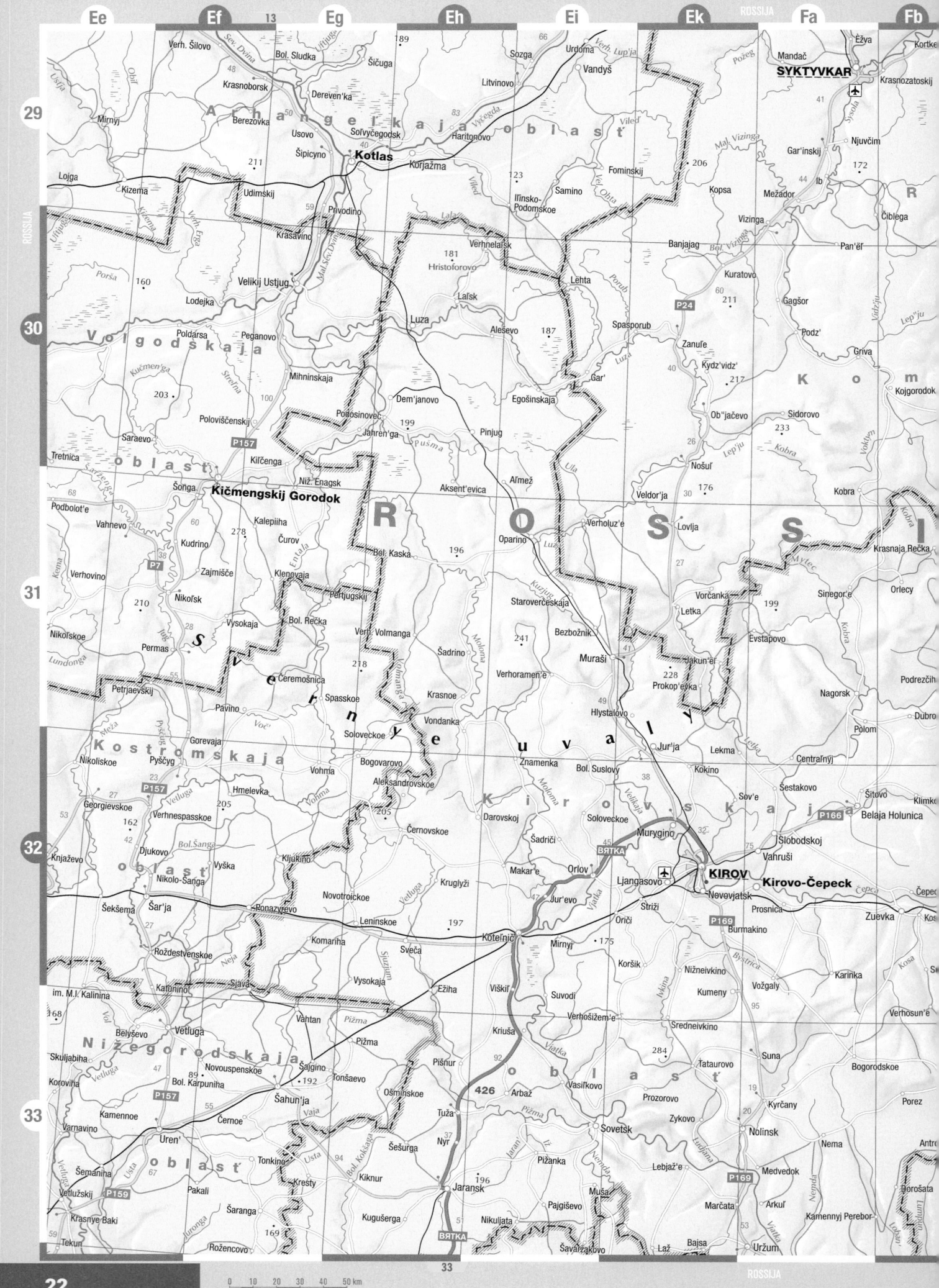

29

ROSSIJA

30

31

32

33

ROSSIJA

33

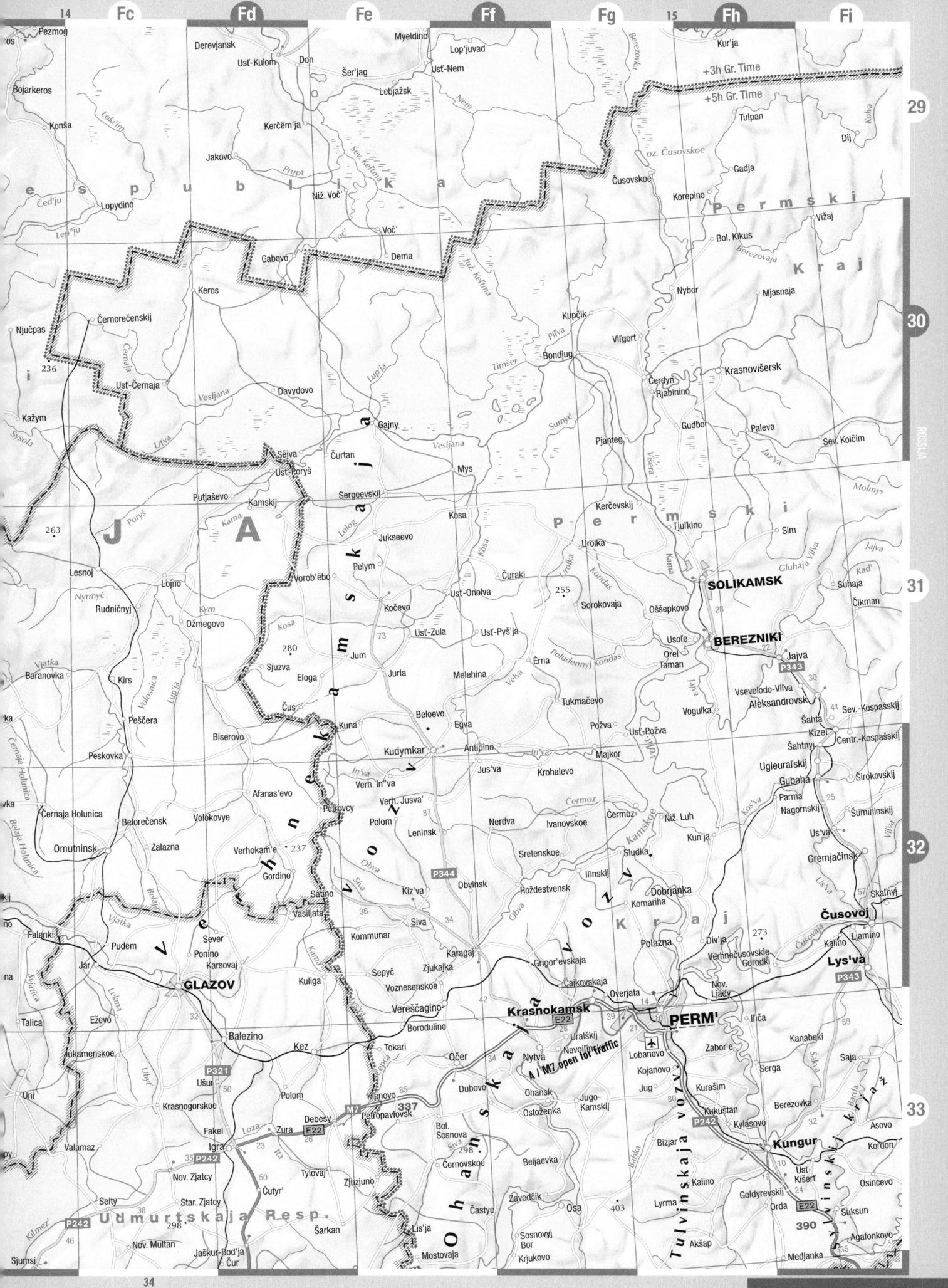

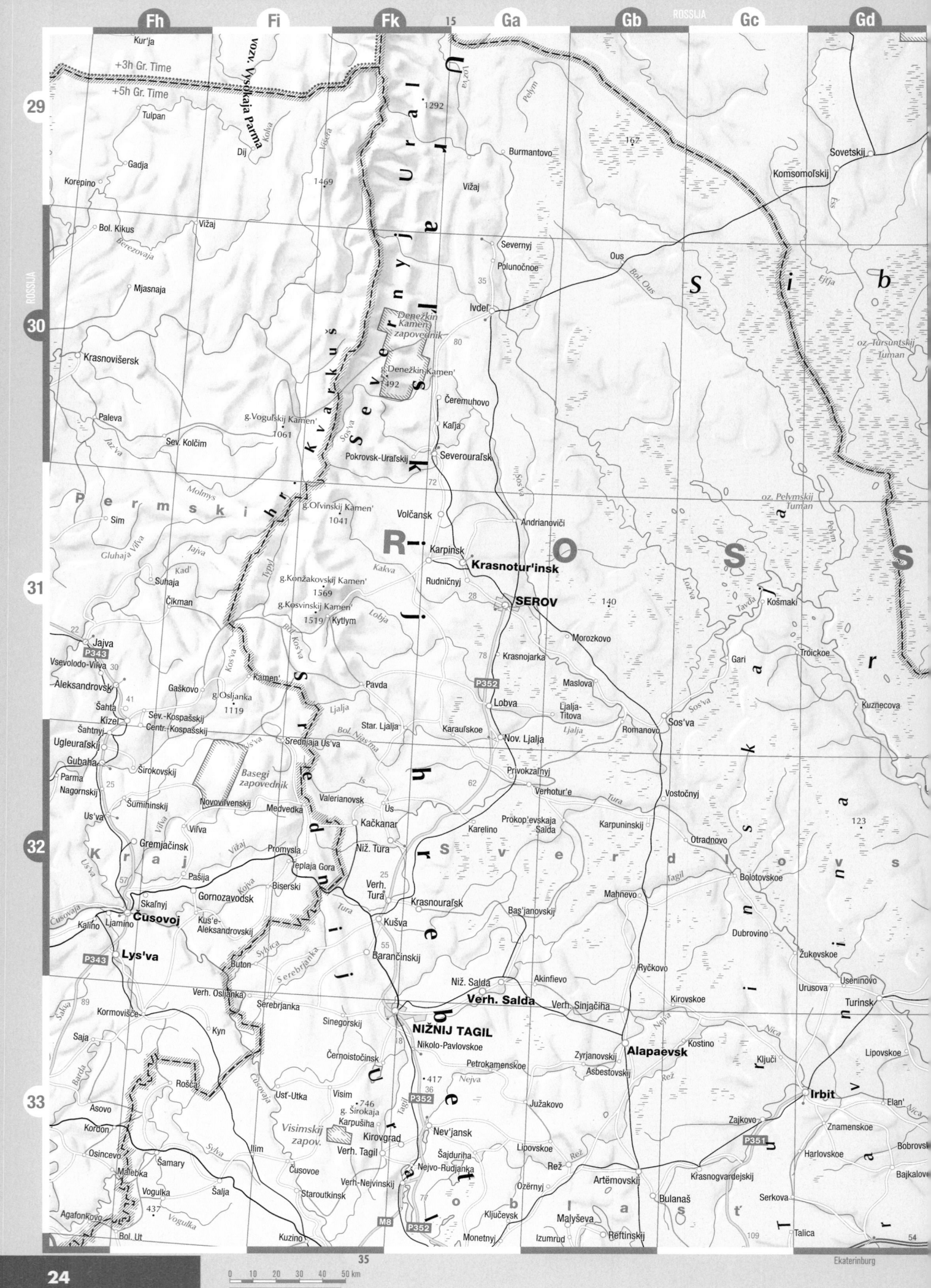

29

+3h Gr. Time
+5h Gr. Time

vozv. Vysokaja parma

Kur'ja

Tulpan

Gadja

Dij

1292

Korepino

Vižaj

Burmantovo

167

Sovetskij

Komsomoľskij

Bol. Kikus

Vižaj

1469

Severnyj

Polunočnoe

Ous

ROSSIJA

Mjasnaja

Ivdeľ

35

Bol. Ous

S   i   b

oz. Türsùntskij
Tuman

Ejtja

30

Krasnovišersk

Denežkin
Kamen'
zapovednik

80

Denežkin Kamen'

492

Čeremuhovo

Kalja

Paleva

g. Vogulskij Kamen'
1061

Sev. Kolčim

Pokrovsk-Uraľskij

Severouraľsk

oz. Pelymskij
Tuman

Sim

g. Olvinskij Kamen'
1041

Volčansk

Andrianoviči

O

S

S

Suhaja

g. Konžakovskij Kamen'
1569
g. Kosvinskij Kamen'
1519

Čikman

Karpinsk

Rudničnyj

Krasnotur'insk

R

Košmaki

31

22

Jajva

Vsevolodo-Vilva

30

Kytlym

28

SEROV

140

Gari

Troickoe

Kuznecova

Aleksandrovsk

Gaškovo

Kamen'

Pavda

78

Krasnojarka

Morozkovo

Šahta

41

g. Osljanka
1119

Ljalja

Lobva

Maslova

Kizel

Sev.-Kospašskij

Srednjaja Us'va

Star. Ljalja

Karauľskoe

Ljalja-
Titova

Romanovo

Sos'va

Šahtnyj

Centr. Kospašskij

Nov. Ljalja

Ugleuraľskij

Gubaha

Širokovskij

Basegi
zapovednik

Valerianovsk

Us

Privokzaľnyj

Verhotur'e

62

Vostočnyj

Parma
Nagornskij

25

Šumihinskij

Medvedka

Kačkanar

Karelino

Prokop'evskaja
Salda

Karpuninskij

Otradnovo

123

Us'va

Viľva

Novovilvenskij

Niž. Tura

32

57

Gremjačinsk

Promysla

Teplaja Gora

25

Bolotovskoe

Pašija

Verh.
Tura

Mahnevo

Gornozavodsk

Biserski

Krasnouraľsk

Baš'janovskij

Dubrovino

Skaľnyj

Kuš'e-
Aleksandrovskij

Kušva

55

Žukovskoe

Čusovoj

Kaliňo

Ljamino

Buton

Barančinskij

Ryčkovo

Useninovo

Lys'va

Niž. Salda

Akinfievo

Kirovskoe

Urusova

Verh. Osljanka

Serebrjanka

Verh. Salda

Verh. Sinjačiha

Turinsk

33

Kormovišče

89

Sinegorskij

NIŽNIJ TAGIL

Zyrjanovskij

Kostino

Ključi

Lipovskoe

Saja

Kyn

Černoistočinsk

Nikolo-Pavlovskoe

Alapaevsk

Asovo

Rošča

Visim

417
36

Petrokamenskoe

Asbestovskij

Južakovo

Irbit

Kordon

Usť-Utka

746
g. Širokaja

Karpušiha

Nev'jansk

Lipovskoe

Zajkovo

Elan'

Znamenskoe

Osincevo

Visimskij
zapov.

Kirovgrad

Rež

Harlovskoe

Malebka

Čusovoe

Verh. Tagil

Šajduriha

Rež

Krasnogvardejskij

Bobrovsk

Šamary

Ilim

Verh-Nejvinskij

Nejvo-Rudjanka

Ozërnyj

Artëmovskij

Serkova

Vogulka

Šalja

437

Staroutkinsk

Ključevsk

Malyševa

Bulanaš

Bajkalovo

Agafonkovo

Kuzino

Monetnyj

Izumrud

Reftinskij

109

Talica

Bol. Ut

35

Ekaterinburg

0  10  20  30  40  50 km

0  10  20  30 miles

zapovednik
Mal. Sos'va

vozv. Belogorskij materik

Konda

H a n t y - m a n s i j s k i j

Njalinskoe
Zenkovo

P404
Hanty-Mansijsk
Surgut

oz. Ajtor

Seul

Irtyš

i  r  s  k  a  j  a     j  a

97. k

oz. Endra
Tjuli
Mal. Salym

a  v  t .     o  k  r  u  g

oz. Syrkovo

RUSSIJA
101

K  o  n  d  i  n  s  k  a  j  a        a

Mulym'ja

Bol. Tap

Šugur
Kama
oz. Ènstor
Čingaly

Jakonda

Uraj
Surgut

Mugen

Konda
Dem'janskoe

L          J          A
Kondinskoe
Dem'janka

oz. Leušinskij Tuman
Katym

Meždurečenskij

118
Uvat

K o n d a        a  v  n  i  n  a

Konda

Turtas

Černaja
n  i  ž  m  e  n  n  o  s  t ,

Kuma

Volčim'ja
Turtas

že-Pavinskoe
Kuma
oz. Andreevskoe
Turtas
Turtas
Bol. Turtas

Kuminskij

Tavda
Noska
Mal. Turtas

k  a  j  a        j  a
Verchnefilatovo

Tabory
v  o  z  v  y  š  e  n  n  o  s  t '

Karabaška
T o b o r s k i j - m a t e r i k

Galkino
oz. Bol. Karas'e
Mendeleevo

Dobrino
Tobol'sk
8

Belojarka
Kuškurgul'
Sumkino
Irtyš
Karelina
Dubrovnoe
Bol. Karagaj

Saragulka  Azanka  Tavda  Gerasimovka
Lajma
Vagaj
Polino-Ašlyk

Košuki
T j u m e n s k a j a
Tobol
P404
oz. Bol. Šyšarym

Žirjakovo
Turnaeva
Toboltura
63
Vagaj

Tura
Tavda
Bajkalovo
Čeburga
Čërnoe

104
Bačelino
40
oz. Kondan
Ašlyk
Syčevo

Turinskaja
Sloboda
Niž. Tavda
o  b  l  a  s  t '
Ašlyk
Kordon

Ahmany
Iska
Ievlevo
Šestovoe
Tuhuzskij
zakaznik

Ust'-Nicinskoe
20
Bor
Lajmy

oz. Bol. Uvat

Jarkovo
Karbany

Kamenka
Tjunevo
Pokrovskoe
106
Tap
Novopetrovo

P351
Jar  Kaskara
Sozonevo
Tura
Tapovskij
zakaznik
Novotapovskij
zakaznik
Malinovka

Tjumen'
Ekaterinburg  Kurgan
P404
P404

29

30

31

32

33

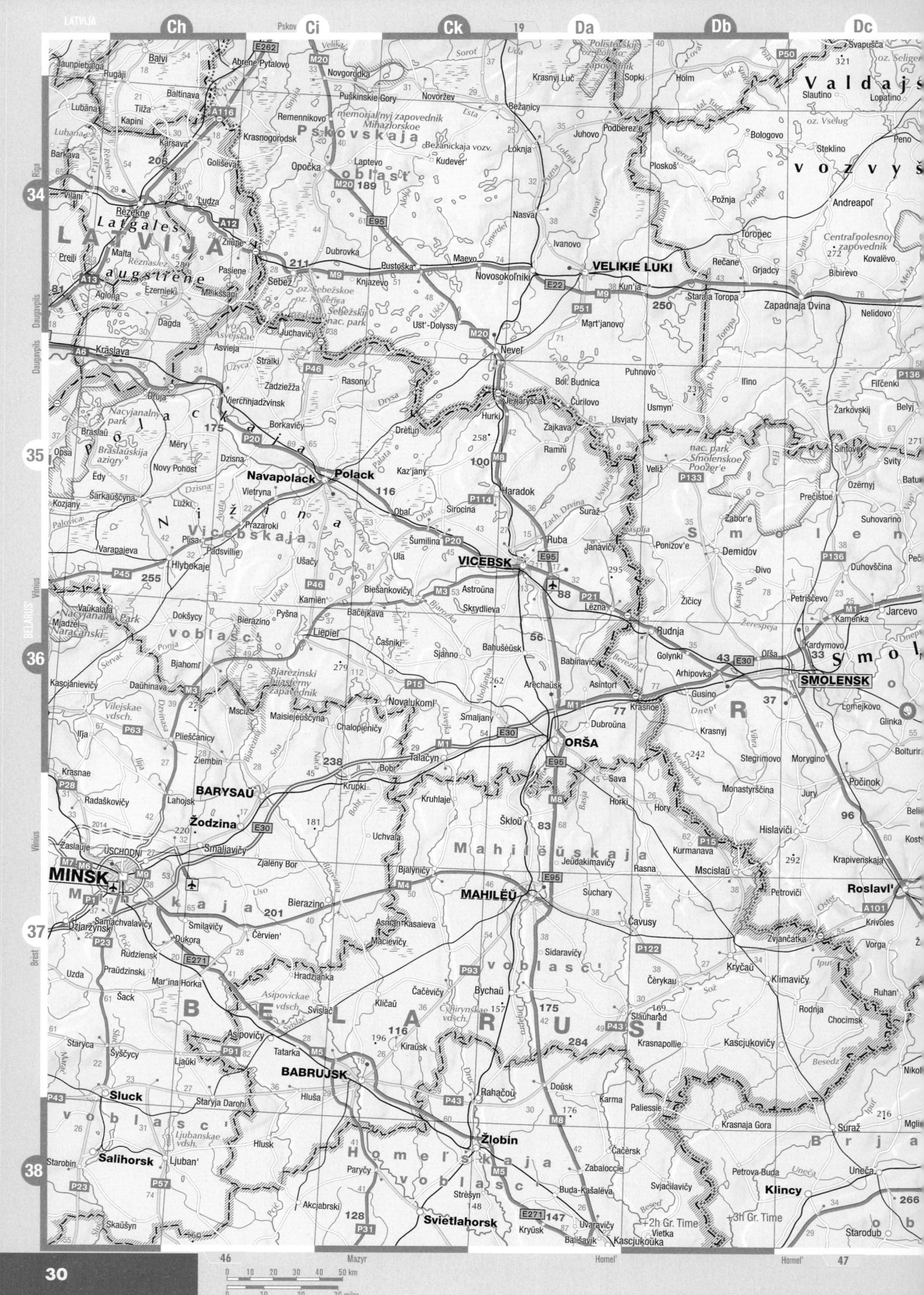

34
35
36
37
38

46          Mazyr          Homel'          Homel'     47

0   10   20   30   40   50 km
0        10        20        30 miles

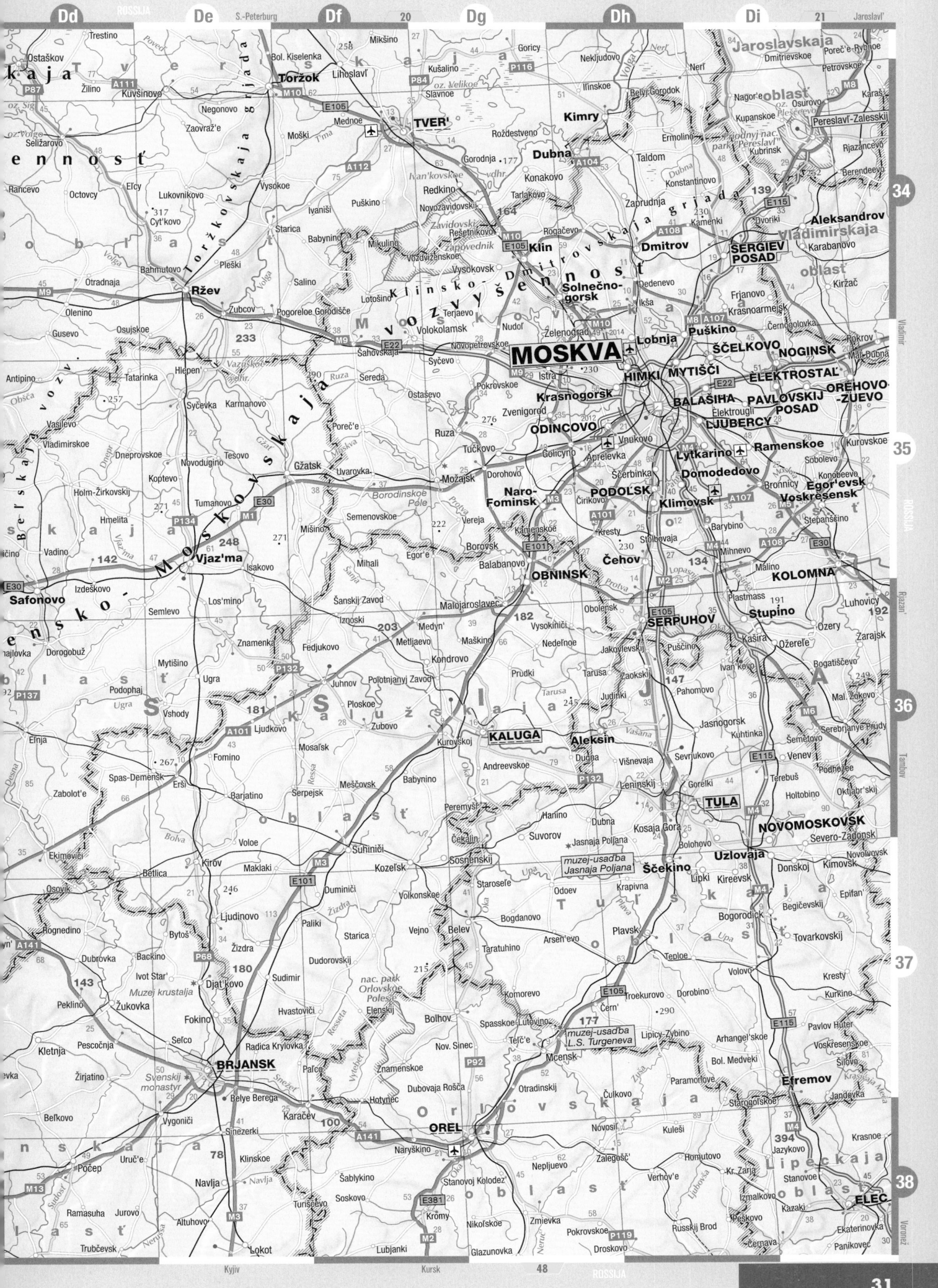

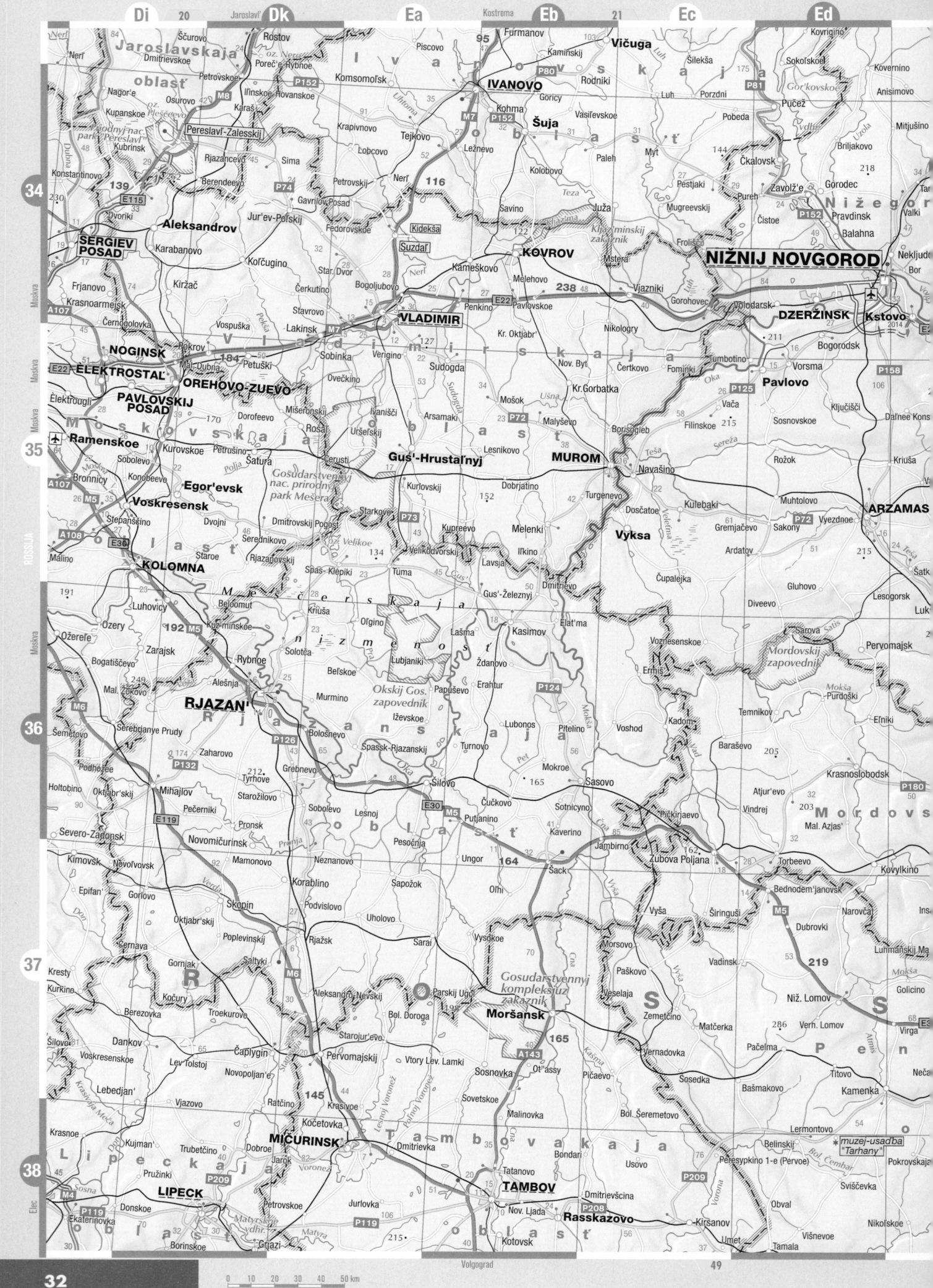

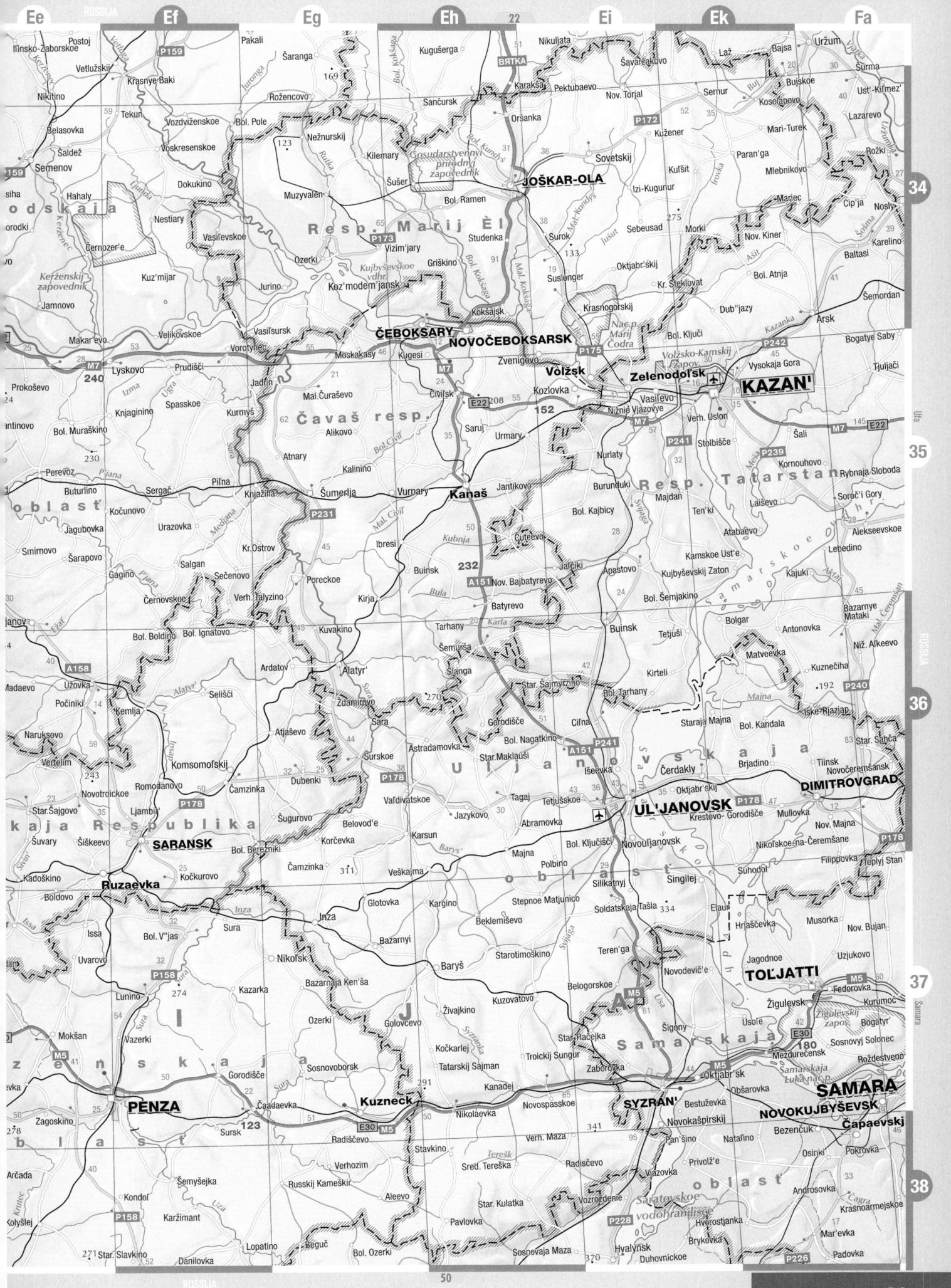

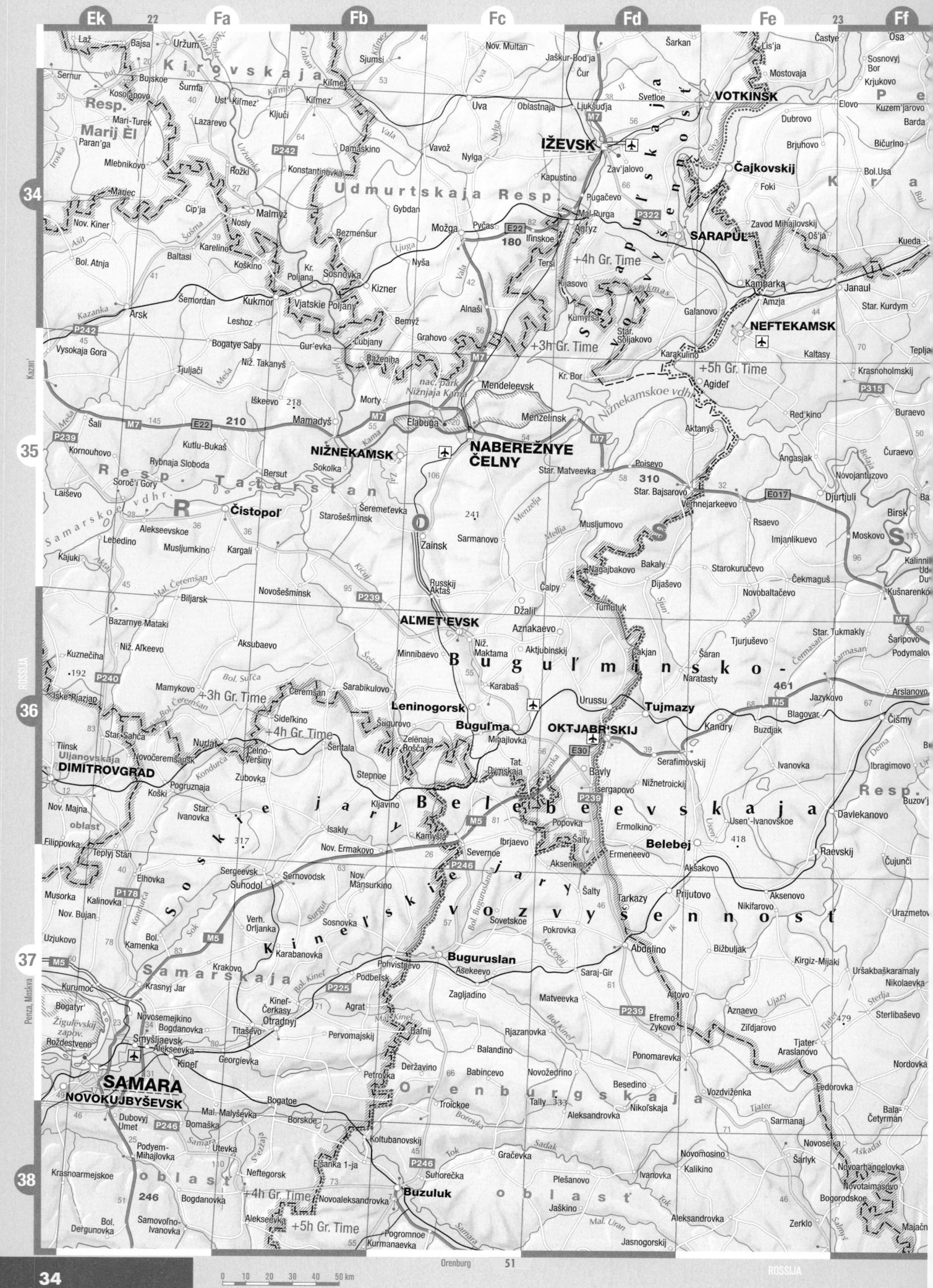

Orenburg 51

0 10 20 30 40 50 km
0 10 20 30 miles

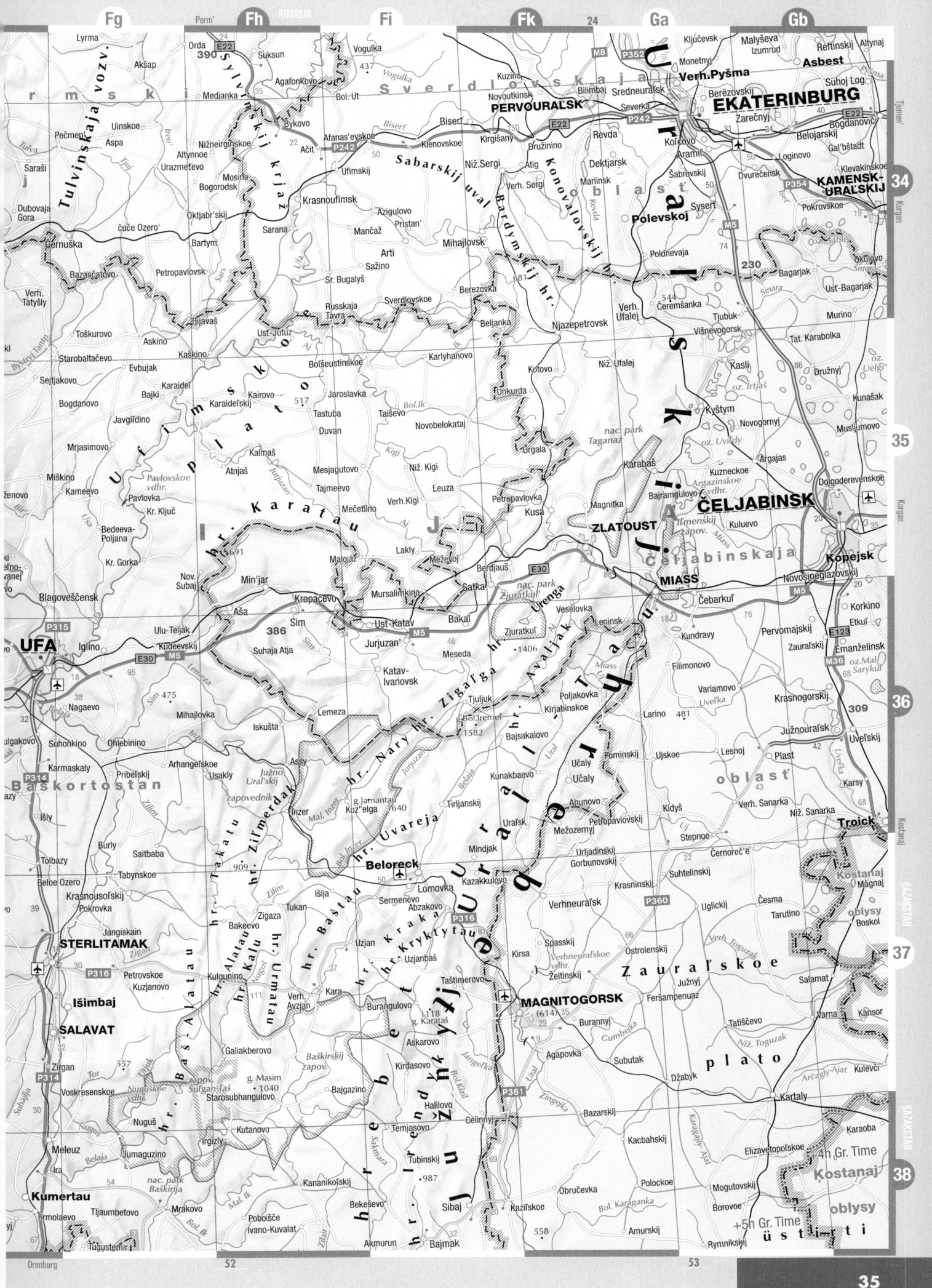

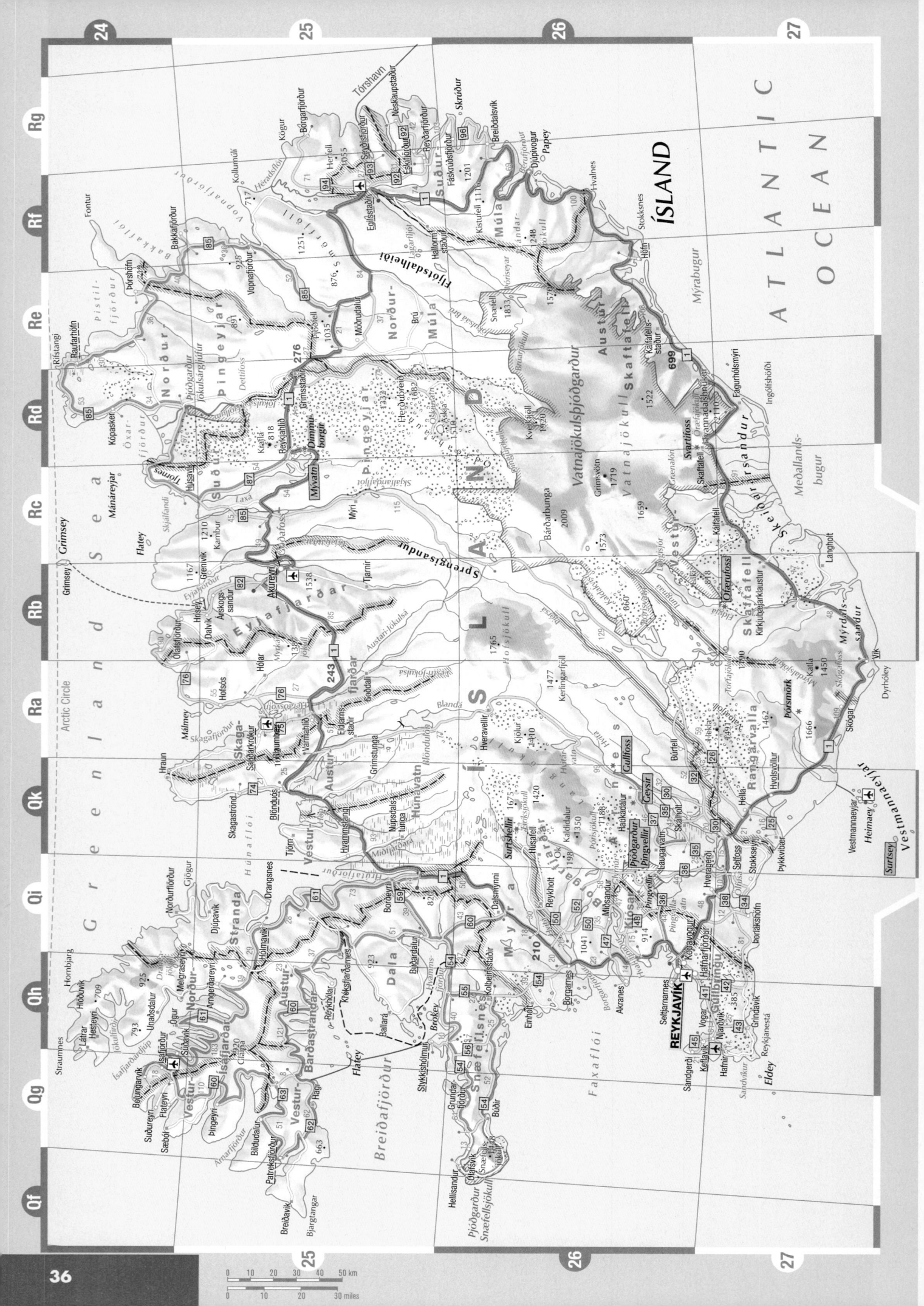

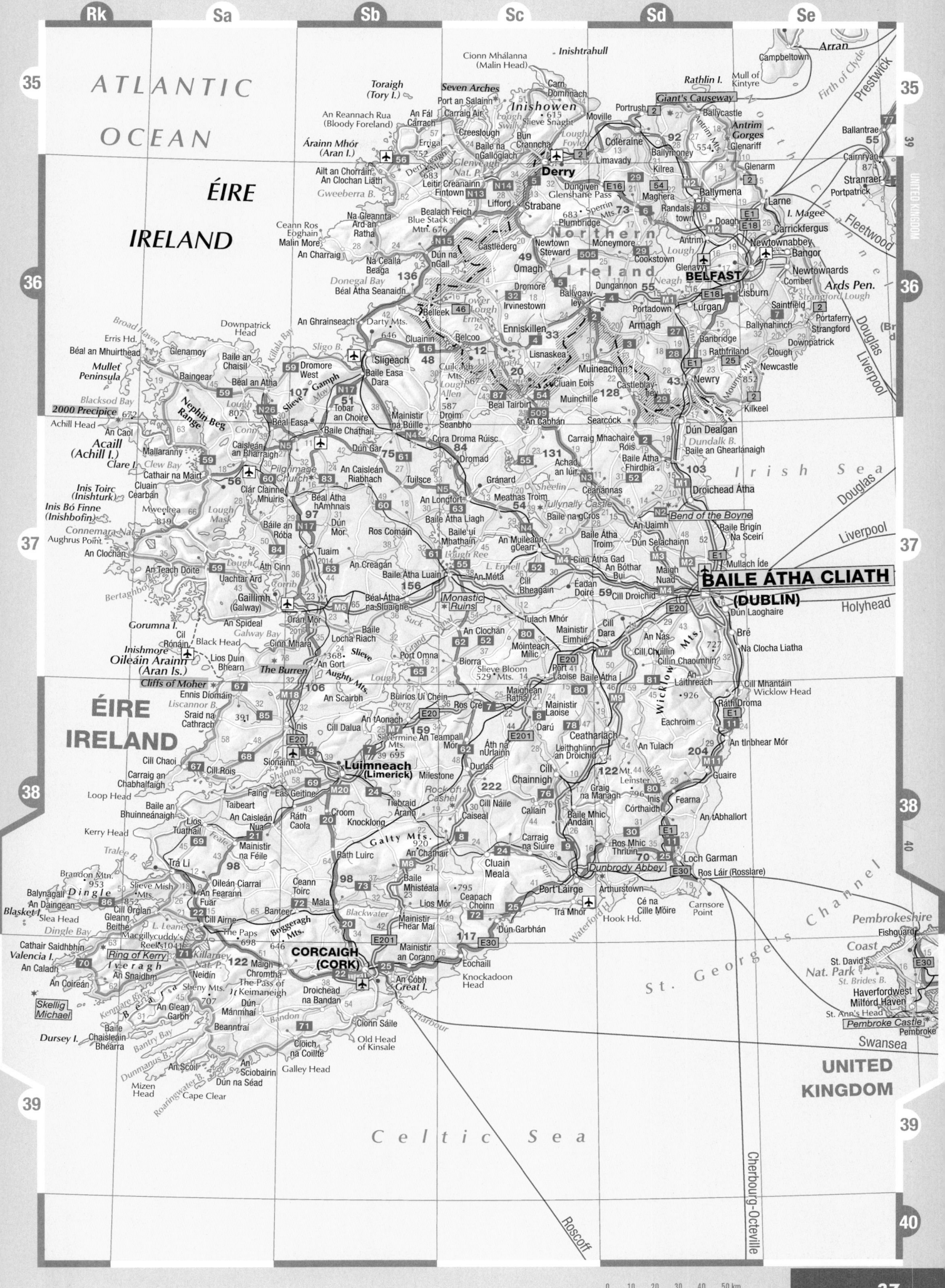

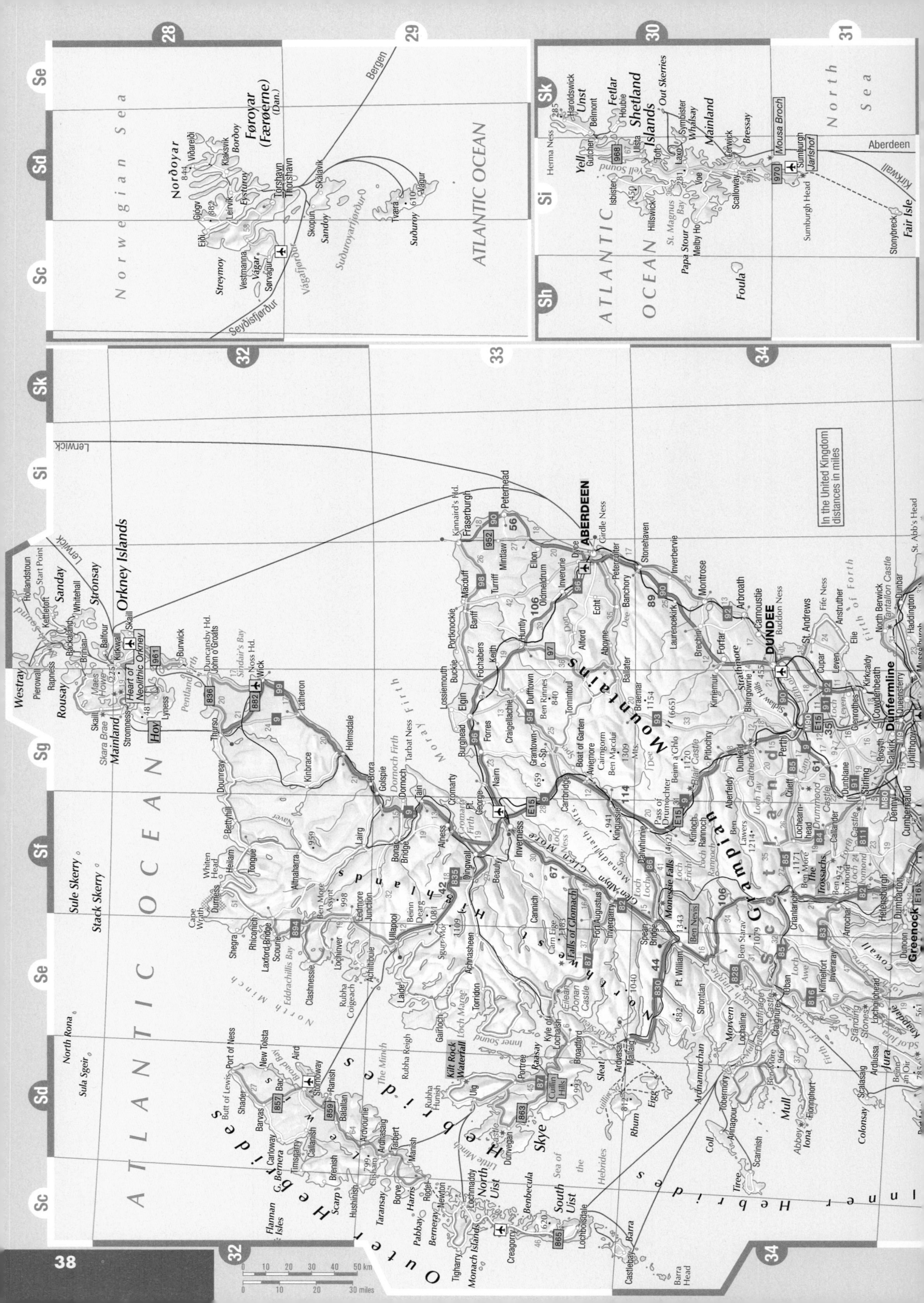

**28**

N o r w e g i a n   S e a

Norðoyar
Viðareiði
844
Eiði
Gjógv
882
Klaksvík
Borðoy
Leirvík
Eysturoy
Streymoy
Vestmanna
Vágar
59
Sørvágur
Tórshavn
Thorshavn
Skopun
Sandoy
Skálavík

Foroyar
(Færøerne)
(Dan.)

Bergen

ATLANTIC OCEAN

**29**

Suðuroyarfjørður
Tvøra
Vágafjørður
Skúvoy
610
Suðuroy

ATLANTIC OCEAN

Seyðisfjørður

**30**

**Sk**
Herma Ness
285
Haroldswick
Unst
Fetlar
Hubie
Belmont
Gutcher
Out Skerries
Yell
968
Shetland
Islands
Isbister
450
Ulsta
Symbister
Mainland
Toft
2931
Lago
Lerwick
Voe
Whalsay
Bressay
Scalloway
291
Mousa Broch
970
Sumburgh
Jarlshof
Sumburgh Head

St. Magnus
Bay
Papa Stour
Hillswick
Melby Ho
Stour

Foula

**Si**

A T L A N T I C

O C E A N

**31**

N o r t h   S e a

Aberdeen

Kirkwall

Stonybreck
Fair Isle

**Sh**

---

**32**

Lerwick

Orkney Islands

Westray
Pierowall
Rousay
Rapness
Sanday
Stronsay
Hollandstoun
Start Point
Kettletoft
Whitehall
Backaland
Balfour
Brinian
Kirkwall
961
Mainland
Stromness
Skara Brae
Skaill
Maes
Howe
Heart of
Neolithic Orkney
481
Hoy
Burwick
Lyness
Pentland Firth
Duncansby Hd.
John o' Groats
Noss Hd.
Sinclair's Bay
Wick
836
20
Thurso
882
9
99
Latheron

**Si**

**33**

Atlantic Ocean

**Sk**

**Sg**

North Rona
Sula Sgeir
Sule Skerry
Stack Skerry

Butt of Lewis
Port of Ness
New Tolsta
Aird
857
Shader
Barvas
Carloway
Stornoway
Bac
Ranish
859
Balallan
G. Bernera
Timsgarry
Callanish
Brenish
Scarp
Harris
Husinish
Tarbert
Manish
Rodel
Lochmaddy
North
Uist
Benbecula
Newton
Pabbay
Berneray

Outer Hebrides

**Sf**

Cape
Wrath
Durness
Whiten
Head
Hellam
Tongue
Bettyhill
Altnaharra
Rhiconich
Laxford Bridge
Scourie
Clashnessie
Ben More
Assynt
998
Lairg
Shegra
Loch Shin
Eddrachillis Bay
Ledmore
Junction
Elphin
Ullapool
Achiltibuie
Beinn
Dearg
1081
Inchnadamph
Loch
Maree
894
Sgurr Mór
1109
Garve
Strath-
carron

Dounreay
Naver
Forsinard
959
Kinbrace
Helmsdale
Brora
Golspie
Dornoch
Dornoch Firth
Bonar
Bridge
Ardgay
Tain
Tarbat Ness
Alness
Dingwall
835
42
18
Beauly
Muir of
Ord
Inverness
Cromarty
Cromarty
Firth
Ft.
George
Nairn
Moray
Firth

**Se**

North Minch
The Minch
Little
Minch
Sea of
the
Hebrides

Eddrachillis Bay
Gairloch
Rubha
Reidh
Torridon
Loch
Carron
Shieldaig
Applecross
Kyle of
Lochalsh
Kyleakin
Broadford
Sleat
Mallaig
Ardvasar

Rubha
Hunish
Uig
Raasay
Portree
Cuillin
Hills
993
Skye
863
87
Kilt Rock
Waterfall
Dunvegan
Castle
799

Inner
Sound

Eilean
Donan
Castle
Glen
Shiel
Falls of Glomach
Cannich
Camich
Spean
Bridge
Invergarry
Fort
Augustus

**Sd**

South
Uist
Lochboisdale
Barra
865
Castlebay
Barra Head
Creagorry
Tigharry
Monach Islands

Eriskay
620
Lochboisdale

Inner Hebrides

Tiree
Coll
Scarinish

Rhum
Eigg
811
812
Muck

Ardnamurchan
Tobermory
Mull
Iona
Abbey
Fionnphort
Colonsay
Scalasaig

Ardtoe
Strontian
Morvern
Lochaline
Loch
Linnhe
Craignure
Castle
Stalker
Oban
816
Kilninver
Seil
Easdale

---

**Scotland**

Grampian Mountains

ABERDEEN

Peterhead
Fraserburgh
Kinnaird's Hd.
18
90
952
56
Mintlaw
27
Ellon
20
106
Oldmeldrum
Inverurie
96
Dyce
Girdle Ness
Stonehaven
17
89
Banchory
Echt
Aboyne
Ballater
Alford
Dee
Don
42
39
Huntly
Keith
Portknockie
Buckie
Fochabers
Rothes
97
Dufftown
Ben Rinnes
840
Tomintoul
Craigellachie
95
Grantown-
o.-Sp.
659
Boat of Garten
Aviemore
Cairngorm
Ben Macdui
1309
Cairngorm
Mts.
Braemar
1154
(665)
33
Blair Castle
Pitlochry
Pass of
Drumochter
941
Dalwhinnie
Kingussie
114
E15
Loch
Ericht
Kinloch
Rannoch
Loch
Rannoch
Aberfeldy
Loch Tay
Ben
Lawers
1214
Crianlarich
Callander
The
Trossachs
Loch
Lomond
974
Ben More
1171
82
Loch
Katrine
Aberdeen
2931

Dufftown
95
E15
Aviemore
Carrbridge
28.9
E15
Tomatin
Daviot
Moy
Loch Moy
67
Glen Mor
Loch Ness
Inverness
Drumnadrochit
Urquhart
Castle
82
Invermoriston
Glen
Moriston
86
Fort
Augustus
Moniliath Mts.
Garva
Bridge
Laggan
Loch
Laggan
Spean
Bridge
1343
Ben Nevis
Ft. William
830
Glen
Nevis
Kinlochleven
44
Ballachulish
Glencoe
1120
Rannoch
Moor
Bridge
of Orchy
Tyndrum
828
Dalmally
Inveraray
Loch
Awe
Lochgilphead
817
Tarbert

Moidart
Acharacle
Glenfinnan
Loch
Shiel
1040
882
Loch Eil
Corran

DUNDEE
Carnoustie
Arbroath
13
90
Montrose
22
Inverbervie
Laurencekirk
Brechin
Forfar
Kirriemuir
Strathmore
Blairgowrie
90
Coupar
Angus
91
Dunkeld
61
85
Crieff
1171
Dunblane
91
Stirling
M80
Denny
Cumbernauld

St. Andrews
Cupar
24
Leven
Elie
Anstruther
Fife Ness
Buddon Ness
Firth of Tay
Perth
35
92
Glenrothes
16
Kinross
Loch
Leven
16
Cowdenbeath
Dunfermline
Rosyth
Queensferry
Firth of Forth
North Berwick
Tantallon Castle
Dunbar
St. Abb's Head
Haddington
Musselburgh
Linlithgow
Falkirk
E16
Helensburgh
Dumbarton
Greenock
E16
Kirkcaldy
Firth of Forth
Ben Ime
974
Arrochar
Loch Long
E16

Drummond
Castle
Doune
Drummond

Duart
Castle
Standing
Stones
Firth of Lorn
Ben Cruachan
1126
Jura
Scalasaig
Craobh
Haven
Crinan
Ben an Oir
Sound of
Jura

**34**

North
Sea

In the United Kingdom
distances in miles

---

0   10   20   30   40   50 km
0        10        20
30 miles

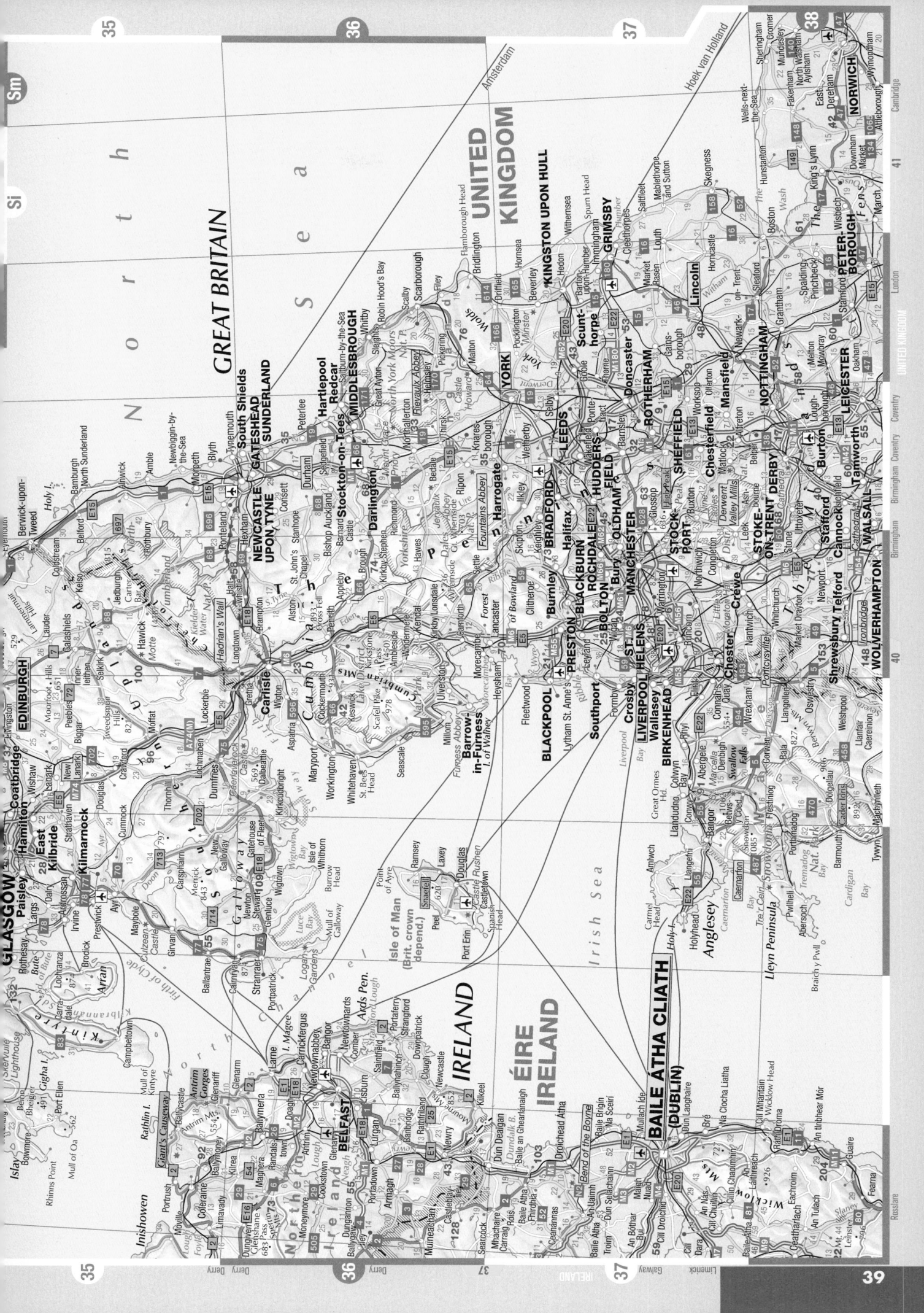

38

39

40

41

42

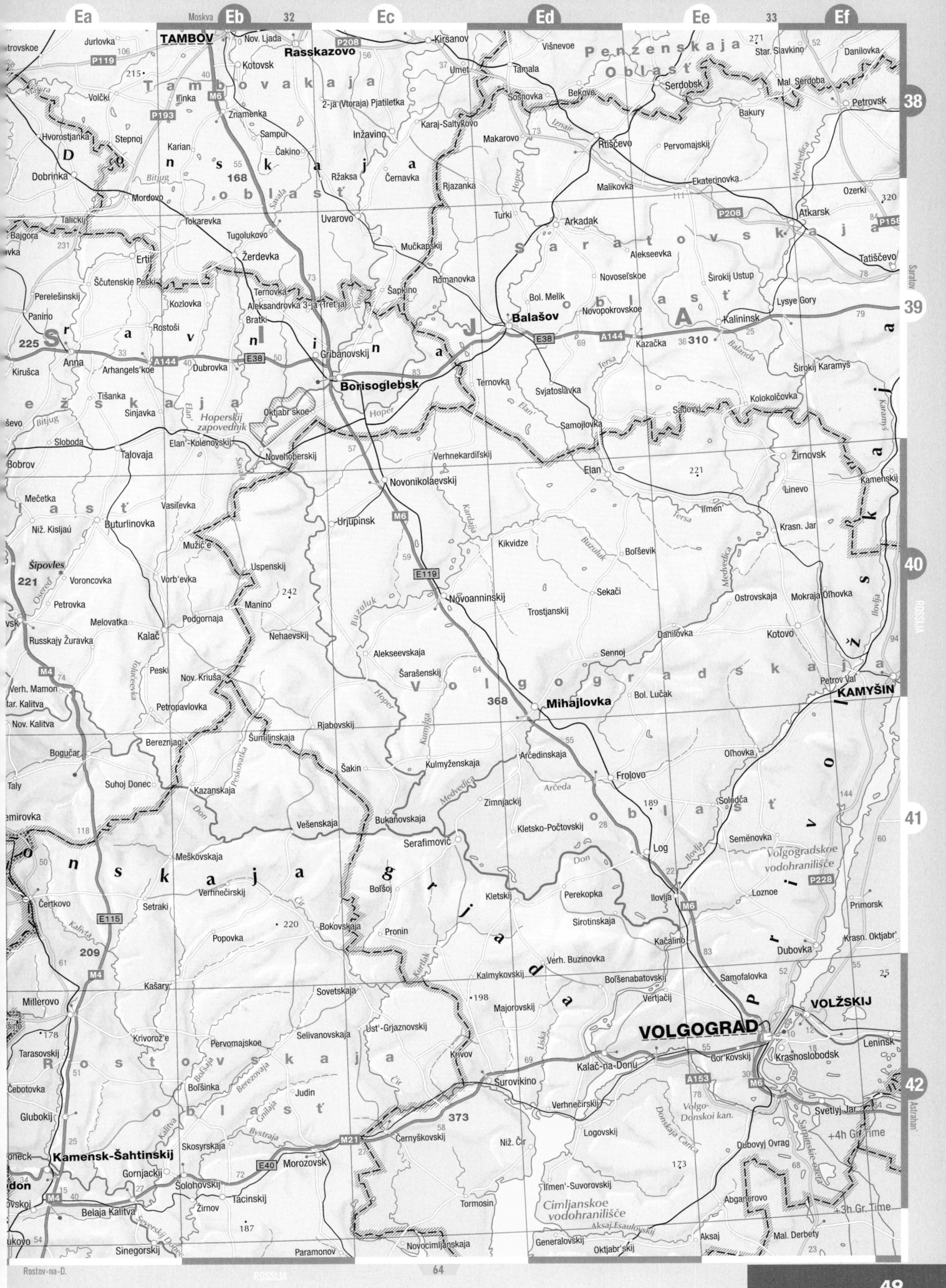

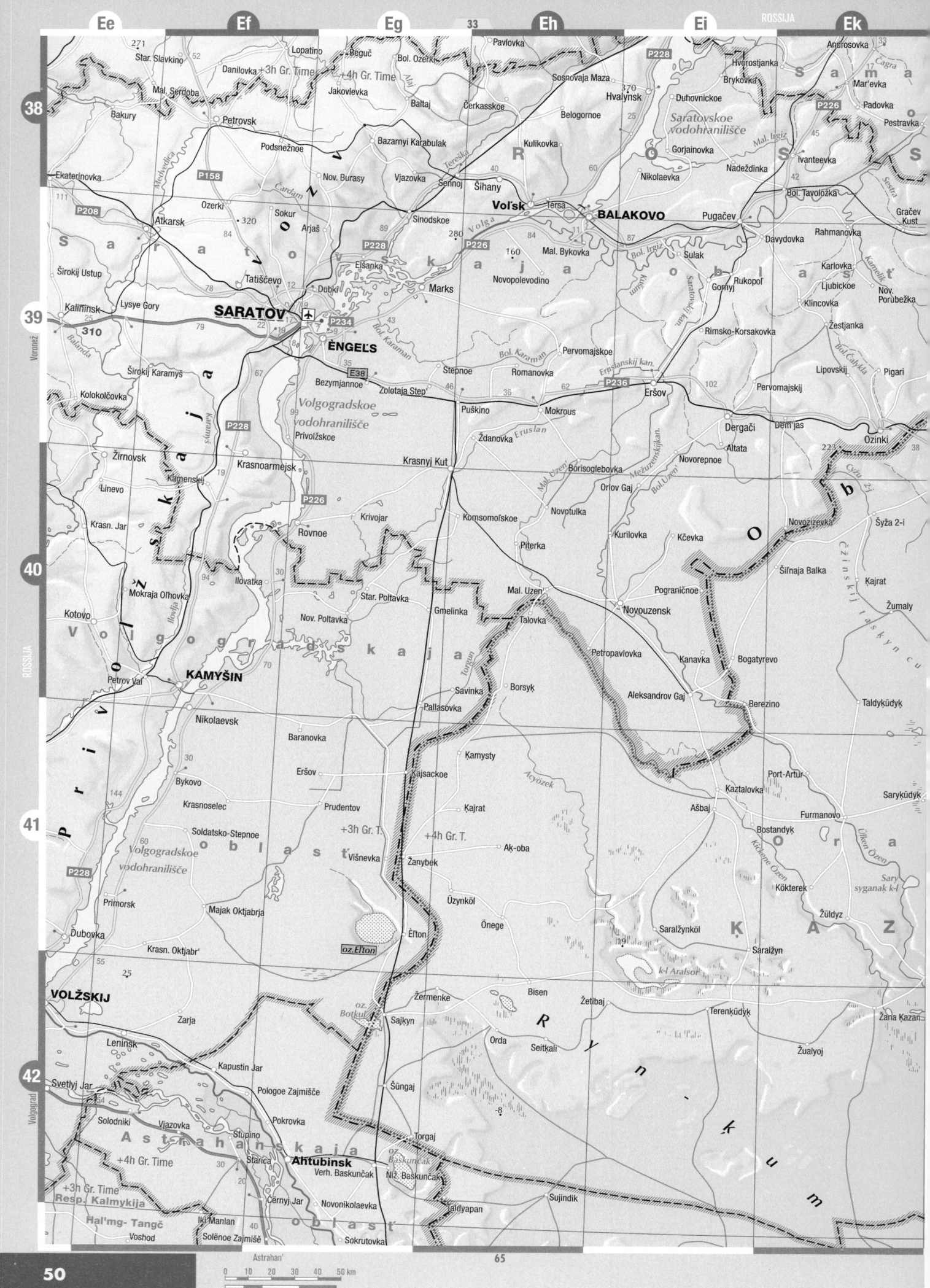

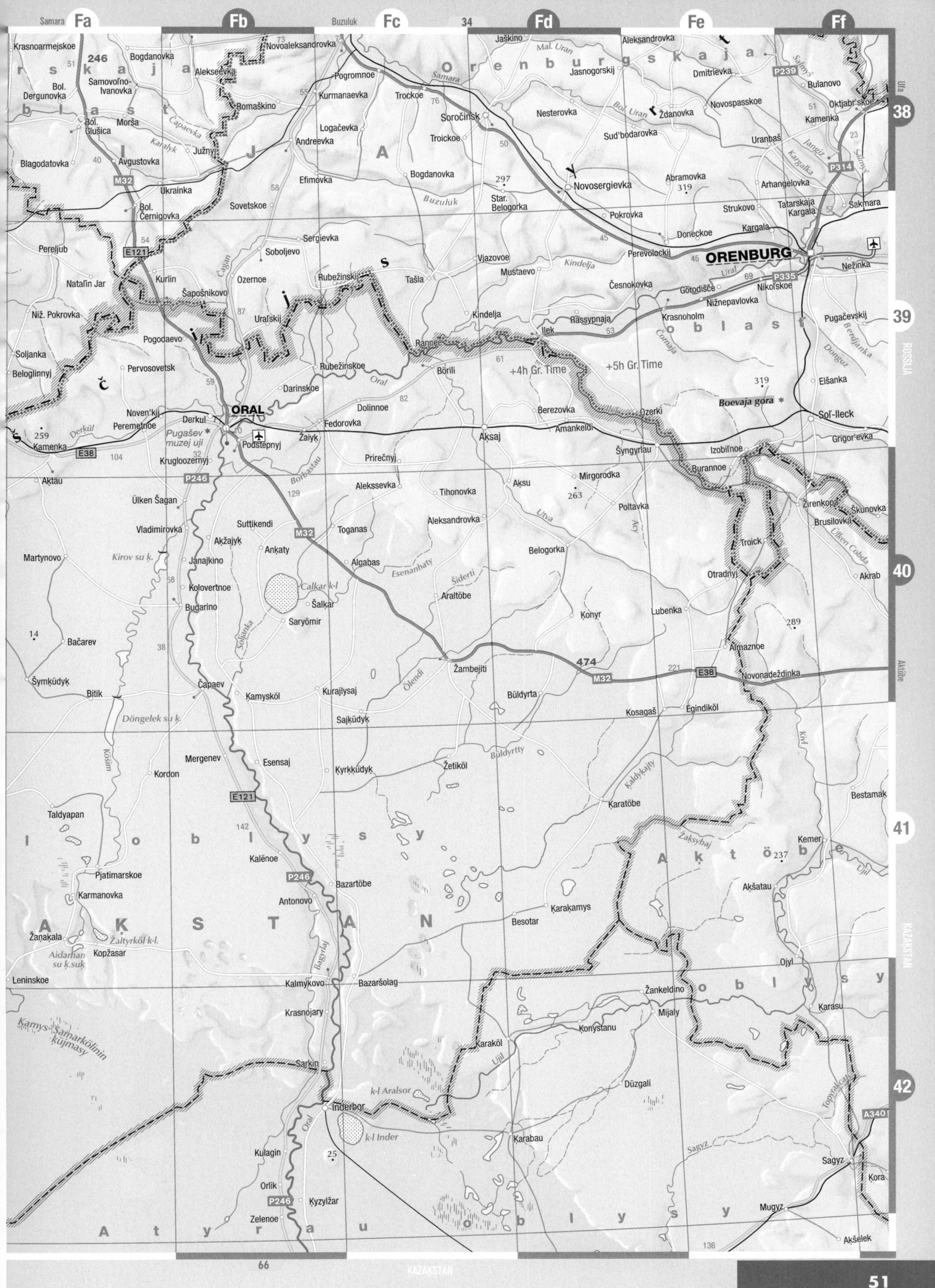

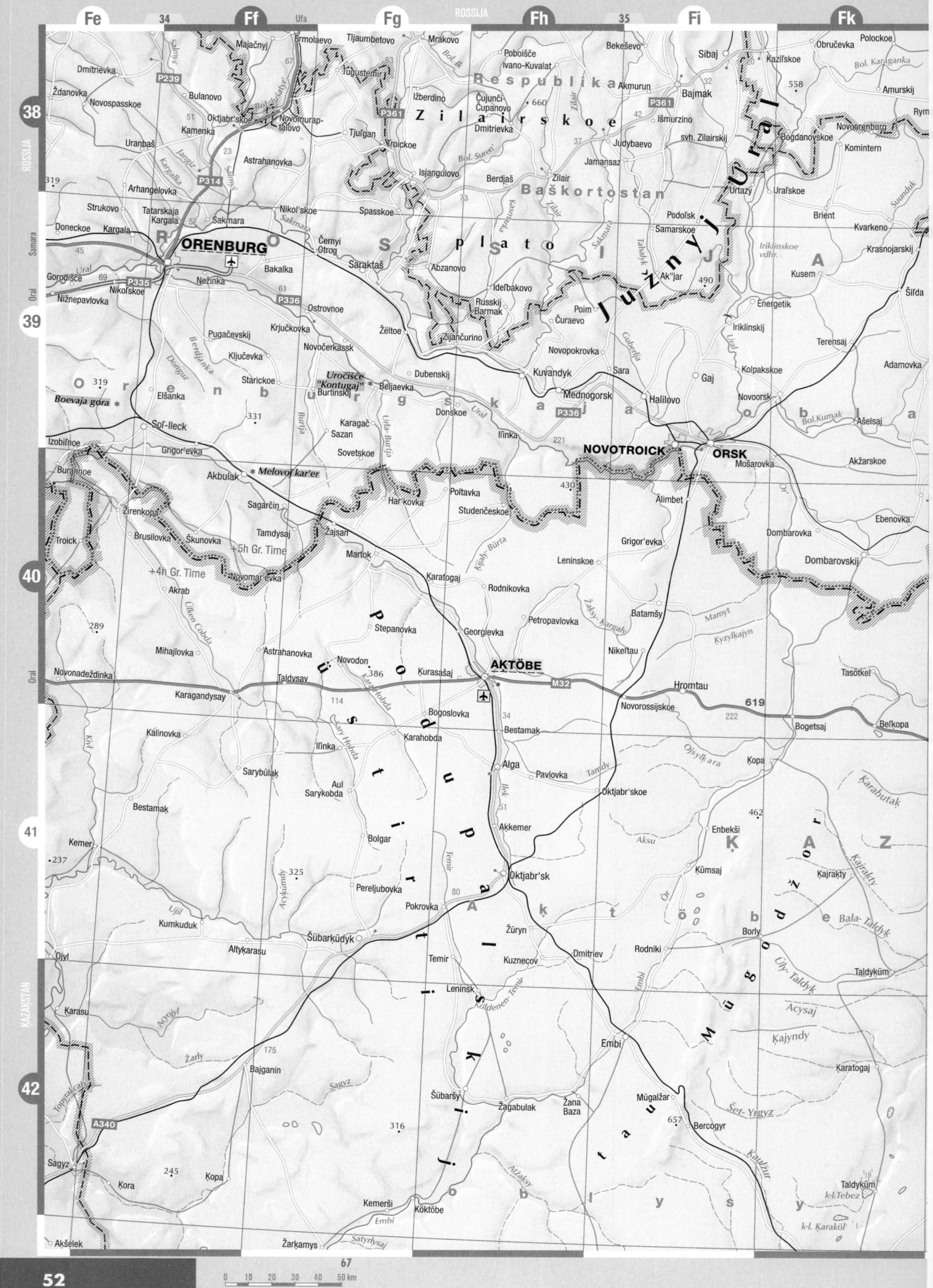

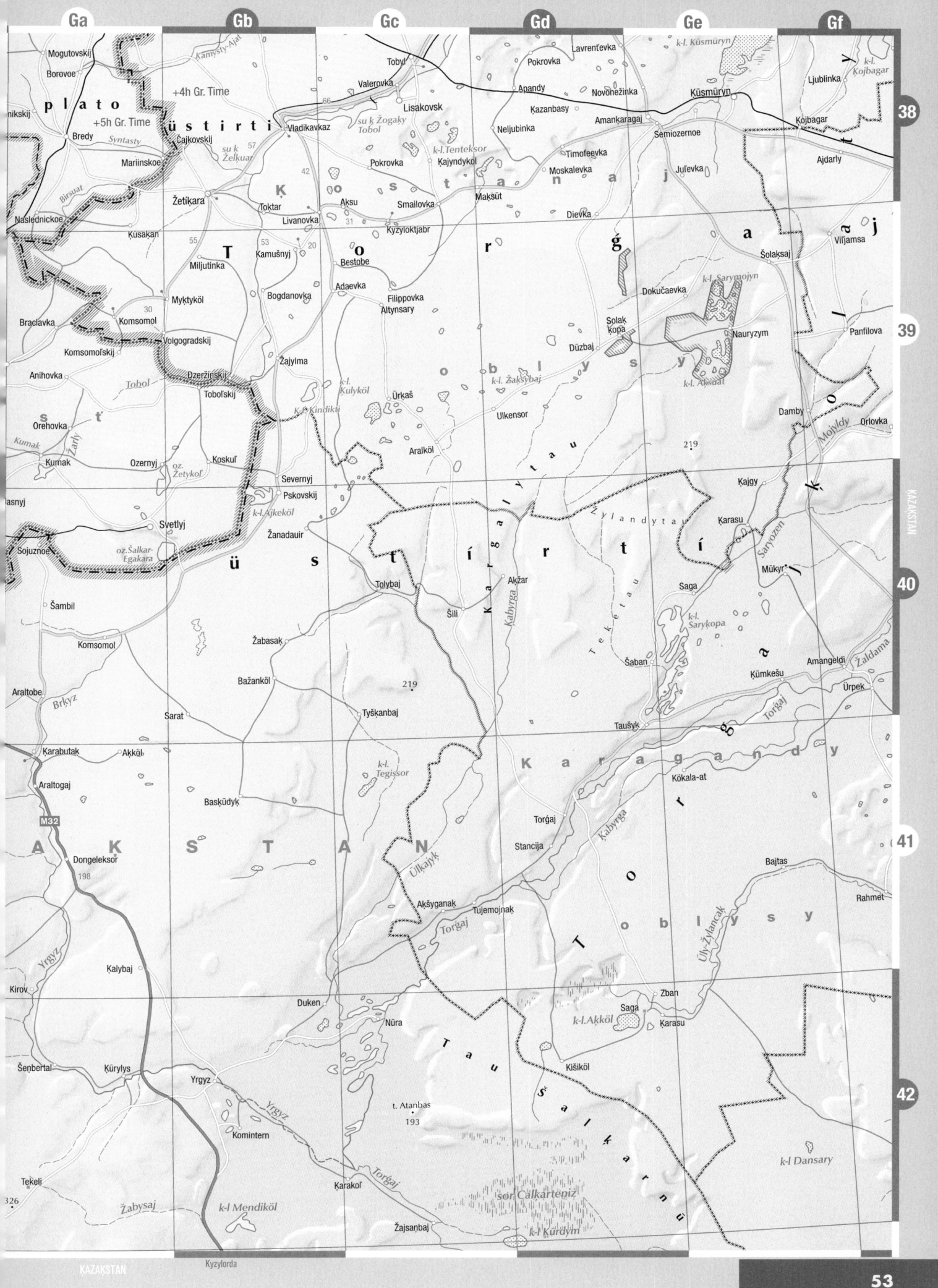

0  10  20  30  40  50 km
0  10  20  30 miles

MAGYARORSZÁG　Mukačeve　　UKRAJINA　Krasnojil's'k　Černivci

Nagykálló 2013　Nagygéc　Negrești-Oaș　Vel. Byčkiv　Rus'ka　Seljatyn　Občina Cereteului　M19　Dorohoi
Nyírbátor 49　Sighetu　Vicovu　Siret　Várfu Câmpului　238　Să
Nagyecsed　Livada　Marmației　de Sus　Rădăuți　85
471　Seini　Hărnicești　18　Vișeu　Șepit　Sucevița　17A　Câmpulung　23　BOTOȘANI
Nyiradony　Carei　Baia　de Sus　Moisei　Borșa　Solca　Gura　Păltinoasa　Botoș
182　Cavnik　Săcel　Pietrosul　Humorului　17　SUCEAVA
Nyíradony　SATU　BAIA　Telciu　1472　Moldovița　Voronet　Fălticeni　128　E58
Létavértes　MARE　MARE　Baia　Rodna　Poiana　Vatra　17B　Gura　103
E671　Țășnad　Sprie　Târgu　Năsăud　(1200) 17　Stampei　Dornei　97 106　Humorului　Poiana　Târgu
Valea lui Mihai　131　19　19B　1C　Lăpuș　Salva　E58　Prundu-　P.N.　Teiului　Neamț
ORADEA　Marghita　Supuru de Jos　E671　Râștoci　Gâlgău　Bârgăului　Călimani　Tulgheș　1907　Girov　Roman
Biharia　Șimleu　Sărmășag　Dej　Beclean　Bistrița　Deda　Parc. Nac.　N. P. Cheile　Bicaz　PIATRA-　E85
76　Aleșd　Silvaniei　Jibou　Surduc　Reghin　Toplița　B.-Hășmaș　Ditrău　NEAMȚ
Roșia　Zalău　Românași　Zimbor　694　Gherla　Monor　15A　1775　Gheorgheni　4568　15
E81　Tinca　Răbăgani　Huedin　Apahida　Sărmășel　Teaca　Sovata　13B　Harghita　54　Buhuși
155　Beiuș　Parc. Nac.　Gilău　CLUJ-　Gara　Zau　Praid　291　E578　Scorteni
233　C. Ponorului　16　NAPOCA　de Câmpie　TÂRGU　Bahnea　Miercurea　12A　Moinești
255 E79　Muntii Dealului　A3　Câmpia　MUREȘ　Vânători　Ciuc　1516　Comănești　11
218　Albac　Turda　Turzii　Ludus　15　Bălăușeri　13　Odorheiu　13A　1077　Târgu
Ștei　Muntele　1826　75　Câmpeni　Aiud　Ocna　Târnăveni　Secuiesc　Frumoasa　226　Ocna
Sebiș　Mare　74　Abrud　Teius　Mureș　Blaj　Sighișoara　39　Bataolt　Micfalău　Onești
Buteni　Vârfurile　113　Zlatna　Mediaș　Biertan　E60　Sfântu　E574
Gurahont　905　Brad　Muntii Metaliferi　ALBA　Copșa　Rupea　Măieruș　Gheorghe　Covasna
7　Ilia　IULIA　Mică　Agnita　Fāgăraș　13　Șercaia　11
Făget　68A　Deva　Simeria　Sebeș　Ocna　Vurpăr　Feldioara　E68　Prejmer　Întorsura
E673　Orăștie　E68　Sibiului　Sāliște　2013　77　Codlea　Hârman　Buzăului
HUNEDOARA　66　Hațeg　67C　SIBIU　Avrig　Victoria　Moldoveanu　BRAȘOV　Săcele
66　M. Cindrel　Tălmaciu　Brașov　2544　Râșnov　Predeal　10
R　Sarmizegetusa　2244　1　Făgărașului　73　Bușteni　1A　Gura Teghii
Caransebeș　E79　Petrila　Pasul Turnu　219　Lacul Vidraru　136　Sinaia　Nehoiu
Teregova　Muntii Retezat　Petroșani　Roșu E81　Câmpulung　E574　143　Buzău
E70　Parcul Nac.　Lupeni　134　Brezoi　Muntii Bucegi　Câmpina　154
Severin　Retezat　2 219　MERIDIONALI　Cozia　Curtea　Domnești　Vălenii　Verneşti
Baia	Bumbești-	de Arges	de M.	BUZĂU
Orșova	de-Aramă	Jiu	RÂMNICU	Cislău
Portile de Fier	67C	VÂLCEA	Băiculești	Urlaţi
Veliki	Târgu	Horezu	Coșești	Mizil
Đerdap	Jiu	Buleta	E81	Târgoviște	154
Brza	Călnic	Târgu	Morăreşti	PLOIEȘTI
Palanka	67	Rovinari	Cărbuneşti	7	Mereşani	72	Ciorani
89	Motru	E79	Sineşti	60	TÂRGOVIȘTE	de Jos	E85
E771 25	Broşteni	65	Hurezani	PITEȘTI	36	Topoloveni	Moreni	56
DROBETA-TURNU	66	C	(288)	Găeşti	A3	Urziceni
SEVERIN	Strehaia	65	Orleşti	A1	Costeşti	Titu	Moara	E60
74	Prunişor	E70	Drăgăşani	E81	114	Buftea	Vlăsiei	63
Kladovo	Filiaşi	Bălceşti	Vedea	Otopeni	2012	Movilița
Vânju Mare	37	Melineşti	Luhca	Negraşi	Bolintin-	Afumaţi
Brẑa	Isalnița	Corbului	Vale	Fundulea
Palanka	Cernăteşti	Slatina	E574	120	Izvoru	Crevedia	BUCUREȘTI
60	44	Bălăcita	Dobriceni	Potcoava	Selaru	Mare	34	Frumuşani	C (83)
Negotin	Radovan	Bals	Şcorniceşti	Costeşti	Adunaţii-	Vidra
Gruia	Orodel	Şerbăneşti	Balaci	Copăceni	Curcani
Vânători	CRAIOVA	Găneasa	Dobroteşti	Trivalea-	Videle	Oltenița
Brẑa	(83)	Coşoveni	Hotărani	Drăgăneşti-	Moşteni	Ghimpaţi	Srebarn
Rgotina	Cetate	Podari	Vâlceni	Nat. Re
Vidin	Giubega	Bratovoeşti	Drăgăneşti-	Băneasa	117
Kula	E79	Segarcea	Căracal	Vlaşca	Prundu	21
60	Calafat	Băileşti	Roşiori	228	Giurgiu	Tutrakan
Vrātarnica	Piscu	Bîrca	Amărăştii	de Vede	RUSE	Tetovo
55	Vechi	55	de Jos	Studina	Alexandria	52	Sveștari
Gramada	Lom	Gighera	Sadova	Toporu	Belica
Dimovo	Arčar	Lunca	Dăbuleni	Corabia	Turnu	52	Străklevo	Car Kalojan
49	Dolni	Bistret	Dunării	Izbiceni	Măgurele	108	Razgrad
E771 107	Lom	Kozloduj	Bechet	Ohaba	Zimnicea	Pietroşani	85	Popovo	ŞUMEN
Smirnenski	Vălčedrăm	Ohavo	Svištov	Nikopol	Levski	E772
Montana	E79	Mihajlovo	Mizija	253	Güljanci	Dojreni	Pavlikeni	Târgovište
SRBIJA	Berkovica	Borovan	Bjala	Priroden Park	Dragomirovo	Obnova	Kamen
Vraca	Červen Brjag	Slatina	Persina	38	Bjala	Opaka
Krivodol	Sadovec	Lukovit	PLEVEN	82	Levski	E85	2013
Bela Palanka	Varčec	Pavlikeni

Sofija　Botevgrad　Sofija　Loveč　75　Vel. Tărnovo　BĂLGARIJA　Vel. Tărnovo

0　10　20　30　40　50 km
0　10　20　30 miles

Zaicani
Rişcani
Costeşti
E583
Glodeni
BĂLȚI
Faleşti
Chişcăreni
Sculeni
Corneşti
Pîrlita
Ungheni
Nisporeni
IAȘI
R42
CHIȘINĂU
Zberoaia
Ialoveni
Lăpuşna
Leuşeni
Hînceşti
Huşi
VASLUI
Dragomireşti
Leova
Puieşti
Bălteşti
Iargara
Cantemir
Baimaclia
Congaz
Ceadîr-Lunga
Comrat
Basarabeasca
BĂRLAD
Popeşti
Murgeni
Bălăbăneşti
Oancea
Târgu Bujor
Taraclia
Cahul
Cervonoarmijs'ke
Adjud
Panciu
Mărăşeşti
Tecuci
Valea Mărului
Giurgiuleşti
Reni
FOCȘANI
E85
Măicăneşti
GALAȚI
BRĂILA
Șuteşti
Ianca
Cilibia
Făurei
Viziru
Pogoanele
Padina
Dudeşti
Insurăței
Amara
Grivita
Giurgeni
Scinteia
Tăndărei
Făcăeni
SLOBOZIA
Dragalina
Movila
Perişoru
Feteşti
Cernavodă
Medgidia
Ovidiu
Mamaia
CĂLĂRAŞI
Oltina
Basarabi
CONSTANȚA
SILISTRA
Ostrov
Băneasa
Cobadin
Topraisar
Tuzla
Eforie Nord
Alfatar
Rosica
Comana
Negru Vodă
Mangalia
Dulovo
Hitovo
Svoboda
Jovkovo
Vama Veche
Tervel
Karapelit
General Toşevo
Vaklino
N. Šabla
Kaolinovo
DOBRIČ
Vranino
Šabla
Novi Pazar
Vălčidol
Obročište
Kavarna
Vetrino
Balčik
N. Kaliakra
Madara
Devnja
VARNA
Varnenski Zaliv

Florești
Cotiujeni
MOLDOVA
Soldăneşti
Rezina
Rîbnița
Bălti
Singerei
Telenești
Orhei
Crasni Okny
Bertuceni
Peresecina
Criuleni
Grigoriopol
Dubăsari
Fiunzivka
Vadul lui Vodă
Cricova
Străşeni
Vel. Mychajlivka
Bucovăţ
Anenii Noi
Căuşeni
Dnestrovsc
TIGHINA (BENDER)
Slobozia
TIRASPOL
Rozdil'na
Pervomajsc
Kam'janka
Cimişlia
Ciucur Mingir
Ştefan Vodă
Volintiri
Borodino
Faraonivka
Starokozače
Tarutyne
Malojaroslavec'
Peršyj
Sarata
Arcyz
Žovtyj Jar
Tuzly
Tatarbunary
Kyrnyčky
Suvorove
Kilija
Vylkove
Izmajil
Tulcea
Isaccea
Somova
Sulina
Luncaviţa
Măcin
Cerna
Nalbant
Murighiol
Agighiol
Sfântu Gheorghe
Ciucurova
Babadag
Topolog
Baia
Jurilovca
Rămnicu de Jos
Istria
Dorobanțu
Mihail Kogălniceanu
Iaşaul
L. Siutghiol
Năvodari
Adamclisi
Cobadin

Balta
Kodyma
Kryve Ozero
Kotovs'k
Tylihul
Trojic'ke
Ljubaševka
Odes'ka
Šyrjajeve
Andrijevo-Ivanivka
Berezivka
Radisne
Petrivka
Berezanka
Sverdlove
Fontanka
Majaky
Velykodolyns'ke
ODESA
Illičivs'k
Ovidiopol
Monaši
Bilhorod-Dnistrovs'kyj
Zatoka
Kulevča
Serhijivka
Kurortne
Alibej
Sahany
Desantne

Vradijivka
Južnoukrajins'k
Brats'ke
Jelaneč
Oleksandrivka
Domanivka
Kujbyševka
Vozsijats'ke
Mykolajivka
Voznesens'k
Veselynove
Nova Odesa
Stepove
Ternivka
UKRAJINA
Petrivka
MYKOLAJIV
Kobleve
Očakiv
Dniprovs'kyj lyman
Čornomors'kyj zapovidnyk
Tendrivs'ka Kosa
Jevpatorija

Dunajs'kyj biosfernyj zapovidnyk

Delta Dunării
Delta du Danube

ČORNOE MORE

BLACK SEA

43
44
45
46
47

Havrylivka
Pokrovs'ke
H15
26
55
Krasnohorivka
Bahatyr
Kurachove
DONEC'K
Snižne
Sohfna
233 M03
77
Novoborovyci
Krasnyj Sulin
18
182
Kumbučja
Oleksandrivka
Ilovajs'k
117
NOVOŠAHTINSK
ŠAHTY
Ternuvate
Vel. Novosilka
Dokučajevs'k
Amvrosijivka
Kujbyševo
Ust'-Doneckij
Konstantinovsk
uljajpole
Uspenivka
Pavlivka
Hovotrojic'ke
Starobeševe
Rostovska
Matveev Kurgan
Rodionovo-Nesvetajskaja
E115
E50
37
M19
Sémikarakorsk
158
Novopetrykivka
Volnovacha
Starobeševe
Uljanivs'ke
Pokrovskoe
Tuzlov
9A
M4
NOVOČERKASSK
Ljubymivka
Andrijivka
Tel'manove
Mychajlivka
archeologičeskij
stanica Bagaevskaja
Čubarivka
Začativka
H20
Fedorovka
zapovednik Tanais
Sultan-Saly
2012
26
Smyrnove
Rozivka
Kujbyševe
98
Nedvigouka–Čaltyr
Aksaj
Staročerkasskaja
Polohy
Kujbyševe
83
Azovs
TAGANROG
ROSTOV-NA-DONU
Batajsk
39
Zapadnenski
lim.
Černihivka
Volodars'ke
ROSTOV-NA-DONU
Batajsk
16
30
Šahaevskij
lim.
Berestove
24
Talakivka
180
Azov
59
Veselyj
oblast'
Manyč
Veselókskoe vdh.
Andrijivka
E58
M14
41
M14
Novoazovs'k
Kirovskaja
12
Azov
Kagalnik
MARIUPOL'
Semibalki
Samarskoe
Kirovskaja
Zernograd
Mečetinskaja
85
P37
M14
39
Margaritovo
Kugej
Kagalnickaja
40
O
elenivka
Osypenko
Ursuf
Aleksandrovka
E50
40
ičná
Hannivka
Dmytrivka
20
Novopetrivka
57
E115
121
Egorlykskaja
Celina
P269
zatoka
202
13
*Petrivs'ka fortec'a
Ejskoe Ukreplenie
121
Kuščevskaja
Sred. Egorlyk
57
58
Prymors'k
Berdjans'ka
Ejsk
Ejskij liman
Kugoevskaja
Sred. Egorlyk
44
očna
zatoka
Berdjans'ka kosa
Dolžanskaja
Staroščerbinovskaja
Skurinskaja
Kisljakovskaja
Krylovskaja
Oktjabr'skaja
Nezamaevskaja
Belaja Glina
Obitočna kosa
Kamyševatskaja
Novoščerbinovskaja
Starominskaja
Sosyka
56
ROSSIJA
Pavlovskaja
Eja
z o v s k o e
Jasenskaja
Novominskaja
Leningradskaja
M4
Belaja Glina
Kopanskaja
Lim.
Kuščevatyj
Novopokrovskaja
oz. Hanskoe
lim.
Sladkij
Kanevskaja
Krylovskaja
39
E50
more
Privolnaja
39
Egorlyk
Kalaly
P268
64
Čelbasskaja
E115
Tihoreck
Ilinskaja
233
Primorsko-Ahtarsk
Priazovskaja
Irklievskaja
Novomalorossijskaja
55
lim. Krasnyj
Bejsug
11
143
Čelbas
lim. Bojkov
lim.
Br'uchoveckaja
Berezanskaja
143
Kirpil'skij
29
Novovladimirovskaja
Bejsug
45
m o r e
Stepnaja
Timaševsk
M4
Vyselki
Kropotkin
Protoka
Grivenskaja
46
Korenovsk
Kirpili
M29
Gul'keviči
Novonikolaevskaja
Kalininskaja
Kirpil'skaja
75
70
lim. Dolgij
Petrovskaja
Staronižesteblievskaja
Kuban'
P251
lim.
Temryjukskij zaliv
Vojskovoj
Ivanovskaja
24
Novotitarovskaja
Dinskaja
Ust'-Labinsk
30
Temrjuk
Krasnoarmejskaja
Voronežskaja
P256
15
26
Slavjansk-na-Kubani
28
Adygé
P251
65
Kuban'
Kalinino
24
M4
71
Zarevo
Košehabl'
KERČ
Tamanskij zaliv
M25
26
Varenikovskaja
Troickaja
KRASNODAR
P253
Kurganinsk
M17
Taman'
Starotitarovskaja
Paškovskij
Krasnodar vdh.
Rjazanskaja
Giaginskaja
48
46
Zavitne
Kiziltaškij
E97
Krymsk
Afipiskij
A146
Adygejsk
Belorečensk
Kužorskaja
49
M29
m. Opuk
liman
Anapa
34
35
26
E592
59
Labinsk
173
60
Abinsk
Holmskij
171
32
Kubanskaja
25
MAJKOP
Jaroslavskaja
NOVOROSSIJSK
20
56
Gorjačij Ključ
115
43
Tuľskij
73
Abrau-Djurso
36
921
Kutais
Apšeronsk
Respublikém
Mostovskoj
E97
Gelendžik
M4
Hadyžensk
P254
Kamennomostskij
114
78
Arzipo-Osipovka
Džubga
57
Hamyski
Psebaj
Novomihajlovskij
Ofginka
Tuapse
KAVKAZ
Sočinskij
193
Aše
136
Čigus
Kaykazskij
Lazarevskoe
prirodnyj
Soloh-Aul
3238
zapovednik
Golovinka
nacional'nyj
Vardane
Krasnaja Poljana
2013
Loo
Macesta
park
DAGOMYS
Ritsis Avadhara
47
SOČI
A148
Nakrdz.
Hosta
Adler
Bzipi
Aresublika
Leselidze
Gagra
Apsny
SAKARTVELO
(GEORGIA)
Bitch'vinda
155
Gudauta

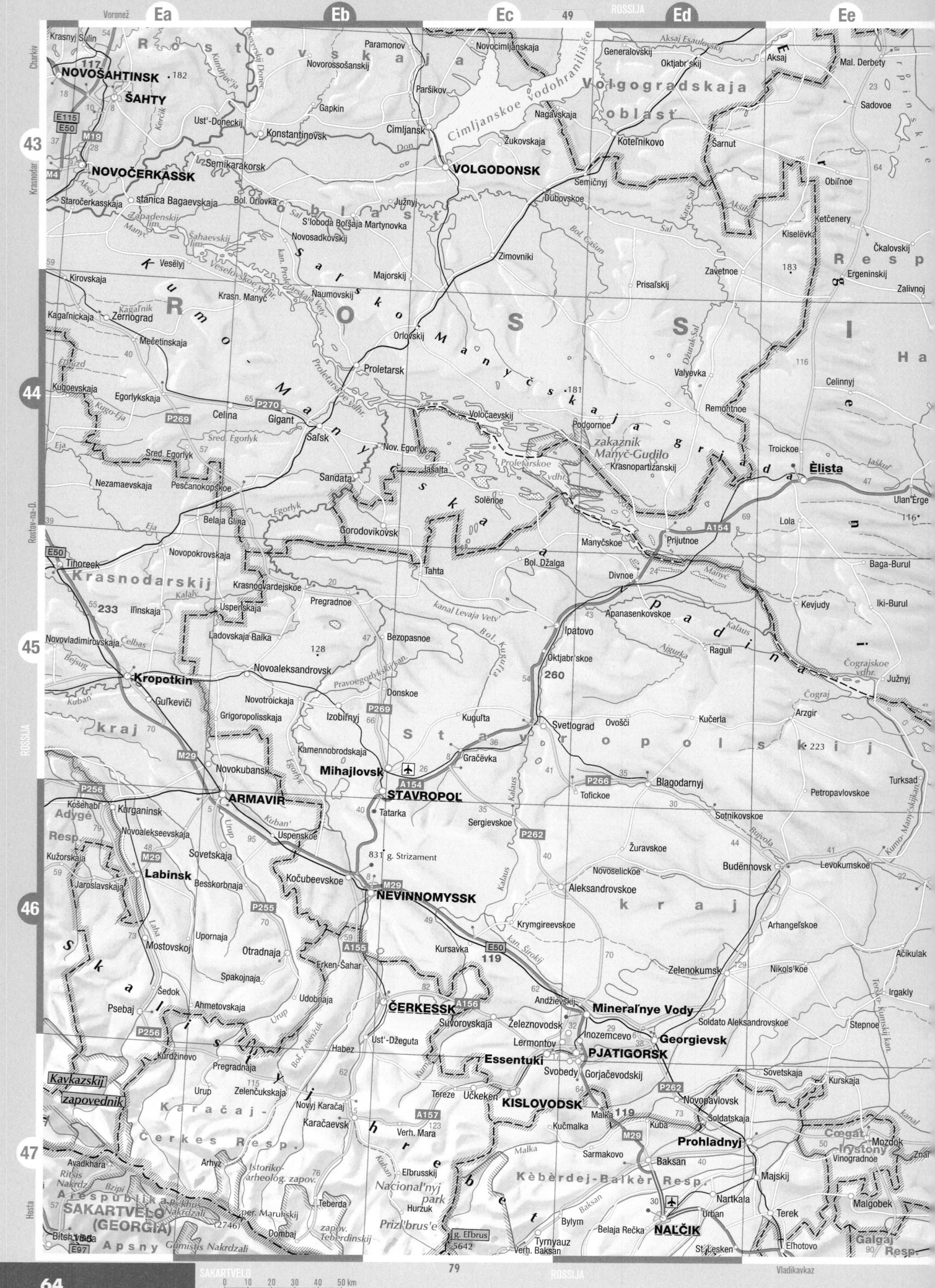

Voronež

Charkiv

Krasnyj Sulin · 182

**NOVOŠAHTINSK**

**ŠAHTY**

E115
E50

**43**

M19

**NOVOČERKASSK**

M4

Staročerkasskaja

stanica Bagaevskaja

Semikarakorsk

Ust'-Doneckij

Konstantinovsk

Paramonov

Novorossošanskij

Paršikov

Gapkin

Cimljansk

Novocimljanskaja

Nagavskaja

Žukovskaja

*Cimljanskoe vodohranilišče*

Don

Generalovskij

Oktjabr'skij

Aksaj Esaulovskij

**Volgogradskaja oblasť**

Aksaj

Mal. Derbety

Sadovoe

23

Kotel'nikovo

Šarnut

64

Obil'noe

Ketčenery

Kiselëvka

Čkalovskij

**VOLGODONSK**

Semičnyj

Dubovskoe

183

R

e

s

p

Rostovskaja

oblasť

S'loboda Bol'šaja Martynovka

Novosadkovskij

Južnyj

Bol. Orlovka

Zimovniki

Majorskij

Zavetnoe

Prisal'skij

Ergeninskij

Zalivnoj

Kirovskaja

Kagal'nickaja

Zernograd

Mečetinskaja

Krasn. Manyč

Naumovskij

Orlovskij

Manyč

Proletarsk

Voločaevskij

Nov. Egorlyk

181

Podgornoe

*zakaznik Manyč-Gudilo*

Krasnopartizanskij

Remontnoe

Valyevka

116

Celinnyj

Troickoe

**Èlista**

47

H

a

l

b

i

n

s

g

r

j

a

d

a

P269

**44**

40

Kugoevskaja

Egorlykskaja

P270

Celina

Gigant

Sal'sk

Sred. Egorlyk

57

Nezamaevskaja

Pešanokopskoe

Sandata

Jašalta

Solënoe

Manyčskoe

Prijutnoe

A154

Lola

Jaškul'

Ulan Ergè

116

Sred. Egorlyk

Belaja Glina

Gorodovikovsk

Egorlyk

Tahta

Bol. Džalga

Divnoe

24

Baga-Burul

Iki-Burul

Kevjudy

Čograjskoe vdhr.

Južnyj

E50

Tihoreck

**Krasnodarskij**

55 233

Il'inskaja

Kalaly

Krasnogvardejskoe

Uspenskaja

Pregradnoe

20

Bezopasnoe

47

Ipatovo

43

Apanasenkovskoe

Ragulí

Arzgir

223

**45**

Novovladimirovskaja

Čelbas

Bejsug

Ladovskaja Balka

128

kanal Levaja Vetv'

Oktjabr'skoe

260

Kučerla

Kalaus

**Kropotkin**

Gul'keviči

Novoaleksandrovsk

Pravoegorlyksk.jkan.

Donskoe

54

Svetlograd

Ovošči

Čograj vdhr.

kraj

Kuban'

Novotroickaja

Grigoropolisskaja

Izobil'nyj

P269

66

Kugul'ta

S        t        a        v        r        o        p        o        l        s        k        i        j

Turksad

70

M29

Kamennobrodskaja

**Mihajlovsk**

A154

26

Gračëvka

36

41

P266

35

**Blagodarnyj**

Sotnikovskoe

Petropavlovskoe

41

Novokubansk

8

**STAVROPOĽ**

Tatarka

Urup

40

35

Sergievskoe

P262

ToFickoe

30

44

**ARMAVIR**

P256

Urup

95

Koševat

Kurganinsk

Novoalekseevskaja

Uspenskoe

831 g. Strizament

Žuravskoe

Novoselickoe

Budënnovsk

Levokumskoe

22

**Adygé Resp.**

48

M29

Sovetskaja

8

M29

Kalaus

900

Aleksandrovskoe

Bujvola

Kužorskaja

**Labinsk**

Besskorbnaja

Kočubeevskoe

**NEVINNOMYSSK**

49

Krymgireevskoe

kraj

Arhangel'skoe

59

Jaroslavskaja

Laba

P255

70

**46**

Mostovskoj

Upornaja

59

A155

Kursavka

E50

119

Ačikulak

Nikol'skoe

Irgakly

Psebaj

Ahmetovskaja

Otradnaja

Spakojnaja

Udobnaja

82

Zelenokumsk

129

Stepnoe

P256

Šedok

Urup

Kurdžinovo

Pregradnaja

Habez

Ust'-Džeguta

62

**ČERKESSK**

A156

Suvorovskaja

Andžievskij

**Mineral'nye Vody**

Železnovodsk

32

Soldato Aleksandrovskoe

**Georgievsk**

Sovetskaja

Kurskaja

**Kavkazskij zapovednik**

K a r a č a j -

Novyj Karačaj

Zelenčukskaja

115

Tereze

Učkeken

Inozemcevo

Lermontov

**Essentuki**

Svobody

**PJATIGORSK**

6

Gorjačevodskij

P262

Novopavlovsk

73

Soldatskaja

Č e r k e s   R e s p.

**Karačaevsk**

A157

123

Verh. Mara

**KISLOVODSK**

Malka

119

Kuba

Kučmalka

M29

**Prohladnyj**

50

Mozdok

Vinogradnoe

Znar

 Avadkhara

Ritsis Nakdzal

Arhyz

Istoriko arheológ. zapov.

76

Teberda

El'brusskij

Sarmakovo

Baksan

**47**

Bzipi

A résublika

SAKARTVELO (GEORGIA)

Dombaj

per. Maruhskij

(2746)

zapov. Teberdinskij

**Nacional'nyj park**

Hurzuk

Prizl'brus'e

g. El'brus

5642

K è b ë r d e j - B a l k ê r   R e s p.

Baksan

Tyrnyauz

Verh. Baksan

Bylym

Belaja Rečka

30

Majskij

**NAĽČIK**

Nartkala

Urban

St.-Lesken

Terek

Majskoe

El'hotovo

Malgobek

90

Galgaj Resp.

Čeçát Iryston

Apsny

Gimistis Nakdzali

E97

Bitsvi ps

Hista

ROSSIJA

Rostov-na-D.

Krasnodar

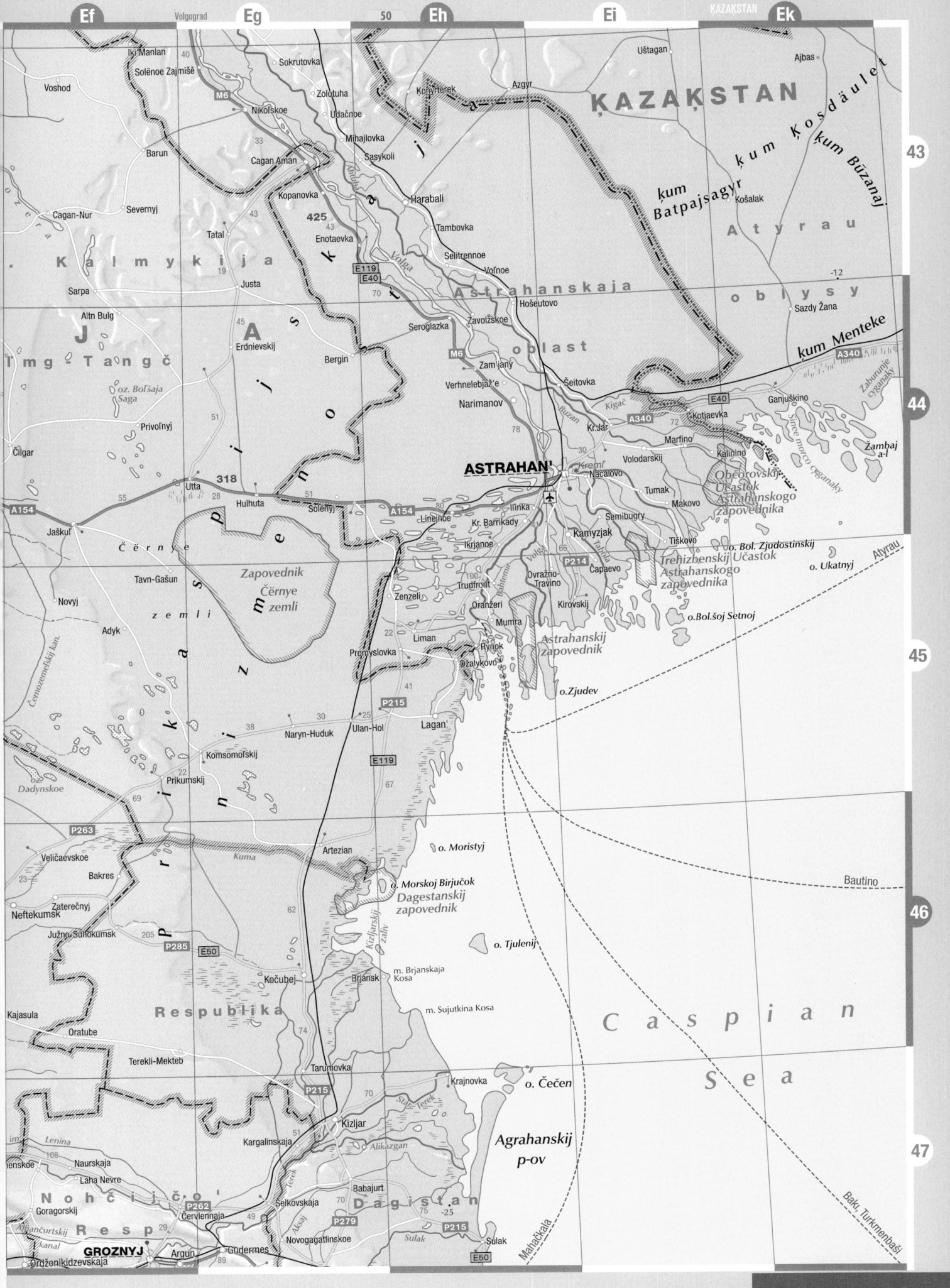

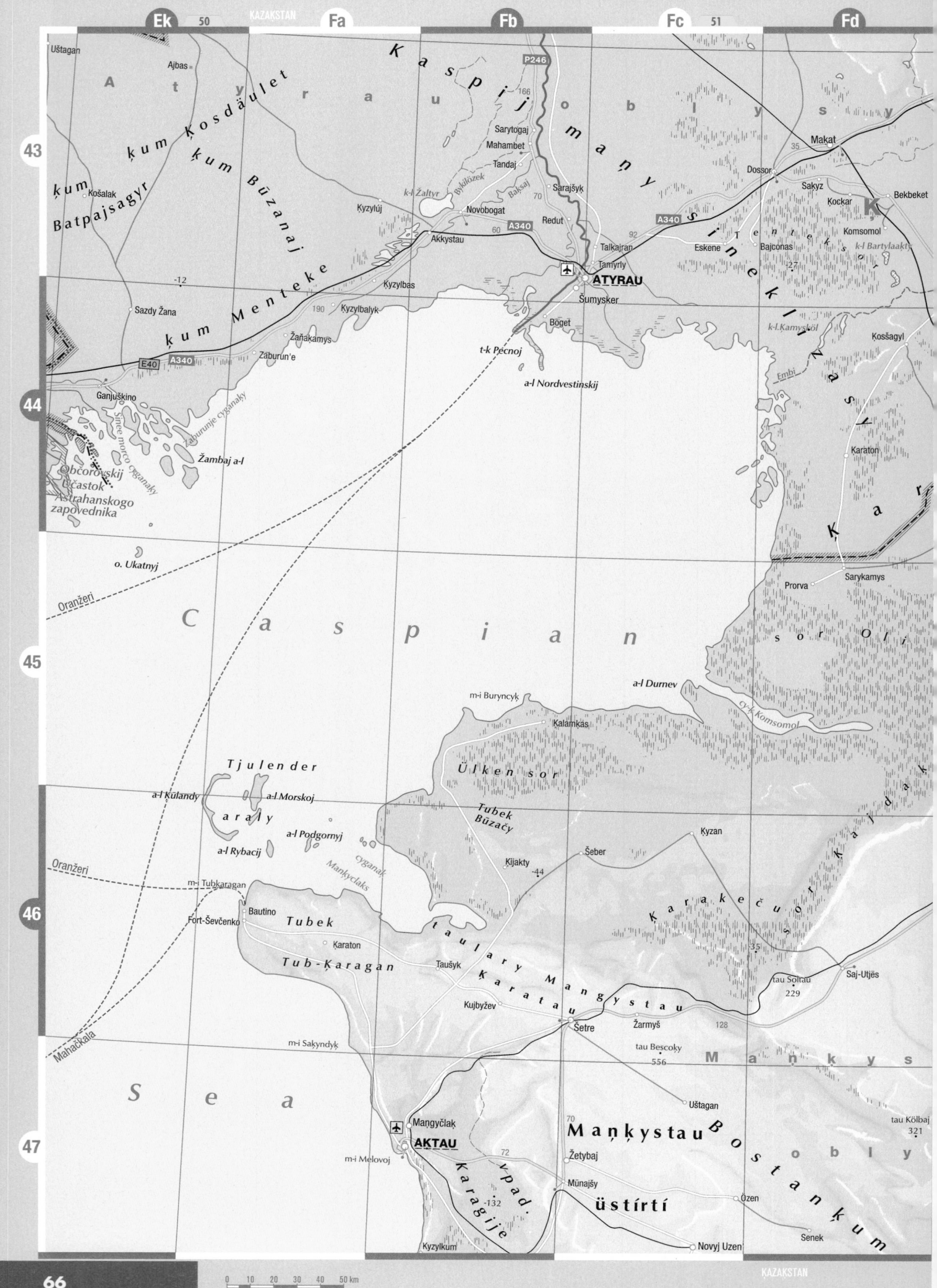

A t y r a u   o b l y s y

Uštagan

Ajbas

K a s p i j   m a ņ y   s i ņ e k l i ņ a s y

P246

166

Sarytogaj

Mahambet

Tandaj

k-l Žaltyr

Byktözek

Bakšaj

Novobogat

Sarajšyk

70

Makat

35

Dossor

Sakyz

Kockar

Komsomol

Bekbeket

K

Redut

A340

60

A340

Akkystau

Talkajran

92

A340

Eskene

Bajconas

T e n t e k s a j

k-l Bartylaakt

Košalak

Kyzylúj

Tamyrly

ATYRAU

127

ķ u m   K o s d ä u l e t

ķ u m   B ū z a n a j

B a t p a j s a g y r

ķ u m

ķ u m

Sumysker

Kyzylbas

Kyzylbalyk

-12

190

Bōget

k-l.Kamystöl

Kossagyl

Sazdy Žana

Žaňakamys

ķ u m   M e n t e k e

Zaburun'e

t-k Pěcnoj

a-l Nordvestinskij

Embi

E40

A340

Ganjuškino

Sinee morco cyganaky

Zaburunje cyganaky

Žambaj a-l

K a r

Karaton

Občorovskij
Učastok
Astrahanskogo
zapovednika

o. Ukatnyj

Oranžeri

C   a   s   p   i   a   n

Sarykamys

Prorva

s o r   O l i

a-l Durnev

cy-k Komsomol

45

m-i Buryncyk

Kalamkas

T j u l e n d e r

Ülken sor

a-l Kúlandy

a-l.Morskoj

a r a l y

Tubek
Būzačy

a-l Podgornyj

cyganak

Mankyclaks

Kyzan

a-l Rybacij

Šeber

Kijakty

-44

Oranžeri

m-i Tubkaragan

Bautino

Fort-Ševčenko

Karaton

Tubek

t a u l a r y   M a ņ g y s t a u

K a r a k e č u   s o r

ķ a j d a k

35

tau Soltau
229

Saj-Utjěs

Tub-Ķaragan

Taušyk

K a r a t a u

Kujbyžev

Šetre

Žarmyš

128

M a ņ k y s

Mahačkala

m-i Sakyndyk

tau Bescoky
556

Uštagan

tau Kölbaj
321

S   e   a

m-i Mělovoj

Maņgyclak

AKTAU

72

M a ņ ķ y s t a u   o b l y s y

Žetybaj

B o s t a n ķ u m

ü s t í r t í

vpad.
Karagije
-132

Mūnajšy

Özen

Senek

Kyzylkum

Novyj Uzen

0 10 20 30 40 50 km
0 10 20 30 miles

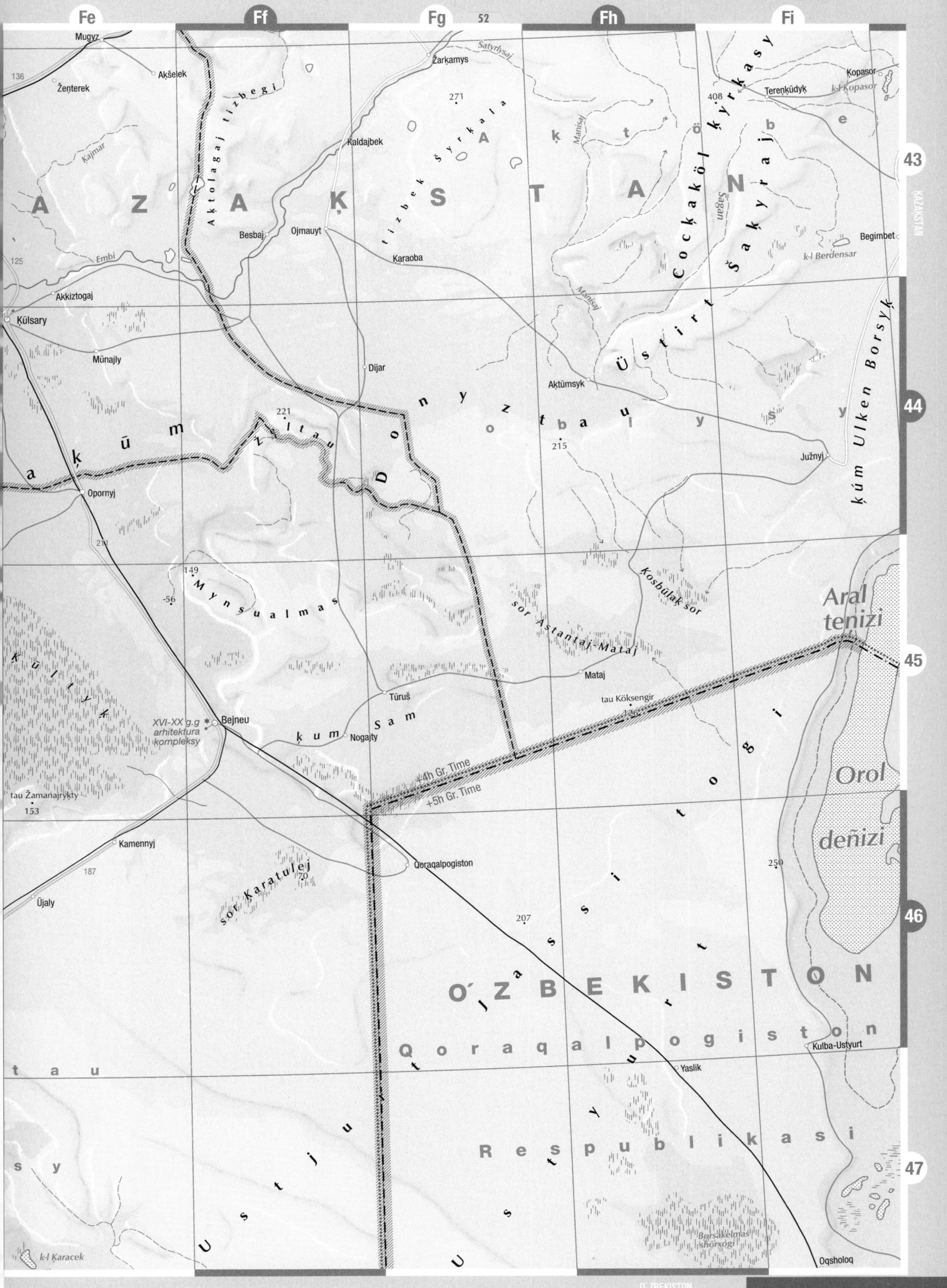

43

44

45

46

47

KAZAKSTAN

Mugyz

Žeņterek

Akšelek

136

Kajmar

125

Embi

Akkiztogaj

Külsary

Münajly

Opornyj

Aktolagaj tizbegi

A   Z   A   Ķ   S   T   A   N

tizbek šyrķala

Žarkamys

Satyrlysaj

271

Kaldajbek

Besbaj

Ojmauyt

Karaoba

Dijar

Aķtöbek šyrķala

Aktūmsyk

215

Cockaköl ķyrkasy

408

Terenkūdyk

Kopasor

k-l Kopasor

Begimbet

k-l Berdensar

Manisaj

Sagan

Üstirt   Šaķyraj

Manisaj

Južnyj

ķúm   Ulken   Borsyķ

D   o   n   y   z   t   b   a   u   l   y   s   y

221

Želtau

D

a   ķ   ū   m

271

149

-56

Mynsualmas

Kúliyk

sor   Astantaj   Mataj

Kosbūlak   sor

Mataj

tau Köksengir

-126

Aral
tenizi

k   u   m   Sam

Tūruš

Nogajty

XVI-XX g.g
arhitektura
kompleksy

Bejneu

tau Žamanajrykty

153

Kamennyj

187

Üjaly

sor   Karatulej

70

+4h Gr. Time

+5h Gr. Time

Qoraqalpogiston

s   s   t   o   g   i

250

Orol
deñizi

207

O´   Z   B   E   K   I   S   T   O   N

Q   o   r   a   q   a   l   p   o   g   i   s   t   o   n

Kulba-Ustyurt

Yaslik

R   e   s   p   u   b   l   i   k   a   s   i

U   s   t   j   u   r   t

t   a   u

s   y

U   s

k-l Karacek

Borsakelmas
shörxóġi

Oqsholoq

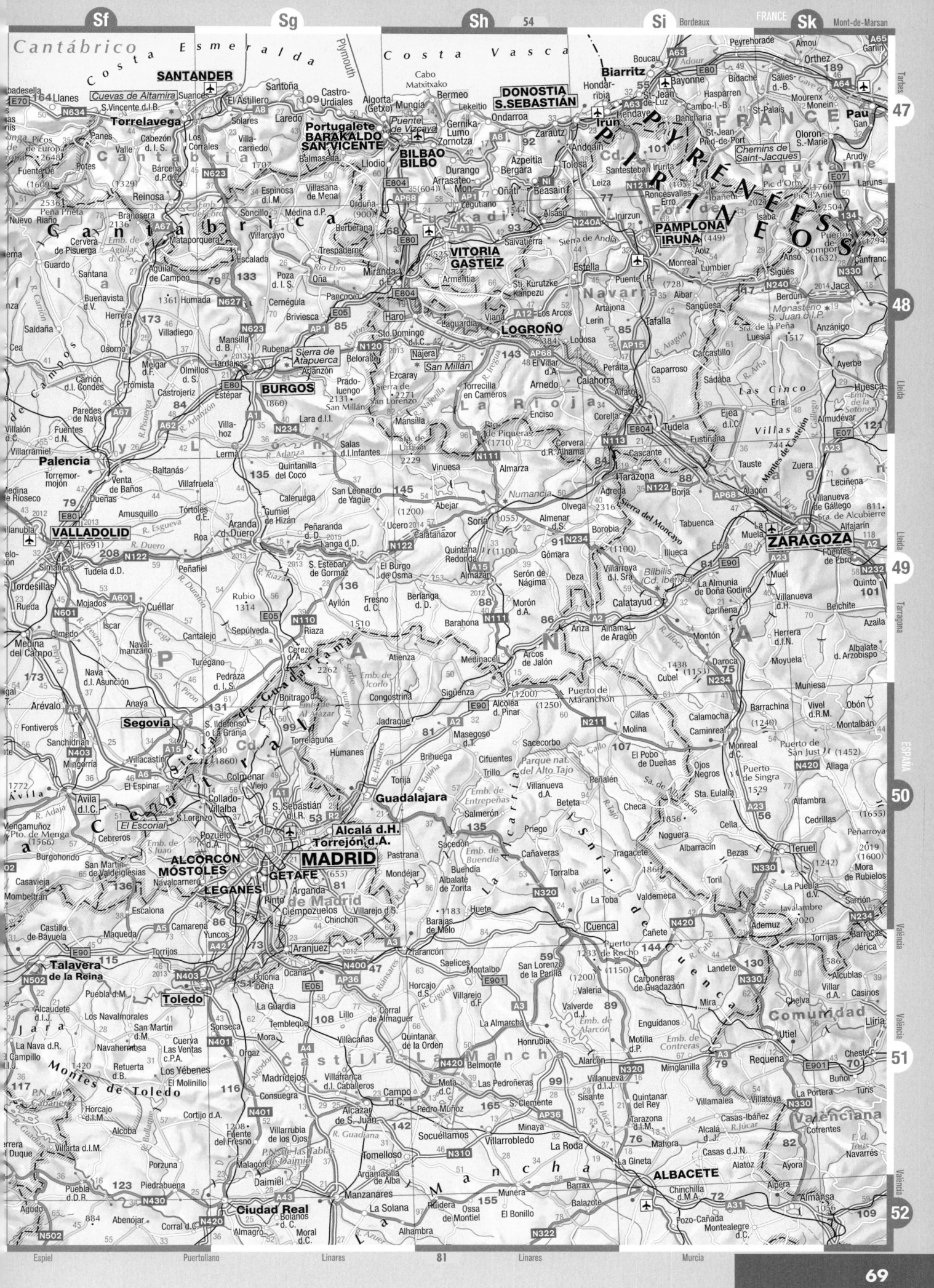

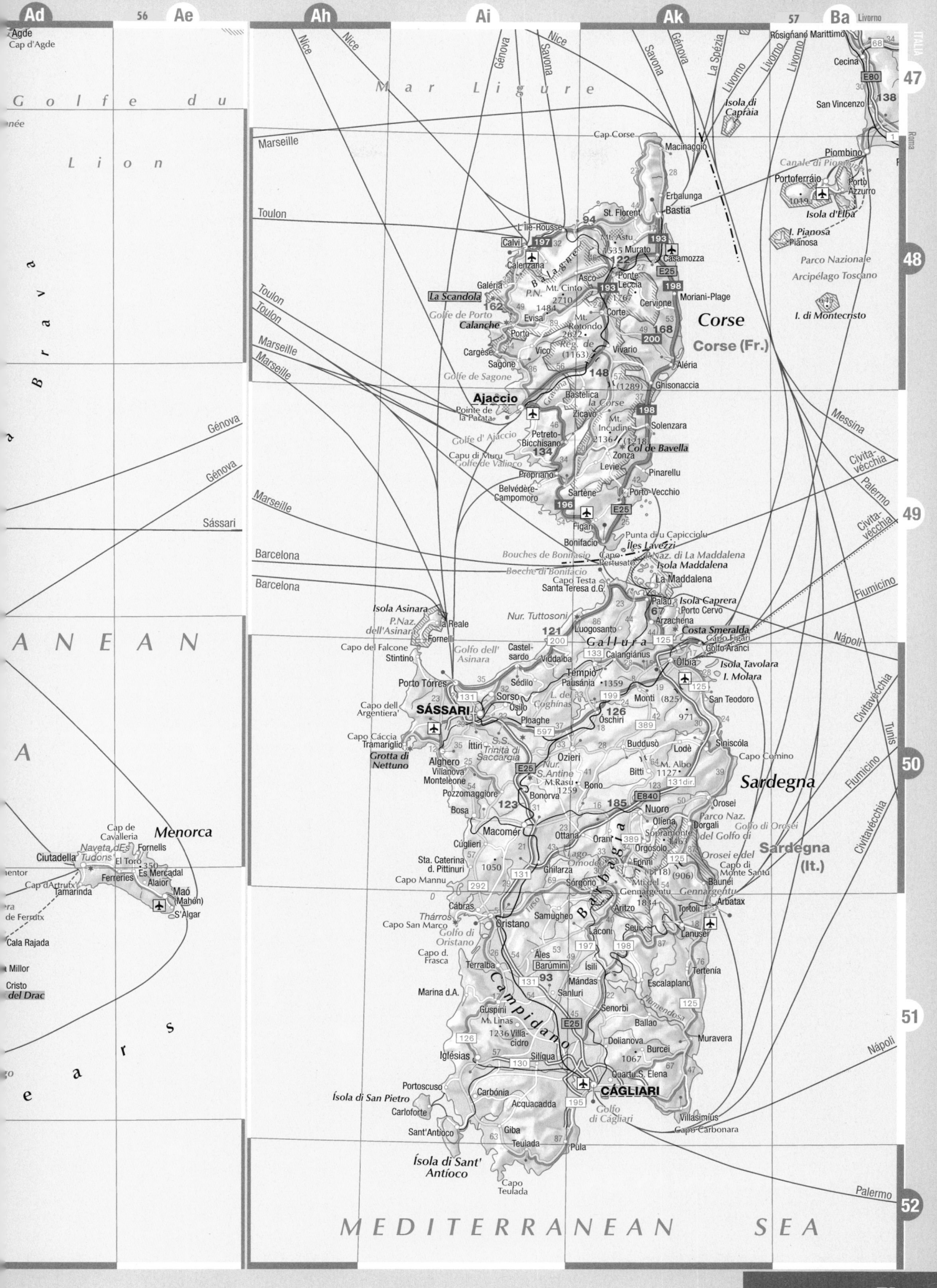

## Page 47

Cap Corse
Macinaggio
St. Florent
Erbalunga
193 Bastia
1535 Murato
122
Ponte Leccia
1767
Cervione
168 Casamozza
Moriani-Plage
E25
198
53
200

**Corse**
**Corse (Fr.)**

Aléria
(1289)
Ghisonaccia
198
Solenzara
(1218)
Col de Bavella
E25
Pinarellu
Porto-Vecchio
Iles Lavezzi
P. Naz. di La Maddalena
Isola Maddalena
La Maddalena
Palau
67 Isola Caprera
Porto Cervo
Arzachena
Costa Smeralda
Capo Figari
125
Golfo Aranci
Olbia
Isola Tavolara
I. Molara
Monti
(825)
San Teodoro
42 971
Lodè
Siniscóla
Capo Comino

**Sardegna**
**Sardegna (It.)**

Nice
Savona
Genova
La Spezia
Livorno
Livorno
Cecina
Pomarance
le Cornate
83
**Colline Metallifere**
**Toscana**
E80
138
1059
Massa Mar.
San Vincenzo
Piombino
G. di Follonica
Follonica
630
Portoferráio
Porto Azzurro
1019
**Isola di Capráia**
**Isola d'Elba**
I. Pianosa
Pianosa
Castiglione d.P.
Grosseto
Scansano

**Parco Nazionale**
**Arcipélago Toscano**
I. di Montecristo
Magliano i.T.
175
Orbetello
P. S. Stéfano
'Cosa
Porto Ércole
I. del Giglio
Gíglio Castello
Montalto di Castro
Tarquínia

Siena
223
Monticiano
S. Galgano
148
Montalcino
276
Pienza
Val d'Orcia
307
M. Amiata
1738
Abbadia S. Salvatore
Arcidosso
57
Pitigliano
Manciano
Viterbo
Tuscánia 168
Vetralla
Montefiascone
L. di Bolsena
71
Marta
Ronciglione
Pso. Farnese
579
Civitavécchia
E80
Ladíspoli
Cervéteri
A12

E78
Sinalunga
Castiglione d.l.
Cortona
Passignano
L. Trasimeno
Città d.P.
854
Marsciano
Todi
3bis
Orvieto
Acquasparta
1121
Narni
204
M. Terminillo
2216
Rieti
Mti. Sabini
1287
Città ducale
Orte
Civita Castellana
Fara i.S.
70
2
L. di Bracciano
Monterotondo
A1d
A24

Fabriano
Gúbbio
68
Gualdo T.
Matélica
Camerino
931
**Perúgia**
Assisi
Nocera Umbra
**Folígno** 264
Montefalco
75
**164**
**Spoleto**
Norcia
Visso
Antrodoco
2455
Gran Sasso d'Itália
(1283)
2912
17 A24
(72) Barisciano
**L'Áquila**
173
Celano
196
A25
2349
Avezzano
Pescina
82
(1400)
Subiaco
2156

Cingoli
Macerata
77
Civitanova Marche
49
Porto S. Giórg.
Fermo
165
S. Ginésio
S. Séverino
P. Naz. dei Monti Sibillini
48
S. Ben.
**Áscoli Piceno**
Arquata
1814
E55
**Téramo**
Atri
4
Isola d. Gr. Sasso
Penne
Popoli
Sulmona
Abruzzo

## Page 50

Ba Bb Bc Bd

**ROMA**
CIVITAS VATICANA
CITTÀ DEL VATICANO
Fiumicino
Óstia
**Lido di Óstia**
Anzio
Aprilia
16
148
**LATINA**
Sabáudia
Parco Naz. del Circeo
S. Felice Circeo
M. Circeo
Golfo di Gaeta
I. Palmarola
Ponza
Isola di Ponza
Isole Ponziane o Pontine
I. Ventotene
Isola d'Íschia
Íschia
Pozz
I. di Prócida

Palestrina
Tívoli
Frascati
Castel Gandolfo
Colli Albani
Velletri
7
Ferentino
193 Sezze
Terracina
148
Gaeta
Formia
213
Mondragone
Sessa
7quat
223

Montecassino
Cassi
Anagni
Alatri
213
Frosinone
Arpino
Sora
Casamad
Ceccano
Priverno
1090
Fondi
1533
630
Fiuggi
Avezzano
Pescina
Marsicano
Celano

**Mare Tirreno**

Barcelona
Tunis
Palermo
Valletta
Messina
Messina
Nápoli

**ITALIA**

## Page 52 / 53 (Sicília)

Bc Bd Be Bf Bg

Cágliari
Civitavécchia
Génova
Tunis
Isola di Ústica
Nápoli
Nápoli
Génova

Isola Alicudi
Isola Filicudi
Malfa
Santa Marina-Salina
Isola Salina
Lípari
Isola Lípari
Porto Levante
Isola Vulcano
I. Panarea
Isola Strómboli
Capo Vaticano
Nicotera
Rosarno
Gióia Táuro
Palmi
Serra S. Bruno
9
Polístena
682
188
Cittanova
Marina d. Gióiosa
E90
Gerace
Locri

Capo San Vito
Mondello
Carini
San Vito l.C.
**PALERMO**
61
Monreale
Baghèria
Bagheria
Termini Imerese
A19
Cefalù
Sant'Ágata d.M.
Capo d'Orlando
Milazzo
Patti
**MESSINA**
Villa S.G.
Mti. Peloritani
A20
116
Novara d.S.
1374
**RÉGGIO D.C.**
Bova Marina
Aspromonte
P. Naz. dell'Aspromonte
1956
106
Bovalino M.
Brancaleone Marina
Mélito d. Porto Salvo
50
111

Trápani
Càstellammare di Golfo
A29
Partinico
102
E933
41
Alcamo
Marineo
Segesta
Calatafími
624
Salemi
94 Belice
E90
Corleone
Prizzi
Lércara Fríddi
Partanna
Chiusa Sclàfani
133
(932)
38 Menfi
M. Cammarata
1579
Sto. Stéfano Quisquina
Ribera
118
169
Sciacca
Castelvetrano
Màzara del Vallo
Marinella
Selinunte
115

Termini Imerese
Sto. Stéfano
113
231
Mistretta
d. Miráglia
(1505)
(1264)
Randazzo
120
Castelbuono
(1107)
**Madonie**
102
Nicosia
Troina
Bronte
Adrano
M. Etna
3323
Zafferana Etnea
52
Leonforte
Agira
Catenanuova
Paternò
Enna
91
L. d. Ogliastro
A19
Villa di Casale
Piazza Armerina
Caltanissetta
68
Barrafranca
Mazzarino
Caltagirone
Scórdia
417
Militello i-V-d Catánia
Francofonte
Nec. di Pantalica
124

**Nébrodi**
186
A18
Giarre
Acireale
Taormina
94
Sta. Teresa d. Riva
E45
Sta.
**CATÁNIA**
114
Lentini
194
Augusta
65
**SIRACUSA**

Favignana
115
Marsala
43
Pantelleria
E90
Marinella
Eraclea Minoa
115 57
**Agrigento**
Porto Empédocle
Canicattí
Raffadali
Campobello d.L.
640
76
E931
Ribera
Butera
Riesi
**Sicília (It.)**
Licata
Gela
Niscemi
Vizzini
Akrai
Palazzolo Acréide
Ragusa
Vittória
91
Scicli
Módica
Noto
Ávola
Marina d. Ragusa
Sta. Croce Camerina
Ispica
Pachino
Capo delle Correnti
Pozállo
Floridia
52
Golfo di Noto
E45
**Sicília**

**MEDITERRANEAN SEA**

Lampedusa
Valletta

## Inset (Malta)

Be
54
Gozo
Ghawdex
Victoria (Rabat)
Ggantija
Mellieha
Mdina
Rabat
Zurrieq
Hal Saflieni
Comino
Génova
Réggio
Pozzallo
Valletta
Tarxien
55
**Malta**
**MALTA**

0 10 20 30 40 50 km
0 10 20 30 miles

N O E   M O R E

A C K   S E A

A   D E N İ Z

İnceburun
Kızılabalı    (18)   **Sinop**
Sinop Br.

Kerempe Br.      İnebolu    Abana    Çatalzeytin    Ayancık    58    Şerefiye    Kabalı   (310)
Akbayır           Doğanyurt                    Türkeli    **158**                010
Çide    96                Bozkurt                              Erfelek   Gerze    69
        Şenpazar    Dikmen D.    88    Çangal                   Çiçekyayla    (1370)    Dranoz
                    1471    Küre    D. 1605    Yenikonak    785    169    Dikman    Bafra Br.
Amasra    86    Meydan            2019    Bürnük                                        Kürtler
        Ant    Azdavay    Karaçam    (1440)              Çakırçay    Çuhali          Bafra
Hisarönü    Bartın    Şahin    Ağlı   **152** Yaralıgöz    63    030    Boyabat    Durağan    Ovası
İnkumu         Pınarbaşı        Dağı                     Gökırmak         70              Ondokuzmayıs   Bafra
Kilimli    Ulus    Seydiler    Devrekâni    765    Direklikaya    Çerçiler    Pelitbüku    1300   Boğazkaya
LDAK    010    Kozcağız    Kumluca    (1550)    Daday    Taşköprü    44    Sarayçık Dağı    Saraydüzü    106    Mezraa    030    Esençay   Sargın
(5)    58    Daday Çayı    14         Kastamonu    775    Akkaya    Ciftlikçay    27    785    Türkmen    Yunddağı   Çakıralan
Çaycuma    86    755    Eflâni    (798)    14    775    Kargı    030   1783    83
Kozlu    38    Karapınar    Kuzlam    40    Araç    68    Kırık    Hacıhamza    Kâmil    Vezirköprü    (940)
Beycuma    Gökçebey    728    Safranbolu    Araç Çayı    Kuzyaka    2587    Akkaya    İskilip    Sarayçık    20    030
KARABÜK    62    İğdir    İhsangazi    Ilgaz Dağı    39    Tosya    228    Osmancık    68   (960)    Havza    030    Lâdik
Ormanlı    Devrek    030    Çavuşlar    Milli Parkı    765    43    775    Harun    Hamamözü    14    Ak Dağ    2062
Dorukhan    Yenice    46    Ovacık    Boyalı    100    Devrez Çayı    Kargın    Asarcık    97    Merzifon    Suluova    48
Eğerci    925    Geç.    77    Soğanlı    Ilgaz    35    36    Kurşunlu    Belören    Yaprakli    İkizören    Bayat    Lâçin    795    Saribuğday    E80    Amasya
Mengen    Gökçesu    İsmetpaşa    Bayramören    Çerkeş    E80    187    Çankırı    180    ÇORUM    Doğantepe    Amasya    180    Kaleköy
Karadürgen    Atkaracalar    Eldivan    Kuzu    180    Seydim    Mecitözü    Gediksaray    180
Gerede    Dağı    Ağaca    Işık D.    Korgun    İkizören    Sağpazar    Hamdi    1791    İbek    Göynücek    Zile    190
Bolu    Kavacık    2015    Sakaevi    Bozkır    84    Uğurludağ    1198    Demirşeyh    Cemilbey    Ortaköy    Aydıncık    74    Boztepe
(725)    E89    Güven    Orta    Tatlı Ç.    21    Karaçay    795    Alaca    Çöplü    Devici Dağı
Çamlıdere    Kızılcahamam    Şabanözü    Karamusa    Termo Ç.    Kızılırmak    Alacahöyük    190    Çekerek
Köroğlu T.    Balcılar    Karagöl    765    Hasayaz    Kızılırmak    Sungurlu    Tasarı Milli    805    Kadışehri
Peçenek    Çeltikçi    750    135    Çubuk    Çandır    Sulakyurt    Kavak    57    Alembeyli    Parkı    Eymir    Beyyurdu
Kibrıscık    Karaşar    138    Pazar    Çubuk    (1365)    45    Delice    190    Boğazkale    Hattusaş    53    Sorgun    795    Yanık
Karaköy    Güdül    54    Kazan    140    İdris D.    Kalecik    Balışeyh    200    Salmanlı    1689    Deremahal    42    Camlık
Çayırhan    Beypazarı    96    Sirkeli    1985    74    52    E88    (700)    E88    1742    Musabeyli    Sorgun    Milli Parkı    228
Yağmurdede    Yenikent    KEÇİÖREN    020    ALTINDAĞ    Delice    Sekili    **Yozgat**    200    Doğanli    200
nyar    Ayaş    SİNCAN    23    MAMAK    Elmadağ    753    Saray    37    Osmanpaşa    Karamgara
Koyunağılı    Kırbaşı    İçmecesi    Polatlı    ÇANKAYA    29    .1862    **KIRIKKALE**    Dinek    Sekili    Aiçi    Hasbek    Akçakışla
Mihalıççık    Ayas    18    29    Gölbaşı    Yahşihan    D.    Akçakent    Yerköy    Gelingüllü    Olüközü    805
Sarayözu    Şabanözü    (850)    020    Koparan    Hacılar    24    Keskin    Çiçekdağı    785    Brj.    Yenipazar    200    Sarıkaya
Biçer    Poyraz    Temelli    Çökören    260    Karaali    Karakeçili    765    Akpınar    Çamalak    Karahasanlı    72    Çayıralan    Ak Dağı    2272
Sazılar    **130**    Kayabaşı    İkizce    63    260    Balâ    Kaman    Göllü    Sırçalı    Çandır
Iğdecik    Yassıhöyük    E90    200    Şeyhali    Oyaca    **158**    Celebi    757    Kaman    Çoğun    Karahanaslı    Fehimli    Boğazlıyan    Çukur
Polatlı    (Gordion)    Çimşit    26    Seyfe    Kozaklı    Akpınar    Oğulcak    Felâhiye
59    Yenimehmetli    Haymana    Yenice    Kesikköprü    61    Aydınlar    G.    Seyfeköy    Büyüköz    Kurşunlu D.    Tuzla
Arayıt D.    Günyüzü    695    Ilıca    Yamak    Yaylâsı    Kaçarlı    46    1808    Seyfeköy    Kozaklı    Himmetdede    Golü
1820    İlyaspaşa    82    Yeşilöz    Çeltikli    .1724    Odunboğazı    Hirfanlı    Boztepe    8    Akpınar    Büyüköz    Kanis    300Gezi
Yarıkkaya    Adatoprakpınar    Çekirge    Karaca D.    17    Yazıçayırı    Brj.    Tokluman    15    **Kırşehir**    Topaklı    (1260)    Erkilet    (1054)
Çeltik    Emirler    Kozanlı    Akın    (978)    Mucur    765    **126**    Özkonak    **KAYSERİ**
Yunak    33    Yeşilyurt    Kulu    Şereflikoç    Kesikköprü    Hacıbektaş    Çallıgedik Geç.    260    22
Hacıfaklı    Harabeköy    Tavşançalı    Tuzyaka    hisar    Hânı    Ağaçören    Gümüşkent    64    E90    Boğazköprü
Yeniceoba    **Cihanbeyli**    905    Savcılı    Bozkır

Novorossijsk

SOČI
DAGOMYS
Loo
Hosta
Macest
Adler
Lese

Č O R N O E   M O R E

B L A C K   S E A

K A R A   D E N İ Z

+2h Gr. Time       +3h Gr. Time

Bafra Br.
Yakakent  Bafra  Harız  Kürtler
Alaçam   Ovası
Sinop   26  Bafra
Ondokuzmayıs
49
Pelitbükü   Boğazkaya
1300
Altınkaya   169   Sargın
Brj.   Esençay
Y u n d d a ğ ı   Çakıralan
SAMSUN
(42)
Çıva Br.
Çarşamba
Ovası
Dikbıyık   Emiryusuf
Themiskira
60   Kavak   Tekkeköy   Çayırkent   Çarşamba   Terme
Köprübaşı   (940)
795   010
Havza   20   030   Şeyhli   Cevizlik   152   94
14   11   Lâdik   54   Asarcık   Salıpazarı   Ünye
Çorum   Hasan Uğurlu   Ayvacık   Çaybaşı   010
Suluova   Ak Dağ   Destek   Brj.   850   21
100   2062   Taşova   Kumru   Fatsa
28   48   Karayaka   Akkuş   Korgan
Amasya   E80   Tekke   Çamiçi
Doğantepe   Çiğdemlik   Esençay   Erbaa   (235)   Gölköy
180   Kaleköy   Kozlu   Niksar   (1570)   Bereketli
69   Aydınca   d a   ğ   l a   r   ı   Yeşilce
Turhal   Dazya-   Yazıtepe   44   Gökdere   Reşadiye
Han   Komana   Almus   Meşudiye
Buzluk Dağ   Yaylacık Dağı   Pontike   Almus   Cilhane   E80   200   Umurca
İğdir   190   Zile   Brj.   Köyülhisar
Dökmetepe   47   Doğan-   Gökçekent
Pazar   Horostepe   Yeşilırmak   şar   290
Tokat   2643   (1925)
(1150)   Yıldız D.   Keşiş D.   Şerefiye
74   Artova   2552   Aşağıa-   2812
Kadışehri   Çiftlik   (623)   sarıcık
Hanı   Çamlıbel   Çırçır   Suşehri   60   100
Yanık   59   Çamlıbel   Geç   Akıncılar
Pazarcık   Sulusaray   Yeşilyurt   Gölova
228   E88   (1646)   Yenihan   163   Hafik   68   Zara   İmranlı
Belcik   Havaalanı   Tekkeköy   E88   200
Oluközü   Yıldızeli   46   Kızıldağ   Akarsu
Akçakışla   Direkli   Beydağı   Geç   Refahiye
Çayıralan   SİVAS   Celâli   95   (2190)   Cengerli
Akdağmadeni   (1275)   2802   Karacaören   Gümüşakar   Çatalarmut
Ak Dağlar   Çallı   850   Karayün   Bulucan   Doğanbeyli   3549
2345   Ortaköy   Akkoç   2688   Bozoğlak   Esence Dağl.
Sizir   Akçakışla   Bedirli   Harmancık   Büyükarmutlu   Erzincan
Çukur   İncebel Dağları   Kayadibi   Ulaş   Beypınarı   Gedikbaşı   Altıntepe   Akbaba
2272   (1180)   Şarkışla   Sincan   İğdeli   İliç   Oğuz   Tepe   Çağlayan
Gemerek   260   Altınyayla   Deliktaş   Kavak   3462   Üzümlü
Sarıoğlan   Karagöl   Divriği   Kemah   Alpköy
Tuzla   K u l m a c   D a ğ l a r ı   (1950)   (750)   Karaşar   3188   Kemâliye   Yeşilyazı   Ovacik
Gölü   2079   Çetinkaya   Mursal   Danişment   Başpınar   Munzur Vadisi
Sultanhanı   Akkışla   Karaca T.   Havuz   Kangal   13   78   84   Dutluca   Karaoğlan   Milli Parkı   Büyükyurt
Bünyan   Örenşehir   Ziyarettepesi   860   850   Alacahan   Calgan   Gedikler   Hozat   Tunceli   105
Kayseri   349   Yılanlı   Geç   Uzun Yayla   60   Yoncalı   Arapgir   Çemişgezek   Dere
Sizir   Kaynar   (1900)   Hasançelebi   Kuluncak   Akçapınar   Pertek   57
Pınarbaşı   Göltepe   300   Köyünlü   Konakpınarı   Ballıkaya   Hekimhan   Taşdelen   Balıbey   Pınarlar

Civa Br. area right: ORDU
Perşembe   Oman Paşa   52   Kabadüz   Pİraziz   Bulancak   Sakarya   171   Eynesil   Vakfıkebir   Fener Br.   Akçakale
Yasun Br.   Çamaş   Ulubey   Gürgen-tepe   Topçam   Bulancak   Kale   Tirebolu   Görele   Beşikdüzü   010   TRABZON
Çamlı   tepe   (1275)   (1940)   Çambaşı Y.   Giresun   Keşap   Espiye   Çanakçı   Şalpazarı   Akçaabat   50
Mele Yrm.   3027   Kovanlık   Yavuz-kemal   Dereli   Yağlıdere   877   Doğankent   Tonya   Düzköy   E97
Karagöl D.   93   Akılbaba T.   Sapmaz   2168   Kürtün   Altındere   Arsin
Yeşilce   2826   865   Torul   883   Altındere   Maçka   88
Ballıca   Giresun   Gümüşhane   Vadisi   E97
Ortakent   (2200)   Alucra   Kara Dağ   Milli   3082
3331   Dağları   Yağlıdere
Köyülhisar   34   040   E97   885   885   Kale   (1900)
290   Kelkit Çayı   Şiran   Dilekyolu   31   Köse   05
(1925)   Şebin-karahisar   84   Çamoluk   Kozağaç   Kelkit   Demir
2812   Gölova   77   Otlukbeli Dağları   885   Başköy   Balıklı
100   Akıncılar   885   Çatalçam   E80   (2160)   100   3549
Suşehri   60   Kızıldağ   (2190)   Refahiye   81   Üzümlü   Tanye

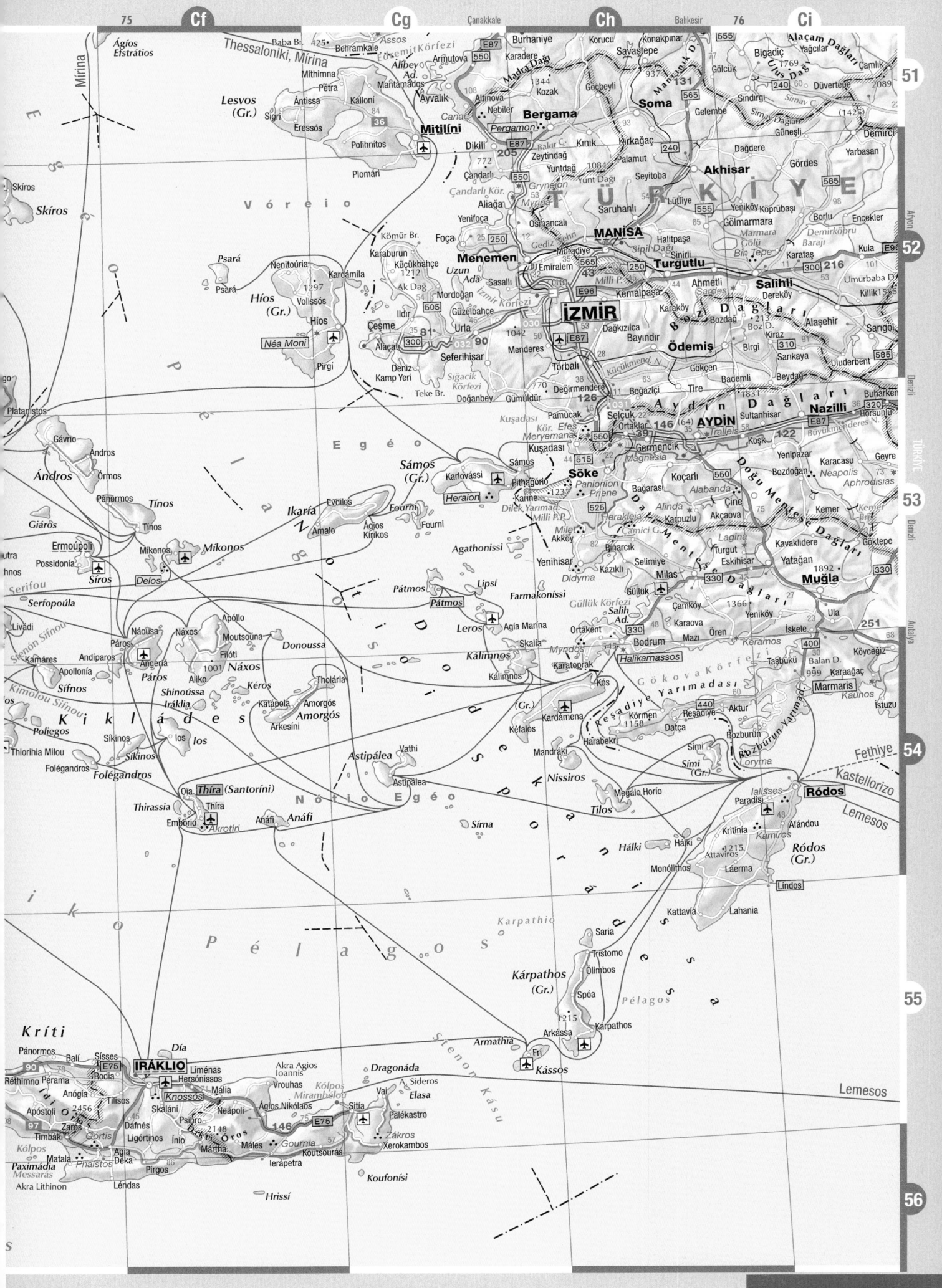

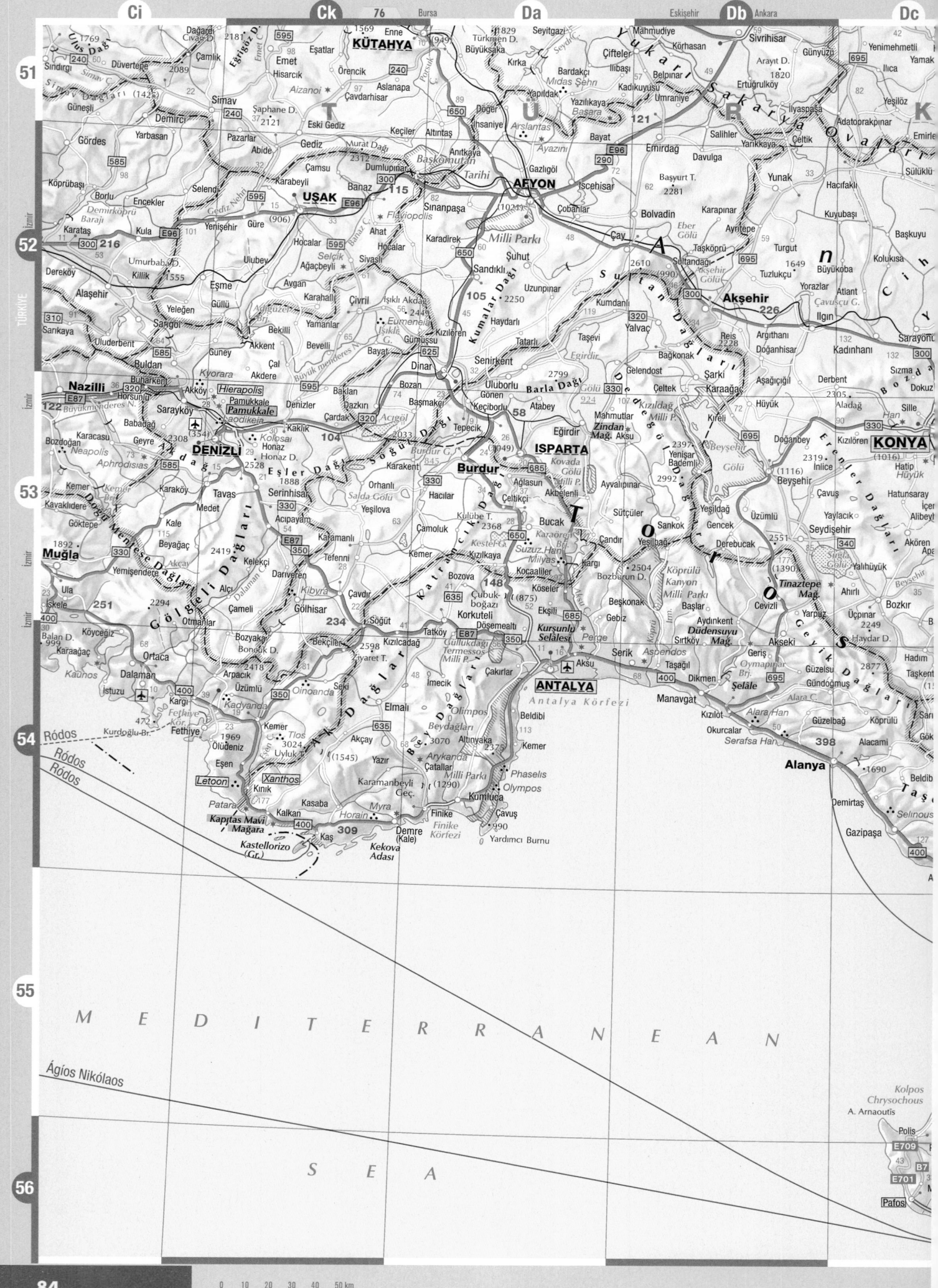

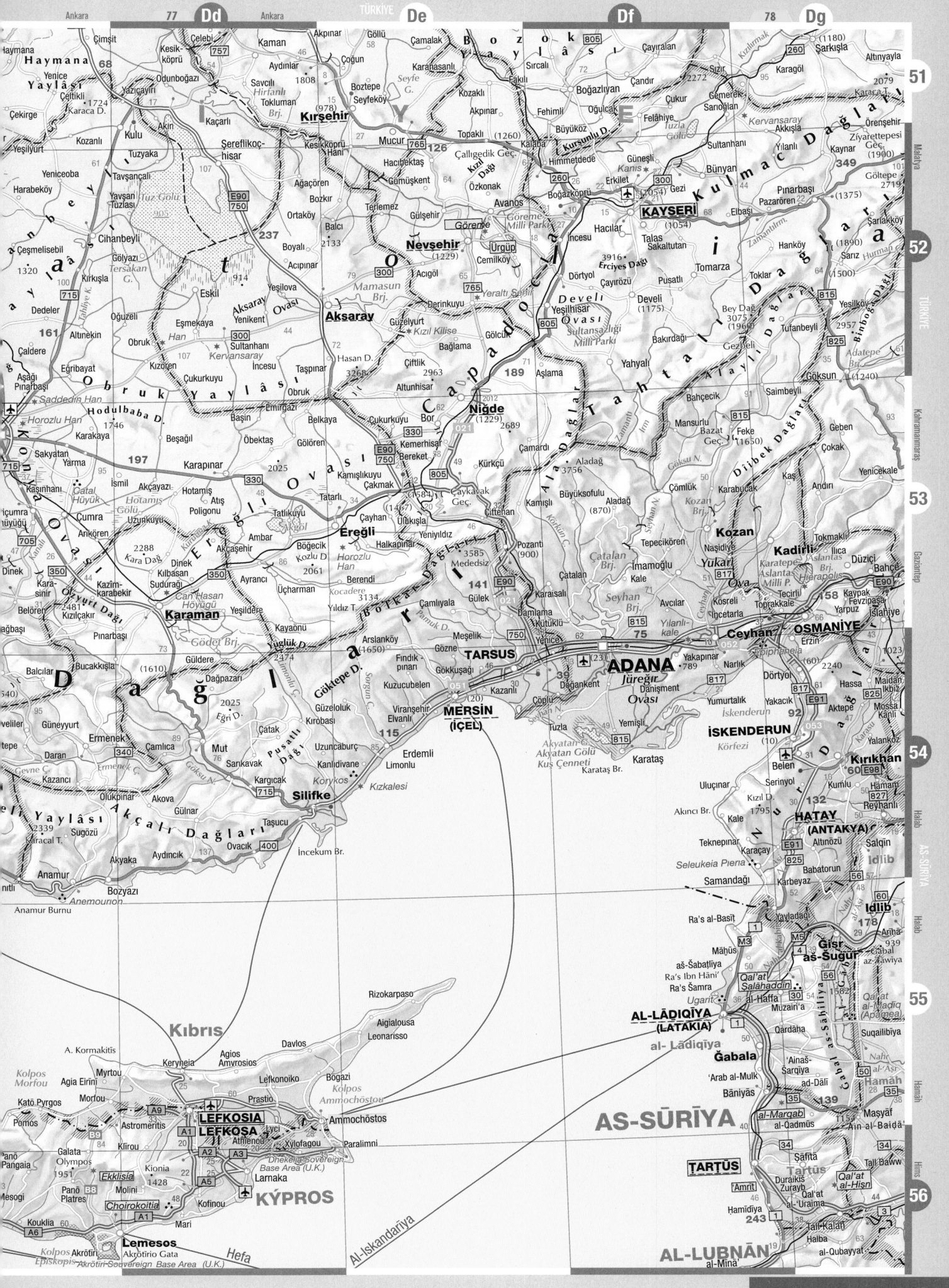

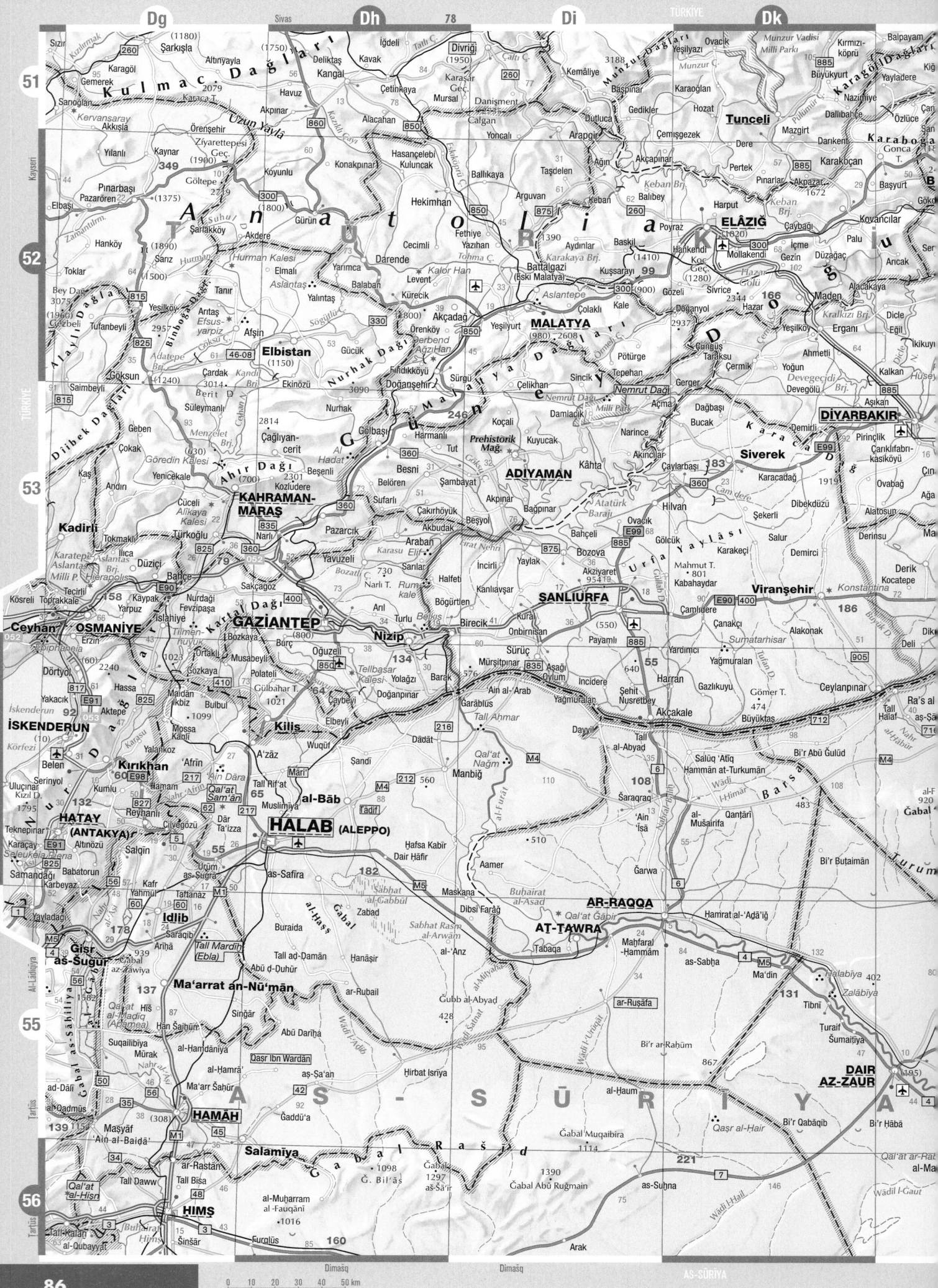

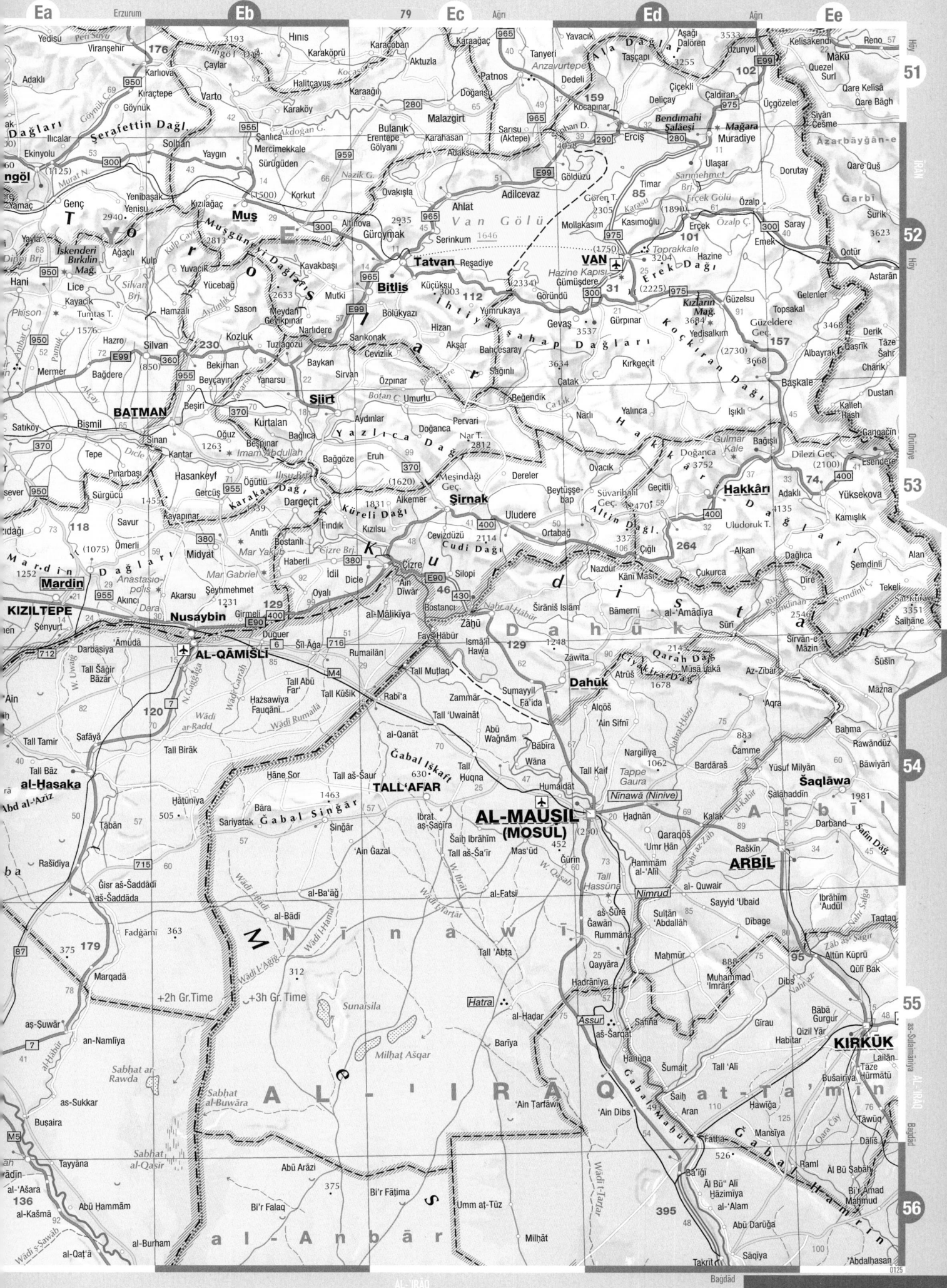

# 1 : 20.000

| GB | F | D | | I | E | NL |
|---|---|---|---|---|---|---|
| Motorway | Autoroute | Autobahn | | Autostrada | Autopista | Autosnelweg |
| Road with four lanes | Route à quatre voies | Vierspurige Straße | | Strada a quattro corsie | Carretera de cuatro carriles | Weg met vier rijstroken |
| Thoroughfare | Route de transit | Durchgangsstraße | | Strada di attraversamento | Carretera de tránsito | Weg voor doorgaand verkeer |
| Main road | Route principale | Hauptstraße | | Strada principale | Carretera principal | Hoofdweg |
| Other roads | Autres routes | Sonstige Straßen | | Altre strade | Otras carreteras | Overige wegen |
| One-way street - Pedestrian zone | Rue à sens unique - Zone piétonne | Einbahnstraße - Fußgängerzone | | Via a senso unico - Zona pedonale | Calle de dirección única - Zona peatonal | Straat met eenrichtingsverkeer - Voetgangerszone |
| Information - Parking place | Information - Parking | Information - Parkplatz | | Informazioni - Parcheggio | Información - Aparcamiento | Informatie - Parkeerplaats |
| Main railway with station | Chemin de fer principal avec gare | Hauptbahn mit Bahnhof | | Ferrovia principale con stazione | Ferrocarril principal con estación | Belangrijke spoorweg met station |
| Other railway | Autre ligne | Sonstige Bahn | | Altra ferrovia | Otro ferrocarril | Overige spoorweg |
| Underground | Métro | U-Bahn | | Metropolitana | Metro | Ondergrondse spoorweg |
| Tramway | Tramway | Straßenbahn | | Tram | Tranvía | Tram |
| Airport bus | Bus d'aéroport | Flughafenbus | | Autobus per l'aeroporto | Autobús al aeropuerto | Vliegveldbus |
| Police station - Post office | Poste de police - Bureau de poste | Polizeistation - Postamt | | Posto di polizia - Ufficio postale | Comisaria de policia - Correos | Politiebureau - Postkantoor |
| Hospital - Youth hostel | Hôpital - Auberge de jeunesse | Krankenhaus - Jugendherberge | | Ospedale - Ostello della gioventù | Hospital - Albergue juvenil | Ziekenhuis - Jeugdherberg |
| Church - Church of interest | Église - Église remarquable | Kirche - Sehenswerte Kirche | | Chiesa - Chiesa interessante | Iglesia - Iglesia de interés | Kerk - Bezienswaardige kerk |
| Synagogue - Mosque | Synagogue - Mosquée | Synagoge - Moschee | | Sinagoga - Moschea | Sinagoga - Mezquita | Synagoge - Moskee |
| Monument - Tower | Monument - Tour | Denkmal - Turm | | Monumento - Torre | Monumento - Torre | Monument - Toren |
| Built-up area, public building | Zone bâtie, bâtiment public | Bebaute Fläche, öffentliches Gebäude | | Caseggiato, edificio pubblico | Zona edificada, edificio público | Bebouwing, openbaar gebouw |
| Industrial area | Zone industrielle | Industriegelände | | Zona industriale | Zona industrial | Industrieterrein |
| Park, forest | Parc, bois | Park, Wald | | Parco, bosco | Parque, bosque | Park, bos |

| DK | S | PL | | CZ | H | RUS |
|---|---|---|---|---|---|---|
| Motorvej | Motorväg | Autostrada | | Dálnice | Autópálya | Автострада |
| Firesporet vej | Väg med fyra körfällt | Droga o czterech pasach ruchu | | Čtyřstopá silnice | Négysávos út | 4-х полосная автодорога |
| Genemmfartsvej | Genomfartsled | Droga przelotowa | | Průjezdní silnice | Átmenő út | Магистральная дорога |
| Hovedvej | Huvudled | Droga główna | | Hlavní silnice | Főút | Главная дорога |
| Andre mindre vejen | Övriga vägar | Drogi inne | | Ostatní silnice | Egyéb utak | Другие дороги |
| Gade med ensrettet kørsel - Gågade | Enkelriktad gata - Gågata | Ulica jednokierunkowa - Strefa ruchu pieszego | | Jednosměrná ulice - Pěší zóna | Egyirányú utca - Sétáló utca | Улица с односторонним движением - Пешеходная зона |
| Information - Parkeringplads | Information - Parkering | Informacja - Parking | | Informace - Parkoviště | Információ - Parkolóhely | Информация - Парковка |
| Hovedjernbanelinie med station | Huvudjärnväg med station | Kolej główna z dworcami | | Hlavní železnice s stanice | Fővasútvonal állomással | Главная железная дорога с вокзалом |
| Anden jernbanelinie | Övrig järnväg | Kolej drugorzędna | | Ostatní železnice | Egyéb vasútvonal | Прочая железная дорога |
| Underjordisk bane | Tunnelbana | Metro | | Metro | Földalatti vasút | Метро |
| Sporvej | Spårväg | Linia tramwajowa | | Tramvaj | Villamos | Трамвай |
| Bus til lufthavn | Flygbuss | Autobus dojazdowy na lotnisko | | Letištní autobus | Repülőtéri autóbusz | Автобус до аэропорта |
| Politistation - Posthus | Poliskontor - Postkontor | Komisariat - Poczta | | Policie - Poštovní úřad | Rendőrség - Postahivatal | Полицейский участок - Почта |
| Sygehus - Vandrerhjem | Sjukhus - Vandrarhem | Szpital - Schronisko młodzieżowe | | Nemocnice - Ubytovna mládeže | Kórház - Ifjúsági szálló | Больница - Туристская база для молодежи |
| Kirke - Seværdig kirke | Kyrka - Sevärd kyrka | Kościół - Kościół zabytkowy | | Kostel - Zajímavý kostel | Templom - Látványos templom | Церковь - Достопримечательная церковь |
| Synagoge - Moské | Synagoga - Moské | Synagoga - Meczet | | Synagoga - Mešita | Zsinagóga - Mecset | Синагога - Мечеть |
| Mindesmærke - Tårn | Monument - Torn | Pomnik - Wieża | | Pomník - Věž | Emlékmű - Torony | Памятник - Башня |
| Bebyggelse, offentlig bygning | Bebyggt område, offentlig byggnad | Obszar zabudowany, budynek użyteczności publicznej | | Zastavěná plocha, veřejná budova | Beépítés, középület | Застройка, обшественное здание |
| Industriområde | Industriområde | Obszar przemysłowy | | Průmyslová plocha | Iparvidék | Промышленная область |
| Park, skov | Park, skog | Park, las | | Park, les | Park, erdő | Парк, лес |

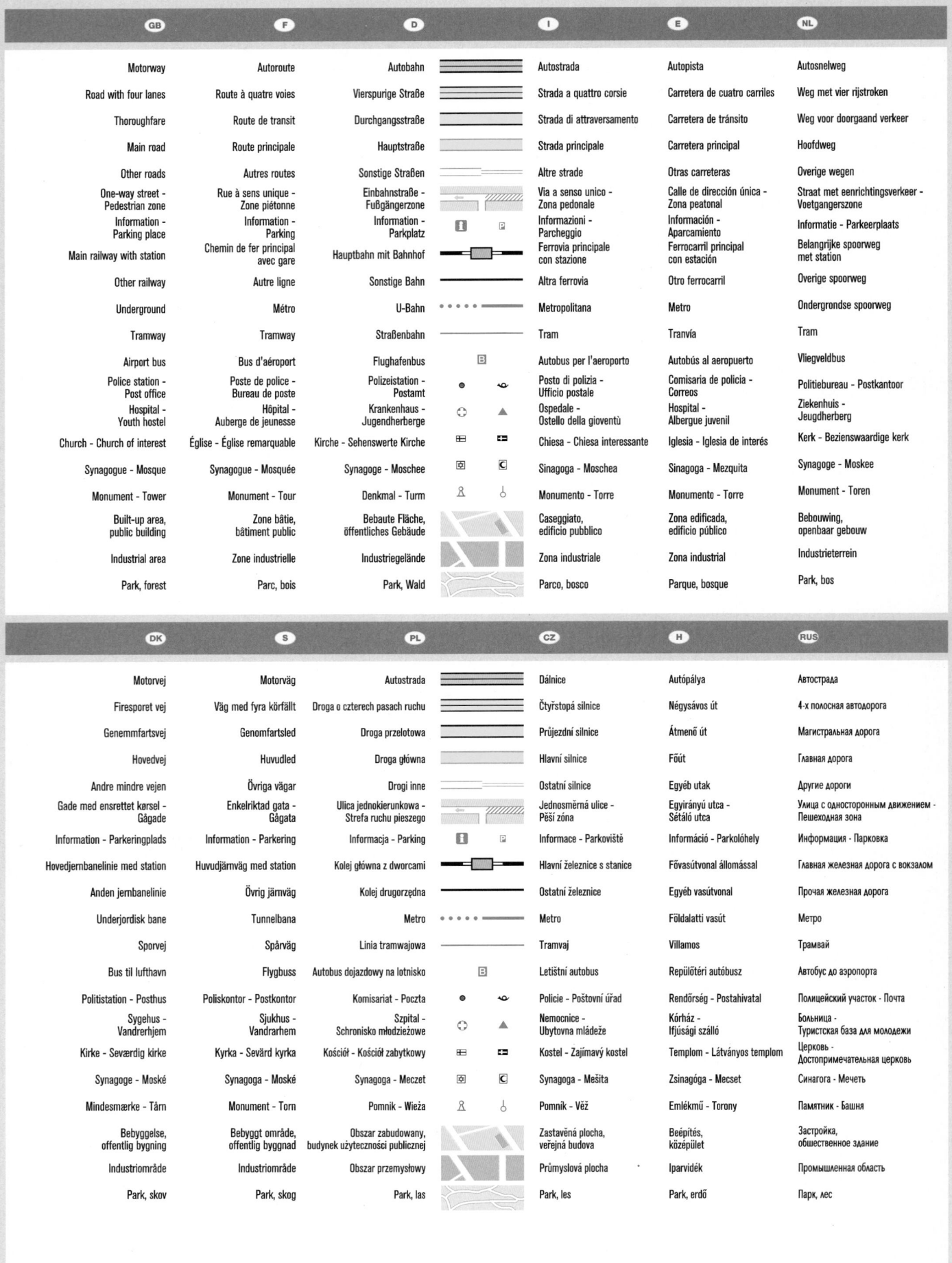

Amsterdam
Ankara
Athína
Barcelona
Belfast
Beograd
Berlin
Bern
Bonn
Bratislava
Brussel / Bruxelles
București
Budapest
Cardiff
Dublin / Baile Átha Cliath
Frankfurt am Main
Genève
Glasgow
Hamburg
Helsinki
İstanbul
Kaliningrad

København
Kyjiv
Leipzig
Lisboa
Ljubljana
London
Luxembourg
Lyon
Madrid
Marseille
Milano
Minsk
Monaco*
Monte Carlo***
Moskva
München
Oslo
Paris
Praha
Reykjavík
Rīga

Roma
Sankt Peterburg
Sarajevo
Sofija
Stockholm
Tallinn
Tiranë

València
Venézia**
Vilnius
Warszawa
Wien
Zagreb
Zürich

**1:20 000 / 1cm = 200m**

* 1:7 500 / 1cm = 75m  |  ** 1:10 000 / 1cm = 100m  |  *** 1: 15 000 / 1cm = 150m

Photo: Altstadt, Stockholm (IFA-Bilderteam/Jon Arnold Images)

ULUS · HISAR · SAMANPAZARI · DÖRTYOL · KURTULUŞ · ANITTEPE · MALTEPE · SIHHIYE · KIZILAY

Hipodrom C · Kazım Karabekir C · Anafartalar C · Hisar C · Bentderesi C · Ankara Kalesi · Celal · Cumhuriyet · Gençlik Parkı · İstiklal C · Atatürk Caddesi · Hasırcılar C · Ulucanlar Caddesi · Talatpaşa Caddesi · Talatpaşa Bulvarı · Anıtkabir · Akdeniz Caddesi · Maraşal Fevzi Çakmak · Celal Bayar Bulvarı · Cemal Gürsel C · Atatürk Mausoleum · Kurtuluş Parkı · Gökalp

FALLS · Shankill · Crumlin Road · Antrim Road · Clifton St. · Great George's St. · Sydenham Road · Falls Road · Grosvenor · Divis Street · Springfield Road · Broadway · Donegall Road · Ormeau Park · River Lagan · Ormeau Road · East Bridge Street · Bridge End · Middlepath St. · Lagan Bridge · Oxford Street · Great Victoria Street · Royal Victoria Hospital · Royal Maternity Hospital · City Hospital · Europa Bus Centre · Opera House · City Hall · Botanic Station · Lagan Bank Road · Queen's Quay · The Odyssey · Abercorn Basin · Queen's Island

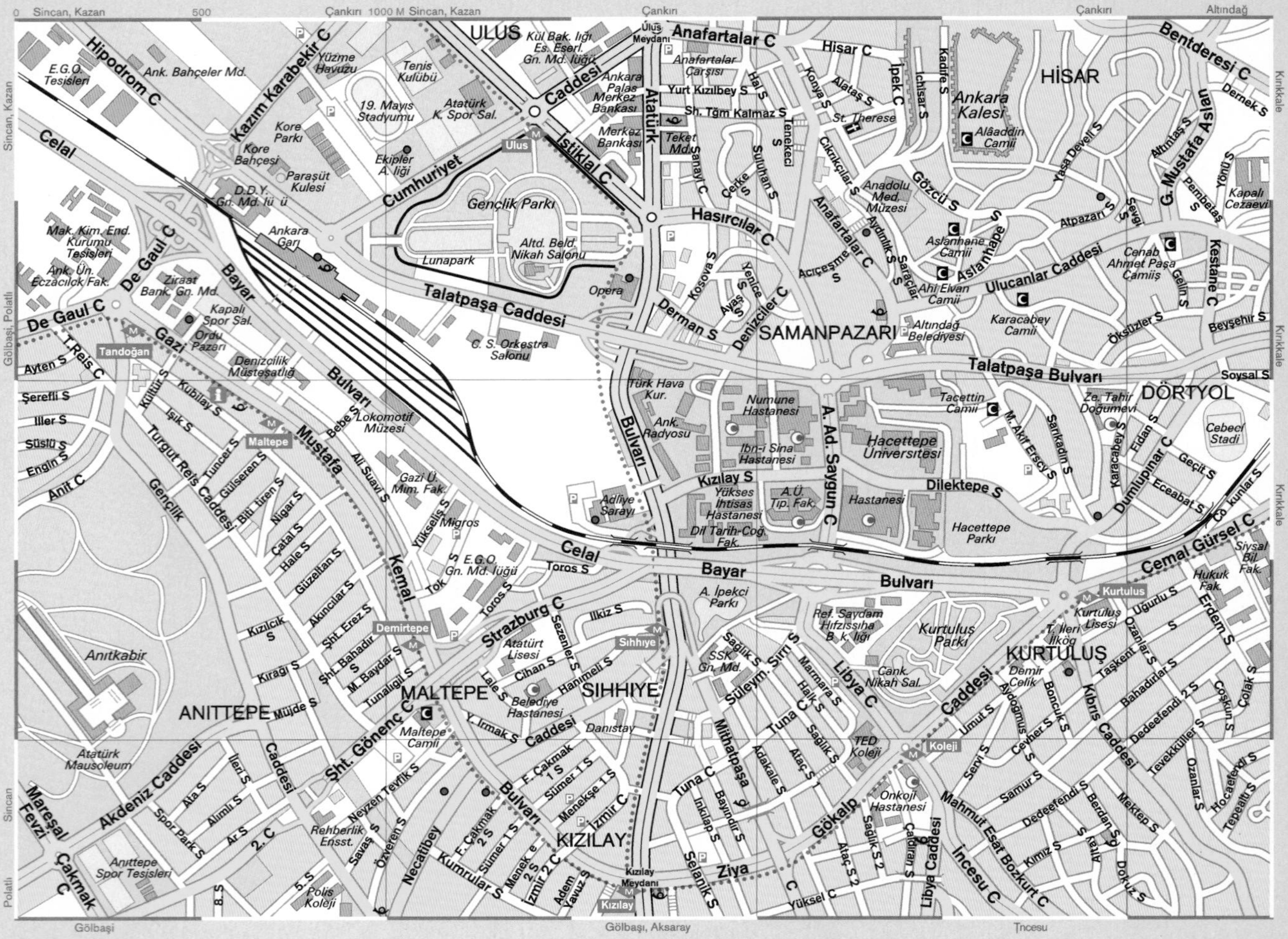

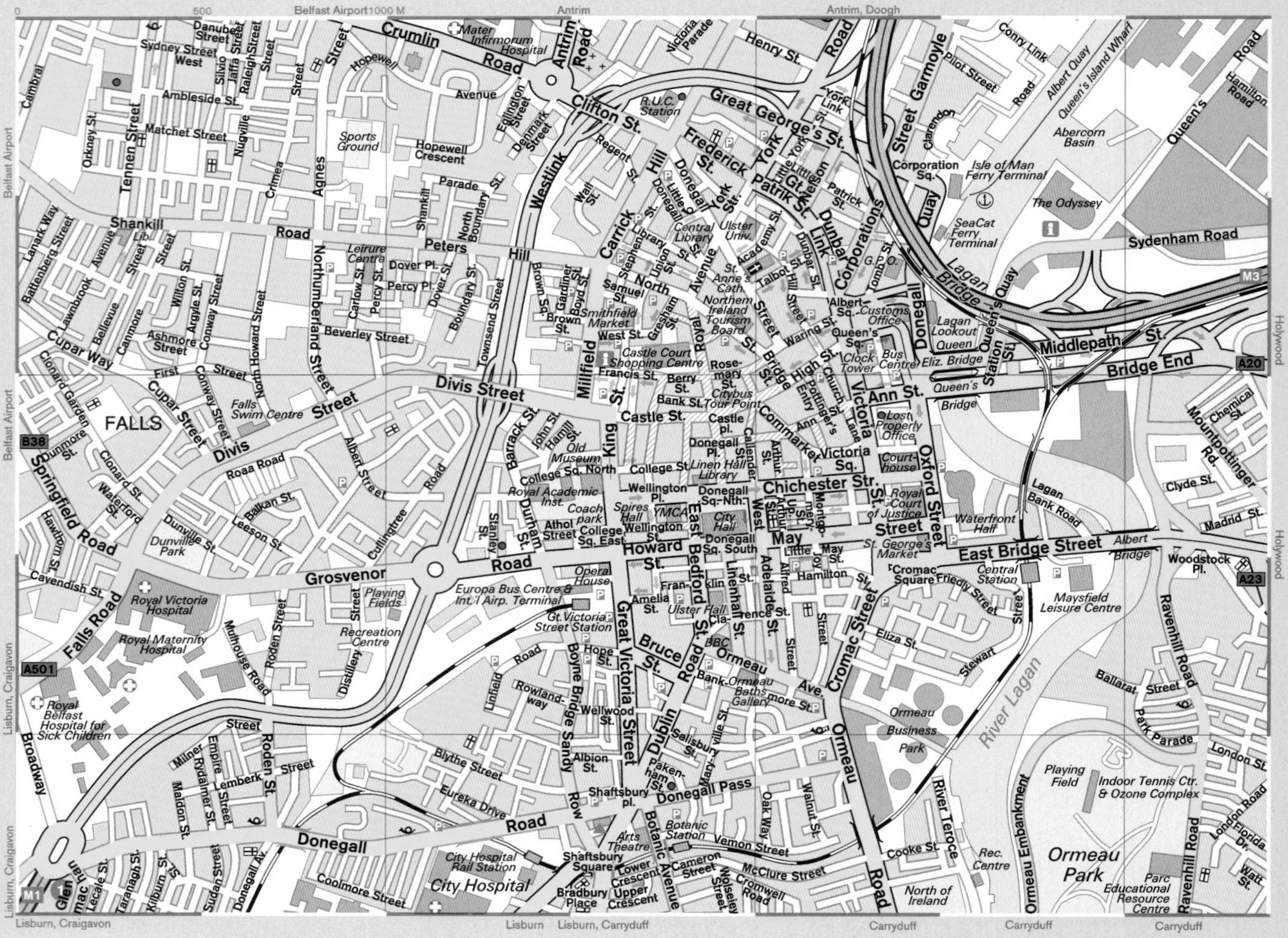

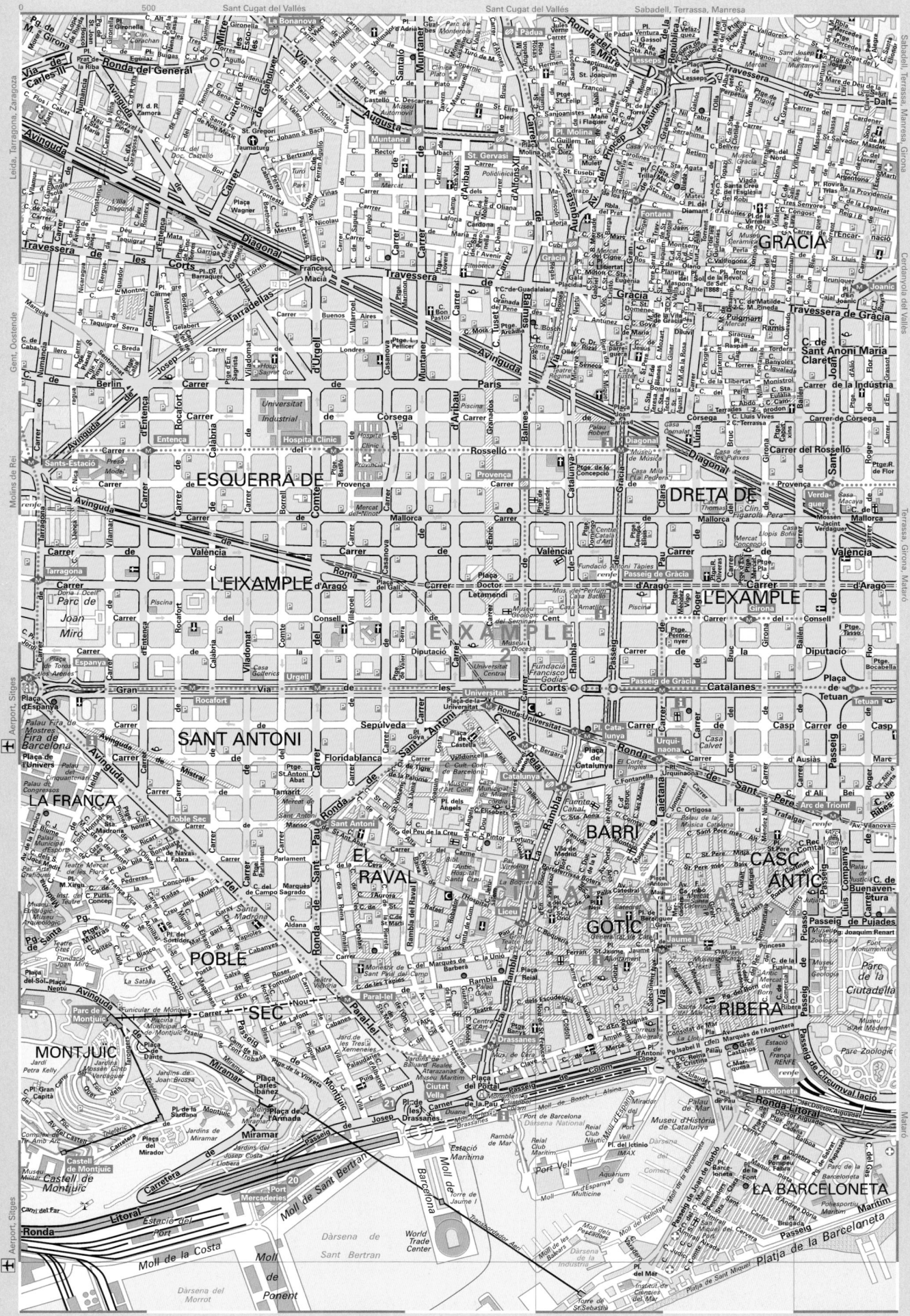

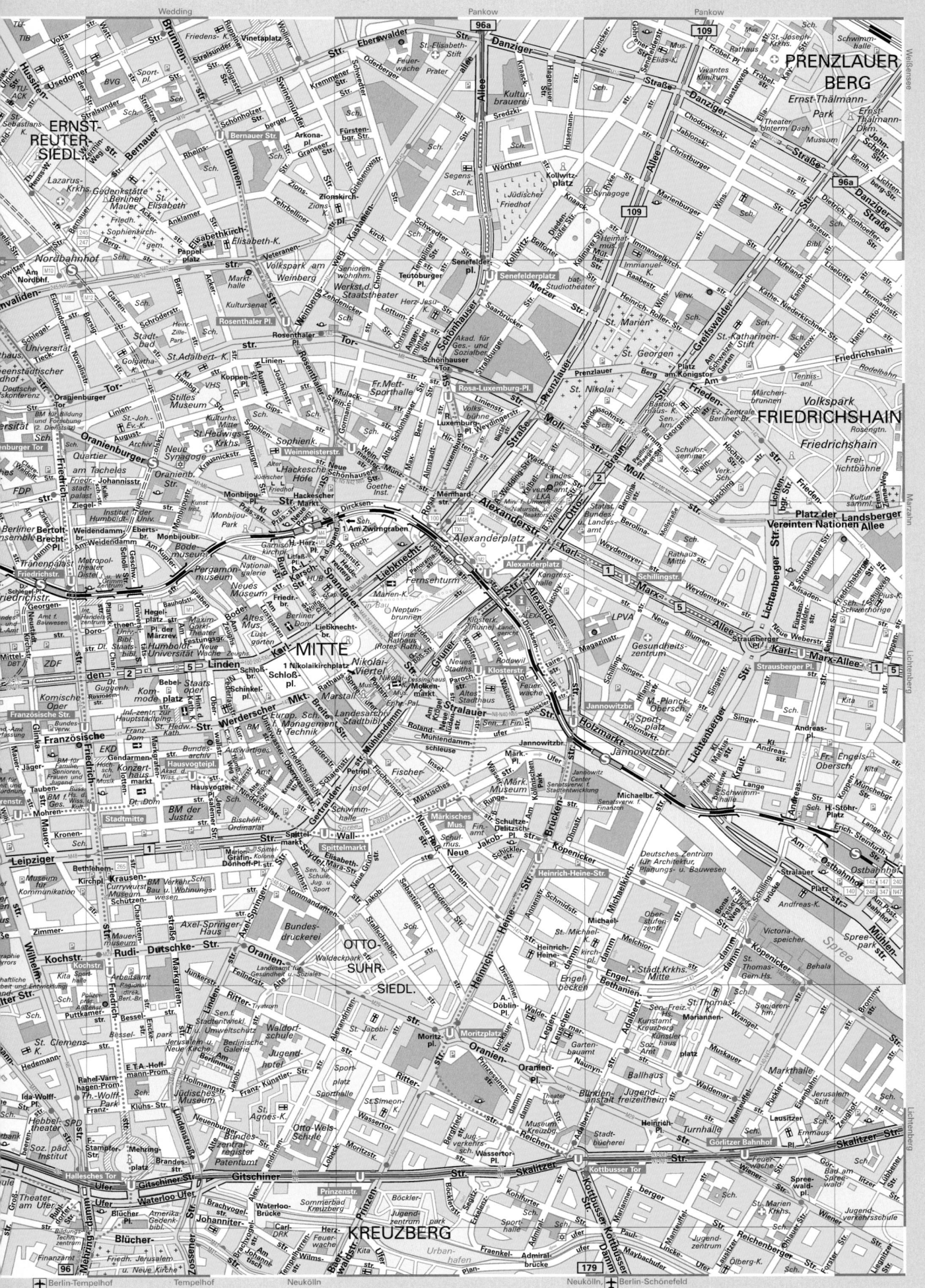

# Beograd SRB-11000

DORĆOL

STARI GRAD

Kalemegdan

29. Novembra

PALILULA

1 Kopernikova
2 Stanoja Stanojevića
3 Boška Palkovljevića

# Bern CH-3000-31

NEUFELD

BRÜCKFELD

LORRAINE

WYLER

BREITFELD

ALLMEND

BERN

LORRAINE

SPITALACKER

BEUNDEN-FELD

STADT-BACH

Haupt bf.

RBS- Bf.

VILLETTE

MARZILI

MONBIJOU

SCHOSS-HALDE

OBST-BERG

KIRCHENFELD

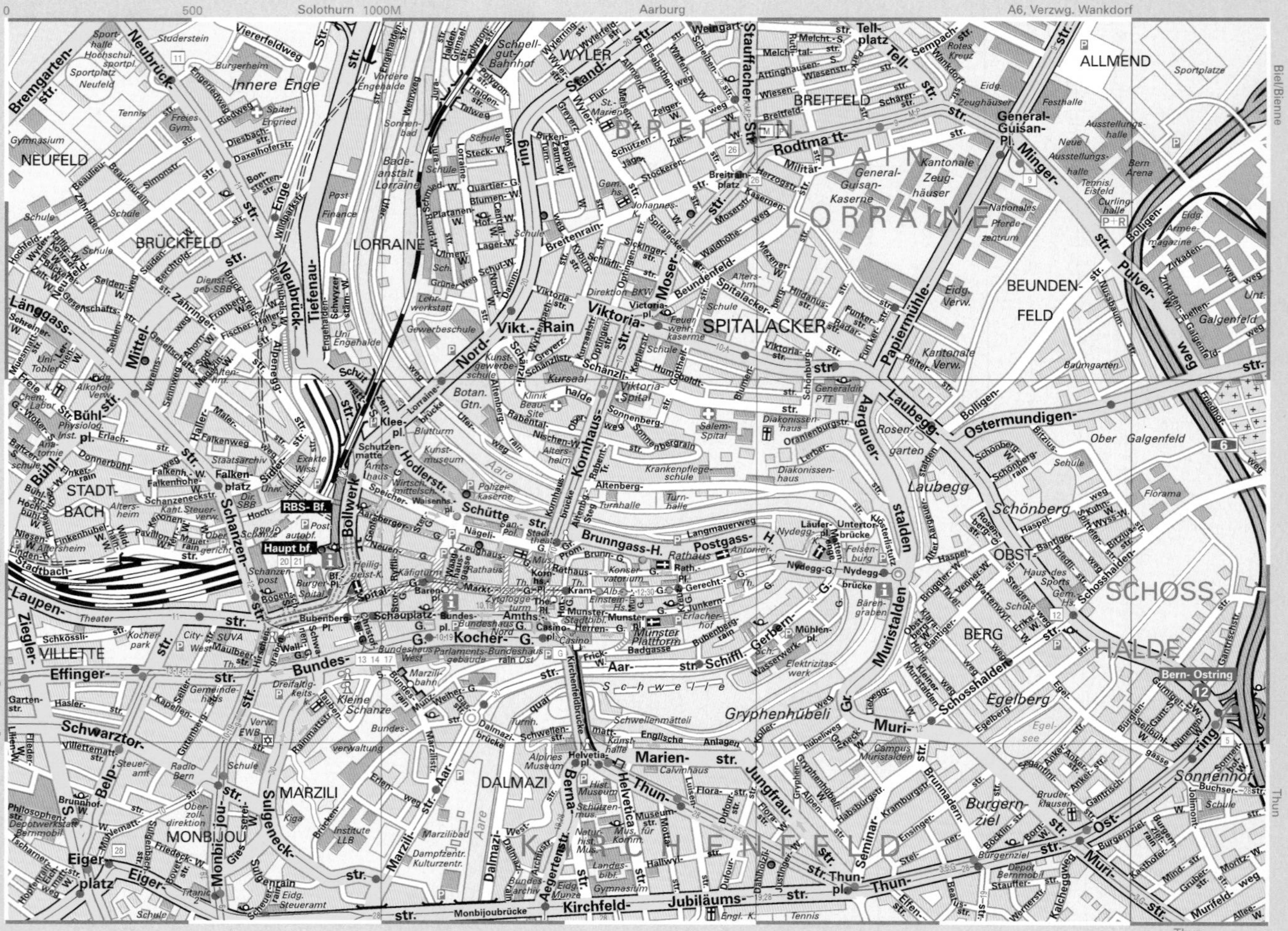

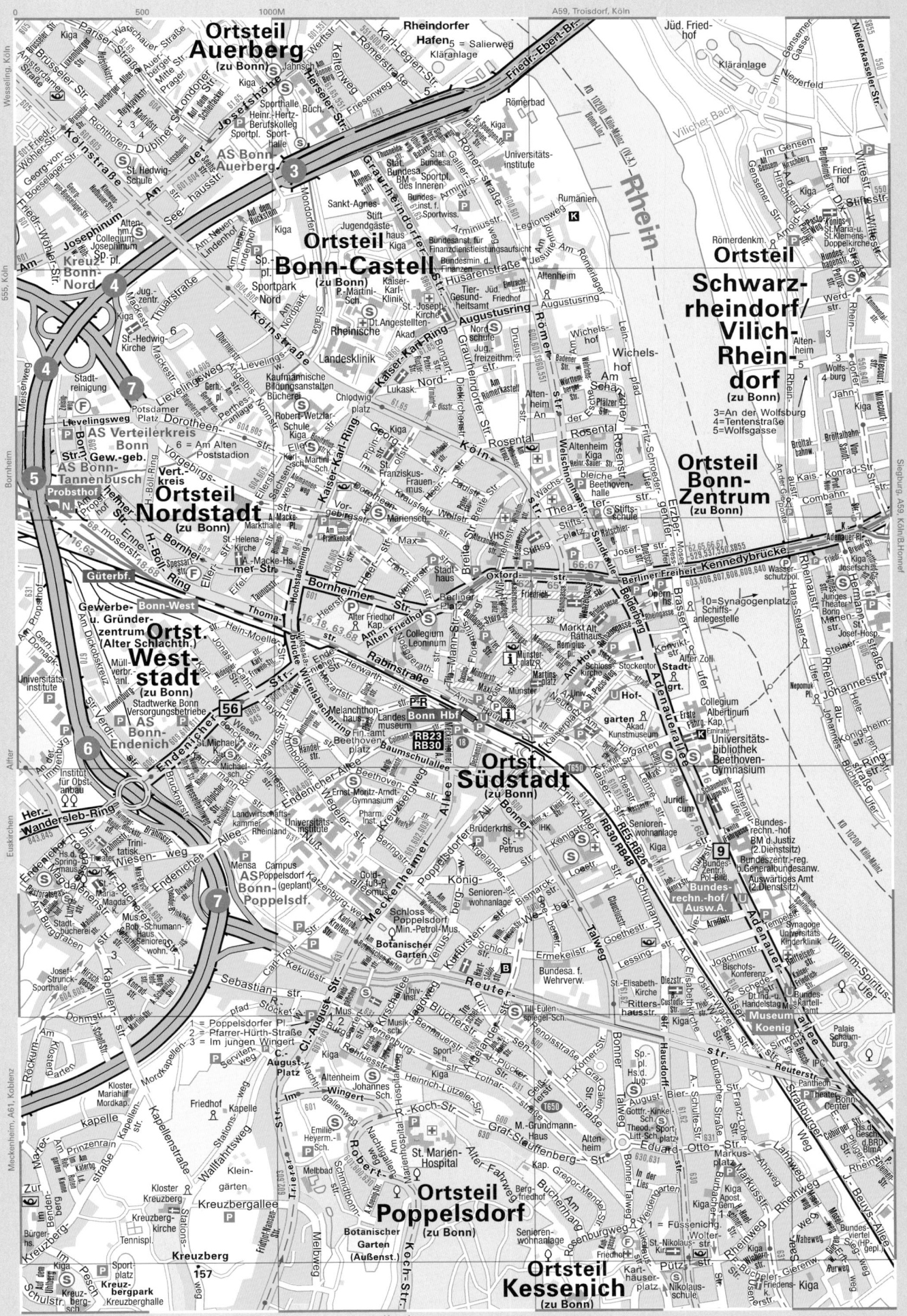

**Ortsteil Auerberg** (zu Bonn)

**Ortsteil Bonn-Castell** (zu Bonn)

Rheindorfer Hafen

**Ortsteil Schwarz-rheindorf/ Vilich-Rheindorf** (zu Bonn)

3=An der Wolfsburg
4=Tentenstraße
5=Wolfsgasse

**Ortsteil Bonn-Zentrum** (zu Bonn)

**Ortsteil Nordstadt** (zu Bonn)

10=Synagogenplatz
= Schiffs-anlegestelle

**Ortst. Weststadt** (zu Bonn)

**Ortst. Südstadt** (zu Bonn)

Bonn Hbf

**Ortsteil Poppelsdorf** (zu Bonn)

1 = Poppelsdorfer Pl.
2 = Pfarrer-Hürth-Straße
3 = Im jungen Wingert

Botanischer Garten (Außenst.)

Kreuzberg

1 = Füssenich

**Ortsteil Kessenich** (zu Bonn)

Museum Koenig

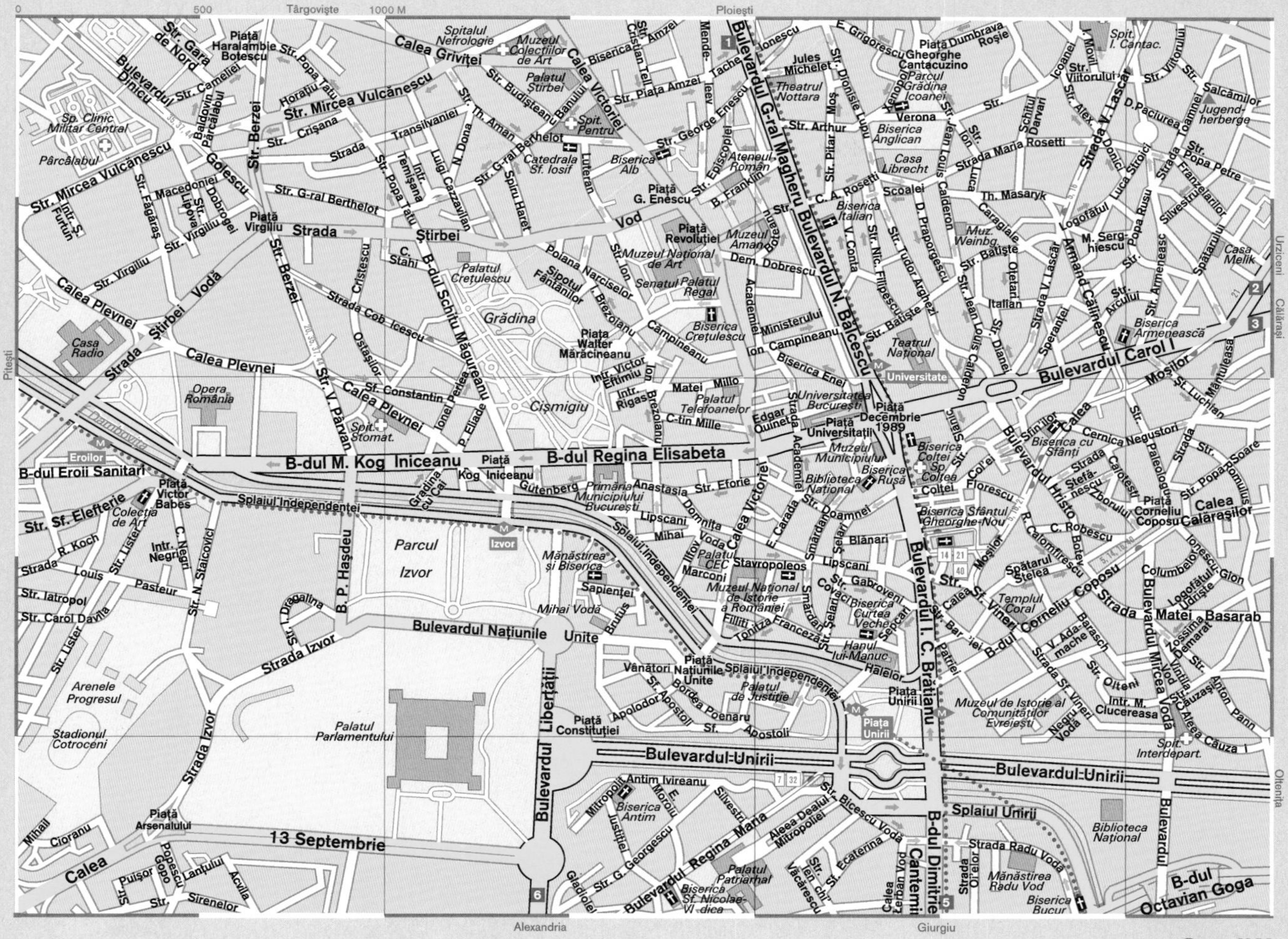
0
500
1000 M
Târgovişte
Ploieşti
Piteşti
Urziceni
Călăraşi
Olteniţa
Alexandria
Giurgiu
Calea Griviţei
Str. Mircea Vulcănescu
Calea Plevnei
Bulevardul Carol I
B-dul M. Kog Iniceanu
B-dul Regina Elisabeta
B-dul Eroii Sanitari
Splaiul Independenţei
Bulevardul Naţiunile Unite
Bulevardul Unirii
Bulevardul Libertăţii
13 Septembrie
Bulevardul G-ral Magheru
Bulevardul N. Bălcescu
Bulevardul I. C. Brătianu
Calea Victoriei
Parcul Izvor
Palatul Parlamentului
Grădina Cişmigiu
Opera Română
Arenele Progresul
Stadionul Cotroceni
Piaţa Unirii
Universitate
Izvor
Eroilor
Strada Izvor
Strada Radu Vodă
B-dul Octavian Goga
B-dul Dimitrie Cantemir
Bulevardul Regina Maria



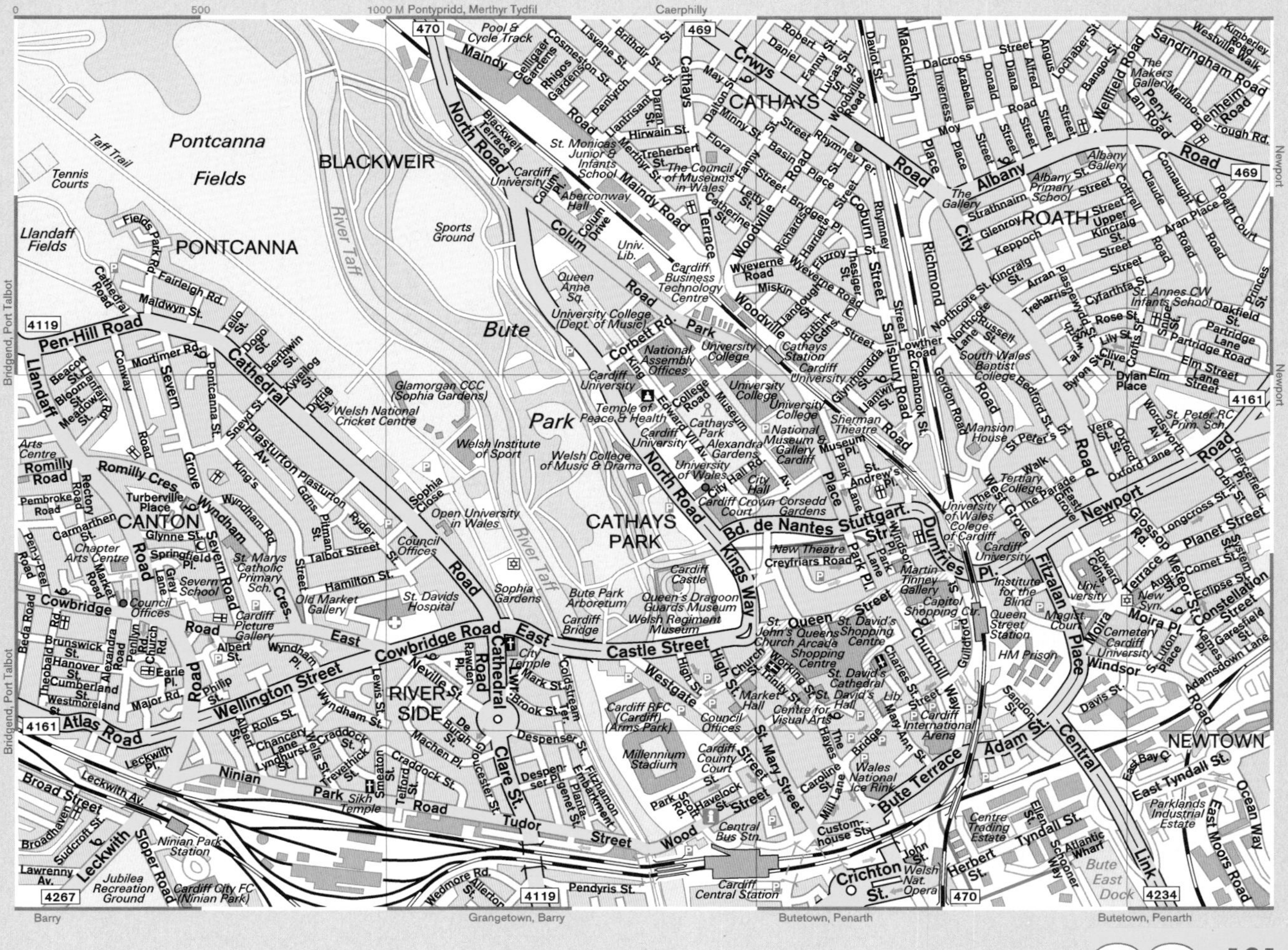
0
500
1000 M
Pontypridd, Merthyr Tydfil
Caerphilly
Newport
Bridgend, Port Talbot
Barry
Grangetown, Barry
Butetown, Penarth
Pontcanna Fields
BLACKWEIR
PONTCANNA
CATHAYS
ROATH
Bute Park
CATHAYS PARK
CANTON
RIVERSIDE
NEWTOWN
River Taff
North Road
Cathedral Road
Cowbridge Road East
Castle Street
Wellington Street
Ninian Park Road
Newport Road
Bd. de Nantes
Kings Way
Millennium Stadium
Cardiff Central Station
Cardiff City FC (Ninian Park)
Bute East Dock

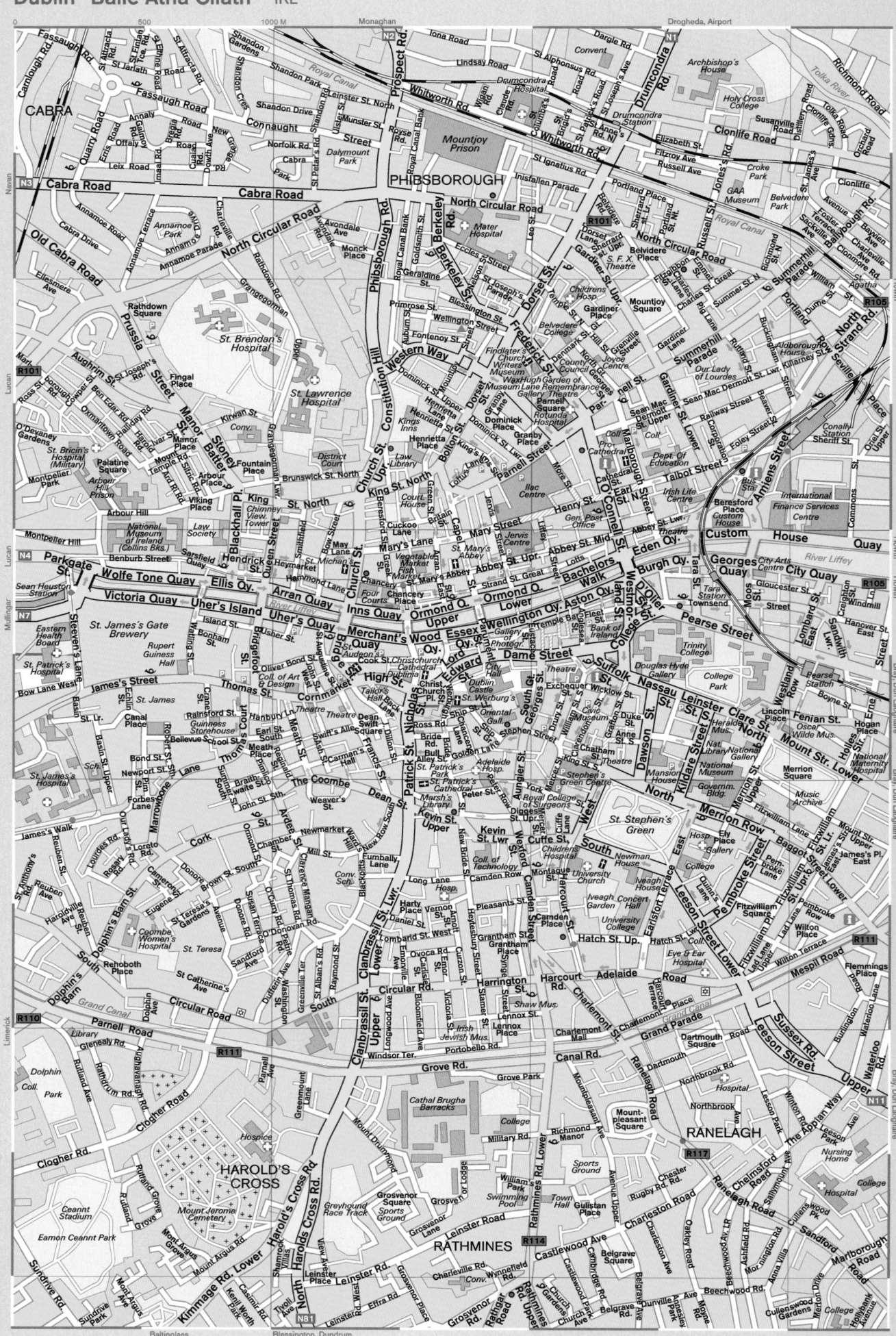

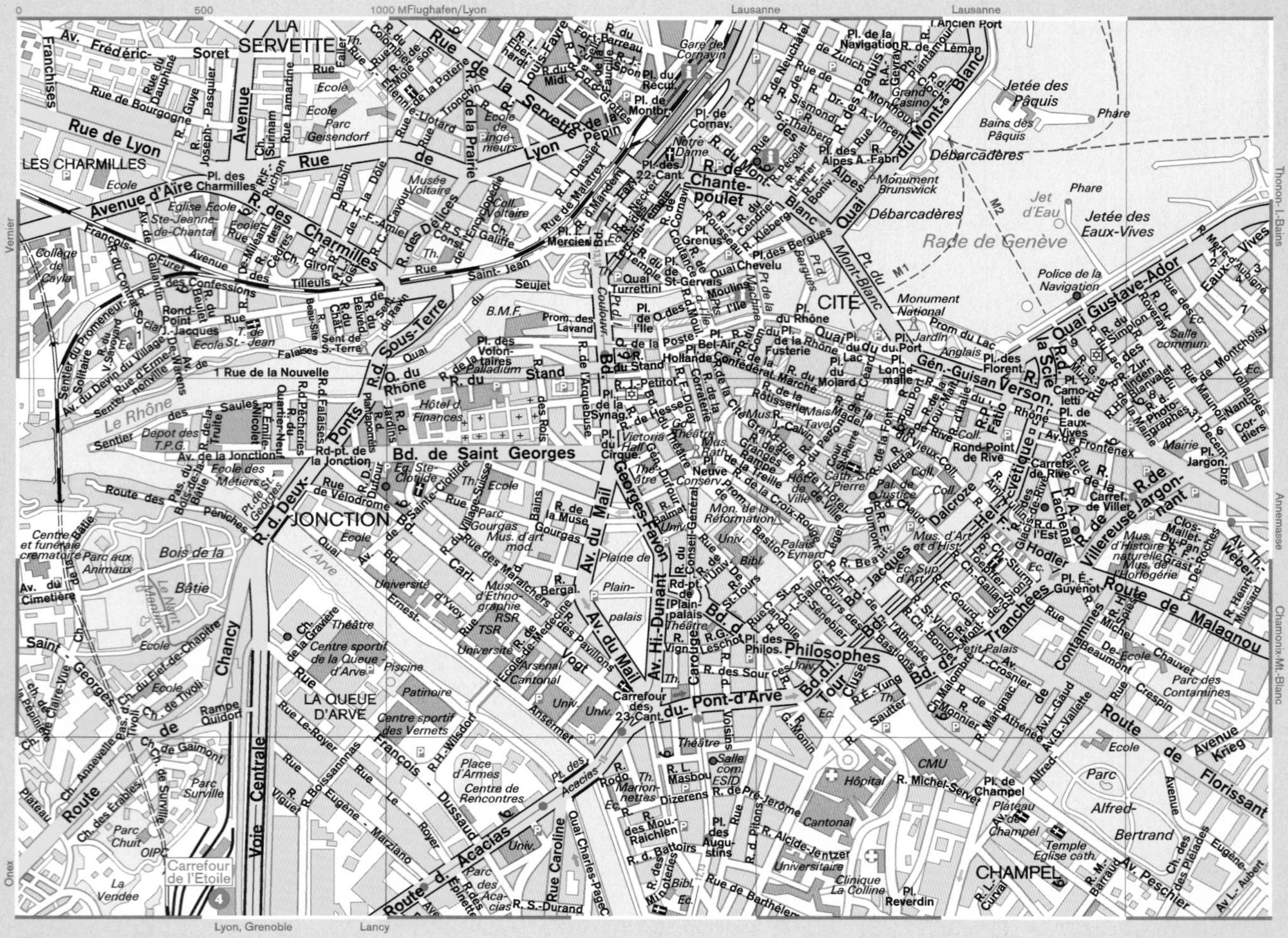

## Glasgow GB

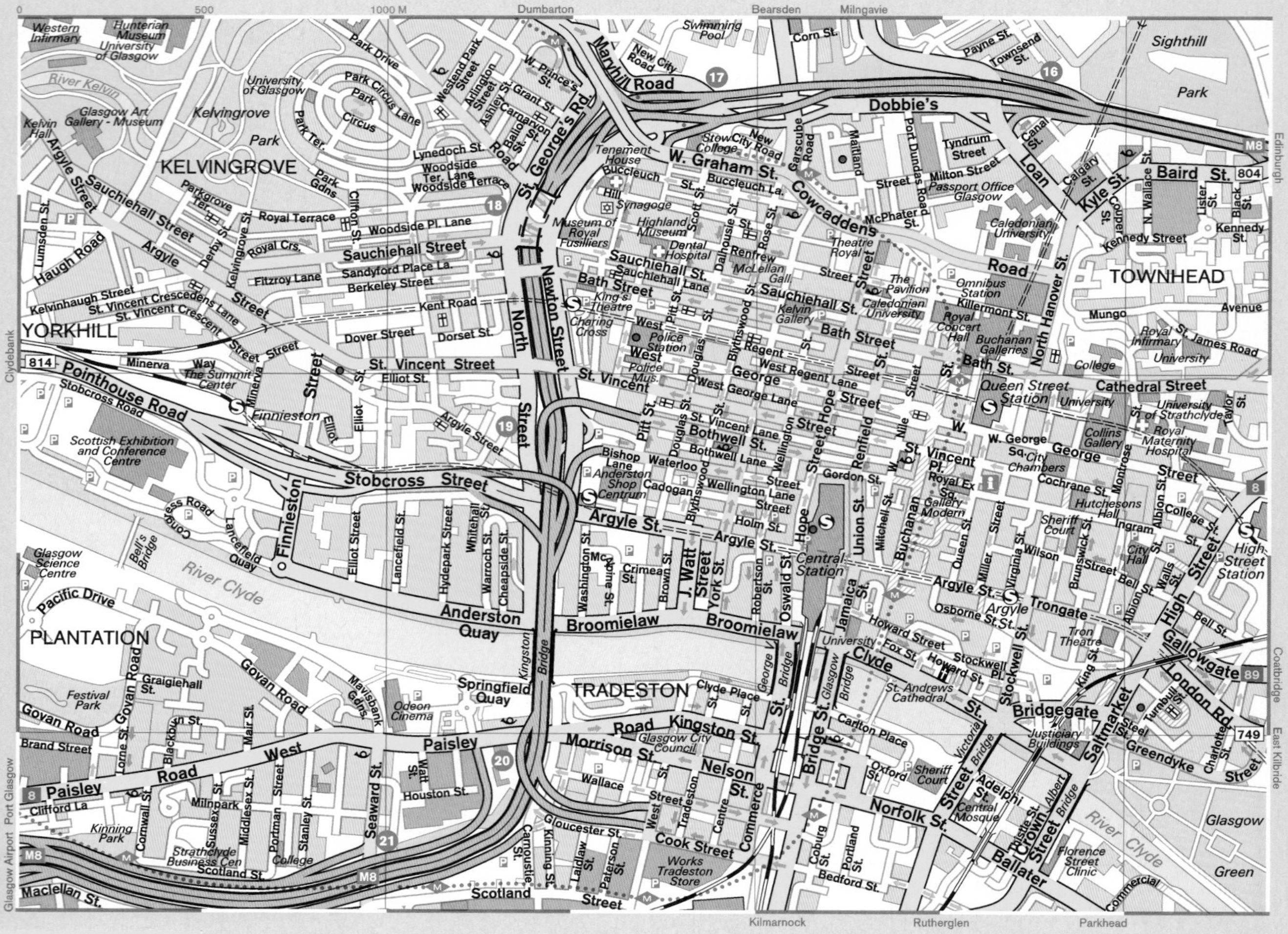

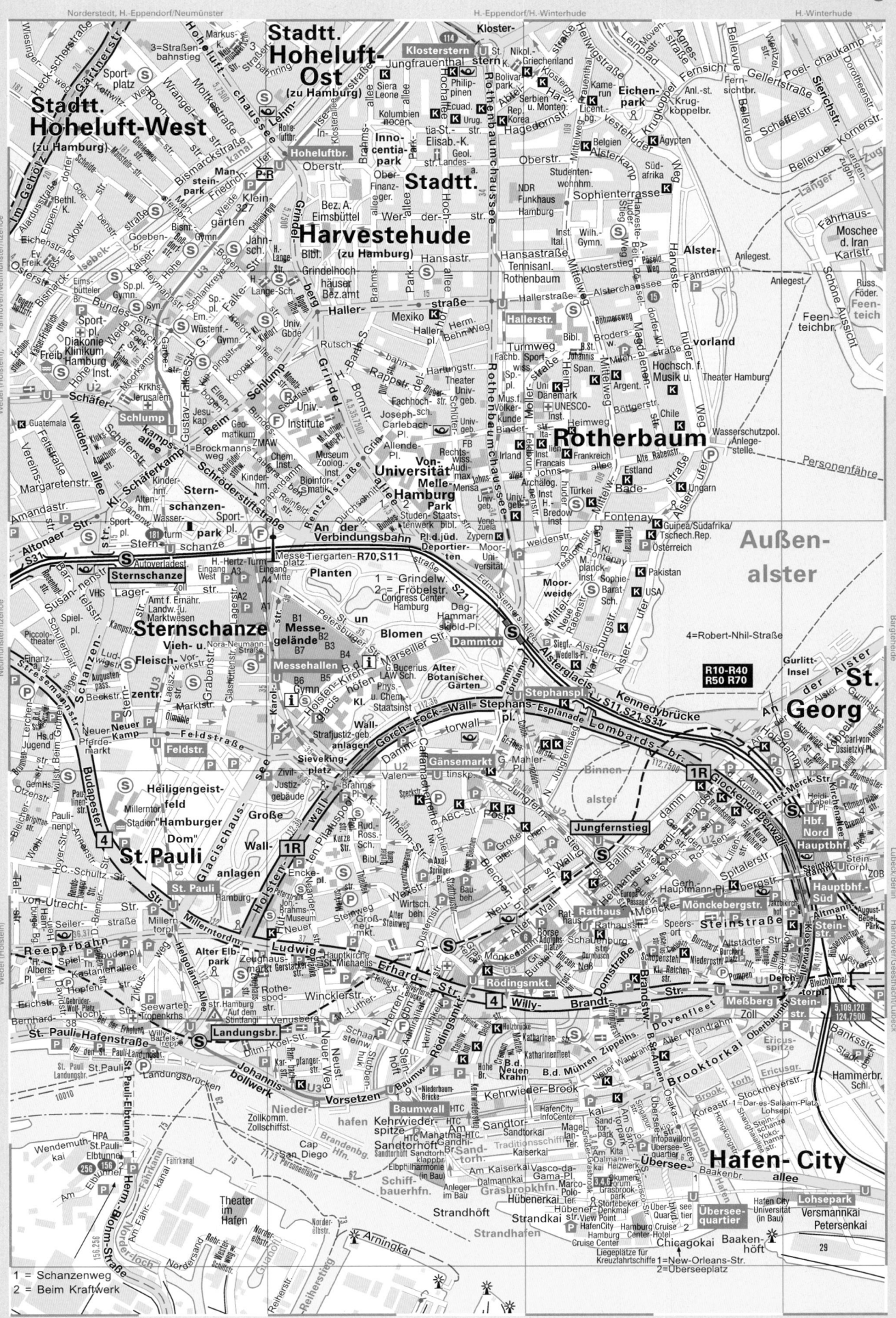

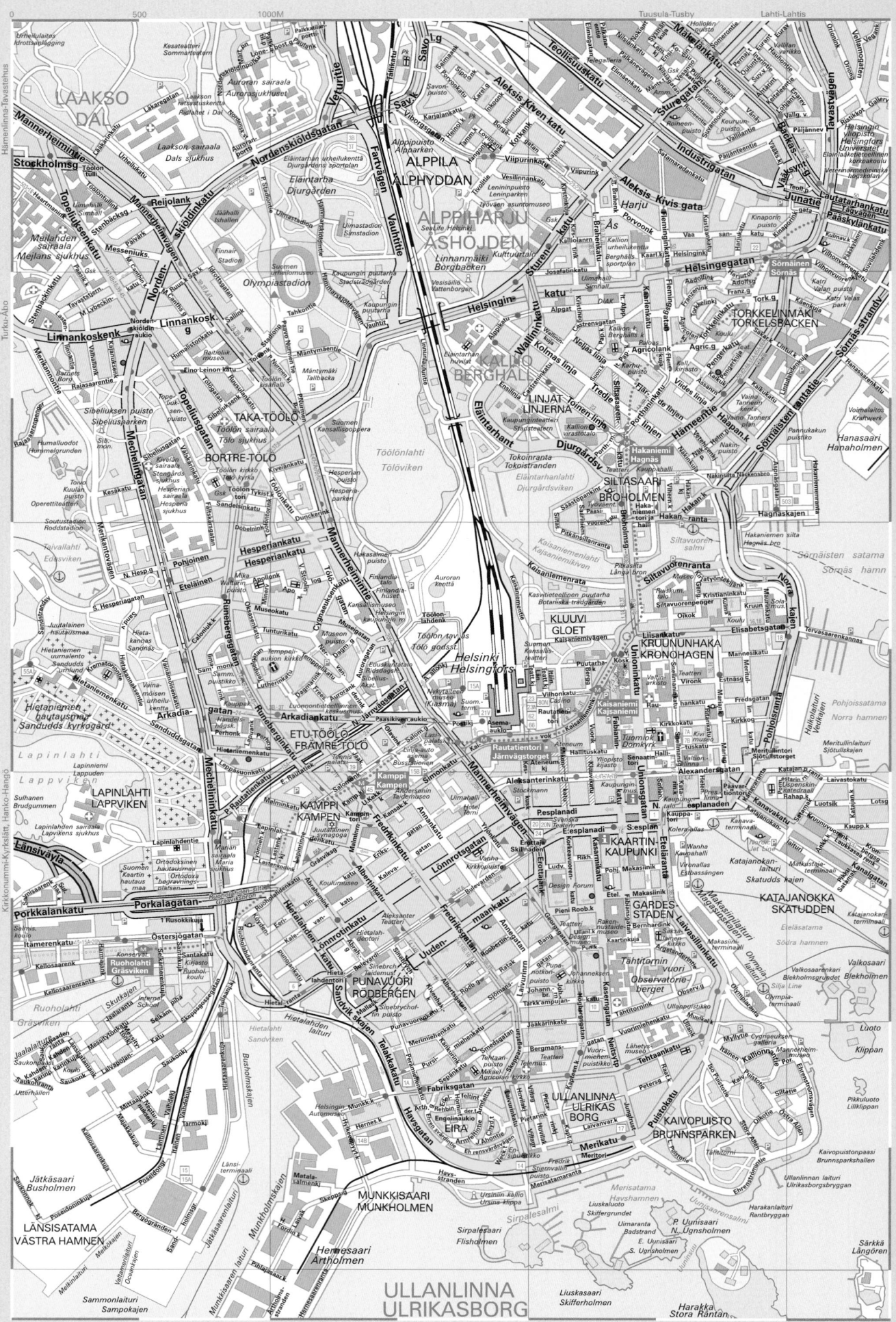

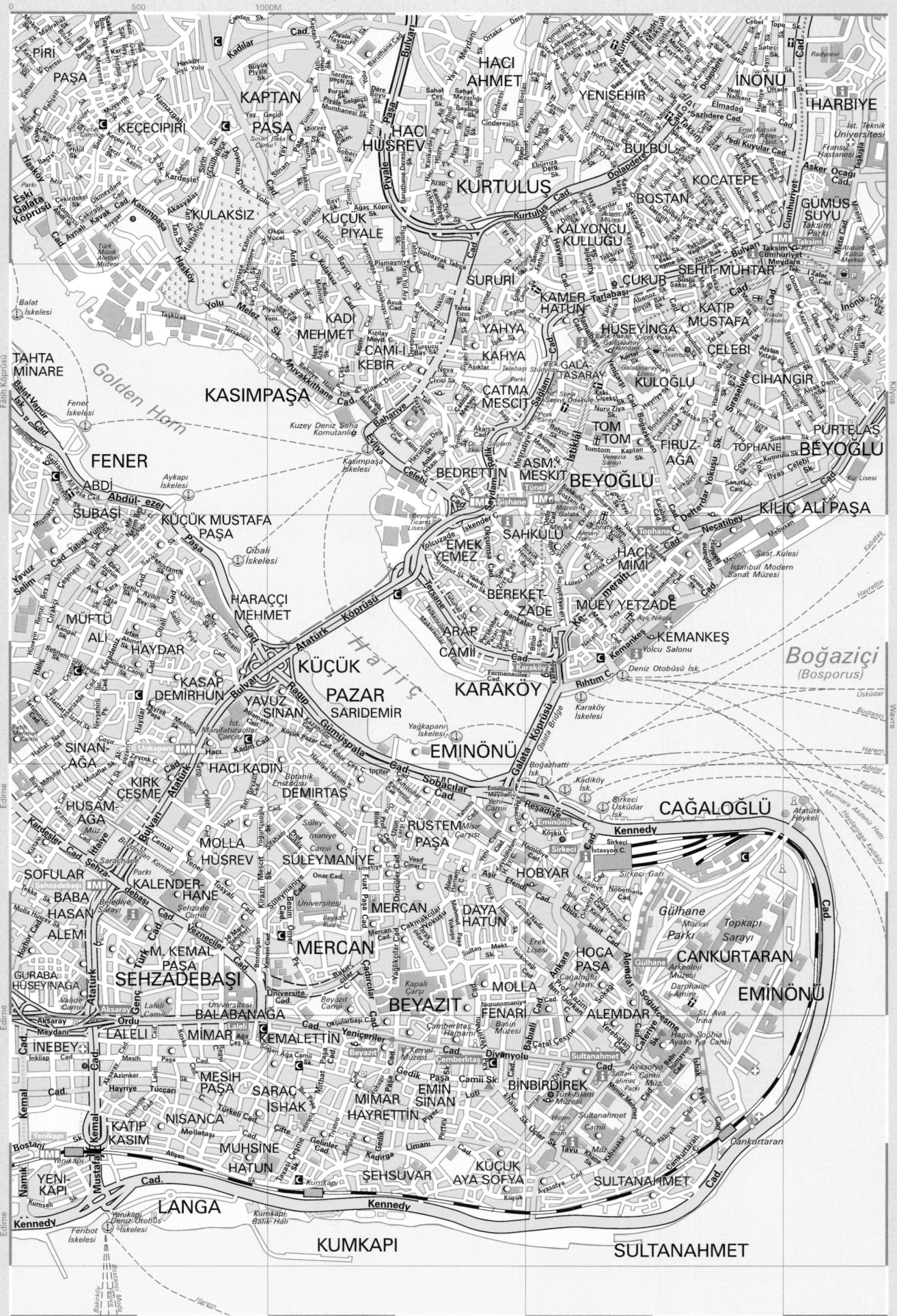

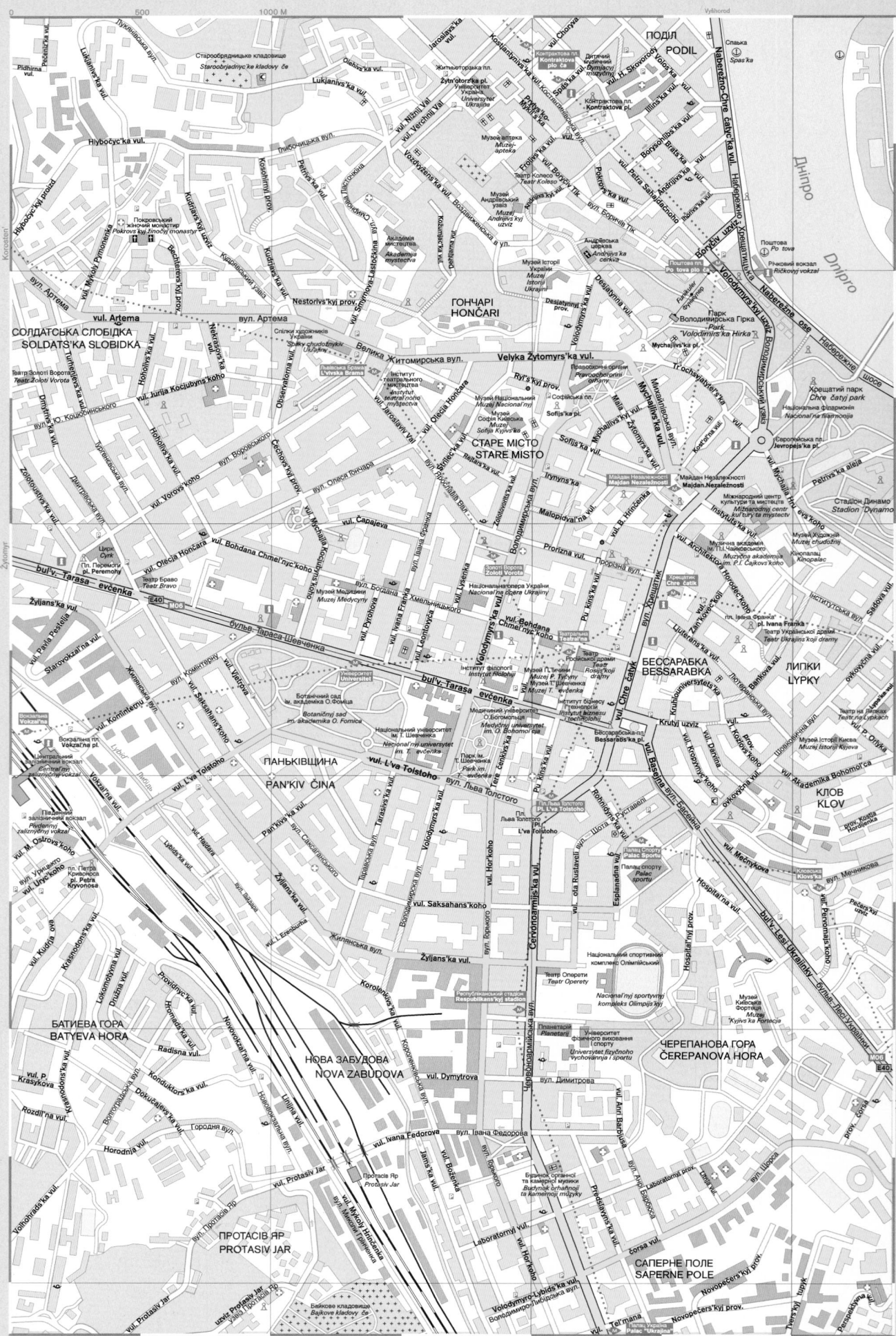

# Kaliningrad RUS-236000

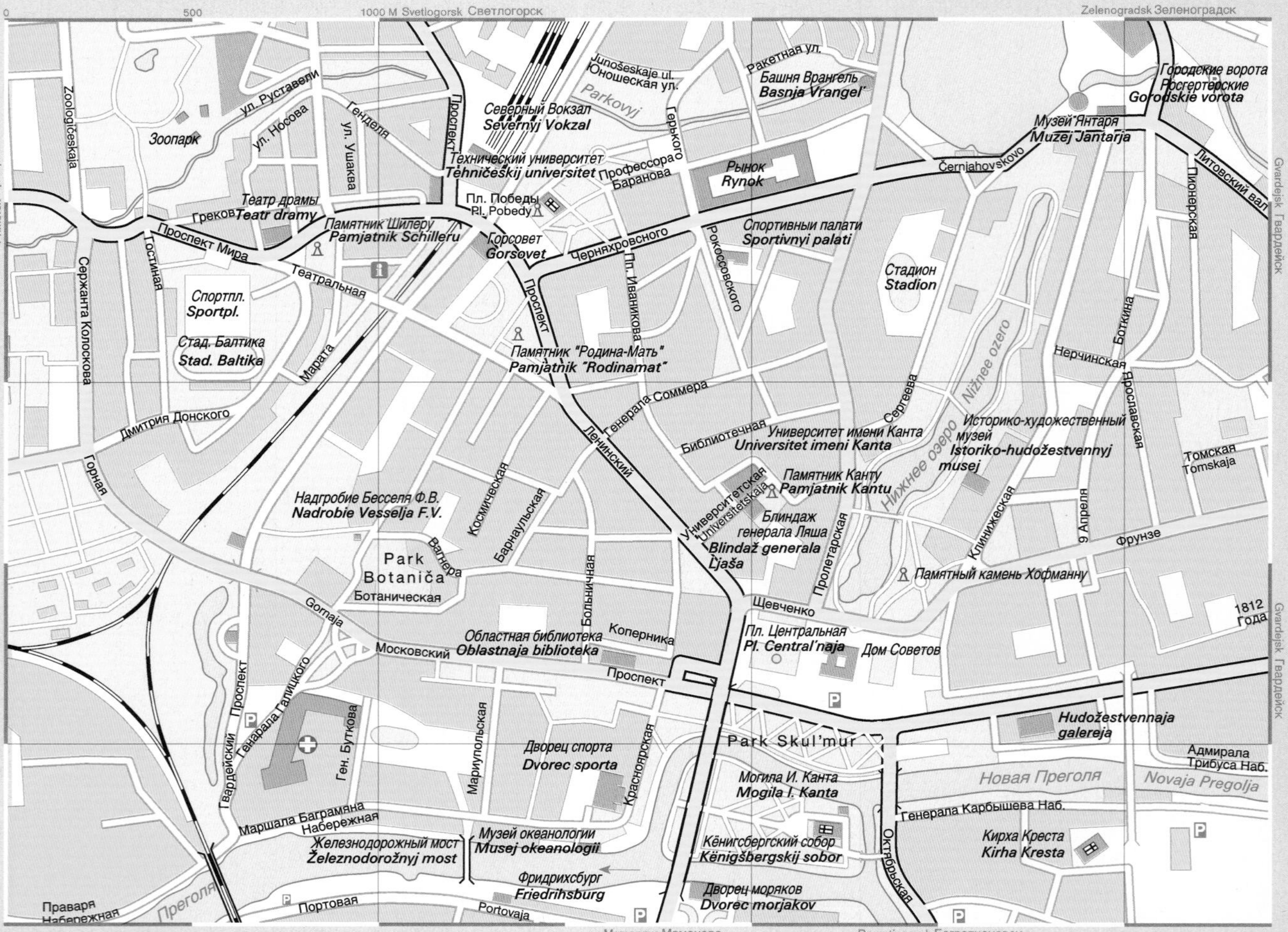

0 500 1000 M Svetlogorsk Светлогорск — Zelenogradsk Зеленоградск

Primorsk Приморск
Gvardejsk Гвардейск

Ракетная ул.
Башня Врангель
Basnja Vrangel'
Городские ворота
Росгертерские
Gorodskie vorota

Юношеская ul.
Юношеская ул.
Parkovyi
Паркový

Зоопарк
Zoopark

ул. Руставели
ул. Носова
ул. Ушакова
Генделя

Музей Янтаря
Muzej Jantarja

Северный Вокзал
Severnyj Vokzal

Технический университет
Těhničeškij universitet Профессора Баранова

Театр драмы
Театр драмы Греков
Teatr dramy

Проспект Мира

Памятник Шиллеру
Pamjatnik Schilleru

Пл. Победы
Pl. Pobedy

Горсовет
Gorsovet

Рынок
Rynok

Спортивный палац
Sportivnyi palaci

Черняховского

Театральная
Гостиная
Сержанта Колоскова

Спортпл.
Sportpl.

Стад. Балтика
Stad. Baltika

Стадион
Stadion

Памятник "Родина-Мать"
Pamjatnik "Rodinamat"

Генерала Соммера

Горная
Дмитрия Донского

Библиотечная
Университет имени Канта
Universitet imeni Kanta

Историко-художественный музей
Istoriko-hudožestvennyj musej

Надгробие Бесселя Ф.В.
Nadrobie Vesselja F.V.

Park
Botaniča
Ботаническая

Университетская
Универси.тетская

Памятник Канту
Pamjatnik Kantu

Блиндаж генерала Ляша
Blindaž generala Ljaša

Нерчинская

Томская
Tomskaja

9 Апреля
Фрунзе

Коперника

Щевченко

Памятный камень Хофманну

Пролетарская

Барнаульская

Космическая
Большая

Областная библиотека
Oblastnaja biblioteka

Московский

Проспект

Пл. Центральная
Pl. Central'naja

Дом Советов

1812 Года

Гвардейск Гвардейск

Генерала Галицкого

Дворец спорта
Dvorec sporta

Park Skul'mur

Могила И. Канта
Mogila I. Kanta

Хуdožestvennaja galereja

Новая Преголя
Novaja Pregolja

Ген. Буткова
Гвардейский Проспект

Мариупольская
Краснодарская

Адмирала Трибуса Наб.

Маршала Баграмяна набережная

Железнодорожный мост
Železnodorožnyj most

Музей океанологии
Musej okeanologii

Кёнигсбергский собор
Kёnigšbergskij sobor

Кёнигсбергский собор

Кирха Креста
Kirha Kresta

Генерала Карбышева Наб.

Праваря Набережная

Преголя
Пригеля

Портовая
Портовая

Фридрихсбург
Friedrihsburg

Дворец моряков
Dvorec morjakov

Mamonova Мамоново — Bagrationovsk Багратионовск

# Ljubljana SLO-1000

0 500 Kranj 1000M Celje, Maribor — Bežigrad — Šmartino

Šišenski hrib 429

Tivolski vrh 387

Sv Jernej
Ulica Milana Majcna
Linhartova
ZELENA JAMA

Bellevue

Železniški muzej

Frankopanska
na

Gospodarsko razstavišče
Quartiere turistico

SRC Tivoli
Pivovarski muzej

Tivoli
Sportni park ing Stanka Bloudka

Hala Tivoli
Palazzo Cekinov grad

Zdravstveni dom

Železniška postaja
Avtobusna postaja

VODMAT

Mednarodni likovni grafični center
Jakopičevo sprehajališče

Trg Os'vobodilne fronte

Masarykova

Gospodarska

Tivolska

Etnografski muzej

TABOR

Ribnik

Jakopičeva galerija
Nar. galerija

Dvorakova

Pražakova

Slomškova

Dalmatinova

RTV Slovenija
Srce Jezusovo
Ledina

Klinični center

Medicinska fakulteta

Cankarjev dom
Narodni muzej
Parlament

Trg
Ajdovščina

Komenskega ulica

Ilirska

Hrvatski trg

Zaloška

Ortoped klinika

Slovenska

Trdinova ul.
Tavčarjeva

Frančiškanski cerkev

Trubarjeva

Klinične bolnišnice

Ljubljanica

Maxi-market
Ursulinska cerkev

Preseren trg
Prešernov trg

Zmajski most

Vodnikov trg

Kapiteljska

CENTER

Subičeva

Magistrat SML

Poljanska

Ambrožev trg
Poljanski trg

POLJANE

Trg republike

Akad.
Drama

Kongresni trg

Ljudsko gledališče
Dvorni trg

Ljubljanski grad

Sv. Jožef
Šola center

Gallery

Tobačni muzej
Tobačna Tovarna

GRADIŠČE
Borštnikov trg

Trg mladinskih delovnih brigad

Filozofska fakulteta

Trg francoske revolucije
Mestni muzej

Levstikov trg

Grad Kodeljevo

Kopališče

Aškerčeva

Zoisova cesta

Sv. Janez
Sv. Florijan

Studentska naselje

Trnovska

Karlovška

Roška

Gruberjev prekop

Tržaška

Fakulteta za elektrotehniko
Elektroinštitut

Park Arturo Toscanini

Institut Jožef Stefan

KRAKOVO

Barjanska

Orlov vrh 356

PRULE

Astronomsko-geofizikalni observatorij

Gradaščica

Novo Mesto, Zagreb

110 RUS SLO

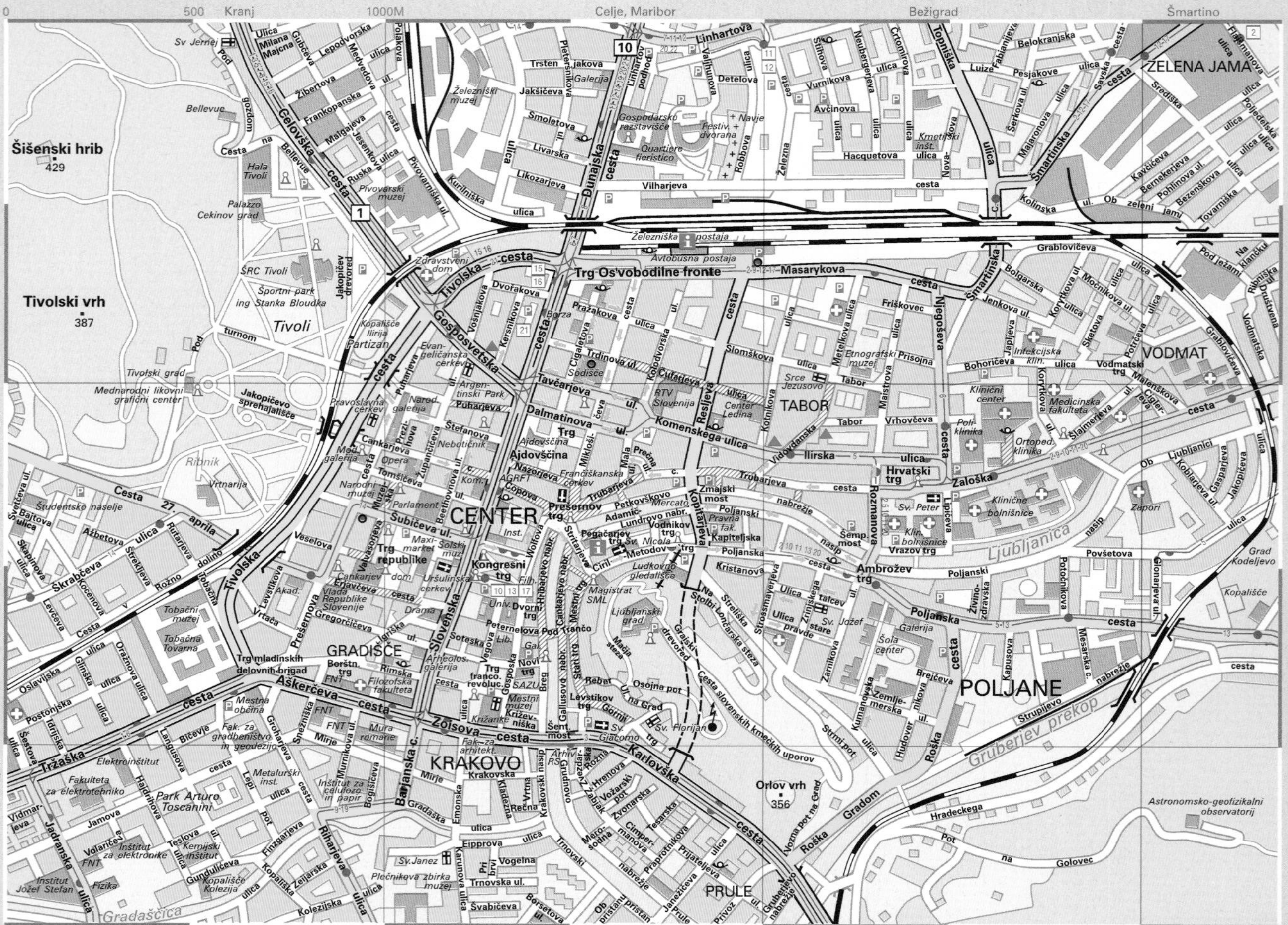

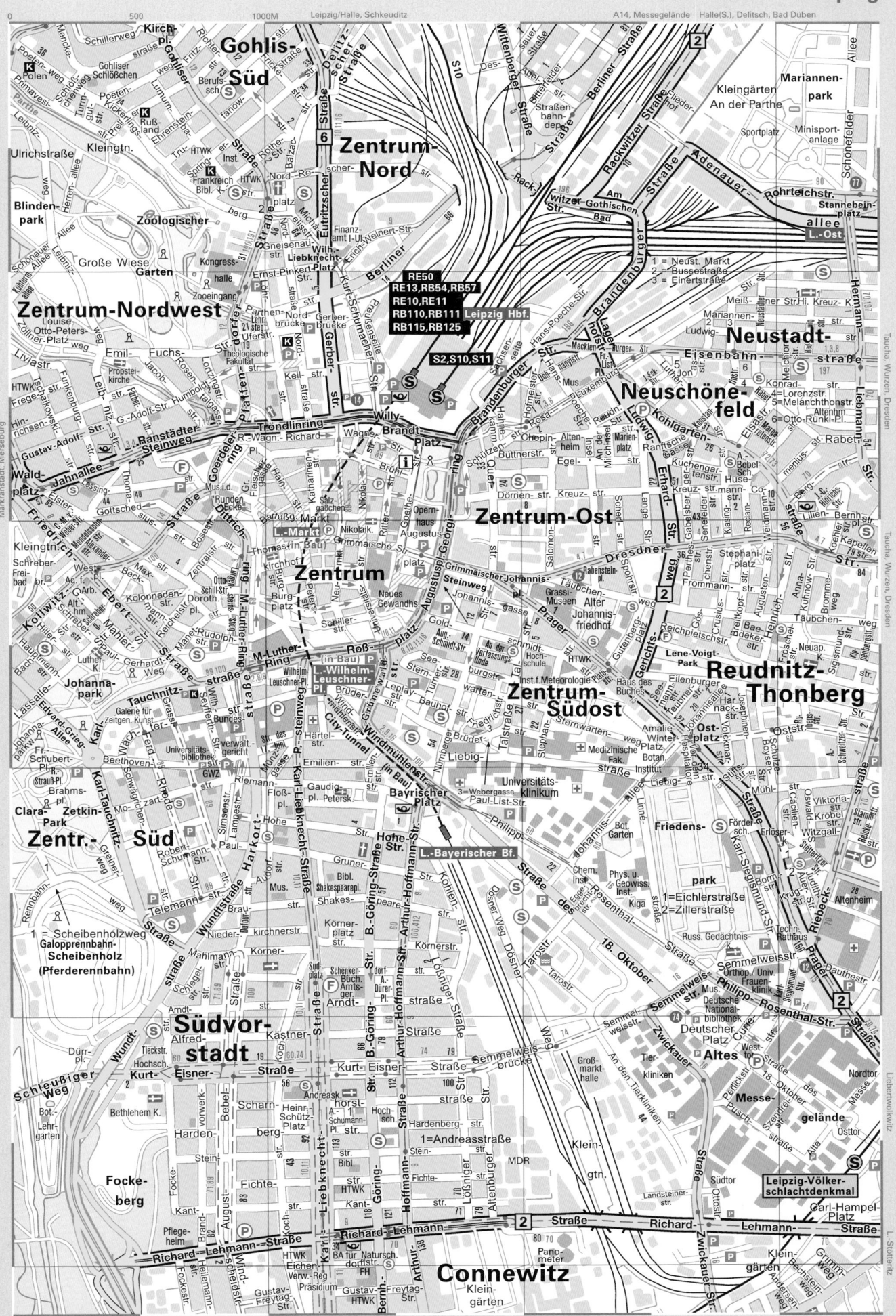

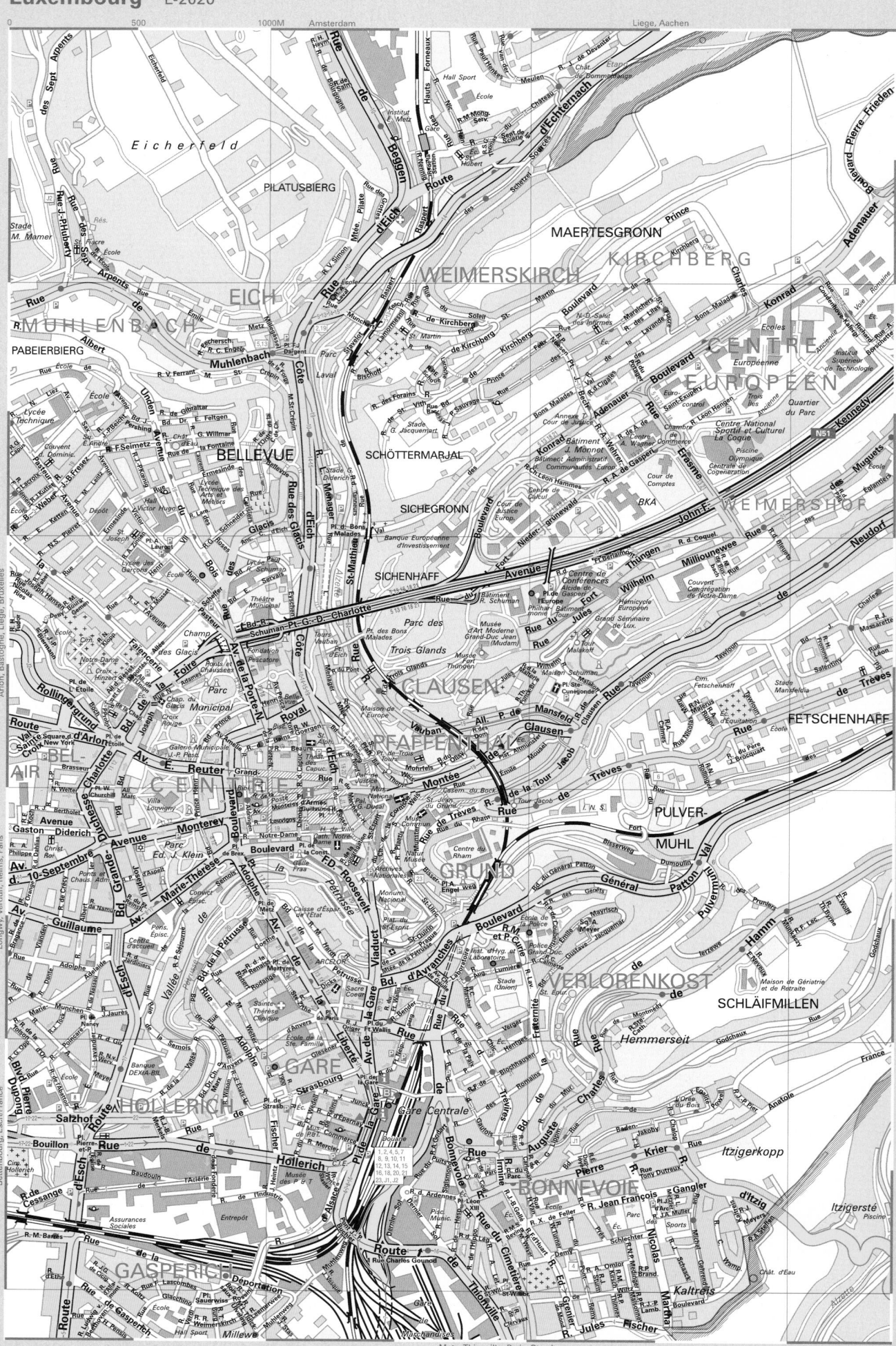

# Luxembourg L-2020

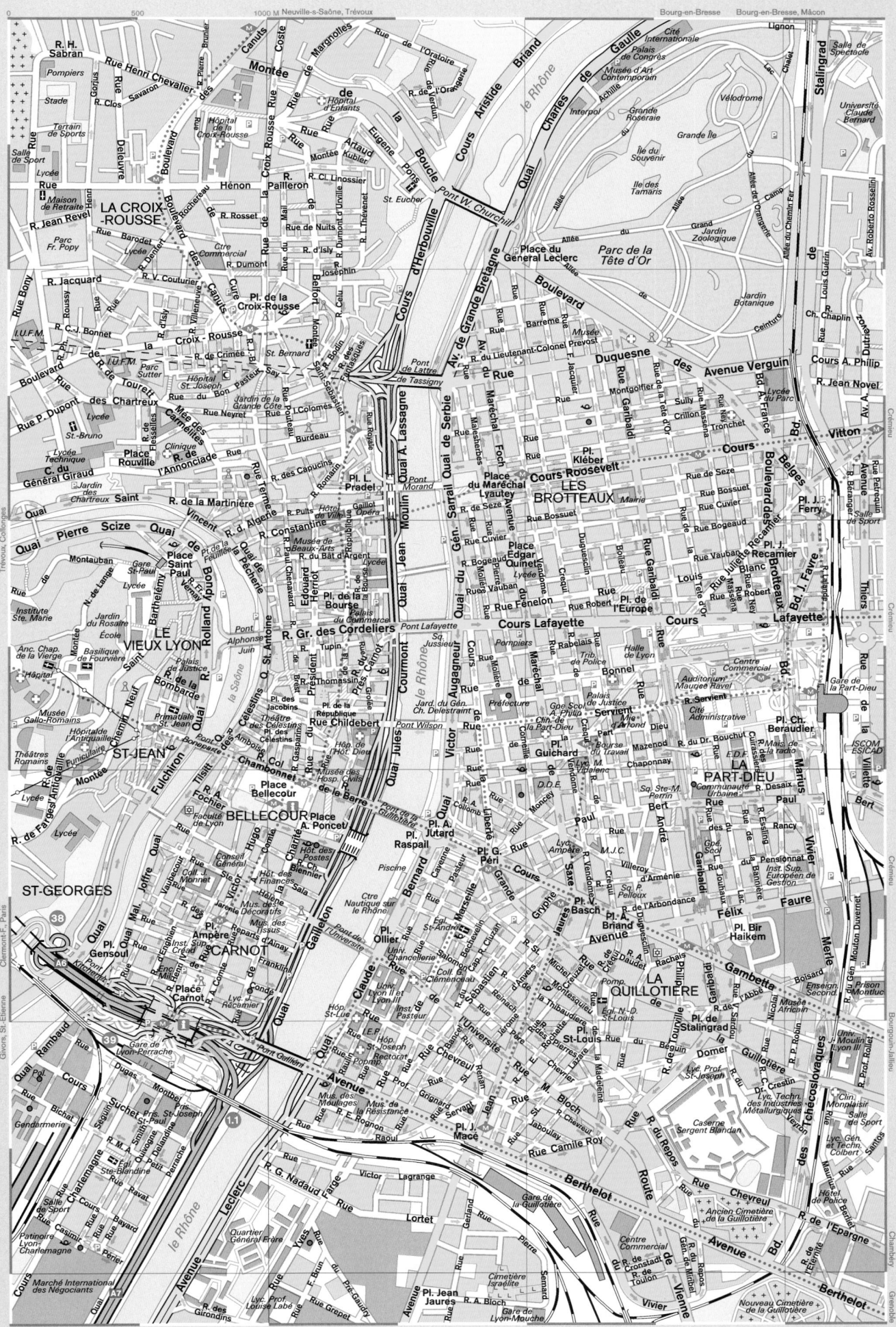

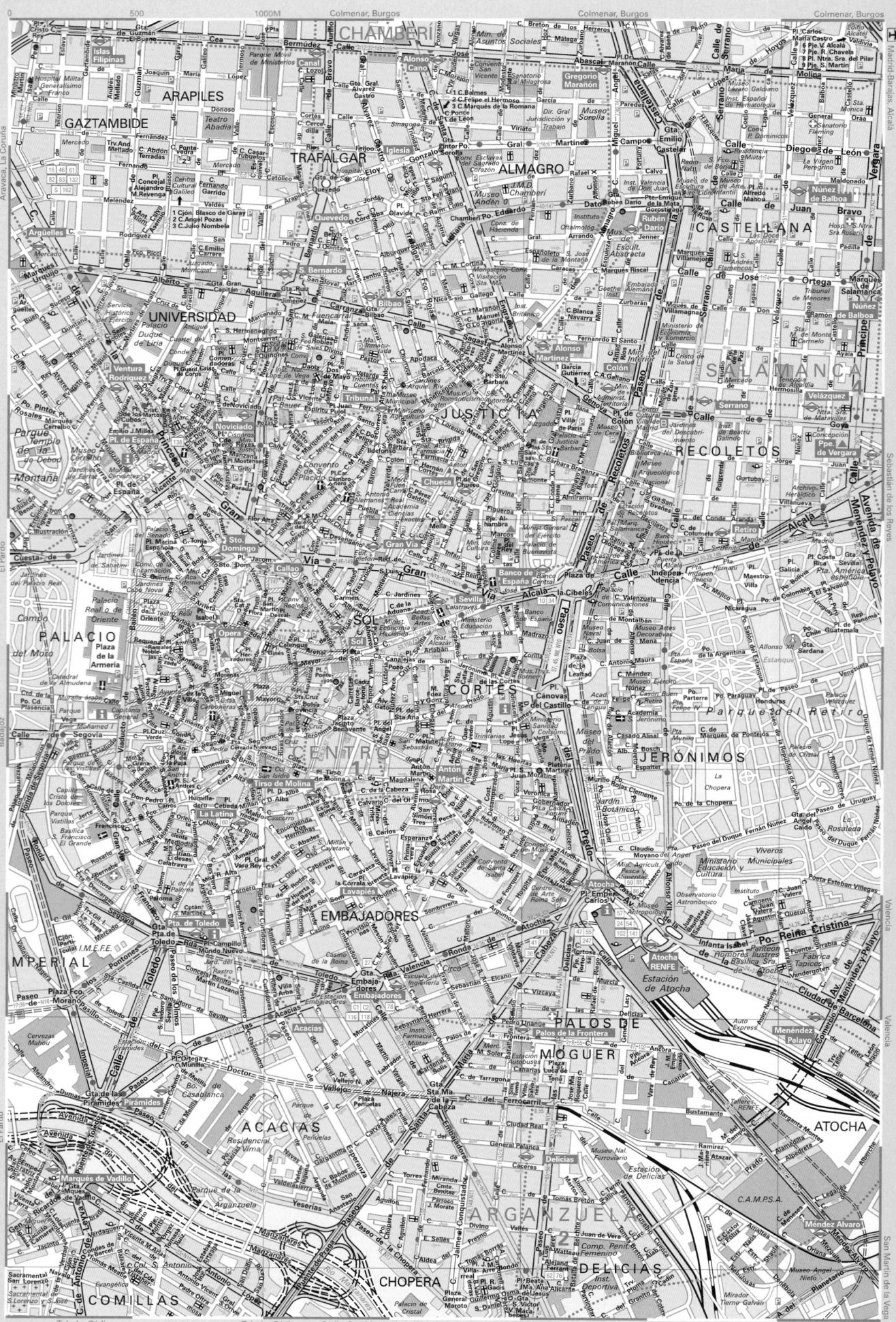

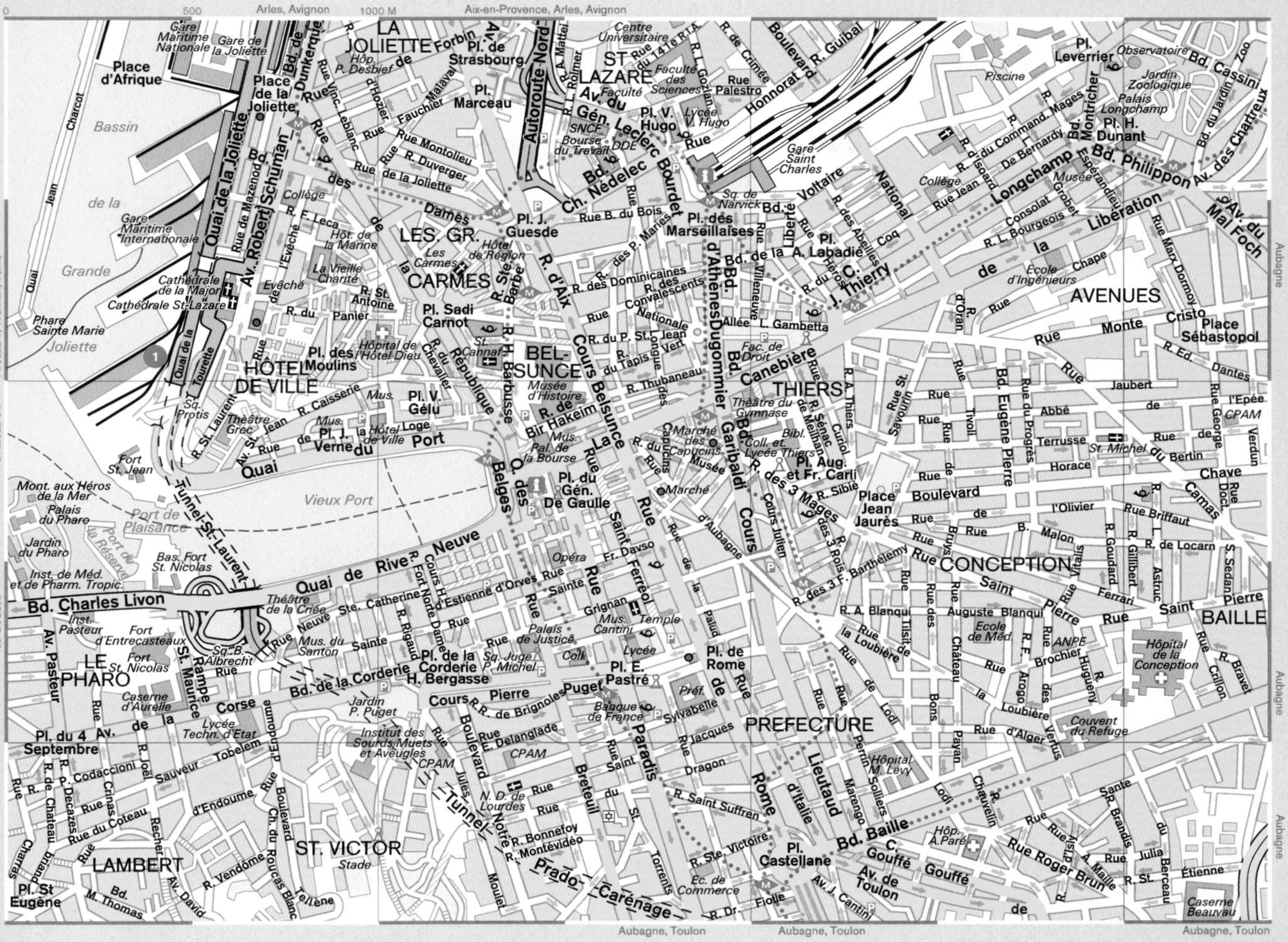
0
500
1000 M
Arles, Avignon
Aix-en-Provence, Arles, Avignon
LA JOLIETTE
ST LAZARE
Place d'Afrique
Bassin de la Grande Joliette
Gare Maritime Nationale
Gare de la Joliette
Place de la Joliette
Gare Maritime Internationale
Cathédrale de la Major
Cathédrale St-Lazare
Phare Sainte Marie
LES GR. CARMES
HÔTEL DE VILLE
BELSUNCE
THIERS
Gare Saint Charles
Pl. J. Guesde
Pl. Sadi Carnot
Pl. des Moulins
Vieux Port
Quai du Port
Quai de Rive Neuve
Bd. Charles Livon
Tunnel St-Laurent
Fort St. Jean
Fort d'Entrecasteaux
Fort St. Nicolas
Palais du Pharo
LE PHARO
Canebière
Pl. du Gén. De Gaulle
Cours Belsunce
Place Jean Jaurès
CONCEPTION
BAILLE
AVENUES
Place Sébastopol
Pl. H. Dunant
Pl. Leverrier
Palais Longchamp
Observatoire
Bd. Philippon
Bd. de la Libération
Pl. des Marseillaises
PREFECTURE
Pl. de Rome
Pl. E. Pastré
Pl. Castellane
Bd. Baille
Rue de Rome
Rue Paradis
Cours Pierre Puget
Bd. de la Corderie
Pl. du 4 Septembre
LAMBERT
ST. VICTOR
Pl. St Eugène
Prado Carénage
Hôpital de la Conception
Hôpital de l'Hôtel Dieu
Opéra
Al-Jazā'ir, Wahrān, Tunis
Château d'If
les Goudes
Aubagne
Aubagne, Toulon



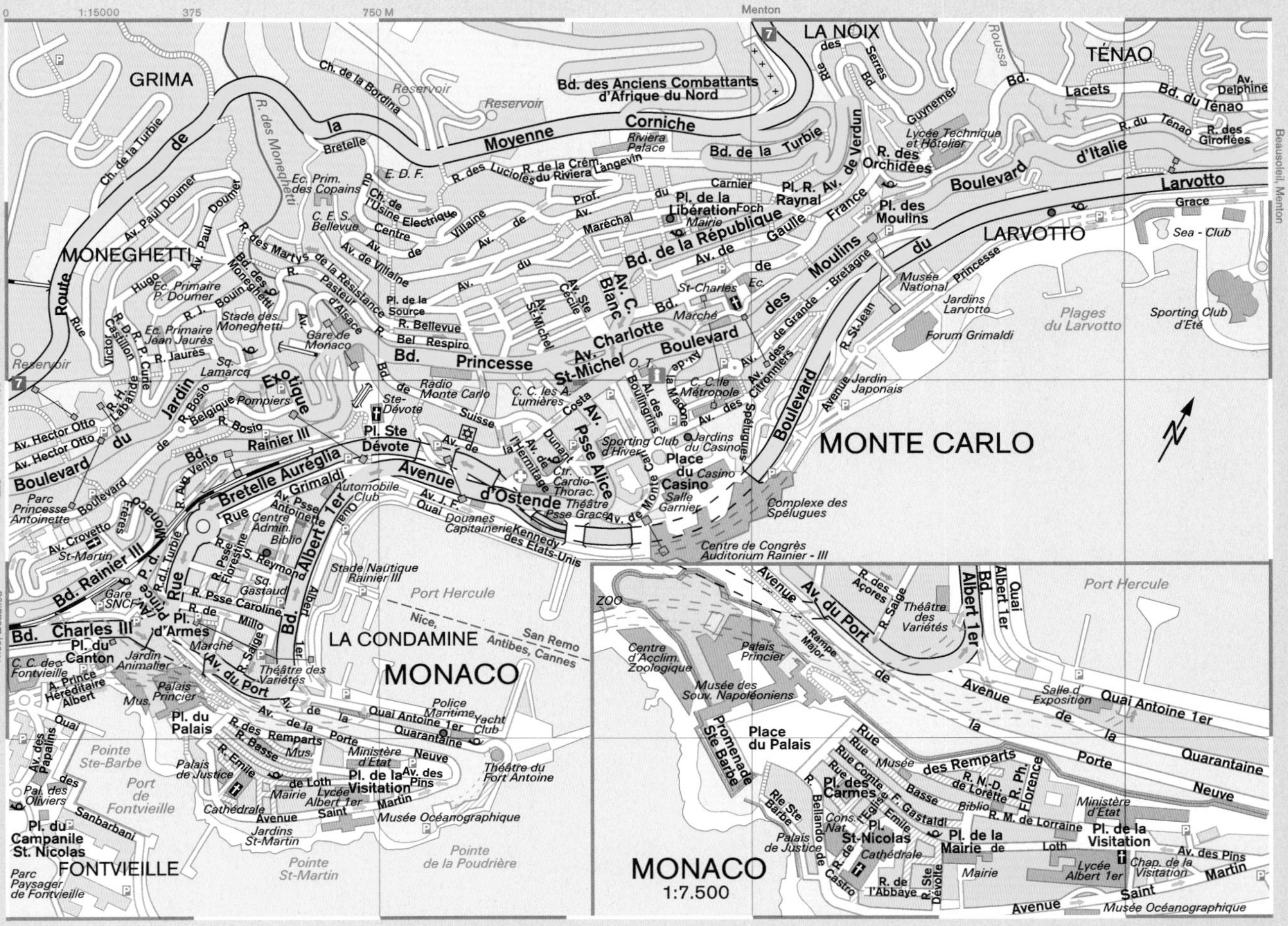
0
1:15000
375
750 M
Menton
GRIMA
LA NOIX
TÉNAO
MONEGHETTI
LARVOTTO
MONTE CARLO
LA CONDAMINE
MONACO
FONTVIEILLE
Moyenne Corniche
Bd. des Anciens Combattants d'Afrique du Nord
Bd. de la Turbie
Boulevard d'Italie
Bd. de la République
Bd. Princesse Charlotte
Av. de Grande Bretagne
Boulevard du Larvotto
Pl. de la Libération
Pl. des Moulins
Pl. Ste Dévote
Boulevard du Jardin Exotique
Bd. Rainier III
Bd. Charles III
Place du Casino
Casino
Jardins Japonais
Plages du Larvotto
Sporting Club d'Eté
Forum Grimaldi
Port Hercule
Stade Nautique Rainier III
Quai Antoine 1er
Avenue d'Ostende
Pl. d'Armes
Pl. du Palais
Palais Princier
Pl. de la Visitation
Musée Océanographique
Cathédrale
Pointe Ste-Barbe
Port de Fontvieille
Pointe St-Martin
Pointe de la Poudrière
Centre de Congrès Auditorium Rainier - III
Nice
Eze
Nice, Beaulieu
Beausoleil, Menton
MONACO
1:7.500
Place du Palais
Promenade Ste Barbe
Centre d'Acclim. Zoologique
Musée des Souv. Napoléoniens
Rue des Remparts
Pl. de la Mairie
Pl. St-Nicolas
Théâtre des Variétés
Avenue de la Porte Neuve
Quai Antoine 1er
Avenue de la Quarantaine

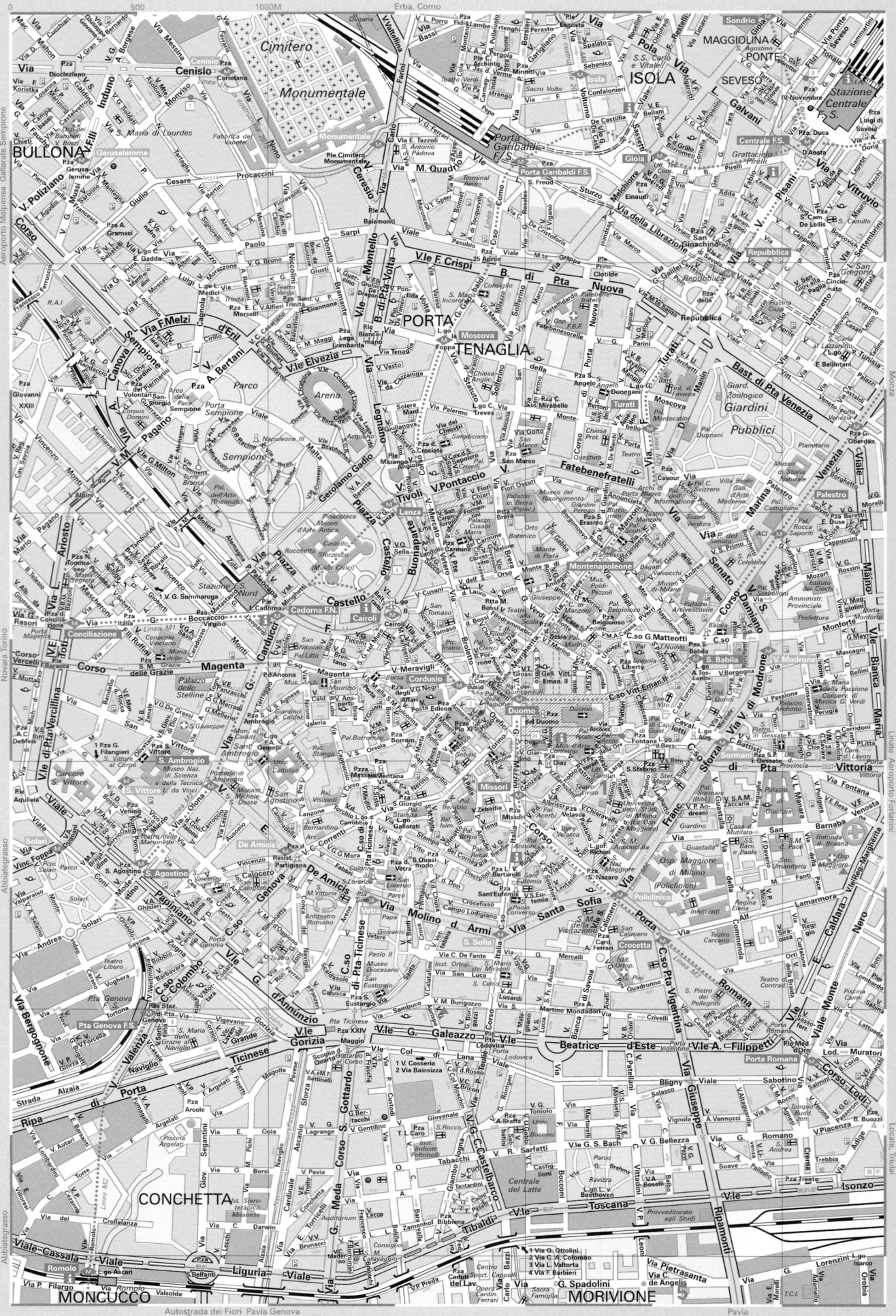

Milano I-20100

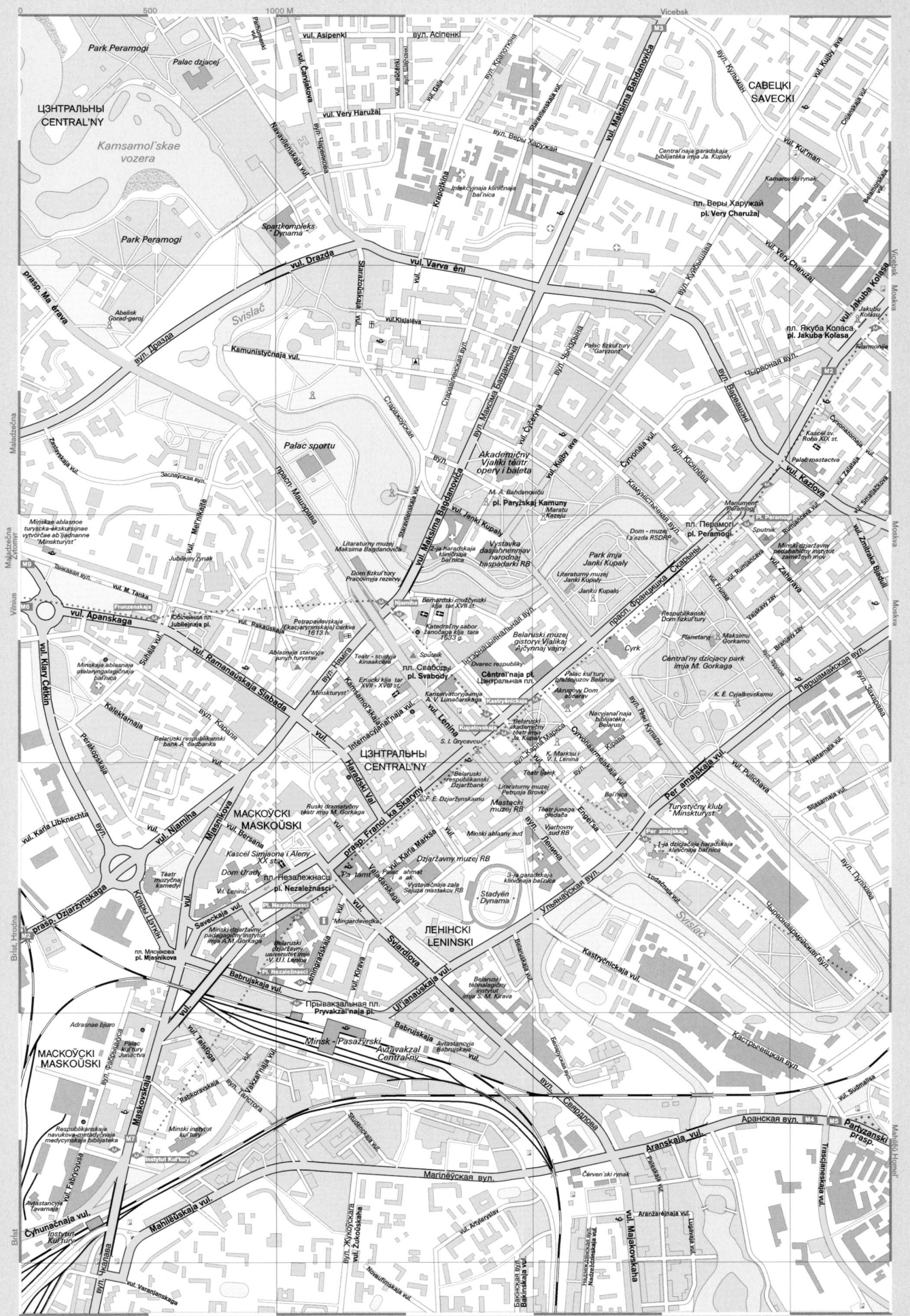

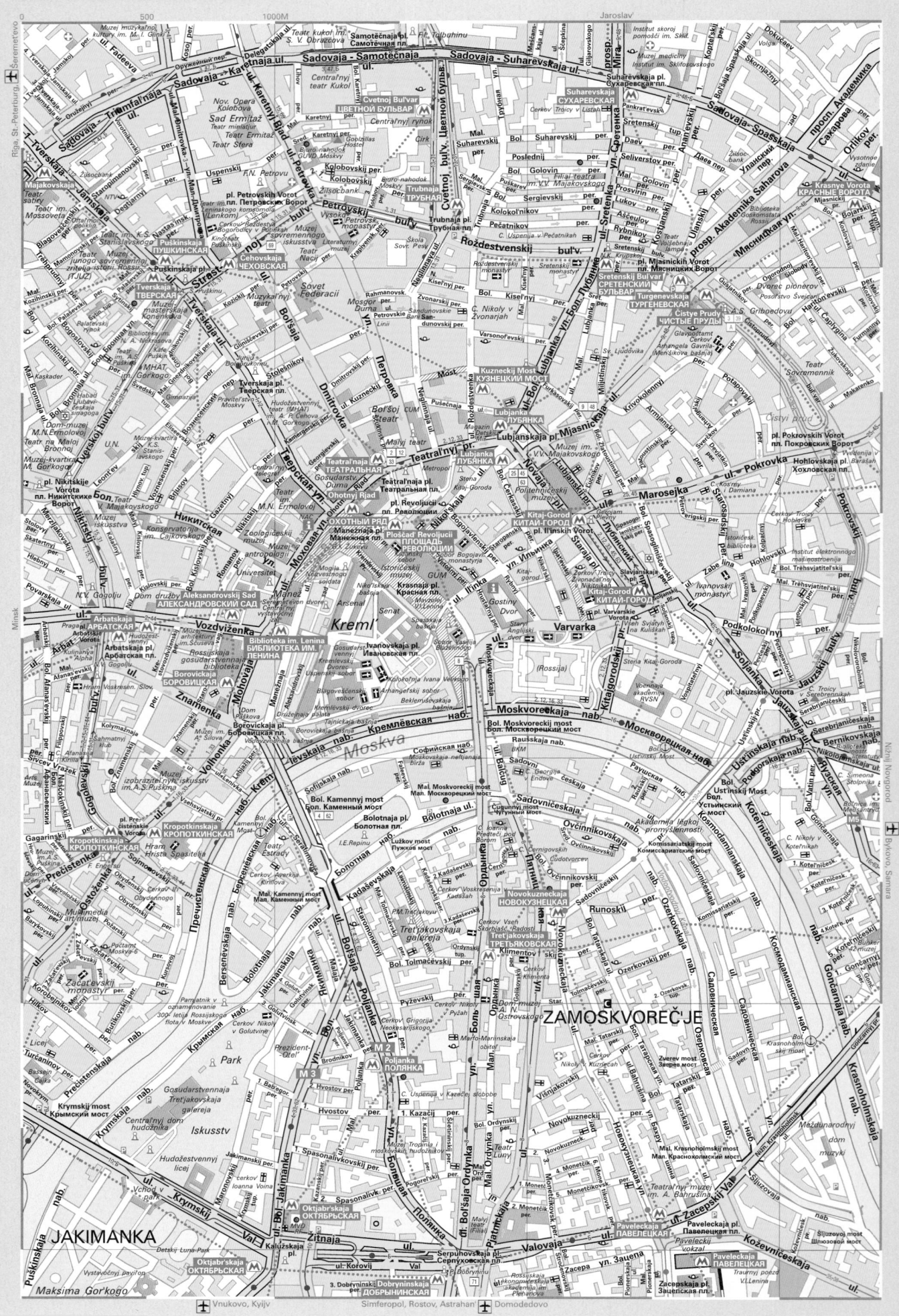

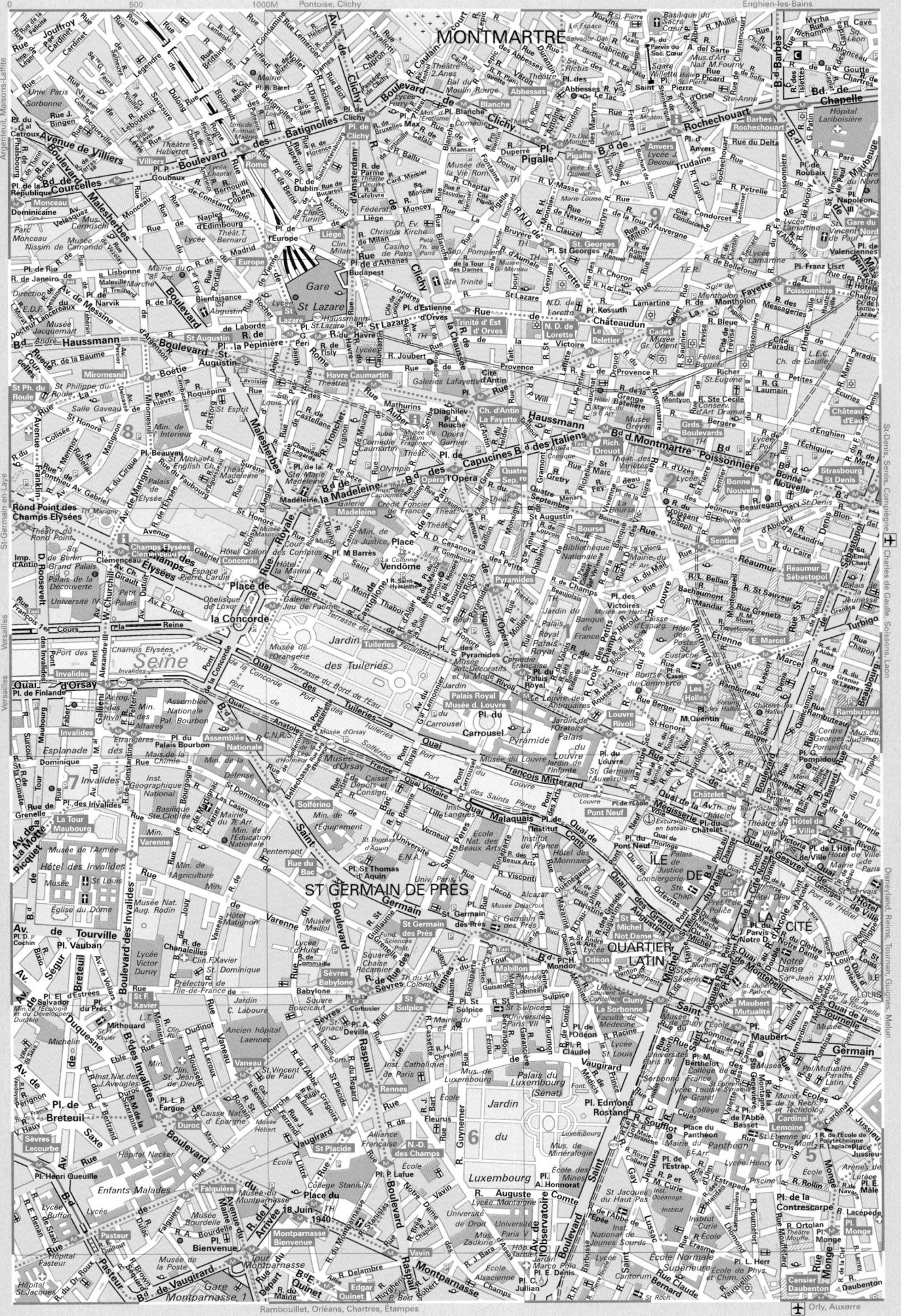

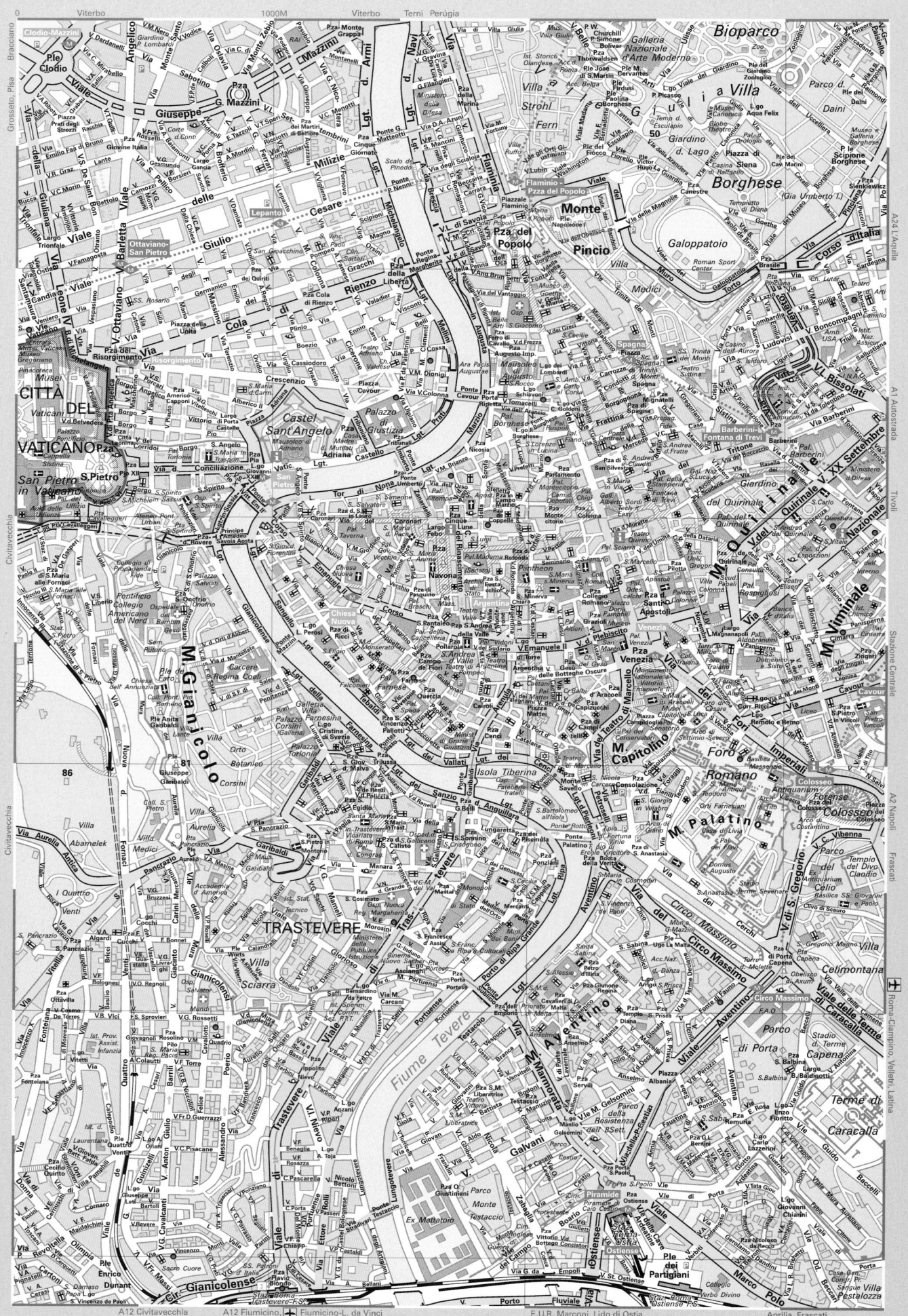

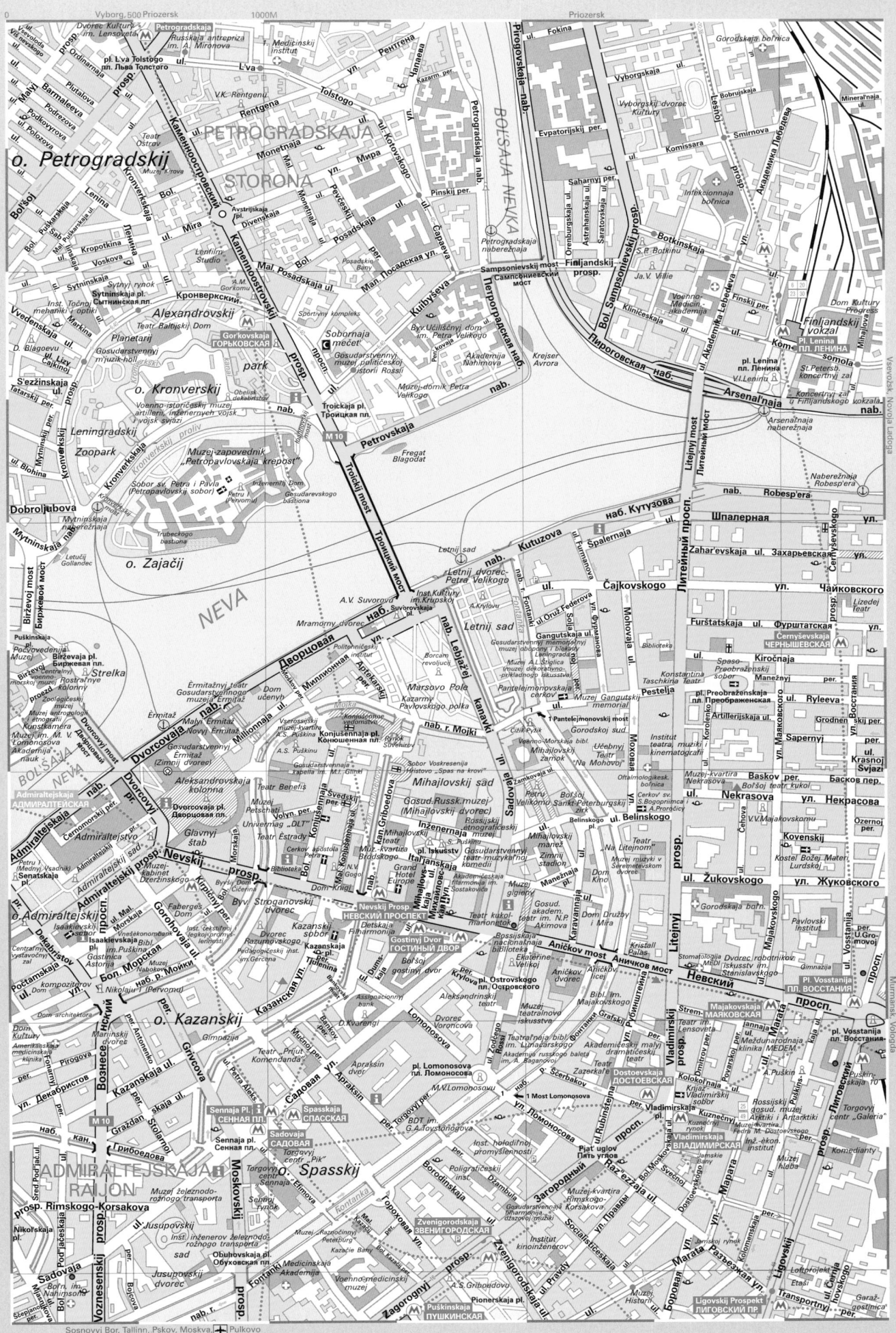

VELEŠIĆI
KOŠEVO
KOŠEVSKO BRDO
BJELAVE
BREKA
Gornja Breka
HRASTOVI
CIGLANE
GORICA
CRNI VRH
MEJTA
Veliki Park
Mali Park
Maršala Tita
Mula Mustafe Bašeskije
CENTAR
BAŠČARŠIJA
Telali
Žel. stanica Novo Sarajevo
Autobuska stanica
Put života
Sarajevo Fakultet
MARINDVOR
Hiseta
Obala
Kulina
SKENDERIJA
MRAKUŠA
Put Mladih Muslimana
BISTRIK
Zmaja od Bosne
Vilsonovo šetalište
Grbavička
Zagrebačka
Stadion Koševo
Zetra
Bolnica Koševo
Fakultet
Gradska bolnica
Alipašina džamija
Narodno pozorište
Univerzitet pravni fak.
Galerija
Srbinje
Zenica, Tuzla

ВЪЗРАЖДАНЕ
VĂZRAŽDANE
OBORIŠTE
ОБОРИЩЕ
Bul. T. Aleksandrov
Бул. Александър
Бул. Тодор
Бул. Хр. Ботев
Bul-Slivnica
Бул. Сливница
Bul. Vasil Levski
Бул. Васил Левски
Bul. Knjaz Aleksandăr Dondukov
Бул. Княз Алекс. Дондуков
Bul. Car Osvoboditel
Bul. Janko Sakăzov
Бул. Янко Сакъзов
Pl. Aleks.
Hram A. Nevski
Nevski
Narodna Biblioteka
Народна Библиотека
Universitet
Stočna Gara
Сточна Гара
Park Oborište
Serdika
Сердика
Vъzraždane
Възраждане
Stamboliiski
Стамболийски
Pl. Vъzraždane
Tel Aviv Aleksandrov
Ген. Ед.И. Тотлебен
Bul. Hristo Botev
Бул. Христо Ботев
Bul. Makedonija
Бул. Македония
Gen.M.D.Skobelev
Bul. Penčo Slavejkov
Бул. Пенчо Славейков
Bul. Patriarh
Евтимий
Bul. Gen. Eduard Totleben
Bul. Gurko
Georgiev
Георгиев
Bul. Evlogi Georgiev
Бул. Евлоги Георгиев
Bul. Carigradsko
Бул. Цариградско
ŽK JAVOROV
ЖК ЯВОРОВ
SREDEC
СРЕДЕЦ
Borisova
Gradina
Nacionalen Stadion Vasil Levski
Национален Стадион Васил Левски
Junak Stadion
Юнак Стадион
Nacionalen Dvorec na Kulturata (NDK)
NDK
НДК
Univ. po Arhitektura
Medic.Universitet Stomatolog.
Vidin

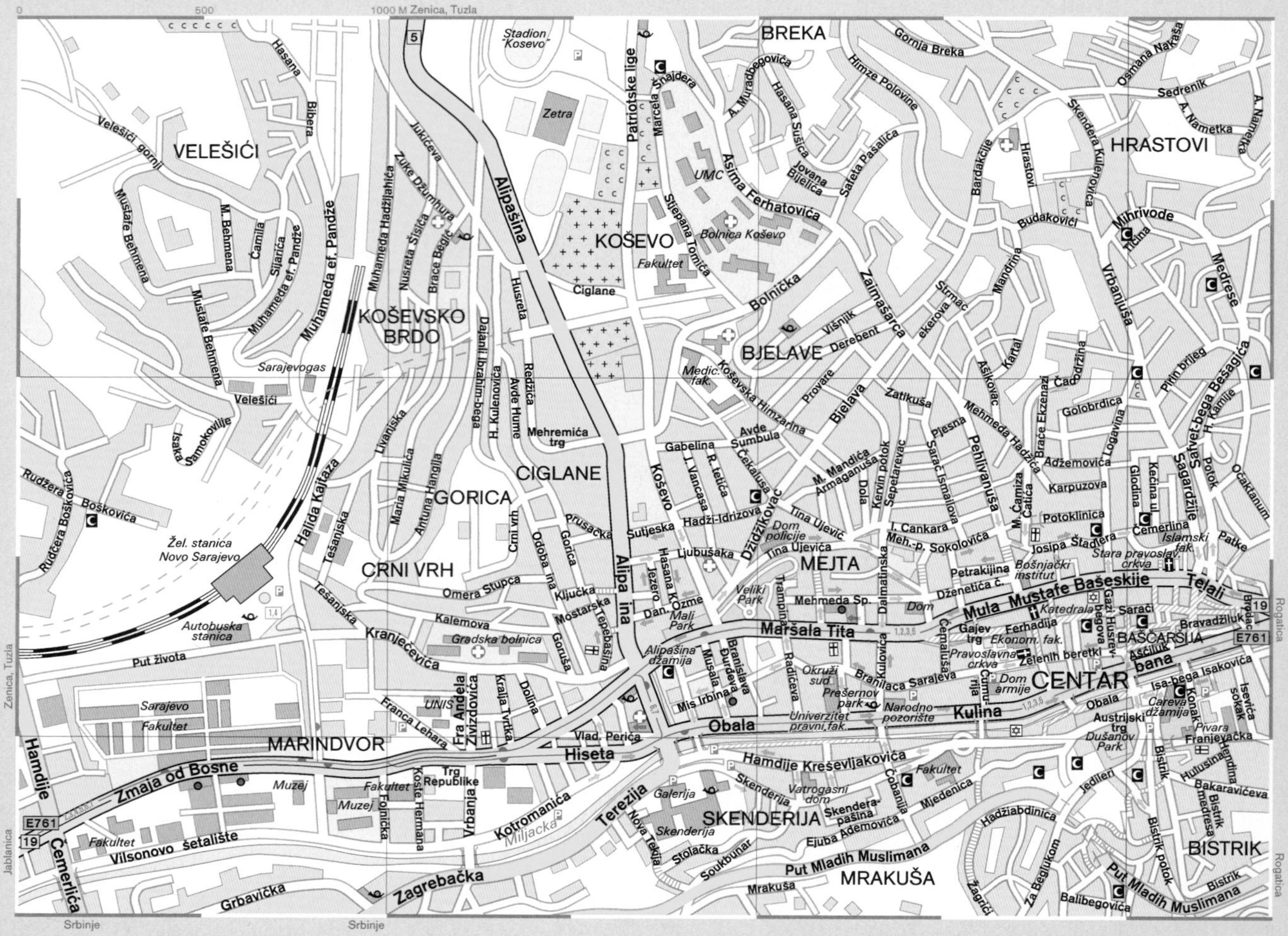

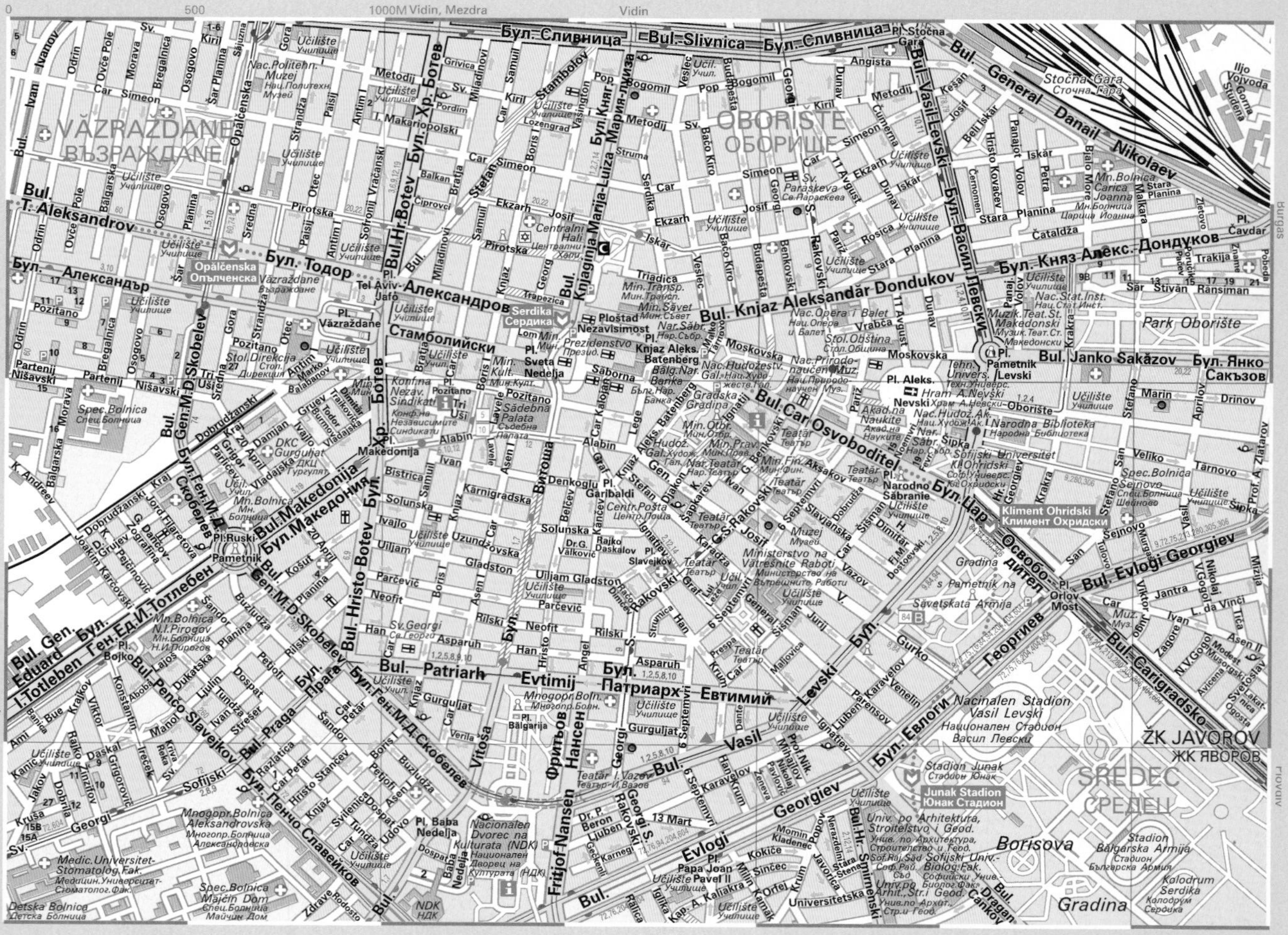

0   500   1000 M

Lastemuseum · Nline · Põhja pst · Põhja pst · Vanasadam · B-terminal · A-terminal · C-terminal · D-terminal · Sadama

Kotzebue · Suur Rannavärav · Rannamäe tee · Rannamäe tee · Merekeskus · Kai · Ahtri · Ahtri · Siimeoni kirik · SADAMA · Löbustuspark · Narva mnt

Balti jaam · Olevista kirik · Linnateater · Kanuti · ALL-LINN · Narva · Pedagoogikaülikool · Narva mnt · A. Welzenbergi · A. Alle

VANALINN · Toompark · Nukuteater · Kino "Coca-Cola Plaza" · Postimaja · Narva · RAUA · Museum

TOOMPEA · Konservatoorium · Toomkirik · Aleksander Nevski Katedraal · Niguliste kirik · Viru-keskus · Gonsiori · Kaubamaja · Kunstiülikool · KOMPASSI · Gonsiori

Kiek in de Kök Museum · Draamateater · Estonia teater · SÜDALINN · Sakala keskus · Politseiised · MAAKRI · Tartu · TORUPILLI · Laagna tee

Toompea loss · Harjumägi · Vanalinna-studio · SIBULAKÜLA · Lembitu park · KELDRIMÄE · K. Türnpu

Rahvus-raamatukogu · VAT teater · TATARI · Kaasani kirik · Pleekmägi · Juhkentali · Oära autobussijaam Bus Station · Sikupilli kaubanduskeskus

TÕNISMÄE · Livalaia · Keskhaigla · Tiigiveski park · Kalevi kesk-staadion · JUHKENTALI

UUS MAAILM · Hostel · Tatari · Spordihall · Siselinna kalmistu · Sõjaväe kalmistu · Üksik-Side-pataljon · Peterburi

Pärnu · Järvevana · Tartu mnt · Tartu, Ülemiste

0   500   1000 M

Don Bosko · Rr. Jordan Misja · Rr. Karl Gega · Rr. Ferit Xhajku · Rruga Bardhyl · Onkologjik · Rr. Kongresi Manastirit · Burrel

Rruga e Durrësit · Rr. Mine Peza · Stacioni Hekurudhor · Reshit Petrela · Rruga e Dibres · Rr. 4 Deshmoret · Rr. Qemal Stafa

Durrës, Shkoder · Rr. Haxhi Hysen Dalliu · Rr. Mine Peza · Rr. Asim Vokshi · Rr. Siri Kodra · Rr. Dervish Hekali · Arkitekt Kaserni

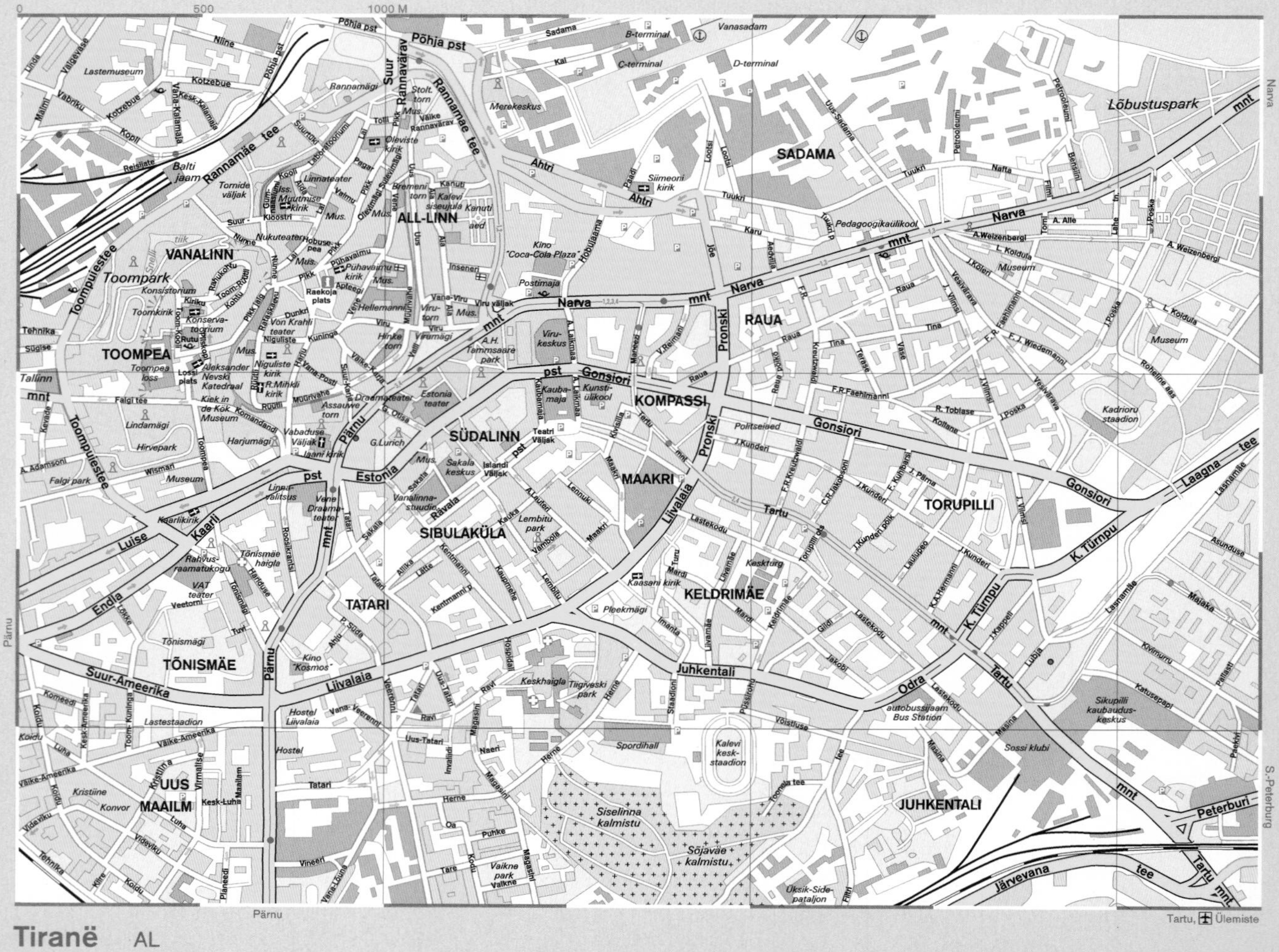

Rr. Muhamet Gjollesha · Rruga e Durrësit · Muzeu Historik Kombetar · Rr. Qemal Stafa · Rr. Hoxha Tasim · Bulevardi Zhane d'Ark

Rr. Skenderbeg · Rr. Gjön · Muzaka · Pallati Kultures · Bulevardi Bajram Curri · Rr. Al Demi

Rr. Frosina Plaku · Rruga e Kavajës · K. Katolike · K. Ortodokse · Luigi Gurakuqi · Agjensia Telegrafike · Todi Shkurti

Konferenca e Pezes · Rr. Myslym Shyri · Telekomi · Ministria · Teatri · Murat Toptani · Sali Nivica

Bulevardi Zhane d'Ark · Bulevardi Bajram Curri · Presidenca · Radio Televizioni Shqiptare · Pieter Budi

Suleiman Delvina · Stadium Selman Stermasi · Rr. Ismail Qemali · Abdyl Frasheri · Pallati Kongreseve · Stadium Qemal Stafa · Rruga e Elbasanit

BLLOKU VASIL SHANTO · Elbasan

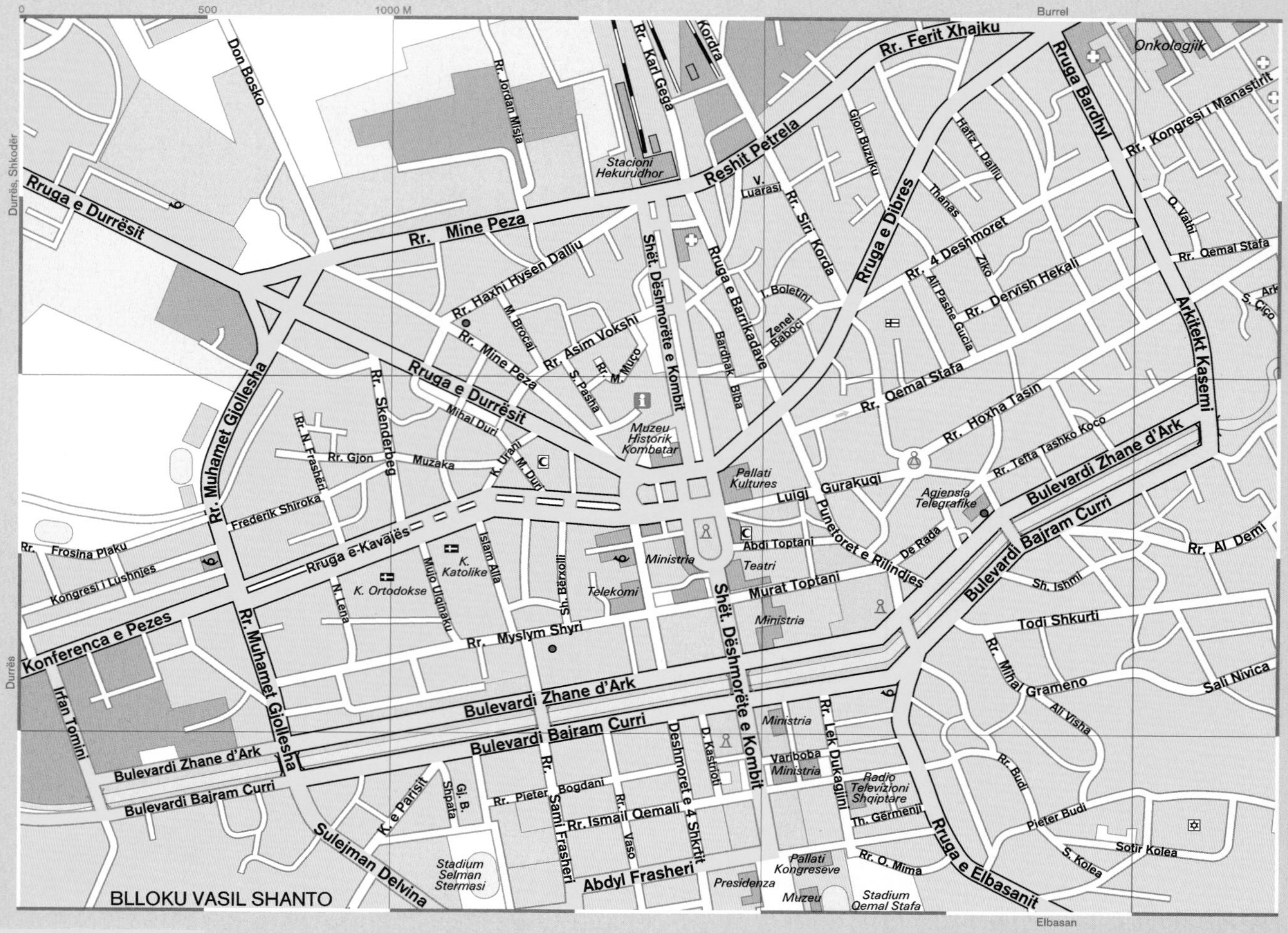

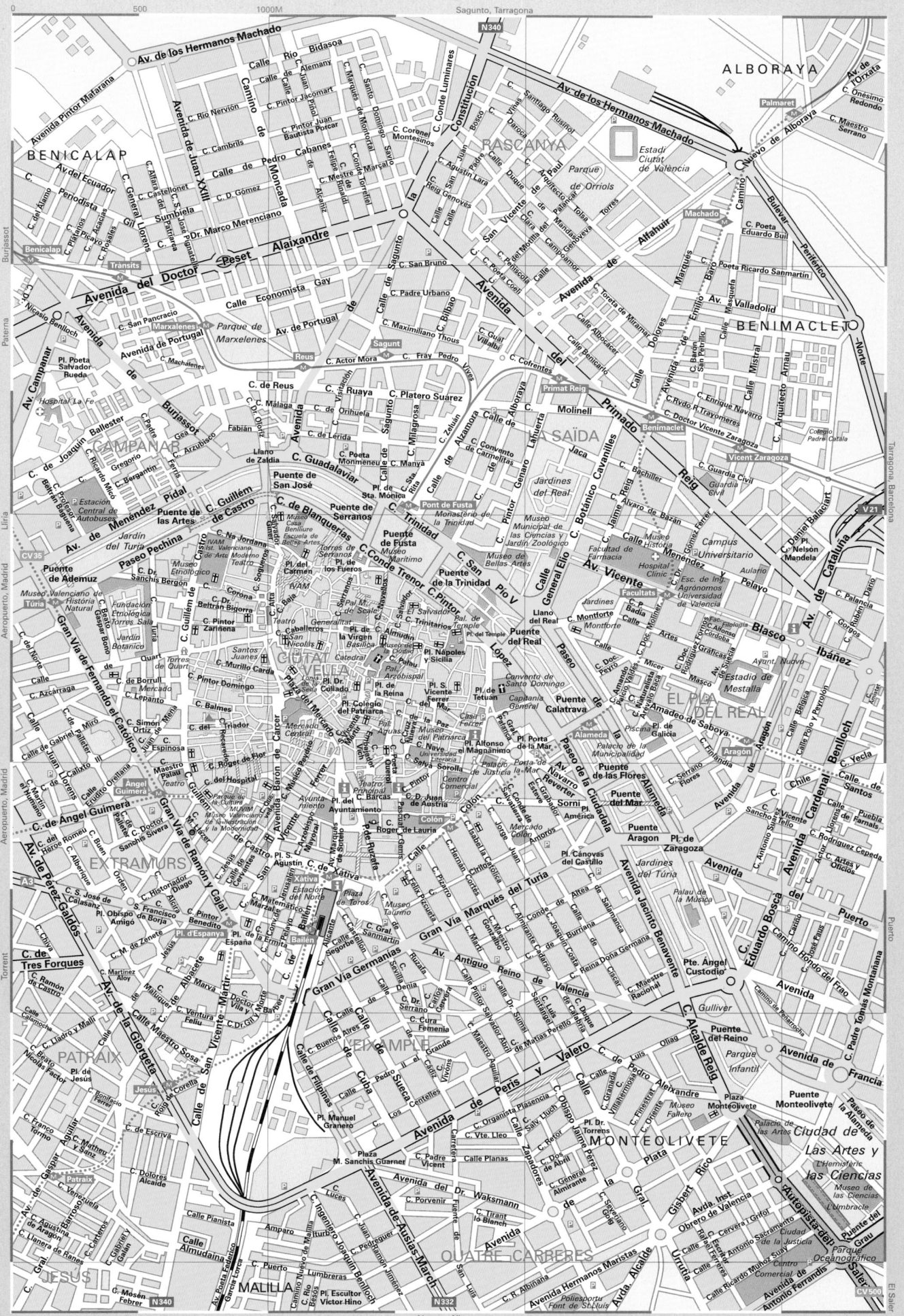

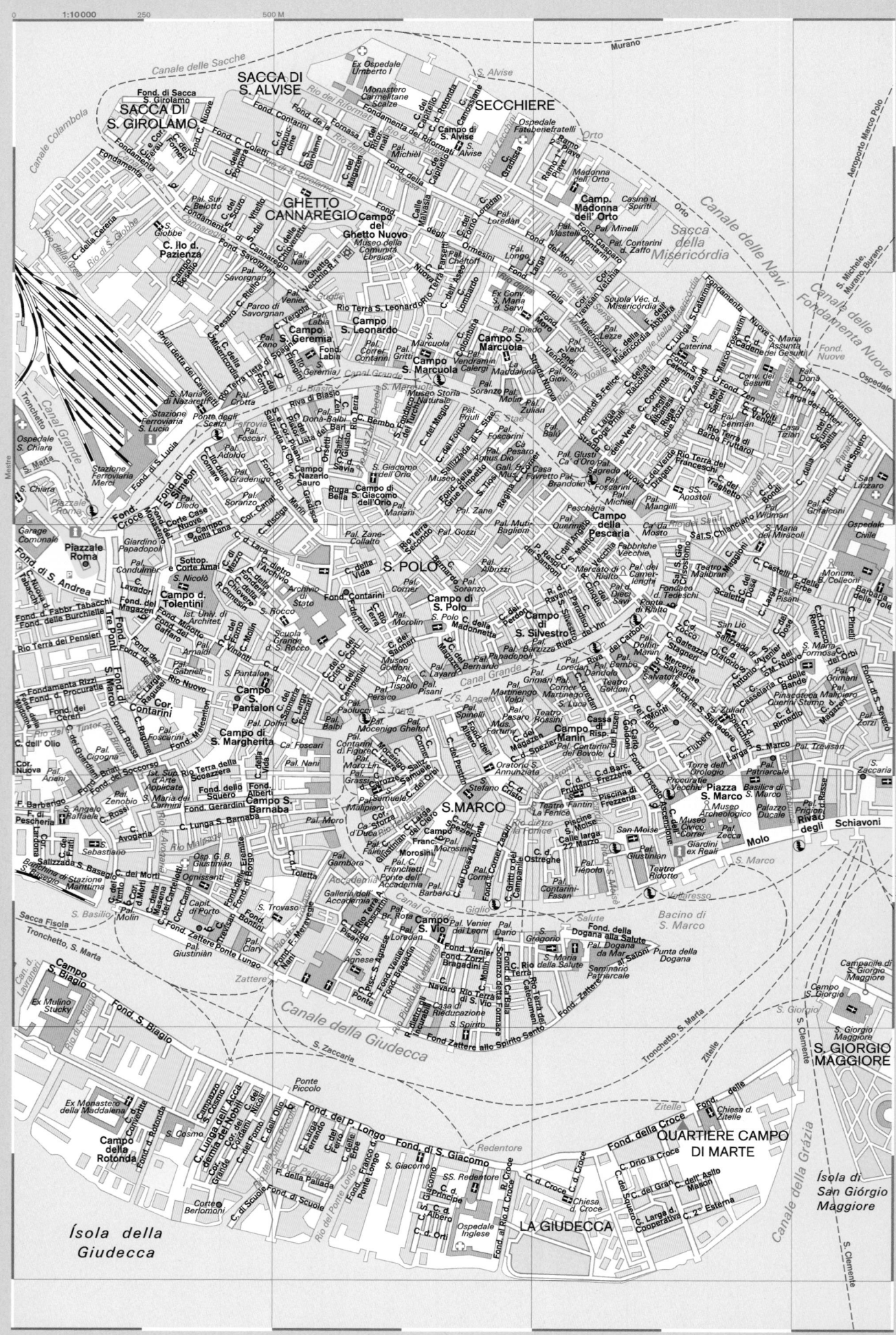

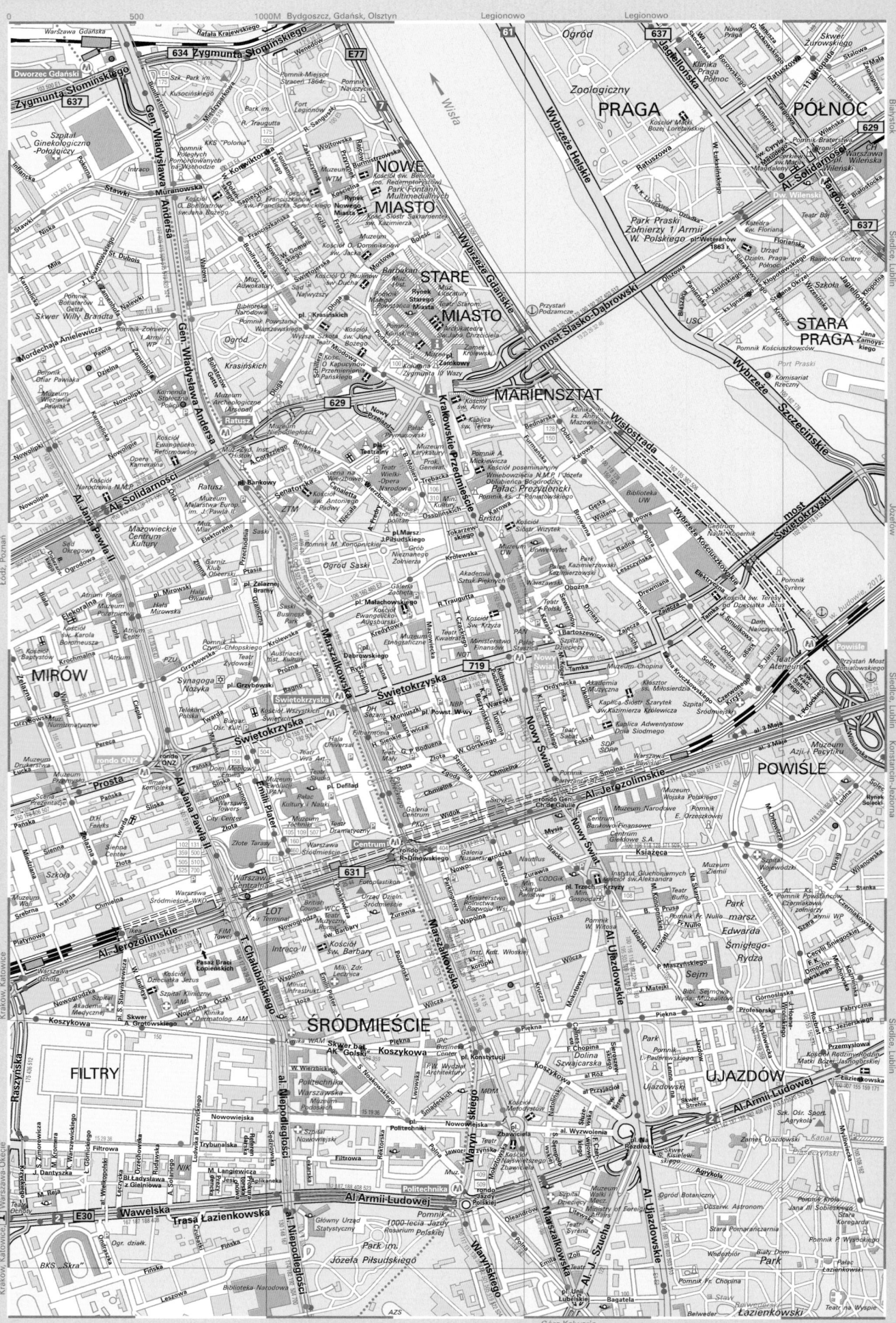

# Zagreb HR-10000

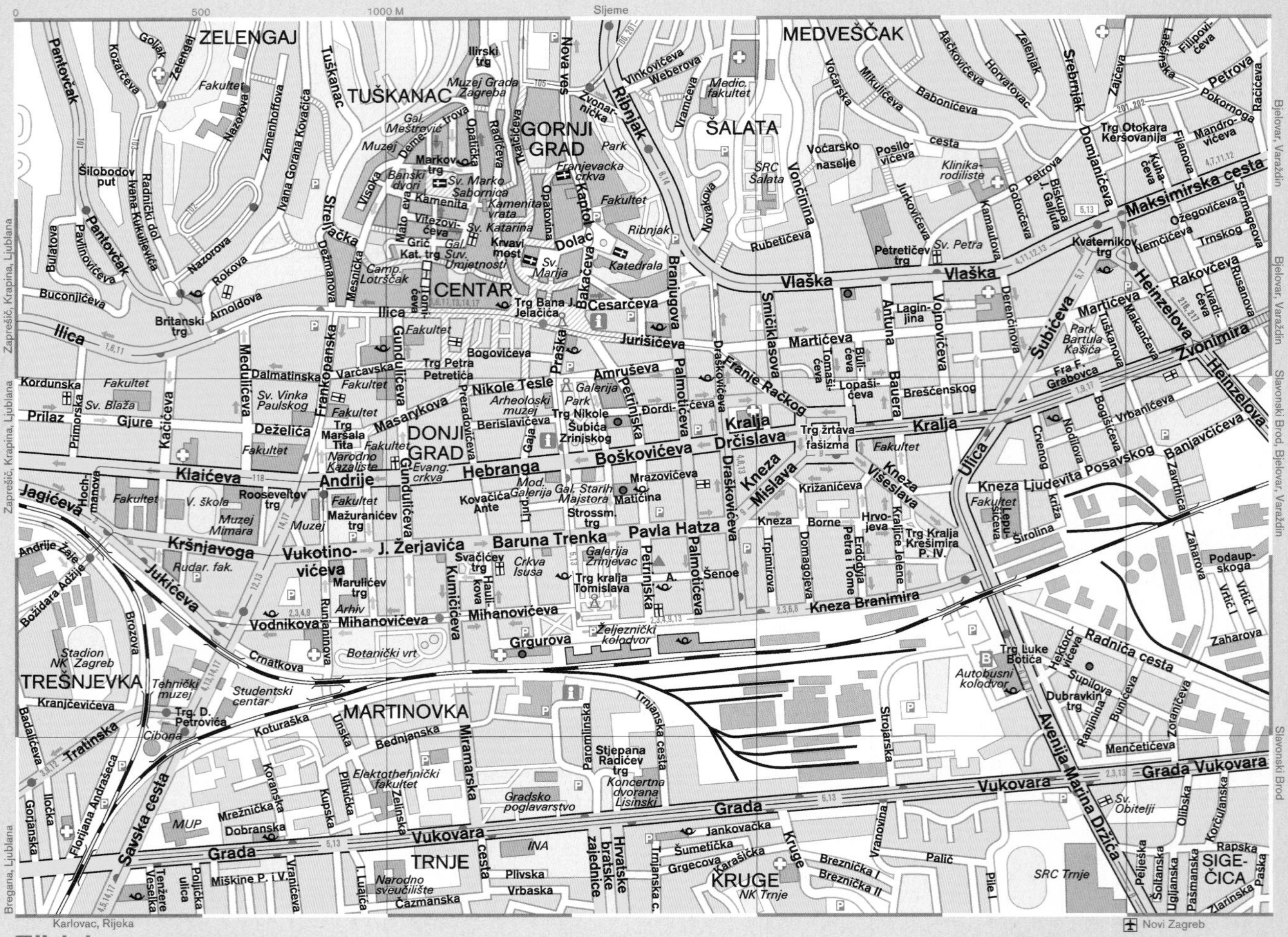

ZELENGAJ  TUŠKANAC  GORNJI GRAD  MEDVEŠČAK  ŠALATA

CENTAR  DONJI GRAD

TREŠNJEVKA  MARTINOVKA  TRNJE  KRUGE  SIGEČICA

Katedrala  Dolac  Trg Bana Jelačića

Željeznički kolodvor  Autobusni kolodvor

Avenija Marina Držića  Grada Vukovara  Vukovara

Maksimirska cesta  Radnička cesta

Botanički vrt  Stadion NK Zagreb

500  1000 M

# Zürich CH-8000-99

LANG-STRASSE  ENGE  HOTTINGER

Hauptbahnhof  Bahnhof Wiedikon  Bahnhof Enge  Bahnhof Stadelhofen

Selnau SZU  Binz SZU  Giesshübel

Zürich Wiedikon

Universitätsspital  Universität

Zürichsee

0 Basel  500  1000M

Badener  Seebahn  Stauffacher  Sihlquai  Museumstr.

Gen-Guisan-Quai  Utoquai  Quaibr.  Bellevue

Opernhaus  Arboretum  Seebad Enge

136  HR  CH

# Index of place names | Index des localités | Ortsnamenverzeichnis
# Plaatsnamenregister | Elenco dei nomi di località | Índice de topónimos
# Stednavnsfortegnelse | Ortnamnsförteckning | Rejstřík sídel
# Skorowidz miejscowości | Helységnévjegyzék | Указатель населенных пунктов

| | ① | ② | ③ | ④ | ⑤ |
|---|---|---|---|---|---|
| Ⓛ | Luxembourg | 1009 * | 42 | Ag 41 |
| ⓇⓊⓈ | Sankt-Peterburg | 190000 * | 18 | Da 31 |
| Ⓝ | Longyearbyen | 9170 | 2 | I Svalbard |

## ①

| | |
|---|---|
| GB | Motor vehicle nationality letters |
| F | Plaques de nationalité |
| D | Internationale Autokennzeichen |
| NL | Internationaale autokentekens |
| I | Targhe automobilistiche internazionali |
| E | Matrículas internacionales |
| DK | Nationalitetsbetegnelser |
| S | Nationalitetsbeteckningar |
| CZ | Poznávací značky aut |
| PL | Międzynarodowe znaki rejestracyjne |
| H | Nemzetközi autójelzesek |
| RUS | Международные опознавательные знаки |

## ②

| | |
|---|---|
| | Place name |
| | Localité |
| | Ortsname |
| | Plaatsnaam |
| | Località |
| | Topónimo |
| | Stednavn |
| | Ortnamn |
| | Jméno obcí |
| | Nazwa miejscowości |
| | Helységnév |
| | Имя населённого пункта |

## ③

| | |
|---|---|
| GB | Postal code |
| F | Code postal |
| D | Postleitzahl |
| NL | Postcode |
| I | Codice postale |
| E | Código postal |
| DK | Postnummer |
| S | Postnummer |
| CZ | Poštovní směrovací číslo |
| PL | Kod pocztowy |
| H | Iranyitoszám |
| RUS | Почтовый индекс |

## *

Lowest postcode number for places having several postcodes
Code postal le plus bas pour les localités à plusieurs codes posteaux
Niedrigste Postleitzahl bei Orten mit mehreren Postleitzahlen
Laagste postcode bij gemeenten met meerdere postcodes

Codice di avviamento postale riferito a città comprendenti più codici di avviamento postale
Código postal más bajo en lugares con varios códigos postales
Laveste postnummer ved byer med flere postnumre
Lägsta postnumret vid uppgifter med flera postnummer

Nejnižší poštovní směrovací číslo v městech s vicenásobnými poštovními směrovacími čísly
Najnyższy kod pocztowy w przypadku miej-scowości z wieloma kodami pocztowymi
Több irányítószámmal rendelkező helységéknél a legalacsonyabb irányítószám
Самый низкий почтовый индекс в случае городов с множеством почсовых индексов

## ④

| | |
|---|---|
| GB | Page number |
| F | Número de página |
| D | Seitenzahl |
| NL | Paginanummer |
| I | Numero di pagina |
| E | Número de página |
| DK | Sidetal |
| S | Sidnummer |
| CZ | Číslo strany |
| PL | Numer strony |
| H | Oldalszám |
| RUS | Число страниц |

## ⑤

| | |
|---|---|
| | Grid search reference |
| | Coordonnées |
| | Suchfeldangabe |
| | Zoekveld-gegevens |
| | Riquadro nel quale si trova il nome |
| | Coordenadas de localización |
| | Kvadratangivelse |
| | Kartrutangivelse |
| | Údaje hledacího čtverce |
| | Współrzędne skorowidzowe |
| | Keresőhálózat megadása |
| | Указатель индексного поля |

## I

| | |
|---|---|
| | Auxiliary map |
| | Carton intérieur |
| | Nebenkarte |
| | Bijkaart |
| | Inserto cartografico |
| | Cartela |
| | Bikort |
| | Bikarta |
| | Vedlejší mapa |
| | Mapa boczna |
| | Melléktérkép |
| | Врезная карта |

A – B – C ...
A – B – C – D – E – F – G – H – I – J – K – L – M – N – O – P – Q – R – S – T – U – V – W – X – Y – Z

## Internationale Autokennzeichen | Motor vehicle nationality letters
## Plaques de nationalité | Internationaale autokentekens
## Targhe automobilistiche internazionali | Matrículas internacionales
## Nationalitetsbetegnelser | Nationalitetsbeteckningar
## Międzynarodowe znaki rejestracyjne | Poznávací značky aut
## Nemzetközi autójelzesek | Международные опознавательные знаки

| (A) | (BG) | (CZ) | (F) | (GBA) |
|---|---|---|---|---|
| Austria | Bulgaria | Czech Republic | France | Alderney |
| Autriche | Bulgarie | République tchèque | France | Alderney |
| Österreich | Bulgarien | Tschechische Republik | Frankreich | Alderney |
| Oostenrijk | Bulgarije | Tsjechische Republiek | Frankrijk | Alderney |
| Austria | Bulgaria | Repubblica ceca | Francia | Alderney |
| Austria | Bulgaria | República Checa | Francia | Alderney |
| Østrig | Bulgarien | Tjekkiske republik | Frankrig | Alderney |
| Österrike | Bulgarien | Tjeckiska republiken | Frankrike | Alderney |
| Rakousko | Bulharsko | Česká republika | Francie | Alderney |
| Austria | Bułgaria | Republika Czeska | Francja | Alderney |
| Ausztria | Bulgária | Cseh Köztársaság | Franciaország | Alderney |
| Австрия | Болгария | Чешская республика | Франция | Олдерни |

| (AL) | (BIH) | (D) | (FIN) | (GBG) |
|---|---|---|---|---|
| Albania | Bosnia and Herzegovina | Germany | Finland | Guernsey |
| Albanie | Bosnie-Herzégovine | Allemagne | Finlande | Guernsey |
| Albanien | Bosnien und Herzegowina | Deutschland | Finnland | Guernsey |
| Albanië | Bosnië en Hercegovine | Duitsland | Finland | Guernsey |
| Albania | Bosnia e Erzegovina | Germania | Finlandia | Guernsey |
| Albania | Bosnia y Herzegovina | Alemania | Finlandia | Guernsey |
| Albanien | Bosnien og Hercegovina | Tyskland | Finland | Guernsey |
| Albanien | Bosnien och Hercegovina | Tyskland | Finland | Guernsey |
| Albánie | Bosna a Hercegovina | Německo | Finsko | Guernsey |
| Albania | Bośnia i Hercegowina | Niemcy | Finlandia | Guernsey |
| Albánia | Bosznia és Hercegovina | Németország | Finnország | Guernsey |
| Албания | Босния и Герцеговина | Германия | Финляидия | Гернси |

| (AND) | (BY) | (DK) | (FL) | (GBJ) |
|---|---|---|---|---|
| Andorra | Belorussia | Denmark | Liechtenstein | Jersey |
| Andorre | Biélorussie | Danemark | Liechtenstein | Jersey |
| Andorra | Weißrussland | Dänemark | Liechtenstein | Jersey |
| Andorra | Wit-Rusland | Denemarken | Liechtenstein | Jersey |
| Andorra | Russia Bianca | Danimarca | Liechtenstein | Jersey |
| Andorra | Bielorusia | Dinamarca | Liechtenstein | Jersey |
| Andorra | Hviderusland | Danmark | Liechtenstein | Jersey |
| Andorra | Vitryssland | Danmark | Liechtenstein | Jersey |
| Andorra | Bělorusko | Dánsko | Lichtenštejnsko | Jersey |
| Andora | Białoruś | Dania | Liechtenstein | Jersey |
| Andorra | Belorusszia | Dánia | Liechtenstein | Jersey |
| Андорра | Беларусь | Дания | Лихтенштейн | Джерси |

| (AX) | (CH) | (E) | (FR) | (GBM) |
|---|---|---|---|---|
| Åland Islands | Switzerland | Spain | Faeroe Islands | Isle of Man |
| Îles d'Aland | Suisse | Espagne | Iles Féroé | Île de Man |
| Ålandinseln | Schweiz | Spanien | Färöer | Insel Man |
| Ålandseilanden | Zwitserland | Spanje | Faeröer | Isle of Man |
| Isole Åland | Svizzera | Spagna | Islas Faeroe | Isola de Man |
| Islas de Åland | Suiza | España | Islas Faeroe | Isla de Man |
| Ålandsøerne | Schweiz | Spanien | Færøerne | Isle of Man |
| Åland | Schweiz | Spanien | Färöarna | Isle of Man |
| Alandské ostrovy | Švýcarsko | Španělsko | Faerské ostrovy | Ostrov Man |
| Wyspy Alandzkie | Szwajcaria | Hiszpania | Wyspy Owcze | Wyspa Man |
| Aland-szigetek | Svájc | Spanyolország | Feröer | Man sziget |
| Аландские острова | Швей ипр Швейцария | Испания | Фарерские острова | Остров мэн |

| (B) | (CY) | (EST) | (GB) | (GBZ) |
|---|---|---|---|---|
| Belgium | Cyprus | Estonia | Great Britain | Gibraltar |
| Belgique | Chypre | Estonie | Grande Bretagne | Gibraltar |
| Belgien | Zypern | Estland | Großbritannien | Gibraltar |
| België | Cyprus | Estland | Groot-Brittanië | Gibraltar |
| Belgio | Cipro | Estonia | Gran Bretagna | Gibraltar |
| Bélgica | Chipre | Estonia | Gran Bretaña | Gibraltar |
| Belgien | Cypern | Estland | Storbritannien | Gibraltar |
| Belgien | Cypern | Estland | Storbritannien | Gibraltar |
| Belgie | Kypr | Estonsko | Velká Británie | Gibraltar |
| Belgia | Cypr | Estonia | Wielka Brytania | Gibraltar |
| Belgium | Ciprus | Észtország | Nagy-Britannia | Gibraltár |
| Белгия | Кипр | Эстония | Великобритания | Гибралтар |

138

| (GR) Greece | (L) Luxembourg | (MK) Macedonia (F.Y.R.O.M.) | (RKS) Kosovo | (SLO) Slovenia |
|---|---|---|---|---|
| Grèce | Luxembourg | Macédonie (F.Y.R.O.M.) | Kosovo | Slovénie |
| Griechenland | Luxemburg | Mazedonien (F.Y.R.O.M.) | Kosovo | Slowenien |
| Griekenland | Luxemburg | Macedonië (F.Y.R.O.M.) | Kosovo | Slovenija |
| Grecia | Lussemburgo | Macedonia (F.Y.R.O.M.) | Kosovo | Eslovenia |
| Grecia | Kuxemburgo | Macedonia (F.Y.R.O.M.) | Kosovo | Slovenien |
| Grækenland | Luxemburg | Makedonien (F.Y.R.O.M.) | Kosovo | Slovenien |
| Grekland | Luxemburg | Makedonien (F.Y.R.O.M.) | Kosovo | Slovinsko |
| Řecko | Lucembursko | Makedonie (F.Y.R.O.M.) | Kosovo | Słowenia |
| Grecja | Luksemburg | Macedonia (F.Y.R.O.M.) | Kosowo | Szlovénia |
| Görögország | Luxemburg | Macedónia (F.Y.R.O.M.) | Koszovó | Словения |
| Греция | Люксембург | Македония (Б.Ю.Р.М.) | Косово | |

| (H) Hungary | (LT) Lithuania | (MNE) Montenegro | (RO) Romania | (SRB) Serbia |
|---|---|---|---|---|
| Hongrie | Lithuanie | Monténégro | Roumanie | Serbie |
| Ungarn | Litauen | Montenegro | Rumänien | Serbien |
| Hongarije | Litouwen | Montenegro | Roemenië | Servië |
| Ungheria | Lituania | Montenegro | Romania | Serbia |
| Hungria | Lituania | Montenegro | Rumania | Serbia |
| Ungarn | Litauen | Montenegro | Rumänien | Serbien |
| Ungern | Litauen | Montenegro | Rumänien | Serbien |
| Mad'arsko | Litva | Černa Hora | Rumunsko | Srbsko |
| Węgry | Litwa | Czarnogóra | Rumunia | Serbia |
| Magyarország | Litvánia | Montenegró | România | Szerbia |
| Венгрия | Литва | Церногория | Румыния | Сербия |

| (HR) Croatia | (LV) Latvia | (N) Norway | (RSM) San Marino | (TR) Turkey |
|---|---|---|---|---|
| Croatie | Lettonie | Norvège | Saint-Marin | Turquie |
| Kroatien | Lettland | Norwegen | San Marino | Türkei |
| Kroatië | Letland | Noorwegen | San Marino | Turkije |
| Croazia | Lettonia | Norvegia | San Marino | Turchia |
| Croacia | Letonia | Norvega | San Marino | Turquía |
| Kroatien | Letland | Norge | San Marino | Tyrkiet |
| Kroatien | Lettland | Norge | San Marino | Turkiet |
| Chorvatsko | Lotyšsko | Norsko | San Marino | Turecko |
| Chorwacja | Łotwa | Norwegia | San Marino | Turcja |
| Horvátország | Lettország | Norvégia | San Marino | Törökország |
| Хорватия | Латвия | Норвегия | Сан-Марино | Турция |

| (I) Italy | (M) Malta | (NL) Netherlands | (RUS) Russia | (UA) Ukrainia |
|---|---|---|---|---|
| Italie | Malte | Pays-Bas | Russie | Ukraine |
| Italien | Malta | Niederlande | Russland | Ukraine |
| Italië | Malta | Nederland | Rusland | Oekraine |
| Italia | Malta | Paesi Bassi | Russia | Ucraina |
| Italia | Malta | Países Bajos | Rusia | Ucraina |
| Italien | Malta | Nederland | Ryssland | Ukraine |
| Italien | Malta | Nederländerna | Ryssland | Ukraina |
| Itálie | Malta | Nizozemsko | Rusko | Ukrajina |
| Włochy | Malta | Holandia | Rosja | Ukraina |
| Olaszország | Málta | Hollandia | Oroszország | Ukrajna |
| Италия | Мальта | Нидерланды | Россия | Украина |

| (IRL) Ireland | (MC) Monaco | (P) Portugal | (S) Sweden | (V) Vatican City |
|---|---|---|---|---|
| Irlande | Monaco | Portugal | Suède | Cité du Vatican |
| Irland | Monaco | Portugal | Schweden | Vatikanstadt |
| Ierland | Monaco | Portugal | Zweden | Vaticaanstad |
| Irlanda | Monaco | Portugal | Svezia | Città del Vaticano |
| Irlanda | Monaco | Portogallo | Suecia | Ciudad del Vaticano |
| Irland | Monaco | Portugal | Sverige | Vatikanet |
| Irland | Monaco | Portugal | Sverige | Vatikanstaten |
| Irsko | Monako | Portugalsko | Švédsko | Vatikán |
| Irlandia | Monaco | Portugalia | Szwecja | Watykan |
| Írország | Monaco | Portugália | Svédország | Vatikán-város |
| Ирландия | Монако | Португалия | Швеция | Ватикан |

| (IS) Iceland | (MD) Moldavia | (PL) Poland | (SK) Slovak Republic | |
|---|---|---|---|---|
| Islande | Moldavie | Pologne | République slovaque | |
| Island | Moldawien | Polen | Slowakische Republik | |
| Ijsland | Moldavië | Polen | Slowaakse Republiek | |
| Islanda | Moldavia | Polonia | Repubblica slovacca | |
| Islandia | Moldavia | Polonia | República Eslovaca | |
| Island | Moldavien | Polen | Slovakiske republik | |
| Island | Moldavien | Polen | Slovakiska republiken | |
| Island | Moldavsko | Polsko | Slovenská republika | |
| Islandia | Moldawia | Polska | Republika Słowacka | |
| Izland | Moldava | Lengyelország | Szlovák Köztársaság | |
| Исландия | Молдова | Польша | Словацкая республика | |

**A B C D E F G H I J K L M N O P Q R S T U V W X Y Z**

# A


(DK) Aabenraa = Åbenrå 6200 26 Ak 35
(DK) Aabybro = Åbybro 9440 16 Ak 33
(D) Aachen 52062* 42 Ag 40
(DK) Aalborg 9000* 16 Ak 33
(D) Aalen 73430* 43 Ba 42
(NL) Aalsmeer 1430* 41 Ae 38
(B) Aalst 3800 41 Ae 40
(NL) Aalten 7120* 42 Ag 39
(B) Aalter 9880 41 Ad 39
(FIN) Äänekoski 44150 10 Cf 28
(S) Aapua 3 Cd 24
(CH) Aarau 5000* 56 Ai 43
(S) Aareavaara 3 Cd 23
(DK) Aarhus 8000* 27 Ba 34
(B) Aarschot 3200 41 Ae 40
(E) Abadín 27730 68 Sc 47
(I) Abano Terme 35031 57 Bb 45
(TR) Abaş 76 Ck 51
(I) Abbadia San Salvatore 53021 72 Bb 48
(S) Abbekås 27404 27 Bd 35
(F) Abbeville 80100* 41 Ab 40
(IRL) Abbeyfeale = Mainistir na Féile 37 Sa 38
(IRL) Abbeyleix = Mainistir Laoise 37 Sc 38
(S) Abborrträsk 93082 10 Bk 25
(RUS) Abdulino 34 Fd 37
(E) Abejar 42146 69 Sh 49
(E) Abenójar 13180 81 Sf 52
(DK) Åbenrå = Aabenraa 26 Ak 35
(GB) Aberaeron SA46 40 Sf 38
(GB) Aberdâr = Aberdare CF44 40 Sg 39
(GB) Aberdare CF44 40 Sg 39
(GB) Aberdaugleddau = Milford Haven SA73 40 Se 39
(GB) Aberdeen AB16 38 Sh 33
(GB) Aberfeldy PH15 38 Sg 34
(GB) Abergavenny NP7 40 Sg 39
(GB) Abergele LL22 39 Sg 37
(GB) Aberhonddu = Brecon LD3 40 Sg 39
(GB) Abermaw = Barmouth LL42 39 Sf 38
(GB) Abersoch LL53 39 Sf 38
(GB) Abertawe = Swansea SA1 40 Sg 39
(GB) Aberteifi = Cardigan SA43 40 Sf 38
(GB) Aberystwyth SY23 40 Sf 38
(RUS) Abez' 7 Gb 24
(RUS) Abganerovo 49 Ee 42
(TR) Abide 17900 75 Cg 50
(TR) Abide 17900 84 Ck 52
(GB) Abington CB1 39 Sg 35
(RUS) Abinsk 63 Di 46
(S) Abisko 98107 2 Bi 22
(F) Ablis 78660 41 Ab 42
(FIN) Åbo = Turku 20002* 18 Cc 30
(H) Abony 2740 59 Ca 43
(GB) Aboyne AB34 38 Sh 33
(RUS) Abramovka 33 Eh 36
(RUS) Abramovka 51 Fe 38
(P) Abrantes 2200-001* 68 Sb 51
(RUS) Abrau-Djurso 63 Dh 46
(LV) Abrene = Pytalovo 29 Ch 33
(F) Abrets, les 38490 56 Af 45
(F) Abriès 05460 56 Ag 46
(RO) Abrud 515100 60 Cd 44
(DK) Åbybro = Aabybro 9100 16 Ak 33
(S) Åbyn 93047 10 Cb 25
(RUS) Abzakovo 35 Fi 37
(RUS) Abzanovo 52 Fg 39
(I) Accéglio 12021 56 Ag 46
(IRL) Achad an Iúir 37 Sc 37
(GB) Achiltibuie IV26 38 Se 32
(D) Achim 28832 26 Ak 37
(GB) Achnasheen IV22 38 Se 33
(TR) Acıgöl 50140 85 De 52
(RUS) Ačikulak 64 Ee 46
(TR) Acıpayam 20800* 84 Ck 53
(TR) Acıpınar 19500 85 Dd 52
(I) Acireale 95024 72 Bf 53
(RUS) Ačit 35 Fh 34
(GB) Acle NR13 41 Ab 38
(TR) Açma 86 Di 52
(I) Acquasparta 05021 72 Bc 48
(I) Ácqui Terme 15011 56 Ai 46
(I) Acri 87041 73 Bg 51
(H) Ács 2941 59 Bi 43
(SRB) Ada 24430 74 Bk 49
(RUS) Adaevka 53 Gc 39
(S) Adak 93072 9 Bi 25
(TR) Adaklı 79 Ea 51
(TR) Adaklı 87 Ee 53
(TR) Adaksu 87 Ec 52
(RO) Adamclisi 907010 61 Ch 46
(E) Adamuz 14430 81 Sf 52
(TR) Adana 01000* 85 Df 54
(TR) Adapazarı = Sakarya 76 Da 50
(TR) Adatoprakpınar 77 Dc 51
(CH) Adelboden 3715 56 Ah 44
(I) Adélfia 70010 73 Bg 50
(TR) Adilcevaz 13500 87 Ec 52
(TR) Adiller 70820 84 Dc 54
(TR) Adıyaman 02000* 86 Di 53
(RO) Adjud 625100 61 Ch 44
(RUS) Adler 63 Dk 47
(A) Admont 8911* 58 Be 43
(S) Adolfsström 2 Bg 24
(D) Adorf 08626 43 Bc 40
(E) Adrall 25797 70 Ab 48
(I) Adrano 95031 72 Be 53
(I) Ádria 45011 57 Bc 45
(RO) Adunaţii-Copăceni 087005 60 Cg 46
(LT) Adutiškis 18039 29 Cg 35
(RUS) Adygejsk 63 Dk 46
(RUS) Adyk 65 Ef 45
(EST) Aegviidu 74501 18 Cf 31
(GR) Aetós 30004 74 Cb 50
(RUS) Afanas'evo 21 Ec 32
(RUS) Afanas'evo 23 Fd 32
(RUS) Afanas'evskoe 35 Fi 34
(GR) Afándou 85103 84 Ci 54
(RUS) Afipinskij 63 Dk 45
(RUS) Afipskij 63 Di 46
(N) Åfjord 7170 8 Ba 27
(RUS) Afrikanda 4 Dc 23
(TR) Afşar 77 Dd 51
(TR) Afşin 46500 86 Dg 52
(RO) Afumaţi 077010 60 Cg 46
(TR) Afyon 03000* 84 Da 52
(TR) Ağaca 18600 77 Dc 50
(TR) Ağaçbeyli 64810 84 Ck 52
(TR) Ağaçlı 21920 87 Ea 52
(TR) Ağaçören 68600 85 Dd 52
(TR) Ağaçsever 87 Ea 53
(RUS) Agafonkovo 23 Fh 33
(RUS) Agapovka 35 Fk 37
(F) Agde 34300* 55 Ad 47
(F) Agen 47000* 54 Aa 46
(DK) Agger 7770 26 Ai 34
(GR) Agía Ána 82 Cc 52
(GR) Agia Déka 82 Ce 55
(CY) Agia Eirini 9610 84 Dc 55
(GR) Agía Galíni 70200 82 Ce 55
(GR) Agía Marína 35101 83 Cg 53
(CY) Agia Napa 5330 85 Dd 56
(GR) Agía Pelagía 71001 82 Cc 54
(GR) Agía Rouméli 73005 82 Cd 55
(GR) Ágias Triás Parnithos 14565 82 Cd 52
(GR) Agía Triáda 21055 82 Cb 53
(RUS) Agidel' 34 Fe 35
(RO) Aghighiol 827236 61 Ci 45
(TR) Ağın 23960 86 Di 52
Agios Amvrosios 85 Dd 55
(GR) Ágios Apóstoli 82 Cd 54
(GR) Ágios Efstrátios 81400 75 Ce 51
(GR) Ágios Harálambos 69400 75 Cf 50
(GR) Ágios Kírikos 83 Cg 53
(GR) Ágios Konstantínos 82 Cc 52
(GR) Ágios Nikólaos 83 Cf 55
(GR) Ágios Pétros 31082 82 Ca 52
(GR) Ágios Theódori 82 Cd 53
(I) Agira 94011 72 Be 53
(TR) Ağlasun 15800 84 Da 53
(LV) Aglona 5304 29 Cg 34
(RO) Agnita 555100 60 Ce 45
(I) Agnone 86081 73 Be 49
(F) Agon-Coutainville 50230 40 Si 41
(E) Agramunt 25310 70 Ab 49
(RUS) Agrat 34 Fb 37
(TR) Ağrı 04000* 79 Ed 51
(I) Agrigento 92100 72 Bd 53
(GR) Agrínio 30100 82 Cb 52
(GR) Agriovótano 34200 75 Cd 51
(I) Agrópoli 84043 73 Be 50
(RUS) Agryz 34 Fd 34
(E) Agudo 13410 69 Sf 52
(P) Águeda 3750-101* 68 Sb 50
(E) Aguilar 33619 81 Sf 53
(E) Aguilar de Campoo 34800 69 Sf 48
(E) Águilas 30880 81 Si 53
(TR) Ağva 34991 76 Ck 49
(TR) Ahat 84 Ck 52
(D) Ahaus 48683 42 Ah 38
(RUS) Ahikovo 21 Ed 31
(GR) Ahíllio 37007 74 Cc 51
(E) Ahillones 06940 80 Se 52
(TR) Ahırlı 42180 84 Dc 53
(GR) Ahladohóri 62300 75 Cd 49
(FIN) Ahlainen 29700 18 Cb 29
(TR) Ahlat 13400 87 Ec 52
(TR) Ahlatlı 39000 79 Eb 50
(D) Ahlbeck 27 Be 37
(D) Ahlen 88524 42 Ah 39
(RUS) Ahmany 25 Ge 33
(TR) Ahmetbey 39770 76 Ch 49
(TR) Ahmetli 83 Ch 52
(TR) Ahmetli 86 Dk 52
(RUS) Ahmetovskaja 64 Eb 46
(FIN) Ahmovaara 83950 11 Ck 27
(D) Ahrensbök 23623 27 Ba 36
(D) Ahrensburg 22926 27 Ba 37
(CY) Ahrotiri 84 Dc 56
(D) Ahrweiler, Bad Neuenahr- 53474 42 Ah 40
(FIN) Ähtäri 63701 10 Ce 28
(RUS) Ahtarsk, Primorsko- 63 Di 44
(EST) Ahtme, Jõhvi- 41541 19 Ch 31
(BG) Ahtopol 8280 76 Ch 48
(RUS) Ahtropovo 21 Ec 32
(RUS) Ahtubinsk 50 Eg 42
(F) Ahun 23150 55 Ac 44
(RUS) Ahunovo 35 Fk 36
(S) Åhus 29600 27 Be 35
(FIN) Ahvenselkä 98630 3 Ci 24
(GR) Aianí 50004 74 Cb 50
(D) Aibling, Bad 83043 57 Bc 43
(D) Aichach 86551 43 Bb 42
(N) Aiddejavrre Fjellstue 3 Cd 22
(A) Aigen im Mühlkreis 4160* 43 Bd 42
Aigialousa 85 De 55
(CH) Aigle 1860 56 Ag 44
(F) Aigle, l' 61300 41 Aa 42
(GR) Aigósthena 82 Cd 52
(F) Aigre 16140 54 Aa 45
(F) Aiguebelle 73220 56 Ag 45
(F) Aigues-Mortes 30220 55 Ae 47
(F) Aiguillon 47190 54 Aa 46
(F) Aigurande 36140 55 Ab 44
(F) Aillant-sur-Tholon 89110 55 Ad 43
(IRL) Ailt an Chorráin 37 Sb 36
(LV) Ainaži 4035 18 Ce 33
(E) Ainsa-Sobrarbe 70 Aa 48
(F) Airaines 80270 41 Ab 41
(GB) Aird HS2 38 Sd 32
(F) Airel 50680 40 Si 41
(F) Aire-sur-l'Adour 40800* 54 Sk 47
(F) Aire-sur-la-Lys 62120 41 Ac 40
(CH) Airolo 6780 56 Ai 44
(F) Airvault 79600 54 Sk 44
(RUS) Aitovo 34 Fe 37
(RO) Aiud 515200 60 Cd 44
(F) Aix-d'Angillon, les 18220 55 Ac 43
(F) Aix-en-Provence 13080* 56 Af 47
(F) Aix-les-Bains 73100* 56 Af 45
(F) Aizenay 85190 54 Si 44
(LV) Aizpute 3456 28 Cb 34
(F) Ajaccio 20000 71 Ai 49
(S) Ajaureforsen 9 Bf 25
(RUS) Ajdar 48 Di 40
(SLO) Ajdovščina 5270 57 Bd 45
(H) Ajka 8400* 58 Bh 43
(RUS) Ajkino 14 Ek 28
(BG) Ajtos 8500 76 Ch 48
(TR) Akarsu 78 Di 51
(TR) Akarsu 87 Eb 53
(FIN) Äkäsjokisuu 95901 3 Cd 23
(FIN) Äkäslompolo 95970 3 Ce 23
(TR) Akbaba 79 Ed 50
(TR) Akbaş 84 Dc 52
(TR) Akbelenli 84 Da 53
(TR) Akbıyıklı 77 De 51
(TR) Akbudak 86 Dh 53
(RUS) Akbulak 52 Ff 39
(TR) Akburun 84 Db 53
(TR) Akçaabat 61300 78 Dk 49
(TR) Akçabelen 42705 84 Db 53
(TR) Akçadağ 44600 86 Dh 52
(TR) Akçagöze 86 Dh 53
(TR) Akçakale 78 Dk 49
(TR) Akçakale 86 Di 54
(TR) Akçakent 77 De 51
(TR) Akçakışla 66660 77 Df 51
(TR) Akcakışla 58420 78 Dg 51
(TR) Akçakoca 14700 76 Db 49
(TR) Akçaova 41620 76 Ck 49
(TR) Akçaova 41620 84 Ci 53
(TR) Akçapınar 17600 86 Di 52
(TR) Akçaşehir 85 Dd 53
(TR) Akçay 21560 79 Ed 50
(TR) Akçay 21560 84 Ck 54
(TR) Akçayazı 85 Dd 53
(BY) Akcjabrski 46 Ci 38
(TR) Akdağmadeni 66300 78 Df 51
(TR) Akdere 33940 84 Ck 52
(TR) Akdere 33940 86 Dg 52
(D) Aken (Elbe) 06385 43 Bc 39
(S) Åkernäs 9 Bg 25
(S) Åkersberga 18400* 17 Bi 31
(TR) Akhisar 29650* 83 Ch 52
(TR) Akın 06965 77 Dd 51
(TR) Akıncı 87 Ea 53
(TR) Akıncılar 02420 78 Di 50
(TR) Akıncılar 02420 86 Di 53
(TR) Akıne 33630 84 Dc 54
(RUS) Akinfievo 24 Gb 32
(DK) Åkirkeby 27 Be 35
(RUS) Ak"jar 52 Fi 39
(TR) Akkaya 06840 77 De 49
(TR) Akkent 20710 84 Ck 52
(TR) Akkışla 38830 78 Dg 51
(TR) Akkoç 78 Dh 51
(TR) Akköprü 84 Ci 54
(TR) Akköy 38800 83 Ch 53
(TR) Akköy 38800 84 Ck 53
(TR) Akkuş 78 Dg 50
(LT) Akmenė 85022 29 Cc 34
(LT) Akmenė, Naujoji 85001 29 Cc 34
(TR) Akmeşe 76 Da 50
(RUS) Akmurun 52 Fi 38
(LV) Akniste 29 Cf 34
(TR) Akören 84 Dc 53
(TR) Akova 33700 85 Dd 54
(TR) Akpazar 62810 86 Dk 52
(TR) Akpınar 76 Da 51
(TR) Akpınar 77 Dd 51
(TR) Akpınar 77 De 50
(TR) Akpınar 78 Dh 51
(TR) Akpınar 84 Ck 52
(TR) Akpınar 86 Di 53
(N) Åkrahamn-Vedavågen 4276 16 Af 31
(IS) Akranes 300 36 Qh 26
(GR) Akráta 25006 82 Cc 52
(GR) Akréfnio 32200 82 Cd 52
(N) Åkrestrømmen 2480 16 Bb 29
(RUS) Aksaj 63 Dk 43
(RUS) Aksaj 64 Ed 43
(TR) Aksakal 10245 76 Ci 50
(RUS) Aksakovo 34 Fe 36
(RUS) Akšap 23 Fg 33
(TR) Akşar 79 Ec 50
(TR) Akşar 87 Ec 52
(TR) Aksaray 68000* 85 De 52
(TR) Aksaz 17200 84 Ck 52
(TR) Akşehir 42550* 84 Db 52
(TR) Akseki 37400 84 Db 53
(RUS) Aksenkino 34 Fd 36
(RUS) Aksenovo 34 Fe 37
(RUS) Aksent'evica 22 Eh 30
(TR) Aksu 25430 84 Da 54
(TR) Aksu 25430 84 Db 53
(RUS) Aksubaevo 34 Fa 36
(RUS) Aktanyš 34 Fe 35
(RUS) Aktarsk 49 Ee 39
(TR) Aktaş 78 Dg 50
(TR) Aktepe 79 Ec 51
(TR) Aktepe 86 Dg 54
(RUS) Aktjubinskij 34 Fc 36
(TR) Aktur 48920 83 Ch 54
(TR) Aktuzla 49430 79 Ec 51
(IS) Akureyri 600* 36 Rb 25
(TR) Akyaka 79 Ed 50
(TR) Akyaka 85 Dd 54
(TR) Akyazı 76 Da 50
(TR) Akyurt 06750 77 Dd 50
(RUS) Akžarskoe 52 Fk 39
(TR) Akziyaret 63180 86 Di 53
(N) Ål 3570 16 Ai 30
(S) Ala 17 Bi 33
(TR) Alaca 25500 77 De 50
(TR) Alaca 25500 79 Ea 51
(TR) Alacahan 58910 78 Dh 51
(TR) Alacakaya 23410 86 Dk 52
(TR) Alacalı 34886 76 Ck 49
(TR) Alacami 84 Dc 54
(E) Alacant 03001 81 Sk 52
(TR) Alaçatı 83 Cg 52
(TR) Aladağ 01720 84 Dc 53
(TR) Aladağ 01720 85 Df 53
(E) Alaejos 47510 68 Se 49
(RUS) Alagir 79 Ee 48
(FIN) Alahärmä 62375 10 Cc 27
(E) Alaior 07730 71 Ae 51
(FIN) Alajärvi 62901 10 Cd 28
(TR) Alakonak 63700 86 Dk 53
(RUS) Alakurtti 4 Da 24
(TR) Alan 87 Ee 53
(E) Alange 06840 80 Sd 52
(E) Alanís 41380 80 Se 52
(TR) Alanya 07400 84 Dc 54
(TR) Alanyurt 76 Da 51
(RUS) Alapaevsk 24 Gb 33
(TR) Alaplı 67850 76 Db 49
(E) Alaraz 37312 68 Se 50
(TR) Alaşehir 45600 83 Ci 52
(S) Alåsen 83060 9 Be 27
(I) Alássio 56 Ai 46
(TR) Alatosun 87 Ea 53
(I) Alatri 03011 72 Bd 49
(EST) Alatskivi 60201 19 Ch 32
(RUS) Alatyr' 33 Eg 36
(FIN) Alavieska 85201 10 Ce 26
(FIN) Ala-Vuokki 89830 11 Ck 26
(FIN) Alavus 63301 10 Cd 28
(TR) Alayurt 76 Da 51
(I) Alba 12051 56 Ai 46
(RO) Albac 517005 59 Cc 44
(E) Albacete 02001* 81 Si 52
(E) Alba de Tormes 37800 68 Se 50
(DK) Ålbæk 6740 16 Ba 33
(RO) Alba Iulia 000510* 60 Cd 44
(E) Albalate de Cinca 22534 70 Aa 49
(E) Albalate del Arzobispo 44540 70 Sk 49
(E) Albalate de Zorita 19117 69 Sh 50
(F) Alban 81250 55 Ac 47
(E) Albanyà 70 Ac 48
(TR) Albayrak 65610 87 Ee 52
(I) Albenga 17031 56 Ai 46
(E) Alberca, La 37624 68 Sd 50
(P) Albergaria-a-Velha 3850-001* 68 Sb 50
(P) Albernoa 7800-601 80 Sc 53
(F) Albert 80300 41 Ac 40
(F) Albertville 73200 56 Ag 45
(F) Albi 81000* 55 Ac 47
(E) Albocásser 70 Aa 50
(DK) Ålborg = Aalborg 9100 16 Ak 33
(E) Albox 04800 81 Sh 53
(D) Albstadt 72458* 42 Ak 42
(E) Albuera, La 06170 80 Sd 52
(P) Albufeira 8200-001* 80 Sb 53
(E) Albuñol 18700 81 Sg 54
(E) Albuquerque 68 Sc 51
(S) Alby 84144 9 Bf 28
(P) Alcácer do Sal 7580-001* 80 Sb 52
(P) Alcáçovas 7090-010* 80 Sb 52
(E) Alcalá de Chivert = Alcalà de Xivert 12570 70 Aa 50
(E) Alcalá de Guadaira 41500 80 Se 53
(E) Alcalá de Henares 28801 69 Sg 50
(E) Alcalà de Xivert 12570 70 Aa 50
(E) Alcalá la Real 23680 81 Sg 53
(I) Álcamo 72 Bc 53
(E) Alcanar 43530 70 Aa 50
(P) Alcanede 2025-030* 68 Sb 51
(E) Alcañices 49500 68 Sd 49
(E) Alcañiz 44600 70 Sk 49
(E) Alcántara 10980 68 Sd 51
(E) Alcantarilla 02489 81 Si 53
(E) Alcaracejos 14480 81 Sf 52
(E) Alcarràs 25180 70 Aa 49
(E) Alcaudete 23660 81 Sf 53
(E) Alcaudete de la Jara 45662 69 Sf 51
(E) Alcázar de San Juan 13600 69 Sg 51
(UA) Alčevs'k 48 Di 42
(TR) Alcı 66700 77 Df 51
(TR) Alçı 84 Ck 53
(TR) Alçiören 78 Dh 51
(E) Alcoba 13116 69 Sf 51
(P) Alcobaça 2460-001* 68 Sb 51
(E) Alcoi 03800 70 Sk 52
(E) Alcolea de Calatrava 13107 81 Sf 52
(E) Alconchel 06131 80 Sc 52
(E) Alcora 70 Sk 50
(E) Alcorcón 28921 69 Sg 50
(E) Alcorisa 44550 70 Sk 50
(P) Alcoutim 2000-791 80 Sc 53
(E) Alcoy = Alcoi 03800 81 Sk 52
(E) Alcublas 46172 70 Sk 51
(E) Alcúdia 07400 70 Ad 51
(E) Aldeadávila de la Ribera 37250 68 Sd 49
(E) Aldea del Rey 13380 81 Sg 52
(E) Aldeanueva del Camino 10740 68 Se 50
(GB) Aldeburgh IP15 41 Ab 38
(GB) Aldershot GU11 40 Sk 39
(MK) Aldinci 1052 74 Cb 49
(RUS) Aleevo 33 Eg 38
(RUS) Alëhovščina 20 Dd 30
(BG) Alekovo 7555 61 Ch 47
(UA) Aleksandrija = Oleksandrivka 47 Dd 42
(RUS) Aleksandro-Nevskij 32 Ea 37
(RUS) Aleksandrov 31 Di 34
(SRB) Aleksandrovac 37230 59 Cb 47
(RUS) Aleksandrov Gaj 50 Ei 40
(RUS) Aleksandrovka 34 Fd 37
(RUS) Aleksandrovka 34 Fe 38
(RUS) Aleksandrovka 48 Dk 41
(RUS) Aleksandrovka 63 Di 44
(RUS) Aleksandrovka Tret'ja 49 Eb 39
(RUS) Aleksandrovsk 23 Fh 31
(RUS) Aleksandrovskij 48 Dg 39
(RUS) Aleksandrovskij, Kus'e- 24 Fi 32
(RUS) Aleksandrovskoe 22 Eh 32
(RUS) Aleksandrovskoe 64 Ec 46
(RUS) Aleksandrovskoe 64 Ed 46
(PL) Aleksandrów Łódzki 95-070 44 Bk 39
(RUS) Alekseevaka 48 Di 40
(RUS) Alekseevka 34 Fa 37
(RUS) Alekseevka 49 Ed 39
(RUS) Alekseevka 51 Fb 38
(RUS) Alekseevka 7 Fg 22
(RUS) Alekseevskaja 49 Ec 40
(RUS) Alekseevskaja, stanica = Alekseevskaja 49 Ec 40
(RUS) Alekseevskoe 34 Fa 35
(RUS) Aleksin 31 Dh 36
(SRB) Aleksinac 18220 59 Cb 47
(S) Älem 38402 28 Bg 34
(TR) Alembeyli 19300 77 De 50
(TR) Alemdar 76 Ck 49
(N) Ålen 7380 8 Bb 28
(F) Alençon 61000* 41 Aa 42
(P) Alenquer 2580-012* 68 Sa 51
(F) Aleria 71 Ak 48
(F) Alès 30100* 55 Ae 46
(I) Áles 09091 71 Ai 51
(RO) Aleşd 415100 59 Cc 43
(RUS) Aleševo 22 Eh 30
(RUS) Aleški 14 Ei 25
(RUS) Alešnja 32 Dk 36
(I) Alessándria 15100 56 Ai 46
(N) Ålesund 6002* 8 Ag 28
(GR) Alexándria 59300 74 Cc 50
(RO) Alexandria 000140* 60 Cf 47
(GR) Alexandroúpoli 68100 75 Cf 50
(P) Alfaiates 6320-081 68 Sd 50
(E) Alfajarín 50172 70 Sk 49
(E) Alfarràs 25120 70 Aa 49
(BG) Alfatar 7570 61 Ch 47
(D) Alfeld (Leine) 31061 42 Ak 39
(I) Alfonsine 48011 57 Bc 46
(GB) Alford AB33 38 Sh 33
(GB) Alfreton DE55 39 Si 37


**140** Aabenraa

(S) Alfta 82201 17 Bg 29
(E) Algaba, La 41980 80 Sd 53
(E) Algar, S' 07713 71 Ae 51
(N) Ålgård-Figgjo 4330 16 Af 32
(E) Algeciras 11101* 80 Se 54
(I) Alghero 07041 71 Ai 50
(S) Älghult 36075 27 Bf 33
(E) Algodonales 11680 80 Se 54
(E) Algorta 48930 54 Sg 47
(E) Alhama de Murcia 30840 81 Si 53
(E) Alhambra 13248 81 Sg 52
(E) Alhaurín el Grande 29120 81 Sf 54
(N) Ålhus 6826 16 Ag 29
(E) Aliaga 44150 70 Sk 50
(TR) Aliağa 33400 83 Cg 52
(GR) Alíartos 32001 82 Cd 52
(TR) Alibeyhüyüğü 42520 84 Dc 53
(SRB) Alibunar 26310 59 Ca 45
(E) Alicante = Alacant 03001 81 Sk 52
(TR) Alıcık 05300 77 Df 50
(I) Alife 81011 73 Be 49
(P) Alijó 5070-471 68 Sc 49
(GR) Aliko 83 Cf 54
(RUS) Alikovo 33 Eg 35
(S) Alingsås 44100* 17 Bc 33
(TR) Alisaray 37400 77 De 49
(E) Aliseda 10550 68 Sd 51
(P) Aljezur 8670-001* 80 Sb 53
(P) Aljustrel 7600-010* 80 Sb 53
(TR) Alkan 87 Ed 53
(TR) Alkemer 87 Ec 53
(NL) Alkmaar 1800* 26 Ae 38
(E) Allariz 32660 68 Sc 48
(N) Alleen 16 Ah 32
(D) Allersberg 90584 43 Bb 41
(DK) Allinge 3770 27 Be 35
(S) Ålloluokta kapell 2 Bk 23
(E) Almacelles 25100 70 Aa 49
(P) Almada 2800-001* 80 Sa 52
(E) Almadén 13400 81 Sf 52
(E) Almadén de la Plata 41240 80 Sd 53
(E) Almagro 13270 81 Sg 52
(E) Almansa 02640 81 Si 52
(E) Almanza 24170 68 Se 48
(E) Almaraz 10350 68 Se 51
(S) Älmeboda 36023 27 Bf 34
(P) Almeida 6355-201 68 Sd 50
(P) Almeirim 2080-001* 68 Sb 51
(NL) Almelo 7600* 42 Ag 38
(E) Almenara 12590 70 Sk 51
(E) Almendralejo 06200 80 Sd 52
(NL) Almere 1300* 42 Af 38
(E) Almería 04001 81 Sh 54
(E) Almerimar 04711 81 Sh 54
(I) Almese 10040 56 Ah 45
(RUS) Al'met'evsk 34 Fc 36
(RUS) Al'mež 22 Ei 30
(S) Älmhult 34301 27 Be 34
(GR) Almirós 37100 74 Cc 51
(P) Almodôvar 7700-011* 80 Sb 53
(E) Almodóvar del Campo 13580 81 Sf 52
(E) Almodóvar del Río 14720 80 Se 53
(E) Almoharín 10132 68 Sd 51
(E) Almonte 21730 80 Sd 53
(S) Älmsta 17 Bi 31
(E) Almudévar 22270 70 Sk 48
(S) Almundsryd 27 Be 34
(S) Almunge 74010 17 Bi 31
(E) Almuradiel 13760 81 Sg 52
(TR) Almus 60900* 78 Dg 50
(S) Almvik 17 Bg 33
(RUS) Alnaši 34 Fc 34
(N) Alnes 8 Af 28
(GB) Alness IV17 38 Sf 33
(GB) Alnwick NE66 39 Si 35
(LV) Aloja 4064 18 Ce 33
(GR) Alónnissos 37005 75 Cd 51
(E) Álora 29500 81 Sf 54
(B) Alost = Aalst 9300 41 Ae 40
(P) Alpalhão 6050-011* 68 Sc 51
(E) Alpera 02690 81 Si 52
(NL) Alphen aan de Rijn 2400* 41 Ae 38
(P) Alpiarça 2090-019* 68 Sb 51
(TR) Alpköy 78 Dk 51
(TR) Alpu 26850 76 Da 51
(TR) Alpullu 39200 76 Ch 49
(DK) Als 27 Ba 34
(D) Alsfeld 36304 42 Ak 40
(N) Ålstad 2 Bf 23
(S) Alsterbro 38044 27 Bf 34
(GB) Alston CA9 39 Sh 36
(LV) Alsunga 3306 28 Cb 34
(N) Alta 9509 3 Cd 21
(I) Altamura 70022 73 Bg 50
(RUS) Altata 50 Ei 39
(CH) Altdorf 84032 56 Ai 44
(D) Altdorf bei Nürnberg 90518 43 Bb 41
(E) Altea 03590 70 Sk 52
(N) Alteidet 3 Cc 20
(D) Altenberg 01773 43 Bd 40
(D) Altenburg 04600 43 Bc 40
(D) Altenkirchen (Westerwald) 57610 42 Ah 40
(D) Altenmarkt an der Alz 83352 43 Bc 43
(D) Altentreptow 17087 27 Bd 37
(P) Alter do Chão 7440-011* 68 Sc 51
(TR) Altındağ 77 Dc 51
(TR) Altındere 78 Dk 50
(TR) Altınekin 42450 84 Dc 52
(TR) Altınoluk 58510 75 Cg 51
(TR) Altınova 10280 75 Cg 51
(TR) Altınova 10280 87 Eb 52
(TR) Altınözü 31750 85 Dg 54
(TR) Altıntaş 24860 76 Da 51
(TR) Altınyaka 07350 84 Da 54
(TR) Altınyayla 58470 78 Dg 51
(F) Altkirch 68130 56 Ah 43
(GB) Altnaharra IV27 38 Sf 32
(RUS) Altn Bulg 65 Ef 44
(D) Altomünster 85250 43 Bb 42
(GB) Alton GU34 40 Sk 39
(D) Altona 22763* 26 Ak 37
(D) Altötting 84503 43 Bc 42
(GB) Altrincham WA14 39 Sh 37
(RUS) Altuhovo 31 De 38
(TR) Altunhisar 85 De 52
(RUS) Altynaj 35 Gb 33
(RUS) Altynnoe 35 Fh 34
(RUS) Altynsary 53 Gc 39
(TR) Alucra 28700 78 Di 50
(LV) Alūksne 4301 19 Ch 33
(S) Alunda 74700 17 Bi 30
(S) Ålundsby 10 Cb 25
(UA) Alupka 62 De 46
(UA) Alušta 62 De 46
(P) Alvalade 7565-011* 80 Sb 53
(S) Älvängen 44600 17 Bc 33
(S) Alvastra 17 Be 32
(N) Alvdal 2560 8 Ba 28
(S) Älvdalen 79601 17 Be 29
(S) Alvesta 34200 27 Be 34
(N) Alvik 8 Ag 28
(P) Alvito 7940-001 80 Sc 52
(S) Älvkarleby 81425 17 Bh 30
(S) Älvros 84201 17 Be 29
(S) Älvsbacka 17 Bd 31
(S) Älvsbyn 94201 10 Cb 25
(S) Älvsered 31063 17 Bc 33
(LT) Alytus 62001* 29 Ce 36
(D) Alzey 55232 42 Ai 41
(E) Alzira 46600 70 Sk 51
(F) Alzonne 11170 55 Ac 47
(S) Åmådalen 17 Be 29
(P) Amadora 2610-001* 68 Sa 52
(S) Åmål 66200 17 Bc 31
(I) Amalfi 84011 73 Be 50
(GR) Amaliáda 27200 82 Cb 53
(I) Amantea 87032 73 Bg 51
(RO) Amara 927020 61 Ch 46
(P) Amarante 4600-001* 68 Sb 49
(RO) Amărăştii de Jos 207020 60 Ce 47
(P) Amareleja 7885-011* 80 Sc 52
(P) Amares 4720-011* 68 Sb 49
(TR) Amasya 77 Df 50
(I) Amatrice 02012 72 Bd 48
(GR) Amaxádes 75 Cf 49
(TR) Ambar 38125 85 Dd 53
(RUS) Ambarnyj 11 Dd 25
(F) Ambazac 87240 55 Ab 45
(GR) Ambeliá 74 Ca 51
(D) Amberg 92224 43 Bb 41
(F) Ambérieu-en-Bugey 01500 56 Af 45
(F) Ambert 63600 55 Ad 45
(GB) Amble NE65 39 Si 35
(GB) Ambleside LA22 39 Sh 36
(F) Amboise 37400* 54 Aa 43
(RUS) Amderma 7 Gb 21
(P) Ameixial 8100-050 80 Sc 53
(F) Amélie-les-Bains-Palalda 66110* 70 Ac 48
(D) Amelinghausen 21385 27 Ba 37
(NL) Amersfoort 3800* 42 Af 38
(GB) Amersham HP7 40 Sk 39
(GR) Amfilohía 30500 82 Cb 52
(GR) Amfissa 33100 82 Cc 52
(F) Amiens 80000* 41 Ac 41
(GR) Amigdalées 51100 74 Cb 50
(GR) Amíndeo 53200 74 Cb 50
(N) Åmli 16 Ai 32
(GB) Amlwch LL68 39 Sf 37
(GB) Ammanford SA18 40 Sg 39
(FIN) Ämmänsaari 89999 11 Ci 26
(S) Ammarnäs 92075 9 Bg 25
Ammochostos 85 Dd 55
(RUS) Amon' 47 De 39
(E) Amorebieta = Zornotza 54 Sh 47
(GR) Amorgós 84008 83 Cf 54
(N) Åmot 3340 16 Ba 30
(S) Åmot 17 Bg 30
(S) Åmotfors 17 Bc 31
(N) Åmot-Geithus 3360 16 Ai 31
(F) Amou 40330 54 Sk 47
(F) Amplepuis 69550 55 Ae 45
(E) Amposta 43870 70 Aa 50
(S) Åmsele 92275 10 Bk 26
(NL) Amsterdam 1000* 41 Ae 38
(A) Amstetten 3300* 43 Be 42
(RUS) Amurskij 52 Fk 38
(E) Amusquillo 47177 69 Sf 49
(UA) Amvrosijivka 63 Di 43
(RUS) Amzja 34 Fe 34
(GR) Anáfi 84009 83 Cf 54
(I) Anagni 03012 72 Bd 49
(GR) Anaharávi 74 Bk 51
(TR) Anaköy 87 Ec 52
(TR) Anamur 33630* 84 Dc 54
(RUS) Anapa 63 Dh 46
(FIN) Anar = Inari 99871 3 Ch 22
(S) Änäset 91534 10 Cb 26
(IRL) An Bóthar Bui 37 Sd 37
(IRL) An Cabhán = Cavan 37 Sc 37
(IRL) An Caisleán Nua = Newcastle West 37 Sa 38
(IRL) An Caisleán Riabhach 37 Sb 37
(IRL) An Caladh 37 Rk 39
(IRL) An Caol = Keel 37 Rk 37
(F) Ancenis 44150 54 Si 43
(IRL) An Charraig 37 Sb 36
(IRL) An Chathair = Caher 37 Sc 38
(RUS) Anciferovskij Bor 12 Dk 27
(IRL) An Clochán 37 Sc 37
(IRL) An Clochán = Clifden 37 Rk 37
(IRL) An Clochan Liath 37 Sb 36
(IRL) An Cóbh = Cobh 37 Sb 39
(IRL) An Coireán = Waterville 37 Rk 39
(I) Ancona 60100* 57 Bd 47
(IRL) An Daingean = Dingle 37 Rk 38
(N) Åndalsnes 6300 8 Ah 28
(RUS) Andeg 6 Fd 23
(F) Andelys, les 27700 41 Ab 41
(N) Andenes 8480 2 Bg 21
(CH) Andermatt 6490 56 Ai 44
(D) Andernach 56626 42 Ah 40
(S) Anderstorp 33401 17 Bd 33
(TR) Andiçen 87 Ed 53
(GR) Andíparos 84400 83 Cf 53
(TR) Andırın 46400 86 Dg 53
(GR) Andírio 30020 82 Cb 52
(E) Andoain 20140 54 Sh 47
(RUS) Andomskij Pogost 20 Dg 29
(E) Andorra 44500 70 Sk 50
(AND) Andorra La Vella AD500 70 Ab 48
(GB) Andover SP10 40 Si 39
(E) Andratx 07150 70 Ac 51
(RUS) Andreapol' 30 Dc 34
(RUS) Andreevka 51 Fb 38
(RUS) Andreevskoe 31 Dg 36
(I) Ándria 70031 73 Bg 49
(RUS) Andrianoviči 24 Ga 31
(UA) Andrijaśivka 47 Dd 40
(MNE) Andrijevica 84 320 74 Bk 48
(UA) Andrijivka 48 Dg 41
(UA) Andrijivka 63 Dg 43
(UA) Andrijivka 63 Dh 43
(GR) Andrítsena 27061 82 Cb 53
(RUS) Andropov = Rybinsk 20 Di 32
(GR) Ándros 84500 82 Ce 53
(RUS) Androsovka 50 Ek 38
(UA) Andruśivka 46 Ck 40
(N) Andselv 9325 2 Bi 21
(E) Andújar 23740 81 Sf 52
(F) Anduze 30140 55 Ad 46
(RUS) Andžiewskij 64 Ed 46
(MD) Anenii Noi 6500 61 Ck 44
(IRL) An Fál Carrach 37 Sb 35
(IRL) An Fearann Fuar 37 Sa 38
(RUS) Angasjak 34 Fe 35
(S) Ånge 84100 9 Bf 28
(S) Ängelholm 26200* 27 Bc 34
(FIN) Angeli 99871 3 Cf 22
(S) Ångelsberg 73790 17 Bg 31
(GR) Angeriá 83 Cf 54
(D) Angermünde 16278 27 Be 37
(F) Angers 49000* 54 Sk 43
(F) Angerville 91670 41 Ab 42
(IRL) An Ghrainseach 37 Sb 36
(IRL) An Glean Garbh 37 Sa 39
(E) Anglès 17160 70 Ac 49
(F) Anglure 51260 41 Ad 42
(IRL) An Gort = Gort 37 Sb 37
(F) Angoulême 16000* 54 Aa 45
(E) Angüés 70 Sk 48
(F) Aniche 59580 41 Ad 40
(RUS) Anihovka 53 Ga 39
(RO) Anina 325100 59 Cb 45
(RUS) Anisimovo 21 Ee 33
(TR) Anıtkaya 03050 84 Da 52
(TR) Anıtlı 33630 84 Dc 54
(TR) Anıtlı 33630 87 Eb 53
(S) Anjans fjällstation 83005 9 Bc 27
(RUS) Anjuša 14 Fa 28
(TR) Ankara 06105* 77 Dc 51
(D) Anklam 17389 27 Bd 37
(IRL) An Láithreach = Laragh 37 Sd 37
(IRL) An Longfort = Longford 37 Sc 37
(IRL) An Móta = Moate 37 Sc 37
(IRL) An Muileann-gCearr = Mullingar 37 Sc 37
(RUS) Anna 49 Ea 39
(D) Annaberg-Buchholz 09456 43 Bd 40
(IRL) An Nás = Naas 37 Sd 37
(N) Anndalsvågen 9 Bc 25
(F) Annecy 74000 56 Ag 45
(FIN) Annel = Angeli 99871 3 Cf 22
(S) Annelund 17 Bd 33
(F) Annemasse 74100 56 Ag 44
(RUS) Annenskij Most 20 Dh 30
(RUS) Annino 20 Dh 31
(UA) Annivka 63 Dg 44
(F) Annonay 07100 55 Ae 45
(D) Annweiler am Trifels 76855 42 Ah 41
(GR) Anógia 23054 82 Ce 55
(GR) Áno Kalendíni 47044 74 Cb 51
(GB) An Ómaigh = Omagh BT79 37 Sc 36
(GR) Áno Poróia 62053 75 Cd 49
(F) Anould 88650 42 Ag 42
(DK) Ansager 6823 26 Ai 35
(D) Ansbach 91522 43 Ba 41
(IRL) An Scairbh 37 Sb 38
(IRL) An Sciobairin 37 Sa 39
(IRL) An Scoil 37 Sa 39
(P) Ansião 3240-101* 68 Sb 51
(IRL) An Snaidhm 37 Rl 39
(E) Ansó 70 Sk 48
(IRL) An Spideal 37 Sa 37
(GB) Anstruther KY10 38 Sh 34
(RO) Ânsurăţei 61 Ch 46
(TR) Ant 77 Dc 49
(IRL) An tAbhallort 37 Sd 38
(TR) Antalya 07000* 84 Da 54
(IRL) An tAonach = Nenagh 37 Sb 38
(IRL) An Teach Doite 37 Sa 37
(IRL) An Teampall Mór 37 Sc 38
(E) Antequera 29200 81 Sf 53
(GR) Anthótopos 50100 74 Cc 51
(F) Antibes 06160* 56 Ah 47
(RUS) Antipino 23 Ff 31
(RUS) Antipino 31 Dd 35
(GR) Ántissa 81103 75 Cf 51
(GB) An tIúr = Newry BT34 37 Sd 36
(S) Antnäs 10 Cb 25
(RUS) Antonovka 33 Ek 36
(BG) Antonovo 7970 75 Cg 47
(RUS) Antonovskaja 20 Di 29
(RO) Antorsura Buzăului 525300 60 Cg 45
(UA) Antracyt 48 Dk 42
(F) Antrain 35560 40 Si 42
(GB) Antrim BT41 37 Sd 36
(I) Antrodoco 02013 72 Bd 48
(RUS) Antropy 22 Fb 33
(EST) Antsla 66403* 18 Cg 33
(S) Anttis 3 Cc 23
(FIN) Anttola 52100 19 Ch 29
(IRL) An Tulach 37 Sd 38
(B) Antwerpen 2000* 41 Ae 39
(IRL) An Uaimh = Navan 37 Sd 37
(RUS) Anufrievo 20 Di 31
(B) Anvers = Antwerpen 2000 41 Ae 39
(RUS) Anyb 14 Fd 29
(LT) Anykščiai 29001 29 Cf 35
(E) Anzánigo 70 Sk 48
(I) Ánzio 00042 72 Bc 49
(I) Aosta 11100 56 Ah 45
(TR) Apa 84 Dc 53
(RO) Apahida 407035 60 Cd 44
(RUS) Apanasenkovskoe 64 Ed 45
(RUS) Apastovo 33 Ei 35
(SRB) Apatin 25260 59 Bi 45
(RUS) Apatity 4 Dd 23
(LV) Ape 4337 18 Cg 33
(NL) Apel, Ter 9561 26 Ah 38
(NL) Apeldoorn 7300* 42 Af 38
(GR) Apolakkiá 85108 83 Ch 54
(D) Apolda 99510 43 Bb 39
(GR) Apóllo 84301 83 Cf 53
(GR) Apollonía 84003 82 Ce 54
(GR) Apóstoli 74061 82 Ce 55
(UA) Apostolove 62 Dd 43
(CH) Appenzell 9050 57 Ak 43
(NL) Appingedam 9900* 26 Ag 37
(GB) Appleby-in-Westmorland CA16 39 Sh 36
(RUS) Apraksin Bor 19 Db 31
(RUS) Aprelevka 31 Dh 35
(I) Apricena 71011 73 Bf 49
(I) Aprília 04011 72 Bc 49
(RUS) Apšeronsk 63 Dk 46
(F) Apt 84400 56 Af 47
(TR) Araban 27550 86 Dh 53
(TR) Araç 37800 77 Dd 49
(E) Aracena 21200 80 Sd 53
(RO) Arad 000310* 59 Cb 44
(E) Arahal, El 41600 80 Se 53
(GR) Aráhova 32004 82 Cc 52
(TR) Araklı 61700 79 Ea 50
(TR) Aralık 76500 79 Ee 51
(RUS) Aramil' 35 Ga 34
(E) Aranda de Duero 09400 69 Sg 49
(SRB) Aranđelovac 34300* 59 Ca 46
(E) Aranjuez 28300 69 Sg 50
(TR) Arapkir 78 Di 51
(TR) Aras 25810 79 Ec 51
(RUS) Araslanovo, Tjater- 34 Fe 37
(EST) Aravete 73501 18 Cf 31
(GR) Aravissos 74 Cc 50
(GR) Áraxos 25200 82 Cb 52
(I) Árbatax 08041 71 Ak 51
(RUS) Arbaž 22 Ei 33
(A) Arbesbach 3925* 43 Be 42
(S) Arboga 73201* 17 Bf 31
(F) Arbois 39600 56 Af 44
(S) Arbrå 82010 17 Bg 29
(F) Arbresle, l' 69210 55 Ae 45
(GB) Arbroath DD11 38 Sh 34
(UA) Arbuzynka 62 Db 43
(F) Arcachon 33120* 54 Si 46
(RUS) Arčedinskaja 49 Ed 41
(F) Arc-et-Senans 25610 56 Af 43
(I) Arcévia 60011 57 Bc 47
(RUS) Archangels'koe 31 Dh 37
(UA) Archanhel's'ke 62 Dd 43
(E) Archena 30600 81 Si 52
(F) Archiac 17520 54 Sk 45
(E) Archidona 29300 81 Sf 53
(I) Arcidosso 58031 72 Bb 48
(F) Arcis-sur-Aube 10700 41 Ae 42
(I) Arco 38062 57 Ba 45
(P) Arco de Baúlhe 4860-041* 68 Sc 49
(E) Arcos de la Frontera 11630 80 Se 54
(P) Arcos de Valdevez 4970-230* 68 Sb 49
(UA) Arcyz 61 Ck 45
(TR) Ardahan 75000 79 Ec 49
(N) Årdal 6826 16 Ah 32
(N) Årdalstangen 6885 16 Ah 29
(IRL) Ard an Ratha 37 Sb 36
(TR) Ardanuç 08300 79 Ec 49
(IRL) Ardara = Ard an Ratha 37 Sb 36
(RUS) Ardatov 32 Ed 35
(RUS) Ardatov 33 Eg 36
(IRL) Ardee = Baile Átha Fhirdhia 37 Sd 37
(F) Ardentes 36120 55 Ab 44
(TR) Ardeşen 53400 79 Eb 49
(GB) Ardhasaig HS3 38 Sd 33
(BG) Ardino 6750 75 Cf 49
(GB) Ardlussa PA60 38 Se 34
(GB) Ard Mhacha = Armagh BT61 37 Sd 36
(RUS) Ardon 79 Ee 47
(GB) Ardrossan KA22 39 Sf 35
(RO) Arduşat 437005 60 Cd 43
(GB) Ardvasar IV44 38 Se 33
(GB) Ardvourlie HS3 38 Sd 33
(S) Åre 83013 9 Bd 27
(BY) Arèchavsk 30 Da 36
(E) Arenal, S' 07600 70 Ac 51
(E) Arenas de San Pedro 05400 68 Se 50
(N) Arendal 4825* 16 Ai 32
(B) Arendonk 2370 42 Af 39
(D) Arendsee (Altmark) 29416* 27 Bb 38
(E) Arenys de Mar 08350 70 Ac 49
(I) Arenzano 16011 56 Ai 46
(GR) Areópoli 23062 82 Cc 54
(F) Arès 33740 54 Si 46
(E) Arévalo 05200 69 Sf 49
(I) Arezzo 52100 57 Bb 47
(GR) Arfará 24007 82 Cc 53
(RUS) Argajas 35 Ga 35
(GR) Argalastí 37006 75 Cd 51
(E) Argamasilla de Alba 13710 69 Sg 51
(E) Arganda 28500 69 Sg 50
(P) Arganil 6120-211 68 Sb 50
(F) Argelès-Gazost 65400 70 Sk 47
(F) Argelès-sur-Mer 66700 70 Ad 48
(I) Argenta 44011 57 Bb 46
(F) Argentan 61200 40 Sk 42
(F) Argenton-Château 79150 54 Sk 44
(F) Argenton-sur-Creuse 36200 55 Ab 44
(F) Argent-sur-Sauldre 18410 55 Ac 43
(TR) Argıthanı 84 Db 52
(GR) Árgos 21201 82 Cc 53
(GR) Árgos Orestikó 52200 74 Cb 50
(GR) Argostóli 28100 82 Ca 52
(RUS) Argun 65 Ef 47
(RUS) Arhangelovka 51 Fe 38
(RUS) Arhangel'sk 12 Ea 26
(RUS) Arhangel'skoe 31 Dh 37
(RUS) Arhangel'skoe 35 Fg 36
(RUS) Arhangels'koe 49 Ea 39
(RUS) Arhangel'skoe 64 Ee 46
(TR) Arhavi 08200 79 Eb 49
(RUS) Arhipo-Osipovka 63 Di 46
(RUS) Arhipovka 30 Db 36
(DK) Århus = Aarhus 8000* 27 Ba 34
(RUS) Arhyz 64 Eb 47
(I) Ariano Irpino 83031 73 Bf 49
(TR) Arıcak 23510 87 Ea 52
(GR) Aridéa 58400 74 Cc 50
(TR) Arıkören 84 Dc 53
(TR) Arıl 86 Dh 53
(SRB) Arilje 31230 59 Ca 47
(GB) Arinagour PA78 38 Sd 34
(LT) Ariogala 60019 29 Cd 35
(GR) Aristoménis 24015 82 Cb 53
(TR) Arıtaş 46540 86 Dg 52
(I) Aritzo 08031 71 Ak 51
(S) Årjäng 67201 17 Bc 31
(RUS) Arjaš 50 Eg 39
(S) Arjeplog 93087 9 Bh 24
(E) Arjona 23760 81 Sf 53
(RUS) Arkadak 49 Ed 39
(GR) Arkássa 85700 83 Ch 55
(GR) Arkesíni 83 Cf 54
(RUS) Arkul' 22 Fa 33


A B C D E F G H I J K L M N O P Q R S T U V W X Y Z

Arkul' 141

(F) Arlanc 63220 55 Ad 45
(E) Arlanzón 69 Sg 48
(F) Arles 13200* 55 Ae 47
(B) Arlon 6700 42 Af 41
(GB) Armagh BT60 37 Sd 36
(RUS) Armavir 64 Eb 45
(RUS) Armavir 64 Eb 46
(GR) Arméni 37500 82 Ce 55
(E) Armentia 09215 69 Sh 48
(F) Armentières 59116 41 Ac 40
(UA) Armjans'k 62 Dd 44
(TR) Armutçuk 76 Db 49
(TR) Armutlu 76 Ci 50
(TR) Armutlu 86 Dh 53
(TR) Armutova 10700 75 Cg 51
(GR) Arna 23054 82 Cc 54
(S) Arnäsvall 89155 9 Bi 27
(F) Arnay-le-Duc 21230 55 Ae 43
(GR) Arnéa 63074 75 Cd 50
(D) Arneburg 39596 27 Bc 38
(N) Årnes 16 Bb 30
(NL) Arnhem 6800* 42 Af 38
(GR) Árnissa 58002 74 Cb 50
(D) Arnsberg 85110 42 Ai 39
(D) Arnstadt 99310 43 Ba 40
(D) Arnstein 97450 42 Ak 41
(D) Arolsen 34454 42 Ak 39
(CH) Arosa 7050 57 Ak 44
(P) Arouca 4540-098* 68 Sb 50
(N) Årøysund 16 Ba 31
(TR) Arpaçay 36730 79 Ed 50
(TR) Arpacık 84 Ck 54
(F) Arpajon 91290 41 Ac 42
(TR) Arpalı 79 Ed 50
(FIN) Arpela 95590 10 Ce 24
(I) Arpino 03033 72 Bd 49
(I) Arquata del Tronto 63043 72 Bd 48
(E) Arquillos 23230 81 Sg 52
(P) Arraiolos 7040-010* 80 Sc 52
(F) Arras 62000* 41 Ac 40
(E) Arrasate-Mondragón 69 Sh 47
(F) Arreau 65240 70 Aa 48
(GR) Arrianá 69300 75 Cf 49
(E) Arriondas 33540 68 Se 47
(GB) Arrochar G83 38 Sf 34
(P) Arronches 7340-001* 68 Sc 51
(E) Arroyo de la Luz 10900 68 Sd 51
(DK) Års 26 Ak 34
(RUS) Arsamaki 32 Ea 35
(RUS) Arsen'evo 31 Dg 37
(TR) Arsin 61900 78 Dk 50
(RUS) Arsk 33 Ek 34
(IS) Árskogssandur 36 Rb 25
(TR) Arslanköy 33000 85 De 53
(RUS) Arslanovo 34 Ff 36
(S) Årsunda 81022 17 Bg 30
(E) Artà 07570 70 Ad 51
(GR) Árta 47101 74 Ca 51
(UA) Artemivka 48 Df 41
(UA) Artemivs'k 48 Di 42
(UA) Artemovsk = Artemivs'k 48 Di 42
(RUS) Artëmovskij 24 Gb 33
(F) Artenay 45410 41 Ab 42
(E) Artesa de Segre 25730 70 Ab 49
(RUS) Artezian 65 Eg 46
(IRL) Arthurstown 37 Sd 38
(RUS) Arti 35 Fi 34
(TR) Artova 60670* 78 Dg 50
(TR) Artvin 08000 79 Eb 49
(F) Arudy 64260 70 Sk 47
(S) Arvidsjaur 93301 10 Bk 25
(S) Arvika 67101* 17 Bc 31
(N) Årviksand 9195 2 Ca 20
(S) Arvträsk 92101 10 Bk 26
(I) Arzachena 07021 71 Ak 49
(RUS) Arzamas 32 Ed 35
(RUS) Arzgir 64 Ee 45
(I) Arzignano 36071 57 Bb 45
(RUS) Arzipo Osipovka 63 Di 46
(F) Arzon 56640 54 Sh 43
(E) Arzúa 15810 68 Sb 48
(RUS) Arzubiha 21 Ea 30
(B) As 3665 42 Af 39
(CZ) Aš 352 01 43 Bc 40
(RUS) Aša 35 Fh 35
(DK) Aså = Asaa 16 Ba 33
(DK) Asaa = Aså 16 Ba 33
(TR) Aşağıasarcık 78 Dh 50
(TR) Aşağıçiğil 42620 84 Db 52
(TR) Aşağı Dalören 79 Ed 51
(TR) Aşağı İrmaklar 79 Ec 49
(TR) Aşağı Karacasu 79 Ec 50
(TR) Aşağı Katırlı 79 Ed 51
(TR) Aşağıköy 86 Di 52
(TR) Aşağı Oylum 86 Di 54
(TR) Aşağı Pınarbaşı 84 Dc 52
(TR) Asarcık 19400 77 De 50
(TR) Asarcık 19400 78 Dg 49
(S) Åsarna 84031 9 Be 28
(RUS) Asbest 35 Gb 33
(RUS) Asbestovskij 24 Gb 33
(I) Ascea 84046 73 Bf 50
(D) Aschaffenburg 63739* 42 Ak 41
(D) Aschersleben 06449 43 Bb 39
(F) Asco 20276 71 Ak 48
(I) Àscoli Piceno 63100 72 Bd 48
(N) Åse 2 Bf 21
(RUS) Aše 63 Dk 47
(S) Åseda 36070 17 Bf 33
(RUS) Asekeevo 34 Fc 37
(S) Åsele 91060 9 Bh 26
(RUS) Ašelsaj 52 Fk 39
(S) Åsen 17 Bd 29
(BG) Asenovgrad 4230* 75 Ce 48
(N) Åseral 4540 16 Ah 32
(RUS) Aševo 19 Ck 33
(GR) Asfáka 45500 74 Ca 51
(N) Åsgårdstrand 3179 16 Ba 31
(GB) Ashbourne DE6 39 Si 37
(GB) Ashby-de-la-Zouch LE65 39 Si 38
(GB) Ashford TN23 41 Aa 39
(TR) Aşıkan 86 Dk 53
(BY) Asintorf 30 Da 36
(BY) Asipovičy 30 Ci 37
(N) Ask 5307 16 Af 30
(FIN) Aska 99550 3 Cg 23
(TR) Aşkale 79 Ea 51
(UA) Askanija-Nova 62 Dd 44
(RUS) Askarovo 35 Fi 37
(IRL) Askeaton = Eas Geitine 37 Sb 38
(N) Asker 1383* 16 Ba 31
(S) Askersund 69601 17 Be 32
(S) Åskiljeby 92195 9 Bh 26
(N) Askim 1807* 16 Bb 31
(RUS) Askino 35 Fg 34
(S) Äsköping 17 Bg 31
(GR) Askós 57016 75 Cd 50
(N) Askøy 16 Af 30
(TR) Aşlama 51050 85 Df 52
(TR) Aslanapa 43210 76 Ck 51
(RUS) Ašlyk 25 Gi 33
(RUS) Ašlyk, Polino- 25 Gk 33
(BY) Asman-Kasaeva 30 Ck 37
(BY) Ašmjany 29 Cf 36
(FIN) Asmunti 93190 10 Cg 25
(I) Àsola 46041 57 Ba 45
(RUS) Asovo 23 Fh 33
(RUS) Aspa 35 Fg 34
(GB) Aspatria CA15 39 Sg 36
(S) Aspeå 89597 9 Bh 27
(F) Aspet 31160 70 Aa 47
(F) Aspres-sur-Buëch 56 Af 46
(NL) Assen 9400* 26 Ag 37
(DK) Assens 9550 26 Ak 35
(DK) Assens 9550 27 Ba 34
(I) Assisi 06081 72 Bc 47
(GR) Ássos 82 Ca 52
(RUS) Assy 35 Fh 36
(F) Astaffort 47220 54 Aa 46
(GR) Astakós 30006 82 Cb 52
(NL) Asten 5720 42 Af 39
(I) Asti 14100 56 Ai 46
(E) Astillero,El 39610 54 Sg 47
(GR) Astipálea 85900 83 Cg 54
(E) Astorga 24700 68 Sd 48
(S) Åstorp 26501 27 Bc 34
(RUS) Astradamovka 33 Eh 36
(RUS) Astrahan' 65 Eh 44
(RUS) Astrahanovka 52 Ff 38
(S) Åsträsk 93061 10 Bk 26
(BY) Astravec 29 Cf 36
(CY) Astromeritis 2722 85 Dd 55
(GR) Ástros 22001 82 Cc 53
(BY) Astrovna 30 Ck 36
(BY) Astryna 29 Ce 37
(BY) Asveja 30 Ci 34
(RUS) Atabaevo 33 Ek 35
(TR) Atabey 32670 84 Da 53
(GR) Atalánti 35200 82 Cc 52
(E) Atarfe 18230 81 Sg 53
(TR) Atça 84 Ci 53
(I) Atessa 66041 73 Be 48
(B) Ath 7800 41 Ad 40
(IRL) Áth Cinn 37 Sa 37
(GR) Athína 10678* 82 Cd 52
(IRL) Athlone = Baile Átha Luain 37 Sc 37
(IRL) Áth na nUrlainn 37 Sc 38
(IRL) Athy = Baile Átha Í 37 Sd 38
(E) Atienza 19270 69 Sh 49
(RUS) Atig 35 Fk 34
(TR) Atış Poligonu 85 Dd 53
(RUS) Atjaševo 33 Eg 36
(RUS) Atjur'evo 32 Ed 36
(TR) Atkaracalar 18310 77 Dd 50
(TR) Atlant 84 Dc 52
(RUS) Atnary 33 Eg 35
(N) Atnbrua 2580 8 Ba 29
(RUS) Atnjaš 35 Fh 35
(S) Åtran 31061 17 Bc 33
(I) Atri 64032 72 Bd 48
(F) Attigny 08130 41 Ae 41
(S) Åtvidaberg 59700 17 Bg 32
(F) Aubagne 13400* 56 Af 47
(F) Aubenas 07200 55 Ae 46
(F) Aubigny-sur-Nère 18700 55 Ac 43
(F) Aubin 12110 55 Ac 46
(F) Aubusson 23200 55 Ac 45
(LV) Auce 3708 29 Cc 34
(F) Auch 32000* 54 Aa 47
(F) Audierne 29770 40 Sf 42
(F) Audincourt 25400 56 Ag 43
(EST) Audru 88301 18 Ce 32
(D) Aue 57319 43 Bc 40
(I) Auer = Ora 39040 57 Bb 44
(D) Auerbach (Vogtland) 08209 43 Bc 40
(D) Auerbach in der Oberpfalz 91275 43 Bb 41
(IRL) Aughrim = Eachroim 37 Sd 38
(D) Augsburg 86150* 43 Ba 42
(I) Augusta 96011 72 Bf 53
(PL) Augustów 16-300* 29 Cc 37
(LT) Aukštadvaris 21034 29 Ce 36
(S) Auktsjaure 10 Bk 25
(I) Auletta 84031 73 Bf 50
(F) Aulnay 17470 54 Sk 44
(F) Ault 80460 41 Ab 40
(F) Aumale 76390 41 Ab 41
(F) Aumont-Aubrac 48130 55 Ad 46
(F) Aunay-sur-Odon 14260 40 Sk 41
(F) Auneau 28700 41 Ab 42
(DK) Auning 8963 27 Ba 34
(FIN) Aura 21381 18 Cc 30
(F) Auray 56400* 54 Sh 43
(N) Aurdal 2910 16 Ak 30
(N) Aure 6690 8 Ai 27
(D) Aurich (Ostfriesland) 26603* 26 Ah 37
(F) Aurignac 31420 70 Aa 47
(F) Aurillac 15000 55 Ac 46
(N) Aurlandsvangen 5743 16 Ah 30
(N) Aursmoen 2000 16 Bb 31
(I) Ausa-Corno 33058 57 Bd 45
(N) Austmarka 2224 17 Bc 30
(N) Austnes 6293 8 Ag 28
(N) Austrheim 5943 16 Ae 30
(F) Autun 71400* 55 Ae 44
(F) Auxerre 89000* 55 Ad 43
(F) Auxi-le-Château 62390 41 Ac 40
(F) Auxon 10130 41 Ad 42
(F) Auxonne 21130 56 Af 43
(F) Auzances 23700 55 Ac 44
(N) Avaldsnes 4262 16 Af 31
(F) Avallon 89200* 55 Ad 43
(S) Avan 93010 10 Cb 25
(TR) Avanos 50500 85 De 52
(S) Avaträsk 91701 9 Bg 26
(S) Avaviken 9 Bi 25
(TR) Avcılar 85 Df 53
(UA) Avdijivka 47 Dc 39
(P) Aveiro 3800-002* 68 Sb 50
(I) Avellino 83100 73 Be 50
(I) Aversa 81031 73 Be 50
(F) Avesnes-sur-Helpe 59440 41 Ad 40
(S) Avesta 77401* 17 Bg 30
(I) Avezzano 67051 72 Bd 48
(TR) Avgan 64910 84 Ck 52
(RUS) Avgustovka 51 Fa 38
(GB) Aviemore PH22 38 Sg 33
(I) Avigliano 85021 73 Bf 50
(F) Avignon 84000* 55 Ae 47
(E) Ávila de los Caballeros 69 Sf 50
(E) Avilés 33400 68 Se 47
(EST) Avinurme 42101 18 Cg 32
(I) Àvio 57 Ba 45
(P) Avis 7480-101* 68 Sc 51
(GR) Avliotes 74 Bk 51
(DK) Avlum 26 Ai 34
(RUS) Avneporog 11 Dd 25
(RUS) Avnjugskij 22 Ef 29
(I) Àvola 96012 72 Bf 54
(S) Avradsberg 17 Bd 30
(F) Avranches 50300* 40 Si 42
(BG) Avren 9135 75 Cf 49
(RO) Avrig 555200 60 Ce 45
(BIH) Avtovac 73 Bi 47
(FIN) Avvil = Ivalo 99801 3 Ch 22
(GR) Axioúpoli 61400 74 Cc 50
(F) Ax-les-Thermes 09110 70 Ab 48
(S) Axmar bruk 17 Bh 29
(TR) Ayaklı 63700 86 Dk 53
(E) Ayamonte 21400 80 Sc 53
(TR) Ayas 33730 77 Dc 50
(TR) Ayaş 06710 77 Dc 50
(TR) Ayaş İçmecesi 06840 77 Dc 50
(TR) Aybastı 52500 78 Dh 50
(TR) Ayder Kablıca 53400 79 Eb 50
(TR) Aydın 83 Ch 53
(TR) Aydınca 05040 78 Dg 50
(TR) Aydıncık 33840 77 Df 50
(TR) Aydıncık 33840 85 Dd 54
(TR) Aydınkent 42280 84 Db 53
(TR) Aydınlar 77 Dd 51
(TR) Aydınlar 86 Di 52
(TR) Aydınlar 87 Ec 53
(TR) Aydıntepe 69500 79 Ea 50
(E) Ayerbe 22800 70 Sk 48
(GB) Aylesbury HP19 40 Sk 39
(E) Ayllón 40520 69 Sg 49
(GB) Aylsham NR11 39 Ab 38
(GB) Ayr KA7 39 Sf 35
(TR) Ayrancı 85 Dd 53
(TR) Ayrıtepe 84 Db 52
(TR) Ayvacık 55550 75 Cg 51
(TR) Ayvacık 55550 78 Dg 50
(TR) Ayvalı 60700 79 Eb 50
(TR) Ayvalık 75 Cg 51
(TR) Ayvalıpınar 32960 84 Db 53
(E) Azaila 44590 70 Sk 49
(RUS) Azanka 25 Ge 32
(RUS) Azapol'e 13 Ef 25
(P) Azaruja 7005-100* 80 Sc 52
(BY) Azaryčy 46 Ck 38
(F) Azay-le-Rideau 37190 54 Aa 43
(BY) Azëry 29 Ce 37
(RUS) Azigulovo 35 Fi 34
(RUS) Azinozero 13 Eb 28
(RUS) Aznaevo 34 Fe 37
(RUS) Aznakaevo 34 Fd 36
(RUS) Azov 63 Dk 43
(E) Azpeitia 20730 54 Sh 47
(E) Azuaga 06920 80 Se 52


## B


(E) Baamonde 27371 68 Sc 47
(B) Baarle-Nassau 2387 41 Ae 39
(RO) Babadag 825100 61 Ci 46
(TR) Babadağ 20480 84 Ci 53
(TR) Babaeski 39200 76 Ch 49
(RUS) Babaevo 20 Df 31
(TR) Babatorun 31000 85 Dg 54
(D) Babenhausen 87727 43 Ba 42
(RO) Băbeni 457020 60 Ce 46
(PL) Babięta 11-710 28 Cb 37
(E) Babilafuente 37330 68 Se 50
(BY) Babinavičy 30 Da 36
(RUS) Babincevo 34 Fc 37
(BY) Babrujsk 30 Ck 37
(LT) Babtai 54059 29 Cd 35
(SRB) Babušnica 18330 59 Cc 47
(RUS) Babynino 31 Df 34
(RUS) Babynino 31 Df 36
(GB) Bac HS2 38 Sd 32
(SRB) Bač 21420 59 Bk 45
(RO) Bacău 000600* 60 Cg 44
(F) Baccarat 54120 42 Ag 42
(BY) Bačėjkava 30 Ck 35
(RUS) Bačelino 25 Gh 33
(RO) Băceşti 737050 61 Ch 44
(UA) Bachčysaraj 62 Dd 46
(UA) Bachmač 47 Dc 39
(GB) Backaland KW17 38 Sh 31
(SRB) Bačka Palanka 21400* 59 Bk 45
(SRB) Bačka Topola 24300* 59 Bk 45
(S) Backe 88050 9 Bg 27
(S) Bäckefors 66840 17 Bc 32
(S) Bäckhammar 17 Be 31
(RUS) Backino 31 Dd 37
(D) Backnang 71522 42 Ak 42
(H) Bácsalmás 6430 59 Bk 44
(D) Bad Aibling 83043 57 Bc 43
(E) Badajoz 06001* 80 Sd 52
(E) Badalona 08910* 70 Ac 49
(A) Bad Aussee 8990* 57 Bd 43
(D) Bad Bederkesa 27624 26 Ai 37
(D) Bad Bentheim 48455 42 Ah 38
(D) Bad Bergzabern 76887 42 Ah 41
(D) Bad Berka 99438 43 Bb 40
(D) Bad Berleburg 57319 42 Ai 39
(D) Bad Bevensen 29549 27 Ba 37
(D) Bad Blankenburg 07422 43 Bb 39
(D) Bad Bramstedt 24576 26 Ak 37
(D) Bad Doberan 18209 27 Bb 36
(D) Bad Düben 04849 43 Bc 39
(D) Bad Dürrenberg 06231 43 Bc 39
(TR) Bademli 75 Cf 50
(TR) Bademli 83 Ci 52
(D) Bad Ems 56130 42 Ah 40
(A) Baden 2500* 58 Bg 43
(CH) Baden 5400* 56 Ai 43
(D) Baden-Baden 76530* 42 Ai 42
(D) Bad Fallingbostel 29683 26 Ak 38
(D) Bad Frankenhausen (Kyffhäuser) 06567 43 Bb 39
(D) Bad Freienwalde (Oder) 16259 27 Be 38
(D) Bad Friedrichshall 74177 42 Ak 41
(A) Bad Gastein 5640* 57 Bd 43
(D) Bad Griesbach im Rottal 94086 43 Bd 42
(D) Bad Harzburg 38667 43 Ba 39
(D) Bad Hersfeld 36251 42 Ak 40
(A) Bad Hofgastein 5630* 57 Bd 43
(D) Bad Homburg vor der Höhe 61348* 42 Ai 40
(D) Bad Honnef 53604 42 Ah 40
(A) Bad Ischl 4820* 57 Bd 43
(D) Bad Kissingen 97688 43 Ba 40
(D) Bad Kleinen 23996 27 Bb 37
(D) Bad Königshofen im Grabfeld 97631 43 Ba 40
(D) Bad Kösen 06628 43 Bb 39
(D) Bad Kötzting 93444 43 Bc 41
(D) Bad Kreuznach 55543* 42 Ah 41
(D) Bad Laasphe 57334 42 Ai 40
(D) Bad Lauterberg im Harz 37431 43 Ba 39
(D) Bad Liebenwerda 04924 43 Bd 39
(D) Bad Lobenstein 07356 43 Bb 40
(D) Bad Meinberg, Horn- 32805 42 Ai 39
(D) Bad Mergentheim 97980 42 Ak 41
(D) Bad Neuenahr-Ahrweiler 53474 42 Ah 40
(D) Bad Neustadt an der Saale 97616 43 Ba 40
(D) Bad Oeynhausen 32545* 42 Ai 38
(D) Bad Oldesloe 23843 27 Ba 37
(D) Bad Orb 63619 42 Ak 40
(D) Bad Pyrmont 31812 42 Ak 39
(A) Bad Radkersburg 8490 58 Bf 44
(D) Bad Reichenhall 83435 57 Bc 43
(D) Bad Rothenfelde 49214 42 Ai 38
(D) Bad Salzdetfurth 31162 43 Ba 38
(D) Bad Salzuflen 32105* 42 Ai 38
(D) Bad Salzungen 36433 43 Ba 40
(A) Bad Sankt Leonhard im Lavanttal 9462 58 Be 44
(D) Bad Schandau 01814 43 Be 40
(D) Bad Schmiedeberg 06905 43 Bc 39
(D) Bad Schussenried 88427 42 Ak 42
(D) Bad Schwartau 23611 27 Ba 37
(D) Bad Segeberg 23795 27 Ba 37
(D) Bad Sobernheim 55566 42 Ah 41
(D) Bad Sülze 18334 27 Bc 36
(D) Bad Tölz 83646 57 Bb 43
(D) Bad Waldsee 88339 57 Ak 43
(D) Bad Wildungen 34537 42 Ak 39
(D) Bad Wilsnack 19336 27 Bb 38
(D) Bad Zwischenahn 26160 26 Ai 37
(GB) Bae Colwyn = Colwyn Bay LL29 39 Sg 37
(E) Baena 14850 81 Sf 53
(E) Baeza 23440 81 Sg 53
(RUS) Baga-Burul 64 Ee 45
(RUS) Bagaevskij = stanica Bagaevskaja 64 Ea 43
(TR) Bağarası 35690 83 Ch 53
(RUS) Bagarjak 35 Gb 34
(RUS) Bagarjak, Ust'- 35 Gb 34
(TR) Bağbaşı 84 Dc 53
(TR) Bağdaşan 79 Ec 49
(TR) Bağdere 21560 87 Ea 52
(DK) Bagenkop 5935 27 Ba 36
(TR) Bağgöze 87 Eb 53
(TR) Bağışlı 30100 87 Ee 53
(TR) Bağkonak 32410 84 Db 52
(TR) Bağlama 85 De 52
(TR) Bağlica 73600 87 Eb 53
(TR) Bağlıca 73600 87 Ec 53
(TR) Bağlum 06840 77 Dc 50
(N) Bagn 2930 16 Ak 30
(F) Bagnères-de-Bigorre 65200* 70 Aa 47
(I) Bagno di Romagna 47021 57 Bb 47
(F) Bagnols-sur-Cèze 30200 55 Ae 46
(TR) Bağpınar 86 Di 53
(RUS) Bagrationovsk 28 Ca 36
(SRB) Bagrdan 35204 59 Cb 46
(UA) Bahatyr 63 Dg 43
(TR) Bahçe 86 Dg 53
(TR) Bahçecik 76 Ck 50
(TR) Bahçecik 85 Df 52
(TR) Bahçeli 86 Di 53
(TR) Bahçesaray 65710 87 Ec 52
(RUS) Bahmutovo 31 De 34
(RO) Bahnea 547055 60 Ce 44
(RO) Baia 317381 61 Ci 46
(RO) Baia de Aramă 225100 59 Cc 46
(RO) Baia Mare 000430* 60 Cd 43
(RO) Baia Sprie 435100 60 Cd 43
(RO) Băicoi 105200 60 Cf 45
(RO) Băiculeşti 117065 60 Ce 45
(IRL) Baile an Bhuinneánaight 37 Sa 38
(IRL) Baile an Chaisil 37 Sa 36
(GB) Baile an Chaistil = Ballycastle BT54 37 Sd 35
(IRL) Baile an Ghearlánaigh 37 Sd 37
(IRL) Báile an Róba 37 Sa 37
(IRL) Baile Átha Cliath = Dublin 37 Sd 37
(IRL) Baile Átha Fhirdhia = Ardee 37 Sd 37
(IRL) Baile Átha Í 37 Sd 38
(IRL) Baile Átha Liagh 37 Sc 37
(IRL) Baile Átha Luain = Athlone 37 Sc 37
(IRL) Baile Átha Troim = Trim 37 Sd 37
(IRL) Baile Brigín = Balbriggan 37 Sd 37
(IRL) Baile Chaisleáin Bhéarra = Castletown Bearhaven 37 Rl 39
(IRL) Baile Chathail = Charlestown 37 Sb 37
(IRL) Baile Easa Dara = Ballycadare 37 Sb 36
(RO) Băile Herculane 325200 59 Cc 46
(IRL) Baile Locha Riach = Loughrea 37 Sb 37
(IRL) Baile Mhic Andáin 37 Sc 38
(IRL) Baile Mhistéala = Mitchelstown 37 Sb 38
(E) Bailén 23710 81 Sg 52
(IRL) Baile na gCros 37 Sc 37
(IRL) Baile na nGallóglach 37 Sc 35
(RO) Băileşti 205100 60 Cd 46
(IRL) Baile uí Mhatháin 37 Sc 37
(F) Bailleul 59270 41 Ac 40
(MD) Baimaclia 7313 61 Ci 44
(F) Bain-de-Bretagne 35470 54 Si 43
(IRL) Baingear 37 Sa 36
(E) Baio Grande 68 Sb 47
(E) Baiona 36300 68 Sb 48
(F) Bais 53160 40 Sk 42
(LT) Baisogala 82025 29 Cd 35


**142** Arlanc

(H) Baja 6500* 59 Bi 44
(H) Bajánsenye 9944 58 Bg 44
(RUS) Bajgazino 35 Fh 37
(SRB) Bajina Bašta 31250 59 Bk 47
(RUS) Bajkalovo 25 Gh 33
(RUS) Bajki 35 Fg 35
(RUS) Bajmak 52 Fi 38
(SRB) Bajmok 59 Bk 45
(MNE) Bajovo Polje 81 432 74 Bi 47
(AL) Bajram Curri 74 Ca 48
(RUS) Bajramgulovo 35 Ga 35
(RUS) Bajsa 33 Ek 33
(RUS) Bajsakalovo 35 Fk 36
(TR) Bakacak 76 Ch 50
(RUS) Bakal 35 Fi 36
(RUS) Bakalka 52 Ff 39
(RUS) Bakaly 34 Fd 35
(RUS) Bakeevo 35 Fh 37
(TR) Bakırdağı 85 Df 52
(TR) Bakırköy 76 Ci 49
(IS) Bakkafjörður 685 36 Rf 24
(N) Bakkejord 2 Bi 21
(N) Bakko 16 Ai 31
(TR) Baklan 20770* 84 Ck 52
(RUS) Baklanka 21 Ea 32
(H) Bakonybél 8427 58 Bh 43
(RUS) Bakres 65 Ef 46
(RUS) Baksan 64 Ed 47
(H) Baktalórántháza 4561 45 Cc 43
(RUS) Bakury 49 Ee 38
(GB) Bala LL23 39 Sg 38
(TR) Balâ 06720 77 Dd 51
(TR) Balaban 61450 86 Dh 52
(RO) Bălăbănești 807010 61 Ch 44
(RUS) Balabanovo 31 Dg 35
(RUS) Bala-Četyrman 34 Ff 37
(UA) Balachivka 47 Dd 42
(RO) Balaci 147005 60 Ce 46
(RO) Bălăcița 227040 60 Cd 46
(RO) Balaciu 927040 60 Cg 46
(E) Balaguer 25600 70 Aa 49
(RUS) Balahna 32 Ed 34
(UA) Balaklija 48 Dg 41
(RUS) Balakovo 50 Eh 38
(GB) Balallan HS2 38 Sd 32
(RUS) Balandino 34 Fc 37
(RUS) Balašiha 31 Dh 35
(RUS) Balašov 49 Ed 39
(H) Balassagyarmat 44 Bk 42
(H) Balatonboglár 58 Bh 44
(H) Balatonföldvár 58 Bh 44
(H) Balatonfüred 58 Bh 44
(H) Balatonfűzfő 8175 59 Bi 43
(H) Balatonszentgyörgy 8710 58 Bh 44
(RO) Bălăușeri 547100 60 Ce 44
(E) Balazote 02320 69 Sh 52
(IRL) Balbriggan = Baile Brigín 37 Sd 37
(RO) Bălcești 245400 60 Cd 46
(TR) Balcı 18320 85 De 52
(BG) Balčik 9600 61 Ci 47
(TR) Balcılar 06890 75 Cg 50
(TR) Balcılar 06890 77 Dc 50
(TR) Balcılar 06890 84 Dc 54
(LV) Baldone 2125 29 Ce 34
(CH) Bâle = Basel 4000* 56 Ah 43
(N) Balestrand 6899 16 Ag 29
(RUS) Balezino 23 Fd 33
(GB) Balfour KW17 38 Sh 31
(BG) Bălgarovo 8110 76 Ch 48
(BG) Bălgarska Poljana 75 Cg 48
(GR) Balí 82 Ce 55
(TR) Balıbey 86 Di 52
(TR) Balıkesir 10000* 76 Ch 51
(TR) Balıklıçeşme 17270 76 Ch 50
(D) Balingen 72336 42 Ai 42
(RO) Balinț 307005 59 Cb 45
(TR) Balışeyh 71520 77 Dd 51
(AL) Ballaban 74 Ca 50
(N) Ballangen 8540 2 Bg 22
(GB) Ballantrae KA26 39 Se 35
(I) Ballao 09040 71 Ak 51
(IS) Ballará 370 36 Qh 25
(S) Ballasviken 2 Bg 24
(GB) Ballater AB35 38 Sg 33
(F) Balleroy 14490 40 Sk 41
(TR) Ballı 59800 76 Ch 50
(TR) Ballıca 73600 78 Di 50
(TR) Ballık 84 Ck 54
(TR) Ballıkaya 73600 86 Di 52
(IRL) Ballina = Béal an Atha 37 Sa 36
(IRL) Ballinasloe = Béal Átha na Sluaighe 37 Sb 37
(IRL) Ballinrobe = Báile an Róba 37 Sa 37
(AL) Ballsh 74 Bk 50
(N) Ballstad 8373 2 Bd 22
(DK) Ballum 26 Ai 35
(IRL) Ballybofey = Bealach Feich 37 Sc 36
(IRL) Ballybunnion = Baile an Bhuinneáight 37 Sa 38
(IRL) Ballycadare 37 Sb 36
(GB) Ballycastle BT54 37 Sd 35
(IRL) Ballycastle = Baile an Chaisil 37 Sa 36
(GB) Ballygawley BT70 37 Sc 36
(IRL) Ballyhaunis = Béal Átha hAmhnais 37 Sb 37
(IRL) Ballymahon = Baile uí Mhatháin 37 Sc 37
(GB) Ballymena BT42 37 Sd 36
(GB) Ballymoney BT53 37 Sd 35
(GB) Ballynahinch BT24 37 Se 36
(IRL) Ballyshannon = Béal Átha Seanaidh 37 Sb 36
(E) Balmaseda 48800 54 Sg 47
(H) Balmazújváros 4060 59 Cb 43
(FIN) Bálojávri = Palojärvi 97240 3 Cd 22
(TR) Balpayam 79 Ea 51
(RO) Balș 235100 60 Ce 46
(BY) Bal'šavik 47 Da 38
(RO) Balta 227030 59 Cc 46
(UA) Balta 61 Ck 43
(RUS) Baltaj 50 Eg 38
(TR) Baltalin 77 Dc 51
(E) Baltanás 34240 69 Sf 49
(RUS) Baltasi 34 Fa 34
(MD) Bălți 3100 61 Ch 43
(RUS) Baltijsk 28 Bk 36
(IRL) Baltimore = Dún na Séad 37 Sa 39
(LV) Baltinava 4594 30 Ch 34
(LV) Balvi 4501 19 Ch 33
(TR) Balya 10840 76 Ch 51
(GB) Balynagall 37 Rk 38
(D) Bamberg 96047* 43 Ba 41
(GB) Bamburgh NE69 39 Si 35
(E) Baña, La 24746 68 Sd 48
(TR) Banarlı 59010 76 Ch 49
(TR) Banaz 64500 84 Ck 52
(GB) Banbridge BT32 37 Sd 36
(GB) Banbury OX16 40 Si 38
(GB) Banchory AB31 38 Sh 33
(E) Bande 32840 68 Sc 48
(DK) Bandholm 4941 27 Bb 36
(TR) Bandırma 10200* 76 Ch 50
(F) Bandol 83150 56 Af 47
(IRL) Bandon = Droichead na Bandan 37 Sb 39
(RO) Băneasa 087010 60 Cg 46
(RO) Băneasa 087010 61 Ch 46
(E) Bañeza, La 24750 68 Se 48
(GB) Banff AB45 38 Sh 33
(GB) Bangor BT3 37 Se 36
(GB) Bangor BT3 39 Sf 37
(IRL) Bangor = Baingear 37 Sa 36
(N) Bangsund 7822 8 Bb 26
(PL) Banie 74-100 27 Be 37
(PL) Banie Mazurskie 19-520 29 Cc 36
(BG) Banja 8239 75 Ce 48
(BG) Banja 8239 76 Ch 48
(RUS) Banjajag 22 Ek 30
(SRB) Banja Koviljača 15316 59 Bk 46
(BIH) Banja Luka 78000* 58 Bh 46
(SRB) Banjani 14214 59 Bk 46
(RKS) Banjska 74 Ca 48
(S) Bankeryd 56420 17 Be 33
(F) Bannalec 29380 54 Sg 43
(F) Banon 04150 56 Af 46
(BIH) Banovići 59 Bi 46
(D) Bansin 17429 27 Be 37
(SK) Banská Bystrica 947 01 44 Bk 42
(SK) Banská Štiavnica 969 01 44 Bi 42
(BG) Bansko 2770 75 Cd 49
(IRL) Banteer 37 Sb 38
(IRL) Bantry = Beanntraí 37 Sa 39
(E) Banyalbufar 07191 70 Ac 51
(E) Banyoles 17820 70 Ac 48
(F) Bapaume 62450* 41 Ac 40
(MNE) Bar 85 000 74 Bk 48
(UA) Bar 46 Ch 41
(E) Barajas de Melo 16460 69 Sh 50
(SRB) Barajevo 11460 59 Ca 46
(TR) Barak 86 Dh 54
(E) Barakaldo 54 Sh 47
(TR) Baraklı 84 Ck 52
(BY) Baranavičy 29 Cg 37
(RUS) Barančinskij 24 Fk 32
(UA) Baranivka 46 Ch 40
(BY) Baranoviči = Baranavičy 29 Cg 37
(RUS) Baranovka 22 Fb 31
(RUS) Baranovka 50 Eg 41
(UA) Baranykivka 48 Dk 41
(RO) Baraolt 525100 60 Cf 44
(RUS) Barašеvo 32 Ec 36
(RUS) Baraški 14 Fc 25
(HR) Barban 57 Bd 45
(E) Barbantes 68 Sb 48
(TR) Barbaros 59020 76 Ch 50
(E) Barbastro 22300 70 Aa 48
(E) Barbate de Franco 80 Se 54
(LV) Bărbele 3905 29 Ce 34
(F) Barbezieux-Saint-Hilaire 16300 54 Sk 45
(RO) Barca 207331 60 Cd 47
(P) Barca de Alva 6440-071 68 Sd 49
(E) Barcarrota 06160 80 Sd 52
(E) Barcelona 08001* 70 Ac 49
(F) Barcelonnette 04400 56 Ag 46
(P) Barcelos 4750-100* 68 Sb 49
(E) Bárcena de Pie de Concha 54 Sf 47
(PL) Barciany 11-410 28 Cb 36
(PL) Barcin 88-190 28 Bh 38
(PL) Barcino 88-190 28 Bg 36
(E) Barco de Ávila, El 05600 68 Se 50
(H) Barcs 7570 58 Bh 45
(PL) Barczewo 11-010 28 Ca 37
(RUS) Barda 34 Ff 34
(TR) Bardakçı 25500 76 Da 51
(SK) Bardejov 085 01 45 Cb 41
(I) Bardonècchia 10052 56 Ag 45
(F) Barentin 76360 41 Aa 41
(N) Barentsburg 9178 2 I Svalbard
(I) Barga 55051 57 Ba 46
(RO) Bărgăului, Mureșenii 60 Ce 43
(GB) Bargoed CF82 40 Sg 39
(I) Bari 70100* 73 Bg 49
(HR) Barić-Draga 58 Bf 46
(I) Barisciano 67021 72 Bd 48
(F) Barjac 48000 55 Ae 46
(RUS) Barjatino 31 De 36
(F) Barjols 83670 56 Ag 47
(N) Barkald 2560 8 Ba 29
(LV) Barkava 4834 29 Cg 34
(TR) Barla 32530 84 Da 52
(RO) Bârlad 000731* 61 Ch 44
(F) Bar-le-Duc 55000* 42 Af 42
(I) Barletta 70051 73 Bg 49
(PL) Barlinek 74-320 27 Bf 38
(GB) Barmouth LL42 39 Sf 38
(GB) Barnard Castle DL12 39 Si 36
(NL) Barneveld 3770* 42 Af 38
(F) Barneville-Carteret 50270 40 Si 41
(GB) Barnsley S70 39 Si 37
(GB) Barnstaple EX31 40 Sf 39
(F) Barr 67140 42 Ah 42
(E) Barracas 12420 70 Sk 50
(I) Barrafranca 94012 72 Be 53
(P) Barrancos 7875-051 80 Sd 52
(E) Barranda 30412 81 Si 52
(P) Barreiro 2830-445 80 Sa 52
(F) Barrême 04330 56 Ag 47
(GB) Barri = Barry CF62 40 Sg 39
(GB) Barrow-in-Furness LA14 39 Sg 36
(GB) Barry CF62 40 Sg 39
(RUS) Barsaniha 20 Df 32
(D) Barsinghausen 30890 42 Ak 38
(F) Bar-sur-Aube 10200 41 Ae 42
(F) Bar-sur-Seine 10110 41 Ae 42
(LV) Bārta 3482 28 Cb 34
(D) Barth 18356 27 Bc 36
(GB) Barton-upon-Humber DN18 39 Sk 37
(PL) Bartoszyce 11-200 28 Ca 36
(RUS) Bartym 35 Fg 34
(I) Barúmini 09021 71 Ak 51
(RUS) Barun 65 Ef 43
(D) Baruth 15837 43 Bd 38
(GB) Barvas HS2 38 Sd 32
(F) Barville, Cany- 76450 41 Aa 41
(UA) Barvinkove 48 Dg 42
(PL) Barwice 78-460 28 Bg 37
(RUS) Barybino 31 Dh 35
(RUS) Baryš 33 Eh 37
(BY) Barysav 30 Ci 36
(UA) Baryšivka 47 Db 40
(SRB) Bašaid 23316 59 Ca 45
(RO) Basarabi 905100 61 Ci 46
(TR) Başbağlar 25530 79 Eb 50
(CH) Basel 4000* 56 Ah 43
(TR) Başgedikler 79 Ed 50
(TR) Başharman 85 Dd 53
(GB) Basildon SS16 41 Aa 39
(TR) Başin 85 Dd 53
(GB) Basingstoke RG23 40 Si 39
(RUS) Bas'janovskij 24 Ga 32
(HR) Baška 58 Be 46
(TR) Başkale 25530 87 Ee 52
(TR) Baskil 23800 86 Di 52
(TR) Başköy 78 Dk 51
(TR) Başköy 79 Ea 50
(TR) Başköy 79 Ea 51
(TR) Başköy 87 Ec 53
(TR) Başkuyu 42820 84 Dc 52
(TR) Başlar 84 Db 53
(TR) Başmakçı 84 Da 53
(RUS) Bašmakovo 32 Ed 37
(TR) Başpınar 78 Di 51
(TR) Başpınar 84 Da 53
(I) Bassano del Grappa 36061 57 Bb 45
(E) Bassella 70 Ab 48
(N) Bassevuovdde 3 Cf 22
(F) Bassoues 32320 54 Aa 47
(D) Bassum 27211 26 Ai 38
(S) Båstad 26901 27 Bc 34
(UA) Baštanka 62 Dc 43
(F) Bastelica 20119 71 Ak 48
(B) Bastenaken = Bastogne 6600 42 Af 40
(F) Bastia 20200 71 Ak 48
(F) Bastide-Puylaurent, la 48250 55 Ad 46
(B) Bastogne 6600 42 Af 40
(S) Bastuträsk 93061 10 Ca 26
(BY) Bastyn' 46 Cg 38
(TR) Başyurt 23610 87 Ec 53
(SRB) Batajnica 59 Ca 46
(RUS) Batajsk 63 Dk 43
(BG) Batak 5228 75 Ce 49
(H) Bátaszék 7140 59 Bi 44
(RUS) Bateckij 19 Da 32
(GB) Bath BA1 40 Sh 39
(TR) Batman 72000* 87 Eb 53
(SRB) Batočina 34220 59 Cb 46
(N) Båtsfjord 9990 3 Ck 20
(S) Båtsjaur 9 Bh 24
(TR) Battalgazi = Eskimalatya 86 Di 52
(I) Battipáglia 73 Be 50
(H) Battonya 5830 59 Cb 44
(RUS) Baturino 30 Dc 35
(UA) Baturyn 47 Dc 39
(RUS) Batyrevo 33 Eh 35
(F) Baud 56150 54 Sg 43
(F) Baugé 49150 54 Sk 43
(F) Baugy 71110 55 Ac 43
(F) Baule-Escoublac, la 54 Sh 43
(F) Baume-les-Dames 25110* 56 Ag 43
(I) Baunei 08040 71 Ak 50
(LV) Bauska 3901 29 Ce 34
(D) Bautzen 02625 43 Be 39
(RUS) Bavly 34 Fd 36
(TR) Bayat 57600 76 Da 51
(TR) Bayat 57600 77 De 50
(TR) Bayat 57600 84 Ck 52
(TR) Bayburt 69000 79 Ea 50
(F) Bayeux 14400* 40 Sk 41
(TR) Bayındır 16860 83 Ch 52
(TR) Bayırköy 84 Ci 54
(TR) Baykan 56460 87 Eb 52
(TR) Bayramiç 17700 75 Cg 51
(TR) Bayramören 18320 77 Dd 50
(D) Bayreuth 95444* 43 Bb 41
(D) Bayrischzell 83735 57 Bc 43
(AL) Baz 74 Bk 49
(E) Baza 18800 81 Sh 53
(UA) Bazalija 46 Cg 41
(UA) Bazalijvka 48 Dg 41
(RUS) Bazančatovo 35 Fg 34
(RUS) Bazarnaja Ken'ša 33 Eg 37
(RUS) Bazarnye Mataki 33 Ek 36
(RUS) Bazarnyi Karabulak 50 Eg 38
(RUS) Bazarnyj Syzgan 33 Eg 37
(RUS) Bazarskij 35 Fk 37
(F) Bazas 33430 54 Sk 46
(RUS) Baženiha 34 Fb 35
(RUS) Baženovo 34 Ff 35
(RO) Baziaș 327366 59 Cb 46
(GB) Beaconsfield HP10 40 Sk 39
(IRL) Béal an Atha = Ballina 37 Sa 36
(IRL) Béal an Mhuirthead = Belmullet 37 Rl 36
(IRL) Béal Átha hAmhnais 37 Sb 37
(IRL) Béal Átha na Sluaighe = Ballinasloe 37 Sb 37
(IRL) Béal Átha Seanaidh = Ballyshannon 37 Sb 36
(IRL) Béal Easa 37 Sa 37
(IRL) Beal Tairbirt 37 Sc 36
(IRL) Beanntraí = Bantry 37 Sa 39
(E) Beasain 20200 69 Sh 47
(E) Beas de Segura 23280 81 Sh 52
(F) Beaucaire 30300 55 Ae 47
(F) Beaugency 45190 55 Ab 43
(F) Beaujeu 69430 55 Ae 44
(GB) Beauly IV4 38 Sf 33
(GB) Beaumaris LL58 39 Sf 37
(B) Beaumont 6500 41 Ae 40
(F) Beaumont 24440 40 Si 41
(F) Beaumont 24440 54 Aa 46
(F) Beaumont-de-Lomagne 82500 54 Aa 47
(F) Beaumont-sur-Oise 95260 41 Ac 41
(F) Beaumont-sur-Sarthe 72170 41 Aa 42
(F) Beaune 21200* 55 Ae 43
(F) Beaupréau 49600 54 Sk 43
(F) Beaurepaire 85500 56 Af 45
(F) Beauvais 60000* 41 Ac 41
(F) Beauvoir-sur-Mer 85230 54 Sh 44
(D) Bebra 36179 42 Ak 40
(LV) Bebrene 5439 29 Cg 34
(GB) Beccles NR34 41 Ab 38
(E) Becedas 05610 68 Se 50
(SRB) Bečej 21220* 59 Ca 45
(E) Becerreá 27640 68 Sc 48
(RUS) Bečevinka 20 Dh 31
(RO) Bechet 207060 60 Cd 47
(E) Becilla de Valderaduey 47670 68 Se 48
(D) Beckum 59269 42 Ai 39
(RO) Beclean 507010 60 Ce 43
(F) Bécon-les-Granits 49370 54 Sk 43
(GB) Bedale DL8 39 Si 36
(F) Bédarieux 34600 55 Ad 47
(RUS) Bedeeva-Poljana 35 Fg 35
(D) Bederkesa, Bad 27624 26 Ai 37
(GB) Bedford MK41 40 Sk 38
(TR) Bedirli 58180 78 Dg 51
(RUS) Bednodem'janovsk 32 Ed 37
(NL) Bedum 9780 26 Ag 37
(NL) Beek 6190 42 Af 40
(D) Beeskow 15848 43 Be 38
(F) Bégard 22140 40 Sg 42
(TR) Beğendik 87 Ec 53
(RUS) Begičevskij 31 Di 37
(N) Begndal 2930 16 Ak 30
(E) Begonte 27373 68 Sc 47
(RUS) Beguč 50 Eg 38
(RUS) Begunicy 19 Ck 31
(TR) Behramkale 17860 75 Cg 51
(NL) Beilen 9410* 26 Ag 38
(N) Beisfjord 8522 2 Bh 22
(RO) Beiuș 415200 59 Cc 44
(P) Beja 7800-001* 80 Sc 52
(E) Béjar 37700 68 Se 50
(N) Bejarn 2 Be 23
(TR) Bekçiler 84 Ck 54
(H) Békés 5630 59 Cb 44
(H) Békéscsaba 5600 59 Cb 44
(RUS) Bekeševo 52 Fi 38
(TR) Bekilli 20930* 84 Ck 52
(TR) Bekirhan 72410 87 Eb 52
(RUS) Beklemiševo 33 Eh 37
(RUS) Bekovo 49 Ed 38
(TR) Bektaşlı 66410 86 Dg 54
(BY) Belaazërsk 46 Cf 38
(SRB) Bela Crkva 26340 59 Cb 46
(RUS) Belaja Berëzka 47 Dd 38
(UA) Belaja Cerkov' = Bila Cerkva 47 Da 41
(RUS) Belaja Glina 64 Ea 44
(RUS) Belaja Holunica 22 Fa 32
(RUS) Belaja Kalitva 49 Ea 42
(RUS) Belaja Rečka 64 Ed 47
(E) Belalcázar 14280 80 Se 52
(SRB) Belanovica 59 Ca 46
(SRB) Bela Palanka 18310 59 Cc 47
(RUS) Belasovka 33 Ee 34
(MD) Bèl'c' = Bălți 3100 61 Ch 43
(TR) Belceğiz 84 Db 52
(PL) Bełchatów 97-400 44 Bk 39
(E) Belchite 50130 70 Sk 49
(TR) Belcik 58540 78 Dg 51
(IRL) Belcoo 37 Sc 36
(MD) Bel'cy = Bălți 3100 61 Ch 43
(TR) Beldibi 07985 84 Da 54
(TR) Beldibi 07985 84 Dc 54
(RUS) Belebej 34 Fe 36
(RUS) Belebelka 19 Da 33
(TR) Belen 31351 85 Dg 54
(RUS) Belenihino 48 Dg 40
(E) Beleño (Ponga) 68 Se 47
(RUS) Belev 31 Dg 37
(GB) Belfast BT18 37 Se 36
(GB) Belford NE70 39 Si 35
(F) Belfort 90000* 56 Ag 43
(D) Belgern 04874 43 Bd 39
(RUS) Belgorod 48 Dg 40
(UA) Belgorod-Dnestrovskij 61 Da 44
(SRB) Belgrad = Beograd 11133* 59 Ca 46
(BG) Belica 5363 60 Cg 47
(BY) Belica 29 Cf 37
(RUS) Belica 48 Df 39
(RUS) Beličaevskoe 65 Ef 46
(RUS) Belik 30 Dc 36
(HR) Beli Manastir 59 Bi 45
(BG) Belimel 3462 59 Cc 47
(F) Belin-Béliet 33830 54 Sk 46
(RUS) Belinskij 32 Ed 38
(RO) Beliș 407075 60 Cd 44
(RUS) Beljaevka 23 Ff 33
(RUS) Beljaevka 52 Fg 39
(RUS) Beljanka 35 Fk 34
(TR) Belkaya 42355 85 Dd 53
(RUS) Bel'kovo 31 Dd 37
(F) Bellac 87300 55 Ab 44
(I) Bellágio 22021 57 Ak 45
(IRL) Belleek 37 Sb 36
(F) Bellegarde 45270 55 Ac 43
(F) Bellegarde-sur-Valserine 01200 56 Af 44
(F) Belle-Isle-en-Terre 22810 40 Sg 42
(F) Bellême 61130 41 Aa 42
(F) Belley 01300 56 Af 45
(CH) Bellinzona 6500* 57 Ak 44
(E) Bellpuig 25250 70 Ab 49
(I) Belluno 32100 57 Bc 44
(E) Bélmez 14240 80 Se 52
(GB) Belmont ZE2 38 Sk 30
(E) Belmonte 16640 68 Sd 47
(E) Belmonte 16640 69 Sh 51
(P) Belmonte 6250-020* 68 Sc 50
(E) Belmonte de Miranda = Belmonte 33830 68 Sd 47
(IRL) Belmullet = Béal an Mhuirthead 37 Rl 36
(RUS) Beloe 21 Dk 32
(RUS) Beloe More 4 Dc 23
(RUS) Beloe Ozero 35 Fg 37
(RUS) Beloevo 23 Fe 31
(RUS) Beloger'e 48 Dk 40
(RUS) Belogornoe 50 Eh 38
(RUS) Belogorskoe 33 Ei 37
(BG) Belogradcik 59 Cc 47
(BG) Belogradčik 3900 59 Cc 47
(RUS) Belojarka 25 Ge 32
(RUS) Belojarskij 35 Gb 34
(SRB) Beloljin 18424 59 Cb 47
(RUS) Belomorsk 12 De 26
(RUS) Beloomut 32 Dk 36
(E) Belorado 09250 69 Sg 48
(RUS) Beloreçensk 23 Fc 32
(RUS) Belorečensk 63 Dk 46
(RUS) Beloreck 35 Fi 37
(TR) Belören 77 Dd 50
(TR) Belören 84 Dc 53


A B C D E F G H I J K L M N O P Q R S T U V W X Y Z

Belören 143

TR Belören 86 Dh 53
BG Beloslav 9178 76 Ch 47
BG Belovo 4470 75 Cd 48
BG Belovo 4470 75 Ce 48
RUS Belovod'e 33 Eg 36
RUS Belozersk 20 Dh 30
GB Belper DE56 39 Si 37
TR Belpınar 76 Db 51
RUS Bel'skoe 32 Ea 36
IRL Belturbet = Beal Tairbirt 37 Sc 36
SK Beluša 018 61 44 Bi 41
RUS Beluš'e 6 Eh 24
SRB Belušić 35263 59 Cb 47
F Belvédère-Campomoro 20110 71 Ai 49
I Belvedere Marittimo 87021 73 Bf 51
F Belvès 24170 55 Ab 46
RUS Belye Berega 31 De 37
RUS Belyi Kolodez' 48 Di 40
RUS Belyj 30 Dc 35
RUS Belyj Gorodok 31 Dh 34
RUS Belyševo 22 Ef 33
PL Bełżec 22-670 45 Cd 40
RUS Bemyž 34 Fb 34
E Benabarre 22580 70 Aa 48
E Benalup de Sidonia 11150 80 Se 54
E Benasque 22440 70 Aa 48
E Benavente 49600 68 Se 48
E Benavides de Órbigo 24280 68 Se 48
MD Bender = Tighina 3200 61 Ck 44
MD Bendery = Tighina 3200 61 Ck 44
D Benediktbeuern 83671 57 Bb 43
CZ Benešov 549 83 43 Be 41
I Benevento 82100 73 Be 49
F Benfeld 67230 42 Ah 42
S Bengtsfors 66600 17 Bc 31
E Benicarló 12580 70 Aa 50
E Benicasim = Benicàssim 12560 70 Aa 50
E Benicàssim 12560 70 Aa 50
E Benidorm 03501* 70 Sk 52
E Benifaió 46450 70 Sk 51
HR Benkovac 58 Bf 46
S Bensbyn 10 Cc 25
D Bentheim, Bad 48455 42 Ah 38
SRB Beograd 11133* 59 Ca 46
SRB Berane 74 Bk 48
AL Berat 74 Bk 50
BY Berazino 30 Ci 36
BY Berazino 30 Ci 37
E Berberana 09511 69 Sg 48
D Berchtesgaden 83471 57 Bc 43
F Berck-Plage 62600 41 Ab 40
UA Berdičev = Berdyčiv 46 Ci 41
TR Berdil 86 Dk 53
UA Berdjans'k 63 Dg 44
UA Berdjansk = Berdjans'k 63 Dg 44
RUS Berdjaš 52 Fh 38
RUS Berdjauš 35 Fk 35
E Berdún 70 Sk 48
UA Berdyčiv 46 Ci 41
RUS Bereg 20 Dh 30
UA Beregove = Berehove 45 Cc 42
UA Berehomet 46 Cf 42
UA Berehove 45 Cc 42
TR Bereket 79 Ed 51
TR Bereket 85 De 53
TR Bereketli 78 Dh 50
RUS Berendeevo 32 Dk 34
TR Berendi 42280 85 De 53
UA Berestečko 46 Cf 40
UA Berestove 63 Dg 43
H Berettyóújfalu 59 Cb 43
RUS Berez' 20 Dg 32
UA Berezan' 47 Db 40
UA Berezanka 62 Db 44
RUS Berezanskaja 63 Dk 45
UA Berežany 45 Ce 41
UA Berezdiv 46 Ch 40
UA Berezine 46 Cg 40
UA Berezivka 61 Da 43
UA Berezna 47 Db 39
RUS Berežnaja 21 Ed 29
UA Berezn'aky 47 Dc 41
UA Bereznehuvate 62 Dc 43
RUS Bereznik 13 Ec 28
RUS Bereznik 13 Ed 26
RUS Berezniki 23 Fg 31
RUS Bereznjagi 49 Eb 41
RUS Berezova 11 Dc 26
RUS Berezovec, Nikolo- 21 Ec 32
RUS Berezovka 22 Ef 29
RUS Berezovka 23 Fh 33
RUS Berezovka 32 Di 37
RUS Berezovka 35 Fi 34
RUS Berezovo 20 Di 30
RUS Berëzovskij 35 Ga 34
RUS Berezy 13 Eb 26
N Berg 2 Bh 21
E Berga 08600 70 Ab 48
TR Bergama 35700 75 Ch 51
I Bérgamo 24100* 57 Ak 45
E Bergara 20570 69 Sh 47
D Bergen 08239 26 Ak 38
D Bergen 5003* 16 Af 30
NL Bergen 08239 26 Ae 38
D Bergen (Rügen) 18528 27 Bd 36
NL Bergen op Zoom 4600* 41 Ae 39
F Bergerac 24100* 54 Aa 46
RUS Bergin 65 Eh 44
D Bergisch Gladbach 51427* 42 Ah 40
S Bergkvara 38502 28 Bg 34
N Berglia 9 Bd 26
F Bergnicourt 08300 41 Ae 41
FIN Bergö 66220 10 Cb 28
S Bergshamra 17 Bi 31
S Bergsjö 9 Bh 29
F Bergues 59380 41 Ac 40
D Bergzabern, Bad 42 Ah 41
B Beringen 3580 42 Af 39
D Berka, Bad 99438 43 Bb 40
N Berkåk 8 Ba 28
BG Berkovica 3500 60 Cd 47
BIH Berkovići 73 Bi 47
E Berlanga 06930 80 Se 52
E Berlanga de Duero 42360 69 Sh 49
D Berleburg, Bad 57319 42 Ai 39
N Berlevåg 9980 3 Ck 20
D Berlin 10115* 43 Bd 38
E Bermeo 48370 54 Sh 47
CH Bern 3000* 56 Ah 44
I Bernalda 75012 73 Bg 50
D Bernau bei Berlin 16321 27 Bd 38
F Bernaville 80370 41 Ac 40
F Bernay 72240 41 Aa 41
D Bernburg (Saale) 06406 43 Bb 39
A Berndorf 2560 58 Bg 43
F Bernières-sur-Mer 14990 40 Sk 41
D Bernkastel-Kues 54470 42 Ah 41
A Bernstein 7434 58 Bg 43
CH Beromünster 6215 56 Ai 43
CZ Beroun 266 01 43 Be 41
MK Berovo 2330 74 Cc 49
F Berre-l'Étang 13130 56 Af 47
UA Beršad' 46 Ck 42
D Bersenbrück 49593 42 Ah 38
RUS Bersut 34 Fa 35
GB Berwick-upon-Tweed TD15 39 Sh 35
UA Beryslav 62 Dd 44
TR Beşağıl 85 Dd 53
E Besalú 70 Ac 48
F Besançon 25000* 56 Ag 43
BY Bešankovičy 30 Ck 35
MD Besarabca 61 Ci 44
MD Besarabjaska = Besarabca 61 Ci 44
RUS Besedino 34 Fd 37
RUS Besedino 48 Dg 39
TR Beşenli 46000 86 Dh 53
TR Beşikdüzü 61800 78 Dk 49
TR Beşiri 72200 87 Eb 53
TR Beşkonak 84 Db 53
RUS Beslan 79 Ee 47
RUS Beslenej 64 Eb 46
TR Besni 02300 86 Dh 53
RUS Bešpagir 64 Ec 45
TR Beşpınar 69400 87 Eb 53
MD Bessarabka = Besarabca 6700 61 Ci 44
RUS Besskorbnaja 64 Eb 46
NL Best 5680* 42 Af 39
RUS Bestobe 53 Gc 39
RUS Bestuževka 33 Ei 37
TR Beşyol 36500 86 Di 53
E Betanzos 15300 68 Sb 47
E Bétera 46117 70 Sk 51
F Béthune 62400 41 Ac 40
HR Betina 58 Bf 47
RUS Betlica 31 Dd 36
S Bettna 64033 17 Bg 33
GB Bettyhill KW14 38 Sf 32
GB Betws-y-Coed LL24 39 Sg 37
F Beuzeville 27210 41 Aa 41
I Bevelli 84 Ck 52
GB Beverley HU17 39 Sk 37
D Beverstedt 27616 26 Ai 37
GB Bexhill TN39 41 Aa 40
TR Beyağaç 20590 84 Ci 53
TR Beyazköy 59600 76 Ch 49
TR Beyçayırı 17800 75 Cg 50
TR Beyçayırı 17800 87 Eb 52
TR Beycuma 67980 76 Db 49
TR Beydağ 35790 83 Ci 52
TR Beydili 76 Da 50
TR Beykoz 34801* 76 Ck 49
TR Beylikova 26750 76 Db 51
TR Beyoba 45240 83 Ch 52
TR Beypazarı 06730 76 Db 50
TR Beypınarı 78 Dh 51
TR Beypınarı 86 Dg 52
TR Beyşehir 42700 84 Db 53
TR Beytüşşebap 73800 87 Ed 53
TR Beyyurdu 77 Df 51
RUS Bežanicy 30 Ck 34
RUS Bezbožnik 22 Ei 31
RUS Bežeck 20 Dg 33
RUS Bezenčuk 33 Ek 38
RUS Bezengi 79 Ed 47
F Béziers 34500* 55 Ad 47
RUS Bezmenšur 34 Fb 34
RUS Bezopasnoe 64 Eb 45
RUS Bezymjannoe 50 Eg 39
PL Biała, Bielsko- 44 Bk 41
PL Biała Piska 12-230 29 Cc 37
PL Biała Podlaska 21-500 45 Cd 38
PL Białogard 78-200 27 Bf 36
PL Biały Bór 78-425 28 Bg 37
PL Białystok 15-900 29 Cd 37
F Biarritz 64200* 54 Si 47
I Bibbiena 52011 57 Bb 47
D Biberach an der Riß 88400 42 Ak 42
RUS Bibirevo 30 Dc 34
UA Bibrka 45 Ce 41
AL Bicaj 74 Ca 49
RO Bicaz 615100 60 Cg 44
F Bicchisano, Petreto- 71 Ai 49
TR Biçer 76 Db 51
GB Bicester OX26 40 Si 39
H Bicske 2060* 59 Bi 43
RUS Bičurino 34 Ff 34
F Bidache 64520 54 Si 47
GB Bideford EX39 40 Sf 39
N Bidjovagge 3 Cc 21
PL Biecz 38-340 45 Cb 41
CH Biel = Bienne 2500* 56 Ah 43
PL Bielawy 99-423 44 Bk 38
D Bielefeld 33602* 42 Ai 38
I Biella 13900 56 Ai 45
E Bielsa 22350 70 Aa 48
PL Bielsk 09-230 44 Bk 38
PL Bielsko-Biała 43-300* 44 Bk 41
PL Bielsk Podlaski 17-100* 29 Cd 38
CH Bienne = Biel 2500* 56 Ah 43
RO Biertan 557045 60 Ce 44
E Biescas 22630 70 Sk 48
D Bietigheim-Bissingen 74321 42 Ak 42
PL Bieżuń 09-320 28 Bk 38
TR Biga 17200 76 Ch 50
TR Bigadiç 10440 76 Ci 51
F Biganos 33380 54 Sk 46
GB Biggar ML12 39 Sg 35
BIH Bihać 58 Bf 46
RO Biharia 417050 59 Cb 43
RUS Bijavaš 35 Fg 34
BIH Bijela 59 Bi 46
BIH Bijeljina 59 Bk 46
MNE Bijelo Polje 81 304 74 Bk 47
SK Bílá 44 Bi 41
UA Bila Cerkva 47 Da 41
E Bilbao = Bilbao 48001* 54 Sh 47
E Bilbo = Bilbao 48001 54 Sh 47
IS Bíldudalur 465 36 Qg 25
BIH Bileća 73 Bi 48
TR Bilecik 76 Ck 50
PL Biłgoraj 23-400 45 Cc 40
UA Bilhorod-Dnistrovs'kyj 61 Da 44
RUS Bilimbaj 35 Fk 34
AL Bilisht 74 Ca 50
RUS Biljarsk 34 Fa 36
F Billom 63160 55 Ad 45
S Billsta 9 Bi 27
DK Billund 7190 26 Ak 35
F Billy 41130 55 Ad 44
UA Bilohir'ja 46 Cg 40
UA Bilohors'k 62 De 45
UA Bilokurakyne 48 Di 41
UA Biloluc'k 48 Dk 41
UA Bilopil'l'a 47 De 39
UA Bilousivka 47 Dc 41
UA Bilovods'k 48 Dk 41
N Bilto 3 Cb 21
UA Biluchivka 48 Df 41
UA Bilyi Kolodjaz' 48 Dh 40
E Binéfar 22500 70 Aa 49
D Bingen am Rhein 55411 42 Ah 41
TR Bingöl 12000 87 Ea 52
D Binz 18609 27 Bd 36
HR Biograd na Moru 58 Bf 47
IRL Biorra = Birr 37 Sc 37
PL Bircza 37-740 45 Cc 41
TR Birecik 86 Dh 53
TR Birgi 35775 83 Ci 52
N Birkeland 4760 16 Ai 32
D Birkenfeld 97834 42 Ah 41
GB Birkenhead CH42 39 Sg 37
DK Birkerød 3460 27 Bc 35
A Birkfeld 8190 58 Bf 43
GB Birmingham B8 40 Si 38
IRL Birr = Biorra 37 Sc 37
RUS Birsk 34 Ff 35
LT Birštonas 59009 29 Ce 36
LT Biržai 41001 29 Ce 34
LV Birži 5214 29 Cf 34
E Bisbal d'Empordà, la 17100 70 Ad 49
F Biscarrosse 40600* 54 Si 46
I Biscéglie 70052 73 Bg 49
A Bischofshofen 5500* 57 Bd 43
D Bischofswerda 01877 43 Be 39
F Bischwiller 67240 42 Ah 42
RUS Biser = Biserski 24 Fi 32
RUS Biserovo 23 Fd 31
RUS Biserski 24 Fi 32
RUS Bisert' 35 Fk 34
GB Bishop Auckland DL14 39 Si 36
GB Bishop's Castle SY9 40 Sg 38
AL Bishtqethm 74 Bk 50
I Bisignano 63040 73 Bg 51
PL Biskupiec 11-300 28 Ca 37
D Bismark (Altmark) 39629 27 Bb 38
TR Bismil 21500 87 Ea 53
S Bispgården 9 Bg 27
RO Bistreț 207065 60 Cd 47
RO Bistrița 000420* 60 Ce 43
RO Bistrița Bârgăului 427005 60 Ce 43
PL Bisztynek 11-230 28 Ca 36
D Bitburg 54634 42 Ag 41
F Bitche 57230 42 Ah 41
TR Bitlis 13000 87 Ec 52
MK Bitola 7000* 74 Cb 49
I Bitonto 70032 73 Bg 49
D Bitterfeld-Wolfen 06749 43 Bc 39
I Bitti 08021 71 Ak 50
RUS Bižbuljak 34 Fe 37
RUS Bizjar 23 Fg 33
BY Bjahoml' 30 Ci 36
BG Bjala 7100 60 Cf 47
BG Bjala 7100 75 Cg 48
BG Bjala 7100 76 Ch 48
BG Bjala Slatina 3200 60 Cd 47
BY Bjalyničy 30 Ck 37
N Bjarkøy 9426 2 Bg 22
BY Bjaroza 45 Ce 38
BY Bjarozavka 29 Cf 37
S Bjärred 24601 27 Bd 35
S Bjästa 89300 9 Bi 27
HR Bjelovar 58 Bg 45
N Bjerka 8643 2 Bd 24
N Bjerkvik 8530 2 Bh 22
DK Bjerringbro 8850 26 Ak 34
N Bjølstad 2676 16 Ak 29
S Björbo 78045 17 Be 30
N Bjordal 16 Af 29
N Bjørkås 2 Bk 22
N Bjørkelangen 1940 16 Bb 31
S Björkliden 98193 2 Bi 22
FIN Björköby 65870 10 Cb 27
S Björköby 17 Be 33
S Björksele 92041 9 Bi 26
S Björkvattnet 84070 9 Bd 26
N Bjorli 2669 8 Ai 28
N Bjørn 2 Bc 24
S Björna 89050 9 Bi 27
N Bjørnevatn 9910 3 Ck 21
S Björnlunda 64050 17 Bh 31
S Björsarv 82700 9 Bg 28
S Bjurholm 91601 10 Bk 27
S Bjursås 79021 17 Bf 30
S Bjuv 26701 27 Bc 34
SRB Blace 18420 59 Cb 47
GB Blackburn AB2 39 Sh 37
GB Blackpool FY1 39 Sg 37
S Blackstad 59094 17 Bg 33
RUS Blagodarnij 64 Ed 45
RUS Blagodarnyj 64 Ed 45
RUS Blagodatovka 51 Fa 38
BG Blagoevgrad 2700* 75 Cd 48
RUS Blagoevo 13 Eh 27
RUS Blagovar 34 Fe 36
RUS Blagoveščensk 34 Ff 35
F Blain 44130 54 Si 43
GB Blairgowrie PH10 38 Sg 34
RO Blaj 515400 60 Cd 44
AL Blakstad 16 Ai 32
F Blanc, le 36300 55 Ab 44
GB Blandford Forum DT11 40 Sh 40
E Blanes 17300 70 Ac 49
F Blangy-sur-Bresle 76340 41 Ab 41
B Blankenberge 8370 41 Ad 39
CZ Blansko 382 41 44 Bg 41
PL Błaszki 98-235 44 Bi 39
S Blattnicksele 9 Bh 25
D Blaubeuren 89143 42 Ak 42
F Blaye 33390 54 Sk 45
D Bleckede 21354 27 Ba 37
D Bleicherode 99752 43 Ba 39
N Bleik 8481 2 Bf 21
N Bleikvassli 9 Bd 25
F Bléneau 89220 55 Ac 43
F Bléré 37150 54 Aa 43
S Blidsberg 52024 17 Bd 33
AL Blinisht 74 Bk 49
F Blois 41000* 55 Ab 43
IS Blönduós 540 36 Qk 25
PL Błonie 55-330 45 Ca 38
A Bludenz 6700* 57 Ak 43
GB Blyth NE24 39 Si 35
UA Blyznjuky 48 Dg 42
N Bø 16 Ak 31
E Boal 33720 68 Sd 47
GB Boat of Garten PH24 38 Sg 33
D Böblingen 71032* 42 Ak 42
PL Bobolice 76-020 28 Bg 37
BY Bobr 30 Ck 36
RUS Bobrava 48 Df 40
RUS Bobrov 48 Dk 39
RUS Bobrovskoe 25 Ge 33
UA Bobrovycja 47 Db 40
PL Bobrowniki 76-231 29 Cd 37
BY Bobrujsk = Babrujsk 30 Ck 37
UA Bobrynec' 47 Dc 42
RUS Bočevo 20 Dd 31
PL Bochnia 32-700 45 Ca 41
D Bocholt 46395* 42 Ag 39
CZ Bochov 364 71 43 Bd 40
D Bochum 44787* 42 Ah 39
S Bockara 57900 17 Bg 33
RO Bocșa 457045 59 Cb 45
RO Bocsig 317055 59 Cb 44
S Boda 17 Bf 29
S Böda 38075 17 Bh 33
S Boden 96100* 10 Cb 25
RUS Bod'ja, Jaškur- 23 Fd 33
GB Bodmin PL31 40 Sf 40
N Bodø 8003* 2 Be 23
TR Bodrum 48400 83 Ch 53
S Bodsjö 9 Be 28
S Bodum 88051 9 Bg 27
PL Bodzanów 48-340 45 Ca 38
F Boën 42130 55 Ae 45
RUS Boeve 48 Dk 39
RUS Bogatiščevo 31 Di 36
RUS Bogatoe 34 Fb 37
RUS Bogatye Saby 34 Fa 35
RUS Bogatyr' 34 Fa 37
Bogazi 85 Dd 55
TR Boğaziçi 35135 83 Ch 52
TR Boğazkale 19310 77 De 50
TR Boğazkaya 77 Df 49
TR Boğazköprü 85 Df 52
TR Boğazlıyan 66400 77 Df 51
RUS Bogdanovka 34 Fa 37
RUS Bogdanovka 51 Fa 38
RUS Bogdanovka 51 Fc 38
RUS Bogdanovo 31 Dg 37
RUS Bogdanovo 35 Fg 35
RUS Bogdanovskoe 52 Fk 38
PL Bogdanów 49-200 44 Bk 39
TR Böğecik 85 Dd 53
N Bogen 8533 2 Bg 22
DK Bogense 5400 27 Ba 35
GB Bognor Regis PO21 40 Sk 40
RUS Bogoljubovo 32 Ea 34
MK Bogomila 1415 74 Cb 49
MK Bogorodica 1482 74 Cc 49
RUS Bogorodick 31 Di 37
RUS Bogorodsk 14 Fc 28
RUS Bogorodsk 32 Ed 34
RUS Bogorodsk 35 Fh 34
RUS Bogorodskoe 20 Dh 33
RUS Bogorodskoe 22 Fa 33
RUS Bogorodskoe 34 Ff 38
RUS Bogovarovo 22 Eh 32
RUS Bogučar 49 Ea 41
TR Böğürtlen 86 Di 52
RUS Boguslav' 20 Dg 32
F Bohain-en-Vermandois 02110 41 Ad 41
SLO Bohinjska Bistrica 4264 57 Bd 44
UA Bohoduchiv 48 Df 40
E Bohonal de Ibor 10320 68 Se 51
H Böhönye 8719 58 Bh 44
UA Bohorodčany 45 Ce 42
BY Bohušèvsk 30 Da 36
UA Bohuslav 47 Da 41
D Boizenburg (Elbe) 19258 27 Ba 37
MK Bojane 1226 74 Cb 48
I Bojano 86021 73 Be 49
PL Bojanowo 63-940 44 Bg 39
RUS Bojarkeros 22 Fb 29
RUS Bojaščina 12 Df 28
BG Bojčinovci 3430 60 Cd 47
BG Bojnica 3840 59 Cc 47
SRB Bojnik 16205 59 Cb 47
SRB Boka 23252 59 Ca 45
RUS Bokovskaja 49 Eb 41
RUS Boksitogorsk 20 Dd 31
HR Bol 58 Bg 47
RUS Bol'šaja Vereika 48 Di 38
E Bolaños de Calatrava 13260 81 Sg 52
TR Bolayır 17350 75 Cg 50
F Bolbec 76210 41 Aa 41
RO Bolboși 217080 60 Cd 46
RO Boldești-Scăeni 105300 60 Cg 45
RUS Boldovo 33 Ee 36
UA Bolechiv 45 Cd 41
PL Bolesławiec 59-700 44 Bf 39
RUS Bolhov 31 Dg 37
UA Bolhrad 61 Ci 45
S Boliden 93601 10 Ca 26
RO Bolintin-Vale 085100 60 Cf 46
MNE Boljanići 59 Bk 47
BG Boljarovo 8720 75 Cg 48
SRB Boljevac 19370 59 Cb 47
F Bollène 84500 55 Ae 46
S Bollnäs 82100* 17 Bg 29
S Bollstabruk 87320 9 Bh 28
E Bollullos Par del Convado 80 Sd 53
S Bolmsö 27 Bd 33
I Bologna 40100* 57 Bb 46
RUS Bologoe 20 De 33
RUS Bologovo 30 Db 34
RUS Bološnevo 32 Ea 36
RUS Bolotovskoe 24 Gc 32
RUS Bol'šaja 21 Dk 30
RUS Bol'šaja Atnja 33 Ek 34


144 Belören

(RUS) Bol'šaja Budnica 30 Da 35
(RUS) Bol'šaja Černigovka 51 Fa 38
(RUS) Bol'šaja Dergunovka 51 Fa 38
(RUS) Bol'šaja Doroga 32 Ea 37
(RUS) Bol'šaja Džalga 64 Ec 45
(RUS) Bol'šaja Glušica 51 Fa 38
(RUS) Bol'šaja Gora 13 Eb 27
(RUS) Bol'šaja Kamenka 34 Fa 37
(RUS) Bol'šaja Kandala 33 Ek 36
(RUS) Bol'šaja Karpuniha 22 Ef 33
(RUS) Bol'šaja Kaskan 22 Eh 31
(RUS) Bol'šaja Kiselenka 20 De 33
(RUS) Bol'šaja Martynovka = S'loboda Bol'šaja Martynovka 64 Eb 43
(RUS) Bol'šaja Nisogora 13 Ef 26
(RUS) Bol'šaja Orlovka 64 Eb 43
(RUS) Bol'šaja Poljana 48 Di 38
(RUS) Bol'šaja Privalovka 48 Dk 39
(RUS) Bol'šaja Rečka 22 Eg 31
(RUS) Bol'šaja Sludka 22 Eg 29
(RUS) Bol'šaja Šonoma 14 Ei 29
(RUS) Bol'šaja Sosnovka 23 Fe 33
(RUS) Bol'šaja Tavoložka 50 Ek 38
(RUS) Bol'šaja Tovra 13 Eb 26
(RUS) Bol'šaja Usa 34 Ff 34
(RUS) Bol'šakovo 28 Cb 36
(UA) Bol'šečernihivka 48 Dk 42
(RUS) Bol'šekrepinskaja 63 Dk 43
(RUS) Bolšelug 14 Fc 28
(I) Bolsena 01023 72 Bb 48
(RUS) Bol'šenabatovskij 49 Ed 42
(RUS) Bol'šetroickoe 48 Dh 40
(RUS) Bol'šeustinskoe 35 Fi 35
(RUS) Bol'ševik 49 Ed 40
(RUS) Bol'šie Berezniki 33 Ef 36
(RUS) Bol'šie Kajbicy 33 Ei 35
(RUS) Bol'šie Ključi 33 Ei 34
(RUS) Bol'šie Ključišči 33 Ei 36
(RUS) Bol'šie Medveki 31 Dh 37
(RUS) Bol'šie Ozerki 50 Eg 38
(RUS) Bol'šie Suslovy 22 Ei 32
(RUS) Bol'šie Tarhany 33 Ei 36
(RUS) Bol'šinka 49 Eb 42
(RUS) Bol'šoe Boldino 33 Ef 36
(RUS) Bol'šoe Gorodišče 48 Dh 40
(RUS) Bol'šoe Ignatovo 33 Ef 35
(RUS) Bol'šoe Muraškino 33 Ee 35
(RUS) Bol'šoe Nagatkino 33 Ei 36
(RUS) Bol'šoe Pole 19 Ci 30
(RUS) Bol'šoe Pole 33 Ef 34
(RUS) Bol'šoe Selo 20 Di 33
(RUS) Bol'šoe Šemjakino 33 Ei 35
(RUS) Bol'šoe Šeremetovo 32 Ec 37
(RUS) Bol'šoe Tokarevo 21 Ec 31
(RUS) Bol'šoe Zaborov'e 20 Dd 32
(RUS) Bol'šoe Žirovo 48 Df 39
(RUS) Bol'šoj 49 Ec 41
(RUS) Bol'šoj Čurki 13 Eh 27
(RUS) Bol'šoj Dvor 20 De 31
(RUS) Bol'šoj Lučak 49 Ed 40
(RUS) Bol'šoj Melik 49 Ed 39
(RUS) Bol'šoj Ramen' 33 Eh 34
(RUS) Bol'šoj Sabsk 19 Ck 31
(RUS) Bol'šoj Ut 35 Fi 33
(RUS) Bol'šoj V'jas 33 Ef 37
(RUS) Bol'šoj V''jas 33 Ef 37
(NL) Bolsward 26 Af 37
(E) Boltaña 22340 70 Aa 48
(GB) Bolton BL1 39 Sh 37
(RUS) Bolturino 30 Dc 36
(TR) Bolu 14000* 76 Db 50
(TR) Bölükyazı 87 Ec 52
(IS) Bolungarvík 415 36 Qg 24
(TR) Bolvadin 03300 84 Db 52
(I) Bolzano = Bozen 39100 57 Bb 44
(I) Bomarzo 01020 72 Bc 48
(E) Boñar 24850 68 Se 48
(GB) Bonar Bridge IV24 38 Sf 33
(RUS) Bondari 32 Ec 38
(I) Bondeno 46023 57 Bb 46
(RUS) Bondjug 23 Fg 30
(RUS) Bonga 20 Dh 30
(F) Bonifacio 20169 71 Ak 49
(E) Bonillo, El 02610 69 Sh 52
(D) Bonn 53111* 42 Ah 40
(F) Bonnétable 72110 41 Aa 42
(F) Bonneval 28800 41 Ab 42
(F) Bonneville 74130 56 Ag 44
(F) Bonny-sur-Loire 45420 55 Ac 43
(I) Bono 07011 71 Ak 50
(I) Bonorva 07012 71 Ai 50
(H) Bonyhád 7150 59 Bi 44
(D) Boppard 56154 42 Ah 40
(CZ) Bor 348 02 43 Bc 41
(RUS) Bor 20 De 32
(RUS) Bor 25 Gh 33
(RUS) Bor 33 Ee 34
(SRB) Bor 19210* 59 Cc 46
(TR) Bor 51700 85 De 53
(S) Borås 50110* 17 Bc 33
(P) Borba 7150-101* 80 Sc 52
(TR) Borçka 08400 79 Eb 49
(F) Bordeaux 33000* 54 Sk 46
(P) Bordeira 8005-423* 80 Sb 53
(IS) Borðeyri 370 36 Qi 25
(S) Borensberg 59030 17 Bf 32
(FIN) Borgå = Porvoo 06500* 18 Cf 30
(IS) Borgarfjörður H. 36 Rg 25
(IS) Borgarnes 310 36 Qi 26
(NL) Borger 9530 26 Ag 38
(E) Borges Blanques, les 25400 70 Aa 49
(S) Borgholm 38701 28 Bg 34
(I) Borgomanero 28021 56 Ai 45
(I) Borgo San Dalmazzo 12011 56 Ah 46
(I) Borgo San Lorenzo 50032 57 Bb 47
(I) Borgo Val di Taro 43043 57 Ak 46
(I) Borgo Valsugana 38051 57 Bb 44
(S) Borgstena 51370 17 Bd 33
(N) Borgund 6854 16 Ah 29
(BG) Borino 4824 75 Ce 49
(RUS) Borinskoe 48 Dk 38
(RUS) Borisoglеb 32 Ec 35
(RUS) Borisoglebovka 50 Eh 39
(RUS) Borisoglebsk 49 Ec 39
(RUS) Borisoglebskij 21 Dk 33
(BY) Borisov = Barysav 30 Ci 36
(RUS) Borisovka 48 Dg 40
(RUS) Borisovo 21 Dk 31
(RUS) Borisovo 21 Ee 31
(RUS) Borisovo-Sudskoe 20 Dg 31
(UA) Borivs'ke 48 Di 42
(S) Börjelsbyn 10 Cc 25
(BY) Borkavičy 30 Ci 35
(D) Borken 04916 42 Ag 39
(N) Borkenes 9475 2 Bg 22
(S) Borlänge 78100* 17 Bf 30
(N) Borlaug 6854 16 Ah 29
(TR) Borlu 45940 84 Ci 52
(I) Bòrmio 23032 57 Ba 44
(D) Borna 04552 43 Bc 39
(F) Borne 43350 55 Ad 45
(RUS) Borodinskoe 19 Ck 29
(UA) Borodjanka 46 Ck 40
(RUS) Borodki 33 Ee 34
(RUS) Borodulino 23 Fe 33
(UA) Borodyno 61 Ck 44
(RUS) Borok 19 Da 32
(RUS) Borok 19 Dc 32
(RUS) Borok 20 Dg 30
(RUS) Borok 20 Dh 32
(RUS) Borok-Suležskij 20 Dg 33
(UA) Boromlja 48 Df 40
(PL) Boronów 42-283 44 Bi 40
(UA) Borova 48 Dh 41
(BG) Borovan 3240 60 Cd 47
(UA) Borove 46 Ch 39
(BG) Borovec 2626 75 Cd 48
(RUS) Borovenka 20 Dd 32
(RUS) Boroviči 19 Ck 33
(RUS) Boroviči 20 Dd 32
(RUS) Borovina 13 Ee 28
(BG) Borovo 2904 60 Cf 47
(RUS) Borovo 14 Ek 27
(RUS) Borovoe 53 Ga 38
(RUS) Borovoj 11 Dc 26
(RUS) Borovsk 31 Dg 35
(RUS) Borovskij 25 Gf 33
(S) Borrby 27621 27 Be 35
(DK) Borre 27 Bc 36
(E) Borriana 12530 70 Sk 51
(IRL) Borrisokane = Buiríos Uí Chéin 37 Sb 38
(S) Börrum 17 Bg 32
(RO) Borșa 707592 60 Ce 43
(UA) Borščiv 46 Cg 42
(N) Børselv 9716 3 Cf 20
(RUS) Borskoe 34 Fb 38
(F) Bort-les-Orgues 19110 55 Ac 45
(S) Börtnan 84035 9 Bd 28
(GB) Borve IV51 38 Sd 33
(UA) Boryslav 45 Cd 41
(UA) Boryspil' 47 Da 40
(UA) Borzna 47 Dc 39
(I) Bosa 08013 71 Ai 50
(BIH) Bosanska Gradiška 58 Bh 45
(BIH) Bosanska Krupa 58 Bg 46
(BIH) Bosanski Brod 58 Bi 45
(BIH) Bosanski Novi 58 Bg 45
(BIH) Bosanski Petrovac 58 Bg 46
(BIH) Bosanski Šamac 59 Bi 45
(BIH) Bosansko Grahovo 58 Bg 46
(GB) Boscastle PL35 40 Sf 40
(BIH) Bosinska Dubica 58 Bg 45
(CZ) Boskovice 680 01 44 Bg 41
(TR) Bostancı 10680 87 Ec 53
(TR) Bostanlı 87 Eb 53
(GB) Boston PE21 39 Sk 38
(S) Boteå 88195 9 Bh 27
(BG) Botevgrad 2140 75 Cd 48
(P) Boticas 5460-502 68 Sc 49
(N) Botngård 7140 8 Ak 27
(RO) Botoșani 000710* 60 Cg 43
(S) Botsmark 92276 10 Ca 26
(F) Boucau 64340 54 Si 47
(P) Bougado 68 Sb 49
(B) Bouillon 6830 42 Af 41
(F) Boulay-Moselle 57220 42 Ag 41
(F) Boulogne-Billancourt 92100* 41 Ac 42
(F) Boulogne-sur-Gesse 31350 54 Aa 47
(F) Boulogne-sur-Mer 62200* 41 Ab 40
(F) Bourbon-Lancy 71140 55 Ad 44
(F) Bourbon-l'Archambault 03160 55 Ad 44
(F) Bourbourg 59630 41 Ac 40
(F) Bourg 33710 54 Sk 45
(F) Bourganeuf 23400 55 Ab 45
(F) Bourg-Argental 42220 55 Ae 45
(F) Bourg-de-Péage 26300 56 Af 45
(F) Bourg-en-Bresse 01000* 56 Af 44
(F) Bourges 18000* 55 Ac 43
(F) Bourg-Lastic 63760 55 Ac 45
(F) Bourg-Madame 66760 70 Ab 48
(F) Bourgneuf-en-Retz 44580 54 Si 43
(F) Bourgoin-Jallieu 38300 56 Af 45
(F) Bourg-Saint-Andéol 07700 55 Ae 46
(F) Bourg-Saint-Maurice 73700 56 Ag 45
(F) Bourgueil 37140 54 Aa 43
(GB) Bournemouth BH1 40 Si 40
(F) Bournezeau 85480 54 Si 44
(F) Bouscat, le 33110 54 Sk 46
(F) Boussac 23600 55 Ac 44
(B) Boussu 7300 41 Ad 40
(F) Bouzonville 57320 42 Ag 41
(I) Bovalino Marina 89034 72 Bg 52
(S) Bovallstrand 45047 16 Bb 32
(I) Bova Marina 89035 72 Bf 53
(SLO) Bovec 5230 57 Bd 44
(E) Bóveda de Toro, La 49155 68 Se 49
(N) Bøverdal 2690 16 Ai 29
(GB) Bowmore PA44 37 Sd 35
(S) Boxholm 59010 17 Bf 32
(NL) Boxmeer 5830 42 Af 39
(NL) Boxtel 5280* 42 Af 39
(TR) Boyabat 57200 77 De 49
(TR) Boyalı 77 Dd 49
(TR) Boyalı 85 Dd 52
(TR) Boyalıca 16870 76 Ck 50
(TR) Boyalık 34232 76 Ci 49
(IRL) Boyle = Mainistir na Búille 37 Sb 37
(TR) Bozan 84 Ck 52
(TR) Bozburun 48710 84 Ci 54
(TR) Bozcaada 17680 75 Cg 51
(TR) Bozd g 84 Ci 52
(TR) Bozdoğan 09760 84 Ci 53
(I) Bozen = Bolzano 39100 57 Bb 44
(TR) Bozkaya 86 Dg 53
(TR) Bozkır 77 Dd 50
(TR) Bozkır 84 Dc 53
(TR) Bozkır 85 De 52
(TR) Bozkurt 37660 84 Ck 53
(TR) Bozlar 17200 76 Ch 50
(TR) Bozoğlak 78 Di 51
(F) Bozouls 12340 55 Ac 46
(TR) Bozova 63850 84 Da 53
(TR) Bozova 63850 86 Di 53
(TR) Boztepe 77 Df 50
(TR) Bozüyük 11300 76 Da 51
(TR) Bozyaka 84 Ck 54
(TR) Bozyazı 33830* 85 Dd 54
(I) Bra 12042 56 Ah 46
(I) Bracciano 00062 72 Bc 48
(F) Bracieux 41250 55 Ab 43
(S) Bräcke 84060 9 Bf 28
(GB) Brackley NN13 40 Si 38
(GB) Bracknell RG12 40 Sk 39
(UA) Braclav 46 Ci 42
(RUS) Braclavka 53 Ga 39
(RO) Brad 335200 59 Cc 44
(GB) Bradford BD9 39 Si 37
(BG) Bradvari 7568 61 Ch 47
(BY) Bradzjacin 45 Cd 39
(DK) Brædstrup 8740 26 Ak 35
(GB) Braemar AB35 38 Sg 33
(P) Braga 4700-001* 68 Sb 49
(P) Bragança 5300-001* 68 Sd 49
(FIN) Brahestad 92100* 10 Ce 26
(BY) Brahin 47 Da 39
(RO) Brăila 000810* 61 Ch 45
(GB) Braintree CM7 41 Aa 39
(UA) Brajiliv 46 Ci 41
(D) Brake (Unterweser) 26919 26 Ai 37
(D) Brakel 33034 42 Ak 39
(S) Bräkne-Hoby 37010 27 Bf 34
(S) Brålanda 46065 17 Bc 32
(GR) Brálos 33057 82 Cc 52
(DK) Bramming 6740 26 Ai 35
(GB) Brampton NR34 39 Sh 36
(D) Bramsche 49565 42 Ah 38
(S) Brånaberg 9 Bg 25
(I) Brancaleone Marina 89036 72 Bg 53
(N) Brandbu 16 Ba 30
(DK) Brande 7330 26 Ak 35
(D) Brandenburg an der Havel 14770* 43 Bc 38
(GB) Brandon IP27 41 Aa 38
(CZ) Brandýs nad Labem-Stará Boleslav 250 01 43 Be 40
(PL) Braniewo 14-500 28 Bk 36
(UA) Br'anka 48 Di 42
(E) Brañosera 34829 69 Sf 48
(PL) Brańsk 17-120 29 Cc 38
(F) Brantôme 24310 54 Aa 45
(BY) Braslav 30 Ch 35
(RO) Brașov 000500* 60 Cf 45
(B) Brasschaat 2930 41 Ae 39
(CH) Brassus, Le 1348 56 Ag 44
(S) Brastad 45420 16 Bb 32
(SK) Bratislava 810 00* 44 Bh 42
(BG) Bratja Daskalovi 6250 75 Cf 48
(RUS) Bratki 49 Eb 39
(RO) Bratovoești 207095 60 Cd 46
(UA) Brats'ke 62 Db 43
(N) Brattvåg 6270 8 Ag 28
(BIH) Bratunac 59 Bk 46
(A) Braunau am Inn 5280* 43 Bd 42
(D) Braunlage 38700 43 Ba 39
(D) Braunschweig 38100* 43 Ba 38
(IRL) Bray = Bré 37 Sd 37
(F) Bray-sur-Seine 77480 41 Ad 42
(E) Brazatortas 13450 81 Sf 52
(BIH) Brčko 59 Bi 46
(PL) Brdów 62-620 44 Bi 38
(IRL) Bré = Bray 37 Sd 37
(F) Brécey 50370 40 Si 42
(GB) Brechin DD9 38 Sh 34
(B) Brecht 2960 41 Ae 39
(CZ) Břeclav 690 02* 44 Bg 42
(GB) Brecon LD3 40 Sg 39
(NL) Breda 4800* 41 Ae 39
(S) Bredaryd 33010 17 Bd 33
(S) Bredbyn 83100 9 Bi 27
(F) Brède, la 33650 54 Sk 46
(S) Bredsel 10 Ca 25
(D) Bredstedt 25821 26 Ai 36
(RUS) Bredy 53 Ga 38
(B) Bree 53150 42 Af 39
(RUS) Bregadnaja 64 Eb 47
(A) Bregenz 6900* 57 Ak 43
(BG) Bregovo 6878 59 Cc 46
(F) Bréhal 50290 40 Si 42
(IS) Breiðavík 36 Qf 25
(IS) Breiðdalsvík 760 36 Rg 26
(D) Breisach am Rhein 79206 42 Ah 42
(N) Breivikbotn 9593 3 Cc 20
(RUS) Brejtovo 20 Dh 32
(N) Brekken 8 Bb 28
(N) Brekkesto 16 Ai 32
(N) Brekksillan 8 Bb 26
(N) Brekstad 7130 8 Ak 27
(N) Bremangerpollen 8 Ae 29
(D) Bremen 28195* 26 Ai 37
(D) Bremerhaven 27568* 26 Ai 37
(D) Bremervörde 27432 26 Ak 37
(E) Brenes 41310 80 Se 53
(GB) Brenish HS2 38 Sc 32
(I) Breno 25043 57 Ba 45
(GB) Brentwood CM13 41 Aa 39
(I) Bréscia 57 Ba 45
(NL) Breskens 4510 41 Ad 39
(I) Bressanone = Brixen 39042 57 Bb 44
(F) Bressuire 79300* 54 Sk 44
(BY) Brèst 45 Cd 38
(F) Brest 29200* 40 Sf 42
(BY) Brest = Brèst 45 Cd 38
(F) Bretenoux 46130 55 Ab 46
(F) Breteuil 60120 41 Aa 42
(F) Breteuil 60120 41 Ac 41
(D) Bretten 75015 42 Ai 41
(N) Brevik 16 Ak 31
(BIH) Breza 59 Bi 46
(SLO) Brežice 8250 58 Bf 45
(RUS) Brežnev = Naberežnye Čelny 34 Fc 35
(BG) Breznica 2972 75 Cd 49
(PL) Brežnica 44 Bk 39
(BG) Breznik 2360 74 Cc 48
(SK) Brezno 977 01 44 Bk 42
(RO) Brezoi 245500 60 Ce 45
(F) Brezolles 28270 41 Ab 42
(SK) Brezová pod Bradlom 906 13 44 Bh 42
(BG) Brezovo 5083 75 Cf 48
(F) Briançon 05100* 56 Ag 46
(HR) Bribir 58 Bf 47
(MD) Bričany = Briceni 5114 46 Ch 42
(MD) Bričen' = Briceni 5154 46 Ch 42
(MD) Briceni 5114 46 Ch 42
(F) Bricquebec 50260 40 Si 41
(GB) Bridgend CF31 40 Sg 39
(GB) Bridgnorth WV15 40 Sh 38
(GB) Bridgwater TA6 40 Sg 39
(GB) Bridlington YO15 39 Sk 36
(GB) Bridport DT6 40 Sh 40
(F) Briec 29510 40 Sf 42
(RUS) Brient 52 Fk 38
(I) Brienza 85050 73 Bf 50
(F) Briey 54150 42 Af 41
(CH) Brig 3900* 56 Ah 44
(GB) Brighton BN2 40 Sk 40
(F) Brignoles 83170 56 Ag 47
(E) Brihuega 19400 69 Sh 50
(RUS) Briljakovo 32 Ed 34
(F) Brillane, la 56 Af 47
(D) Brilon 59929 42 Ai 39
(N) Brimnes 16 Ag 30
(I) Bríndisi 72100 73 Bh 50
(GB) Brinian KW17 38 Sh 31
(HR) Brinje 58 Bf 46
(RUS) Brin-Navolok 13 Eb 27
(F) Brionne 27800 41 Aa 41
(F) Brioude 43100 55 Ad 45
(F) Brioux-sur-Boutonne 79170 54 Sk 44
(F) Briouze 61220 40 Sk 42
(I) Brisighella 48013 57 Bb 46
(GB) Bristol BS4 40 Sh 39
(F) Brive-la-Gaillarde 19100 55 Ab 45
(E) Briviesca 09240 69 Sg 48
(I) Brixen = Bressanone 39042 57 Bb 44
(GB) Brixham TQ5 40 Sg 40
(F) Brizeaux 55250 42 Af 41
(RUS) Brjadino 33 Ek 36
(UA) Brjanka = Br'anka 48 Di 42
(RUS) Brjansk 31 De 37
(RUS) Brjansk 65 Eg 46
(RUS) Brjuhovo 34 Fe 34
(CZ) Brno 60010* 44 Bg 41
(GB) Broadford IV49 38 Se 33
(S) Broby 28060 27 Be 34
(LV) Brocēni 3851 29 Cc 34
(MK) Brod 6259 74 Cb 49
(SRB) Brodarevo 31305 74 Bk 47
(S) Broddebo 59700 17 Bg 32
(UA) Brodec'ke 46 Ci 41
(GB) Brodick KA27 39 Se 35
(PL) Brodnica 87-300 28 Bk 37
(UA) Brody 46 Cf 40
(F) Broglie 27270 41 Aa 41
(FIN) Bromarv 10570 18 Cd 31
(D) Brome 38465 43 Ba 38
(S) Bromölla 29500 27 Be 34
(S) Brömsebro 37045 27 Bf 34
(GB) Bromsgrove 40 Sh 38
(DK) Brønderslev 9700 16 Ak 33
(RUS) Bronnicy 31 Di 35
(N) Brønnøysund 8900 9 Bc 25
(I) Bronte 95034 72 Be 53
(F) Broons 22250 40 Sh 42
(GB) Brora KW9 38 Sg 32
(N) Brøstadbotn 9311 2 Bh 21
(RO) Broșteni 217346 59 Cc 46
(E) Broto 22370 70 Sk 48
(F) Brou 28160 41 Ab 42
(GB) Brough CA17 39 Sh 36
(CZ) Broumov 550 01 44 Bg 40
(UA) Brovary 47 Da 40
(DK) Brovst 9460 26 Ak 33
(E) Brozas 10950 68 Sd 51
(IS) Bru 36 Re 25
(N) Bru 4158 16 Af 29
(F) Bruay-en-Artois 41 Ac 40
(RUS) Br'uchoveckaja 63 Di 45
(D) Bruchsal 76646 42 Ai 41
(A) Bruck an der Großglocknerstraße 5671* 57 Bc 43
(A) Bruck an der Leitha 2460 58 Bg 43
(A) Bruck an der Mur 8600* 58 Bf 43
(D) Brüel 19412 27 Bb 37
(B) Bruges = Brugge 8000 41 Ad 39
(CH) Brugg 5200* 56 Ai 43
(B) Brugge 8000 41 Ad 39
(N) Bruheim 16 Ah 29
(D) Brühl 68782 42 Ag 40
(F) Brumath 67170 42 Ah 42
(N) Brumunddal 2380 16 Ba 30
(I) Bruneck = Brunico 39031 57 Bb 44
(S) Brunflo 83401 9 Be 27
(I) Brunico = Bruneck 39031 57 Bb 44
(D) Brunsbüttel 25541 26 Ak 37
(CZ) Bruntál 792 01 44 Bh 41
(SRB) Brus 37220 59 Cb 47
(RUS) Brusenica 12 Ea 26
(CH) Brúsio 7743 57 Ba 44
(B) Brussel = Bruxelles 1000* 41 Ae 40
(PL) Brusy 89-632 28 Bh 37
(UA) Brusyliv 46 Ck 40
(B) Bruxelles = Brussel 1000 41 Ae 40
(F) Bruyères 88600 42 Ag 42
(F) Bruz 35170 40 Si 42
(RUS) Brykalansk 14 Fe 25
(RUS) Brykovka 50 Ei 38
(UA) Brylivka 62 Dd 44
(N) Bryne 4340 16 Af 32
(SRB) Brza Palavka 59 Cc 46
(PL) Brzeg 49-300 44 Bh 40
(PL) Brzeg Dolny 56-120 44 Bg 39
(PL) Brześć Kujawski 87-880 44 Bi 38
(PL) Brzesko 74-200 45 Ca 41
(PL) Brzoza 86-061 28 Bi 37
(LT) Bubiai 80016 29 Cd 35
(UA) Buča 47 Da 40
(UA) Bučač 46 Cf 41
(TR) Bucak 33590 84 Da 53
(TR) Bucak 33590 86 Dk 53
(TR) Bucakkışla 70000 85 Dd 54
(D) Buchenwald 43 Bb 39
(D) Buchholz in der Nordheide 21244 26 Ak 37
(D) Buchloe 86807 43 Ba 42
(AL) Buçimas (Shënmëri) 74 Ca 49
(SRB) Bučje 59 Cc 47
(D) Bückeburg 31675 42 Ak 38
(D) Bücken 27333 26 Ak 38
(GB) Buckhafen KY8 38 Sg 34
(GB) Buckie AB56 38 Sh 33



Buckie 145

(F) Carvin 62220 41 Ac 40
(UA) Caryčanka 47 De 42
(E) Casa del Puerto 81 Si 52
(I) Casale Monferrato 15033 56 Ai 45
(I) Casamássima 70010 73 Bg 50
(F) Casamozza 20290 71 Ak 48
(E) Casares 29690 80 Se 54
(E) Casavieja 05450 69 Sf 50
(P) Cascais 2750-001* 80 Sa 52
(I) Caserta 81100 73 Be 49
(IRL) Cashel = Caiseal 37 Sc 38
(E) Casinos 46171 70 Sk 51
(UA) Časiv Jar 48 Dh 42
(CZ) Čáslav 286 01 44 Bf 41
(GB) Casnewydd = Newport NP19 40 Sh 39
(BY) Čašniki 30 Ck 36
(I) Cásoli 73 Be 48
(RUS) Časovenskoe 20 Dd 30
(RUS) Časovo 14 Fa 28
(E) Caspe 50700 70 Sk 49
(F) Cassel 59670 41 Ac 40
(I) Cassino 03043 72 Bd 49
(F) Cassis 13260 56 Af 47
(E) Castañar de Ibor 10340 68 Se 51
(P) Castanheira de Pêra 3280-007* 68 Sb 50
(I) Castelbuono 90013 72 Be 53
(I) Castel di Sangro 67031 73 Be 49
(I) Castelfranco Véneto 57 Bb 45
(I) Castel Gandolfo 00040 72 Bc 49
(F) Casteljaloux 47700 54 Aa 46
(I) Castellabate 84048 73 Be 50
(I) Castellammare del Golfo 72 Bc 52
(I) Castellammare di Stábia 80053 73 Be 50
(F) Castellane 04120 56 Ag 47
(E) Castellar de Santiago 13750 81 Sg 52
(E) Castellar de Santisteban 23260 81 Sg 52
(E) Castelldans 25154 70 Aa 49
(E) Castelldefels 08860 70 Ab 49
(E) Castell de Ferro 18740 81 Sg 54
(GB) Castell-nedd = Neath SA11 40 Sg 39
(E) Castelló de la Plana 12001 70 Sk 51
(E) Castellón de la Plana = Castelló de la Plana 12001 70 Sk 51
(E) Castellote 44560 70 Sk 50
(F) Castelnaudary 11400* 55 Ab 47
(F) Castelnau-Magnoac 65230 54 Aa 47
(I) Castelnovo ne'Monti 42035 57 Ba 46
(I) Castelnuovo Berardenga 53019 57 Bb 47
(I) Castelnuovo di Garfagnana 55032 57 Ba 46
(P) Castelo Branco 6005-001 68 Sc 51
(F) Castelsarrasin 82100* 55 Ab 46
(I) Casteltérmini 92025 72 Bd 53
(I) Castelvetrano 91022 72 Bc 53
(F) Castets 40300 54 Si 47
(I) Castiglioncello 57012 57 Ba 47
(I) Castiglione del Lago 06061 72 Bc 47
(I) Castiglione della Pescáia 72 Ba 48
(I) Castiglion Fiorentino 52043 57 Bb 47
(E) Castilblanco 06680 68 Se 51
(E) Castilblanco de los Arroyos 41230 80 Se 53
(E) Castillo, O (Salvaterra de Miño) 68 Sb 48
(E) Castillo de Bayuela 45641 69 Sf 50
(F) Castillon-en-Couserans 09800 70 Ab 48
(F) Castillon-la-Bataille 33350 54 Sk 46
(F) Castillonnès 47330 54 Aa 46
(IRL) Castlebar = Caisleán an Bharraigh 37 Sa 37
(GB) Castlebay HS9 38 Sc 34
(IRL) Castlebellingham = Baile an Ghearlánaigh 37 Sd 37
(IRL) Castleblayney 37 Sd 36
(GB) Castlederg BT81 37 Sc 36
(IRL) Castleisland = Oileán Ciarrai 37 Sa 38
(IRL) Castlepollard = Baile na gCros 37 Sc 37
(IRL) Castlerea = An Caisleán Riabhach 37 Sb 37
(GBM) Castletown IM9 39 Sf 36
(IRL) Castletown Bearhaven = Baile Chaisleáin Bhéarra 37 Rl 39
(F) Castres 81100* 55 Ac 47
(NL) Castricum 1900 41 Ae 38
(E) Castril 18816 81 Sh 53
(P) Castro Daire 3600-069* 68 Sc 50
(E) Castrojeriz 09110 69 Sf 48
(E) Castropol 33760 68 Sc 47
(E) Castro-Urdiales 39700 54 Sg 47
(P) Castro Verde 7780-090* 80 Sb 53
(I) Castrovillari 87012 73 Bg 51
(E) Castuera 06420 80 Se 52
(RUS) Častye 23 Ff 33
(TR) Çat 79 Ea 51
(TR) Çatak 76 Da 50
(TR) Çatak 85 Dd 54
(TR) Çatak 87 Ed 52
(TR) Çatalan 01790 85 Df 53
(TR) Çatalarmut 78 Dk 51
(TR) Çatalca 34540* 76 Ci 49
(TR) Çatalçam 78 Di 51
(TR) Çatallar 84 Da 54
(RO) Cataloi 827076 61 Ci 45
(I) Catánia 95100 72 Bf 53
(I) Catanzaro 88100 73 Bg 52
(I) Catanzaro Lido 73 Bg 52
(F) Cateau-Cambrésis, le 59360 41 Ad 40
(I) Catenanuova 94010 72 Be 53
(IRL) Cathair na Mairt = Westport 37 Sa 37
(IRL) Catheir Saidhbhin 37 Rk 39
(TR) Çatköy 86 Dg 54
(I) Cattólica 57 Bc 47
(F) Caudry 59540 41 Ad 40
(F) Caulnes 22350 40 Sh 42
(F) Caunes-Minervois 11160 55 Ac 47
(MD) Căuşeni 4300 61 Ck 44
(F) Caussade 82300 55 Ab 46
(F) Cauterets 65110 70 Sk 48
(F) Cavaillon 84300 56 Af 47
(F) Cavalerie, la 12230 55 Ad 46
(IRL) Cavan = An Cabhán 37 Sc 37
(RUS) Čavan'ga 12 Dh 24
(I) Cavárzere 30014 57 Bc 45
(TR) Çavdar 83 Ch 53
(TR) Çavdarhisar 43710 76 Ck 51
(TR) Çavdır 15900 84 Ck 53
(HR) Cavtat 73 Bi 48
(TR) Çavuş 55420 84 Db 53
(TR) Çavuşçugöl 84 Db 52
(TR) Çavuşköy 84 Da 54
(TR) Çavuşlar 77 Dc 49
(BY) Čavusy 30 Da 37
(TR) Çay 37270 84 Db 52
(TR) Çayağzı 34886 76 Ck 49
(TR) Çayarası 36500 79 Ec 50
(TR) Çaybağı 86 Dk 52
(TR) Çaybaşı 05300 78 Dh 49
(TR) Çaybeyi 27700 86 Dh 54
(TR) Çaycuma 67900 77 Dc 49
(TR) Çayeli 53200 79 Ea 49
(F) Cayeux-sur-Mer 80410 41 Ab 40
(TR) Çayhan 42335 85 De 53
(TR) Çayır 55700 77 Df 49
(TR) Çayıralan 66600 77 Df 51
(TR) Çayırbaşı 36000 79 Ec 50
(TR) Çayırhan 06922 76 Db 50
(TR) Çayırkent 55300 78 Dg 49
(TR) Çayırlı 47510 79 Ea 51
(TR) Çayırözü 25900 85 Df 52
(TR) Çaykara 79 Ea 50
(TR) Çaylar 49610 79 Eb 51
(F) Caylar, le 34520 55 Ad 47
(TR) Çaylarbaşı 86 Dk 53
(F) Caylus 82160 55 Ab 46
(TR) Çayönü 78 Dh 50
(TR) Çaytepe 21560 87 Ea 52
(E) Cazalla de la Sierra 41370 80 Se 53
(F) Cazaubon 64700 54 Sk 47
(F) Cazères 31220 70 Ab 47
(BIH) Cazin 58 Bf 46
(HR) Čazma 58 Bg 45
(E) Cazorla 23470 81 Sg 53
(E) Cea 24174 68 Se 48
(MD) Ceadîr-Lunga 6101 61 Ci 44
(IRL) Ceanánnas 37 Sd 37
(IRL) Ceann Toirc 37 Sb 38
(IRL) Ceapach Choinn 37 Sc 38
(IRL) Ceatharlach = Carlow 37 Sd 38
(RUS) Čebarkul' 35 Ga 35
(TR) Cebeci 37400 79 Ed 50
(RUS) Čeboksary 33 Eh 34
(RUS) Čebotovka 48 Dk 42
(SK) Čebovce 991 25 44 Bk 42
(E) Cebreros 05260 69 Sf 50
(RUS) Čebsara 20 Di 31
(RUS) Čeburga 25 Gi 33
(I) Ceccano 03023 72 Bd 49
(H) Cece 7013 59 Bi 44
(UA) Čečel'nyk 46 Ck 42
(TR) Cecimli 86 Dh 52
(I) Cecina 57 Ba 47
(E) Cedeira 15350 68 Sb 47
(E) Cedillo 10513 68 Sc 51
(E) Cedrillas 44147 70 Sk 50
(I) Cefalù 90015 72 Be 52
(RUS) Čegem Pervyj 64 Ed 47
(LV) Ceģi 18 Cc 33
(H) Cegléd 2700 59 Bk 43
(I) Céglie Messápico 73 Bh 50
(MK) Čegrane 1237 74 Ca 49
(E) Cehegín 30430 81 Si 52
(RUS) Čehov 31 Dh 35
(GB) Ceinewydd = New Quay SA45 40 Sf 38
(RUS) Čekalin 31 Dg 36
(TR) Çekerek 66500 77 Df 50
(TR) Çekirge 77 Dc 51
(RUS) Čekmaguš 34 Fe 35
(RUS) Čekšino 21 Ea 31
(TR) Celâli 78 Dh 51
(I) Celano 67043 72 Bd 48
(E) Celanova 32800 68 Sc 48
(RUS) Čelbasskaja 63 Dk 45
(IRL) Celbridge = Cill Droichid 37 Sd 37
(TR) Çelebi 71810 77 Dd 51
(BIH) Čelić 59 Bi 46
(TR) Çelikhan 02600 86 Di 52
(RUS) Celina 64 Eb 44
(RUS) Celinnyj 35 Fi 37
(RUS) Celinnyj 64 Ee 44
(RUS) Čeljabinsk 35 Gb 35
(BY) Celjachany 46 Cf 38
(SLO) Celje 3000* 58 Bf 44
(H) Celldömölk 9500 58 Bh 43
(D) Celle 29221* 43 Ba 38
(RUS) Čelno-Veršiny 34 Fb 36
(P) Celorico da Beira 6360-287* 68 Sc 50
(TR) Çeltek 84 Db 52
(TR) Çeltik 76 Db 51
(TR) Çeltikçi 77 Dc 50
(TR) Çeltikçi 84 Da 53
(TR) Çeltikli 77 Dc 51
(TR) Cemilbey 19050 77 Df 50
(TR) Cemilköy 50420 85 De 52
(TR) Çemişgezek 62600 78 Di 51
(IRL) Cé na Cille Móire 37 Sd 38
(TR) Cengerli 78 Di 51
(TR) Cengilli 36500 79 Ec 50
(F) Cenon 33150 54 Sk 46
(E) Centelles 08540 70 Ac 49
(I) Cento 44042 57 Bb 46
(RUS) Central'no-Kospašskij 23 Fh 31
(RUS) Central'nyj 22 Fa 31
(RUS) Čepeck, Kirovo- 22 Fa 32
(RUS) Čepeckij 22 Fb 32
(BG) Čepelare 4850 75 Ce 49
(HR) Čepin 59 Bi 45
(TR) Çepni 76 Db 50
(SLO) Čepovan 5253 57 Bd 44
(BY) Čerachavka 47 Db 38
(F) Cerbère 66290 70 Ad 48
(P) Cercal 7555-101 80 Sb 53
(I) Cerchiara di Calábria 87070 73 Bg 51
(TR) Çerçiler 77 Df 49
(F) Cercy-la-Tour 58340 55 Ad 44
(RUS) Čerdakly 33 Ei 36
(E) Cerdedo 36130 68 Sb 48
(F) Cerdon 45620 55 Ac 43
(RUS) Čerdyn' 23 Fg 30
(RUS) Čerelennye Buruny 65 Ef 46
(RUS) Čeremošnica 22 Eg 31
(RUS) Čeremšan 34 Fb 36
(RUS) Čeremšanka 35 Ga 34
(RUS) Čeremuhovo 24 Ga 30
(RUS) Čerencovo 19 Dc 31
(RUS) Čerenskoe 20 Df 32
(RUS) Čerepovec 20 Dh 31
(I) Céres 10070 56 Ah 45
(F) Céret 66400 70 Ac 48
(RUS) Cerevkovo 13 Ef 29
(E) Cerezo de Abajo 40591 69 Sg 49
(I) Cerignola 71042 73 Bf 49
(F) Cérilly 03350 55 Ac 44
(F) Cerizay 79140 54 Sk 44
(UA) Čerkas'ke 48 Dh 42
(RUS) Čerkasskoe 50 Eh 38
(UA) Čerkassy = Čerkasy 47 Dc 41
(UA) Čerkasy 47 Dc 41
(TR) Çerkeş 18600 77 Dc 50
(RUS) Čerkessk 64 Ec 46
(TR) Çerkezköy 59500 76 Ci 49
(SLO) Cerknica 1380 58 Be 45
(BG) Čerkovica 5959 60 Ce 47
(RUS) Čerkutino 32 Dk 34
(RO) Cermei 317075 59 Cb 44
(RUS) Čermenino 21 Ed 31
(TR) Çermik 21600 86 Dk 52
(RUS) Čermoz 23 Fg 32
(RUS) Čern' 31 Dg 37
(RO) Cerna 827045 61 Ci 45
(RUS) Černaja, Ust'- 23 Fc 30
(RUS) Černaja Holunica 22 Fb 32
(RO) Cernăteşti 207185 60 Cd 46
(RUS) Černava 32 Dk 37
(RUS) Černavka 49 Ec 38
(RO) Cernavodă 905200 61 Ci 46
(F) Cernay 68700 56 Ah 43
(E) Cernégula 69 Sg 48
(RUS) Černevo 19 Ci 32
(UA) Černigov = Černihiv 47 Db 39
(RUS) Černigovskaja 63 Dk 46
(UA) Černihiv 47 Db 39
(UA) Černivci 46 Cf 42
(UA) Černjachiv 46 Ci 40
(RUS) Černjahovsk 28 Cb 36
(RUS) Černjanka 48 Dh 40
(RUS) Černoborskaja 14 Fd 25
(RUS) Černoe 22 Eg 33
(RUS) Černoe 25 Gk 33
(RUS) Černogolovka 31 Di 34
(RUS) Černoistočinsk 24 Fk 33
(RUS) Černoreč'e 35 Ga 36
(RUS) Černorečenskij 23 Fc 30
(UA) Černovcy = Černivci 46 Cf 42
(RUS) Černovskoe 22 Eh 32
(RUS) Černovskoe 23 Fe 33
(RUS) Černovskoe 33 Ef 35
(RUS) Černozer'e 33 Ee 34
(RUS) Černuška 35 Fg 34
(RUS) Černut'evo 14 Ei 27
(UA) Černyhivka 63 Dg 43
(RUS) Černyj Jar 50 Eg 42
(RUS) Černyj Otrog 52 Fg 39
(RUS) Černyškovskij 49 Ec 42
(AL) Cërrik 74 Bk 49
(I) Certaldo 50052 57 Bb 47
(RUS) Čertkovo 32 Ec 35
(RUS) Čertkovo 49 Ea 41
(RUS) Čerusti 32 Ea 35
(RUS) Červa 14 Ei 28
(BY) Čèrven' 30 Ci 37
(BG) Červen Brjag 5980 60 Ce 47
(E) Cervera 25200 70 Ab 49
(E) Cervera de Pisuerga 34840 69 Sf 48
(I) Cervéteri 00052 72 Bc 49
(I) Cérvia 48015 57 Bc 46
(I) Cervignano del Friuli 33052 57 Bd 45
(I) Cervinara 83012 73 Be 49
(F) Cervione 20221 71 Ak 48
(E) Cervo 68 Sc 47
(UA) Červone 47 De 39
(UA) Červonoarmijs'k 46 Cf 40
(UA) Červonoarmijs'k 46 Ci 40
(UA) Červonoarmijs'ke 61 Ci 45
(UA) Červonograd = Červonohrad 45 Ce 40
(UA) Červonohrad 45 Ce 40
(UA) Červonozavods'ke 47 Dd 40
(UA) Červonoznam'janka 61 Da 43
(BY) Čèrykav 30 Db 37
(I) Cesena 47023 57 Bc 46
(I) Cesenático 57 Bc 46
(LV) Cēsis 4101 18 Cf 33
(CZ) Česká Kamenice 407 21 43 Be 40
(CZ) Česká Lípa 470 01* 43 Be 40
(CZ) Česká Třebová 560 02* 44 Bg 41
(CZ) České Budějovice 370 01* 43 Be 42
(CZ) Český Brod 282 01 43 Be 40
(CZ) Český Krumlov 381 01 43 Be 42
(CZ) Český Těšín 735 61* 44 Bi 41
(RUS) Česma 35 Ga 37
(TR) Çeşme 35930 83 Cg 52
(TR) Çeşmelisebil 42445 84 Dc 52
(SRB) Čestobrodica 31210 59 Ca 47
(LV) Cesvaine 4871 29 Cg 34
(RO) Cetate 207190 60 Cd 46
(MNE) Cetinje 81 250 74 Bi 48
(TR) Çetinkaya 58920 78 Dh 51
(I) Cetraro 87022 73 Bf 51
(RUS) Četyrman, Bala- 34 Ff 37
(E) Ceuta (Sebta) 80 Se 55
(I) Ceva 12073 56 Ai 46
(TR) Cevizdüzü 73400 87 Ec 53
(TR) Cevizli 84 Db 53
(TR) Cevizlik 78 Dg 49
(TR) Cevizlik 87 Ec 52
(MNE) Čevo 81 258 74 Bi 48
(TR) Ceyhan 01920* 85 Df 53
(TR) Ceylanpınar 63570 87 Ea 54
(F) Chabanais 16150 54 Aa 45
(F) Chabeuil 26120 56 Af 46
(F) Chablis 89800 55 Ad 43
(F) Chabris 36210 55 Ab 43
(F) Chagny 71150 55 Ae 44
(F) Chaise-Dieu, la 43160 55 Ad 45
(F) Chalais 36370 54 Aa 45
(F) Châlette-sur-Loing 45120 41 Ac 42
(F) Challans 85300 54 Si 44
(F) Chalonnes-sur-Loire 49290 54 Sk 43
(F) Châlons-en-Champagne 51000 41 Ae 42
(F) Châlons-sur-Marne = Châlons-en-Champagne 41 Ae 42
(F) Chalon-sur-Saône 71100* 55 Ae 44
(BY) Chalopeničy 30 Ci 36
(F) Châlus 87230 54 Aa 45
(D) Cham 93413 43 Bc 41
(F) Chambéry 73000* 56 Af 45
(F) Chambon-sur-Lignon, le 43400 55 Ae 45
(F) Chambord 41250 55 Ab 43
(F) Chamborêt 87140 55 Ab 44
(F) Chamonix-Mont-Blanc 74400* 56 Ag 45
(F) Champagne-Mouton 16350 54 Aa 45
(F) Champagnole 39300* 56 Af 44
(F) Champaubert 51270 41 Ad 42
(CH) Champéry 1874 56 Ag 44
(F) Champlitte 70600 56 Af 43
(I) Champoluc 11020 56 Ah 45
(E) Chantada 27500 68 Sc 48
(F) Chantilly 60500 41 Ac 41
(F) Chantôme, Eguzon- 55 Ab 44
(F) Chantonnay 85110 54 Si 44
(F) Chapelle-d'Angillon, la 18380 55 Ac 43
(GB) Chard TA20 40 Sh 40
(F) Charité-sur-Loire, la 58400* 55 Ad 43
(UA) Charkiv 48 Dg 41
(UA) Charkow = Charkiv 48 Dg 41
(B) Charleroi 6000 41 Ae 40
(IRL) Charlestown = Baile Chathail 37 Sb 37
(F) Charleville-Mézières 08000* 41 Ae 41
(S) Charlottenberg 67301 17 Bc 31
(F) Charmes 88130 42 Ag 42
(F) Charny 89120 55 Ad 43
(F) Charolles 71120 55 Ae 44
(F) Chartres 28000* 41 Ab 42
(F) Chasseneuil-sur-Bonnieure 16260 54 Aa 45
(F) Châtaigneraie, la 85130 54 Sk 44
(F) Château-Arnoux 04160 56 Ag 46
(F) Châteaubriant 56500 54 Si 43
(F) Château-Chinon 58120 55 Ad 43
(CH) Château-d'Oex 1837 56 Ah 44
(F) Château-d'Oléron, Le 17480 54 Si 45
(F) Château-du-Loir 72500 54 Aa 43
(F) Châteaudun 28200 41 Ab 42
(F) Château-Gontier 53200* 54 Sk 43
(F) Château-Landon 77570 41 Ac 42
(F) Château-la-Vallière 37330 54 Aa 43
(F) Châteaulin 29150 40 Sf 42
(F) Châteaumeillant 18370 55 Ac 44
(F) Châteauneuf-de-Randon 48170 55 Ad 46
(F) Châteauneuf-du-Faou 29520 40 Sg 42
(F) Châteauneuf-en-Thymerais 28170 41 Ab 42
(F) Châteauneuf-sur-Charente 16120 54 Sk 45
(F) Châteauneuf-sur-Loire 45110 55 Ac 43
(F) Châteauneuf-sur-Sarthe 49330 54 Sk 43
(F) Châteauponsac 87290 55 Ab 44
(F) Château-Renault 37110 54 Aa 43
(F) Châteauroux 36000* 55 Ab 44
(F) Château-Salins 57170 42 Ag 42
(F) Château-Thierry 02400* 41 Ad 41
(F) Châteauvillain 52120 41 Ae 42
(F) Châtelaillon-Plage 17340 54 Si 44
(B) Châtelet 6200 41 Ae 40
(F) Châtellerault 86100 54 Aa 44
(I) Châtillon 11024 56 Ah 45
(F) Châtillon-Coligny 45230 55 Ac 43
(F) Châtillon-en-Bazois 58110 55 Ad 43
(F) Châtillon-en-Diois 26410 56 Af 46
(F) Châtillon-sur-Chalaronne 01400 55 Ae 44
(F) Châtillon-sur-Indre 36700 55 Ab 44
(F) Châtillon-sur-Seine 21400* 55 Ae 43
(F) Châtre, la 86390 55 Ab 44
(F) Chaudes-Aigues 15110 55 Ad 46
(F) Chauffailles 71170 55 Ae 44
(F) Chaumont 52000* 42 Af 42
(F) Chaumont 52000* 55 Ab 44
(F) Chauny 02300* 41 Ad 41
(F) Chauvigny 86300 54 Aa 44
(CH) Chaux-de-Fonds, La 2300* 56 Ag 43
(P) Chaves 5000-215 68 Sc 49
(CZ) Cheb 350 02 43 Bc 40
(F) Chef-Boutonne 79110 54 Sk 44
(E) Cheles 06105 80 Sc 52
(PL) Chełm 22-100 45 Cd 39
(PL) Chełmno 62-660 28 Bi 37
(GB) Chelmsford CM2 41 Aa 39
(PL) Chełmża 87-140 28 Bi 37
(GB) Cheltenham GL50 40 Sh 39
(E) Chelva 46176 70 Sk 51
(F) Chemillé 49120 54 Sk 43
(D) Chemnitz 09111* 43 Bc 40
(GB) Chepstow NP16 40 Sh 39
(F) Cherbourg-Octeville 50100 40 Si 41
(MD) Cherman 61 Ch 43
(F) Chéroy 89690 41 Ad 42
(UA) Cherson 62 Dc 44
(GB) Chertsey KT15 40 Sk 39
(E) Cheste 46380 70 Sk 51
(GB) Chester CH1 39 Sh 37
(GB) Chesterfield CT5 39 Si 37
(F) Chevagnes 03230 55 Ad 44
(F) Chevillon 52170 42 Af 42
(F) Chevilly 45520 41 Ab 42
(F) Chey 79120 54 Sk 44
(F) Cheylard, le 07160 55 Ae 46
(I) Chiaravalle 60033 57 Bd 47
(I) Chiaravalle Centrale 88064 73 Bg 52
(I) Chiari 25032 57 Ak 45
(I) Chiávari 16043 57 Ak 46
(I) Chiavenna 23022 57 Ak 44
(GB) Chichester PO19 40 Sk 40
(E) Chiclana de la Frontera 11130 80 Sd 54
(I) Chieri 10023 56 Ah 45
(I) Chieti 66100 73 Be 48
(B) Chimay 6460 41 Ae 40
(E) Chinchilla de Monte Aragón 02520 81 Si 52
(E) Chinchón 28370 69 Sg 50
(F) Chinon 37500 54 Aa 43
(I) Chióggia 30015 57 Bc 45
(MD) Chiperceni 61 Ci 43
(E) Chipiona 11550 80 Sd 54
(GB) Chippenham SN15 40 Sh 39
(GB) Chipping Sodbury BS37 40 Sh 39
(E) Chirivel 04825 81 Sh 53
(MD) Chişinău 2000 61 Ci 43
(RO) Chişineu-Criş 315100 59 Cb 44
(I) Chiusi 53043 57 Bb 47
(I) Chivasso 10034 56 Ah 45
(UA) Chlystunivka 47 Db 41
(UA) Chmeliv 47 Dd 40
(UA) Chmel'nyc'kyj 46 Cg 41
(UA) Chmel'nyc'kyj, Perejaslav- 47 Db 40
(PL) Chmielnik 36-016 45 Ca 40
(UA) Chmil'nyk 46 Ch 41
(CZ) Choceň 565 01 44 Bg 41
(BY) Chocimsk 30 Dc 37
(PL) Chociwel 73-120 27 Bf 37
(UA) Chočyne 46 Ch 39
(PL) Chodecz 87-860 44 Bk 38




Chodecz 147

(TR) Dağbaşı 61720 78 Dk 50
(TR) Dağbaşı 61720 86 Dk 53
(LV) Dagda 5674 30 Ch 34
(TR) Dağdere 46300 83 Ci 52
(D) Dagebüll 25899 26 Ai 36
(TR) Dağkızılca 83 Ch 52
(TR) Dağlıca 30340 87 Ee 53
(RUS) Dagomys 63 Dk 47
(TR) Dağpazarı 61950 85 Dd 54
(TR) Dağyolu 78 Dk 51
(D) Dahlenburg 21368 27 Ba 37
(D) Dahme 15936 27 Bb 36
(D) Dahme 15936 43 Bd 39
(E) Daimiel 13250 69 Sg 51
(RKS) Đakovica = Gyakovë 74 Ca 48
(HR) Đakovo 59 Bi 45
(S) Dala-Järna 78051 17 Be 30
(TR) Dalaman 48770 84 Ci 54
(S) Dalavardo 2 Bf 24
(GB) Dalbeattie DG5 39 Sg 36
(BG) Dălbok Izvor 4280 75 Cf 48
(BG) Dălbok Izvor 75 Cf 48
(S) Dalby 27 Bd 35
(N) Dale 16 Af 29
(N) Dale 16 Af 30
(N) Dale 16 Ai 32
(N) Dalen 16 Ai 31
(S) Dalfors 17 Bf 29
(BG) Dălgopol 9250 61 Ch 47
(E) Dalías 04750 81 Sh 54
(TR) Dallıbahçe 78 Dk 51
(RUS) Dal'nee Konstantinovo 33 Ee 35
(RUS) Dal'nij 14 Ek 28
(RUS) Dal'nij 14 Ff 28
(RUS) Dal'nij 34 Fc 37
(RUS) Dal'nije Zelency 4 Dg 21
(GB) Dalry KA24 39 Sf 35
(FIN) Dalsbruk 25860 18 Cc 30
(IS) Dalsmynni 370 36 Qi 26
(IS) Dalvík 620* 36 Rb 25
(GB) Dalwhinnie PH19 38 Sf 34
(TR) Dalyan 48840 84 Ci 54
(TR) Damal 79 Ec 49
(RUS) Damaskino 34 Fb 34
(TR) Dambaslar 59400 76 Ch 49
(TR) Damlacık 02430 86 Di 53
(TR) Damlama 33590 85 De 53
(S) Danasjö 9 Bg 25
(F) Dancharia 64310 69 Si 47
(RUS) Danilkovo 20 Dh 31
(RUS) Danilov 21 Ea 32
(MNE) Danilovgrad 81 410 74 Bk 48
(RUS) Danilovka 49 Ee 40
(RUS) Danilovka 50 Ef 38
(TR) Danışment 10845 76 Ch 51
(TR) Danişment 69000 78 Di 51
(TR) Danişment 69000 85 Df 54
(RUS) Dankov 32 Dk 37
(D) Dannenberg (Elbe) 29451 27 Bb 37
(RO) Darabani 715100 46 Cg 42
(TR) Daran 84 Dc 54
(TR) Darende 44700 86 Dh 52
(TR) Dargeçit 47530 87 Eb 53
(D) Dargun 17159 27 Bc 37
(TR) Darıca 61345 76 Ck 50
(TR) Darıkent 62820 86 Dk 52
(TR) Darıveren 20830 84 Ck 53
(GB) Darlington DL1 39 Si 36
(PL) Darłowo 76-150 28 Bg 36
(RO) Dărmănești 137185 60 Cf 46
(D) Darmstadt 64283* 42 Ai 41
(F) Darnétal 76160 41 Ab 41
(RUS) Darovskoe 22 Eh 32
(GB) Dartford DA1 41 Aa 39
(GB) Dartmouth TQ6 40 Sg 40
(IRL) Darú 37 Sc 38
(HR) Daruvar 58 Bh 45
(GB) Darwen BB3 39 Sh 37
(UA) Dašiv 46 Ck 41
(BG) Dăskotna 8561 76 Ch 48
(D) Dassow 23942 27 Ba 37
(TR) Datça 48900 83 Ch 54
(LT) Daugai 64009 29 Ce 36
(LV) Daugavpils 5401* 29 Cg 35
(D) Daun 54550 42 Ag 40
(GB) Daventry NN11 40 Si 38
(BY) Davhinava 30 Ch 36
(RUS) Davlekanovo 34 Fe 36
(BY) Davljady 46 Ck 39
Davlos 85 Dd 55
(CH) Davos 7270 57 Ak 44
(TR) Davulga 76 Db 51
(BY) Davyd-Haradok 46 Ch 38
(UA) Davydiv Brid 62 Dd 43
(RUS) Davydovka 48 Dk 39
(RUS) Davydovka 50 Ek 39
(RUS) Davydovo 23 Fd 30
(F) Dax 40100* 54 Si 47
(TR) Dazkırı 03950 84 Ck 53
(GB) Deal CT14 41 Ab 39
(F) Deauville 14800 41 Aa 41
(UA) Debal'ceve 48 Di 42
(MK) Debar 1250 74 Ca 49
(RUS) Debesy 23 Fd 33
(PL) Dębica 39-200 45 Cb 40
(PL) Dęblin 08-530 45 Cb 39
(PL) Dębno 74-400 27 Be 38
(SRB) Debrc 15214 59 Bk 46
(H) Debrecen 4000* 59 Cb 43
(MK) Debrešte 7537 74 Cb 49
(PL) Debrzno 77-310 28 Bh 37
(RKS) Deçan = Dečani 51000 74 Ca 48
(RKS) Dečani = Deçan 51000 74 Ca 48
(F) Decazeville 12300 55 Ac 46
(CZ) Děčín 405 01* 43 Be 40
(F) Decize 58300 55 Ad 44
(RO) Deda 547205 60 Ce 44
(TR) Dedeler 84 Dc 52
(TR) Dedeli 66840 79 Ed 51
(RUS) Dedenevo 31 Dh 34
(RUS) Dedoviči 19 Ck 33
(RUS) Dedovsk 31 Dh 35
(H) Dég 8135 59 Bi 44
(S) Degeberga 29701 27 Be 35
(S) Degerfors 69301 17 Be 31
(D) Deggendorf 94469 43 Bc 42
(TR) Değirmendere 83 Ch 52
(LT) Degučiai 83022 29 Cg 35
(RO) Dej 405200 60 Cd 43
(S) Deje 66920 17 Bd 31
(RUS) Dektjarsk 35 Ga 34
(MK) Delčevo 2320 74 Cc 49
(CH) Delémont 2800* 56 Ah 43
(NL) Delft 2600* 41 Ae 38
(NL) Delfzijl 9930 26 Ag 37
(TR) Deli 47800 87 Ea 53
(TR) Deliçay 79 Ed 51
(TR) Delice 77 De 51
(I) Deliceto 71026 73 Bf 49
(TR) Delihasan 79 Ed 51
(TR) Deliktaş 58930 78 Dh 51
(D) Delitzsch 04509 43 Bc 39
(F) Delle 90100 56 Ag 43
(D) Delmenhorst 27749* 26 Ai 37
(HR) Delnice 58 Be 45
(CH) Delsberg = Delémont 2800* 56 Ah 43
(S) Delsbo 82060 9 Bg 29
(AL) Delvinë 74 Ca 51
(RUS) Dema 23 Fe 30
(RUS) Demensk, Spas- 31 De 36
(RUS) Demidov 30 Db 35
(TR) Demirci 76 Ci 51
(TR) Demirci 85 De 52
(TR) Demirci 86 Dk 52
(TR) Demirci 86 Dk 53
(TR) Demirkent 08830 79 Eb 50
(TR) Demirköy 11800 76 Ch 49
(TR) Demirli 86 Dk 53
(TR) Demirözü 69400 78 Dk 50
(TR) Demirşeyh 19600 77 De 50
(TR) Demirtaş 16245 76 Ck 50
(TR) Demirtaş 16245 84 Dc 54
(RUS) Dem'janovo 22 Eh 30
(RUS) Demjansk 19 Dc 33
(RUS) Dem'janskoe 25 Gk 31
(RUS) Dem'jas 50 Ek 39
(D) Demmin 17109 27 Bd 37
(UA) Demuryne 48 Dg 42
(F) Denain 59220 41 Ad 40
(GB) Denbigh LL16 39 Sg 37
(NL) Den Burg 1790 26 Ae 37
(NL) Den Haag = 's-Gravenhage 2500 41 Ae 38
(NL) Den Helder 1780 26 Ae 38
(RUS) Denislav'e 12 Ea 28
(RUS) Denisovska 7 Ff 24
(TR) Deniz Kamp Yeri 83 Cg 52
(TR) Denizler 20740 84 Ck 53
(TR) Denizli 17200 76 Ch 50
(TR) Denizli 17200 84 Ck 53
(GB) Denny FK6 38 Sg 34
(NL) Den Oever 1779 26 Af 38
(B) De Panne 8660 41 Ac 39
(UA) Deražnja 46 Ch 41
(TR) Derbent 84 Dc 52
(GB) Derby DE23 39 Si 38
(TR) Dere 86 Dk 52
(TR) Derebaşı 33700 83 Ch 52
(TR) Derebucak 42480 84 Db 53
(TR) Dereköy 76 Ch 49
(TR) Dereköy 76 Ck 51
(TR) Dereler 87 Ec 53
(TR) Dereli 78 Di 50
(TR) Deremahal 77 De 51
(TR) Derepazarı 53900 79 Ea 49
(TR) Derepazarı 53900 79 Ea 49
(RUS) Dereven'ka 22 Eg 29
(RUS) Derevjanka 20 De 29
(RUS) Derevjannoe 20 De 29
(RUS) Derevjansk 14 Fd 29
(RUS) Dergači 50 Ei 39
(UA) Derhačy 48 Dg 40
(UA) Derijivka 47 Dd 42
(TR) Derik 47800 87 Ea 53
(TR) Derinkuyu 85 De 52
(TR) Derinsu 47800 87 Ea 53
(BG) Dermanci 5780 75 Ce 47
(TR) Dernekpazarı 61950 79 Ea 50
(GB) Derry BT48 37 Sc 36
(GB) Derry Doire = Londonderry 37 Sc 36
(F) Derval 44590 54 Si 43
(BIH) Derventa 58 Bh 46
(RUS) Deržavino 34 Fc 37
(UA) Desantne 61 Ck 45
(F) Descartes 37160 54 Aa 44
(I) Desenzano del Garda 25015 57 Ba 45
(GR) Deskáti 51200 74 Cb 51
(SRB) Despotovac 35213 59 Cb 46
(D) Dessau-Roßlau 06844 43 Bc 39
(TR) Destek 05830 78 Dg 50
(F) Desvres 62240 41 Ab 40
(RO) Deta 305200 59 Cb 45
(D) Detmold 32756* 42 Ai 39
(NL) Deurne 5750 42 Af 39
(RO) Deva 000330* 59 Cc 45
(TR) Devecikonağı 16520 76 Ci 51
(TR) Devegölü 86 Dk 52
(TR) Develi 85 Df 52
(NL) Deventer 7400* 42 Ag 38
(BG) Devin 4800 75 Ce 49
(GB) Devizes SN10 40 Si 39
(RUS) Devjatiny 20 Dg 30
(TR) Devletliağaç 39000 76 Ch 49
(BG) Devnja 9160 61 Ch 47
(TR) Devrek 67800 76 Db 49
(CY) Dhekelia Sovereign Base Area (GB) 85 Dd 56
(AL) Dhërmi 74 Bk 50
(AL) Dhivër 74 Ca 51
(CH) Diablerets, Les 1865 56 Ah 44
(GR) Diafáni 85700 83 Ch 55
(I) Diano Marina 18013 56 Ai 47
(GR) Diavatá 57008 74 Cc 50
(TR) Dibekdüzü 86 Dk 53
(UA) Dibrivka 46 Ch 40
(TR) Dicle 73200 87 Ea 52
(TR) Dicle 73200 87 Ec 53
(GB) Didcot OX11 40 Si 39
(GR) Didimótiho 68300 75 Cg 49
(F) Die 26150 56 Af 46
(D) Dieburg 64807 42 Ai 41
(L) Diekirch 9205* 42 Ag 41
(D) Diepholz 49356 42 Ai 38
(F) Dieppe 76200 41 Ab 41
(NL) Dieren 6950 42 Ag 38
(F) Dieulefit 26220 56 Af 46
(F) Dieuze 57260 42 Ag 42
(LT) Dieveniškės 17008 29 Cf 36
(N) Digermulen 8324 2 Bf 22
(F) Digne-les-Bains 04000* 56 Ag 46
(F) Digoin 71160 55 Ae 44
(TR) Digor 36670 79 Ed 50
(RUS) Digora 79 Ee 47
(RUS) Dij 24 Fi 29
(RUS) Dijaševo 34 Fd 35
(F) Dijon 21000* 56 Af 43
(RUS) Dijur 14 Fd 25
(S) Dikanäs 91094 9 Bf 25
(TR) Dikbıyık 55510 78 Dg 49
(TR) Dikili 75 Cg 51
(TR) Dikkaya 61500 78 Dk 50
(TR) Dikmen 57660 84 Db 54
(TR) Dikmen 57660 87 Ea 53
(B) Diksmuide 8600 41 Ac 39
(TR) Dilekyolu 29600 78 Dk 50
(GR) Dílesi 32009 82 Cd 52
(UA) Diljatyn 45 Ce 42
(D) Dillenburg 35683* 42 Ai 40
(D) Dillingen an der Donau 89407 43 Ba 42
(GR) Dímitra 40003 74 Cc 51
(RUS) Dimitrievka 32 Ea 38
(BG) Dimitrovgrad 6400* 75 Cf 48
(RUS) Dimitrovgrad 33 Ek 36
(SRB) Dimitrovgrad 18320 74 Cc 47
(GR) Dimitsána 22007 82 Cc 53
(GB) Dimovo 4757 59 Cc 47
(F) Dinan 22100* 40 Sh 42
(B) Dinant 5500 41 Ae 40
(TR) Dinar 03400 84 Da 52
(F) Dinard 35800* 40 Sh 42
(GB) Dinbych = Denbigh LL16 39 Sg 37
(GB) Dinbych-y-pysgodm = Tenby SA70 40 Sf 39
(TR) Dinek 76 Db 51
(TR) Dinek 84 Dc 53
(TR) Dinek 85 Dd 53
(D) Dingelstädt 37351 43 Ba 39
(IRL) Dingle = An Daingean 37 Rk 38
(D) Dingolfing 84130 43 Bc 42
(GB) Dingwall IV15 38 Sf 33
(D) Dinkelsbühl 91550 43 Ba 41
(RUS) Dinskaja 63 Dk 45
(D) Dinslaken 46535* 42 Ag 39
(F) Diou 03290 55 Ad 44
(GR) Dipótamos 64009 75 Ce 49
(TR) Direkli 78 Dg 51
(GR) Dirráhi 22023 82 Cc 53
(CH) Disentis/Mustér 7180 56 Ai 44
(GB) Diss IP22 41 Ab 38
(GR) Dístrato 44019 74 Cb 50
(RO) Ditrău 537090 60 Cf 44
(RUS) Diveevo 32 Ed 35
(F) Dives-sur-Mer 14160* 40 Sk 41
(RUS) Div'ja 23 Fg 32
(RUS) Divnoe 64 Ed 45
(RUS) Divnogor'e 48 Dk 40
(RUS) Divo 30 Db 35
(TR) Divriği 58300 78 Di 51
(TR) Diyadin 04900 79 Ed 51
(TR) Diyarbakır 21000* 87 Ea 53
(RUS) D'jakonovo 21 Ea 31
(RUS) D'jakovo, Verhovino- 21 Ed 31
(RUS) Djat'kovo 31 De 37
(RUS) Djukovo 22 Ef 32
(BG) Djulino 9108 76 Ch 48
(IS) Djúpavík 510 36 Qi 25
(IS) Djúpivogur 765 36 Rf 26
(N) Djupvik 2 Ca 21
(S) Djurås 17 Bf 30
(RUS) Djurtjuli 34 Fe 35
(RUS) Dmitrievka 51 Fe 38
(RUS) Dmitrievka 52 Fh 38
(RUS) Dmitriev-L'govskij 48 Df 38
(RUS) Dmitrievo 32 Eb 35
(RUS) Dmitrievšcina 49 Ec 38
(RUS) Dmitrievskoe 31 Di 33
(RUS) Dmitrov 31 Dh 34
(RUS) Dmitrovskij Pogost 32 Dk 35
(UA) Dmytrivka 27 Dc 40
(UA) Dmytrivka 48 Dg 42
(UA) Dmytrivka 63 Dg 44
(UA) Dneprodzeržinsk = Dniprodzeržyns'k 47 De 42
(UA) Dnepropetrovsk = Dnipropetrovs'k 48 Df 42
(RUS) Dneprovskoe 31 Dd 35
(MD) Dnestrovsc 3352 61 Ck 44
(UA) Dniprodzeržyns'k 47 De 42
(UA) Dnipropetrovs'k 48 Df 42
(UA) Dniprorudne 62 De 43
(RUS) Dno 19 Ck 33
(GB) Doagh BT39 37 Sd 36
(I) Dobbiaco = Toblach 39034 57 Bc 44
(LV) Dobele 3701* 29 Cd 34
(D) Döbeln 04720 43 Bd 39
(PL) Dobiegniew 66-520 27 Bf 38
(BIH) Doboj 74000* 59 Bi 46
(PL) Dobra 37-530 27 Bf 37
(RO) Dobra 337215 60 Cf 46
(SRB) Dobra 12224 59 Cb 46
(PL) Dobre Miasto 11-040 28 Ca 37
(BG) Dobrič 9300* 61 Ch 47
(RO) Dobriceni 247629 60 Ce 46
(RUS) Dobrinka 49 Ea 38
(RUS) Dobrino 25 Ge 32
(CZ) Dobříš 263 01 43 Be 41
(BY) Dobrjanka 47 Db 38
(RUS) Dobrjanka 23 Fg 32
(RUS) Dobrjatino 32 Eb 35
(PL) Dobrodzień 46-380 44 Bi 40
(RUS) Dobroe 32 Dk 38
(UA) Dobromyl' 45 Cc 41
(UA) Dobron' 45 Cc 42
(UA) Dobropil'l'a 48 Dh 42
(BIH) Dobro Polje 59 Bi 47
(RO) Dobrotești 147115 60 Ce 46
(UA) Dobrovelyčkivka 47 Db 42
(UA) Dobrovil'l'a 48 Dg 42
(RUS) Dobrovol'sk 29 Cc 36
(RUS) Dobruči 19 Ch 32
(BIH) Dobrun 59 Bk 47
(BY) Dobruš 47 Db 38
(PL) Dobrzyń nad Wisłą 87-610 44 Bk 38
(S) Docksta 87033 9 Bi 27
(GR) Dodóni 45500 74 Ca 51
(TR) Dodurga 19060 76 Ck 51
(TR) Dodurga 19060 77 De 50
(NL) Doetinchem 7001* 42 Ag 39
(TR) Doğanbey 42980 83 Cg 52
(TR) Doğanbey 42980 84 Db 53
(TR) Doğanbeyli 24450 78 Dk 51
(TR) Doğanca 37800 87 Ec 53
(TR) Doğanca 37800 87 Ed 53
(TR) Doğançay 47510 76 Da 50
(TR) Doğançayır 26960 76 Da 51
(TR) Doğanhisar 42930 84 Db 52
(TR) Doğankent 66740 78 Di 50
(TR) Doğankent 66740 85 Df 54
(TR) Doğanlı 14370 77 Df 51
(TR) Doğanoğlu 26860 76 Db 51
(TR) Doğanpınar 27920 86 Dk 54
(TR) Doğanşar 58780 78 Dh 50
(TR) Doğanşehir 44500 86 Dh 52
(TR) Doğansu 04530 79 Ec 51
(TR) Doğantepe 05070 77 Df 50
(TR) Doğanyol 44880 86 Dk 52
(TR) Doğanyurt 78 Dg 50
(TR) Döğer 76 Da 51
(I) Dogliani 12063 56 Ah 46
(TR) Doğruyol 79 Ed 49
(TR) Doğubayazıt 04400 79 Ee 51
(BG) Dojrenci 5550 60 Ce 47
(N) Dokka 2870 16 Ba 30
(NL) Dokkum 9100 26 Af 37
(TR) Dökmetepe 60800 78 Dg 50
(CZ) Doksy 472 01 43 Be 40
(BY) Dokšycy 30 Ch 36
(RO) Doktor Petru Groza = Ştei 415600 59 Cc 44
(UA) Dokučaevs'k 63 Dh 43
(RUS) Dokukino 33 Ef 34
(TR) Dokuz 11130 84 Dc 52
(TR) Dokuzyol 85 Dd 53
(F) Dol-de-Bretagne 35120 40 Si 42
(F) Dole 39100* 56 Af 43
(MK) Dolenci 7244 74 Cb 49
(GB) Dolgellau LL40 39 Sg 38
(RUS) Dolgie Budy 48 Df 39
(RUS) Dolgoderevenskoe 35 Gb 35
(RUS) Dolgoe 48 Dh 38
(RUS) Dolgorukovo 28 Ca 36
(RUS) Dolgorukovo 48 Di 38
(RUS) Dolgoščel'e 13 Ed 24
(I) Dolianova 09041 71 Ak 51
(RUS) Dolina Karzanov 64 Ec 47
(RUS) Dolina Narzanov 64 Ec 47
(SRB) Doljevac 59 Cb 47
(BG) Dolna Dikanja 2420 75 Cd 48
(BG) Dolna Mitropolia 5855 60 Ce 47
(BG) Dolni Čiflik 9120 76 Ch 48
(BG) Dolni Dăbnik 5870 60 Ce 47
(BG) Dolni Lom 3958 59 Cc 47
(SK) Dolný Kubín 026 01 44 Bk 41
(E) Dolores 81 Sk 52
(TR) Doluca 86 Dg 53
(UA) Dolyna 45 Ce 42
(UA) Dolyns'ka 47 Dc 42
(UA) Dolyns'ke 61 Ck 43
(RUS) Dolžanskaja 63 Dh 44
(TR) Domaniç 43850 76 Ck 51
(UA) Domanivka 62 Db 43
(PL) Domaradz 36-230 45 Cb 41
(RUS) Domaška 34 Fa 38
(CZ) Domažlice 344 01 43 Bc 41
(RUS) Dombaj 64 Eb 47
(RUS) Dombarovka 52 Fi 40
(RUS) Dombarovskij 52 Fk 40
(N) Dombås 2660 8 Ak 28
(F) Dombasle-sur-Meurthe 54110 42 Ag 42
(H) Dombóvár 7200 59 Bi 44
(H) Dombrád 4492 45 Cb 42
(F) Domérat 03410 55 Ac 44
(F) Domfront 61700 40 Sk 42
(D) Dömitz 19303 27 Bb 37
(RO) Domnești 077090 60 Ce 45
(GR) Domnísta 82 Cb 52
(RUS) Domodedovo 31 Dh 35
(I) Domodóssola 28845 56 Ai 44
(F) Dompaire 88270 42 Ag 42
(F) Dompierre-sur-Besbre 03290 55 Ad 44
(SLO) Domžale 1230 58 Be 44
(RUS) Don 23 Fd 29
(D) Donaueschingen 78166 56 Ai 43
(D) Donauwörth 86609 43 Ba 42
(E) Don Benito 06400 68 Se 52
(GB) Doncaster DN1 39 Si 37
(MD) Dondjušany = Dondușeni 5106 46 Ch 42
(MD) Dondușeni 5106 46 Ch 42
(RUS) Doneck 48 Dk 42
(UA) Donec'k 63 Dh 43
(UA) Doneck = Donec'k 63 Dh 43
(RUS) Doneckij, Ust'- 64 Ea 43
(RUS) Doneckoe 51 Fe 39
(UA) Donec'kyj 48 Di 42
(IRL) Donegal = Dún na nGall 37 Sb 36
(TR) Dönemeç 87 Ed 52
(HR) Donja Brela 58 Bg 47
(HR) Donja Konjšćina 58 Bg 44
(SRB) Donja Rudnica 59 Ca 47
(HR) Donja Stupnica 58 Bg 45
(HR) Donji Lapac 58 Bf 46
(HR) Donji Miholjac 59 Bi 45
(SRB) Donji Milanovac 19220 59 Cc 46
(HR) Donji Muć 58 Bg 47
(HR) Donji Srb 58 Bg 46
(BIH) Donji Vakuf 58 Bh 46
(F) Donjon, le 03130 55 Ad 44
(E) Donostia-San Sebastián 20001 54 Si 47
(RUS) Donskoe 48 Di 38
(RUS) Donskoe 52 Fh 39
(RUS) Donskoe 64 Eb 45
(RUS) Donskoj 31 Di 37
(F) Donzère 26290 55 Ae 46
(F) Donzy 58220 55 Ad 43
(B) Doornik = Tournai 7500 41 Ad 40
(RUS) Dor 21 Eb 32
(F) Dorat, le 87210 55 Ab 44
(GB) Dorchester OX10 40 Sh 40
(NL) Dordrecht 3300* 41 Ae 39
(D) Dorfen 84405 43 Bc 42
(A) Dörfles 2115 44 Bg 42
(I) Dorgali 08022 71 Ak 50
(GR) Dório 24011 82 Cb 53
(GR) Dorísko 68500 75 Cg 50
(GB) Dorking RH4 40 Sk 39
(D) Dormagen 41539* 42 Ag 39
(F) Dormans 51700 41 Ad 41
(RO) Dor Mărunt 917055 60 Cg 46
(A) Dornbirn 6850* 57 Ak 43
(GB) Dornoch IV25 38 Sf 33




Dornoch 149

(RO) Dorobanţu 827070 ... 61 Ci 46
(RUS) Dorobino ... 31 Dh 37
(RUS) Dorofeevo ... 32 Dk 35
(RUS) Dorogobuž ... 31 Dd 36
(RUS) Dorogorskoe ... 13 Ee 25
(RO) Dorohoi 715200 ... 60 Cg 43
(RUS) Dorohovo ... 31 Dg 35
(RUS) Dorošata ... 22 Fb 33
(S) Dorotea 91701 ... 9 Bg 26
(D) Dorsten 46282* ... 42 Ag 39
(TR) Dörtdivan ... 77 Dc 50
(D) Dortmund 44135* ... 42 Ah 39
(TR) Dörtyol 05800 ... 85 Df 52
(TR) Dörtyol 05800 ... 85 Dg 54
(D) Dorum 27632 ... 26 Ai 37
(TR) Dorutay ... 87 Ee 52
(RUS) Doščatoe ... 32 Ec 35
(TR) Döşemealtı ... 84 Da 53
(E) Dos Hermanas 41700 ... 80 Se 53
(BG) Dospat 4831 ... 75 Ce 49
(F) Douai 59500 ... 41 Ad 40
(F) Douarnenez 29100 ... 40 Sf 42
(F) Douchy 45220 ... 55 Ad 43
(F) Doudeville 76560 ... 41 Aa 41
(F) Doué-la-Fontaine 49700 ... 54 Sk 43
(GB) Douglas ML12 ... 39 Sg 35
(GBM) Douglas IM1 ... 39 Sf 36
(F) Doullens 80600 ... 41 Ac 40
(GB) Dounreay KW14 ... 38 Sg 32
(F) Dourdan 91410 ... 41 Ac 42
(GB) Dover CT16 ... 41 Ab 39
(UA) Dovhe ... 45 Cd 42
(N) Dovre 2662 ... 8 Ak 29
(BY) Dovsk ... 30 Da 37
(GB) Downham Market PE38 ... 41 Aa 38
(GB) Downpatrick BT30 ... 37 Se 36
(GR) Doxāto ... 75 Ce 49
(UA) Drabiv ... 47 Dc 41
(NL) Drachten 9200* ... 26 Ag 37
(RO) Dragalina 917080 ... 61 Ch 46
(RO) Drăgăneşti-Olt 235400 ... 60 Ce 46
(RO) Drăgăneşti-Vlaşca 147135 ... 60 Cf 46
(BG) Draganovo 9349 ... 60 Cf 47
(RKS) Dragaš = Dragash 22000 ... 74 Ca 48
(RKS) Dragash = Dragaš 22000 ... 74 Ca 48
(RO) Drăgăşani 245700 ... 60 Ce 46
(SRB) Draglica 31317 ... 59 Bk 47
(AL) Dragoç ... 74 Bk 48
(BG) Dragoman 2210 ... 74 Cc 48
(RO) Dragomireşti 617165 ... 61 Ch 44
(BG) Dragomirovo 5285 ... 60 Cf 47
(FIN) Dragsfjärd 25870 ... 18 Cc 30
(F) Draguignan 83300* ... 56 Ag 47
(RUS) Dragunskoe ... 48 Dg 40
(RO) Drăguşeni 807115 ... 60 Cg 43
(BY) Drahičyn ... 46 Cf 38
(GR) Drakótripa 43060 ... 74 Cb 51
(GR) Dráma 66100 ... 75 Ce 49
(N) Drammen 3004* ... 16 Ba 31
(N) Drangedal 3750 ... 16 Ak 31
(IS) Drangsnes 510 ... 36 Qi 25
(PL) Drawsko Pomorskie 78-500 ... 27 Bf 37
(PL) Drążdżewo 06-214 ... 28 Cb 37
(BG) Drenovec 3920 ... 59 Cc 47
(D) Dresden 01067* ... 43 Bd 39
(BY) Drètun' ... 30 Ck 35
(F) Dreux 28100* ... 41 Ab 42
(N) Drevsjø 2443 ... 9 Bc 29
(PL) Drezdenko 66-530 ... 27 Bf 38
(BIH) Drežnica ... 57 Bd 44
(GB) Driffield YO25 ... 39 Sk 36
(GR) Drimó ... 82 Cc 54
(GR) Drimós 57200 ... 74 Cc 50
(BG) Drjanovo 6493 ... 75 Cf 48
(RUS) Drjazgi ... 48 Dk 38
(HR) Drniš ... 58 Bg 47
(N) Drøbak 1440 ... 16 Ba 31
(RO) Drobeta-Turnu Severin 000220* . 59 Cc 46
(MD) Drochia 5200 ... 46 Ch 42
(IRL) Drogheda = Droichead Átha ... 37 Sd 37
(UA) Drogobyč = Drohobyč ... 45 Cd 41
(UA) Drohobyč ... 45 Cd 41
(IRL) Droichead Átha = Drogheda ... 37 Sd 37
(IRL) Droichead na Bandan = Bandan 37 Sb 39
(IRL) Droim Seanbho ... 37 Sb 36
(IRL) Dromad ... 37 Sc 37
(IRL) Dromod = Dromad ... 37 Sc 37
(GB) Dromore BT78 ... 37 Sc 36
(IRL) Dromore West ... 37 Sb 36
(I) Dronero 12025 ... 56 Ah 46
(NL) Dronten 8250* ... 42 Af 38
(A) Drosendorf Stadt-Zissersdorf 2095 ... 44 Bf 42
(RUS) Droskovo ... 48 Dg 38
(GR) Drossopigí 47043 ... 74 Cb 51
(UA) Drozdyn' ... 46 Ch 39
(SRB) Drume ... 74 Bk 48
(IRL) Drumshanbo = Droim Seanbho . 37 Sb 36
(LT) Druskininkai 66001 ... 29 Cd 36
(UA) Družba ... 47 Dd 38
(UA) Družbivka ... 62 De 44
(RUS) Družinino ... 35 Fk 34
(UA) Družkivka ... 48 Dh 42
(UA) Družkovka = Družkivka ... 48 Dh 42
(RUS) Družnyj ... 35 Gb 35
(HR) Drvenik ... 73 Bh 47
(P) Duas Igrejas 3560-048* ... 68 Sd 49
(MD) Dubăsari 4500 ... 61 Ck 43
(RUS) Dubec ... 20 Di 32
(D) Düben, Bad 04849 ... 43 Bc 39
(RUS) Dubenki ... 33 Eg 36
(RUS) Dubenskij ... 52 Fg 39
(MD) Dubèsar' = Dubăsari 4500 ... 61 Ck 43
(RUS) Dub"jazy ... 33 Ek 34
(RUS) Dubki ... 50 Eg 39
(IRL) Dublin = Baile Átha Cliath ... 37 Sd 37
(RUS) Dubna ... 31 Dg 36
(RUS) Dubna ... 31 Dh 34
(UA) Dubno ... 46 Cf 40
(MD) Dubossary = Dubăsari 4500 ... 61 Ck 43
(BIH) Duboštica ... 59 Bi 46
(SRB) Dubovac 26224 ... 59 Cb 46
(RUS) Dubovaja Gora ... 34 Ff 34
(RUS) Dubovaja Rošča ... 31 Dg 37
(UA) Dubove ... 45 Cd 42
(UA) Dubovjazivka ... 47 Dd 39
(RUS) Dubovka ... 49 Ee 41
(RUS) Dubovo ... 23 Ff 33
(RUS) Dubovskoe ... 64 Ec 43
(RUS) Dubovyj Ovrag ... 49 Ee 42
(RUS) Dubovyj Umet ... 34 Fa 38
(RUS) Dubrovino ... 24 Gc 32
(RUS) Dubrovka ... 22 Fb 31
(RUS) Dubrovka ... 30 Ci 34
(RUS) Dubrovka ... 31 Dd 37
(RUS) Dubrovka ... 49 Eb 39
(RUS) Dubrovki ... 32 Ed 37
(BY) Dubrovna ... 30 Da 36
(HR) Dubrovnik ... 73 Bi 48
(RUS) Dubrovnoe ... 25 Gk 33
(RUS) Dubrovo ... 20 Dh 31
(RUS) Dubrovo ... 34 Fe 34
(UA) Dubrovycja ... 46 Cg 39
(F) Ducey 50220 ... 40 Si 42
(UA) Duchanivka ... 47 Dd 39
(CZ) Duchcov 419 01 ... 43 Bd 40
(L) Dudelange 3401 ... 42 Ag 41
(D) Duderstadt 37115 ... 43 Ba 39
(RO) Dudeşti 817040 ... 61 Ch 46
(GB) Dudley DY3 ... 40 Sh 38
(RUS) Dudorovskij ... 31 Df 37
(E) Dueñas 34210 ... 69 Sf 49
(GB) Dufftown AB55 ... 38 Sg 33
(SRB) Duga Poljana 36312 ... 59 Ca 47
(HR) Duga Resa ... 58 Bf 45
(RUS) Dugna ... 31 Dg 36
(HR) Dugo Selo ... 58 Bg 45
(RUS) Duhovnickoe ... 50 Ei 38
(RUS) Duhovščina ... 30 Dc 35
(F) Duingt 74410 ... 56 Ag 45
(I) Duino-Aurisina 34013 ... 57 Bd 45
(D) Duisburg 47051* ... 42 Ag 39
(AL) Dukëz ... 74 Bk 50
(PL) Dukla 38-450 ... 45 Cb 41
(BY) Dukora ... 30 Ch 37
(LT) Dūkštas 30042 ... 29 Cg 35
(RUS) Duljapino ... 21 Ea 33
(D) Dülmen 48249 ... 42 Ah 39
(BG) Dulovo 7650 ... 61 Ch 47
(GB) Dumbarton G82 ... 39 Sf 35
(GB) Dumfries DG1 ... 39 Sg 35
(RUS) Duminiči ... 31 Df 37
(TR) Dumlu ... 79 Eb 50
(TR) Dumluca 26600 ... 76 Db 51
(TR) Dumlupınar 43820 ... 84 Ck 52
(H) Dunaföldvár 7020 ... 59 Bi 44
(UA) Dunajivci ... 46 Cg 41
(UA) Dunajivci ... 46 Cg 42
(SK) Dunajská Streda 929 01 ... 58 Bh 43
(H) Dunaszekcső ... 59 Bi 44
(H) Dunaújváros 2400 ... 59 Bi 44
(BG) Dunavci 6145 ... 59 Cc 47
(GB) Dunbar EH42 ... 39 Sh 35
(GB) Dunblane FK15 ... 38 Sg 34
(LV) Dundaga 3270 ... 18 Cc 33
(IRL) Dundalk = Dún Dealgan ... 37 Sd 36
(IRL) Dún Dealgan = Dundalk ... 37 Sd 36
(GB) Dundee DD3 ... 38 Sh 34
(GB) Dunfermline KY11 ... 38 Sg 34
(GB) Dungannon BT71 ... 37 Sd 36
(IRL) Dún Gar ... 37 Sb 37
(IRL) Dún Garbhán = Dungarvan ... 37 Sc 38
(IRL) Dungarvan = Dún Garbhán ... 37 Sc 38
(GB) Dungiven BT47 ... 37 Sd 36
(IRL) Dunglow = An Clochán Liath ... 37 Sb 36
(MK) Dunje 7506 ... 74 Cb 49
(GB) Dunkeld ... 38 Sg 34
(F) Dunkerque 59140* ... 41 Ac 39
(IRL) Dún Laoghaire ... 37 Sd 37
(IRL) Dunleary = Dún Laoghaire ... 37 Sd 37
(IRL) Dún Mánmhaí ... 37 Sa 39
(IRL) Dunmanway = DúnMńmhaí ... 37 Sa 39
(IRL) Dún Mor ... 37 Sb 37
(IRL) Dunmore = Dún Mor ... 37 Sb 37
(IRL) Dún na nGall ... 37 Sb 36
(IRL) Dún na Séad = Baltimore ... 37 Sa 39
(GB) Dunoon PA23 ... 39 Sf 35
(IRL) Dún Selachainn ... 37 Sd 37
(IRL) Dunshaughlin = Dún Selachainn 37 Sd 37
(F) Dun-sur-Auron 18130 ... 55 Ac 44
(F) Dun-sur-Meuse 55110 ... 42 Af 41
(GB) Dunvegan IV55 ... 38 Sd 33
(BG) Dupnica 2600 ... 75 Cd 48
(TR) Durağan 57700 ... 77 Df 49
(TR) Durak 01470 ... 76 Ci 51
(E) Durango 48200 ... 54 Sh 47
(F) Duras 47120 ... 54 Aa 46
(LV) Durbe 3440 ... 28 Cb 34
(HR) Đurđenovac ... 59 Bi 45
(HR) Đurđevac ... 58 Bh 44
(D) Düren 52349* ... 42 Ag 40
(GB) Durham DH1 ... 39 Si 36
(TR) Durhasan ... 84 Ci 52
(IRL) Durlas = Thurles ... 37 Sc 38
(GB) Durness IV27 ... 38 Sf 32
(A) Dürnstein 3601 ... 44 Bf 42
(D) Dürrenberg, Bad 06231 ... 43 Bc 39
(AL) Durrës ... 74 Bk 49
(IRL) Durrow = Darú ... 37 Sc 38
(TR) Dursunbey 10800 ... 76 Ci 51
(F) Durtal 49430 ... 54 Sk 43
(TR) Durusu 34557 ... 76 Ci 49
(LT) Dusetos 32029 ... 29 Cf 35
(BIH) Dusina ... 58 Bh 47
(D) Düsseldorf 40210* ... 42 Ag 39
(TR) Dutluca ... 78 Di 51
(RUS) Dutovo ... 15 Fg 27
(RUS) Duvan ... 35 Fh 35
(RUS) Duvanej, Udel'no- ... 34 Ff 35
(TR) Düvertepe ... 76 Ci 51
(BIH) Duvno ... 58 Bh 47
(TR) Düzağaç ... 86 Dk 52
(TR) Düzbağ 46000 ... 86 Dh 53
(TR) Düzce ... 76 Db 50
(TR) Düzgeçit ... 79 Ed 50
(TR) Düziçi 01970 ... 86 Dg 53
(TR) Düzköy 61390 ... 78 Dk 50
(BG) Dve Mogili 7150 ... 60 Cf 47
(RUS) Dvinskoj ... 13 Ef 28
(RUS) Dvojni ... 32 Dk 35
(HR) Dvor ... 58 Bg 45
(UA) Dvorična ... 48 Dh 41
(RUS) Dvoriki ... 31 Di 34
(RUS) Dvorišči ... 20 Df 32
(RUS) Dvurečensk ... 35 Gb 34
(CZ) Dvůr Králové nad Labem 544 01* ... 44 Bf 40
(GB) Dyce AB21 ... 38 Sh 33
(UA) Dykan'ka ... 47 De 41
(UA) Dymer ... 47 Da 40
(RUS) Dymnica ... 21 Ec 33
(UA) Dymytrove ... 47 Dc 42
(PL) Dynów 36-065 ... 45 Cc 41
(N) Dyrnes ... 8 Ah 27
(RUS) Džabyk ... 35 Ga 37
(RUS) Džalil' ... 34 Fc 35
(RUS) Džalykovo ... 65 Eh 45
(UA) Džankoj ... 62 De 45
(RUS) Dzeržinsk ... 32 Ed 34
(UA) Dzeržyns'k ... 48 Dh 42
(PL) Działdowo 13-200 ... 28 Ca 37
(PL) Dzierzgoń 82-440 ... 28 Bk 37
(PL) Dzierżoniów 58-200 ... 44 Bg 40
(RUS) Dzinaga ... 79 Ed 48
(BY) Dzisna ... 30 Ci 35
(BY) Dzivin ... 45 Ce 39
(BY) Dzjarečyn ... 29 Ce 37
(BY) Dzjaržynsk ... 30 Ch 37
(BY) Dzjatlava ... 29 Cf 37
(RUS) Džubga ... 63 Di 46
(UA) Džuryn ... 46 Ci 42
(PL) Dźwierzuty 12-120 ... 28 Ca 37


# E


(IRL) Eachroim ... 37 Sd 38
(IRL) Éadan Doire = Edenderry ... 37 Sc 37
(FIN) Eanodat = Enontekiö 99401 ... 3 Cd 22
(IRL) Eas Geitine ... 37 Sb 38
(GB) Eastbourne BN20 ... 41 Aa 40
(GB) East Dereham ... 41 Aa 38
(GB) East Kilbride G74 ... 39 Sf 35
(F) Eauze 32800 ... 54 Aa 47
(TR) Ebecik ... 84 Ci 53
(DK) Ebeltoft 8400 ... 27 Ba 34
(D) Eberbach 69412 ... 42 Ai 41
(D) Ebersbach-Neugersdorf 04643 .. 43 Be 39
(A) Eberstein 9372 ... 58 Be 44
(D) Eberswalde 16225 ... 27 Bd 38
(I) Éboli 84025 ... 73 Bf 50
(D) Ebstorf 29574 ... 27 Ba 37
(TR) Eceabat 17900 ... 75 Cg 50
(GB) Echt AB32 ... 38 Sh 33
(L) Echternach 6408* ... 42 Ag 41
(E) Écija 41400 ... 80 Se 53
(D) Eckernförde 24340 ... 26 Ak 36
(AX) Eckerö 22271 ... 18 Bk 30
(F) Ecommoy ... 54 Aa 43
(F) Ecueillé 36240 ... 55 Ab 43
(S) Ed ... 16 Bb 32
(NL) Ede 6710 ... 42 Af 38
(S) Edefors 83070 ... 10 Ca 24
(IRL) Edenderry = Éadan Doire ... 37 Sc 37
(GR) Édessa 58200 ... 74 Cc 50
(IRL) Edgeworthstown = Meathas Troim ... 37 Sc 37
(GB) Edinburgh KY11 ... 39 Sg 35
(TR) Edincik 10640 ... 76 Ch 50
(MD) Edincy = Edineţ 4600 ... 46 Ch 42
(MD) Edinec = Edineţ 4600 ... 46 Ch 42
(MD) Edineţ 4600 ... 46 Ch 42
(TR) Edirne 22000* ... 75 Cg 49
(I) Èdolo 25048 ... 57 Ba 44
(TR) Edremit 65170 ... 75 Ch 51
(S) Edsbro 76031 ... 17 Bi 31
(S) Edsbruk 59098 ... 17 Bg 32
(S) Edsbyn 82801 ... 17 Bf 29
(S) Edsele 88041 ... 9 Bg 27
(S) Edsvalla 66052 ... 17 Bd 31
(BY) Ëdy ... 30 Ch 35
(B) Eeklo 9900 ... 41 Ad 39
(TR) Efeköy ... 84 Da 52
(A) Eferding 4070 ... 43 Be 42
(RUS) Efimovka ... 51 Fc 38
(RUS) Efimovskij ... 20 De 31
(GR) Efíra 27069 ... 82 Cb 53
(TR) Eflâni 67180 ... 77 Dc 49
(RO) Eforie Nord 905350 ... 61 Ci 46
(RUS) Efremov ... 31 Di 37
(RUS) Efremo-Zykovo ... 34 Fd 37
(RUS) Efrosimovka ... 48 Dg 38
(S) Egby 38701 ... 28 Bg 34
(H) Eger ... 59 Ca 43
(TR) Eğerci 67840 ... 76 Db 49
(N) Egersund 4370 ... 16 Ag 32
(N) Eggedal 3359 ... 16 Ak 30
(D) Eggenfelden 84307 ... 43 Bc 42
(B) Eghezée 5310 ... 41 Ae 40
(PL) Egiertowo 83-314 ... 28 Bi 36
(TR) Eğil 21360 ... 87 Ea 52
(IS) Egilsstaðir 700* ... 36 Rf 25
(GR) Egínio 59032 ... 74 Cc 50
(GR) Égio 25100 ... 82 Cc 52
(TR) Eğirdir 32500 ... 84 Da 53
(F) Egletons 19300 ... 55 Ac 45
(NL) Egmond aan Zee 1930 ... 26 Ae 38
(RUS) Egor'e ... 31 Dg 35
(RUS) Egor'evsk ... 32 Dk 35
(RUS) Egorlykskaja ... 64 Ea 44
(RUS) Egorovo ... 6 Eh 24
(RUS) Egošinskaja ... 22 Ei 30
(TR) Eğribayat ... 84 Dc 52
(DK) Egtved 6040 ... 26 Ak 35
(F) Eguzon-Chatôme ... 55 Ab 44
(RUS) Egva ... 23 Fe 31
(D) Ehingen (Donau) 89584 ... 42 Ak 42
(GR) Ehīnos ... 75 Ce 49
(N) Ehodak ... 3 Cd 22
(A) Eichgraben 3032 ... 44 Bf 42
(D) Eichstätt 85072 ... 43 Bb 42
(N) Eide 6409 ... 8 Ah 28
(N) Eidfjord 5783 ... 16 Ah 30
(FR) Eiði 470 ... 38 Sc 28
(N) Eidsdal 6215 ... 8 Ah 28
(N) Eidskog ... 17 Bc 30
(N) Eidsvåg 6636 ... 8 Ai 28
(N) Eidsvoll 2080 ... 16 Bb 30
(N) Eikefjord 6940 ... 16 Af 29
(D) Eilenburg 04838 ... 43 Bc 39
(N) Eina 2843 ... 16 Ba 30
(D) Einbeck 37547 ... 42 Ak 39
(NL) Eindhoven 5600* ... 42 Af 39
(IS) Einholt 310 ... 36 Qh 26
(D) Eisenach 99817 ... 43 Ba 40
(A) Eisenerz 8790 ... 58 Be 43
(D) Eisenhüttenstadt 15890 ... 43 Be 38
(A) Eisenkappel 9135 ... 58 Be 44
(A) Eisenstadt 7000* ... 58 Bg 43
(D) Eisfeld 98673 ... 43 Ba 40
(LT) Eišiškės 17017 ... 29 Cf 36
(D) Eisleben, Lutherstadt 06295 ... 43 Bb 39
(N) Eivindvik 5966 ... 16 Af 30
(E) Eivissa 07800 ... 70 Ab 52
(FR) Ejde = Eiði 470 ... 38 Sc 28
(RUS) Ėjna ... 4 Dc 21
(RUS) Ejsk ... 63 Di 44
(RUS) Ejskoe Ukreplenie ... 63 Di 44
(RUS) Ekaterinburg ... 35 Ga 34
(RUS) Ekaterinovka ... 48 Di 38
(RUS) Ekaterinovka ... 48 Dk 40
(RUS) Ekaterinovka ... 49 Ee 38
(FIN) Ekenäs 10600* ... 18 Cd 31
(S) Ekenäs ... 17 Bd 32
(B) Ekeren 2180 ... 41 Ae 39
(RUS) Ekimoviči ... 31 Dd 36
(TR) Ekinözü 46360 ... 86 Dh 52
(TR) Ekinyolu ... 87 Ea 52
(S) Ekshärad 68050 ... 17 Bd 30
(TR) Ekşili 07145 ... 84 Da 53
(S) Eksjö 57501* ... 17 Be 33
(RUS) Elabuga ... 34 Fc 35
(GR) Elafónissos 23053 ... 82 Cc 54
(RUS) Elan' ... 24 Gd 33
(RUS) Elan' ... 49 Ed 40
(RUS) Elan'-Kolenovskij ... 49 Eb 39
(GR) Elassóna 40200 ... 74 Cc 51
(RUS) Elat'ma ... 32 Eb 36
(RUS) Elaur ... 33 Ei 37
(TR) Elâzığ 23000* ... 86 Dk 52
(AL) Elbasan ... 74 Ca 49
(TR) Elbaşı 38610 ... 85 Df 52
(F) Elbeuf 76500 ... 41 Aa 41
(TR) Elbeyli ... 86 Dh 54
(TR) Elbistan 46300 ... 86 Dh 52
(PL) Elbląg 82-300 ... 28 Bk 36
(RUS) Él'brus ... 64 Ec 47
(RUS) El'brus ... 79 Ec 47
(RUS) El'brusskij ... 64 Ec 47
(E) Elche = Elx 03201 ... 81 Sk 52
(RUS) El'cy ... 31 Dd 34
(E) Elda 03600 ... 70 Sk 52
(TR) Eldîvan ... 77 Dd 50
(IS) Eldjarnsstaðir 540 ... 36 Ql 25
(RUS) Elec ... 48 Di 38
(RUS) Eleckaja Lozovka ... 48 Dk 38
(GR) Elefsína 19201 ... 82 Cd 52
(GR) Eleftheroupoli ... 75 Ce 50
(RUS) Elegino ... 21 Eb 32
(LV) Eleja 3023 ... 29 Cd 34
(H) Elek 5742 ... 59 Cb 44
(LT) Elektrėnai 26001 ... 29 Ce 36
(RUS) Èlektrostal' ... 31 Di 35
(RUS) Èlektrougli ... 31 Di 35
(BG) Elena 5070 ... 75 Cf 48
(RUS) Elenovka ... 52 Fk 40
(RUS) Elenskij ... 31 Df 37
(TR) Eleşkirt 04600 ... 79 Ec 51
(N) Elgå ... 8 Bb 28
(GB) Elgin IV30 ... 38 Sg 33
(RUS) Él'hotovo ... 64 Ee 47
(RUS) El'hotovo ... 79 Ee 47
(RUS) Elhovka ... 34 Fa 37
(BG) Elhovo 6064 ... 75 Cg 48
(GB) Elie KY9 ... 38 Sh 34
(FIN) Elimäki 47201 ... 18 Cg 30
(RUS) Elionka ... 47 Dc 38
(RUS) Èlista ... 64 Ee 44
(N) Elistranda ... 8 Ba 27
(RUS) Elizavetopol'skoe ... 53 Ga 38
(PL) Ełk 19-300 ... 29 Cc 37
(RUS) El'kib ... 14 Ei 27
(GB) Ellon AB41 ... 38 Sh 33
(S) Ellös 47401 ... 16 Bb 32
(D) Ellwangen (Jagst) 73479 ... 43 Ba 42
(TR) Elmadağ 06780 ... 77 Dd 51
(TR) Elmalı ... 75 Cg 50
(TR) Elmalı ... 79 Ea 51
(TR) Elmalı ... 84 Ck 54
(TR) Elmalı ... 85 Df 52
(TR) Elmalı ... 86 Dh 52
(TR) Elmalıdere ... 79 Ec 51
(D) Elmshorn 25335* ... 26 Ak 37
(F) Elne 66200* ... 70 Ac 48
(N) Elnesvågan 6409 ... 8 Ah 28
(RUS) El'niki ... 32 Ed 36
(RUS) El'nja ... 31 Dd 36
(RUS) Eloga ... 23 Fd 31
(RUS) Elovo ... 34 Fe 33
(RUS) Elšanka ... 50 Eg 39
(RUS) Elšanka ... 52 Ff 39
(RUS) Elšanka Pervaja ... 34 Fb 38
(N) Elsfjord 8672 ... 9 Bd 24
(BY) El'sk ... 46 Ck 39
(N) Elstad ... 16 Ba 29
(D) Elsterwerda 04910 ... 43 Bd 39
(D) Eltmann 97483 ... 43 Ba 41
(EST) Elva 61503* ... 18 Cg 32
(TR) Elvanlı 33730 ... 85 De 54
(P) Elvas 7350-001* ... 80 Sc 52
(F) Elven 56250 ... 54 Sh 43
(N) Elverum 2406* ... 16 Bb 30
(E) Elx = Elche ... 81 Sk 52
(GB) Ely CB6 ... 41 Aa 38
(D) Elze 31008 ... 42 Ak 38
(S) Emådalen ... 17 Be 29
(RUS) Emanželinsk ... 35 Gb 36
(GR) Embório 85200 ... 83 Cf 54
(LV) Embūte 3436 ... 28 Cb 34
(RUS) Emca ... 12 Ea 27
(D) Emden 26721* ... 26 Ah 37
(RUS) Emeck ... 13 Eb 27
(TR) Emek ... 87 Ed 52
(RUS) Emel'janovka ... 11 Da 27
(RUS) Emel'janovskaja ... 13 Eb 26
(TR) Emet 43700 ... 76 Ck 51
(TR) Emiralem 35670 ... 83 Ch 52
(TR) Emirdağ 03600 ... 76 Db 51
(TR) Emirgazi 42910 ... 85 Dd 53
(TR) Emirler ... 77 Dc 51
(TR) Emirler ... 86 Dg 53
(TR) Emiryusuf ... 78 Dg 49
(D) Emlichheim 49824 ... 42 Ag 38
(S) Emmaboda 36101 ... 27 Bf 34
(EST) Emmaste 92001 ... 18 Cc 32
(NL) Emmeloord 8300* ... 26 Af 38
(NL) Emmen 7722 ... 26 Ag 38
(D) Emmendingen 79312 ... 42 Ah 42
(D) Emmerich am Rhein 46446 ... 42 Ag 39
(BG) Emona 8252 ... 76 Ch 48


**150** **Dorobanţu**

(GR) Empessós 30017 74 Cb 51
(I) Émpoli 50053 57 Ba 47
(D) Ems, Bad 56130 42 Ah 40
(D) Emsdetten 48282 42 Ah 38
(RUS) Emva 14 Fa 28
(RUS) Ëna 4 Db 23
(UA) Enakievo = Jenakijeve 48 Di 42
(S) Enånger 82519 17 Bh 29
(TR) Encekler 84 Ci 52
(N) Endrespless 9 Bd 25
(RUS) Ènergetik 52 Fi 39
(TR) Enez 22700 75 Cg 50
(IRL) Enfield = An Bóthar Bui 37 Sd 37
(CH) Engelberg 6390 56 Ai 44
(A) Engelhartszell 4090* 43 Bd 42
(RUS) Èngel's 50 Eg 39
(N) Engjan 8 Ai 27
(RUS) Engozero 11 Dd 25
(LV) Engure 3113 18 Cd 33
(RUS) Enjukovo 20 Dh 31
(NL) Enkhuizen 1600 26 Af 38
(S) Enköping 74500* 17 Bh 31
(I) Enna 94100 72 Be 53
(TR) Enne 76 Ck 51
(IRL) Ennis = Inis 37 Sb 38
(IRL) Enniscorthy = Inis Córthaidh 37 Sd 38
(IRL) Ennis Díomáin 37 Sa 38
(GB) Enniskillen BT74 37 Sc 36
(IRL) Ennistymon = Ennis Díomáin 37 Sa 38
(A) Enns 4470* 43 Be 42
(FIN) Eno 81201 11 Da 28
(N) Enodden 8 Ba 28
(FIN) Enonkoski 58175 11 Ci 28
(FIN) Enontekiö 99401 3 Cd 22
(RUS) Enotaevka 65 Eg 43
(NL) Enschede 7500* 42 Ag 38
(F) Entrains-sur-Nohain 58410 55 Ad 43
(F) Entraygues-sur-Truyère 12140 55 Ac 46
(F) Entrevaux 04320 56 Ag 47
(P) Entroncamento 2330-001* 68 Sb 51
(H) Enying 8130 59 Bi 44
(IRL) Eochaill = Youghal 37 Sc 39
(GR) Epanomí 57500 74 Cc 50
(NL) Epe 48599 42 Af 38
(F) Épernay 51200* 41 Ad 41
(RUS) Epifan' 31 Di 37
(F) Épinac 71360 55 Ae 44
(F) Épinal 88000* 42 Ag 42
(CY) Episkopi Bay 84 Dc 56
(D) Eppingen 75031 42 Ai 41
(GB) Epsom KT19 40 Sk 39
(I) Eraclea 30020 57 Bc 45
(RUS) Erahtur 32 Eb 36
(TR) Erarslan 05000 77 Df 50
(GR) Erátini 33058 82 Cc 52
(GR) Erátira 50003 74 Cb 50
(TR) Erbaa 60500* 78 Dg 50
(F) Erbalunga 20222 71 Ak 48
(TR) Erçek 65210 87 Ed 52
(TR) Erciş 65400 79 Ed 51
(H) Érd 2030 59 Bi 43
(TR) Erdek 10500 76 Ch 50
(TR) Erdemli 33730* 85 De 54
(F) Erdeven 56410 54 Sg 43
(D) Erding 85435 43 Bb 42
(RUS) Erdnievskij 65 Eg 44
(TR) Ereğli 42310* 76 Db 49
(TR) Ereğli 42310* 85 De 53
(TR) Erentepe 49510 79 Ec 51
(GR) Eressós 81105 75 Cf 51
(GR) Erétria 37400 82 Cd 52
(N) Erfjord 16 Ag 31
(D) Erfurt 99084* 43 Bb 40
(TR) Erganı 86 Dk 52
(RUS) Ergeninskij 64 Ee 43
(LV) Ērgļi 4840 29 Cf 34
(P) Ericeira 2655-001* 68 Sa 52
(TR) Erikli 57800 75 Cg 50
(S) Eriksund 84196 9 Bf 28
(S) Eriksmåla 36194 27 Bf 34
(S) Eringsboda 37017 27 Bf 34
(GR) Erithrés 19008 82 Cd 52
(RUS) Erken-Šahar 64 Eb 46
(TR) Erkilet 38170 85 Df 52
(E) Erla 50611 70 Sk 48
(D) Erlangen 91052* 43 Bb 41
(A) Erlsbach 9963 57 Bc 44
(RUS) Ermakovo 21 Dk 32
(RUS) Ermeneevo 34 Fd 36
(TR) Ermenek 70400 84 Dc 54
(P) Ermesinde 4445-274* 68 Sb 49
(RUS) Ërmica 6 Fc 24
(GR) Ermióni 21051 82 Cd 53
(RUS) Ermiš' 32 Ec 36
(RUS) Ermolaevo 52 Ff 38
(RUS) Ermolino 31 Dh 34
(RUS) Ermolkino 34 Fd 36
(GR) Ermoúpoli 84100 82 Ce 53
(RUS) Èrna 23 Ff 31
(F) Ernée 53500 40 Sk 42
(RO) Ernei 547215 60 Ce 44
(F) Erquy 22430 40 Sh 42
(AL) Ersekë 74 Ca 50
(RUS) Erši 31 De 36
(RUS) Eršov 50 Eg 41
(RUS) Eršov 50 Ei 39
(RUS) Eršovo 20 Di 31
(F) Erstein 67150 42 Ah 42
(RUS) Ertil' 49 Ea 39
(RUS) Ërtoma 13 Eh 27
(TR) Ertuğrul 76 Ch 51
(TR) Ertuğrulköy 76 Db 51
(TR) Eruh 87 Ec 53
(HR) Ervenik 58 Bf 46
(TR) Erzin (Yeşilkent) 85 Dg 54
(TR) Erzurum 25000* 79 Eb 51
(LT) Eržvilkas 74021 29 Cc 35
(TR) Eşatlar 76 Ck 51
(DK) Esbjerg 6700* 26 Ai 35
(FIN) Esbo = Espoo 02002* 18 Ce 30
(E) Escala, l' 17130 70 Ad 48
(E) Escalada 69 Sg 48
(I) Escalaplano 08043 71 Ak 51
(E) Escalona 22363 69 Sf 50
(E) Escatrón 50790 70 Sk 49
(D) Eschede 29348 42 Ba 38
(L) Esch-sur-Sûre 9635 42 Af 41
(D) Eschwege 37269 43 Ba 39
(E) Escorial, El 28280 69 Sf 50
(TR) Eşen 84 Ck 54
(TR) Esençay 05810 77 Df 49
(TR) Esençay 05810 78 Dg 50
(TR) Esençe 76 Ci 50
(TR) Esenköy 11640 84 Ci 53
(TR) Esenlik 79 Ed 51
(RUS) Esenoviči 20 De 33
(D) Esens 26427 26 Ah 37
(TR) Esenyurt 76 Ci 49
(TR) Esenyurt 78 Dg 51
(RUS) Esinskaja 21 Eb 30
(IS) Eskifjörður 735 36 Rf 25
(TR) Eski Gediz 76 Ck 51
(TR) Eskihisar 83 Ci 53
(TR) Eskil 68800 85 Dd 52
(S) Eskilstuna 63003* 17 Bg 31
(TR) Eski Malalatya 44210 86 Di 52
(RUS) Eskino 20 Df 32
(TR) Eskipazar 67200 77 Dc 50
(TR) Eskişehir 26000* 76 Da 51
(S) Eslöv 24110* 27 Bd 35
(TR) Eşme 84 Ci 52
(TR) Eşmekaya 68150 85 Dd 52
(TR) Esmer 79 Ec 51
(F) Espalion 12500 55 Ac 46
(D) Espelkamp 32339 42 Ai 38
(E) Espiel 14220 80 Se 52
(E) Espinar, El 40400 69 Sf 50
(P) Espinho 3885-201* 68 Sb 49
(E) Espinosa de los Monteros 09560 69 Sg 47
(TR) Espiye 28600 78 Di 50
(FIN) Espoo 02002* 18 Ce 30
(P) Esposende 4740-001* 68 Sb 49
(S) Esrange 3 Cb 23
(F) Essarts, les 85140 54 Si 44
(B) Essen 45127* 41 Ae 39
(D) Essen 45127* 42 Ah 39
(RUS) Essentuki 64 Ec 46
(GR) Essími 68100 75 Cf 49
(D) Esslingen am Neckar 73728* 42 Ak 42
(RUS) Èssojla 11 Dd 29
(F) Essones, Corbeil- 41 Ac 42
(RUS) Estapovo 22 Fa 31
(P) Estarreja 3860-201* 68 Sb 50
(E) Estépar 69 Sg 48
(E) Estepona 29680 80 Se 54
(F) Esternay 51310 41 Ad 42
(E) Esterri d'Àneu 70 Ab 48
(E) Esterri de Aneu = Esterri d'Àneu 70 Ab 48
(F) Estissac 10190 41 Ad 42
(E) Estivella 46590 70 Sk 51
(P) Estói 8005-449* 80 Sc 53
(E) Estrada, A 36680 68 Sb 48
(P) Estremoz 7100-100* 68 Sc 52
(H) Esztergom 59 Bi 43
(F) Étain 55400 42 Af 41
(F) Étampes 91150* 41 Ac 42
(TR) Etili 17420 75 Cg 51
(RUS) Etkul' 35 Gb 36
(N) Etne 5590 16 Af 31
(F) Etrépagny 27150 41 Ab 41
(F) Étretat 76790 41 Aa 41
(BG) Etropole 2180 75 Ce 48
(F) Eu 76260 41 Ab 40
(B) Eupen 4700 42 Ag 40
(FIN) Eura 27511 18 Cc 29
(FIN) Eurajoki 27101 18 Cb 29
(D) Euskirchen 53879* 42 Ag 40
(D) Eutin 23701 27 Ba 36
(N) Evanger 5707 16 Ag 30
(F) Evaux-les-Bains 23110 55 Ac 44
(RUS) Evbujak 35 Fg 35
(RUS) Evcaniči 20 Dd 32
(TR) Evciler 33630 75 Cg 51
(TR) Evciler 33630 77 Dd 51
(TR) Evciler 33630 84 Ck 52
(BY) Evdakimavičy 30 Da 36
(GR) Evdilos 83 Cg 53
(RUS) Evdino 14 Fa 27
(B) Evergem 9940 41 Ad 39
(S) Evertsberg 17 Bd 29
(GB) Evesham WR11 40 Si 38
(RUS) Evgora 11 Dd 27
(F) Évian-les-Bains 74500 56 Ag 44
(FIN) Evijärvi 62501 10 Cd 27
(I) Evisa 20126 71 Ai 48
(N) Evje 4735 16 Ah 32
(RUS) Evlanovo 48 Dh 38
(P) Évora 7100-300 80 Sc 52
(UA) Evpatorija = Jevpatorija 62 Dd 45
(TR) Evrese 17350 75 Cg 50
(F) Évreux 27000* 41 Ab 41
(F) Evron 53600* 40 Sk 42
(GR) Evrostína 20009 82 Cc 52
(F) Évry 91000 41 Ac 42
(RUS) Evsinskaja 20 Dh 29
(RUS) Evsjutino 21 Eb 31
(UA) Evsuh 48 Dk 41
(GB) Exeter EX4 40 Sg 40
(F) Exideuil 54 Aa 45
(GB) Exmouth EX8 40 Sg 40
(N) Eydehamn 16 Ai 32
(GB) Eyemouth TD14 39 Sh 35
(F) Eygurande 19340 55 Ac 45
(F) Eymet 24500 54 Aa 46
(F) Eymoutiers 87120 55 Ab 45
(TR) Eynesil 28850 78 Dk 49
(E) Ezcaray 26280 69 Sg 48
(LV) Ezere 3891 29 Cc 34
(LV) Ezernieki 5692 30 Ch 34
(RUS) Ëževo 23 Fc 32
(RUS) Ëžiha 22 Eh 32
(TR) Ezine 17600 75 Cg 51
(BY) Ezjaryšča 30 Ck 35
(RUS) Ëžva 22 Fa 29


## F


(DK) Faaborg = Fåborg 5600 27 Ba 35
(N) Fåberg 2625 16 Ba 29
(DK) Fåborg = Faaborg 5600 27 Ba 35
(I) Fabriano 60044 57 Bc 47
(RO) Făcăeni 927110 61 Ch 46
(I) Faenza 48018 57 Bb 46
(P) Fafe 4820-002* 68 Sb 49
(RO) Făgăraş 505200 60 Ce 45
(S) Fågelberget 83086 9 Be 26
(S) Fågelsjö 9 Be 29
(N) Fagernes 2900 16 Ak 30
(N) Fagernes 2900 2 Bk 21
(S) Fagersta 73701* 17 Bf 30
(RO) Făget 607207 59 Cc 45
(IS) Fagurhólsmýri 880 36 Rd 27
(IRL) Faing 37 Sa 38
(RUS) Fakel 23 Fd 33
(GB) Fakenham NR21 39 Aa 38
(TR) Fakılı 77 Df 51
(BIH) Fakovići 59 Bk 46
(DK) Fakse 4640 27 Bc 35
(F) Falaise 14700 40 Sk 42
(IRL) Falcarragh = An Fál Carrach 37 Sb 35
(I) Falconara Marittima 57 Bd 47
(RUS) Falenki 22 Fb 32
(MD) Fălești 5901 61 Ch 43
(MD) Falešty = Fălești 5901 61 Ch 43
(S) Falkenberg 31101* 27 Bc 34
(D) Falkenberg (Elster) 04895 43 Bd 39
(D) Falkensee 14612 43 Bd 38
(S) Falköping 52101* 17 Bd 32
(S) Fällfors 91501 10 Ca 25
(D) Fallingbostel, Bad 29683 26 Ak 38
(GB) Falmouth 40 Se 40
(E) Falset 43730 70 Aa 49
(RO) Fălticeni 725200 60 Cg 43
(S) Falun 79101* 17 Bf 30
(N) Fanahammaren 16 Af 30
(N) Fannrem 7320 8 Ak 27
(I) Fano 61032 57 Bd 47
(N) Fanrem 8 Ak 27
(F) Faouët, le 56320 40 Sg 42
(I) Fara in Sabina 02032 72 Bc 48
(S) Färgelanda 45801 16 Bb 32
(S) Färila 9 Bf 29
(GB) Faringdon SN7 40 Si 39
(S) Färjestaden 38601 28 Bg 34
(GR) Farkadóna 42031 74 Cc 51
(RO) Fărliug 327200 59 Cb 45
(P) Faro 8700-152* 80 Sc 53
(S) Fårösund 62035 17 Bk 33
(IRL) Farrenfore = An Fearann Fuar 37 Sa 38
(GR) Fársala 40300 74 Cc 51
(N) Farsund 4550 16 Ag 32
(I) Fasano 72015 73 Bh 50
(IS) Fáskrúðsfjörður 750 36 Rg 26
(UA) Fastiv 46 Ck 40
(UA) Fastov = Fastiv 46 Ck 40
(E) Fatela, La 68 Sd 50
(RUS) Fatež 48 Df 38
(TR) Fatih 34080* 76 Ci 49
(P) Fátima 2495-551* 68 Sb 51
(TR) Fatsa 52400 78 Dh 49
(F) Faulquemont 57380 42 Ag 41
(RO) Făurei 815100 61 Ch 45
(N) Fauske 8200 2 Bf 23
(F) Faute-sur-Mer, la 85460 54 Si 44
(N) Fåvang 2634 16 Ba 29
(F) Faverney 70160 56 Ag 43
(GB) Faversham ME13 41 Aa 39
(I) Favignana 91023 72 Bc 53
(GB) Fawley SO45 40 Si 40
(F) Fayl-la-Forêt 52500 56 Af 43
(E) Fayón 50795 70 Aa 49
(IRL) Fearna 37 Sd 38
(F) Fécamp 76400 41 Aa 41
(N) Fedje 5947 16 Ae 30
(RUS) Fedjukovo 31 Df 36
(RUS) Fedorovka 33 Ek 37
(RUS) Fedorovka 34 Ff 37
(RUS) Fëdorovka 63 Di 43
(RUS) Fedorovskoe 32 Dk 34
(RUS) Fedotovo 21 Ec 30
(RUS) Fedovo 12 Dk 28
(TR) Fehimli 77 Df 51
(D) Fehmarn 23769 27 Bb 36
(D) Fehrbellin 16833 27 Bc 38
(A) Feistritz an der Drau 9710 57 Bd 44
(TR) Feke 01660 85 Df 53
(TR) Felâhiye 38750* 77 Df 51
(E) Felanitx 07200 70 Ad 51
(A) Feldbach 8330 58 Bf 44
(D) Feldberg 17258 27 Bd 37
(RO) Feldioara 507065 60 Cf 45
(A) Feldkirch 6800* 57 Ak 43
(A) Feldkirchen in Kärnten 9560 58 Be 44
(MD) Fèlešt' = Falešti 61 Ch 43
(GB) Felixstowe IP11 41 Ab 39
(F) Felletin 23500 55 Ac 45
(I) Feltre 32032 57 Bb 44
(I) Fenestrelle 10060 56 Ah 45
(UA) Fenevyči 47 Da 40
(UA) Feodosija 62 Df 45
(RUS) Ferapontovo 20 Di 31
(F) Fère, la 02800 41 Ad 41
(F) Fère-Champenoise 51230 41 Ad 42
(F) Fère-en-Tardenois 02130 41 Ad 41
(I) Ferentino 03013 72 Bd 49
(RKS) Ferizaj = Uroševac 70000* 74 Cb 48
(TR) Ferizli 54110 76 Da 50
(A) Ferlach 9170* 58 Be 44
(LT) Ferma 25001 29 Ce 35
(I) Fermo 63023 57 Bd 47
(E) Fermoselle 49220 68 Sd 49
(IRL) Fermoy = Mainistir Fhear Maí 37 Sb 38
(IRL) Ferns = Fearna 37 Sd 38
(I) Ferrandina 75013 73 Bg 50
(I) Ferrara 44100 57 Bb 46
(P) Ferreira do Alentejo 7900-195* 80 Sb 52
(E) Ferreries 07750 71 Ae 51
(I) Ferriere 29024 57 Ak 46
(E) Ferrol 15510 68 Sb 47
(RUS) Feršampenuaz 35 Fk 37
(F) Ferté-Bernard, la 72400 41 Aa 42
(F) Ferté-Macé, la 61600 40 Sk 42
(F) Ferté-Saint-Aubin, la 45240 55 Ab 43
(F) Ferté-sous-Jouarre, la 77260 41 Ad 42
(N) Festvåg 2 Be 23
(RO) Fetești 925100 61 Ch 46
(TR) Fethiye 48300 84 Ck 54
(TR) Fethiye 48300 86 Di 52
(N) Fetsund 1900 16 Bb 31
(D) Feuchtwangen 91555 43 Ba 41
(F) Feurs 42110 55 Ae 45
(N) Fevik 4870 16 Ai 32
(TR) Fevzipaşa 27830 86 Dg 53
(GB) Ffestiniog LL41 39 Sg 38
(I) Fiastra 62035 72 Bd 47
(I) Ficulle 05016 72 Bc 48
(I) Fidenza 43036 57 Ba 46
(RO) Fieni 137100 60 Cf 45
(AL) Fier 74 Bk 50
(AL) Fierzë 74 Ca 48
(CH) Fiesch 3984 56 Ai 44
(I) Fiésole 50014 57 Bb 47
(F) Figari 20114 71 Ak 49
(F) Figeac 46100* 55 Ac 46
(S) Figeholm 57205 17 Bg 33
(N) Figgjo, Ålgård- 16 Af 32
(I) Figline 59100 57 Bb 47
(P) Figueira da Foz 3080-011* 68 Sb 50
(P) Figueira de Castelo Rodrigo 6440-100* 68 Sd 50
(P) Figueiró dos Vinhos 3260-305* 68 Sb 51
(E) Figueres 17600 70 Ac 48
(RUS) Fil'čenki 30 Dc 35
(BG) Filevo 75 Cf 48
(GB) Filey YO14 39 Sk 36
(GR) Filí 13601 82 Cd 52
(RO) Filiaşi 205300 60 Cd 46
(GR) Filiatrá 24300 82 Cb 53
(RUS) Filimonovo 35 Ga 36
(RUS) Filinskoe 32 Ec 35
(RUS) Filippovka 33 Ek 36
(RUS) Filippovka 53 Gc 39
(S) Filipstad 68201 17 Be 31
(N) Fillan 7240 8 Ai 27
(I) Finale Lígure 17024 56 Ai 46
(E) Fiñana 04500 81 Sh 53
(AX) Finby 22530 18 Ca 30
(TR) Fındık 87 Eb 53
(TR) Fındıkköyü 86 Dg 52
(TR) Fındıklı 05000 75 Cg 50
(TR) Fındıklı 05000 79 Eb 49
(TR) Fındıkpınarı 33730 85 De 54
(TR) Finike 07740 84 Da 54
(GR) Finikounda 24006 82 Cb 54
(D) Finnentrop 57413 42 Ah 39
(N) Finnskog 17 Bc 30
(N) Finnsnes 9300 2 Bh 21
(S) Finspång 61201* 17 Bf 32
(D) Finsterwalde 03238 43 Bd 39
(IRL) Fintown 37 Sb 36
(GB) Fionnphort PA76 38 Sd 34
(I) Firenze 50100* 57 Bb 47
(I) Firenzuola 50033 57 Bb 46
(F) Firminy 42700 55 Ae 45
(RUS) Firovo 20 Dd 33
(GB) Fishguard SA65 40 Sf 39
(N) Fiskå 4122 8 Af 28
(N) Fiskebøl 2 Be 22
(F) Fismes 51170 41 Ad 41
(GR) Fitíes 30009 82 Cb 52
(I) Fiuggi 03014 72 Bd 49
(I) Fivizzano 54013 57 Ba 46
(N) Fjærland 6848 16 Ag 29
(S) Fjällbacka 45071 16 Bb 32
(S) Fjällnes 84098 9 Bc 28
(DK) Fjellerup 5856 27 Ba 34
(DK) Fjerritslev 9690 26 Ak 33
(N) Fjordgård 2 Bh 21
(N) Flå 3539 16 Ak 30
(N) Flakstad 2 Bd 22
(N) Flåm 5743 16 Ah 30
(IS) Flateyri 425 36 Qg 24
(N) Flatval 8 Ai 27
(F) Flèche, la 72200* 54 Sk 43
(GB) Fleetwood FY7 39 Sg 37
(N) Flekkefjord 4400 16 Ag 32
(S) Flen 17 Bg 31
(D) Flensburg / Flensborg 24937* 26 Ak 36
(F) Flers 61100 40 Sk 42
(N) Flesberg 3620 16 Ak 31
(F) Fleurance 32500 54 Aa 47
(GB) Flint CH6 39 Sg 37
(N) Flisa 2270 17 Bc 30
(E) Flix 43750 70 Aa 49
(S) Floby 52040 17 Bd 32
(S) Floda 17 Bc 33
(D) Flöha 09557 43 Bd 40
(F) Florac 48400 55 Ad 46
(I) Florenz = Firenze 50100 57 Bb 47
(MD) Floreşt' = Floreşti 61 Ci 43
(MD) Floreşti 5000 61 Ci 43
(MD) Floreşty = Floreşti 5000 61 Ci 43
(I) Florídia 96014 72 Bf 53
(GR) Flórina 53100 74 Cb 50
(N) Flornes 7525 8 Bb 27
(N) Florø 6900 16 Af 29
(BIH) Foča 59 Bi 47
(TR) Foça 35680 83 Cg 52
(GB) Fochabers IV32 38 Sg 33
(RO) Focşani 000620* 61 Ch 45
(I) Fóggia 71100 73 Bf 49
(F) Foix 09000* 70 Ab 48
(BIH) Fojnica 58 Bh 47
(RUS) Foki 34 Fe 34
(RUS) Fokino 31 De 37
(N) Foldereid 7985 9 Bc 26
(GR) Folégandros 84011 82 Ce 54
(I) Foligno 06034 72 Bc 48
(GB) Folkestone CT18 41 Ab 39
(N) Follafoss 7796 8 Bb 27
(N) Folldal 2580 8 Ak 28
(N) Follebu 2656 16 Ba 29
(S) Föllinge 83060 9 Be 27
(I) Follónica 72 Ba 48
(RUS) Fominki 32 Ec 35
(RUS) Fomino 31 De 36
(RUS) Fominskij 35 Fk 36
(RUS) Fominskoe 21 Eb 29
(RUS) Fominskoe 21 Ec 31
(I) Fondi 36012 72 Bd 49
(I) Fonni 08023 71 Ak 50
(E) Fonsagrada, A 27100 68 Sc 47
(F) Fontainebleau 77300* 41 Ac 42
(UA) Fontanka 61 Da 44
(F) Fontenay-le-Comte 85200 54 Sk 44
(E) Fontiveros 05310 69 Sf 50
(IS) Fontur 36 Rf 24
(H) Fonyód 8640 58 Bh 44
(F) Forbach 76596 42 Ag 41
(F) Forcalquier 04300 56 Af 47
(D) Forchheim 91301 43 Bb 41
(N) Førde 6826 16 Af 29
(N) Førde 6826 16 Af 31
(PL) Fordon 85-900 28 Bi 37
(I) Fordongiánus 09083 71 Ai 51
(GB) Forfar DD8 38 Sh 34
(F) Forges-les-Eaux 76440 41 Ab 41
(I) Forli 57 Bc 46


A B C D E F G H I J K L M N O P Q R S T U V W X Y Z

Forli 151

(GB) Formby L37 ... 39 Sg 37
(I) Formia 04023 ... 72 Bd 49
(RUS) Forminskij ... 22 Ei 29
(E) Fornells ... 71 Ae 50
(I) Fornovo di Taro 43045 ... 57 Ak 46
(UA) Foros ... 62 Dd 46
(GB) Forres IV36 ... 38 Sg 33
(S) Forshaga 66701 ... 17 Bd 31
(S) Forshällan ... 2 Bk 24
(S) Forsmo 88101 ... 9 Bh 27
(N) Forsnes 7246 ... 8 Ai 27
(FIN) Forssa 32003 ... 18 Cd 30
(D) Forst (Lausitz) 03149 ... 43 Be 39
(GB) Fort Augustus PH32 ... 38 Sf 33
(GB) Fort George IV1 ... 38 Sf 33
(E) Fortuna 30620 ... 81 Si 52
(GB) Fort William PH33 ... 38 Se 34
(N) Forvik ... 9 Bc 25
(N) Fosnavåg 6090 ... 8 Af 28
(I) Fossano 12045 ... 56 Ah 46
(N) Fossbakken 9350 ... 2 Bh 22
(I) Fossombrone 61034 ... 57 Bc 47
(GR) Fotiná 60100 ... 74 Cc 50
(F) Fouesnant 29170 ... 54 Sf 43
(F) Fougères 35300* ... 40 Si 42
(F) Fougerolles 70220 ... 56 Ag 43
(F) Fourchambault 58600 ... 55 Ad 43
(F) Fourmies 59610 ... 41 Ae 40
(GR) Fourni ... 83 Cg 53
(IRL) Foxford = Béal Easa ... 37 Sa 37
(IRL) Foynes = Faing ... 37 Sa 38
(E) Foz 27780 ... 68 Sc 47
(E) Fraga 22520 ... 70 Aa 49
(GR) Fraglista ... 82 Cb 52
(B) Fraiture 6690 ... 42 Af 40
(I) Francavilla Fontana 72021 ... 73 Bh 50
(I) Francavilla in Sinni 85034 ... 73 Bg 50
(F) Francescas 47600 ... 54 Aa 46
(I) Francofonte 96015 ... 72 Be 53
(NL) Franeker = Frjentsjer ... 26 Af 37
(D) Frankenberg (Eder) 35066 ... 42 Ai 39
(D) Frankenthal (Pfalz) 67227 ... 42 Ai 41
(D) Frankfurt (Oder) 15230* ... 43 Be 38
(D) Frankfurt am Main 60311* ... 42 Ai 40
(S) Frankrike 83051 ... 9 Bd 27
(S) Fränsta 84012 ... 9 Bg 28
(D) Franzburg 18461 ... 27 Bc 36
(I) Frascati 00044 ... 72 Bc 49
(GB) Fraserburgh AB43 ... 38 Sh 33
(CH) Frauenfeld 8500* ... 56 Ai 43
(DK) Fredericia 7000 ... 26 Ak 35
(DK) Frederikshavn 9900 ... 16 Ba 33
(DK) Frederikssund 3600 ... 27 Bc 35
(DK) Frederiksværk 3300 ... 27 Bc 35
(S) Fredrika 91050 ... 9 Bi 26
(S) Fredriksberg 77010 ... 17 Be 30
(N) Fredrikstad-Sarpsborg 1604* ... 16 Ba 31
(E) Fregenal de la Sierra 06340 ... 80 Sd 52
(D) Freiberg 09599 ... 43 Bd 40
(CH) Freiburg = Fribourg 1700* ... 56 Ah 44
(D) Freiburg im Breisgau 79098* ... 56 Ah 43
(D) Freienwalde, Bad ... 27 Be 38
(A) Freiland 3183 ... 58 Bf 43
(D) Freilassing 83395 ... 57 Bc 43
(D) Freising 85354* ... 43 Bb 42
(A) Freistadt 4240* ... 43 Be 42
(D) Freital 01705 ... 43 Bd 40
(F) Fréjus 83600* ... 56 Ag 47
(IRL) Frenchpark = Dún Gar ... 37 Sb 37
(CZ) Frenštát pod Radhoštěm 744 01 ... 44 Bi 41
(E) Fresno-Alhándiga ... 68 Se 50
(E) Fresno de Caracena 42311 ... 69 Sg 49
(N) Fresvik 6896 ... 16 Ag 29
(F) Fréteval 41160 ... 55 Ab 43
(F) Fretigney-et-Velloreille 70130 ... 56 Af 43
(D) Freudenstadt 72250 ... 42 Ai 42
(F) Frévent 62270 ... 41 Ac 40
(D) Freyung 94078 ... 43 Bd 42
(GR) Frí 85800 ... 83 Cg 55
(CH) Fribourg = Freiburg 1700* ... 56 Ah 44
(A) Friedberg 86316 ... 58 Bg 43
(D) Friedberg (Hessen) 61169 ... 42 Ai 40
(D) Friedland 37133 ... 27 Bd 37
(D) Friedrichshafen 88045* ... 57 Ak 43
(D) Friedrichshall, Bad 74177 ... 42 Ak 41
(D) Friedrichstadt 25840 ... 26 Ak 36
(A) Friesach 9360 ... 58 Be 44
(D) Friesoythe 26169 ... 26 Ah 37
(S) Friggesund 82700 ... 9 Bg 29
(GR) Frikes ... 82 Ca 52
(S) Fristad 51300 ... 17 Bd 33
(S) Fritsla 51110 ... 17 Bc 33
(D) Fritzlar 34560 ... 42 Ak 39
(RUS) Frjanovo ... 31 Di 34
(NL) Frjentsjer = Franeker ... 26 Af 37
(RUS) Frolišči ... 32 Ec 34
(RUS) Frolovo ... 20 Dh 31
(RUS) Frolovo ... 49 Ed 41
(GB) Frome BA11 ... 40 Sh 39
(E) Frómista 34440 ... 69 Sf 48
(F) Frontignan 34110* ... 55 Ad 47
(I) Frosinone 03100 ... 72 Bd 49
(S) Frösö ... 9 Be 27
(I) Frosolone 86095 ... 73 Be 49
(GR) Frossíni ... 74 Ca 51
(N) Frosta 7633 ... 8 Ba 27
(S) Frostviksbränna ... 9 Bd 26
(RO) Frumoasa 147140 ... 60 Cf 44
(RO) Frumuşani 917100 ... 60 Cg 46
(UA) Frunze ... 62 De 44
(UA) Frunzivka ... 61 Ck 43
(CH) Frutigen 3714 ... 56 Ah 44
(CZ) Frýdek-Místek 738 01* ... 44 Bi 41
(CZ) Frýdlant 464 01 ... 44 Bf 40
(E) Fuengirola 29640 ... 81 Sf 54
(E) Fuente-Álamo 02651 ... 81 Si 53
(E) Fuente Dé 39588 ... 54 Sf 47
(E) Fuente de Cantos 06240 ... 80 Sd 52
(E) Fuente del Arco 06980 ... 80 Se 52
(E) Fuente del Fresno 29315 ... 69 Sg 51
(E) Fuente de San Esteban, La ... 68 Sd 50
(E) Fuente Obejuna 14290 ... 80 Se 52
(E) Fuentesaúco 49400 ... 68 Se 49
(E) Fuentes de Ebro 50740 ... 70 Sk 49
(E) Fuentes de Nava 34337 ... 69 Sf 48
(DK) Fuglebjerg 4250 ... 27 Bb 35
(D) Fulda 36037* ... 42 Ak 40
(S) Fulunäs ... 17 Bd 29
(F) Fumel 47500 ... 54 Aa 46
(S) Funäsdalen 84095 ... 9 Bc 28
(P) Fundão 6100-820* ... 68 Sc 50
(RO) Fundulea 915200 ... 60 Cg 46
(H) Fünfkirchen = Pécs ... 59 Bi 44
(RO) Furculeşti 147145 ... 60 Cf 47
(RUS) Furmanov ... 21 Eb 33
(B) Furnes = Veurne 8630 ... 41 Ac 39
(D) Fürstenau 49584 ... 42 Ah 38
(D) Fürstenberg (Havel) 16798 ... 27 Bd 37
(A) Fürstenfeld 8280 ... 58 Bf 43
(D) Fürstenfeldbruck 82256 ... 43 Bb 42
(D) Fürstenwalde (Spree) 15517 ... 43 Be 38
(D) Fürth 64658 ... 43 Ba 41
(D) Furth im Wald 93437 ... 43 Bc 41
(D) Furtwangen im Schwarzwald 78120 ... 42 Ai 42
(S) Furudal 79070 ... 17 Bf 29
(N) Furuflaten 9062 ... 2 Ca 21
(S) Furuvik 81491 ... 17 Bh 30
(N) Fusa 5641 ... 16 Af 30
(A) Fusch an der Großglocknerstraße 5672 ... 57 Bc 43
(AL) Fushë-Arrëz ... 74 Ca 48
(AL) Fushë-Krujë ... 74 Bk 49
(D) Füssen 87629 ... 57 Ba 43
(DK) Fynshav 6440 ... 26 Ak 36
(N) Fyresdal 3870 ... 16 Ai 31


## G


(BG) Gabare 3265 ... 60 Cd 47
(RUS) Gabovo ... 23 Fd 30
(BG) Gabreševci 2557 ... 74 Cc 48
(RKS) Gabrica ... 74 Cb 48
(BG) Gabrovo 5300* ... 75 Cf 48
(F) Gacé 61230 ... 41 Aa 42
(BIH) Gacko ... 73 Bi 47
(S) Gäddede 83090 ... 9 Be 26
(D) Gadebusch 19205 ... 27 Bb 37
(RUS) Gadja ... 23 Fh 29
(BY) Gadjač = Hadjač ... 47 Dd 40
(RO) Găeşti 135200 ... 60 Cf 46
(I) Gaeta 04024 ... 72 Bd 49
(RUS) Gagino ... 33 Ef 35
(RUS) Gagrino ... 20 De 31
(RUS) Gagšor ... 22 Fa 30
(LV) Gaiķi 3872 ... 29 Cc 34
(D) Gaildorf 74405 ... 42 Ak 41
(F) Gaillac 81600* ... 55 Ab 47
(IRL) Gaillimh = Galway ... 37 Sa 37
(GB) Gainsborough DN21 ... 39 Sk 37
(GR) Gaïou ... 74 Ca 51
(GB) Gairloch IV21 ... 38 Se 33
(HR) Gaj ... 58 Bh 45
(RUS) Gaj ... 52 Fi 39
(RUS) Gajny ... 23 Fe 30
(RUS) Gajutino ... 20 Di 32
(RUS) Gakugsa ... 20 Dg 29
(BG) Gălăbovo 2784 ... 75 Cf 48
(RUS) Galanovo ... 34 Fe 34
(GB) Galashiels TD1 ... 39 Sh 35
(CY) Galata 2827 ... 84 Dc 55
(GR) Galatás ... 82 Cd 53
(RO) Galaţi 000800* ... 61 Ci 45
(I) Galatina 73013 ... 73 Bi 50
(GR) Galátista 63073 ... 75 Cd 50
(E) Galera 18840 ... 81 Sh 53
(F) Galeria ... 71 Ai 48
(RO) Gălgău 457140 ... 60 Cd 43
(RUS) Galiakberovo ... 35 Fh 37
(RUS) Galič ... 21 Ec 32
(RO) Galicea 247205 ... 60 Ce 46
(MK) Galičnik 1256 ... 74 Ca 49
(RUS) Galkino ... 25 Ge 32
(I) Gallarate 21013 ... 56 Ai 45
(I) Gallípoli 73014 ... 73 Bh 50
(S) Gällivare 98201 ... 2 Ca 23
(S) Gällö 84050 ... 9 Bf 28
(IRL) Galway = Gaillimh ... 37 Sa 37
(RUS) Gam ... 14 Ek 28
(F) Gamaches 80220 ... 41 Ab 41
(S) Gamleby 59401 ... 17 Bg 33
(S) Gammelstaden 97100 ... 10 Cc 25
(N) Gamvik 9775 ... 3 Ci 19
(F) Gan 64290 ... 54 Sk 47
(B) Gand = Gent 9000 ... 41 Ad 39
(D) Ganderkesee 27777 ... 26 Ai 37
(D) Gandersheim, Bad 37581 ... 43 Ba 39
(E) Gandesa 43780 ... 70 Aa 49
(E) Gandía 46700 ... 70 Sk 52
(RO) Găneasa 237185 ... 60 Ce 46
(F) Ganges 34190 ... 55 Ad 47
(F) Gannat 03800 ... 55 Ad 44
(A) Gänserndorf 2230 ... 44 Bg 42
(RUS) Gapkin ... 64 Eb 43
(RUS) Gar' ... 22 Ei 30
(BG) Gara Hitrino 9780 ... 60 Cg 47
(D) Garbsen 30823* ... 42 Ak 38
(I) Garda 37016 ... 57 Ba 45
(F) Gardanne 13120 ... 56 Af 47
(S) Gardby 38701 ... 28 Bg 34
(D) Gardelegen 39638 ... 43 Bb 38
(GR) Gardíki 46200 ... 74 Cb 51
(GR) Gardíki 46200 ... 82 Cb 52
(S) Gärdnäs 83086 ... 9 Bf 26
(I) Gardone Val Trómpia ... 57 Ba 45
(S) Gärdsjö ... 17 Bf 30
(HR) Garešnica ... 58 Bg 45
(GR) Gargaliáni 24400 ... 82 Cb 53
(S) Gargnäs 92073 ... 9 Bh 25
(LT) Gargždai 96001 ... 28 Cb 35
(RUS) Gari ... 24 Gc 31
(RUS) Gar'inskij ... 22 Fa 29
(I) Garlasco 27026 ... 56 Ai 45
(LT) Garliava 53030 ... 29 Cd 36
(F) Garlin 64330 ... 54 Sk 47
(D) Garmisch-Partenkirchen 82467 ... 57 Bb 43
(N) Garmo 2685 ... 8 Ai 29
(E) Garrovillas 10940 ... 68 Sd 51
(E) Garrucha 04630 ... 81 Si 53
(S) Gärsnäs 27203 ... 27 Be 35
(D) Gartz (Oder) 16307 ... 27 Be 37
(RUS) Garusovo ... 20 Df 33
(N) Gårva ... 3 Cf 21
(P) Garvão 7670-121* ... 80 Sb 53
(PL) Garwolin 08-400 ... 45 Cb 39
(D) Garz 17419 ... 27 Bd 36
(RUS) Gaškovo ... 24 Fi 31
(RO) Gătaia 307185 ... 59 Cb 45
(RUS) Gatčina ... 19 Da 31
(GB) Gatehouse of Fleet DG7 ... 39 Sf 36
(GB) Gateshead NE11 ... 39 Si 36
(I) Gattinara 13045 ... 56 Ai 45
(E) Gaucín 29480 ... 80 Se 54
(N) Gaupne 6868 ... 16 Ah 29
(F) Gavarnie 65120 ... 70 Sk 48
(P) Gavião 6050-201 ... 68 Sc 51
(S) Gävle 80002* ... 17 Bh 30
(F) Gavray 50450 ... 40 Si 42
(RUS) Gavrilkovo ... 21 Ea 31
(RUS) Gavrilov-Jam ... 21 Dk 33
(RUS) Gavrilov Posad ... 32 Ea 34
(GR) Gávrio 84501 ... 82 Ce 53
(S) Gavsele 91060 ... 9 Bh 26
(S) Gävunda ... 17 Be 30
(TR) Gazi Antep ... 86 Dh 53
(TR) Gaziler ... 79 Ec 50
(TR) Gaziler ... 79 Ed 50
(TR) Gazipaşa ... 84 Dc 54
(TR) Gazlıgöl ... 84 Da 52
(TR) Gazlıkuyu ... 86 Dk 54
(PL) Gdańsk 80-009* ... 28 Bi 36
(RUS) Gdov ... 19 Ch 32
(PL) Gdynia 81-004* ... 28 Bi 36
(TR) Geben 46420 ... 86 Dg 53
(TR) Gebiz 07540 ... 84 Da 53
(TR) Gebze 41400* ... 76 Ck 50
(TR) Geçitli ... 87 Ed 53
(TR) Gedikbaşı ... 78 Di 51
(TR) Gedikdere 24860 ... 79 Ea 51
(TR) Gedikler 62630 ... 78 Di 51
(TR) Gedikli ... 85 Df 52
(TR) Gediksaray 05910 ... 77 Df 50
(B) Gedinne 5575 ... 41 Ae 41
(TR) Gediz 43600 ... 84 Ck 52
(DK) Gedser 4874 ... 27 Bb 36
(B) Geel 2440 ... 42 Af 39
(D) Geilenkirchen 52511 ... 42 Ag 40
(N) Geilo 3580 ... 16 Ai 30
(D) Geisenfeld 85290 ... 43 Bb 42
(D) Geislingen an der Steige 73312 ... 42 Ak 42
(N) Geiterygghytta ... 16 Ah 30
(N) Geithus, Åmot- 3360 ... 16 Ai 31
(I) Gela 93012 ... 72 Be 53
(D) Geldern 47608 ... 42 Ag 39
(TR) Gelembe ... 76 Ch 51
(TR) Gelendost 32900 ... 84 Db 52
(RUS) Gelendžik ... 63 Di 46
(TR) Gelenler ... 87 Ee 52
(TR) Gelibolu 48700 ... 75 Cg 50
(D) Gelnhausen 63571 ... 42 Ak 40
(D) Gelsenkirchen 45879* ... 42 Ah 39
(D) Gelting 24395 ... 26 Ak 36
(B) Gembloux 5030 ... 41 Ae 40
(TR) Gemerek 58840 ... 78 Dg 51
(TR) Gemlik 16600 ... 76 Ck 50
(I) Gemona del Friuli 33013 ... 57 Bd 44
(F) Gémozac 17260 ... 54 Sk 45
(D) Gemünden am Main 97737 ... 42 Ak 40
(TR) Genç 12500 ... 87 Ea 52
(TR) Gencek 42482 ... 84 Db 53
(RUS) Generalovskij ... 64 Ed 43
(BG) General Toševo 9500 ... 61 Ci 47
(CH) Genève 1200* ... 56 Ag 44
(CH) Genf = Genève 1200* ... 56 Ag 44
(B) Genk 3600 ... 42 Af 40
(F) Genlis 21110 ... 56 Af 43
(NL) Gennep 6590 ... 42 Ag 39
(F) Gennes 49350 ... 54 Sk 43
(I) Génova 16100 ... 56 Ai 46
(B) Gent 9000 ... 41 Ad 39
(D) Genthin 39307 ... 43 Bc 38
(I) Genua = Génova ... 56 Ai 46
(I) Genzano di Lucánia 85013 ... 73 Bg 50
(RUS) Georgievka ... 34 Fa 37
(RUS) Georgievsk ... 64 Ed 46
(RUS) Georgievskoe ... 20 Dg 31
(RUS) Georgievskoe ... 22 Ef 32
(RUS) Georgiu-Dež = Liski ... 48 Dk 40
(D) Gera 07545* ... 43 Bc 40
(B) Geraardsbergen 9500 ... 41 Ad 40
(I) Gerace 89040 ... 73 Bg 52
(GR) Gérakas 23070 ... 82 Cd 54
(GR) Geráki 23058 ... 82 Cc 54
(F) Gérardmer 88400* ... 42 Ag 42
(RUS) Gerasimovka ... 25 Gf 32
(TR) Gercüş 72300 ... 87 Eb 53
(TR) Gerede 14900 ... 77 Dc 50
(E) Gerena 41860 ... 80 Sd 53
(E) Gérgal 04550 ... 81 Sh 53
(TR) Gerger ... 86 Dk 52
(TR) Geriş 07635 ... 84 Db 54
(TR) Germencik 09700 ... 83 Ch 53
(D) Germersheim 76726 ... 42 Ai 41
(E) Gernika-Lumo 48300 ... 54 Sh 47
(GR) Geroliménas 23071 ... 82 Cc 54
(E) Gerona = Girona 17001 ... 70 Ac 49
(D) Geseke 59590 ... 42 Ai 39
(S) Gesunda ... 17 Be 30
(AX) Geta 22340 ... 18 Bk 30
(E) Getafe 28901* ... 69 Sg 50
(S) Getinge 31044 ... 27 Bc 34
(TR) Gevaş 65700 ... 87 Ed 52
(MK) Gevgelija 1480* ... 74 Cc 49
(F) Gex 01170 ... 56 Ag 44
(TR) Geyikli 61500 ... 75 Cg 51
(TR) Geyikpınar ... 87 Eb 52
(TR) Geyre 09385 ... 84 Ci 53
(TR) Geyve 54700 ... 76 Da 50
(TR) Gezi 38180 ... 85 Df 52
(TR) Gezin ... 86 Dk 52
(AL) Gëziq ... 74 Bk 49
(A) Gföhl 3542* ... 44 Bf 42
(I) Ghedi 25016 ... 57 Ba 45
(RO) Gheorghe Gheorghiu-Dej = Oneşti 000601* ... 60 Cg 44
(RO) Gheorgheni 535500 ... 60 Cf 44
(RO) Gherla 405300 ... 60 Cd 43
(I) Ghilarza 09074 ... 71 Ai 50
(RO) Ghimpaţi 087095 ... 60 Cf 46
(F) Ghisonaccia 20240 ... 71 Ak 48
(RUS) Giaginskaja ... 63 Ea 46
(F) Giandola, la 06540 ... 56 Ah 47
(GR) Giannitsá 58100 ... 74 Cc 50
(I) Giarre 95014 ... 72 Bf 53
(F) Giat 63620 ... 55 Ac 45
(I) Giba 09010 ... 71 Ai 51
(N) Gibostad 9372 ... 2 Bi 21
(E) Gibraleón 21500 ... 80 Sd 53
(GBZ) Gibraltar ... 80 Se 54
(S) Gideå 89037 ... 10 Bk 27
(F) Gien 45500* ... 55 Ac 43
(F) Gières 38610 ... 56 Af 45
(D) Gießen 35390* ... 42 Ai 40
(NL) Gieten 9460 ... 26 Ag 37
(NL) Giethoorn 8355 ... 26 Ag 38
(D) Gifhorn 38518 ... 43 Ba 38
(RUS) Gigant ... 64 Eb 44
(A) Giggl 6553 ... 57 Ba 43
(RO) Gighera 207285 ... 60 Cd 47
(I) Gíglio Castello ... 72 Ba 48
(F) Gignac 34150 ... 55 Ad 47
(E) Gijón = Xixón 03200* ... 68 Se 47
(RO) Gilău 407310 ... 60 Cd 44
(FIN) Gilbbesjavri = Kilpisjärvi 99460 ... 2 Ca 21
(DK) Gilleleje 3250 ... 27 Bc 34
(S) Gillesnuole ... 9 Bg 25
(GB) Gillingham SP8 ... 41 Aa 39
(S) Gimo 74702 ... 17 Bi 30
(RUS) Gimoly ... 11 Dc 28
(F) Gimont 32200 ... 54 Aa 47
(I) Gióia del Colle 70023 ... 73 Bg 50
(I) Gióia Táuro 89013 ... 72 Bf 52
(GR) Giokaréika ... 82 Cc 53
(RUS) Gir, Saraj- ... 34 Fd 37
(TR) Giresun 28000* ... 78 Di 50
(I) Girifalco 88024 ... 73 Bg 52
(TR) Girmeli 47330 ... 87 Eb 53
(E) Girona 17001 ... 70 Ac 49
(E) Gironella 08680 ... 70 Ab 48
(RO) Girov 617210 ... 60 Cg 44
(GB) Girvan KA26 ... 39 Sf 35
(RUS) Girvas ... 11 Dd 28
(RUS) Girvas ... 4 Da 23
(S) Gislaved 33201 ... 17 Bd 33
(F) Gisors 27140 ... 41 Ab 41
(GR) Githio 23200 ... 82 Cc 54
(S) Gittun ... 2 Bi 24
(RO) Giubega 207290 ... 60 Cd 46
(I) Giulianova 64021 ... 72 Bd 48
(RO) Giurgeni 927135 ... 61 Ch 46
(RO) Giurgiu 000080* ... 60 Cf 47
(MD) Giurgiuleşti 5318 ... 61 Ci 45
(DK) Give 7323 ... 26 Ak 35
(F) Givet 08600 ... 41 Ae 40
(F) Givors 69700 ... 55 Ae 45
(RUS) Gizel' ... 79 Ee 48
(F) Gizeux 37340 ... 54 Aa 43
(PL) Giżycko 11-500* ... 28 Cb 36
(N) Gjerstad 4980 ... 16 Ak 32
(N) Gjersvik ... 9 Bd 26
(N) Gjesvær 9765 ... 3 Cf 19
(RKS) Gjilan = Gnjilane 60000* ... 74 Cb 48
(AL) Gjirokastër ... 74 Ca 50
(FR) Gjógv 476 ... 38 Sd 28
(AL) Gjormë ... 74 Bk 50
(FR) Gjøv = Gjógv 476 ... 38 Sd 28
(N) Gjøvik ... 16 Ba 30
(RUS) Glad' ... 19 Dc 31
(N) Gladstad ... 8 Bb 25
(BIH) Glamoč ... 58 Bg 46
(N) Glåmos 7372 ... 8 Bb 28
(DK) Glamsbjerg 5620 ... 27 Ba 35
(CH) Glarus 8750 ... 57 Ak 43
(GB) Glasgow G40 ... 39 Sf 35
(GB) Glastonbury BA16 ... 40 Sh 39
(D) Glauchau 08371 ... 43 Bc 40
(IS) Glaumbær ... 36 Ql 25
(HR) Glavace ... 58 Bf 46
(BIH) Glavatičevo ... 59 Bi 47
(BG) Glavinica 4409 ... 60 Cg 47
(RUS) Glazaniha ... 12 Di 27
(RUS) Glazov ... 23 Fc 32
(RUS) Glazunovka ... 48 Dg 38
(IRL) Gleann Beithe ... 37 Rl 38
(A) Gleisdorf 8200* ... 58 Bf 43
(IRL) Glenamoy ... 37 Sa 36
(GB) Glenariff BT44 ... 37 Sd 35
(GB) Glenarm BT44 ... 37 Se 36
(GB) Glenavy BT29 ... 37 Sd 36
(IRL) Glenbeigh = Gleann Beithe ... 37 Rl 38
(IRL) Glengarriff = An Glean Garbh ... 37 Sa 39
(GB) Glenluce DG8 ... 39 Sf 36
(GB) Glenrothes KY6 ... 38 Sg 34
(IRL) Glenties = Na Gleannta ... 37 Sb 36
(GR) Glifa 35013 ... 82 Cc 52
(S) Glimåkra 28064 ... 27 Be 34
(HR) Glina ... 58 Bg 45
(RUS) Glinka ... 30 Dc 36
(PL) Glinojeck 06-450 ... 28 Ca 38
(PL) Gliwice 44-100* ... 44 Bi 40
(AL) Gllavë ... 74 Bk 50
(MD) Glodeni 4900 ... 61 Ch 43
(A) Gloggnitz 2640* ... 58 Bf 43
(PL) Głogów 67-200* ... 44 Bg 39
(N) Glomfjord 8160 ... 2 Bd 24
(S) Glommersträsk 93081 ... 10 Bk 25
(GB) Glossop SK13 ... 39 Si 37
(RUS) Glotovka ... 33 Eg 37
(RUS) Glotovo ... 14 Ek 27
(GB) Gloucester GL2 ... 40 Sh 39
(PL) Główczyce 76-220 ... 28 Bh 36
(PL) Głowno 11-040 ... 44 Bk 39
(PL) Głubczyce 48-100 ... 44 Bh 40
(RUS) Glubokij ... 49 Ea 42
(PL) Głuchołazy 48-340 ... 44 Bh 40
(D) Glückstadt 25348 ... 26 Ak 37
(RUS) Gluhovo ... 32 Ed 35
(BY) Gluša ... 30 Ci 37
(RUS) Gluškovo ... 47 De 39
(RUS) Gmelinka ... 50 Eg 40
(A) Gmünd 9853 ... 43 Be 42
(A) Gmünd 9853 ... 57 Bd 44
(A) Gmunden 4810* ... 43 Bd 43
(S) Gnarp 82077 ... 9 Bh 28
(D) Gnarrenburg 27442 ... 26 Ak 37
(PL) Gniew 83-140 ... 28 Bi 37
(PL) Gniewkowo 88-140 ... 28 Bi 38
(PL) Gniezno 62-200* ... 44 Bh 38
(RKS) Gnjilane = Gjilan 60000* ... 74 Cb 48
(D) Gnoien 17179 ... 27 Bc 37
(TR) Göçbeyli 35700 ... 76 Ch 51
(BG) Goce Delčev 2900 ... 75 Cd 49
(D) Goch 47574 ... 42 Ag 39
(IS) Goðdali 560 ... 36 Ql 25
(BG) Godeč 2240 ... 75 Cd 47
(F) Goderville 76110 ... 41 Aa 41
(PL) Godętowo 84-218 ... 28 Bh 36
(H) Gödöllő ... 59 Bk 43
(PL) Godziszewo 83-209 ... 28 Bi 36


**152** Formby

(UA) Hadjač ... 47 Dd 40
(DK) Hadsten 8370 ... 27 Ba 34
(DK) Hadsund 9560 ... 27 Ba 34
(RUS) Hadyžensk ... 63 Dk 46
(N) Hægeland 4720 ... 16 Ah 32
(TR) Hafik 58760 ... 78 Dh 51
(IS) Hafnarfjörður 220* ... 36 Qi 26
(IS) Hafnir 230 ... 36 Qh 27
(D) Hagen 58089* ... 42 Ah 39
(D) Hagenow 19230 ... 27 Bb 37
(F) Hagetmau 40700 ... 54 Sk 47
(S) Hagfors 68301 ... 17 Bd 30
(S) Häggenås 83030 ... 9 Be 27
(S) Häggnäset 83090 ... 9 Be 26
(S) Häggsjöbränna ... 9 Bc 27
(IS) Hagi 801 ... 36 Qg 25
(F) Haguenau 67500* ... 42 Ah 42
(RUS) Hahaly ... 33 Ee 34
(H) Hahót 8771 ... 58 Bg 44
(FIN) Hailuoto 90480 ... 10 Ce 25
(A) Hainfeld 3170 ... 44 Bf 42
(D) Hainichen 09661 ... 43 Bd 40
(H) Hajdúböszörmény 4220 ... 59 Cb 43
(H) Hajdúnánás 4080 ... 59 Cb 43
(H) Hajdúszoboszló 4200 ... 59 Cb 43
(PL) Hajnówka 17-200 ... 29 Cd 38
(UA) Hajsyn ... 46 Ck 42
(TR) Hakkâri 30000 ... 87 Ed 53
(S) Hakkas 98041 ... 3 Cb 24
(N) Hakkstabben 9532 ... 3 Cd 20
(GR) Halandrítsa 25008 ... 82 Cb 52
(D) Halberstadt 38820* ... 43 Bb 39
(N) Halden 1763* ... 16 Bb 31
(D) Haldensleben 39340 ... 43 Bb 38
(GB) Halesworth IP19 ... 41 Ab 38
(TR) Halfeti 63950 ... 86 Dh 53
(GB) Halifax HX2 ... 39 Si 37
(TR) Halilkaya 25900 ... 79 Ea 50
(RUS) Halilovo ... 35 Fi 37
(RUS) Halilovo ... 52 Fi 39
(TR) Halitçavuş ... 79 Eb 51
(TR) Halitpaşa 45850 ... 83 Ch 52
(EST) Haljala 45301 ... 18 Cg 31
(TR) Halkapınar 42280 ... 85 De 53
(GR) Hálki 40009 ... 83 Ch 54
(GR) Halkiādes ... 74 Cc 51
(GR) Halkída 34100 ... 82 Cd 52
(GR) Halkidó ... 74 Cc 50
(S) Hälla 91060 ... 9 Bh 27
(B) Halle 37620 ... 41 Ae 40
(D) Halle (Saale) 06108* ... 43 Bb 39
(D) Halle (Westfalen) 33790 ... 42 Ai 38
(S) Hällefors 71201 ... 17 Be 31
(A) Hallein 5400* ... 57 Bd 43
(S) Hällekis 53304 ... 17 Bd 32
(S) Hallen 83001 ... 9 Be 27
(S) Hällestad ... 17 Bf 32
(A) Hall in Tirol 6060 ... 57 Bb 43
(S) Hällnäs ... 10 Bk 26
(IS) Hallormstaður ... 36 Rf 25
(S) Hallsberg 69401 ... 17 Bf 31
(S) Hallstavik 76300 ... 17 Bi 30
(S) Halmstad 30004* ... 27 Bc 34
(DK) Hals 9370 ... 27 Ba 33
(N) Halsa 8178 ... 8 Ai 27
(BY) Hal'šany ... 29 Cg 36
(FIN) Halsua 69510 ... 10 Ce 27
(D) Haltern am See 45721 ... 42 Ah 39
(RUS) Halturin ... 22 Ei 32
(GB) Haltwhistle NE49 ... 39 Sh 36
(UA) Halyč ... 45 Ce 41
(F) Ham 80400 ... 41 Ad 41
(TR) Hamam ... 86 Dg 54
(TR) Hamamözü 05700 ... 77 Df 50
(N) Hamar 2315* ... 16 Bb 30
(D) Hamburg 20099* ... 27 Ba 37
(S) Hamburgsund 45070 ... 16 Bb 32
(TR) Hamdi 19600 ... 77 De 50
(FIN) Hämeenkyrö 39101 ... 18 Cd 29
(FIN) Hämeenlinna 13100* ... 18 Ce 29
(D) Hameln 31785* ... 42 Ak 38
(TR) Hamidiye ... 75 Cg 49
(TR) Hamidiye ... 76 Da 51
(GB) Hamilton ... 39 Sf 35
(FIN) Hamina 49461 ... 19 Ch 30
(D) Hamm 59063* ... 42 Ah 39
(S) Hammarstrand 84070 ... 9 Bg 27
(FIN) Hammaslahti = Pyhäselkä 82200* ... 11 Ck 28
(DK) Hammel 8450 ... 26 Ak 34
(D) Hammelburg 97762 ... 42 Ak 40
(S) Hammerdal 83070 ... 9 Bf 27
(N) Hammerfest 9600 ... 3 Cd 20
(DK) Hammershøj 9460 ... 26 Ak 34
(N) Hamneidet 9181 ... 2 Ca 21
(B) Hamont-Achel 3930 ... 42 Af 39
(S) Hamra 82051 ... 17 Be 29
(S) Hamrånge ... 17 Bh 30
(TR) Hamur 04850 ... 79 Ec 51
(RUS) Hamyski ... 63 Ea 46
(TR) Hamzalar ... 79 Eb 51
(TR) Hamzalı 50900 ... 87 Eb 52
(TR) Hanak 75900 ... 79 Ec 49
(D) Hanau 63450* ... 42 Ai 40
(BY) Hancavičy ... 29 Cg 38
(S) Handen ... 17 Bi 31
(S) Handöl 83019 ... 9 Bc 27
(N) Hanestad 2478 ... 8 Ba 29
(FIN) Hangö 10900* ... 18 Cc 31
(TR) Hani 21800 ... 87 Ea 52
(GR) Haniá 73101 ... 82 Ce 55
(RUS) Hanino ... 31 Dg 36
(FIN) Hankasalmen asema 41521 ... 10 Cg 28
(TR) Hankendi 23130 ... 86 Dk 52
(FIN) Hanko = Hangö 10900* ... 18 Cc 31
(TR) Hanköy ... 85 Dg 52
(D) Hann. Münden 34346 ... 42 Ak 39
(D) Hannover 30159* ... 42 Ak 38
(BIH) Han Pijesak ... 59 Bi 46
(RUS) Hanskaja ... 63 Dk 46
(DK) Hanstholm 7730 ... 16 Ai 33
(RUS) Hanty-Mansijsk ... 25 Gk 29
(SK) Hanušovce nad Topl'ou 094 31 ... 45 Cb 41
(S) Haparanda 95301 ... 10 Ce 25
(N) Håra ... 16 Ag 31
(RUS) Harabali ... 65 Eh 43
(TR) Harabeköy ... 84 Dc 52
(TR) Harabekri = Knidos Harabekri ... 83 Ch 54
(TR) Harabeleri 48980 ... 83 Ch 54
(BY) Haradok ... 30 Ck 35
(BY) Haradok, Davyd- ... 46 Ch 38
(BY) Haradzeja ... 29 Cg 37
(BY) Haradzišča ... 29 Cg 37
(GR) Haravgí 50200 ... 74 Cb 50
(DK) Harborø ... 26 Ai 34
(D) Harburg 21073* ... 26 Ak 37
(D) Harburg (Schwaben) 86655 ... 43 Ba 42
(N) Hardbakke 6924 ... 16 Ae 29
(NL) Hardenberg 7770 ... 42 Ag 38
(NL) Harderwijk 3840* ... 42 Af 38
(N) Hareid 6060 ... 8 Ag 28
(D) Haren (Ems) 49733 ... 26 Ah 38
(N) Harestua 2743 ... 16 Ba 30
(RUS) Harino ... 21 Ed 31
(RUS) Haritonovo ... 22 Eh 29
(H) Harkány 7815 ... 59 Bi 45
(UA) Har'kov = Charkiv ... 48 Dg 41
(RUS) Har'kovka ... 52 Fg 40
(RUS) Harlamovskaja ... 20 Dh 32
(RO) Hârlău 705100 ... 60 Cg 43
(GB) Harleston IP20 ... 41 Ab 38
(DK) Hårlev 4652 ... 27 Bc 35
(NL) Harlingen = Harns ... 26 Af 37
(RUS) Harlovka ... 4 Dh 22
(RUS) Harlovskoe ... 24 Gd 33
(GB) Harlow CM17 ... 41 Aa 39
(RO) Hărman 507085 ... 60 Cf 45
(TR) Harmancık ... 76 Ck 51
(TR) Harmancık ... 78 Dh 51
(S) Harmånger 82075 ... 9 Bh 29
(FIN) Härmänkyla ... 11 Ck 26
(BG) Harmanli 6450 ... 75 Cf 49
(TR) Harmanlı ... 86 Dh 53
(S) Härnösand 87101* ... 9 Bh 28
(NL) Harns = Harlingen ... 26 Af 37
(E) Haro 26200 ... 69 Sh 48
(GB) Haroldswick ZE2 ... 38 Sk 30
(RUS) Harovsk ... 21 Ea 31
(D) Harpstedt 27243 ... 26 Ai 38
(TR) Harput 23140 ... 86 Dk 52
(N) Harran 7873 ... 9 Bc 26
(TR) Harran ... 86 Dk 54
(GB) Harrogate HG3 ... 39 Si 37
(D) Harsefeld 21698 ... 26 Ak 37
(RO) Hârşova ... 61 Ch 46
(N) Harstad 9402* ... 2 Bg 22
(N) Harsvik ... 8 Ba 26
(A) Hartberg 8230* ... 58 Bf 43
(GB) Hartlepool TS24 ... 39 Si 36
(FIN) Hartola 19601 ... 18 Cg 29
(TR) Harun ... 77 De 50
(GB) Harwich CO12 ... 41 Ab 39
(D) Harzburg, Bad 38667 ... 43 Ba 39
(D) Harzgerode 06493 ... 43 Bb 39
(TR) Hasanağa ... 76 Ci 50
(TR) Hasançelebi 44420 ... 86 Dh 52
(TR) Hasankeyf 72350 ... 87 Eb 53
(TR) Hasanoğlan 06850 ... 77 Dd 50
(TR) Hasbek 66670 ... 77 Df 51
(D) Haselünne 49740 ... 26 Ah 38
(BG) Haskovo 6300* ... 75 Cf 49
(TR) Hasköy 22500 ... 75 Cg 49
(TR) Hasköy 22500 ... 79 Ec 50
(GB) Haslemere GU27 ... 40 Sk 39
(DK) Haslev 4690 ... 27 Bb 35
(F) Hasparren 64240 ... 54 Si 47
(TR) Hassa 31700 ... 86 Dg 54
(S) Hassela 82078 ... 9 Bg 28
(B) Hasselt 3500 ... 42 Af 40
(D) Haßfurt 97437 ... 43 Ba 40
(D) Haßlau, Wilkau- 08112 ... 43 Bc 40
(S) Hässleholm 28101* ... 27 Bd 34
(GB) Hastings TN34 ... 41 Aa 40
(S) Hästveda 28023 ... 27 Bd 34
(N) Hasvik 9590 ... 3 Cc 20
(TR) Hatay (Antakya) ... 85 Dg 54
(RO) Haţeg 335500 ... 59 Cc 45
(GB) Hatfield AL9 ... 40 Sk 39
(TR) Hatip 42215 ... 84 Dc 53
(N) Hatlestrand ... 16 Af 30
(N) Hattfjelldal 8690 ... 9 Bd 25
(FIN) Hattuselkonen 81950 ... 11 Da 27
(FIN) Hattuvaara 81650 ... 11 Db 28
(TR) Hatunsaray 42220 ... 84 Dc 53
(H) Hatvan 3000* ... 59 Bk 43
(N) Haugesund 5514* ... 16 Af 31
(N) Haugland ... 16 Ae 30
(FIN) Hauho 14700 ... 18 Ce 29
(IS) Haukadalur 810 ... 36 Qk 26
(N) Haukeligrend ... 16 Ah 31
(FIN) Haukipudas 90840 ... 10 Cf 25
(FIN) Haukivuori 51601 ... 11 Ch 28
(S) Haurida 57874 ... 17 Be 33
(FIN) Hausjärvi 12520 ... 18 Ce 30
(FIN) Hautajärvi 98995 ... 3 Ck 24
(RUS) Hautavaara ... 11 Dc 28
(D) Hauzenberg 94051 ... 43 Bd 42
(TR) Havaalanı ... 78 Dg 51
(GB) Havant PO9 ... 40 Sk 40
(D) Havelberg 39539 ... 27 Bc 38
(GB) Haverfordwest SA61 ... 40 Sf 39
(GB) Haverhill CB9 ... 41 Aa 38
(CZ) Havlíčkův Brod 580 01 ... 44 Bf 41
(N) Havøysund 9690 ... 3 Ce 19
(TR) Havran 10560 ... 76 Ch 51
(F) Havre, Le 76600 ... 41 Aa 41
(UA) Havrylivka ... 48 Dg 42
(TR) Havsa 22500 ... 75 Cg 49
(S) Havsnäs 83081 ... 9 Bf 26
(TR) Havuz 58940 ... 78 Dh 51
(TR) Havza 55700 ... 77 Df 50
(GB) Hawes DL8 ... 39 Sh 36
(GB) Hawick TD9 ... 39 Sh 35
(F) Hayange 57700 ... 42 Ag 41
(TR) Haydarlı 03480 ... 84 Da 52
(TR) Haydere ... 84 Ci 53
(F) Haye-du-Puits, La 50250 ... 40 Si 41
(TR) Haymana 06860 ... 77 Dc 51
(TR) Hayrabolu 59400 ... 76 Ch 49
(TR) Hayrat 61450 ... 79 Ea 50
(GB) Haywards Heath TR21 ... 40 Sk 39
(TR) Hazar ... 86 Dk 52
(F) Hazebrouck 59190 ... 41 Ac 40
(TR) Hazine ... 87 Ed 52
(TR) Hazro 21560 ... 87 Ea 52
(IRL) Headfort = Áth Cinn ... 37 Sa 37
(NL) Hearrenfean, It = Heerenveen 8411* ... 26 Af 38
(S) Heby 74401 ... 17 Bg 31
(D) Hechingen 72379 ... 42 Ai 42
(N) Hedal 2930 ... 16 Ak 30
(S) Hede ... 9 Bd 28
(S) Hedemora 77601 ... 17 Bf 30
(S) Hedenäset 95795 ... 10 Cd 24
(DK) Hedensted 8722 ... 26 Ak 35
(S) Hedesunda 81040 ... 17 Bg 30
(S) Hedeviken 84092 ... 9 Bd 28
(GB) Hedon HU12 ... 39 Sk 37
(NL) Heerenveen = It Hearrenfean 8411* ... 26 Af 38
(NL) Heerlen 6400* ... 42 Af 40
(H) Hegyeshalom 9222 ... 58 Bh 43
(D) Heide 25746 ... 26 Ak 36
(D) Heidelberg 69115* ... 42 Ai 41
(D) Heidenheim an der Brenz 89518* ... 43 Ba 42
(A) Heidenreichstein 3860* ... 44 Bf 42
(FIN) Heikkilä 27511 ... 11 Ck 25
(GB) Heilam IV27 ... 38 Sf 32
(D) Heilbad Heiligenstadt 37308 ... 43 Ba 39
(D) Heilbronn 74072* ... 42 Ak 41
(A) Heiligenblut am Großglockner 9844* ... 57 Bc 43
(D) Heiligenhafen 23774 ... 27 Ba 36
(D) Heiligenstadt, Heilbad 37308 ... 43 Ba 39
(NL) Heiloo 1850 ... 26 Ae 38
(N) Heimdal 7072 ... 8 Ba 27
(FIN) Heinävesi 79701 ... 11 Ci 28
(FIN) Heinola 18200 ... 18 Cg 29
(B) Heist, Knokke- 8300 ... 41 Ad 39
(B) Heist-op-den-Berg 2220 ... 41 Ae 39
(FIN) Heituinlahti 54770 ... 19 Ch 29
(S) Hejde 62020 ... 17 Bi 33
(TR) Hekimdağ ... 76 Da 51
(TR) Hekimhan 44400 ... 86 Dh 52
(PL) Hel 84-150 ... 28 Bi 36
(S) Helagsstugorna 84035 ... 9 Bc 28
(NL) Helder, Den 1783 ... 26 Ae 38
(GB) Helensburgh G84 ... 38 Sf 34
(S) Helgum 88293 ... 9 Bg 27
(IS) Hella 850 ... 36 Qk 27
(N) Helle, Vadfoss- ... 16 Ak 32
(N) Helleland 4376 ... 16 Ag 32
(N) Hellemobotn ... 2 Bg 23
(N) Hellesvik ... 8 Ai 27
(N) Hellesylt 6218 ... 8 Ag 28
(NL) Hellevoetsluis 3220* ... 41 Ae 39
(E) Hellín 02400 ... 81 Si 52
(IS) Hellisandur 360 ... 36 Qg 26
(N) Hellnessund ... 2 Be 23
(NL) Helmond 5700* ... 42 Af 39
(GB) Helmsdale KW8 ... 38 Sg 32
(GB) Helmsley YO62 ... 39 Si 36
(D) Helmstedt 38350 ... 43 Ba 38
(S) Helsingborg 25002* ... 27 Bc 34
(FIN) Helsingfors = Helsinki 00002* ... 18 Ce 30
(DK) Helsingør 3000 ... 27 Bc 34
(FIN) Helsinki 23311 ... 18 Ce 30
(GB) Helston TR13 ... 40 Se 40
(S) Hemavan ... 9 Bf 25
(GB) Hemel Hempstead HP1 ... 40 Sk 39
(F) Heming 57830 ... 42 Ag 42
(S) Hemling 89051 ... 9 Bi 27
(S) Hemmingsmark 94493 ... 10 Cb 25
(N) Hemnes 1970 ... 16 Bb 31
(N) Hemnesberget 8640 ... 2 Bd 24
(S) Hemse 62012 ... 17 Bi 33
(N) Hemsedal 3560 ... 16 Ai 30
(S) Hemsö 87010 ... 9 Bi 28
(S) Henån 47301 ... 16 Bb 32
(F) Hendaye 64700* ... 54 Si 47
(TR) Hendek 54300 ... 76 Da 50
(NL) Hengelo 7255* ... 42 Ag 38
(UA) Heničes'k ... 62 De 44
(GB) Henley-on-Thames RG9 ... 40 Sk 39
(F) Hennebont 56700 ... 54 Sg 43
(D) Hennigsdorf 16761 ... 43 Bd 38
(N) Henningsvær ... 2 Be 22
(N) Heradsbygd 2415 ... 16 Bb 30
(F) Herbault 41190 ... 55 Ab 43
(F) Herbiers, les 85500 ... 54 Si 44
(F) Herbignac 44410 ... 54 Sh 43
(PL) Herby 42-284 ... 44 Bi 40
(MNE) Herceg-Novi 85 340 ... 73 Bi 48
(SRB) Hercegovačka Goleša = Pribojska Goleša ... 59 Bk 47
(N) Herefoss 4766 ... 16 Ai 32
(TR) Hereke 41800 ... 76 Ck 50
(IS) Herfell ... 36 Rf 25
(D) Herford 32049* ... 42 Ai 38
(F) Héricourt 70400 ... 56 Ag 43
(CH) Herisau 9100* ... 57 Ak 43
(D) Herleshausen 37293 ... 43 Ba 39
(A) Hermagor-Pressegger See 9620 ... 57 Bd 44
(D) Hermannsburg 29320 ... 27 Ba 38
(N) Hermansverk 6863 ... 16 Ag 29
(DK) Herning 7400 ... 26 Ai 34
(N) Herøy ... 9 Bc 25
(N) Herre 3965 ... 16 Ak 31
(D) Herrenberg 71083 ... 42 Ai 42
(E) Herrera del Duque 06670 ... 68 Se 51
(E) Herrera de Pisuerga 34400 ... 69 Sf 48
(E) Herreruela 10560 ... 68 Sd 51
(N) Herringbotn ... 9 Bd 25
(S) Herrljunga 52401 ... 17 Bd 32
(D) Hersbruck 91217 ... 43 Bb 41
(D) Hersfeld, Bad 36251 ... 42 Ak 40
(UA) Herson = Cherson ... 62 Dc 44
(NL) Hertogenbosch, 's- 5248 ... 42 Af 39
(D) Herzberg (Elster) 04916 ... 43 Bd 39
(D) Herzberg am Harz 37412 ... 43 Ba 39
(F) Hesdin 62140 ... 41 Ac 40
(N) Hessfjord ... 2 Bk 21
(D) Hessisch Lichtenau 37235 ... 42 Ak 39
(IS) Hesteyri 400 ... 36 Qh 24
(FIN) Hetekylä 91300 ... 10 Cg 25
(RUS) Hetolambina ... 4 Dd 24
(RUS) Hetovo ... 13 Ec 27
(H) Heves 3360 ... 59 Ca 43
(CZ) Hevlín 671 69 ... 44 Bg 42
(GB) Hexham NE46 ... 39 Sh 36
(GB) Heysham LA3 ... 39 Sh 36
(RUS) Hibiny ... 4 Dd 23
(H) Hidasnémeti 3876 ... 45 Cb 42
(D) Hiddensee ... 27 Bd 36
(A) Hieflau 8920* ... 58 Be 43
(FIN) Hietapera 88901 ... 11 Ck 26
(GB) High Wycombe HP12 ... 40 Sk 39
(FIN) Hiirola 51520 ... 11 Ch 29
(E) Híjar 44530 ... 70 Sk 49
(D) Hildburghausen 98646 ... 43 Ba 40
(D) Hildesheim 31134* ... 42 Ak 38
(GR) Hiliomódi 20008 ... 82 Cc 53
(NL) Hillegom 2180 ... 41 Ae 38
(DK) Hillerød 3400 ... 27 Bc 35
(S) Hillerstorp 33033 ... 17 Bd 33
(GB) Hillswick ZE2 ... 38 Si 30
(TR) Hilvan 63900 ... 86 Di 53
(NL) Hilversum 1200* ... 42 Af 38
(FIN) Himanka 68100 ... 10 Cd 26
(AL) Himarë ... 74 Bk 50
(RUS) Himki ... 31 Dh 35
(TR) Himmetdede 38420 ... 85 Df 52
(MD) Hînceşti 3400 ... 61 Ci 44
(GB) Hinckley LE10 ... 40 Si 38
(S) Hindås 43063 ... 17 Bc 33
(TR) Hınıs 25600 ... 79 Eb 51
(FIN) Hinnerjoki 27600 ... 18 Cb 30
(E) Hinojosa del Duque 14270 ... 80 Se 52
(GR) Híos 82100 ... 83 Cg 52
(D) Hirschberg 59581 ... 43 Bb 40
(FIN) Hirsilä 35320 ... 18 Ce 29
(F) Hirson 02500 ... 41 Ae 41
(MD) Hîrtop ... 61 Ci 44
(DK) Hirtshals 9850 ... 16 Ak 33
(FIN) Hirvas 97130 ... 3 Cf 24
(TR) Hisar 73400 ... 77 Dd 51
(TR) Hisarcık 43780 ... 76 Ck 51
(BG) Hisarja 4180 ... 75 Ce 48
(RUS) Hislaviči ... 30 Dc 36
(BG) Hitovo 9433 ... 61 Ch 47
(TR) Hizan 13600 ... 87 Ec 52
(DK) Hjallerup 9320 ... 16 Ba 33
(N) Hjellestad 5259 ... 16 Af 30
(N) Hjellset ... 8 Ah 28
(N) Hjelmeland ... 16 Ag 31
(N) Hjerkinn 2661 ... 8 Ak 28
(S) Hjo 54401 ... 17 Be 32
(DK) Hjørring 9800 ... 16 Ba 33
(S) Hjortkvarn 69793 ... 17 Bf 32
(UA) Hlavani ... 61 Ck 45
(BG) Hlebarovo = Car Kalojan 7280 ... 60 Cg 47
(RUS) Hlepen' ... 31 De 35
(UA) Hlevacha ... 47 Da 40
(CZ) Hlinsko 370 01 ... 44 Bf 41
(UA) Hlobyne ... 47 Dd 41
(SK) Hlohovec 920 01 ... 44 Bh 42
(UA) Hluchiv ... 47 Dd 39
(BY) Hluša ... 30 Ci 37
(BY) Hlusk ... 30 Ci 38
(BY) Hluškavičy ... 46 Ch 39
(UA) Hlyboka ... 46 Cf 42
(BY) Hlybokae ... 30 Ch 35
(UA) Hlyns'k ... 47 Dc 42
(RUS) Hlystalovo ... 22 Ek 31
(RUS) Hmelevka ... 22 Eg 32
(RUS) Hmelita ... 31 Dd 35
(UA) Hmel'nickij = Chmel'nyc'kyj ... 46 Cg 41
(UA) Hnivan' ... 46 Ci 41
(SK) Hnúšt'a 981 01 ... 44 Bk 42
(DK) Hobro 9500 ... 26 Ak 34
(TR) Hocabey ... 78 Dg 51
(TR) Hocalar 03530 ... 84 Ck 52
(D) Höchstadt an der Aisch 91315 ... 43 Ba 41
(H) Hódmezővásárhely ... 59 Ca 44
(CZ) Hodonín 695 01 ... 44 Bh 42
(RUS) Hodovariha ... 6 Fd 22
(NL) Hoek van Holland 3150 ... 41 Ae 39
(D) Hof 04758 ... 43 Bb 40
(IS) Höfðakaupstaður = Skagaströnd ... 36 Qk 25
(D) Hofgeismar 34369 ... 42 Ak 39
(IS) Höfn 780 ... 36 Re 26
(S) Hofors 81301 ... 17 Bg 30
(IS) Hofsós 565* ... 36 Ql 25
(NL) Hof van Twente 7470* ... 42 Ag 38
(S) Höganäs 26300* ... 27 Bc 34
(S) Högby 38075 ... 17 Bh 33
(S) Högbynäs 83081 ... 9 Bf 26
(S) Högland 91494 ... 9 Bf 26
(S) Höglekardalen 83001 ... 9 Bd 27
(S) Högsäter ... 17 Bc 32
(S) Högsby 57900 ... 17 Bg 33
(N) Høgstadgård ... 2 Bk 22
(H) Hőgyész ... 59 Bi 44
(A) Hohenems 6845* ... 57 Ak 43
(D) Hohenwestedt 24594 ... 26 Ak 36
(UA) Hoholiv ... 47 Db 40
(RUS) Hohol'skij ... 48 Di 39
(DK) Højer 6280 ... 26 Ai 36
(N) Hokksund 3300 ... 16 Ak 31
(N) Hol 3576 ... 16 Ai 30
(RUS) Hol, Ulan- ... 65 Eg 45
(UA) Hola Prystan' ... 62 Dc 44
(IS) Hólar 551 ... 36 Ql 25
(DK) Holbæk 8950 ... 27 Bb 35
(CZ) Holešov 769 01 ... 44 Bh 41
(CZ) Holice 783 71 ... 44 Bf 40
(S) Höljes 68065 ... 17 Bc 30
(A) Hollabrunn 2020* ... 44 Bg 42
(GB) Hollandstrom ... 38 Sh 31
(N) Høllen ... 16 Ah 32
(H) Hollókő 3176 ... 59 Bk 43
(S) Höllviken 23601 ... 27 Bc 35
(IRL) Hollywood = Cillín Chaoimhín ... 37 Sd 37
(FIN) Holm 25488 ... 10 Cc 27
(RUS) Holm 25488 ... 19 Db 33
(S) Holm 30279 ... 9 Bg 28
(S) Holmajärvi ... 2 Bk 23
(IS) Hólmavík 510* ... 36 Qi 25
(RUS) Holmeči ... 47 De 38
(N) Holmedal 6982 ... 16 Af 29
(N) Holmenkollen 0010* ... 16 Ba 31
(N) Holmestrand 3080 ... 16 Ba 31
(RUS) Holmogorskaja ... 12 Ea 27
(RUS) Holmogory ... 13 Eb 26
(RUS) Holmskij ... 63 Di 46
(S) Holmsund 91301 ... 10 Ca 27
(S) Holmsveden 82392 ... 17 Bg 29
(RUS) Holm-Žirkovskij ... 31 Dd 35
(UA) Holoby ... 46 Cf 39
(UA) Holovkivka ... 47 Dc 41
(N) Holøydal 2540 ... 8 Bb 28
(DK) Holstebro 7500 ... 26 Ai 34
(DK) Holsted 6670 ... 26 Ai 35
(GB) Holsworthy EX22 ... 40 Sf 40
(RUS) Holtobino ... 31 Di 36
(NL) Holwerd ... 26 Af 37
(GB) Holyhead LL65 ... 39 Sf 37
(GB) Holy Island TD15 ... 39 Si 35


**154** Hadjač

- (BY) Ivanava 46 Cf 38
- (CZ) Ivančice 664 91 44 Bg 41
- (HR) Ivanec 58 Bg 44
- (RUS) Ivangorod 19 Ci 31
- (MNE) Ivangrad = Berane 84 300 74 Bk 48
- (UA) Ivanhorod 47 Dc 39
- (HR) Ivanič Grad 58 Bg 45
- (RUS) Ivanišči 32 Ea 35
- (RUS) Ivaniši 31 Df 34
- (UA) Ivanivka 45 Cc 42
- (UA) Ivanivka 48 Di 42
- (UA) Ivanivka 62 De 44
- (SRB) Ivanjica 32250 59 Ca 47
- (BIH) Ivanjska 58 Bh 46
- (UA) Ivankiv 46 Ck 40
- (RUS) Ivan'kovo 31 Dh 36
- (UA) Ivano-Frankivs'k 45 Ce 42
- (UA) Ivano-Frankove 45 Cd 41
- (UA) Ivano-Frankovsk = Ivano-Frankivs'k 45 Ce 42
- (RUS) Ivano-Kuvalat 52 Fh 38
- (UA) Ivanopil' 46 Ci 41
- (RUS) Ivanovka 34 Fd 38
- (RUS) Ivanovka 34 Fe 36
- (BG) Ivanovo 6465 60 Cf 47
- (RUS) Ivanovo 30 Da 34
- (RUS) Ivanovo 32 Ea 34
- (RUS) Ivanovsk, Katav- 35 Fi 36
- (RUS) Ivanovskaja 63 Di 45
- (RUS) Ivanovskoe 21 Ee 32
- (RUS) Ivanovskoe 23 Ff 32
- (RUS) Ivanovskoe, Usen'- 34 Fe 36
- (BG) Ivanski 9810 61 Ch 47
- (RUS) Ivanteevka 50 Ek 38
- (RUS) Ivanteevo 20 Dd 33
- (RUS) Ivaševo 21 Ec 33
- (BY) Iv'e 29 Cf 37
- (RO) Iveşti 737320 61 Ch 45
- (BY) Ivjanec 29 Cg 37
- (RUS) Ivlevskaja 13 Ec 28
- (RUS) Ivnja 48 Dg 39
- (RUS) Ivot Star' 31 De 37
- (I) Ivrea 10015 56 Ah 45
- (TR) İvrindi 10770 76 Ch 51
- (TR) İyidere 53600 79 Ea 49
- (RUS) Ižberdino 52 Fg 38
- (PL) Izbica Kujawska 87-865 44 Bi 38
- (RO) Izbiceni 237230 60 Ce 47
- (RUS) Izborsk 19 Ch 33
- (RUS) Izdeškovo 31 Dd 35
- (P) Izeda 5300-591* 68 Sd 49
- (RUS) Iževsk 34 Fd 34
- (RUS) Iževskoe 32 Ea 36
- (RUS) Izi-Kugunur 33 Ei 34
- (UA) Izjum 48 Dh 41
- (RUS) Ižma 14 Fd 25
- (UA) Izmail = Izmajil 61 Ci 45
- (UA) Izmajil 61 Ci 45
- (RUS) Izmajlovo 2-e(Vtoroe) 20 Di 32
- (RUS) Izmalkovo 48 Dh 38
- (TR) İzmir 35000* 83 Ch 52
- (TR) İzmit = Kocaeli 76 Ck 50
- (TR) İznik 16860 76 Ck 50
- (RUS) Iznoski 31 De 35
- (RUS) Izobil'noe 51 Fe 39
- (RUS) Izobil'nyj 64 Eb 45
- (SLO) Izola 6310 57 Bd 45
- (H) Izsák 6070 59 Bk 44
- (RUS) Izumrud 24 Gb 33
- (BG) Izvor 8153 74 Cc 48
- (MK) Izvor 1414 74 Cb 49
- (RO) Izvoru 117405 60 Cf 46


## J


- (FIN) Jaakonvaara 81430 11 Da 27
- (FIN) Jaala 47710 18 Cg 29
- (BIH) Jablan Do 73 Bi 48
- (BG) Jablanica 5750 75 Ce 47
- (BIH) Jablanica 58 Bh 47
- (CZ) Jablonec nad Nisou 466 01* 44 Bf 40
- (PL) Jabłonna 62-067 45 Ca 38
- (PL) Jabłonowo Pomorskie 87-330 28 Bh 37
- (SRB) Jabukovac 19304 59 Cc 46
- (E) Jaca 22700 70 Sk 48
- (CZ) Jáchymov 362 51 43 Bc 40
- (E) Jadraque 19240* 69 Sh 50
- (RUS) Jadrin 33 Eg 35
- (E) Jaén 23001 81 Sg 53
- (BG) Jagoda 6167 75 Cf 48
- (SRB) Jagodina 35000* 59 Cb 47
- (RUS) Jagodnoe 33 Ek 37
- (RUS) Jagubovka 33 Ee 35
- (UA) Jahotyn 47 Db 40
- (RUS) Jahren'ga 22 Eg 30
- (F) Jailleu, Bourgoin- 38300 56 Af 45
- (BIH) Jajce 58 Bh 46
- (RUS) Jajva 23 Fh 31
- (S) Jäkkvik 2 Bg 24
- (FIN) Jakobstad 68600* 10 Cc 27
- (RUS) Jakolevo 48 Dg 40
- (BG) Jakoruda 2790 75 Cd 48
- (RUS) Jakovlevka 50 Eg 38
- (RUS) Jakovlevo 31 Dh 36
- (RUS) Jakovlevskaja 13 Ed 28
- (RUS) Jakovlevskij 31 Dh 36
- (RUS) Jakovo 23 Fd 29
- (RUS) Jakša 15 Fg 29
- (RUS) Jakšino 14 Fc 24
- (RUS) Jakšino 20 Dh 30
- (RUS) Jakun'ël' 22 Ek 31
- (RUS) Jakunvara 11 Db 28
- (UA) Jakymivka 62 Df 44
- (FIN) Jalasjärvi 61601 10 Cc 28
- (RUS) Jal'čiki 33 Ei 35
- (RUS) Jalguba 12 De 29
- (F) Jaligny-sur-Besbre 03220 55 Ad 44
- (UA) Jalta 62 De 46
- (UA) Jama 48 Di 42
- (RUS) Jamansaz 52 Fi 38
- (RUS) Jambirno 32 Ec 36
- (BG) Jambol 8600* 75 Cg 48
- (SRB) Jamena 59 Bk 46
- (FIN) Jämijärvi 38800 10 Cc 29
- (S) Jämjö 37300 27 Bf 34
- (RUS) Jamkino 19 Ck 33
- (RUS) Jamnovo 33 Ee 34
- (UA) Jampil' 46 Cg 41
- (UA) Jampil' 47 Dd 39
- (FIN) Jämsä 42120 10 Cf 29
- (RUS) Janaul 34 Fe 34
- (BY) Janavičy 30 Da 35
- (RUS) Jandovka 31 Di 37
- (RUS) Jangiskain 35 Fg 37
- (RUS) Janiševo 20 Dh 29
- (RUS) Janiskoski 3 Ci 22
- (HR) Janjina 73 Bh 48
- (S) Jänkisjärvi 3 Cd 24
- (H) Jánoshalma 6440 59 Bk 44
- (PL) Janów Lubelski 23-300 45 Cc 40
- (PL) Janów Podlaski 21-505 45 Cd 38
- (S) Jänsmässholmen 83051 9 Bd 27
- (RUS) Jantarnyj 28 Bk 36
- (RUS) Jantikovo 33 Eh 35
- (F) Janzé 35150 54 Si 43
- (RUS) Jar 23 Fc 32
- (RUS) Jar 25 Gf 33
- (E) Jaraicejo 10380 68 Se 51
- (E) Jaraiz de la Vera 10400 68 Se 50
- (E) Jarandilla de la Vera 10450 68 Se 50
- (RUS) Jaransk 22 Eh 33
- (S) Järbo 17 Bg 30
- (RUS) Jarcevo 30 Dc 35
- (RUS) Jarega 14 Fd 27
- (RUS) Jarenga 14 Ek 28
- (RUS) Jarensk 14 Ek 28
- (F) Jargeau 45150 55 Ac 43
- (S) Jarhois 3 Cd 24
- (RUS) Jarkovo 25 Gg 33
- (D) Jarmen 17126 27 Bd 37
- (UA) Jarmolynci 46 Cg 41
- (S) Järna 15300 17 Bh 31
- (S) Järna, Dala- 17 Be 30
- (F) Jarnac 16200 54 Sk 45
- (S) Järnäsklubb 91401 10 Bk 27
- (RUS) Jarnema 12 Dk 28
- (S) Järnforsen 57081 17 Bf 33
- (F) Jarny 54800 42 Af 41
- (PL) Jarocin 63-200 44 Bh 39
- (RUS) Jarok 32 Ea 38
- (CZ) Jaroměř 551 01 44 Bf 40
- (RUS) Jaroslaviči 20 De 30
- (RUS) Jaroslavka 35 Fh 35
- (RUS) Jaroslavl' 21 Dk 33
- (RUS) Jaroslavskaja 64 Ea 46
- (PL) Jarosław 37-500 45 Cc 40
- (S) Järpås 53104 17 Bc 32
- (S) Järpen 83005 9 Bd 27
- (EST) Järva-Jaani 73301 18 Cf 31
- (EST) Järvakandi 79101 18 Ce 32
- (FIN) Järvenpää 73901 10 Cb 28
- (FIN) Järvenpää 73901 18 Cf 30
- (S) Järvsö 82040 17 Bg 29
- (RUS) Jašalta 64 Ec 44
- (SRB) Jaša Tomić 23230 59 Ca 45
- (UA) Jasenivs'kyj 48 Dk 42
- (RUS) Jasenki 48 Di 39
- (RUS) Jasenskaja 63 Di 44
- (UA) Jasinja 45 Ce 42
- (LT) Jašiūnai 17038 29 Cf 36
- (RUS) Jaškino 34 Fd 38
- (RUS) Jaškul' 65 Ef 44
- (RUS) Jaškur-Bod'ja 23 Fd 33
- (PL) Jasło 38-200 45 Cb 41
- (RUS) Jasnaja Poljana 31 Dh 36
- (RUS) Jasnogorsk 31 Dh 36
- (RUS) Jasnogorskij 51 Fd 38
- (RUS) Jasnoje 28 Cb 35
- (RUS) Jasnyj 52 Fk 40
- (PL) Jastarnia 84-140 28 Bi 36
- (HR) Jastrebarsko 58 Bf 45
- (PL) Jastrowie 64-915 28 Bg 37
- (RUS) Jasunt 15 Ga 26
- (UA) Jasynuvata 48 Dh 42
- (H) Jászapáti 5130 59 Ca 43
- (H) Jászárokszállás 5123 59 Bk 43
- (H) Jászberény 5100 59 Bk 43
- (LV) Jaungulbene 4420 18 Cg 33
- (LV) Jaunjelgava 5134 29 Cf 34
- (LV) Jaunpiebalga 4125 29 Cg 33
- (LV) Jaunpils 3145 29 Cd 34
- (RUS) Javgil'dino 35 Fg 35
- (UA) Javkyne 62 Dc 43
- (UA) Javoriv 45 Cd 41
- (S) Jävre 94401 10 Cb 25
- (F) Javron-les-Chapelles 53250 40 Sk 42
- (RUS) Javzora 13 Ef 27
- (PL) Jawor 56-330 44 Bg 39
- (PL) Jaworzno 43-600 44 Bk 40
- (RUS) Jažel'bicy 19 Dc 32
- (RUS) Jazevec 13 Eg 25
- (RUS) Jažma 5 Ee 24
- (RUS) Jazykovo 31 Dh 38
- (RUS) Jazykovo 33 Eh 36
- (RUS) Jazykovo 34 Fe 36
- (GB) Jedburgh TD8 39 Sh 35
- (PL) Jedwabne 18-420 29 Cc 37
- (LV) Jēkabpils 5201* 29 Cf 34
- (RUS) Jekaterinburg = Ekaterinburg 35 Ga 34
- (N) Jektvika 2 Bd 24
- (UA) Jelanec' 62 Db 43
- (PL) Jelenia Góra 58-500 44 Bf 40
- (LV) Jelgava 3001* 29 Cd 34
- (DK) Jelling 7300 26 Ak 35
- (DK) Jels 6630 26 Ak 35
- (HR) Jelsa 73 Bg 47
- (SK) Jelšava 049 16 45 Ca 42
- (UA) Jelyzavethradka 47 Dc 42
- (UA) Jemil'čyne 46 Ch 40
- (D) Jena 07743* 43 Bb 40
- (UA) Jenakijeve 48 Di 42
- (A) Jenbach 6200* 57 Bb 43
- (UA) Jenerhodar 62 De 43
- (FIN) Jeppo 66850 10 Cc 27
- (FIN) Jepua = Jeppo 66850 10 Cc 27
- (E) Jerez de la Frontera 11401* 80 Sd 54
- (E) Jerez de los Caballeros 06380 80 Sd 52
- (E) Jérica 12450 70 Sk 51
- (D) Jerichow 39319 43 Bc 38
- (LV) Jersika 5315 29 Cg 34
- (SLO) Jesenice 4270 58 Be 44
- (CZ) Jeseník 790 01 44 Bh 40
- (SK) Jesenské 980 02 45 Ca 42
- (I) Jesi 60035 57 Bd 47
- (I) Jésolo 30016 57 Bc 45
- (D) Jessen (Elster) 06917 43 Bc 39
- (N) Jessheim 2050* 16 Bb 30
- (F) Jeumont 59460 41 Ae 40
- (D) Jever 26441 26 Ah 37
- (N) Jevnaker 3520 16 Ba 30
- (UA) Jevpatorija 62 Dd 45
- (HR) Jezerane 58 Bf 45
- (BIH) Jezero 58 Bh 46
- (PL) Jeziorany 11-320 28 Ca 37
- (RO) Jibou 455200 60 Cd 43
- (CZ) Jičín 506 01* 44 Bf 40
- (LT) Jieznas 59058 29 Ce 36
- (CZ) Jihlava 586 01 44 Bf 41
- (E) Jijona = Xixona 03100 70 Sk 52
- (CZ) Jilemnice 514 01 44 Bf 40
- (S) Jiltjer 9 Bg 25
- (RO) Jimbolia 305400 59 Ca 45
- (E) Jimena de la Frontera 11330* 80 Se 54
- (CZ) Jindřichův Hradec 377 01 44 Bf 41
- (CZ) Jirkov 431 11* 43 Bd 40
- (D) Joachimsthal 16247 27 Bd 38
- (E) Jócar 81 Sg 53
- (S) Jock 3 Cc 24
- (FIN) Joensuu 80100* 11 Ck 28
- (S) Joesjö 9 Be 25
- (EST) Jõgeva 48303* 18 Cg 32
- (D) Johanngeorgenstadt 08349 43 Bc 40
- (GB) John o'Groats KW1 38 Sg 32
- (EST) Jõhvi-Ahtme 41541 19 Ch 31
- (F) Joigny 89300* 41 Ad 43
- (F) Joinville 52300* 42 Af 42
- (S) Jokkmokk 96201 2 Bk 24
- (AX) Jomala 22151 18 Bk 30
- (N) Jondal 5627 16 Ag 30
- (LT) Joniškėlis 39027 29 Ce 34
- (LT) Joniškis 84001 29 Cd 34
- (S) Jönköping 55001* 17 Be 33
- (BG) Jonkova 7450 60 Cg 47
- (E) Jonquera, La 17700 70 Ac 48
- (F) Jonzac 17500 54 Sk 45
- (N) Jordet 2430 17 Bc 29
- (N) Jorgastak 3 Cf 21
- (AL) Jorgucat 74 Ca 51
- (S) Jormlien 9 Bd 26
- (S) Jörn 93055 10 Ca 25
- (FIN) Joroinen 79601 11 Ch 28
- (N) Jørpeland 4100 16 Ag 31
- (RUS) Joškar-Ola 33 Eh 34
- (HR) Jospidol 58 Bf 45
- (S) Jössefors 17 Bc 31
- (N) Jøssund 7746 8 Ba 26
- (FIN) Joukokylä 89320 11 Ch 25
- (FIN) Joutsa 19651 18 Cg 29
- (FIN) Joutseno 54101 19 Ci 29
- (FIN) Joutsijärvi 98710 3 Ch 24
- (N) Jovik 2 Bk 21
- (BG) Jovkovo 9531 61 Ci 47
- (F) Joyeuse 07260 55 Ae 46
- (FIN) Juankoski 73501 11 Ci 27
- (A) Judenburg 8750* 58 Be 43
- (RUS) Judin 49 Eb 42
- (RUS) Judinki 31 Dh 36
- (RUS) Judybaevo 52 Fh 38
- (DK) Juelsminde 7130 27 Ba 35
- (RUS) Jug 23 Fg 33
- (RUS) Jugo-Kamskij 23 Ff 33
- (RUS) Jugydtydor 14 Fd 28
- (RUS) Juhnevo 21 Ec 29
- (RUS) Juhnov 31 Df 36
- (RUS) Juhoviči 30 Ci 34
- (RUS) Juhovo 30 Da 34
- (RO) Jui, Bumbeşti- 215100 60 Cd 45
- (F) Juillac 19350 55 Ab 45
- (RUS) Jukamenskoe 23 Fc 33
- (S) Jukkasjärvi 98191 2 Ca 23
- (RUS) Jukseevo 23 Fe 31
- (S) Juktfors 92070 9 Bh 25
- (N) Jule 9 Bd 26
- (D) Jülich 52428 42 Ag 40
- (RUS) Jum 23 Fe 31
- (RUS) Juma 11 Dd 25
- (RUS) Jumaguzino 35 Fg 38
- (F) Jumelles, Longué- 49160 54 Sk 43
- (E) Jumilla 30520 81 Si 52
- (FIN) Juminen 73230 11 Ch 27
- (FIN) Jumisko 97870 3 Ci 24
- (UA) Junakivka 48 Df 39
- (S) Junosuando 98062 3 Cc 23
- (E) Junquera, La = La Jonquera 17700 70 Ac 48
- (S) Junsele 88037 9 Bg 27
- (FIN) Juntusranta 89770 11 Ck 25
- (LT) Juodrantė 28 Cb 35
- (LT) Juodupė 42063 29 Cf 34
- (S) Juoksengi 95723 3 Cd 24
- (FIN) Juoksenki 95640 3 Cd 24
- (FIN) Juorkuna 91630 10 Cg 26
- (BY) Juratiški 29 Cf 36
- (LT) Jurbarkas 74001 29 Cc 35
- (RUS) Jur'evec 21 Ed 33
- (RUS) Jur'evo 22 Ei 32
- (RUS) Jur'ev-Pol'skij 32 Dk 34
- (RO) Jurilovca 827115 61 Ci 46
- (RUS) Jurino 33 Eg 34
- (RUS) Jur'ja 22 Ek 31
- (UA) Jurjivka 48 Dg 42
- (RUS) Jurjuzan' 35 Fi 36
- (RUS) Jurkino 21 Dk 33
- (RUS) Jurkovka 65 Eg 46
- (RUS) Jurla 23 Fe 31
- (RUS) Jurlovka 49 Ea 38
- (LV) Jūrmala 3015 29 Cd 34
- (RUS) Juroma 13 Ef 25
- (RUS) Jurovo 21 Ed 33
- (RUS) Jurovo 31 Dd 38
- (FIN) Jurva 66301 10 Cb 28
- (RUS) Jury 30 Dc 36
- (RUS) Jušala 25 Ge 33
- (RUS) Jušino 6 Fe 22
- (RUS) Juškozero 11 Dc 26
- (F) Jussey 70500 56 Af 43
- (RUS) Justa 65 Eg 43
- (RUS) Justozero 11 Dd 28
- (RUS) Jus'va 23 Ff 32
- (D) Jüterbog 14913 43 Bd 39
- (RUS) Jutuz, Ust'- 35 Fh 34
- (FIN) Juuka 83901 11 Ck 27
- (FIN) Juuma 93850 3 Ck 24
- (FIN) Juva 23101 11 Ch 29
- (F) Juvigné 53380 40 Si 42
- (F) Juvisy-sur-Orge 91200 41 Ac 42
- (RUS) Juža 32 Ec 34
- (RUS) Južakovo 24 Gb 33
- (RUS) Južno Suhokumsk 65 Ef 46
- (RUS) Južno-Suhokumsk 65 Ef 46
- (UA) Južnoukrains'k 62 Db 43
- (RUS) Južnoural'sk 35 Gb 36
- (RUS) Južnyj 35 Ga 37
- (RUS) Južnyj 51 Fb 38
- (RUS) Južnyj 64 Eb 43
- (RUS) Južnyj 64 Ee 45
- (DK) Jyderup 4560 27 Bb 35
- (FIN) Jyrkkä 74380 11 Ch 27
- (FIN) Jyväskylä 40100* 10 Cf 28


## K


- (FIN) Kaamanen 99910 3 Ch 21
- (FIN) Kaamasmukka 99950 3 Cg 21
- (FIN) Kaaresuvanto 99460 3 Cc 22
- (FIN) Kaarina 20781 18 Cc 30
- (FIN) Kaavi 73601 11 Ci 28
- (TR) Kabaca 76 Db 50
- (TR) Kabadüz 78 Dh 50
- (TR) Kabahaydar 86 Dk 53
- (UA) Kabanne 48 Di 41
- (S) Kåbdalis 96205 10 Bk 24
- (BY) Kabeliaj pervyj 29 Ce 37
- (BG) Kableškovo 9488 76 Ch 48
- (UA) Kača 62 Dd 46
- (RUS) Kačalino 49 Ee 41
- (RKS) Kaçanik = Kačanik 71000 74 Cb 48
- (RKS) Kačanik = Kaçanik 71000 74 Cb 48
- (RUS) Kačanovo 19 Ch 33
- (TR) Kaçarlı 06956 77 Dd 51
- (RUS) Kacbahskij 35 Fk 38
- (UA) Kachovka 62 Dd 44
- (RUS) Kačkanar 24 Fk 32
- (MD) Kačul = Cahul 3900 61 Ci 45
- (CZ) Kadaň 432 01 43 Bd 40
- (H) Kadarkút 7530 58 Bh 44
- (UA) Kadijivka 48 Di 42
- (TR) Kadiköy = Evrese 17350 75 Cg 50
- (TR) Kadıkuyusu 76 Db 51
- (TR) Kadınhanı 42800 84 Dc 52
- (TR) Kadirli 80750* 85 Dg 53
- (TR) Kadışehri 66540 77 Df 50
- (RUS) Kadnikov 21 Ea 31
- (RUS) Kadnikovskij 21 Ea 30
- (RUS) Kadom 32 Ec 36
- (RUS) Kadoškino 33 Ee 36
- (RUS) Kaduj 20 Dh 31
- (RUS) Kadyj 21 Ed 33
- (RUS) Kadžerom 14 Ff 26
- (N) Kåfjord 3 Cf 20
- (N) Kåfjordbotn 2 Ca 21
- (RUS) Kagal'nickaja 64 Ea 44
- (S) Kåge 93401 10 Ca 26
- (TR) Kağızman 36700 79 Ed 50
- (TR) Kağnılı 79 Ed 51
- (UA) Kaharlyk 47 Da 41
- (TR) Kahramanlar 25000 79 Eb 51
- (TR) Kahramanmaraş 46000* 86 Dg 53
- (TR) Kâhta 02400 86 Di 53
- (MD) Kahul = Cahul 3900 61 Ci 45
- (EST) Käina 92101 18 Cc 32
- (S) Kainulasjärvi 98065 3 Cc 22
- (RUS) Kairovo 35 Fh 35
- (D) Kaiserslautern 67655* 42 Ah 41
- (LT) Kaišiadorys 56001 29 Ce 36
- (S) Kaitum 2 Ca 23
- (FIN) Kajaani 87100* 11 Ch 26
- (RUS) Kajasula 65 Ef 46
- (BG) Kajnardža 7550 61 Ch 47
- (RUS) Kajsackoe 50 Eg 41
- (RUS) Kajuki 33 Ek 35
- (RUS) Kajvaksa 20 Dd 31
- (BIH) Kakanj 59 Bi 46
- (TR) Kaklık 20340 84 Ck 53
- (TR) Kalaba 06121 85 De 52
- (RUS) Kalač 49 Eb 40
- (RUS) Kalač-na-Donu 49 Ed 42
- (FIN) Kalajoki 85101 10 Cd 26
- (N) Kalak 3 Ch 20
- (FIN) Kalakoski 61650 10 Cd 28
- (GR) Kalamariá 55101* 74 Cc 50
- (GR) Kalamáta 24100 82 Cc 53
- (GR) Kalambáka 42200 74 Cb 51
- (GR) Kalamiá 74 Ca 51
- (GR) Kalamitsi 63081 75 Cd 51
- (GR) Kalamos 83 Cf 53
- (EST) Kalana 92212 18 Cc 32
- (UA) Kalančak 62 Dd 44
- (GR) Kalándra 63077 75 Cd 51
- (MD) Kalaraš = Călăraşi 4400 61 Ci 43
- (S) Kälarne 9 Bg 28
- (RUS) Kalašnikov 20 Df 33
- (GR) Kalávrita 25001 82 Cc 52
- (SLO) Kalce 1370 58 Be 45
- (N) Kaldfarnes 9395 2 Bg 21
- (TR) Kale 78 Dk 50
- (TR) Kale 84 Ci 53
- (TR) Kale 84 Da 54
- (TR) Kale 85 Df 53
- (TR) Kale 85 Df 54
- (TR) Kale 86 Di 52
- (TR) Kalecik 77 Dd 50
- (TR) Kaleköy 77 Df 50
- (RUS) Kalepiiha 22 Ef 31
- (EST) Kaleste 18 Cc 32
- (RUS) Kalevala 11 Db 25
- (IS) Kálfafell 880 36 Rc 27
- (IS) Kálfafellsstaður 780 36 Re 26
- (RUS) Kal'i 13 Ec 27
- (GR) Kaliáni 20016 82 Cc 53
- (RUS) Kalikino 34 Fe 38
- (GR) Kálimnos 85200 83 Cg 54
- (RUS) Kalinin = Tver' 31 Df 34
- (RUS) Kaliningrad 28 Ca 36
- (RUS) Kalinino 33 Eg 35
- (RUS) Kalinino 63 Di 45
- (RUS) Kalininsk 49 Ee 39
- (RUS) Kalininskaja 63 Di 45
- (BY) Kalinkavičy 46 Ck 38
- (RUS) Kalinniki 34 Ff 35
- (RUS) Kalino 23 Fg 33
- (RUS) Kalino 23 Fh 32
- (BIH) Kalinovik 59 Bi 47
- (RUS) Kalinovka 34 Fa 37
- (PL) Kalisz 62-800 44 Bi 39
- (PL) Kalisz Pomorski 78-540 27 Bf 37
- (GR) Kalives 64004 75 Ce 50
- (GR) Kalivia 82 Cc 53


156 Ivanava

(S) Kalix 95200 10 Cd 25
(S) Kalixforsbron 2 Ca 23
(RUS) Kal'ja 24 Ga 30
(RUS) Kaljazin 20 Dh 33
(TR) Kalkan 84 Ck 54
(TR) Kalkan 87 Ea 52
(TR) Kalkandere 53500 79 Ea 50
(D) Kalkar 47546 42 Ag 39
(TR) Kalkım 76 Ch 51
(S) Kall 83005 9 Bd 27
(EST) Kallaste 60103* 19 Ch 32
(EST) Kalli 88403 18 Ce 32
(FIN) Kallislahti 58810 11 Ci 29
(GR) Kalloní 84200 74 Cb 50
(GR) Kalloní 84200 75 Cg 51
(FIN) Kalmankaltio 99430 3 Ce 22
(S) Kalmar 28 Bg 34
(RUS) Kalmaš 35 Fh 35
(RUS) Kalmykovskij 49 Ec 42
(SRB) Kalna 19353 59 Cc 47
(SK) Kalná nad Hronom 935 32 44 Bi 42
(LV) Kalnciems 29 Cd 34
(H) Kalocsa 6300 59 Bi 44
(BY) Kalodna 46 Cg 39
(BG) Kalojanovo 8881 75 Ce 48
(BY) Kalonija 45 Ce 38
(GR) Kalpáki 44004 74 Ca 51
(LT) Kaltanėnai 18028 29 Cf 35
(RUS) Kaltasy 34 Fe 34
(D) Kaltenkirchen 24568 26 Ak 37
(D) Kaltennordheim 36452 43 Ba 40
(LT) Kaltinėnai 75044 29 Cc 35
(RUS) Kaluga 31 Dg 36
(DK) Kalundborg 4400 27 Bb 35
(UA) Kaluš 45 Ce 41
(N) Kalvåg 6729 8 Ae 29
(LT) Kalvarija 69030 29 Cd 36
(FIN) Kälviä 68301 10 Cd 27
(FIN) Kalvola 14530 18 Ce 29
(S) Kalvträsk 93027 10 Bk 26
(A) Kalwang 8775 58 Be 43
(UA) Kalynivka 46 Ci 41
(UA) Kalynivka 47 Da 40
(UA) Kalynivka 62 Dc 43
(UA) Kalyta 47 Db 40
(TR) Kaman 40300 77 Dd 51
(GR) Kamáres 70002 82 Ce 54
(RUS) Kambarka 34 Fe 34
(GR) Kámbos 85500 83 Cg 53
(RUS) Kamčuga 21 Ed 30
(RUS) Kameevo 35 Fg 35
(BG) Kamen 59174 60 Cf 47
(BY) Kamen' 30 Ci 35
(RUS) Kamen' 24 Fi 31
(UA) Kamenec-Podol'skij = Kam'janec'-Podil'skyj 46 Cg 42
(BIH) Kamenica 59 Bk 47
(RUS) Kamenka 25 Gf 33
(RUS) Kamenka 30 Dc 35
(RUS) Kamenka 33 Ee 37
(RUS) Kamenka 48 Dk 40
(RUS) Kamenka 52 Ff 38
(RUS) Kamenka 6 Fa 23
(RUS) Kamenki 31 Dh 34
(RUS) Kamennnyj Perebor 22 Fb 33
(RUS) Kamennobrodskaja 64 Eb 45
(RUS) Kamennoe 13 Ee 29
(RUS) Kamennoe 22 Ef 33
(RUS) Kamennogorsk 19 Ck 30
(RUS) Kamennomostskij 63 Ea 46
(BG) Kameno 8120 76 Ch 48
(RUS) Kamenskij 50 Ef 40
(RUS) Kamenskoe 31 Dg 35
(RUS) Kamensk-Šahtinskij 49 Ea 42
(RUS) Kamensk-Ural'skij 35 Gb 34
(D) Kamenz 01917 43 Be 39
(RUS) Kameškovo 32 Eb 34
(RUS) Kamešnaja 21 Dk 30
(PL) Kamienna, Skarżysko- 26-100 45 Ca 39
(PL) Kamienna Góra 58-400 44 Bg 40
(PL) Kamień Pomorski 72-400 27 Be 37
(PL) Kamieńsk 97-360 44 Bk 39
(TR) Kâmil 19500 77 De 49
(UA) Kamin'-Kašyrs'kyj 45 Ce 39
(RUS) Kaminskij 21 Eb 33
(TR) Kamışlı 85 De 53
(TR) Kamışlık 87 Ee 53
(TR) Kamışlıkuyu 85 De 53
(BY) Kamjanec 45 Cd 38
(UA) Kam'janec'-Podil'skyj 46 Cg 42
(UA) Kamjanka 47 Dc 41
(UA) Kam'janka 48 Dk 41
(UA) Kam'janka 61 Da 44
(UA) Kamjanka-Buz'ka 45 Ce 40
(UA) Kamjans'ka Sloboda 47 Dd 38
(UA) Kam'janske 45 Cc 42
(SLO) Kamnik 1241 58 Be 44
(NL) Kampen 8260* 42 Af 38
(RUS) Kamskij 23 Fd 31
(RUS) Kamskoe Ust'e 33 Ek 35
(RUS) Kamyševatskaja 63 Dh 44
(RUS) Kamyšin 50 Ef 40
(RUS) Kamyšla 34 Fc 36
(UA) Kamyšuvacha 62 Df 43
(RUS) Kamyzjak 65 Ei 44
(RUS) Kanabeki 23 Fh 33
(RUS) Kanadej 33 Eh 37
(GR) Kanála 84006 82 Ce 53
(GR) Kanália 38500 74 Cc 51
(RUS) Kananikol'skij 35 Fh 38
(RUS) Kanaš 33 Eh 35
(RUS) Kanavka 50 Ei 40
(RUS) Kandalakša 4 Dc 23
(LV) Kandava 3120 29 Cc 33
(D) Kandel 76870 42 Ai 41
(TR) Kandilli 25680 87 Ed 52
(TR) Kandıra 41600 76 Da 49
(RUS) Kandry 34 Fe 36
(EST) Kanepi 63101 18 Cg 33
(RUS) Kanevka 5 Dk 23
(RUS) Kanevskaja 63 Di 44
(GR) Kangádio 25200 82 Cb 52
(TR) Kangal 58900 78 Dh 51
(FIN) Kangaslampi 79480 11 Ci 28
(FIN) Kangasniemi 51201 10 Cg 29
(S) Kangos 98063 3 Cc 23
(FIN) Kangosjärvi 99360 3 Cd 23
(RUS) Kanin Nos 5 Ed 22
(UA) Kaniv 47 Db 41
(SRB) Kanjiža 24420 59 Ca 44
(FIN) Kankaanpää 38701 10 Cc 29
(FIN) Kankainen 41410 10 Cg 28
(TR) Kanlıavşar 86 Di 53
(TR) Kanlıdivane 33730 85 De 54
(FIN) Kannonkoski 43300 10 Cf 28
(FIN) Kannonsaha 43340 10 Cf 28
(FIN) Kannus 69101 10 Cd 27
(FIN) Kantala 77380 11 Ch 28
(TR) Kantar 87 Eb 53
(TR) Kantarma 86 Dh 52
(RUS) Kantemirovka 48 Dk 41
(N) Kantornes 2 Bk 21
(IRL) Kanturk = Ceann Toirc 37 Sb 38
(BG) Kaolinovo 9960 61 Ch 47
(SRB) Kaona 32234 59 Ca 47
(SRB) Kaonik 37256 59 Cb 47
(BY) Kapatkevičy 46 Ci 38
(LT) Kapčiamiestis 67039 29 Cd 36
(B) Kapellen 47608 41 Ae 39
(A) Kapfenberg 8605* 58 Bf 43
(LV) Kapini 30 Ch 34
(CZ) Kaplice 382 41* 43 Be 42
(H) Kaposvár 7400 58 Bh 44
(N) Kapp 2849 16 Ba 30
(D) Kappel 55483 42 Ah 40
(S) Kappellskär 17 Bk 31
(D) Kappeln 24376 26 Ak 36
(S) Kappelshamn 17 Bi 33
(GR) Kapsorráhi 30015 82 Cb 52
(TR) Kaptanpaşa 53350 79 Ea 50
(RUS) Kapustin Jar 50 Ef 42
(RUS) Kapustino 34 Fc 34
(RUS) Kapustnoe 4 De 23
(UA) Kapustynci 47 De 40
(H) Kapuvár 9330 58 Bh 43
(BY) Kapyl' 29 Ch 37
(RUS) Kara 35 Fh 37
(TR) Karaağa 42950 84 Dc 54
(TR) Karaağaç 79 Ec 51
(TR) Karaağaç 84 Ci 54
(TR) Karaağıl 49550 79 Ec 51
(RUS) Karabanovka 34 Fb 37
(RUS) Karabanovo 31 Di 34
(RUS) Karabaš 34 Fc 36
(RUS) Karabaš 35 Ga 35
(RUS) Karabaška 25 Gf 32
(TR) Karabeyli 84 Ck 52
(TR) Karabiga 17950 76 Ch 50
(TR) Karabucak 85 Df 53
(TR) Karabük 07350 77 Dc 49
(RUS) Karabulak 64 Ee 47
(TR) Karaburun 34558 76 Ci 49
(TR) Karaburun 34558 83 Cg 52
(TR) Karacaali 16670 76 Ck 50
(TR) Karacabey 16700 76 Ci 50
(TR) Karacadağ 76 Ch 49
(TR) Karacadağ 86 Dk 53
(RUS) Karačaevsk 64 Eb 47
(TR) Karacagür 75 Cg 49
(TR) Karacahisar 84 Db 53
(RUS) Karačaj Tereze 64 Ec 47
(TR) Karacaköy 48700 76 Ci 49
(TR) Karacaören 78 Di 51
(TR) Karacasu 14020 84 Ci 53
(TR) Karaçay 19300 77 Dc 50
(TR) Karaçayır 78 Dg 51
(RUS) Karačev 31 Df 37
(TR) Karaçoban 25620 79 Ec 51
(TR) Karadere 10700 76 Ch 51
(TR) Karadere 10700 76 Da 50
(TR) Karadirek 03550 84 Da 52
(RUS) Karagač 52 Fg 39
(RUS) Karagaj 23 Ff 32
(TR) Karagöl 31825 77 Dc 50
(TR) Karagöl 31825 78 Dg 51
(TR) Karahallı 64700 84 Ck 52
(TR) Karahasan 52700 79 Ec 51
(TR) Karahasanlı 50610 77 De 51
(RUS) Karaidel' 35 Fg 35
(RUS) Karaidel'skij 35 Fh 35
(TR) Karaisalı 33830 85 Df 53
(RUS) Karaja Masel'ga 12 De 27
(RUS) Karaj-Saltykovo 49 Ec 38
(TR) Karakale 79 Ed 49
(TR) Karakaya 76 Db 50
(TR) Karakaya 84 Dc 53
(TR) Karakeçi 63620 86 Dk 53
(TR) Karakeçili 71500 77 Dd 51
(TR) Karakent 84 Da 53
(TR) Karakoç 87 Ed 52
(TR) Karakoçan 23600 87 Ea 52
(TR) Karaköprü 05000 79 Eb 51
(TR) Karaköy 76 Db 50
(TR) Karaköy 79 Eb 51
(TR) Karaköy 83 Ch 52
(TR) Karaköy 84 Ci 53
(TR) Karakoyunlu 79 Ee 51
(RUS) Karakša 33 Eh 33
(TR) Karakulak 24860 79 Ea 51
(RUS) Karakulino 34 Fd 34
(TR) Karakurt 79 Ec 50
(TR) Karamağara = Saraykent 66320 77 Df 51
(TR) Karaman 70000* 85 Dd 53
(TR) Karamanlı 46000 84 Ck 53
(TR) Karamürsel 41500 76 Ck 50
(TR) Karamusa 77 Dd 50
(RUS) Karamyševo 19 Ci 33
(TR) Karaoğlan 78 Dk 51
(TR) Karaova 48200 83 Ch 53
(TR) Karapazar 77 Dc 50
(BG) Karapelit 9390 61 Ch 47
(TR) Karapınar 84 Db 52
(TR) Karapınar 85 Dd 53
(TR) Karapürçek 76 Da 50
(RUS) Karaš 32 Dk 34
(TR) Karaşar 18600 77 Dc 50
(FIN) Karasavvon = Kaaresuvanto 99460 3 Cc 22
(TR) Karasinir 84 Dc 53
(N) Karasjok 9730 3 Cf 21
(TR) Karasu 54500 76 Da 49
(UA) Karasyn 46 Cf 39
(RUS) Karatajka 7 Gb 22
(TR) Karataş 84 Ci 52
(TR) Karataş 85 Df 54
(TR) Karatoprak = Turgutreis 48960 83 Ch 54
(S) Karats 2 Bi 24
(RUS) Karaul'skoe 24 Ga 31
(TR) Karaurgan 36520 79 Ec 50
(BY) Karavacičy 47 Da 38
(GR) Karavás 82 Cc 54
(BG) Karavelovo 4350 75 Cg 48
(TR) Karayaka 60540 78 Dg 50
(TR) Karayazı 25830 79 Ec 51
(TR) Karayün 78 Dh 51
(RUS) Karbany 25 Gg 33
(TR) Karbeyaz 31000 85 Dg 54
(S) Kårböle 82043 9 Bf 29
(DK) Karby 7960 26 Ai 34
(H) Karcag 5300 59 Ca 43
(GR) Kardakáta 82 Ca 52
(GR) Kardámena 85300 83 Ch 54
(GR) Kardámila 82300 83 Cg 52
(GR) Kardamíli 82 Cc 54
(HR) Kardeljevo = Ploče 73 Bh 47
(GR) Kardítsa 43101 74 Cb 51
(EST) Kärdla 92411* 18 Cc 32
(RUS) Kardymovo 30 Dc 36
(BG) Kărdžali 6600* 75 Cf 49
(BG) Kărdžali 75 Cf 49
(RUS) Kardžin 64 Ee 47
(RUS) Karelakša 11 Dc 25
(BY) Karèličy 29 Cg 37
(RUS) Karelina 25 Gi 33
(RUS) Karelino 24 Ga 32
(RUS) Karelino 34 Fa 34
(RUS) Karel'skaja Masel'ga 11 Dd 27
(RUS) Karepol'e 13 Ed 25
(S) Karesuando 98016 3 Cc 22
(RUS) Kargala 51 Fe 39
(RUS) Kargali 34 Fa 35
(TR) Kargı 19900 77 De 49
(TR) Kargı 19900 84 Ck 54
(TR) Kargı 19900 84 Da 53
(TR) Kargıcak 48200 85 Dd 54
(TR) Kargın 58510 77 De 50
(TR) Kargın 58510 84 Da 53
(RUS) Kargino 33 Eh 37
(RUS) Kargopol' 20 Di 29
(PL) Kargowa 66-120 44 Bf 38
(FIN) Karhukangas 86480 10 Cf 26
(FIN) Karhula 48810 18 Cg 30
(RUS) Karian 49 Eb 38
(GR) Kariés 23067 75 Ce 50
(FIN) Karigasniemi 99950 3 Cf 21
(EST) Karilatsi 63501 18 Cg 32
(FIN) Karinainen 21840 18 Cc 30
(TR) Karine 83 Ch 53
(RUS) Karinka 22 Fa 32
(GR) Káristos 34001 82 Ce 52
(FIN) Karjaa = Karis 10300* 18 Cd 30
(FIN) Karjalaisenniemi 97890 3 Ci 24
(FIN) Karjalan kirkonkylä 18 Cc 30
(GR) Karkinágri 83 Cg 53
(FIN) Karkkila 03620 18 Ce 30
(FIN) Kärkölä 16610 18 Cf 30
(EST) Karksi-Nuia 69104 18 Cf 32
(FIN) Karleby = Kokkola 67100* 10 Cd 27
(PL) Karlino 78-230 27 Bf 36
(TR) Karlıova 12900 79 Eb 51
(UA) Karlivka 48 Df 41
(HR) Karlobag 58 Bf 46
(UA) Karlo-Libknehtovsk = Soledar 48 Di 42
(HR) Karlovac 58 Bf 45
(GR) Karlovássi 83200 83 Cg 53
(RUS) Karlovka 50 Ek 39
(BG) Karlovo 4300 75 Ce 48
(CZ) Karlovy Vary 360 01* 43 Bc 40
(S) Karlsborg 10 Cd 25
(S) Karlsborg 17 Be 32
(S) Karlshamn 37400* 27 Be 34
(S) Karlskoga 69101* 17 Be 31
(S) Karlskrona 37100* 27 Bf 34
(D) Karlsruhe 76131* 42 Ai 41
(S) Karlstad 65001* 17 Bd 31
(D) Karlstadt 97753 42 Ak 41
(RUS) Karlyhanovo 35 Fi 35
(BY) Karma 30 Da 37
(RUS) Karmanovo 31 De 35
(RUS) Karmaskaly 35 Fg 36
(BG) Kărnare 4337 75 Ce 48
(BG) Karnobat 8400 75 Cg 48
(PL) Karpacz 58-540 44 Bf 40
(FIN) Kärpänkylä 93990 11 Ck 25
(GR) Kárpathos 85700 83 Ch 55
(GR) Karpeníssi 36100 82 Cb 52
(GR) Karperó 42200 74 Cb 51
(RUS) Karpinsk 24 Ga 31
(RUS) Karpogory 13 Ee 26
(RUS) Karpuninskij 24 Gb 32
(RUS) Karpušiha 24 Fk 33
(TR) Karpuzlu 75 Cg 50
(TR) Karpuzlu 83 Ch 53
(TR) Kars 36000* 79 Ed 50
(FIN) Kärsämäki 86710 10 Cf 27
(LV) Kārsava 5717 30 Ch 34
(RUS) Karsovaj 23 Fd 32
(FIN) Karstula 43501 10 Ce 28
(RUS) Karsun 33 Eg 36
(RUS) Karsy 35 Gb 36
(RUS) Kartaël' 14 Fd 26
(RUS) Kartaly 35 Ga 37
(FIN) Karttula 72101 10 Cg 28
(PL) Kartuzy 83-300 28 Bi 36
(S) Karungi 95393 10 Cd 24
(FIN) Karunki 95530 10 Ce 24
(DK) Karup 7470 26 Ak 34
(FIN) Kärväskylä 44910 10 Cf 27
(FIN) Karvia 39930 10 Cc 28
(CZ) Karviná 733 01* 44 Bi 41
(FIN) Karvio 11 Ci 28
(RUS) Karžimant 33 Ef 38
(TR) Kaş 84 Ck 54
(TR) Kaş 85 Dg 53
(TR) Kasaba 07580 84 Ck 54
(FIN) Kasaböle = Kasala 29901 10 Cb 29
(FIN) Kasala 29901 10 Cb 29
(BY) Kašalëvo, Buda- 30 Da 38
(RUS) Kašary 49 Ea 41
(BY) Kascjanevičy 30 Ch 36
(BY) Kascjukovičy 30 Dc 37
(BY) Kascjukovka 47 Da 38
(S) Kåseberga 27 Be 35
(RUS) Kašhatau 64 Ed 47
(TR) Kasımoğlu 87 Ed 52
(RUS) Kasimov 32 Eb 36
(RUS) Kašin 20 Dh 33
(TR) Kaşınhanı 42206 84 Dc 53
(RUS) Kašira 31 Di 36
(RUS) Kaskara 25 Gf 33
(RUS) Kaškarancy 4 Dg 24
(FIN) Kaskinen 64260 10 Cb 28
(RUS) Kaškino 35 Fh 34
(FIN) Kaskö = Kaskinen 64260 10 Cb 28
(RUS) Kasli 35 Ga 35
(UA) Kašperivka 46 Ci 41
(RUS) Kaspijskij = Lagan' 65 Eh 45
(GR) Kassándria 63077 75 Cd 50
(GR) Kassandrinó 75 Cd 50
(D) Kassel 63599 42 Ak 39
(GR) Kassiópi 49100 74 Bk 51
(TR) Kastamonu 37000* 77 Dd 49
(GR) Kastanía 60100 74 Cc 50
(GR) Kastéli 82 Cd 55
(GR) Kastoriá 52100 74 Cb 50
(RUS) Kastornoe 48 Di 39
(UA) Kašyrs'kyj, Kamin'- 45 Ce 39
(GR) Katákolo 27100 82 Cb 53
(GR) Katastári 29090 82 Ca 53
(RUS) Katav, Ust'- 35 Fi 36
(RUS) Katav-Ivanovsk 35 Fi 36
(GR) Kateríni 60100 74 Cc 50
(UA) Katerynopil' 47 Da 42
(MK) Katlanovo 1044 74 Cb 49
(GR) Kátō Ahaía 82 Cb 52
(GR) Káto Alepohóri 19012 82 Cd 52
(GR) Káto Figália 27054 82 Cb 53
(GR) Káto Glikóvrisi 82 Cc 54
(GR) Káto Kateliós 82 Ca 52
(GR) Káto Nevrokópi 66033 75 Cd 49
(CY) Kato Pyrgos 84 Dc 55
(GR) Káto Samikó 82 Cb 53
(GR) Káto Soúnio 19500 82 Ce 53
(PL) Katowice 40-001 44 Bk 40
(S) Katrineholm 64101* 17 Bg 32
(GR) Kattavía 85019 83 Ch 55
(S) Katterjåkk 2 Bi 22
(S) Katthammarsvik 17 Bi 33
(S) Kattilasaari 10 Cd 25
(S) Kattisavan 92195 9 Bi 26
(BG) Katunci 2830 75 Cd 49
(RUS) Katunino 22 Ef 32
(NL) Katwijk aan Zee 2225 41 Ae 38
(D) Kaufbeuren 87600 57 Ba 43
(FIN) Kauhajoki 61801 10 Cc 28
(FIN) Kauhava 62201 10 Cd 27
(FIN) Kaukonen 99110 3 Ce 23
(EST) Kauksi 41001 19 Ch 32
(LT) Kaunas 44001* 29 Cd 36
(N) Kaupanger 6854 16 Ah 29
(MD) Kaušany = Căușeni 4300 61 Ck 44
(FIN) Kaustinen 69601 10 Cd 27
(N) Kautokeino 3 Cd 21
(TR) Kavacık 76 Ci 51
(TR) Kavacık 77 Dc 50
(MK) Kavadarci 1430* 74 Cc 49
(AL) Kavajë 74 Bk 49
(TR) Kavak 75 Cg 50
(TR) Kavak 77 De 50
(TR) Kavak 78 Dg 49
(TR) Kavak 78 Dh 51
(TR) Kavakbaşı 13730 87 Eb 52
(TR) Kavakıdere 48570 84 Ci 53
(GR) Kavála 65000 75 Ce 50
(BG) Kavarna 9650 61 Ci 47
(LT) Kavarskas 29021 29 Ce 35
(RUS) Kaverino 32 Eb 36
(S) Kävlinge 24401 27 Bd 35
(GR) Kávos 49080 74 Ca 51
(RUS) Kavra 13 Ed 27
(S) Kaxås 83051 9 Bd 27
(TR) Kayabaşı 77 Dc 51
(TR) Kayacık 87 Ea 52
(TR) Kayadibi 37400 78 Dg 51
(TR) Kayaönü 85 Dd 53
(TR) Kayapınar 87 Eb 53
(FIN) Käylä 93850 3 Ck 24
(S) Käymäjärvi 3 Cc 23
(TR) Kaymaz 26640 76 Da 50
(TR) Kaymaz 26640 76 Db 51
(TR) Kaynar 38710 86 Dg 52
(TR) Kaynarca 16900 76 Ck 50
(TR) Kaynarca 16900 76 Da 49
(TR) Kaypak 01970 86 Dg 53
(TR) Kayrak 37620 85 Dd 54
(TR) Kayseri 38000* 85 Df 52
(UA) Kazača Lopan' 48 Dg 40
(RUS) Kazačka 49 Ed 39
(RUS) Kazaki 48 Di 38
(RUS) Kazakkulovo 35 Fi 37
(RUS) Kazan' 33 Ek 35
(TR) Kazan 77 Dc 50
(TR) Kazancı 18400 84 Dc 54
(TR) Kazancı 18400 87 Ea 53
(UA) Kazanka 62 Dc 43
(BG) Kazanlăk 6100* 75 Cf 48
(TR) Kazanlı 37600 85 De 54
(RUS) Kazanskaja 49 Eb 41
(RUS) Kazarka 33 Ef 37
(RUS) Kazenščina 13 Eb 27
(TR) Kazıklı 48400 83 Ch 53
(RUS) Kazil'skoe 52 Fi 38
(TR) Kâzımkarabekir 84 Dc 53
(RUS) Kazinaka 48 Dh 40
(BY) Kaz'jany 29 Cg 35
(BY) Kaz'jany 30 Ck 35
(LT) Kazlų Rūda 29 Cd 36
(RUS) Kažma 12 De 28
(LT) Kažukas = Marijampole 29 Cd 36
(RUS) Kažym 22 Fb 30
(RUS) Kčevka 50 Ei 40
(PL) Kcynia 89-240 28 Bh 38
(TR) Keban 23700 86 Di 52
(S) Kebnekaise fjällstation 2 Bi 23
(H) Kecel 6237 59 Bk 44
(TR) Keçiborlu 32700 84 Da 53
(TR) Keçiler 84 Ck 52
(TR) Keçiören 55810 77 Dc 50
(H) Kecskemét 6000 59 Bk 44
(LT) Kėdainiai 57001* 29 Cd 35
(GR) Kédra 36072 74 Cb 51
(GR) Kédros 43300 74 Cc 51
(RUS) Kedrozero 12 De 28
(PL) Kędzierzyn 47-200 44 Bi 40
(PL) Kędzierzyn-Koźle 47-200 44 Bi 40
(IRL) Keel = An Caol 37 Rk 37
(GR) Kéfalos 85301 83 Cg 54
(TR) Kefken 41610 76 Da 49
(IS) Keflavík 415 36 Qh 26
(D) Kehl 77694 42 Ah 42


A B C D E F G H I J K L M N O P Q R S T U V W X Y Z

A B C D E F G H I J K L M N O P Q R S T U V W X Y Z

A B C D E F G H I J K L M N O P Q R S T U V W X Y Z

RUS Majkop 63 Ea 46
RUS Majkor 23 Ff 31
RUS Majna 33 Eh 36
RUS Majorovskij 49 Ed 42
RUS Majorskij 64 Ec 43
BY Majseevščyna 30 Ci 36
RUS Majskij 64 Ee 47
RUS Makar'e 22 Ei 32
RUS Makar'ev 21 Ed 33
RUS Makar'evo 33 Ef 34
RUS Makar'evskaja 20 Df 30
UA Makariv 46 Ck 40
RUS Makarov Dvor 21 Ea 29
RUS Makarovo 49 Ed 38
HR Makarska 58 Bh 47
UA Makeevka = Makijivka 48 Di 42
UA Makijivka 47 Db 40
UA Makijivka 48 Di 42
FIN Makkola 51201 11 Ci 29
RUS Maklaki 31 De 36
H Makó 6900 59 Ca 44
SK Makov 023 56 44 Bi 41
RUS Makovo 65 Ei 44
PL Maków Mazowiecki 06-200 28 Cb 38
GR Makrakómi 35011 82 Cc 52
BY Makrany 45 Ce 39
GR Makriráhi 37001 75 Cd 51
GR Makrirráhi 37001 74 Cc 51
FIN Maksamaa = Maxmo 66640 10 Cc 27
RUS Maksatiha 20 Df 33
UA Maksymec' 45 Ce 42
S Malå 93070 9 Bi 25
IRL Mala = Mallow 37 Sb 38
SK Malacky 901 01 44 Bh 42
BY Maladzečna 29 Cg 36
E Málaga 29001 81 Sf 54
E Malagón 13420 69 Sg 51
IRL Malahide = Mullach Íde 37 Sd 37
RUS Malaja Azjas' 32 Ed 36
RUS Malaja Bykovka 50 Eh 39
RUS Malaja Dubna 31 Di 35
RUS Malaja Malyševka 34 Fa 37
RUS Malaja Purga 34 Fd 34
RUS Malaja Serdoba 49 Ee 38
RUS Malaja Višera 19 Dc 32
RUS Malaja Žokovo 31 Di 36
BG Malăk Izvor 6394 75 Cf 49
BY Malaryta 45 Ce 39
TR Malatya 44000* 86 Di 52
F Malaucène 84340 56 Af 46
UA Mala Vovča 48 Dh 40
UA Mala Vyska 47 Db 42
FIN Malax 66100* 10 Cb 28
TR Malazgirt 49400 79 Ec 51
PL Malbork 82-200* 28 Bk 36
I Malcesine 37018 57 Bb 45
RUS Mal'cevo 25 Ge 33
D Malchin 17139 27 Bc 37
D Malchow 17213 27 Bc 37
B Maldegem 9990 41 Ad 39
GB Maldon CM9 41 Aa 39
I Malè 38027 57 Ba 44
RUS Malebka 23 Fh 33
GR Máleme 73006 82 Cd 55
RUS Malen'ga 12 Dg 27
D Malente 23714 27 Ba 36
S Målerås 38042 27 Bf 34
GR Máles 72056 83 Cf 55
F Malesherbes 45330 41 Ac 42
GR Malesína 35001 82 Cd 52
F Malestroit 56140 54 Sh 43
BG Malevo 6392 75 Cf 49
I Malfa 98050 72 Be 52
RUS Malgobek 64 Ee 47
E Malgrat de Mar 08380 70 Ac 49
GR Mália 70007 83 Cf 55
F Malicorne-sur-Sarthe 72200 54 Sk 43
RUS Malikovka 49 Ed 38
S Målilla 57082 17 Bf 33
HR Mali Lošinj 58 Be 46
BG Malina 9559 76 Ch 48
B Malines = Mechelen 2800 41 Ae 39
S Malingsbo 17 Bf 31
RUS Malino 31 Di 35
RUS Malinovka 12 Ea 27
RUS Malinovka 25 Gi 33
RUS Malinovka 32 Eb 37
HR Malinska 58 Be 45
AL Maliq 74 Ca 50
RUS Malka 64 Ed 47
TR Malkara 59300 75 Cg 50
BG Malko Gradište 6558 75 Cf 49
BG Malko Tărnovo 76 Ch 49
BG Malko Tărnovo 8162 76 Ch 49
GB Mallaig PH41 38 Se 33
IRL Mallaranny 37 Sa 37
CH Malleray 2735 56 Ah 43
D Mallersdorf-Pfaffenberg 84066 43 Bc 42
IRL Mallow = Mala 37 Sb 38
N Malm 7790 8 Bb 26
S Malmbäck 57021 17 Be 33
S Malmberget 98320* 2 Ca 23
B Malmédy 4960 42 Ag 40
S Malmköping 64032 17 Bg 31
S Malmö 20001* 27 Bc 35
RUS Malmyž 34 Fa 34
RUS Maloarhangel'sk 48 Dg 38
RUS Maloe Čuraševo 33 Eg 35
RUS Malojaroslavec 31 Dg 35
UA Malojaroslavec' Peršyj 61 Ck 44
RUS Malojaz 35 Fi 35
RUS Malokirsanovka 63 Di 43
N Måløy 6700 8 Af 29
RUS Maložujka 12 Dh 27
E Malpartida de Plasencia 10680 68 Sd 51
E Malpica 15113 68 Sb 47
TR Maltepe 34845* 83 Cg 52
GB Malton YO17 39 Sk 36
S Malung 78201 17 Bd 30
S Malungen 82078 9 Bg 28
N Malvik 7563 8 Ba 27
RUS Malye Derbety 64 Ee 43
RUS Malyj Uzen' 50 Eh 40
UA Malyn 46 Ck 40
UA Malyns'k 46 Cg 39
RUS Malyševa 24 Gb 33
RUS Malyševo 32 Eb 35
RUS Mamadyš 34 Fb 35
RO Mamaia 900001 61 Ci 46
TR Mamak 06261 77 Dc 51
F Mamers 72600 41 Aa 42
RUS Mamonovo 32 Dk 37
AL Mamurras 74 Bk 49
RUS Mamykovo 34 Fa 36
E Manacor 07500 70 Ad 51
FIN Manamansalo 88340 11 Ch 26
RO Mânăstirea 917170 60 Cg 46
TR Manavgat 07600 84 Db 54
RUS Mančaž 35 Fi 34
GB Manchester M5 39 Sh 37
I Manciano 58014 72 Bb 48
RUS Mandač 22 Fa 29
N Mandal 4513 16 Ah 32
I Mándas 09040 71 Ak 51
GR Mándra 19600 75 Ce 50
GR Mandráki 85303 83 Ch 54
I Mandúria 74024 73 Bh 50
UA Manevyči 46 Cf 39
I Manfredónia 71043 73 Bf 49
RO Mangalia 905500 61 Ci 47
S Mångsbodarna 17 Bd 29
P Mangualde 3530-092* 68 Sc 50
I Maniago 33085 57 Bc 44
RUS Manino 49 Eb 40
TR Manisa 45000* 83 Ch 52
E Manises 46940 70 Sk 51
GB Manish HS3 38 Sd 33
UA Man'kivka 47 Da 42
RUS Manlan, Iki 65 Ef 43
E Manlleu 08560 70 Ac 48
D Mannheim 68159* 42 Ai 41
IRL Manorhamilton = Cluainin 37 Sb 36
F Manosque 04100 56 Af 47
E Manresa 08241* 70 Ab 49
D Mansfeld 06343 43 Bb 39
GB Mansfield NG18 39 Si 37
E Mansilla 40591 69 Sh 48
E Mansilla de Burgos 69 Sg 48
E Mansilla de las Mulas 24210 68 Se 48
F Mansle 16230 54 Aa 45
TR Mansurlu 85 Df 53
GR Mantamádos 75 Cg 51
TR Mantarlı 86 Dk 53
GR Mantasiá 74 Cc 51
P Manteigas 6260-014* 68 Sc 50
F Mantes-la-Jolie 78520 41 Ab 42
I Mantova 46100 57 Ba 45
FIN Mäntsälä 04601 18 Cf 30
FIN Mänttä 35820 10 Ce 28
RUS Manturovo 21 Ee 32
FIN Mäntyharju 52701 18 Cg 29
FIN Mantyjärvi 97901 3 Ch 24
TR Manyas 10470 76 Ch 50
RUS Manyčskoe 64 Ed 44
E Manzanares 13200 81 Sg 52
E Maó 07701 71 Ae 51
E Maqueda 45515 69 Sf 50
TR Maradit 79 Eb 49
F Marans 49500 54 Si 44
RO Mărăşeşti 625200 61 Ch 45
P Marateca 2900-001 80 Sb 52
GR Marathónas 19007 82 Cd 52
F Marbache 54820 42 Ag 42
E Marbella 14880 81 Sf 54
D Marburg (Lahn) 35037* 42 Ai 40
H Marcali 8700 58 Bh 44
RUS Marčata 22 Fa 33
GB March PE15 41 Aa 38
B Marche-en-Famenne 6900 42 Af 40
E Marchena 41620 80 Se 53
F Marcigny 71110 55 Ae 44
F Marcillac-Vallon 12330 55 Ac 46
LT Marcinkonys 65027 29 Ce 36
E Mar de Cristal 30384 81 Sk 53
TR Mardin 47000* 87 Ea 53
F Marennes 17320 54 Si 45
F Mareuil 24340 54 Aa 45
RUS Mar'evka 50 Ek 38
RUS Marevo 19 Dc 33
RUS Marfino 65 Ei 44
UA Marganec = Marhanec' 62 De 43
RUS Margaritovo 63 Di 44
GB Margate CT9 41 Ab 39
I Margherita di Savòia 71044 73 Bg 49
RO Marghita 415300 59 Cc 43
UA Marhanec' 62 De 43
CY Mari 7736 85 Dd 56
E María 04838 81 Sh 53
DK Mariager 9550 26 Ak 34
P Marialva 6430-081* 68 Sc 50
S Mariannelund 57030 17 Bf 33
CZ Mariánské Lázně 353 01 43 Bc 41
A Mariazell 8630 58 Bf 43
DK Maribo 4930 27 Bb 36
SLO Maribor 2000* 58 Bf 44
BG Marica 2044 75 Cf 48
RUS Mariec 33 Ek 34
S Mariefred 64701 17 Bh 31
AX Mariehamn 22100* 18 Bk 30
S Mariestad 54201* 17 Bd 32
F Marignane 13700 56 Af 47
RUS Mariinsk 35 Fk 34
RUS Mariinskoe 53 Gb 38
LT Marijampolė 68001* 29 Cd 36
E Marín 36900 68 Sb 48
I Marina di Campo 57034 72 Ba 48
I Marina di Gioiosa Jónica 73 Bg 52
I Marina di Léuca 73040 73 Bi 51
I Marina di Pisa 56013 57 Ba 47
I Marina di Ragusa 97010 72 Be 54
I Marina di Ravenna 48023 57 Bc 46
BY Mar'ina Horka 30 Ci 37
I Marinella 72 Bc 53
I Marineo 90035 72 Bd 52
F Marines 95640 41 Ab 41
F Maringues 63350 55 Ad 45
P Marinha Grande 2430-034* 68 Sb 51
RUS Mar'insko 19 Ci 32
RUS Mari-Turek 33 Ek 34
UA Mariupol' = Maryupol' 63 Dh 43
EST Märjamaa 78301 18 Ce 32
UA Marjans'ke 62 Dd 43
S Markaryd 28501 27 Bd 34
GB Market Drayton TF9 39 Sh 38
GB Market Harborough LE16 40 Sk 38
GB Market Rasen LN8 39 Sk 37
RUS Marki 48 Dk 40
D Märkisch Buchholz 15748 43 Bd 38
UA Markivka 48 Dk 41
D Markkleeberg 04416 43 Bc 39
GR Markópoulo 19003 82 Cd 53
SRB Markovac 35210 59 Cb 46
BG Markovo 4108 61 Ch 47
RUS Markovo 20 Dg 30
RUS Marks 50 Eg 39
D Marktheidenfeld 97828 42 Ak 41
D Marktredwitz 95615 43 Bc 40
GB Marlborough SN8 40 Si 39
F Marle 02250 41 Ad 41
F Marmande 47200* 54 Aa 46
TR Marmara 10360 76 Ch 50
TR Marmara Ereğlisi 59000 76 Ch 50
TR Marmaraereğlisi 59000 76 Ch 50
TR Marmaris 48700 84 Ci 54
GR Mármaro 82300 83 Cg 52
S Marmaskogen 17 Bh 30
F Marnay 86160 56 Af 43
D Marne 25709 26 Ak 37
F Marquise 62250 41 Ab 40
I Marradi 50034 57 Bb 46
I Marsala 91025 72 Bc 53
RUS Maršavicy 19 Ci 33
I Marsciano 06055 72 Bc 48
F Marseille 13001* 56 Af 47
F Marseille-en-Beauvaisis 60690 41 Ab 41
F Mars-la-Tour 54800 42 Af 41
S Märsta 19500* 17 Bh 31
DK Marstal 5960 27 Ba 36
N Marstein 6310 8 Ah 28
TR Mart 77 Dd 50
I Martano 73025 73 Bi 50
F Martel 46600 55 Ab 46
GR Mártha 70015 83 Cf 55
F Martigné-Ferchaud 35640 54 Si 43
CH Martigny 1920 56 Ah 44
F Martigues 13500 56 Af 47
SK Martin 036 01 44 Bi 41
I Martina Franca 74015 73 Bh 50
A Martinsberg 3664* 44 Bf 42
I Martinsicuro 64014 72 Bd 48
RUS Mart'janovo 30 Da 34
DK Martofte 5390 27 Ba 35
E Martorell 08760 70 Ab 49
E Martos 23600 81 Sg 53
FIN Martti 98830 3 Ci 23
FIN Marttila 21490 18 Cc 30
P Marvão 7330-339 68 Sc 51
F Marvejols 48100 55 Ad 46
GB Maryport CA15 39 Sg 36
UA Maryupol' 63 Dh 43
F Mas-d'Azil, le 09290 70 Ab 47
E Masegoso de Tajuña 19490 69 Sh 50
RUS Masel'gskaja 12 De 27
UA Maševe 47 Dc 38
N Masfjorden 5994 16 Af 30
N Masi 3 Cd 21
UA Mašivka 47 De 41
RUS Maškino 31 Dg 36
FIN Masku 21251 18 Cc 30
RUS Maslova 24 Gb 31
BIH Maslovare 58 Bh 46
I Massa 54100 57 Ba 46
I Massafra 74016 73 Bh 50
I Massa Maríttima 72 Ba 47
I Massarosa 55054 57 Ba 47
F Massat 09320 70 Ab 48
F Massay 18120 55 Ab 43
F Masseube 32140 54 Aa 47
F Massiac 15500 55 Ad 45
BY Masty 29 Ce 37
S Masugnsbyn 3 Cc 23
N Måsvik 2 Bi 21
PL Maszewo 72-130 27 Bf 37
PL Maszewo Lęborskie 84-315 28 Bh 36
GR Matala 70200 82 Ce 56
E Mataporquera 39410 69 Sf 48
E Mataró 08301 70 Ac 49
FIN Mätäsvaara 81850 11 Ck 27
RUS Matčerka 32 Ec 37
I Matélica 62024 57 Bd 47
I Matera 75100 73 Bg 50
H Mátészalka 4700 59 Cc 43
S Matfors 86401 9 Bh 28
F Matha 17160 54 Sk 45
F Matignon 22550 40 Sh 42
LV Mat'iši 4210 18 Cf 33
LV Matīši 29 Cg 35
GB Matlock DE4 39 Si 37
RUS Matoksa 19 Da 30
P Matosinhos 4450-001* 68 Sb 49
A Matrei in Osttirol 9971* 57 Bc 44
RUS Matrosy 11 Dd 29
A Mattersburg 7210* 58 Bg 43
A Mattighofen 5230 43 Bd 42
S Mattmar 83002 9 Bd 27
S Mattsmyra 82050 17 Bf 29
RUS Matveevskaja 21 Ee 30
RUS Matveevka 33 Ek 36
RUS Matveevka 34 Fd 37
RUS Matveev Kurgan 63 Di 43
RUS Matveevskoe 21 Dk 31
UA Matvijivka 62 Df 43
F Maubeuge 59600 41 Ad 40
D Maulbronn 75433 42 Ai 41
F Mauléon 79700 54 Sk 44
F Maulévrier 49360 54 Sk 43
S Maunu 3 Cc 22
F Mauriac 15200 55 Ac 45
F Mauron 56430 40 Sh 42
F Maurs 15600 55 Ac 46
A Mauterndorf 5570 57 Bd 43
F Mauvezin 65130 54 Aa 47
F Mauzé-sur-le-Mignon 79210 54 Sk 44
BY Mavčadz' 29 Cf 37
GR Mavrothálassa 62049 75 Cd 50
FIN Maxmo 66640 10 Cc 27
GB Maybole KA19 39 Sf 35
D Mayen 56727 42 Ah 40
F Mayenne 53100* 40 Sk 42
F Mayet-de-Montagne, le 03250 55 Ad 44
IRL Maynooth = Maigh Nuad 37 Sd 37
E Mayorga 47680 68 Se 48
A Mayrhofen 6290* 57 Bb 43
E Mazagón 80 Sd 53
E Mazamet 81200 55 Ac 47
I Mazara del Vallo 91026 72 Bc 53
E Mazarrón 30870 81 Si 53
LT Mažeikiai 89001* 29 Cc 34
TR Mazgirt 62800 78 Dk 51
TR Mazı 48200 83 Ch 53
TR Mazıdağı 47700 87 Ea 53
LV Mazirbe 3273 18 Cc 33
LV Mazsalaca 4215 18 Cf 33
BY Mazyr 46 Ck 38
RUS Mcensk 31 Dg 37
M Mdina 72 Be 55
P Mealhada 3050-006* 68 Sb 50
IRL Meathas Troim 37 Sc 37
F Meaux 77100 41 Ac 42
RUS Mečetinskaja 64 Ea 44
RUS Mečetka 49 Ea 40
RUS Mečetlino 35 Fh 35
B Mechelen 2800 41 Ae 39
TR Mecitözü 19700 77 Df 50
BG Mečka 5843 60 Ce 47
HR Medank 58 Bf 46
NL Medemblik 1670 26 Af 38
BIH Medena Selišta 58 Bg 46
TR Medet 84 Ck 53
S Medevi 17 Be 32
RO Medgidia 905600 61 Ci 46
RO Mediaş 000551* 60 Ce 44
I Medicina 40059 57 Bb 46
E Medina del Campo 47400 69 Sf 49
E Medina de Pomar 09500 69 Sg 48
E Medina de Ríoseco 47800 68 Se 49
E Medina-Sidonia 11170 80 Se 54
LT Medininkai 13019 29 Cf 36
RUS Medjanka 23 Fh 33
S Medle 93100 10 Ca 26
RUS Mednoe 31 Df 34
RUS Mednogorsk 52 Fh 39
BIH Međugorje 73 Bh 47
SRB Medveđa 16240 74 Cb 48
RUS Medvedka 24 Fk 32
RUS Medvedok 22 Fa 33
RUS Medvenka 48 Dg 39
RUS Medvež'egorsk 12 De 28
RUS Medvežka 6 Fc 24
RUS Medvežskaja 15 Fh 26
PL Medyka 37-732 45 Cc 41
RUS Medyn' 31 Df 36
LV Medze 3461 28 Cb 34
SK Medzilaborce 068 01 45 Cb 41
UA Medžybiž 46 Ch 41
EST Meeksi 65302 19 Ch 32
GR Megalí Panagía 75 Cd 50
GR Méga Livádi 84005 82 Ce 53
GR Megálo Horío 83 Ch 54
GR Megalópoli 22200 82 Cc 53
GR Megara 82 Cd 53
N Megard 7760 9 Bc 26
F Megève 74120 56 Ag 45
RUS Megorskij Pogost 20 Df 30
RUS Megra 13 Eb 24
RUS Megrozero 20 Dd 29
N Mehamn 9770 3 Ch 19
TR Mehmetli 01970 86 Dg 53
F Mehun-sur-Yèvre 55 Ac 43
D Meinberg, Bad Horn- 42 Ai 39
D Meiningen 98617 43 Ba 40
E Meira 27240 68 Sc 47
D Meißen 01662 43 Bd 39
N Melbu 8445 2 Be 22
GB Melby Ho ZE2 38 Si 30
N Meldal 7336 8 Ak 27
D Meldorf 25704 26 Ak 36
I Melegnano 20077 57 Ak 45
RUS Melehina 23 Ff 31
RUS Melehovo 32 Eb 34
SRB Melenci 23269* 59 Ca 45
RUS Melenki 32 Eb 35
RUS Melent'evo 14 Ei 27
RUS Meleuz 34 Ff 38
I Melfi 85025 73 Bf 50
N Melfjordbotn 8182 2 Bd 24
P Melgaço 4960-578* 68 Sb 48
E Melgar de Fernamental 09100 69 Sf 48
IS Melgraseyri 36 Qh 24
N Melhus 7224 8 Ba 27
E Melide 15800 68 Sb 48
P Melides 7570-600* 80 Sb 52
GR Melíki 59031 74 Cc 50
E Melílla = Melilla 81 Sh 55
E Melilla 52001 81 Sh 55
RO Melineşti 207385 60 Cd 46
I Mélito di Porto Salvo 89063 72 Bf 53
UA Melitopol' 62 Df 44
GR Melívia 40003 74 Cc 51
A Melk 3390 44 Bf 42
FIN Mellakoski 95690 3 Ce 24
S Mellansel 89042 9 Bi 27
S Mellanström 93092 9 Bi 25
D Melle 49324* 42 Ai 38
F Melle 49324* 54 Sk 44
S Mellerud 46401 17 Bc 32
M Melliera 72 Be 55
FIN Mellilä 32300 18 Cc 30
D Mellrichstadt 97638 43 Ba 40
CZ Mělník 276 01 43 Be 40
UA Mel'nycja-Podil's'ka 46 Cg 42
RUS Melovatka 49 Ea 40
FIN Meltaus 97340 3 Cf 24
GB Melton Mowbray LE14 39 Sk 38
FIN Meltosjärvi 95675 3 Ce 24
F Melun 77000 41 Ac 42
E Membrío 68 Sc 51
D Memmingen 87700 57 Ba 43
UA Mena 47 Dc 39
F Mende 48000 55 Ad 46
RUS Mendeleevo 25 Gi 32
RUS Mendeleevsk 34 Fc 35
TR Menderes 35470 83 Ch 52
TR Menemen 35660 83 Ch 52
B Menen 8930 41 Ad 40
FIN Menesjärvi 99880 3 Cg 22
F Ménestérol, Montpon- 24700 54 Aa 45
I Menfi 92013 72 Bc 53
E Mengamuñoz 05131 69 Sf 50
TR Mengen 14840 77 Dc 50
E Mengíbar 23620 81 Sg 53
GR Menídi 30016 74 Cb 51
FIN Menisjärvi = Menesjärvi 99880 3 Cg 22
F Mens 38710 56 Af 46
RUS Men'šikovo 47 De 39
F Menton 06500* 56 Ah 47
RUS Menzelinsk 34 Fd 35
NL Meppel 7940 26 Ag 38
D Meppen 49716 26 Ah 38
E Mequinenza 50170 70 Aa 49




Mequinenza 163

(F) Mer 41500 55 Ab 43
(N) Meråker 7530 8 Bb 27
(I) Meran = Merano 39012 57 Bb 44
(I) Merano = Meran 39012 57 Bb 44
(E) Mercadal, Es 07740 71 Ae 51
(TR) Mercimekkale 49090 87 Eb 52
(F) Merdrignac 22230 40 Sh 42
(UA) Merefa 48 Dg 41
(B) Merelbeke 9820 41 Ad 40
(D) Mergentheim, Bad 97980 42 Ak 41
(TR) Meriç 22600 75 Cg 49
(BG) Meričleri 6430 75 Cf 48
(E) Mérida 06800 80 Sd 52
(F) Mérignac 33700 54 Sk 46
(FIN) Merijärvi 86220 10 Ce 26
(FIN) Merikarvia 29901 10 Cb 29
(FIN) Merimasku 21160 18 Cb 30
(RO) Merişani 117455 60 Ce 46
(LT) Merkinė 65035 29 Ce 36
(F) Merlerault, le 61240 41 Aa 42
(TR) Mermer 87 Ea 52
(H) Mernye 7453 58 Bh 44
(L) Mersch 7409* 42 Ag 41
(D) Merseburg 06217 43 Bb 39
(TR) Mersin = İçel 85 De 54
(LV) Mērsrags 3284 18 Cd 33
(GB) Merthyr Tydfil CF47 40 Sg 39
(P) Mértola 7750-320* 80 Sc 53
(F) Méru 60110 41 Ac 41
(BY) Mëry 30 Ch 35
(TR) Merzifon 05300 77 Df 50
(D) Merzig 66663 42 Ag 41
(I) Mesagne 72023 73 Bh 50
(GR) Mesagrós 19005 82 Cd 53
(D) Meschede 59872 42 Ai 39
(RUS) Meščovsk 31 Df 36
(RUS) Meseda 35 Fi 36
(S) Meselefors 91060 9 Bg 26
(TR) Meşelik 33590 85 De 53
(RUS) Mesjagutovo 35 Fi 35
(RUS) Meškovskaja 49 Eb 41
(F) Meslay-du-Maine 53170 54 Sk 43
(TR) Mesudiye 78 Dh 50
(SRB) Mešnik 59 Bk 47
(CH) Mesocco 6563 57 Ak 44
(CY) Mesogi 8280 84 Dc 56
(GR) Mesohóri 74 Cc 51
(I) Mésola 44026 57 Bc 46
(GR) Mesopótamo 48062 74 Ca 51
(I) Messina 98100* 72 Bf 52
(GR) Messíni 24200 82 Cc 53
(S) Messlingen 84035 9 Bc 28
(GR) Messolóngi 30200 82 Cb 52
(GR) Mestá 82102 83 Cf 52
(E) Mestanza 13592 81 Sf 52
(GR) Mésti 68100 75 Cf 50
(I) Mestre 30175* 57 Bc 45
(RUS) Mešura 14 Fa 27
(I) Metaponto 75010 73 Bg 50
(GR) Méthana 18030 82 Cd 53
(GR) Methóni 60066 82 Cb 54
(HR) Metković 73 Bh 47
(SLO) Metlika 8330 58 Bf 45
(GR) Metóhi 82 Cd 53
(FIN) Metsäkylä 56730 11 Ci 25
(FIN) Metsälä = Ömossa 64440 10 Cb 28
(FIN) Metsämaa 32270 18 Cd 30
(GR) Métsovo 44200 74 Cb 51
(B) Mettet 5640 41 Ae 40
(F) Metz 57000* 42 Ag 41
(F) Meung-sur-Loire 45130 55 Ab 43
(F) Meximieux 01800 56 Af 45
(TR) Meydan 87 Eb 52
(TR) Meydancık 79 Ec 49
(D) Meyenburg 16945 27 Bc 37
(F) Meymac 19250 55 Ac 45
(F) Meyrueis 48150 55 Ad 46
(RUS) Mežador 22 Fa 29
(BG) Mezdra 3100 75 Cd 47
(RUS) Meždurečensk 33 Ek 37
(RUS) Mezen' 13 Ee 25
(UA) Mezenivka 48 Df 40
(RUS) Meževoj 35 Fi 35
(RUS) Mezga 20 Dg 32
(F) Mézier, Charleville- 41 Ae 41
(F) Mézières-sur-Issoire 87330 54 Aa 44
(F) Mézin 47170 54 Aa 46
(RUS) Mežog 14 Ek 28
(H) Mezőkövesd 59 Ca 43
(F) Mézos 40170 54 Si 46
(H) Mezőtúr 59 Ca 43
(UA) Mežova 48 Dg 42
(RUS) Mežozernyj 35 Fk 36
(TR) Mezraa 55900 77 Df 49
(TR) Mezraa 55900 79 Ed 50
(I) Mezzaselva = Mittewald 57 Bb 44
(RUS) Mga 19 Db 31
(RUS) Mglin 30 Dc 37
(E) Miajadas 10100 68 Se 51
(PL) Mianowice 76-231 28 Bh 36
(RUS) Miass 35 Ga 35
(RUS) Miasskoe 35 Gb 35
(PL) Miastko 77-200* 28 Bg 36
(RO) Micfalău 527115 60 Cf 44
(SK) Michalovce 071 01 45 Cb 42
(D) Michelstadt 64720 42 Ak 41
(RUS) Mičurinsk 32 Ea 38
(RUS) Mičurinskoe 19 Ck 30
(NL) Middelburg 4330* 41 Ad 39
(DK) Middelfart 5500 26 Ak 35
(NL) Middelharnis 3240 41 Ae 39
(B) Middelkerke 8430 41 Ac 39
(GB) Middlesbrough TS5 39 Si 36
(GB) Midhurst GU29 40 Sk 40
(IRL) Midleton = Mainistir an Corann 37 Sb 39
(IS) Miðsandur 340 36 Qi 26
(N) Midsund 6475 8 Ag 28
(TR) Midyat 47510 87 Eb 53
(PL) Miechów 32-200 45 Ca 40
(PL) Międzychód 64-400 44 Bf 38
(PL) Międzyrzec Podlaski 21-560* 45 Cc 39
(PL) Międzyrzecz 66-300 44 Bf 38
(PL) Międzyzdroje 72-500 27 Be 37
(F) Miélan 32170 54 Aa 47
(PL) Mielec 39-300 45 Cb 40
(RO) Miercurea-Ciuc 000530* 60 Cf 44
(E) Mieres 33600 68 Se 47
(N) Mieron 3 Cd 21
(PL) Mieszkowice 74-505 27 Be 38
(FIN) Mietaa 61301 10 Cc 28
(FIN) Mietoinen 23120 18 Cb 30
(F) Migennes 89400 55 Ad 43
(I) Migliónico 75010 73 Bg 50
(RUS) Migološči 20 De 32
(RO) Mihăileşti 085200 60 Cf 46
(RO) Mihăileşti 085200 60 Cg 46
(RO) Mihail Kogălniceanu 927165 61 Ci 46
(RUS) Mihajlov 32 Dk 36
(BG) Mihajlovgrad = Montana 3400* 60 Cd 47
(RUS) Mihajlovka 21 Ed 30
(RUS) Mihajlovka 30 Dc 36
(RUS) Mihajlovka 34 Fc 36
(RUS) Mihajlovka 35 Fh 36
(RUS) Mihajlovka 49 Ed 40
(RUS) Mihajlovka 65 Eh 43
(RUS) Mihajlovka, Podyem- 51 Fa 38
(BG) Mihajlovo 3355 60 Cd 47
(RUS) Mihajlovsk 35 Fk 34
(RUS) Mihajlovskoe 20 Dd 32
(RUS) Mihajlovskoe 33 Ef 34
(TR) Mihalgazi (Gümele) 26880 76 Da 50
(RUS) Mihali 31 De 35
(TR) Mihalıççık 26900 76 Db 51
(GR) Mihas 82 Cb 52
(RUS) Miheevo 21 Eb 31
(RUS) Mihnevo 31 Dh 35
(RUS) Mihninskaja 22 Eg 30
(RUS) Mijaki, Kirgiz- 34 Fe 37
(BY) Mikaševičy 46 Ch 38
(FIN) Mikkeli 50100* 19 Ch 29
(N) Mikkelvik 2 Bk 20
(UA) Mikolajivka 61 Da 43
(GR) Míkonos 84600 83 Cf 53
(BG) Mikrevo 2826 75 Cd 49
(GR) Mikró Dério 75 Cg 49
(RUS) Mikšino 20 Df 33
(RUS) Mikulino 31 Df 34
(CZ) Mikulov 692 01 44 Bg 42
(RUS) Mikun' 14 Fa 28
(RUS) Mila 13 Ef 28
(PL) Miłakowo 14-310 28 Ca 36
(I) Milano 20100* 57 Ak 45
(TR) Milas 48200 83 Ch 53
(I) Milazzo 98057 72 Bf 52
(IRL) Milestone 37 Sb 38
(GB) Milford NE61 40 Sk 39
(GB) Milford Haven SA73 40 Se 39
(PL) Milicz 56-300 44 Bh 39
(F) Millas 66170 70 Ac 48
(F) Millau 12100* 55 Ad 46
(RUS) Millerovo 49 Ea 42
(IRL) Millford = Baile na nGallóglach 37 Sc 35
(GB) Millom LA18 39 Sg 36
(IRL) Milltown Malbay = Sraid na Cathrach 37 Sa 38
(HR) Milna 58 Bg 47
(GR) Milopótamos 80100 82 Cc 54
(GR) Mílos 84800 82 Ce 54
(SRB) Miloševa Kula 59 Cc 46
(AL) Milot 74 Bk 49
(D) Miltenberg 63897 42 Ak 41
(GB) Milton Keynes MK6 40 Sk 38
(F) Mimizan 40200 54 Sk 46
(CZ) Mimoň 471 24 43 Be 40
(P) Mina de São Domingos 7750-120* 80 Sc 53
(D) Mindelheim 87719 43 Ba 42
(D) Minden 32423* 42 Ai 38
(RUS) Mindjak 35 Fi 36
(GB) Minehead TA24 40 Sg 39
(RUS) Mineral'nye Vody 64 Ed 46
(E) Mingorría 69 Sf 50
(SRB) Minićevo 19340 59 Cc 47
(RUS) Min'jar 35 Fh 35
(RUS) Min'kino 21 Dk 32
(RUS) Minnibaevo 34 Fc 36
(BY) Minsk 30 Ch 37
(PL) Mińsk Mazowiecki 05-300* 45 Cb 38
(GB) Mintlaw AB42 38 Si 33
(SRB) Mionica 14242 59 Ca 46
(MNE) Mioska 81 214 74 Bk 48
(I) Mira 30034 57 Bc 45
(P) Mira 3070-301* 68 Sb 50
(F) Miramas 13140 56 Af 47
(F) Mirambeau 17270 54 Sk 45
(F) Miramont-de-Guyenne 47800 54 Aa 46
(E) Miranda de Ebro 09200 69 Sh 48
(P) Miranda do Douro 5210-001* 68 Sd 49
(F) Mirande 32300 54 Aa 47
(P) Mirandela 5370-200* 68 Sc 49
(I) Mirándola 41037 57 Bb 46
(I) Mirano 30035 57 Bc 45
(AL) Miras 74 Ca 50
(F) Mirebeau 86110 54 Aa 44
(F) Mirebeau 86110 56 Af 43
(F) Mirecourt 88500 42 Ag 42
(F) Mirepoix 09500 70 Ab 47
(GR) Mírina 81400 75 Cf 51
(RUS) Mirnyj 12 Ea 28
(RUS) Mirnyj 21 Ee 29
(RUS) Mirnyj 22 Ei 32
(SRB) Miroševce 16204 74 Cb 48
(PL) Mirosławiec 78-650 28 Bg 37
(D) Mirow 17252 27 Bc 37
(RUS) Mišeronskij 32 Dk 35
(FIN) Misi 97580 3 Cg 24
(RUS) Mišino 31 De 35
(RUS) Miškino 34 Ff 35
(H) Miskolc 45 Ca 42
(A) Mistelbach an der Zaya 2130 44 Bg 42
(UA) Mistky 48 Di 41
(I) Mistretta 98073 72 Be 53
(N) Misvær 8100 2 Bf 23
(IRL) Mitchelstown = Baile Mhistéala 37 Sb 38
(GR) Míthimna 81108 75 Cg 51
(GR) Mitilíni 81100 75 Cg 51
(RUS) Mitino 20 Dg 30
(RUS) Mitjušino 33 Ee 34
(RUS) Mitrofanovka 48 Dk 41
(RUS) Mitrofanovo 15 Fg 27
(RKS) Mitrovicë = Kosovska Mitrovica 74 Ca 48
(A) Mittelberg 6993* 57 Ba 43
(A) Mittersill 5730* 57 Bc 43
(I) Mittewald = Mezzaselva 39045 57 Bb 44
(UA) Mižhir'a 45 Cd 42
(BG) Mizija 3330 60 Cd 47
(RO) Mizil 105800 60 Cg 45
(RUS) Mizur 79 Ee 48
(BY) Mjadzel 29 Cg 36
(RUS) Mjaksa 20 Di 32
(RUS) Mjakur'e 13 Eb 27
(S) Mjällom 87031 9 Bi 28
(RUS) Mjasnaja 23 Fh 30
(RUS) Mjatlevo 31 Df 36
(S) Mjöback 17 Bc 33
(S) Mjölby 59501* 17 Bf 32
(N) Mjølfjell 5700 16 Ag 30
(N) Mjøndalen 3050 16 Ba 31
(CZ) Mladá Boleslav 293 01 43 Be 40
(SRB) Mladenovac 11400* 59 Ca 46
(PL) Mława 06-500 28 Ca 37
(RUS) Mlebnikovo 34 Fa 34
(BIH) Mlinište 58 Bg 46
(UA) Mlyniv 46 Cf 40
(CZ) Mnichovo Hradiště 295 01 43 Be 40
(N) Mo 6210 16 Bb 30
(RO) Moara Vlăsiei 077130 60 Cg 46
(IRL) Moate = An Móta 37 Sc 37
(F) Modane 73500 56 Ag 45
(I) Modena 41100 57 Ba 46
(I) Módica 97015 72 Be 54
(A) Mödling 2340 44 Bg 42
(SK) Modra 900 01* 44 Bh 42
(BIH) Modriča 59 Bi 46
(MK) Modrište 74 Cb 49
(N) Moelv 2390 16 Ba 30
(N) Moen 9321 2 Bi 21
(D) Moers 47441* 42 Ag 39
(GB) Moffat DG10 39 Sg 35
(P) Mogadouro 5200-010 68 Sd 49
(BY) Mogilev = Mahilëv 30 De 37
(PL) Mogilno 88-300 44 Bh 38
(I) Mógoro 09095 71 Ai 51
(E) Moguer 21800 80 Sd 53
(RUS) Mogutovskij 53 Ga 38
(H) Mohács 7700 59 Bi 44
(S) Moheda 34036 27 Be 33
(CZ) Mohelnice 789 85 44 Bg 41
(F) Mohon 56490 40 Sh 42
(UA) Mohyliv-Podil's'kyj 46 Ch 42
(N) Moi 4460 16 Ag 32
(P) Moimenta da Beira 3620-300* 68 Sc 50
(RO) Moineşti 605400 60 Cg 44
(IRL) Móinteach Milic 37 Sc 37
(N) Mo i Rana 8610* 2 Be 24
(F) Moirans-en-Montagne 39260 56 Af 44
(EST) Mõisaküla 69302* 18 Cf 32
(RUS) Moiseevskaja 21 Eb 30
(RO) Moisei 437195 60 Ce 43
(FIN) Moisiovaara 89540 11 Ck 26
(F) Moissac 82200 55 Ab 46
(E) Mojácar 04638 81 Si 53
(E) Mojados 47250 69 Sf 49
(MNE) Mojkovac 84 205 74 Bk 48
(RUS) Mokraja Ol'hovka 50 Ef 40
(UA) Mokra Kalihyrka 47 Db 42
(BG) Mokren 8994 75 Cg 48
(SRB) Mokrin 23305 59 Ca 45
(RUS) Mokroe 32 Eb 36
(RUS) Mokrous 50 Eh 39
(RUS) Mokšan 33 Ee 37
(UA) Mokvin 63 Dh 43
(B) Mol 2400 42 Af 39
(I) Mola di Bari 70042 73 Bh 49
(N) Molde 6444* 8 Ah 28
(LT) Molėtai 33001 29 Cf 35
(I) Molfetta 70056 73 Bg 49
(F) Molières 82220 55 Ab 46
(E) Molina de Segura 30500 81 Si 52
(CY) Molini 85 Dd 56
(I) Molini di Tures = Mühlen in Taufers 57 Bb 44
(E) Molinillo, El 18183 69 Sf 51
(I) Moliterno 85047 73 Bf 50
(S) Molkom 66060 17 Bd 31
(TR) Mollafeneri 41800 76 Ck 50
(TR) Mollakasım 87 Ed 52
(TR) Mollakendi 23250 86 Dk 52
(AL) Mollas 74 Ca 50
(A) Möllbrücke 9813 57 Bd 44
(S) Mölle 26042 27 Bc 34
(E) Mollerusa = Mollerussa 25230 70 Aa 49
(E) Mollerussa 25230 70 Aa 49
(D) Mölln 23879 27 Ba 37
(S) Mollösund 47402 16 Bb 32
(S) Mölltorp 54672 17 Be 32
(S) Mölndal 43100* 17 Bc 33
(S) Mölnlycke 43500 17 Bc 33
(UA) Moločans'k 62 Df 43
(RUS) Moločnoe 21 Dk 31
(BY) Molodečno = Maladzečna 29 Cg 36
(RUS) Molokovo 20 Dg 32
(GR) Mólos 35009 82 Cc 52
(RUS) Moloskovicy 19 Ck 31
(F) Molsheim 67120 42 Ah 42
(RUS) Molvoticy 19 Dc 33
(E) Mombeltrán 05410 68 Se 50
(E) Mombuey 49310 68 Sd 48
(BG) Momčilgrad 6800 75 Cf 49
(DK) Mommark 6470 27 Ba 36
(MC) Monaco 56 Ah 47
(IRL) Monaghan = Muineachán 37 Sd 36
(UA) Monaši 61 Da 44
(I) Monasterace Marina 89040 73 Bg 52
(IRL) Monasterevin = Mainistir Eimhin 37 Sc 37
(RUS) Monastyr' 13 Eg 28
(RUS) Monastyrščina 30 Db 36
(UA) Monastyršče 46 Ck 42
(UA) Monastyršče 47 Dc 40
(UA) Monastyrys'ka 46 Cf 41
(E) Moncada 46113 70 Sk 51
(I) Moncalieri 10024 56 Ah 45
(P) Monção 4925-577* 68 Sb 48
(RUS) Mončegorsk 4 Dc 23
(D) Mönchengladbach 41061* 42 Ag 39
(P) Monchique 8550-421* 80 Sb 53
(F) Moncontour 86330 40 Sh 42
(F) Moncoutant 79320 54 Sk 44
(E) Mondéjar 19110 69 Sg 50
(I) Mondello 90151 72 Bd 52
(P) Mondim de Basto 4880-231* 68 Sc 49
(E) Mondoñedo 27740 68 Sc 47
(F) Mondoubleau 41170 54 Aa 43
(I) Mondovì 12084 56 Ah 46
(I) Mondragone 81034 72 Bd 49
(A) Mondsee 5310 57 Bd 43
(F) Monein 64360 54 Sk 47
(GR) Monemvassía 23070 82 Cd 54
(E) Monesterio 06260 80 Sd 52
(RUS) Monetnyj 35 Ga 33
(GB) Moneymore BT45 37 Sd 36
(I) Monfalcone 34074 57 Bd 45
(P) Monforte 7450-101* 68 Sc 51
(E) Monforte (Monforte de Lemos) 68 Sc 48
(F) Monistrol-sur-Loire 43120 55 Ae 45
(PL) Mońki 19-100 29 Cc 37
(GB) Monmouth NP25 40 Sh 39
(GR) Monodéndri 44007 74 Ca 51
(GR) Monólithos 85108 83 Ch 54
(I) Monópoli 70043 73 Bh 50
(H) Monor 2200 59 Bk 43
(RO) Monor 427175 60 Ce 44
(E) Monóvar 03640 81 Sk 52
(I) Monreale 90046 72 Bd 52
(E) Monroy 10194 68 Sd 51
(E) Monroyo 44652 70 Sk 50
(B) Mons 7000 41 Ad 40
(P) Monsanto 6060-085* 68 Sc 50
(P) Monsaraz 80 Sc 52
(D) Monschau 52156 42 Ag 40
(I) Monsélice 35043 57 Bb 45
(D) Montabaur 56410 42 Ah 40
(F) Montagnac 34530 55 Ad 47
(I) Montagnana 35044 57 Bb 45
(F) Montaigu 85600 54 Si 44
(E) Montalbán 44700 70 Sk 50
(E) Montalbo 16440 69 Sh 51
(I) Montalcino 53024 72 Bb 47
(P) Montalegre 5470-471 68 Sc 49
(I) Montalto di Castro 01014 72 Bb 48
(I) Montalto Uffugo 87046 73 Bg 51
(E) Montamarta 49149 68 Se 49
(BG) Montana 3400* 60 Cd 47
(E) Montánchez 10170 68 Sd 51
(E) Montanejos 12448 70 Sk 50
(P) Montargil 7400-201 68 Sb 51
(F) Montargis 19700 55 Ac 43
(F) Montataire 60160 41 Ac 41
(F) Montauban 82000* 40 Sh 42
(F) Montauban 82000* 55 Ab 46
(F) Montbard 21500* 55 Ae 43
(F) Montbazon 37250 54 Aa 43
(F) Montbéliard 25200* 56 Ag 43
(E) Montblanc 43400 70 Ab 49
(F) Montbrison 42600* 55 Ae 45
(F) Montceau-les-Mines 71300 55 Ae 44
(F) Montchanin 71210 55 Ae 44
(F) Montcuq 46800 55 Ab 46
(F) Mont-de-Marsan 40000* 54 Sk 47
(F) Montdidier 80500 41 Ac 41
(F) Mont-Dore, le 55 Ac 45
(E) Montealegre del Castillo 02650 81 Si 52
(I) Montebelluna 31044 57 Bc 45
(MC) Monte-Carlo 56 Ah 47
(I) Montecatini Terme 51016 57 Ba 47
(F) Montech 82700 55 Ab 47
(I) Montefalco 06036 72 Bc 48
(I) Montefalcone nel Sánnio 73 Be 49
(I) Montefiorino 41045 57 Ba 46
(E) Montefrío 18270 81 Sf 53
(F) Montéglin, Laragne- 05300 56 Af 46
(E) Montehermoso 10810 68 Sd 50
(F) Montélimar 26200* 55 Ae 46
(I) Montella 83048 73 Bf 50
(E) Montellano 41770 80 Se 54
(P) Montemor-o-Novo 7050-001* 80 Sb 52
(F) Montendre 17130 54 Sk 45
(I) Montepulciano 53045 72 Bb 47
(F) Montereau-faut-Yonne 41 Ac 42
(I) Monteriggioni 53035 57 Bb 47
(I) Monterotondo 00015 72 Bc 48
(E) Monterrubio de la Serena 06427 80 Se 52
(I) Montesano sulla Marcellana 84033 73 Bf 50
(I) Monte Sant'Ángelo 71037 73 Bf 49
(I) Montesárchio 82016 73 Be 49
(F) Montesquieu-Volvestre 31310 70 Ab 47
(I) Montevarchi 52025 57 Bb 47
(F) Montfaucon-en-Velay 43290 55 Ae 45
(F) Montfort 64190 40 Si 42
(F) Montfort-le-Rotrou 41 Aa 42
(F) Montguyon 17270 54 Sk 45
(I) Monti 07020 71 Ak 50
(I) Monticiano 53015 72 Bb 47
(F) Montier-en-Der 52220 41 Ae 42
(F) Montignac 24320 55 Ab 45
(F) Montigny-le-Roi 52140 42 Af 43
(E) Montijo 06480 80 Sd 52
(P) Montijo 2870-001* 80 Sb 52
(E) Montilla 14550 81 Sf 53
(F) Montivilliers 76290 41 Aa 41
(F) Mont-Louis 66210 70 Ac 48
(F) Montluçon 03100* 55 Ac 44
(F) Montmarault 03390 55 Ac 44
(F) Montmirail 72320 41 Ad 42
(F) Montmoreau-Saint-Cybard 16190 54 Aa 45
(F) Montmorillon 86500 54 Aa 44
(F) Montoire-sur-le-Loir 41800 54 Aa 43
(E) Montoro 14600 81 Sf 52
(F) Montpellier 34000* 55 Ad 47
(F) Montpon-Ménestérol 24700 54 Aa 45
(F) Montréjeau 31210 70 Aa 47
(F) Montreuil 62170 41 Ab 40
(F) Montreuil-Bellay 49260 54 Sk 43
(CH) Montreux 1820* 56 Ag 44
(F) Montrichard 41400 55 Ab 43
(GB) Montrose DD10 38 Sh 34
(E) Montroy 46193 70 Sk 51
(F) Mont-Saint-Michel, le 40 Si 42
(E) Montseny 70 Ac 49
(F) Mont-sous-Vaudrey 39380 56 Af 44
(F) Montsûrs 53150 40 Sk 42
(E) Montuïri 07230 70 Ac 51
(F) Montville 76710 41 Ab 41
(I) Monza 20052 57 Ak 45
(E) Monzón 22400 70 Aa 49
(D) Moormerland 26802 26 Ah 37
(D) Moosburg an der Isar 85368 43 Bb 42
(I) Moos in Passeier = Moso in Passiria 39013 57 Bb 44
(A) Mooskirchen 8562 58 Bf 44
(H) Mór 8060 59 Bi 43
(E) Mora 45400 69 Sg 51
(P) Mora 7490-420 68 Sb 52
(S) Mora 79201* 17 Be 29
(E) Móra d'Ebre 43740 70 Aa 49
(E) Mora de Rubielos 44400* 70 Sk 50
(PL) Morag 14-300* 28 Bk 37
(MNE) Moraice 84 210 59 Bk 47

GR Moraïtika 74 Bk 51
MNE Morakovo 81 400 74 Bk 48
E Moral, El 30413 81 Sh 53
E Moral de Calatrava 13350 81 Sg 52
E Moraleja 10840 68 Sd 50
I Morano Cálabro 87016 73 Bg 51
RO Morărești 117495 60 Ce 45
E Moratalla 14749 81 Si 52
RO Moravița 307280 59 Cb 45
CZ Moravská Třebová 569 21* 44 Bg 41
CZ Moravské Budějovice 676 02 44 Bf 41
PL Morawica 26-026 45 Ca 40
D Morbach 54497 42 Ah 41
I Morbegno 23017 57 Ak 44
S Mörbylånga 38062 28 Bg 34
F Morcenx 40110 54 Sk 46
TR Mordoğan 35970 83 Cg 52
RUS Mordovo 49 Ea 38
RUS Mor'e 19 Db 30
GB Morecambe LA3 39 Sh 36
E Moreda 33684 81 Sg 53
E Morella 12300 70 Sk 50
RO Moreni 135300 60 Cf 46
I Moretta 12033 56 Ah 46
F Moreuil 80110 41 Ac 41
GR Mórfi 46200 74 Ca 51
Morfou 84 Dc 55
CY Morfou Bay 84 Dc 55
CH Morges 1110 56 Ag 44
F Moriani-Plage 20230 71 Ak 48
RUS Morino 19 Da 33
S Morjärv 95042 10 Cc 24
N Morkabygd 8 Bb 27
RUS Morki 33 Ek 34
RUS Morkiny Gory 20 Dg 33
CZ Morkovice-Slížany 768 33 44 Bh 41
S Mörkret 79091 17 Bc 29
F Morlaàs 64160 54 Sk 47
F Morlaix 29600* 40 Sg 42
I Mormanno 87026 73 Bf 51
UA Moročne 46 Cf 39
E Morón de la Frontera 41530 80 Se 53
RUS Morozkovo 24 Gb 31
RUS Morozovsk 49 Eb 42
GB Morpeth NE61 39 Si 35
RUS Morša 51 Fa 38
RUS Moršank 32 Eb 37
FIN Mörskom = Myrskylä 07600* 18 Cf 30
DK Morsø 26 Ai 34
RUS Morsovo 32 Ec 37
N Mørsvikbotn 8266 2 Bf 23
UA Moršyn 45 Cd 41
F Mortagne-au-Perche 61400 41 Aa 42
F Mortagne-sur-Sèvre 85130 54 Sk 44
I Mortara 27036 56 Ai 45
F Morteau 25500 56 Ag 43
F Mortrée 61570 41 Aa 42
RUS Morty 34 Fb 35
RUS Morygino 30 Dc 36
RUS Mosal'sk 31 De 36
D Mosbach 74821 42 Ak 41
N Mosby 4619 16 Ah 32
HR Mošćenička Draga 58 Be 45
RUS Moseevo 13 Eg 25
RUS Moseevo 21 Ec 30
PL Mosina 62-050 44 Bg 38
RUS Mosino 35 Fh 34
N Mosjøen 8655* 9 Bd 25
RUS Moskakasy 33 Eg 34
RUS Moški 31 Df 34
S Moskosel 93086 10 Bk 25
RUS Moskovo 34 Ff 35
RUS Moskva 31 Dh 35
RUS Mošnikovskaja 20 Dg 30
UA Mošny 47 Db 41
I Moso in Passiria = Moos in Passeier 39013 57 Bb 44
RUS Mošok 32 Eb 35
H Mosonmagyaróvár 58 Bh 43
N Moss 1511* 16 Ba 31
CZ Most 434 01* 43 Bd 40
RUS Most 12 Dk 28
BIH Mostar 88000* 58 Bh 47
RO Moșteni, Trivalea- 147410 60 Cf 46
E Móstoles 28931 69 Sg 50
RUS Mostovaja 23 Fe 33
RUS Mostovskoj 64 Ea 46
UA Mostys'ka 45 Cd 41
E Mota del Cuervo 16630 69 Sh 51
E Mota del Marqués 47120 68 Se 49
BY Motal' 46 Cf 38
S Motala 59100* 17 Bf 32
F Mothe-Achard, la 85150 54 Si 44
GB Motherwell ML1 39 Sg 35
E Motril 18600 81 Sg 54
RO Motru 215200 59 Cc 46
I Móttola 74017 73 Bh 50
CH Moudon 1510 56 Ag 44
GR Moúdros 75 Cf 51
F Mougins 06250 56 Ag 47
FIN Mouhijärvi 38460 18 Cc 29
F Moulins 35680 55 Ad 44
IRL Mount Bellew Bridge = An Creagán 37 Sb 37
IRL Mountmellick = Móinteach Mílic 37 Sc 37
IRL Mountrath = Maighean Rátha 37 Sc 37
P Moura 7860-001* 80 Sc 52
P Mourão 7885-011 80 Sc 52
F Mourenx 64150 54 Sk 47
GR Mourési 37001 75 Cd 51
F Moustiers-Sainte-Marie 04360 56 Ag 47
F Moûtiers 73600 56 Ag 45
F Moutiers-les-Mauxfaits 85540 54 Si 44
GR Moutsoúna 84302 83 Cf 53
F Mouy 60250 41 Ac 41
GR Mouzáki 43060 74 Cb 51
RO Movila 927175 61 Ch 46
RO Movila Miresii 817100 61 Ch 45
RO Movilița 927180 60 Cg 46
IRL Moville 37 Sc 35
GR Movríki 32200 82 Cd 52
F Moyeuvre-Grande 57250 42 Ag 41
E Moyuela 50143 70 Sk 49
RUS Možaisk 31 Dg 35
RUS Mozdok 64 Ee 47
RUS Možga 34 Fc 34
BY Mozyr' = Mazyr 46 Ck 38
PL Mrągowo 11-700* 28 Cb 37
RUS Mrakovo 52 Fg 38
SRB Mrčajevci 32210 59 Ca 47
MK Mrežičko 7508 74 Cb 49
RUS Mrjasimovo 35 Fg 35
BIH Mrkalji 59 Bi 46
BIH Mrkonjić Grad 58 Bh 46
PL Mrzeżyno 72-330 27 Bf 36
BY Mscislav 30 Db 36
BY Msciž 30 Ci 36
RUS Mšinskaja 19 Ck 31
RUS Msta 20 De 33
RUS Mstera 32 Eb 34
PL Mszczonów 96-320 45 Ca 39
RUS Mučkapskij 49 Ec 39
RUS Mučkas 14 Ei 26
TR Mucur 40500 77 De 51
TR Mudanya 16940 76 Ci 50
RUS Mud'juga 12 Dk 27
TR Mudurnu 14800 76 Db 50
RUS Muezerskij 11 Dc 27
RUS Muftjuga 13 Eg 26
I Múggia 57 Bd 45
TR Muğla 48000 84 Ci 53
RUS Mugreevskij 32 Ec 34
D Mühlacker 75417 42 Ai 42
D Mühldorf am Inn 84453 43 Bc 42
I Mühlen in Taufers = Molini di Tures 57 Bb 44
D Mühlhausen/Thüringen 99974 43 Ba 39
FIN Muhos 91501 10 Cg 26
RUS Muhtolovo 32 Ed 35
IRL Muinchille 37 Sc 36
IRL Muineachán = Monaghan 37 Sd 36
GB Muir of Ord IV6 38 Sf 33
UA Mukačeve 45 Cc 42
UA Mukačevo = Mukačeve 45 Cc 42
E Mula 30170 81 Si 52
F Mulhouse 68050* 56 Ah 43
IRL Mullach Íde 37 Sd 37
D Müllheim 79379 56 Ah 43
IRL Mullingar = An Muileann-gCearr 37 Sc 37
RUS Mullovka 33 Ek 36
S Mullsjö 56501 17 Bd 33
FIN Multia 42601 10 Ce 28
RUS Mumra 65 Eh 45
D Münchberg 95213 43 Bb 40
D Müncheberg 15374 43 Be 38
D München 80331* 43 Bb 42
D Münden = Hann Münden 34346 42 Ak 39
GB Mundesley NR11 39 Ab 38
E Mungía 48100 54 Sh 47
E Muniesa 44780 70 Sk 49
S Munka-Ljungby 26620 27 Bc 34
S Munkedal 45501 16 Bb 32
S Munkfors 68401 17 Bd 31
CH Münsingen 72525 56 Ah 44
D Munster 29633 27 Ba 38
D Münster 48143* 42 Ah 39
F Munster 29633 42 Ah 42
CH Münster = Müstair 7537 57 Ba 44
S Munsvattnet 83090 9 Be 26
RO Munți, Rușii- 547505 60 Ce 44
S Muodoslompolo 98495 3 Cd 23
FIN Muonio 99301 3 Cd 23
TR Muradiye 65500 83 Ch 52
TR Muradiye 65500 87 Ed 52
RUS Muraši 22 Ei 31
F Murat 15300 55 Ac 45
TR Murat 79 Ed 51
TR Muratlı 63570 76 Ch 49
F Murato 20239 71 Ak 48
F Murat-sur-Vèbre 81320 55 Ac 47
A Murau 8850 58 Be 43
I Muravera 09043 71 Ak 51
P Murça 5090-101* 68 Sc 49
E Murcia 30001* 81 Si 53
F Mur-de-Barrez 12600 55 Ac 46
F Mur-de-Bretagne 40 Sh 42
F Mure, la 38350 56 Af 46
A Mureck 8480* 58 Bf 44
TR Mürefte 59800 76 Ch 50
RO Mureșenii Bârgăului 60 Ce 43
F Muret 31600* 55 Ab 47
RO Murgeni 737370 61 Ci 44
TR Murgul 79 Eb 49
RUS Murino 35 Gb 34
S Murjek 96033 2 Ca 24
RUS Murmansk 4 Dd 22
RUS Murmaši 4 Dc 22
RUS Murmino 32 Ea 36
E Muro 07440 70 Ad 51
E Muro del Acoy = Muro del Comtat 70 Sk 52
FIN Murole 34410 10 Cd 29
I Muro Lucano 85054 73 Bf 50
RUS Murom 32 Ec 35
RUS Murom 48 Dg 40
E Muros 33138 68 Sa 48
UA Murovani Kurylivci 46 Ch 42
PL Murowana Goślina 62-095* 44 Bh 38
D Murrhardt 71540 42 Ak 42
TR Mursal 78 Dh 51
RUS Mursalimkino 35 Fi 35
TR Mürşitpınar 86 Di 54
SLO Murska Sobota 9000* 58 Bg 44
FIN Murtovaara 81810 11 Ck 25
RUS Murygino 22 Ek 32
A Mürzzuschlag 8680* 58 Bf 43
TR Muş 49000* 87 Eb 52
RUS Muša 22 Ei 33
TR Musabeyli 77 De 51
TR Musabeyli 86 Dg 54
RUS Musljumkino 34 Fa 35
RUS Musljumovo 34 Fd 35
RUS Musljumovo 35 Gb 35
RUS Musorka 33 Ek 37
GB Musselburgh EH15 39 Sg 35
F Mussidan 24400 54 Aa 45
RUS Mustaevo 51 Fd 39
TR Mustafakemalpaşa 76 Ci 50
CH Müstair = Münster 7537 57 Ba 44
CH Mustér, Disentis/ 7180 56 Ai 44
EST Mustjala 93601 18 Cc 32
EST Mustla 69701 18 Cf 32
EST Mustvee 49603* 18 Cg 32
PL Muszyna 33-370 45 Ca 41
TR Mut 33600 85 Dd 54
TR Mutki 13700 87 Eb 52
RUS Mutnyj Materik 14 Ff 25
TR Muttalıp 26555 76 Da 51
UA Mutyn 47 Dd 39
FIN Muurasjärvi 44880 10 Cf 27
FIN Muurola 49760 3 Cf 24
FIN Muuruvesi 73460 11 Ch 27
E Muxía 15124 68 Sa 47
RUS Mužič'e 49 Eb 40
F Muzillac 56190 54 Sh 43
RUS Muzyvalen 33 Eg 34
UA Mychajlivka 48 Df 42
UA Mychajlivka 62 Df 43
UA Mychajlivka 63 Di 43
S Myckelgensjö 37034 9 Bh 27
RUS Myeldino 14 Fe 29
SK Myjava 907 01 44 Bh 42
N Mykland 16 Ai 32
UA Mykolajiv 45 Cd 41
UA Mykolajiv 62 Db 44
UA Mykolajivka 47 De 42
UA Mykolajivka 62 Dd 46
RUS Myla 14 Fa 25
FIN Mynämäki 23101 18 Cb 30
N Myrdal 5718 16 Ah 30
N Myre 8430 2 Bf 22
S Myrheden 10 Ca 25
UA Myrhorod 47 Dd 41
IS Mýri 660 36 Rc 25
UA Myrne 62 Dd 44
UA Myronivka 47 Da 41
FIN Myrskylä 07601 18 Cf 30
Myrtou 84 Dc 55
S Myrviken 9 Be 28
RUS Mys 23 Fe 30
N Mysen 1850 16 Bb 31
RUS Myškin 20 Di 33
RUS Myškino = Myškin 20 Di 33
PL Myślenice 32-400 44 Bk 41
PL Myślibórz 74-300 27 Be 38
PL Mysłowice 41-400* 44 Bk 40
PL Myszyniec 07-430 28 Cb 37
RUS Myt 32 Ec 34
RUS Mytišči 31 Dh 35
RUS Mytišino 31 De 36

# N

FIN Naantali 21110 18 Cc 30
FIN Naarajärvi 76851 11 Ch 28
NL Naarden 1410 42 Af 38
FIN Naarva 81470 11 Db 27
IRL Naas = An Nás 37 Sd 37
FIN Näätämö 99940 3 Ck 21
D Nabburg 92507 43 Bc 41
RUS Nabereżnye Čelny 34 Fc 35
RUS Načalovo 65 Ei 44
IRL Na Ceala Beaga 37 Sb 36
CZ Náchod 390 01 44 Bg 40
IRL Na Clocha Liatha 37 Sd 37
RUS Nadeždinka 50 Ei 38
RO Nădlac 315500 59 Ca 44
RUS Nadporož'e 20 Di 31
UA Nadvirna 45 Ce 42
RUS Nadvojcy 12 De 27
N Nærbø 4365 16 Af 32
DK Næstved 4700 27 Bb 35
GR Náfpaktos 30300 82 Cb 52
GR Náfplio 21100 82 Cc 53
RUS Nagaevo 35 Fg 36
RUS Nagajbakovo 34 Fd 35
RUS Nagavskaja 64 Ec 43
S Naggen 84013 9 Bf 28
D Nagold 72202 42 Ai 42
RUS Nagor'e 31 Di 34
RUS Nagornskij 23 Fh 32
RUS Nagorsk 22 Fa 31
RUS Nagutskoe 64 Ec 46
H Nagyatád 7500 58 Bh 44
H Nagygéc 59 Cc 43
H Nagykálló 4320 59 Cb 43
H Nagykanizsa 8800 58 Bg 44
H Nagykáta 2760 59 Bk 43
H Nagykőrös 59 Bk 43
H Nagyszénás 5931 59 Ca 44
D Naila 95119 43 Bb 40
F Naintré 86530 54 Aa 44
GB Nairn IV12 38 Sg 33
F Najac 12270 55 Ab 46
E Nájera 26300 69 Sh 48
RUS Najstenjarvi 11 Dc 28
PL Nakło nad Notecią 89-100* 28 Bh 37
DK Nakskov 4900 27 Bb 36
RO Nalbant 827160 61 Ci 45
RUS Nal'čik 64 Ed 47
BY Nalibaki 29 Cg 37
FIN Näljänkä 89670 11 Ci 25
TR Nallıhan 06920 76 Db 50
B Namen = Namur 5000 41 Ae 40
SK Námestovo 029 01 44 Bk 41
N Namsos 7800 8 Bb 26
N Namsskogan 7890 9 Bd 26
N Namsvassgardan 9 Bd 26
B Namur 5000 41 Ae 40
PL Namysłów 46-100 44 Bh 39
F Nancy 54000* 42 Ag 42
F Nangis 77370 41 Ad 42
N Nannestad 16 Bb 30
F Nant 12230 55 Ad 46
F Nanterre 92000 41 Ac 42
F Nantes 44000* 54 Si 43
F Nanteuil-le-Haudouin 60440 41 Ac 41
GB Nantwich CW5 39 Sh 37
GR Náousa 84401 83 Cf 53
GR Náoussa 59200 74 Cc 50
RO Napoca, Cluj- 000400* 60 Cd 44
I Nápoli 80100* 73 Be 50
BY Narač 29 Cg 36
RUS Naratasty 34 Fd 36
RUS Naratasty 34 Fe 36
GB Narberth SA67 40 Sf 39
F Narbonne 11100* 70 Ac 47
N Narbuvoll 2540 8 Bb 28
I Nardò 73048 73 Bi 50
BG Narečenski Bani 4239 75 Ce 49
RUS Narezka 19 Dc 33
RUS Narimanov 65 Eh 44
TR Narince 02440 86 Di 53
RUS Nar'jan-Mar 6 Fc 23
TR Narlı 10510 86 Dh 53
TR Narlı 10510 87 Ec 53
TR Narlıdere 13040 87 Eb 52
TR Narlık 19600 85 Df 54
TR Narman 25530 79 Eb 50
I Narni 05035 72 Bc 48
UA Narodyči 46 Ck 39
RUS Naro-Fominsk 31 Dg 35
RUS Narovčat 32 Ed 37
BY Narovlja 46 Ck 39
FIN Närpes 64260 10 Cb 28
FIN Närpiö = Närpes 64260 10 Cb 28
RUS Nartkala 64 Ed 47
RUS Naruksovo 33 Ee 36
EST Narva 20103* 19 Ci 31
FIN Narva 37370 18 Cd 29
EST Narva-Jõesuu 29021* 19 Ci 31
N Narvik 8514* 2 Bh 22
RUS Naryn-Huduk 65 Eg 45
RUS Naryškino 31 Df 38
S Nasafjäll 2 Bf 24
S Näsåker 88030 9 Bg 27
RO Năsăud 425200 60 Ce 43
IRL Na Sceiri 37 Sd 37
HR Našice 59 Bi 45
TR Naşidiye 85 Df 53
PL Nasielsk 05-190 45 Ca 38
RUS Naslednickoe 53 Ga 38
A Nassereith 6465 57 Ba 43
S Nässjö 88041 17 Be 33
S Nastansjö 91201 9 Bg 26
FIN Nastola 15561 18 Cf 30
RUS Nasva 30 Da 34
RUS Natal'in Jar 51 Fa 39
RUS Natal'ino 33 Ek 38
S Nattavaara 98206 2 Ca 24
I Naturno = Naturns 39025 57 Ba 44
I Naturns = Naturno 39025 57 Ba 44
F Naucelle 12800 55 Ac 46
UA Naučnyj 62 De 46
D Nauen 14641 43 Bc 38
LT Naujoji Akmenė 85001 29 Cc 34
D Naumburg (Saale) 06618 43 Bb 39
RUS Naumovskaja 21 Ed 30
RUS Naumovskij 64 Eb 43
S Nausta 2 Bk 24
N Naustdal 6817 16 Af 29
S Nautijaur 2 Bk 24
RUS Nautsi 3 Ck 21
E Nava 33520 68 Se 47
BY Navacëlki 46 Ci 38
E Nava de la Asunción 40450 69 Sf 49
E Nava del Rey 47500 68 Se 49
E Nava de Ricomalillo, La 45670 69 Sf 51
E Nava de Santiago, La 06486 68 Sd 51
BY Navael'nja 29 Cf 37
E Navahermosa 45150 69 Sf 51
BY Navahrudak 29 Cf 37
E Navalcarnero 28600 69 Sf 50
E Navalmanzano 40280 69 Sf 49
E Navalmoral de la Mata 10300 68 Se 51
E Navalmorales, Los 45140 69 Sf 51
E Navalvillar de Pela 06760 68 Se 51
IRL Navan = An Uaimh 37 Sd 37
BY Navapolack 30 Ci 35
E Navarrés 46823 70 Sk 51
E Navas de la Concepción, Las 41460 80 Se 53
E Navas del Madroño 10930 68 Sd 51
BY Navasëlki 29 Cg 38
RUS Navašino 32 Ec 35
RUS Navesnoe 48 Dh 38
E Navia 33710 68 Sd 47
RUS Navlja 31 De 38
RO Năvodari 905700 61 Ci 46
RUS Navoloki 21 Eb 33
GR Náxos 84300 83 Cf 53
F Nay-Bourdettes 64800 70 Sk 47
P Nazaré 2450-100* 68 Sa 51
RUS Nazija 19 Db 31
TR Nazilli 09800* 84 Ci 53
TR Nazimiye 62950 78 Dk 51
GR Néa Apolonía 75 Cd 50
GR Néa Kalikrátia 63080 75 Cd 50
GR Néa Mákri 19005 82 Cd 52
GR Néa Mihanióna 57004 74 Cc 50
GR Néa Moudania 75 Cd 50
RO Neamț, Piatra- 000610* 60 Cg 44
I Neapel = Nápoli 73 Be 50
GR Neápoli 23053 74 Cb 50
GR Neápoli 23053 82 Cd 54
GR Neápoli 23053 83 Cf 55
GR Néa Potídea 75 Cd 50
GB Neath SA11 40 Sg 39
GR Néa Zíhni 62042 75 Cd 49
TR Nebiler 35980 75 Cg 51
RUS Nebolči 20 Dd 31
RUS Nečaevka 33 Ee 37
UA Nechvoroša 47 De 41
D Neckargemünd 69151 42 Ai 41
E Neda 15510 68 Sb 47
BG Nedelino 4990 75 Cf 49
RUS Nedel'noe 31 Dg 36
UA Nedobojivci 46 Cg 42
UA Nedryhajliv 47 Dd 40
N Nedstrand 5560 16 Af 31
RUS Nedvigouka 63 Dk 43
RUS Neftegorsk 34 Fb 38
RUS Neftegorsk 63 Dk 46
RUS Neftekamsk 34 Fe 34
RUS Neftekumsk 64 Ee 46
RUS Neftekumsk 65 Ef 46
RUS Negonovo 31 De 34
SRB Negotin 19300* 59 Cc 46
MK Negotino 1235 74 Cc 49
RO Negrași 117535 60 Cf 46
E Negreira 15830 68 Sb 48
F Nègrepelisse 82800 55 Ab 46
RO Negrești-Oaș 445200 60 Cd 43
RO Negru Vodă 905800 61 Ci 47
RUS Nehaevskij 49 Eb 40
RO Nehoiu 125100 60 Cg 45
N Neiden 9930 3 Ck 21
IRL Neidín = Kenmare 37 Sa 39
RUS Neja 21 Ed 32
RUS Nejvinskij, Verh- 24 Ga 33
RUS Nejvo-Rudjanka 24 Ga 33
RUS Nekljudovo 20 Dh 33
RUS Nekljudovo 32 Ed 34
RUS Nekrasovo 35 Gb 34
RUS Nekrasovskoe 21 Ea 33
DK Neksø 27 Bf 35
P Nelas 3505-172* 68 Sc 50
RUS Nelidovo 30 Dc 34
FIN Nellim 99860 3 Ci 22



Nellim 165

MK Novo Selo 2434* 74 Cc 49
RUS Novosel'skoe 49 Ed 39
UA Novoselycja 46 Cg 42
RUS Novosemejkino 34 Fa 37
RUS Novosergievka 51 Fd 38
RUS Novošešminsk 34 Fb 35
RUS Novosil' 31 Dh 38
RUS Novosil'skoe 48 Di 39
RUS Novosineglazovskij 35 Gb 35
RUS Novosokol'niki 30 Da 34
RUS Novospasskoe 33 Eh 37
RUS Novospasskoe 51 Fe 38
UA Novosvitlivka 48 Dk 42
RUS Novotaimasovo 34 Ff 38
RUS Novotitarovskaja 63 Di 45
RUS Novot'jalovo 25 Gg 33
RUS Novotroick 52 Fi 39
RUS Novotroickaja 64 Eb 45
RUS Novotroickoe 22 Eh 32
RUS Novotroickoe 33 Ee 36
UA Novotroji'cke 62 De 44
RUS Novotulka 50 Eh 40
UA Novoukrajinka 47 Db 42
RUS Novoul'janovsk 33 Ei 36
RUS Novouspenskoe 22 Eg 33
RUS Novoutkinsk 35 Fk 34
RUS Novouzensk 50 Ei 40
UA Novovasylivka 62 Df 44
UA Novov'azivs'ke 48 Df 42
RUS Novovil'venskij 24 Fi 32
RUS Novovjatsk 22 Ek 32
RUS Novovladimirovskaja 64 Ea 45
UA Novovolyns'k 45 Ce 40
UA Novovolynsk = Novovolyns'k 45 Ce 40
UA Novovoroncovka 62 Dd 43
RUS Novozavidovskij 31 Dg 34
RUS Novožedrino 34 Fd 37
RUS Novozizevka 50 Ei 40
BY Novozybkov 47 Db 38
HR Novska 58 Bg 45
CZ Nový Bor 473 01 43 Be 40
CZ Nový Bydžov 504 01 44 Bf 40
MD Novye Aneny = Anenii Noi 6500 61 Ck 44
RUS Novye Burasy 50 Eg 38
RUS Novye Ljady 23 Fg 32
RUS Novye Selo 20 Dd 31
RUS Novye Zjatcy 23 Fc 33
RUS Novyi Oskol 48 Dh 40
RUS Novyj 65 Ef 45
RUS Novyj Bor 6 Fc 24
UA Novyj Buh 62 Dc 43
RUS Novyj Bujan 34 Fa 37
RUS Novyj Byt 32 Eb 35
RUS Novyj Egorlyk 64 Eb 44
CZ Nový Jičín 741 01* 44 Bi 41
RUS Novyj Karačaj 64 Eb 47
RUS Novyj Kiner 33 Ek 34
RUS Novyj Multan 23 Fc 33
RUS Novyj Nekouz 20 Di 33
UA Novyj Rozdol 45 Ce 41
RUS Novyj Sinec 31 Dg 37
RUS Novyj Skrebel' 20 Dd 33
RUS Novyj Subaj 35 Fh 35
RUS Novyj Tap 25 Gh 33
RUS Novyj Tor"jal 22 Ei 33
BY Novy Pahost 30 Ch 35
PL Nowa Karczma 83-404 28 Bi 36
PL Nowa Ruda 57-400* 44 Bg 40
PL Nowa Sól 67-100* 44 Bf 39
PL Nowe 86-170 28 Bi 37
PL Nowe Brzesko 32-120 45 Ca 40
PL Nowe Miasteczko 67-124 44 Bf 39
PL Nowe Miasto Lubawskie 13-300 28 Bk 37
PL Nowe Miasto nad Pilicą 26-420 45 Ca 39
PL Nowe Warpno 72-022 27 Be 37
PL Nowogard 72-200 27 Bf 37
PL Nowogród Bobrzański 66-010 44 Bf 39
PL Nowy Dwór Gdański 82-100 28 Bk 36
PL Nowy Dwór Mazowiecki 05-100* 45 Ca 38
PL Nowy Sącz 33-300 45 Ca 41
PL Nowy Targ 34-400* 45 Ca 41
PL Nowy Tomyśl 64-300 44 Bg 38
F Noyant 49490 54 Aa 43
F Noyers 89310 55 Ad 43
F Noyon 60400 41 Ad 41
F Nozay 44170 54 Si 43
RUS Nudol' 31 Dg 34
E Nuevo Riaño 24900 69 Sf 48
RUS Nuguš 35 Fg 37
F Nuits-Saint-Georges 21700 55 Ae 43
E Nules 12520 70 Sk 51
GB Nuneaton CV10 40 Si 38
FIN Nunnanen 99430 3 Ce 22
NL Nunspeet 8070 42 Af 38
FIN Nuorgam 99990 3 Ch 20
I Nuoro 08100 71 Ak 50
IS Núpsdalstunga 531 36 Qk 25
RUS Nur, Cagan- 65 Ef 43
TR Nurhak 46370 86 Dh 53
RUS Nurlat 34 Fa 36
RUS Nurlaty 33 Ei 35
FIN Nurmes 75531 11 Ck 27
FIN Nurmijärvi 81950 11 Ck 27
FIN Nurmijärvi 81950 18 Ce 30
D Nürnberg 90402* 43 Bb 41
D Nürtingen 72622 42 Ak 42
TR Nusaybin 47300 87 Eb 53
FIN Nuvvus = Nuuvos 3 Cg 21
S Nyåker 91494 10 Bk 27
N Ny Ålesund 9173 2 I Svalbard
N Nybergsund 2422 17 Bc 29
RUS Nybor 23 Fg 30
DK Nyborg 5800 27 Ba 35
S Nyborg 95281 10 Cd 25
S Nybro 38201* 27 Bf 34
H Nyékládháza 3433 59 Ca 43
S Nyhammar 77014 17 Be 30
H Nyirád 58 Bh 43
H Nyíradony 4254 59 Cb 43
H Nyírbátor 4300 59 Cc 43
H Nyíregyháza 4400 59 Cb 43
FIN Nykarleby 66900 10 Cc 27
N Nykirke 3180 16 Ba 30
DK Nykøbing Falster 4800 27 Bb 36
DK Nykøbing Mors 7900 26 Ai 34
DK Nykøbing Sjælland 4500 27 Bb 35
S Nyköping 61100* 17 Bh 32
S Nykroppa 68090 17 Be 31
S Nyland 87052 9 Bh 27
RUS Nylga 34 Fc 34
CZ Nymburk 288 02 44 Bf 40
N Nymoen 9 Be 25
S Nynäshamn 14900* 17 Bh 32
N Nyneset 7870 9 Bc 26
CH Nyon 1260 56 Ag 44
F Nyons 26110 56 Af 46
RUS Nyr 22 Eh 33
RUS Nyrud 3 Ck 21
PL Nysa 48-300* 44 Bh 40
RUS Nyša 34 Fb 34
S Nysäter 17 Bc 31
DK Nysted 4880 27 Bb 36
RUS Nytva 23 Ff 33
N Nyvoll 3 Cd 20
UA Nyžankovyči 45 Cc 41
UA Nyžni Sirohozy 62 De 44
UA Nyžni Torhaji 62 De 44
UA Nyžni Vorota 45 Cd 42
UA Nyžn'ohirs'kyj 62 De 45

## O

GB Oakham LE15 39 Sk 38
RO Oancea 807235 61 Ci 45
BY Obal' 30 Ck 35
GB Oban PA34 38 Se 34
S Obbola 91341 10 Ca 27
TR Öbektaş 29650 85 Dd 53
LT Obeliai 42006 29 Cf 35
D Oberammergau 82487 57 Bb 43
A Oberdrauburg 9781 57 Bc 44
D Oberhausen 46045* 42 Ag 39
D Oberkirch 77704 42 Ai 42
F Obernai 67210 42 Ah 42
A Oberndorf bei Salzburg 5110 43 Bc 43
A Oberpullendorf 7350 58 Bg 43
D Oberstdorf 87561 57 Ba 43
D Oberstein, Idar- 55743 42 Ah 41
A Obervellach 9821 57 Bd 44
A Oberwart 7400* 58 Bg 43
A Oberwölz Stadt 8832 58 Be 43
A Oberzeiring 8762 58 Be 43
P Óbidos 2510-001* 68 Sa 51
RUS Obil'noe 64 Ee 43
RUS Ob"jačevo 22 Ek 30
RUS Oblastnaja 34 Fc 34
RUS Obninsk 31 Dg 35
BG Obnova 5922 60 Ce 47
UA Obodivka 46 Ck 42
RUS Obojan 48 Dg 39
RUS Obolensk 31 Dh 36
UA Obolon' 47 Dc 41
E Obón 70 Sk 50
PL Oborniki 64-600* 44 Bg 38
PL Oborniki Śląskie 55-120 44 Bg 39
RUS Obozerskij 12 Ea 27
SRB Obrenovac 11500* 59 Ca 46
BG Obročište 9630 61 Ci 47
HR Obrovac 58 Bf 46
RUS Obručevka 52 Fk 38
TR Obruk 85 Dd 52
RUS Obšarovka 33 Ei 37
UA Obuchiv 47 Da 40
RUS Obval 32 Ed 38
RUS Obvinsk 23 Fe 32
RUS Obža 19 Dc 30
BG Obzon 76 Ch 48
UA Očakiv 62 Db 44
TR Ocaklı 25500 79 Ed 50
E Ocaña 45300 69 Sg 51
RUS Očer 23 Fe 33
UA Očeretuvate 62 Df 43
BIH Očevlje 59 Bi 46
D Ochsenfurt 97199 43 Ba 41
D Ochtrup 48607 42 Ah 38
UA Ochtyrka 47 De 40
S Ockelbo 81601 17 Bg 30
RO Ocna Mureş 515700 60 Cd 44
RO Ocna Sibiului 555600 60 Ce 45
F Octeville, Cherbourg- 40 Si 41
RUS Octovcy 31 Dd 34
N Odda 5750 16 Ag 30
DK Odder 8300 27 Ba 35
P Odeceixe 8670-320* 80 Sb 53
P Odeleite 8950-351* 80 Sc 53
P Odemira 7630-121* 80 Sb 53
TR Ödemiş 18000 83 Ch 52
H Ödenburg = Sopron 58 Bg 43
S Odensbacken 71501 17 Bf 31
DK Odense 5000* 27 Ba 35
I Oderzo 31046 57 Bc 45
UA Odesa 61 Da 44
S Ödeshög 59901 17 Be 32
UA Odessa = Odesa 61 Da 44
RUS Odincovo 31 Dh 35
RO Odobeşti 137345 61 Ch 45
RUS Odoev 31 Dg 37
RUS Odomlja 20 Df 33
RO Odorheiu Secuiesc 535600 60 Cf 44
PL Odrzywół 26-425 45 Ca 39
TR Odunboğazı 77 Dd 51
SRB Odžaci 25250 59 Bk 45
BIH Odžak 59 Bi 45
D Oebisfelde-Weferlingen 39646 43 Ba 38
P Oeiras 2780-001* 80 Sa 52
D Oelsnitz 08606 43 Bc 40
D Oettingen in Bayern 86732 43 Ba 42
NL Oever, Den 1779 26 Af 38
TR Of 61830 79 Ea 50
D Offenbach am Main 63065* 42 Ai 40
D Offenburg 77652* 42 Ah 42
F Offranville 76550 41 Ab 41
RUS Ogarkovo 20 Di 32
TR Öğdem 79 Eb 50
RUS Ogorelyši 12 Df 27
LV Ogre 5001* 29 Ce 34
TR Oğulcak 77 Df 51
HR Ogulin 58 Bf 45
IS Ögur 420 36 Qh 24
TR Öğütlü 87 Eb 53
TR Oğuz 78 Di 51
TR Oğuz 87 Eb 53
RUS Ohansk 23 Ff 33
RUS Ohlebinino 35 Fg 36
RUS Ohotino 20 Di 33
MK Ohrid 6000* 74 Ca 49
RUS Ohtoma 21 Eb 29
FIN Ohtsejohka = Utsjoki 99981 3 Ch 21
FIN Oijärvi 95160 10 Cf 25
FIN Oikarainen 97610 3 Cg 24
IRL Oileán Ciarrai 37 Sa 38
F Oissel 76350 41 Ab 41
FIN Öja 68550 10 Cc 27
S Öje 78061 17 Bd 30
S Öjung 82801 17 Bf 29
GB Okehampton EX20 40 Sf 40
RUS Okladnevo 20 Dd 32
BG Okorš 7680 61 Ch 47
S Oksajärvi 3 Cc 23
DK Oksbøl 6430 26 Ai 35
DK Oksby 6857 26 Ai 35
N Øksfjord 9550 3 Cc 20
RUS Oksino 6 Fc 23
RUS Oksovskij 12 Dk 28
RUS Oktarbr'skij 48 Dg 40
RUS Oktjabr'sk 33 Ei 37
RUS Oktjabr'skaja 12 Dg 28
RUS Oktjabr'skaja 63 Dk 44
RUS Oktjabr'skij 20 Dg 29
RUS Oktjabr'skij 21 Ed 29
RUS Oktjabr'skij 31 Di 36
RUS Oktjabr'skij 32 Dk 37
RUS Oktjabr'skij 33 Ei 34
RUS Oktjabr'skij 33 Ei 36
RUS Oktjabr'skij 34 Fd 36
RUS Oktjabr'skij 35 Fh 34
RUS Oktjabr'skij 4 De 23
RUS Oktjabr'skij 64 Ed 43
RUS Oktjabr'skoe 49 Eb 39
RUS Oktjabr'skoe 52 Ff 38
RUS Oktjabr'skoe 64 Ec 45
HR Okučani 58 Bh 45
HR Okuklje 73 Bh 48
RUS Okulovka 20 Dd 32
RUS Okulovo 13 Ee 24
RUS Okulovo 35 Gb 34
RUS Okulovskaja 21 Ed 30
RUS Okunev Nos 6 Fc 24
TR Okurcalar 07415 84 Db 54
RUS Ola, Joškar- 33 Eh 34
IS Ólafsfjörður H 36 Rb 24
IS Ólafsvík 355 36 Qg 26
LV Olaine 2114 29 Cd 34
F Olargues 34390 55 Ac 47
PL Oława 55-200 44 Bh 40
D Olbernhau 09526 43 Bd 40
I Ólbia 07026 71 Ak 50
N Olden 6788 8 Ag 29
D Oldenburg 26121* 26 Ai 37
D Oldenburg (Holstein) 23758 27 Ba 36
N Olderdalen 9146 2 Ca 21
N Olderfjord 3 Cf 20
N Oldervik 9034 2 Bk 21
GB Oldham OL1 39 Sh 37
GB Oldmeldrum AB51 38 Sh 33
PL Olecko 19-400 29 Cc 36
E Oleiros 68 Sb 47
P Oleiros 6160-011 68 Sc 51
UA Oleksandrivika, Lozno- 48 Di 41
UA Oleksandrivka 47 Db 42
UA Oleksandrivka 47 Dc 42
UA Oleksandrivka 47 Dd 42
UA Oleksandrivka 48 Dg 42
UA Oleksandrivka 62 Db 43
UA Oleksandrivka 62 Dc 44
UA Oleksandrivka 63 Dh 43
RUS Olema 13 Eg 26
N Ølen 5580 16 Af 31
RUS Olenica 4 Df 24
RUS Olenino 31 Dd 34
UA Olenivka 62 Dc 45
UA Olenivka 63 Dh 43
RUS Olenogorsk 4 Dd 22
UA Oles'ko 45 Ce 41
PL Oleśnica 28-220* 44 Bh 39
PL Olesno 33-210 44 Bi 40
UA Olevs'k 46 Ch 39
RUS Ol'ginka 63 Di 46
RUS Ol'gino 32 Ea 36
DK Ølgod 6870 26 Ai 35
P Olhão 8700-152* 80 Sc 53
FIN Olhava 91140 10 Cf 25
RUS Ol'hi 32 Eb 37
RUS Ol'hovatka 48 Dk 40
UA Ol'hovatka 48 Dh 40
RUS Ol'hovka 49 Ee 41
HR Olib 58 Be 46
I Olíena 08025 71 Ak 50
GR Olimbía 27065 82 Cb 53
GR Ólimbos 85700 83 Ch 55
S Olingskog 17 Be 29
E Oliva 46780 70 Sk 52
E Oliva de la Frontera 06120 80 Sd 52
P Oliveira de Azeméis 3720-001* 68 Sb 50
P Oliveira do Hospital 3400-056* 68 Sc 50
E Olivenza 06100 80 Sc 52
PL Olkusz 32-300 44 Bk 40
GB Ollerton NG22 39 Sk 37
E Olmedo 47410 69 Sf 49
E Olmillos de Sasamón 69 Sf 48
S Olofström 29300 27 Be 34
CZ Olomouc 771 00* 44 Bh 41
RUS Olonec 19 Dc 30
F Olonzac 34210 55 Ac 47
F Oloron-Sainte-Marie 64400* 70 Sk 47
E Olot 17800 70 Ac 48
BIH Olovo 59 Bi 46
D Olpe 57462 42 Ah 39
RUS Ol'ša 30 Db 36
RUS Ol'šanka 48 Dh 40
PL Olsztyn 10-900 28 Ca 37
PL Olsztynek 11-015 28 Ca 37
RO Olt, Drăgăneşti 60 Ce 46
N Oltedal 4333 16 Ag 32
CH Olten 4600* 56 Ah 43
RO Olteniţa 915400 60 Cg 46
RO Oltina 907215 61 Ch 46
TR Oltu 25400 79 Ec 50
TR Ölüdeniz 84 Ck 54
TR Oluközü 66300 77 Df 51
TR Olukpınar 84 Dc 54
TR Olur 25650 79 Ec 50
RUS Olymskij 48 Di 39
RUS Oma 6 Eg 24
GB Omagh BT79 37 Sc 36
I Omegna 28887 56 Ai 45
UA Omel'nyk 47 Dd 41
TR Ömerli 76 Ck 49
TR Ömerli 87 Ea 53
HR Omiš 58 Bg 47
RUS Omitrovsk-Orlovskij 48 Df 38
NL Ommen 7730 42 Ag 38
GR Omólio 40007 74 Cc 51
SRB Omoljica 26230 59 Ca 46
FIN Ömossa 64930 10 Cb 28
BG Omurtag 7900 75 Cg 47
RUS Omutninsk 23 Fc 32
E Oña 09530 69 Sg 48
E Oñati 20560 69 Sh 47
TR Onbirnisan 86 Di 53
E Onda 12200 70 Sk 51
E Ondarroa 48700 54 Sh 47
TR Ondokuzmayıs 55420 78 Dg 49
RUS Ondozero 11 Dd 27
RUS Onega 12 Dk 27
RO Oneşti 000601* 60 Cg 44
RUS Onež'e 14 Fa 28
FIN Onkamo 82360 11 Da 28
RUS Onolva, Ust'- 23 Fe 31
E Ontinyent 46870 70 Sk 52
FIN Ontojoki 88640 11 Ci 26
E Ontur 02652 81 Si 52
B Oostende 8400 41 Ac 39
NL Oosterhout 4900* 41 Ae 39
BG Opaka 7840 60 Cg 47
TR Opanözü 76 Ck 51
RUS Oparino 22 Ei 31
HR Opatija 58 Be 45
PL Opatów 42-152 45 Cb 40
CZ Opava 44 Bh 41
RUS Opečenskij Posad 20 De 32
MK Opejica 74 Ca 49
UA Opišn'a 47 De 41
RUS Opočka 30 Ci 34
PL Opoczno 26-300 45 Ca 39
PL Opole 45-076 44 Bh 40
PL Opole Lubelskie 24-300 45 Cb 39
N Oppdal 7340 8 Ak 28
D Oppenheim 55276 42 Ai 41
N Oppstryn 8 Ah 29
BY Opsa 29 Cg 35
I Ora = Auer 39040 57 Bb 44
RO Oradea 000410* 59 Cb 43
RKS Orahovac = Rahovec 21000* 74 Ca 48
BIH Orahov Do 73 Bh 48
HR Orahovica 58 Bh 45
F Orange 84100* 55 Ae 46
I Orani 08026 71 Ak 50
D Oranienburg 16515 27 Bd 38
IRL Oran Mór 37 Sb 37
IRL Oranmore = Oran Mór 37 Sb 37
RUS Oranžeri 65 Eh 45
BIH Orašje 59 Bi 45
RO Orăştie 335700 60 Cd 45
UA Orativ 46 Ck 41
FIN Oravainen = Oravais 66800 10 Cc 27
FIN Oravais 66800 10 Cc 27
RO Oraviţa 325600 59 Cb 45
D Orb, Bad 63619 42 Ak 40
DK Ørbæk 5853 27 Ba 35
RO Orbeasca de Jos 147237 60 Cf 46
F Orbec 14290 41 Aa 41
I Orbetello 58015 72 Bb 48
F Orchies 59310 41 Ad 40
RUS Orda 23 Fg 33
TR Ördekçi 84 Db 52
E Ordes 15680 68 Sb 47
TR Ordu 52000* 78 Dh 50
E Orduña 48460 69 Sg 48
UA Ordžonikidze 62 De 43
RUS Ordžonikidze = Vladikavkaz 79 Ee 48
RUS Ordžonikidzevskij 64 Eb 47
HR Orebić 73 Bh 48
S Örebro 70002* 17 Bf 31
RUS Oredež 19 Da 32
S Öregrund 74071 17 Bi 30
RUS Orehovka 53 Ga 39
RUS Orehovo-Zuevo 31 Di 35
RUS Orel 23 Fg 31
RUS Orel 31 Dg 38
E Orellana la Vieja 06740 68 Se 51
TR Ören 28850 83 Ch 53
RUS Orenburg 52 Ff 39
TR Örencik 76 Ck 51
TR Örenköy 86 Dh 52
E Orense = Ourense 32001 68 Sc 48
TR Örenşehir 86 Dg 51
GR Orestiáda 68200 75 Cg 49
GR Orfáni 64008 75 Cd 50
GB Orford IP12 41 Ab 38
GR Orgáni 69500 75 Cf 49
E Organyà 70 Ab 48
E Orgaz 45450 69 Sg 51
MD Orgeev = Orhei 3500 61 Ci 43
I Orgósolo 08027 71 Ak 50
TR Örgütlü 86 Di 53
TR Orhaneli 16980 76 Ci 51
TR Orhangazi 16800 76 Ck 50
TR Orhanlı 84 Ck 53
MD Orhei 3500 61 Ci 43
MD Orhej = Orhei 3500 61 Ci 43
GR Orhomenós 22002 82 Cc 52
E Oria 04810 81 Sh 53
UA Orichiv 62 Df 43
RUS Oriči 22 Ek 32
E Orihuela 03300 81 Sk 52
UA Oril'ka 48 Dg 42
FIN Orimattila 16301 18 Cf 30
FIN Oripää 32500 18 Cc 30
EST Orissaare 94601 18 Cd 32
I Oristano 09170 71 Ai 51
FIN Orivesi 35301 18 Ce 29
BG Orjahovo 6555 60 Cd 47
N Ørje 1870 16 Bb 31
E Órjiva 18400 81 Sg 54
N Orkanger 7300 8 Ak 27
S Örkelljunga 28601 27 Bd 34
H Örkény 2377 59 Bk 43
F Orléans 45000* 55 Ab 43
RUS Orlecy 22 Fb 31
RO Orleşti 247450 60 Ce 46
UA Orlivka 61 Ci 45
RUS Orlov Gaj 50 Ei 40
RUS Orlovo 48 Dk 39
RUS Orlovskij 64 Ec 44
RUS Orlovskij, Omitrovsk- 48 Df 38
GR Órma 58400 74 Cb 50
TR Ormanlı 76 Db 49
TR Ormanözü 05000 77 Df 50



Ormanözü 167

(E) Pedro Muñoz 10630 69 Sh 51
(E) Pedroñeras, Las 16660 69 Sh 51
(E) Pedroso, El 41360 80 Se 53
(GB) Peebles EH45 39 Sg 35
(GBM) Peel IM5 39 Sf 36
(D) Peenemünde 17449 27 Bd 36
(RUS) Peganovo 22 Eg 30
(D) Pegau 04523 43 Bc 39
(D) Pegnitz 91257 43 Bb 41
(E) Pego 03780 70 Sk 52
(RUS) Pegyš 14 Fa 27
(MK) Pehčevo 2326 74 Cc 49
(TR) Pehlivanköy 39210 75 Cg 49
(D) Peine 31224* 43 Ba 38
(FIN) Peipohja 32810 18 Cc 29
(D) Peitz 03185 43 Be 39
(RKS) Pejë = Peć 30000* 74 Ca 48
(RUS) Peklino 31 Dd 37
(RUS) Pektubaevo 33 Ei 33
(GR) Pelasgía 35013 82 Cc 52
(CZ) Pelhřimov 350 02 44 Bf 41
(TR) Pelitbükü 55700 77 Df 49
(FIN) Pelkosenniemi 98500 3 Ch 23
(FIN) Pello 95701 3 Cd 24
(BG) Pelovo 5870 60 Ce 47
(FIN) Peltovuoma 99420 3 Ce 22
(RUS) Pelym 23 Fe 31
(TR) Pembecik 33700 85 Dd 54
(GB) Pembroke SA71 40 Sf 39
(E) Peñafiel 47300 69 Sf 49
(P) Penafiel 4560-450* 68 Sb 49
(E) Peñaflor 33829 80 Se 53
(P) Penamacor 6090-508* 68 Sc 50
(E) Peñaranda de Bracamonte 37300 68 Se 50
(E) Peñaranda de Duero 09410 69 Sg 49
(E) Peñarroya-Pueblonueva 14200 80 Se 52
(GB) Penarth CF64 40 Sg 39
(E) Peñas de San Pedro 02120 81 Si 52
(E) Peñausende 49178 68 Se 49
(GR) Pendéli 15236 82 Cd 52
(P) Penela 3230-249* 68 Sb 50
(GB) Penfro = Pembroke SA71 40 Sf 39
(P) Peniche 2520-200* 68 Sa 51
(D) Penig 09322 43 Bc 40
(RUS) Peninga 11 Dc 27
(RUS) Penkino 32 Ea 34
(F) Penmarc'h 29760 54 Sf 43
(I) Penne 65017 72 Bd 48
(RUS) Peno 30 Dc 34
(GB) Penrith CA11 39 Sh 36
(GR) Pentálofos 50007 74 Cb 50
(RUS) Penza 33 Ef 37
(GB) Penzance TR18 40 Se 40
(D) Penzberg 82377 57 Bb 43
(AL) Peqin 74 Bk 49
(H) Pér 9099 58 Bh 43
(P) Pêra 80 Sb 53
(GR) Perahóra 20300 82 Cc 52
(E) Peraleda de la Mata 10335 68 Se 51
(E) Peraleda de Zaucejo 06919 80 Se 52
(GR) Pérama 74052 82 Ce 55
(FIN) Peranka 89770 11 Ci 25
(E) Peranzanes 24429 68 Sd 48
(FIN) Perä-Posio 97820 3 Ch 24
(FIN) Peräseinäjoki 61101 10 Cd 28
(GR) Pérdika 46100 74 Ca 51
(GR) Pérdika 46100 82 Cd 53
(UA) Perečyn 45 Cc 42
(UA) Perehins'ke 45 Ce 42
(UA) Perejaslav-Chmel'nyc'kyj 47 Db 40
(RUS) Perejaslovskaja 63 Dk 45
(RUS) Perekopka 49 Ed 41
(RUS) Perelešinskij 49 Ea 39
(RUS) Pereljub 51 Fa 39
(UA) Peremoha 47 Db 40
(RUS) Peremyšl' 31 Dg 36
(UA) Peremyšljany 45 Ce 41
(UA) Pereščepyne 48 Df 41
(MD) Peresecina 3541 61 Ci 43
(RUS) Pereslavl'-Zalesskij 31 Di 34
(RUS) Peresypkino Pervoe 32 Ec 38
(RUS) Per'evo 21 Dk 31
(RUS) Perevolockij 51 Fe 39
(RUS) Perevoz 33 Ee 35
(I) Pèrgine Valsugana 38057 57 Bb 44
(I) Pérgola 57 Bc 47
(FIN) Perho 31140 10 Ce 27
(RO) Periam 307315 59 Ca 44
(F) Périers 50190 40 Si 41
(RO) Perieți 927190 61 Ch 46
(F) Périgueux 24000* 54 Aa 45
(RO) Perişoru 917195 61 Ch 46
(D) Perleberg 19348 27 Bb 37
(RUS) Perlevka 48 Di 39
(RUS) Perm' 23 Fg 32
(RUS) Permas 22 Ef 31
(AL) Përmet 74 Ca 50
(BG) Pernik 2300* 75 Cd 48
(FIN) Perniö 25501 18 Cd 30
(F) Péronne 80200 41 Ac 41
(AL) Përparim 74 Bk 51
(F) Perpignan 66000* 70 Ac 48
(F) Perros-Guirec 22700 40 Sg 42
(S) Persåsen 9 Be 28
(TR) Perşembe 52750 78 Dh 49
(RUS) Peršinskaja 21 Ea 30
(UA) Peršotravneve = Mokvin 63 Dh 43
(UA) Peršotravnevce = Mokvin 63 Dh 43
(S) Perstorp 28401 27 Bd 34
(TR) Pertek 86 Dk 52
(GB) Perth PH1 38 Sg 34
(RUS) Pertjugskij 22 Eg 31
(RUS) Pertominsk 12 Di 26
(F) Pertuis 84120 56 Af 47
(FIN) Pertunmaa 52730 18 Cg 29
(I) Perúgia 06100 72 Bc 47
(HR) Perušić 58 Bf 46
(TR) Pervari 56700 87 Ec 53
(RUS) Pervoavgustovskij 48 Df 38
(UA) Pervomaiskyj 48 Dg 41
(RUS) Pervomajsk 32 Ed 36
(UA) Pervomajs'k 47 Da 42
(UA) Pervomajs'k 48 Di 42
(UA) Pervomajsk = Pervomajs'k 47 Da 42
(UA) Pervomajs'ke 62 Dc 43
(UA) Pervomajs'ke 62 Dd 45
(RUS) Pervomajskij 21 Ee 29
(RUS) Pervomajskij 32 Ea 37
(RUS) Pervomajskij 34 Fb 37
(RUS) Pervomajskij 35 Gb 36
(RUS) Pervomajskij 49 Ee 38
(RUS) Pervomajskij 50 Eh 41
(RUS) Pervomajskij 51 Fb 39
(RUS) Pervomajskoe 19 Ck 30
(RUS) Pervomajskoe 49 Eb 42
(RUS) Pervomajskoe 50 Eh 39
(RUS) Pervoural'sk 35 Fk 34
(I) Pésaro 61100 57 Bc 47
(RUS) Pesčanoe 12 Df 28
(RUS) Pesčanokopskoe 64 Eb 44
(I) Pescara 65100* 73 Be 48
(RUS) Peščera 23 Fc 31
(I) Péschici 71010 73 Bg 49
(I) Peschiera del Garda 37019 57 Ba 45
(I) Pescina 67057 72 Bd 48
(RUS) Pescočnja 31 Dd 37
(RUS) Pesenec 13 Ec 28
(AL) Peshkëpi 74 Bk 50
(AL) Peshkopi 74 Ca 49
(FIN) Pesiökylä 89640 11 Ci 26
(RUS) Peski 31 Di 35
(RUS) Peski 49 Ea 40
(RUS) Peskovka 23 Fc 31
(RUS) Peškovo 48 Dh 38
(MK) Pesočani 6342 74 Ca 49
(RUS) Pesočnja 32 Ea 36
(RUS) Pesocnoe 19 Ck 30
(P) Peso da Régua 5050-208* 68 Sc 49
(F) Pessac 33600 54 Sk 46
(MK) Peštani 6323 74 Ca 49
(BG) Peštera 4754 75 Ce 48
(RUS) Pestjaki 32 Ec 34
(RUS) Pestovo 20 Df 32
(RUS) Pestravka 50 Ek 38
(FIN) Petäiskylä 75930 11 Ck 27
(FIN) Petäjävesi 41901 10 Cf 28
(FIN) Petalax 66240 10 Cb 28
(GR) Petalidi 24005 82 Cb 54
(GB) Peterborough PE3 40 Sk 38
(GB) Peterculter 38 Sh 33
(GB) Peterhead AB42 38 Si 33
(GB) Peterlee SR8 39 Si 36
(GB) Petersfield GU32 40 Sk 39
(H) Pétervására 3250 45 Ca 42
(E) Petín 68 Sc 48
(F) Petit-Quevilly, le 76140 41 Ab 41
(FIN) Petkula 99670 3 Cg 23
(FIN) Petolahti = Petalax 66240 10 Cb 28
(GR) Pétra 60100 75 Cg 51
(F) Petreto-Bicchisano 20140 71 Ai 49
(BG) Petrič 2850 75 Cd 49
(RO) Petrila 335800 60 Cd 45
(HR) Petrinja 58 Bg 45
(RUS) Petriščevo 30 Dc 35
(UA) Petrivka 47 Db 40
(UA) Petrivka 48 Dk 42
(UA) Petrivka 61 Da 44
(UA) Petrivka 62 De 44
(RUS) Petrjaevskij 22 Ef 31
(RUS) Petrodvorec 19 Ck 31
(RUS) Petrokamenskoe 24 Ga 33
(RUS) Petrokrepost' = Šlissel'burg 19 Db 31
(A) Petronell-Carnuntum 2404 44 Bg 42
(UA) Petropavlika 48 Dh 41
(UA) Petropavlivka 48 Dg 42
(RUS) Petropavlovka 35 Fk 35
(RUS) Petropavlovka 49 Ea 40
(RUS) Petropavlovka 50 Eh 40
(RUS) Petropavlovsk 23 Fe 33
(RUS) Petropavlovsk 35 Fh 34
(RUS) Petropavlovskij 35 Fk 36
(RUS) Petropavlovskoe 64 Ee 45
(RO) Petroşani 000332* 60 Cd 45
(RUS) Petrova 13 Ed 26
(BY) Petrova Buda 30 Db 38
(SRB) Petrovac 12300 59 Cb 46
(MNE) Petrovac na moru 85 300 74 Bi 48
(RUS) Petrovcy 23 Fd 32
(UA) Petrove 47 Dd 42
(RUS) Petroviči 30 Dc 37
(RUS) Petrovka 34 Fb 37
(RUS) Petrovka 49 Ea 40
(RUS) Petrovo 20 Df 32
(RUS) Petrovsk 50 Ef 38
(RUS) Petrovskaja 63 Dh 45
(RUS) Petrovskij 32 Ea 34
(RUS) Petrovskoe 32 Dk 33
(RUS) Petrovskoe 35 Fg 37
(RUS) Petrovskoe 49 Ea 38
(RUS) Petrov Val 50 Ef 40
(RUS) Petrozavodsk 12 De 29
(RUS) Petrušino 32 Dk 35
(BY) Petrykav 46 Ci 38
(UA) Petrykivka 47 De 42
(RUS) Petuški 32 Dk 35
(A) Peuerbach 4722 43 Bd 42
(F) Peyrehorade 40300 54 Si 47
(AL) Pezë e Vogël 74 Bk 49
(F) Pézenas 34120 55 Ad 47
(CZ) Pezinok 44 Bh 42
(RUS) Pezmog 14 Fb 29
(D) Pfaffenberg, Mallersdorf- 84066 43 Bc 42
(D) Pfarrkirchen 84347 43 Bc 42
(D) Pforzheim 75172* 42 Ai 42
(D) Pfullendorf 88630 57 Ak 43
(A) Pfunds 6542 57 Ba 44
(F) Phalsbourg 57370* 42 Ah 42
(B) Philippeville 5600 41 Ae 40
(I) Piacenza 29100 57 Ak 45
(I) Piadena 26034 57 Ba 45
(I) Pianoro 40065 57 Bb 46
(I) Pianosa 57036 72 Ba 48
(P) Pias 7860-001 80 Sc 52
(PL) Piaseczno 74-110 45 Cb 38
(PL) Piaski 63-820 45 Cc 39
(PL) Piątek 99-120 44 Bk 38
(RO) Piatra 907197 60 Cf 47
(RO) Piatra-Neamț 000610* 60 Cg 44
(I) Piazza Armerina 94015 72 Be 53
(I) Piazza Brembana 24014 57 Ak 45
(RUS) Pičaevo 32 Ec 37
(RUS) Pičiha 21 Dk 30
(GB) Pickering YO18 39 Sk 36
(RUS) Pičkirjaevo 32 Ec 36
(D) Picnjo = Peitz 03185 43 Be 39
(F) Picquigny 80310 41 Ac 41
(UA) Pidhajci 46 Cf 41
(RUS) Pid'ma 20 De 30
(I) Piedimonte Matese 81016 73 Be 49
(E) Piedrabuena 13100 69 Sf 51
(E) Piedrahita 68 Se 50
(FIN) Pieksämäki 76150 11 Ch 28
(FIN) Pielavesi 72430 10 Cg 27
(PL) Pieniężno 14-520 28 Ca 36
(PL) Pieńsk 59-930 44 Bf 39
(I) Pienza 53026 72 Bb 47
(GB) Pierowall KW17 38 Sh 31
(F) Pierrefort 15230 55 Ac 46
(F) Pierrelatte 26700 55 Ae 46
(SK) Piešťany 44 Bh 42
(FIN) Pietarsaari = Jakobstad 68600* 10 Cc 27
(I) Pietra Ligure 56 Ai 46
(I) Pietrasanta 55045 57 Ba 47
(RO) Pietroşani 147250 60 Cf 47
(I) Pieve di Teco 18026 56 Ah 46
(RUS) Pigari 50 Ek 39
(FIN) Pihlajavesi 42910 10 Ce 28
(FIN) Pihtipudas 44801 10 Cf 27
(FIN) Piippola 92620 10 Cf 26
(FIN) Piittisjärvi 97630 3 Cg 24
(RUS) Pikalevo 20 De 31
(EST) Pikasilla 18 Cg 32
(PL) Piła 64-920 28 Bg 37
(RUS) Pil'na 33 Ef 35
(GR) Pilorí 51100 74 Cb 50
(GR) Pílos 24001 82 Cb 54
(LV) Piltene 3620 18 Cb 33
(PL) Pilzno 39-220 45 Cb 41
(TR) Pınarbaşı 85 Dd 53
(TR) Pınarbaşı 86 Dg 52
(TR) Pınarbaşı 87 Ea 53
(TR) Pınarcık 83 Ch 53
(F) Pinarellu 20144 71 Ak 49
(TR) Pınarhisar 39300 76 Ch 49
(TR) Pınarlar 86 Dk 52
(PL) Pińczów 28-400 45 Ca 40
(RUS) Pinduši 12 De 28
(RUS) Pinega 13 Ed 26
(I) Pinerolo 10064 56 Ah 46
(I) Pineto 64025 73 Be 48
(F) Piney 10220 41 Ae 42
(P) Pinhel 4485-431 68 Sc 50
(RUS) Pinjug 22 Eh 30
(D) Pinneberg 25421 26 Ak 37
(E) Pinoso 03650 81 Si 52
(BY) Pinsk 46 Cg 38
(FIN) Pintamo 93290 11 Ch 25
(E) Pinto 28320 69 Sg 50
(I) Piombino 57025 72 Ba 48
(RUS) Pionerskij 28 Ca 36
(PL) Piotrków Trybunalski 97-300 44 Bk 39
(I) Piove di Sacco 35028 57 Bc 45
(F) Pipriac 35550 54 Si 43
(AL) Piqeras 74 Bk 50
(TR) Piraziz 28340 78 Di 50
(GR) Pireás 18547 82 Cd 53
(GR) Pirgi 82102 83 Cf 52
(GR) Pírgos 70010 82 Cb 53
(GR) Pírgos 70010 83 Cf 55
(TR) Pirinçlik 53400 87 Ea 53
(RUS) Pirinem 13 Ee 26
(UA) Pirki 47 Da 39
(FIN) Pirkkiö 95470 10 Ce 25
(MD) Pîrlița 3641 61 Ch 43
(D) Pirmasens 66953* 42 Ah 41
(D) Pirna 01796 43 Bd 40
(SRB) Pirot 18300* 59 Cc 47
(HR) Pirovac 58 Bf 47
(GR) Pirsógiani 44015 74 Ca 50
(FIN) Pirttikoski 14450 3 Ch 24
(I) Pisa 56100* 57 Ba 47
(HR) Pisarovina 58 Bf 45
(UA) Pišča 45 Cd 39
(UA) Piščane 47 Db 41
(UA) Piščanka 46 Ci 42
(UA) Piščanyj Brid 47 Db 42
(RUS) Piscovo 21 Ea 33
(RO) Piscu Vechi 207455 60 Cd 47
(CZ) Písek 397 01 43 Be 41
(UA) Piski-Rad'kivs'ki 48 Dh 41
(UA) Piskivka 46 Ck 40
(RUS) Pišnur 22 Eh 33
(GR) Pisses 82 Ce 53
(F) Pissos 40410 54 Sk 46
(I) Pisticci 75015 73 Bg 50
(I) Pistóia 57 Ba 47
(PL) Pisz 12-200 28 Cb 37
(S) Piteå 94101* 10 Cb 25
(RUS) Pitelino 32 Eb 36
(RUS) Piterka 50 Eh 40
(RO) Pitești 110323 60 Ce 46
(GR) Pithagório 83103 83 Cg 53
(F) Pithiviers 45300 41 Ac 42
(I) Pitigliano 58017 72 Bb 48
(GR) Pitítsa 82 Cb 52
(RUS) Pitkjaranta 19 Db 29
(RUS) Pitkul' 4 Dd 23
(GB) Pitlochry PH16 38 Sg 34
(HR) Pitomača 58 Bh 45
(SLO) Pivka 6257 58 Be 45
(PL) Piwniczna-Zdrój 45 Ca 41
(RUS) Pižanka 22 Ei 33
(RUS) Pižma 22 Eh 33
(I) Pizzo 89812 73 Bg 52
(RUS) Pjalica 12 Dk 24
(RUS) Pjalka 5 Ea 24
(RUS) Pjal'ma 12 Df 28
(RUS) Pjanda 13 Ec 28
(RUS) Pjanteg 23 Fg 30
(RUS) Pjaozerskij 11 Db 25
(RUS) Pjašnica 20 Dg 31
(RUS) Pjatigorsk 64 Ed 46
(UA) Pjatychatky 47 Dd 42
(RUS) Pjaželka 20 Df 30
(GR) Pláka 81401 75 Cf 50
(GR) Pláka 81401 82 Cc 53
(BIH) Plana 73 Bi 48
(F) Plancoët 22940 40 Sh 42
(SRB) Plandište 26360 59 Cb 45
(UA) Planers'ke 62 Df 46
(AL) Plasë 74 Ca 50
(E) Plasencia 10600 68 Sd 50
(HR) Plaški 58 Bf 45
(N) Plassen 2427 17 Bc 29
(RUS) Plast 35 Ga 36
(RUS) Plastmass 31 Dh 36
(GR) Platanistós 34001 82 Ce 52
(D) Plattling 94447 43 Bc 42
(D) Plau 27 Bc 37
(D) Plauen 08523* 43 Bc 40
(MNE) Plav 84 325 74 Bk 48
(LV) Plavinas 29 Cf 34
(RUS) Plavsk 31 Dh 37
(F) Pleaux 15700 55 Ac 45
(RUS) Ples 21 Eb 33
(RUS) Plešanovo 34 Fd 38
(BY) Pleščanicy 30 Ch 36
(RUS) Pleseck 12 Ea 28
(RUS) Pleški 31 De 34
(RUS) Plëso 20 Df 31
(PL) Pleszew 63-300 44 Bh 39
(HR) Pleternica 58 Bh 45
(BG) Pleven 5800* 60 Ce 47
(F) Pleyben 29190 40 Sg 42
(BY) Plisa 30 Ch 35
(HR) Plitvica 58 Bf 46
(MNE) Pljevlja 84 210* 59 Bk 47
(RUS) Pljussa 19 Ck 32
(HR) Ploče 73 Bh 47
(PL) Płock 09-400 44 Bk 38
(F) Ploërmel 56800 54 Sh 43
(RO) Ploiești 000100* 60 Cg 46
(GR) Plomári 81200 83 Cg 52
(D) Plön 24306 27 Ba 36
(PL) Płońsk 09-100 45 Ca 38
(RUS) Ploska 21 Ee 33
(RUS) Ploskoe 31 Df 36
(RUS) Ploskoš' 30 Db 34
(RUS) Plotniki 20 Dg 33
(PL) Płoty 72-310 27 Bf 37
(F) Plouaret 22420 40 Sg 42
(F) Plouay 56240 54 Sg 43
(F) Ploudalmézeau 29830 40 Sf 42
(F) Plouézec 22470 40 Sh 42
(F) Plouguer, Carhaix- 29270 40 Sg 42
(F) Plouha 22580 40 Sh 42
(BG) Plovdiv 4000* 75 Ce 48
(F) Plozévet 29710 40 Sf 43
(GB) Plumbridge BT79 37 Sc 36
(LT) Plungė 90001 28 Cb 35
(F) Pluvigner 56330 54 Sg 43
(GB) Plymouth PL9 40 Sf 40
(CZ) Plzeň 301 00* 43 Bd 41
(PL) Pniewy 62-045 44 Bg 38
(BG) Pobeda 8679 75 Cg 48
(RUS) Pobeda 32 Ec 34
(RUS) Pobedino 29 Cc 36
(E) Pobla de Lillet, la 08696 70 Ab 48
(E) Pobla de Segur, la 25500 70 Aa 48
(RUS) Poboišče 52 Fh 38
(UA) Pobuz'ke 47 Da 42
(RUS) Poča 12 Di 28
(UA) Počajiv 46 Cf 40
(UA) Počapynci 47 Da 41
(RUS) Počep 31 Dd 38
(RUS) Počiniki 33 Ee 36
(RUS) Počinok 20 De 33
(RUS) Počinok 30 Dc 36
(BIH) Počitelj 73 Bh 47
(GB) Pocklington YO42 39 Sk 37
(RUS) Počtovskij, Kletsko- 49 Ed 41
(RO) Podari 207465 60 Cd 46
(RUS) Podbel'sk 34 Fb 37
(RUS) Podberez'e 19 Dg 32
(RUS) Podberez'e 30 Da 34
(RUS) Podbolot'e 21 Ee 31
(CZ) Podbořany 441 01 43 Bd 40
(RUS) Podborka 12 Ea 26
(RUS) Podborov'e 19 Ci 33
(MNE) Podbožur 74 Bi 48
(RUS) Podčer'e 15 Fh 27
(PL) Poddębice 99-200 44 Bi 39
(RUS) Poddor'e 19 Dd 33
(CZ) Poděbrady 290 01 44 Bf 40
(HR) Podgorac 59 Bi 45
(RUS) Podgorenskij 48 Dk 40
(MNE) Podgorica 81 101* 74 Bk 48
(AL) Podgorje 74 Ca 50
(RUS) Podgornaja 49 Eb 40
(RUS) Podgornoe 64 Ed 44
(RUS) Podhožee 31 Di 36
(BIH) Podhum 58 Bh 47
(UA) Podil 47 Dd 41
(RUS) Podjuga 21 Ea 29
(BG) Podkova 6880 75 Cf 49
(GR) Podogorá 30018 82 Cb 52
(RUS) Podol'sk 31 Dh 35
(RUS) Podol'sk 52 Fi 38
(RUS) Podol'skaja 13 Eg 28
(RUS) Podomskoe, Il'insko- 22 Eh 29
(RUS) Podophaj 31 Dd 36
(RUS) Podora 14 Fe 28
(RUS) Podosinovec 22 Eg 30
(RUS) Podporož'e 20 De 30
(HR) Podravska Slatina 58 Bh 45
(RUS) Podrezčiha 22 Fb 31
(BIH) Podromanija 59 Bi 47
(RUS) Podsnežnoe 50 Ef 38
(RO) Podu Iloaiei 707365 61 Ch 43
(RKS) Podujevë = Podujevo 74 Cb 48
(RKS) Podujevo = Podujevë 74 Cb 48
(RO) Podu Turcului 607450 61 Ch 44
(RUS) Podvislovo 32 Ea 37
(RUS) Podvoloč'e 12 Ea 28
(RUS) Podyem-Mihajlovka 34 Fa 38
(RUS) Podymalovo 34 Ff 36
(RUS) Podyvot'e 47 De 38
(RUS) Podz' 22 Fa 30
(RUS) Pogar 47 Dd 38
(I) Poggibonsi 53036 57 Bb 47
(I) Póggio Rusco 46025 57 Bb 46
(RO) Pogoanele 125200 60 Cg 46
(RUS) Pogorelec 13 Ef 25
(RUS) Pogorelka 20 Dh 31
(RUS) Pogoreloe Gorodišče 31 De 34
(RUS) Pogost 12 Di 29
(RUS) Pogost 13 Eb 27
(AL) Pogradec 74 Ca 50
(RUS) Pograničnoe 50 Ei 40
(RUS) Pogromnoe 51 Fc 38
(RUS) Pogruznaja 34 Fa 36
(FIN) Pohjaslahti 97630 10 Ce 28
(FIN) Pohjois-li 10 Cf 25
(CZ) Pohořelice 691 23 44 Bg 42
(UA) Pohrebyšče 46 Ck 41
(RUS) Pohvistnevo 34 Fc 37
(RO) Poiana Mare 207470 60 Cd 47
(RO) Poiana Stampei 727430 60 Cf 43
(RO) Poiana Teiului 617340 60 Cf 43



Poiana Teiului 169

- RUS Pulonga 5 Dk 24
- RUS Pulozero 4 Dd 22
- E Pulpí 04640 81 Si 53
- S Pulsujärvi 3 Cb 22
- PL Pułtusk 06-100 28 Cb 38
- TR Pülümür 78 Dk 51
- RUS Pummanki 4 Db 21
- LT Pumpėnai 39012 29 Ce 35
- FIN Punkaharju 58501 19 Ck 29
- FIN Punkalaidun 31901 18 Cd 29
- FIN Punkasalmi = Punkaharju 58450* 19 Ck 29
- E Punta Umbría 21100 80 Sd 53
- FIN Puoddopohki = Patoniva 99981 3 Ch 21
- FIN Puokio 91750 11 Ch 26
- FIN Puolanka 89201 11 Ch 26
- S Puoltikasvaara 3 Cb 23
- S Puottaure 10 Ca 24
- E Purchena 04870 81 Sh 53
- RUS Purdoški 32 Ed 36
- RUS Pureh 32 Ed 34
- NL Purmerend 1440* 41 Ae 38
- RUS Purnema 12 Dh 26
- TR Pusatlı 38950 85 Df 52
- RUS Puščino 31 Dh 36
- RUS Puškin 19 Da 31
- RUS Puškino 31 Df 34
- RUS Puškino 31 Dh 34
- RUS Puškino 50 Eh 39
- RUS Puškinskie Gory 30 Ci 33
- RUS Pušlahta 12 Dg 26
- RUS Pušnoj 12 De 26
- H Püspökladány 4150 59 Cb 43
- RUS Pustaja Guba 4 Dd 23
- I Pusterno 57 Bb 45
- RUS Pustoška 30 Ck 34
- D Putbus 18581 27 Bd 36
- RO Putineiu 145200 60 Ce 47
- RUS Putjanino 32 Eb 36
- RUS Putjaševo 23 Fd 30
- D Putlitz 16949 27 Bc 37
- D Puttgarden 23769 27 Bb 36
- UA Putyvl' 47 Dd 39
- FIN Puukkokumpu 95255 10 Cf 25
- FIN Puumala 52201 19 Ci 29
- F Puy-en-Velay, le 43000* 55 Ad 45
- F Puy-L'Evêque 46700 55 Ab 46
- RUS Puzači 48 Dh 39
- GB Pwllheli LL53 39 Sf 38
- RUS Pyčas 34 Fc 34
- FIN Pyhäjärvi 98510 10 Cf 27
- FIN Pyhäjärvi 98510 3 Ch 23
- FIN Pyhäjoki 27920 10 Ce 26
- FIN Pyhäkylä 89770 11 Ci 25
- FIN Pyhäntä 92930 10 Cg 26
- FIN Pyhäranta 23950 18 Cb 30
- FIN Pyhäselkä 82200* 11 Ck 28
- FIN Pyhtää 49270 18 Cg 30
- RUS Pylema 13 Ef 26
- RUS Pylemec 6 Fc 23
- FIN Pylkönmäki 43440 10 Ce 28
- N Pyramiden 9179 2 I Svalbard
- UA Pyrižky 46 Ck 40
- UA Pyrjatyn 47 Dc 40
- D Pyrmont, Bad 31812 42 Ak 39
- PL Pyrzyce 74-200 27 Be 37
- RUS Pyščug 22 Ef 32
- RUS Pyš'ja, Ust'- 23 Ff 31
- PL Pyskowice 44-120 44 Bi 40
- UA Pys'menne 48 Df 42
- BY Pyšna 30 Ci 36
- RUS Pytalovo = Abrene 29 Ch 33
- RUS Pytalovo = Abrene 30 Ch 33
- FIN Pyttis = Pyhtää 49270 18 Cg 30
- PL Pyzdry 62-310 44 Bh 38


# Q


- AL Qaf-Mollë 74 Bk 49
- AL Qeparo 74 Bk 50
- D Quakenbrück 49610 26 Ah 38
- P Quarteira 8125-001* 80 Sb 53
- I Quartu Sant'Elena 09045 71 Ak 51
- D Quedlinburg 06484 43 Bb 39
- GB Queensferry EH30 39 Sg 35
- F Quelaines-Saint-Gault 53360 54 Sk 43
- D Querfurt 06268 43 Bb 39
- F Quettehou 50630 40 Si 41
- F Quiberon 56170* 54 Sg 43
- D Quickborn 25451 26 Ak 37
- F Quillan 11500 70 Ac 48
- F Quimper 29000* 40 Sf 43
- F Quimperlé 29300 54 Sg 43
- E Quintana del Castillo 24397 68 Sd 48
- E Quintanar de la Orden 45800 69 Sg 51
- E Quintanilla del Coco 09348 69 Sg 49
- F Quintin 22800 40 Sh 42
- E Quinto 50770 70 Sk 49
- F Quissac 30260 55 Ae 47
- AL Qukës-Skënderbej 74 Ca 49
- AL Qyrsaç 74 Bk 48
- AL Qyteti Stalin = Kuçovë 74 Bk 50


# R


- H Raab = Győr 58 Bh 43
- A Raabs an der Thaya 3820 44 Bf 42
- FIN Raahe 92150 10 Ce 26
- FIN Rääkkylä 82301 11 Ck 28
- NL Raalte 8100 42 Ag 38
- FIN Raanujärvi 97250 3 Ce 24
- FIN Raattama 99340 3 Ce 22
- HR Rab 58 Be 46
- RO Răbăgani 417400 59 Cc 44
- M Rabat 72 Be 55
- M Rabat = Victoria 72 Be 54
- PL Rabka-Zdrój 34-700 44 Bk 41
- RUS Rabočeostrovsk 12 De 26
- SRB Rabrovo 12254 59 Cb 46
- RO Răcăciuni 607480 60 Cg 44
- RO Răcășdia 327315 59 Cb 46
- UA Rachiv 45 Ce 42
- PL Raciąż 09-140 28 Ca 38
- PL Racibórz 47-400 44 Bi 40
- BY Radaškovičy 30 Ch 36
- RO Rădăuți 725400 60 Cf 43
- D Radeberg 01454 43 Bd 39
- SLO Radeče 1433 58 Bf 44
- UA Radechiv 45 Ce 40
- RUS Radica-Krylovka 31 De 37
- RUS Radiščevo 33 Eg 37
- RUS Radiščevo 33 Eh 38
- UA Rad'kivs'ki, Piski- 48 Dh 41
- BG Radnevo 6260 75 Cf 48
- BIH Radohova 58 Bh 46
- D Radolfzell am Bodensee 78315 56 Ai 43
- PL Radom 26-600 45 Cb 39
- BG Radomir 2400 74 Cc 48
- RO Radomirești 237365 60 Ce 46
- PL Radomsko 97-500 44 Bk 39
- UA Radomyšľ 46 Ck 40
- RO Radovan 207485 60 Cd 46
- BG Radovec 6564 75 Cg 49
- MK Radoviš 2420* 74 Cc 49
- A Radstadt 5550 57 Bd 43
- LT Radviliškis 82001 29 Cd 35
- PL Radymno 37-550 45 Cc 41
- PL Radziejów 88-200 44 Bi 38
- PL Radzyń Chełmiński 87-220 28 Bi 37
- PL Radzyń Podlaski 21-300 45 Cc 39
- D Raesfeld 46348 42 Ag 39
- RUS Raevskij 34 Fe 36
- I Raffadali 92015 72 Bd 53
- GR Rafína 19009 82 Ce 52
- LV Ragana 2144 18 Ce 33
- RUS Raglicy 19 Da 32
- RUS Raguli 64 Ed 45
- I Ragusa 97100 72 Be 54
- BY Rahačav 30 Da 37
- D Rahden 32369 42 Ai 38
- RUS Rah'ja 19 Da 30
- RUS Rahmanovka 50 Ek 38
- RUS Rahmanovka 50 Ek 39
- N Råholt 2070 16 Bb 30
- RKS Rahovec = Orahovac 21000* 74 Ca 48
- D Rain 86641 43 Ba 42
- FIN Raisio 21280 18 Cc 30
- FIN Raivala 39610 10 Cc 29
- FIN Raja-Jooseppi 99801 3 Ci 22
- FIN Rajala 99650 3 Cg 23
- UA Rajhorodka 48 Di 42
- BY Rakav 30 Ch 37
- BG Rakitovo 4640 75 Ce 49
- N Rakkestad 1890 16 Bb 31
- BG Rakovica 3820 59 Cc 47
- CZ Rakovník 269 01* 43 Bd 40
- RUS Rakovskaja 13 Eb 28
- BG Rakovski 4150 75 Ce 48
- EST Rakvere 44306* 18 Cg 31
- UA Rakytne 47 Da 41
- SRB Ralja 11233 59 Ca 46
- FIN Ralppaluoto = Repolt 10 Cb 27
- E Ramales de la Victoria 39800 54 Sg 47
- RUS Ramasuha 31 Dd 38
- F Rambervillers 88700 42 Ag 42
- F Rambouillet 78120* 41 Ab 42
- RUS Ramen'e 20 Df 33
- RUS Ramen'e 21 Ea 32
- RUS Ramenskoe 31 Di 35
- A Rammersdorf 3231 44 Bf 42
- S Ramnäs 73060 17 Bg 31
- N Ramnes 3175 2 Bg 22
- BY Ramni 30 Da 35
- RO Râmnicu de Jos 907073 61 Ci 46
- RO Râmnicu Sărat 125300 61 Ch 45
- RO Râmnicu Vâlcea 000240* 60 Ce 45
- RUS Ramon' 48 Dk 39
- S Ramsberg 71198 17 Bf 31
- S Ramsele 88037 9 Bg 27
- GB Ramsey IM8 39 Sf 36
- GB Ramsgate CT11 41 Ab 39
- S Ramsjö 82700 9 Bf 28
- S Ramundberget 84097 9 Bc 28
- RUS Ramuševo 19 Db 33
- S Ramvik 87016 9 Bh 28
- LT Ramygala 38031 29 Ce 35
- RUS Rancevo 31 Dd 34
- GB Randalstown BT41 37 Sd 36
- I Randazzo 95036 72 Be 53
- S Rånddalen 84093 9 Bd 28
- DK Randers 8900 27 Ba 34
- S Randijaur 2 Bk 24
- S Råneå 95501 10 Cc 25
- N Ranemsletta 8 Bb 26
- GB Ranish HS2 38 Sd 32
- RUS Rannee 51 Fc 39
- S Rånön 10 Cc 25
- S Rantajärvi 3 Cd 24
- FIN Rantasalmi 58901 11 Ci 28
- FIN Rantsila 92501 10 Cf 26
- FIN Ranua 97701 10 Cg 25
- I Rapallo 16035 57 Ak 46
- EST Räpina 64503* 19 Ch 32
- EST Rapla 79512* 18 Ce 31
- CH Rapperswil-Jona (SG) 8640 56 Ai 43
- HR Raša 58 Be 45
- LT Raseiniai 60001 29 Cd 35
- SRB Raška 36350* 59 Ca 47
- BY Rasna 30 Db 37
- RO Râșnov 505400 60 Cf 45
- BY Rasony 30 Ci 35
- RO Rasova 907250 61 Ch 46
- RUS Rasskazovo 49 Eb 38
- RUS Rassypnaja 51 Fd 39
- D Rastatt 76437 42 Ai 42
- D Rastede 26180 26 Ai 37
- RO Răstoci 457202 60 Cd 43
- S Rätansbyn 84030 9 Be 28
- RUS Ratčino 32 Dk 37
- IRL Ráth Caola 37 Sb 38
- IRL Ráth Droma 37 Sd 38
- IRL Rathdrum = Ráth Droma 37 Sd 38
- D Rathenow 14712 43 Bc 38
- GB Rathfriland BT34 37 Sd 36
- IRL Rathkeale = Ráth Caola 37 Sb 38
- IRL Rath Luirc 37 Sb 38
- D Ratingen 40878* 42 Ag 39
- UA Ratne 45 Ce 39
- A Ratten 8673* 58 Bf 43
- A Rattenberg 6240* 57 Bb 43
- S Rättvik 79501 17 Bf 30
- D Ratzeburg 23909 27 Ba 37
- LT Raudonė 74057 29 Cd 35
- IS Raufarhöfn 675 36 Re 24
- N Raufoss 2830 16 Ba 30
- N Rauland 3864 16 Ai 31
- FIN Rauma 27003 18 Cb 29
- FIN Rautalampi 77701 10 Cg 28
- FIN Rautavaara 73901 11 Ci 27
- FIN Rautjärvi 19 Ck 29
- UA Rava-Rus'ka 45 Cd 40
- S Rävemåla 36023 27 Bf 34
- I Ravenna 48100 57 Bc 46
- D Ravensburg 88212* 57 Ak 43
- PL Rawa Mazowiecka 96-200 45 Ca 39
- PL Rawicz 63-900 44 Bg 39
- MD Razeni 7727 61 Ci 44
- RUS Razgort 14 Ei 27
- BG Razgrad 7200* 60 Cg 47
- BG Razlog 2760 75 Cd 49
- GB Reading RG1 40 Sk 39
- I Reale, la 07042 71 Ai 49
- F Réalmont 81120 55 Ac 47
- RUS Reboly 11 Da 27
- P Rebordelo 5320-164 68 Sc 49
- BG Rebrovo 2294 75 Cd 48
- RUS Rečane 30 Db 34
- RO Recaș 307340 59 Cb 45
- F Recey-sur-Ource 21290 55 Ae 43
- BY Rečica = Rèčyca 47 Da 38
- D Recke 49509 42 Ah 38
- D Recklinghausen 45657* 42 Ah 39
- B Recogne 6800 42 Af 41
- BY Rèčyca 47 Da 38
- PL Recz 73-210 27 Bf 37
- PL Reda 84-240 28 Bi 36
- GB Redcar TS10 39 Si 36
- GB Redditch B97 40 Si 38
- H Rédics 8978 58 Bg 44
- RUS Redkino 31 Dg 34
- RUS Red'kino 34 Fe 35
- F Redon 35600* 54 Sh 43
- E Redondela 68 Sb 48
- P Redondo 7005-760 80 Sc 52
- TR Refahiye 24300 78 Di 51
- S Reftele 33021 17 Bd 33
- RUS Reftinskij 24 Gb 33
- D Regen 94209 43 Bd 42
- D Regensburg 93047* 43 Bc 41
- D Regenstauf 93128 43 Bc 41
- I Réggio di Calábria 89100 72 Bf 52
- I Réggio nell'Emilia 42100 57 Ba 46
- RO Reghin 545300 60 Ce 44
- S Regna 17 Bf 32
- FIN Reguby 18 Cc 31
- P Reguengos de Monsaraz 80 Sc 52
- D Rehau 95111 43 Bc 40
- D Rehburg-Loccum 31547 42 Ak 38
- D Rehna 19217 27 Bb 37
- GB Reigate RH2 40 Sk 39
- F Reims 51100* 41 Ae 41
- D Reinbek 21465 27 Ba 37
- N Reine 8390 2 Bd 23
- E Reinosa 39200 54 Sf 47
- N Reinsvoll 2840 16 Ba 30
- TR Reis 42580 84 Db 52
- FIN Reisjärvi 85900 10 Ce 27
- PL Rękoraj 97-310 44 Bk 39
- SRB Rekovac 35260 59 Cb 47
- E Relleu 03578 70 Sk 52
- F Rémalard 61110 41 Aa 42
- RUS Remennikovo 30 Ci 34
- FIN Remeskylä 74940 10 Cg 27
- F Remiremont 88200* 42 Ag 42
- RUS Remontnoe 64 Ed 44
- D Remscheid 42853* 42 Ah 39
- N Rena 2450 16 Bb 29
- B Renaix = Ronse 9600 41 Ad 40
- S Renålandet 82064 9 Bf 26
- LV Renceni 4232 18 Cf 33
- LV Renda 3319 18 Cc 33
- D Rendsburg 24768 26 Ak 36
- UA Reni 61 Ci 45
- N Rennebu 7391 8 Ak 28
- F Rennes 35000* 40 Si 42
- S Rensjön 88041 2 Bk 22
- GR Rentína 43068 74 Cb 51
- GR Rentína 43068 75 Cd 50
- F Réole, la 33190* 54 Sk 46
- H Répcelak 9653 58 Bh 43
- RUS Rep'evka 48 Di 39
- RUS Repino 19 Ck 30
- FIN Replot 65930 10 Cb 27
- N Reppen 2 Bd 24
- N Repvåg 9768 3 Cf 20
- F Réquista 12170 55 Ac 46
- TR Reşadiye 78 Dh 50
- TR Reşadiye 87 Ec 52
- BIH Resanovci 58 Bg 46
- SRB Resavica 35237 59 Cb 46
- BG Resen 5060 60 Cf 47
- MK Resen 7310 74 Cb 49
- P Resende 4660-211* 68 Sc 49
- RUS Rešetnikovo 31 Dg 34
- UA Rešetylivka 47 De 41
- RO Reşiţa 000320* 59 Cb 45
- PL Resko 72-315 27 Bf 37
- PL Reszel 11-440 28 Cb 36
- F Rethel 08300* 41 Ae 41
- GR Réthimno 74100 82 Ce 55
- F Retiers 35240 54 Si 43
- F Retournac 43130 55 Ae 45
- E Retuerta del Bullaque 13194 69 Sf 51
- A Retz 2070* 44 Bf 42
- E Reus 43201* 70 Ab 49
- RUS Reutec 48 Df 39
- D Reuterstadt Stavenhagen 17153 27 Bc 37
- D Reutlingen 72760* 42 Ak 42
- RUS Revda 35 Fk 34
- RUS Revda 4 De 23
- F Revel 31250 55 Ac 47
- F Revigny-sur-Ornain 55800 41 Ae 42
- F Revin 08170 41 Ae 41
- IS Reyðarfjörður 36 Rf 25
- TR Reyhanlı 31500 86 Dg 54
- IS Reykhólar 380 36 Qh 25
- IS Reykholt 311 36 Qi 26
- IS Reykjahlíð 36 Rd 25
- IS Reykjavík 150* 36 Qi 26
- RUS Rež 24 Gb 33
- F Rezé 44400 54 Si 43
- LV Rēzekne 4601* 30 Ch 34
- MD Rezina 5400 61 Ci 43
- BG Rezovo 8281 76 Ch 48
- SRB Rgotina 19214 59 Cc 46
- GB Rhayader LD6 40 Sg 38
- D Rheda-Wiedenbrück 33378 42 Ai 39
- D Rheine 48429* 42 Ah 38
- D Rheinfelden (Baden) 79618 56 Ah 43
- D Rheinsberg 16831 27 Bc 37
- GB Rhiconich IV27 38 Sf 32
- D Rhinow 14728 27 Bc 38
- I Rho 20017 57 Ak 45
- GB Rhondda CF41 40 Sg 39
- GB Rhydaman = Ammanford SA18 40 Sg 39
- GB Rhyl LL18 39 Sg 37
- GR Riákia 60100 74 Cc 50
- E Riaza 40500 69 Sg 49
- E Ribadavia 32400 68 Sb 48
- E Ribadeo 27700 68 Sc 47
- E Ribadesella 33560 68 Se 47
- SRB Ribare 37259 59 Cb 47
- BG Ribarica 5720 75 Ce 48
- SRB Ribariće 36309 74 Ca 48
- DK Ribe 6760 26 Ai 35
- F Ribeauvillé 68150* 42 Ah 42
- P Ribeira de Pena 4870-150* 68 Sc 49
- I Ribera 92016 72 Bd 53
- F Ribérac 24600 54 Aa 45
- E Ribes de Freser 17534 70 Ac 48
- BIH Ribnica 59 Bi 46
- SLO Ribnica 6240 58 Be 45
- MD Ribnița 5500 61 Ck 43
- D Ribnitz-Damgarten 18311 27 Bc 36
- BG Ribnovo 2967 75 Cd 49
- E Ricabo 68 Se 47
- CZ Říčany 664 82 43 Be 41
- I Riccione 47838 57 Bc 46
- F Riceys, les 10340 41 Ae 43
- F Richelieu 37120 54 Aa 43
- GB Richmond TW10 39 Si 36
- D Riedenburg 93339 43 Bb 42
- A Ried im Innkreis 4910* 43 Bd 42
- D Riedlingen 88499 42 Ak 42
- D Riesa 01587* 43 Bd 39
- I Riesi 93016 72 Be 53
- LT Rietavas 90018 28 Cb 35
- I Rieti 02100 72 Bc 48
- F Rieumes 31370 55 Ab 47
- F Riez 04500 56 Ag 47
- LV Rīga 1001* 29 Ce 34
- RUS Rigozero 12 De 27
- EST Riguldi 91202 18 Cd 31
- FIN Riihimäki 11910 18 Ce 30
- FIN Riistavesi 71161 11 Ci 28
- HR Rijeka 58 Be 45
- NL Rijsenburg, Driebergen- 3972 42 Af 38
- BG Rila 2630 75 Cd 48
- SK Rimavská Sobota 979 01 45 Ca 42
- S Rimbo 76200 17 Bi 31
- S Rimforsa 59041 17 Bf 32
- I Rímini 47900 57 Bc 46
- RUS Rimsko-Korsakovka 50 Ei 39
- N Rindal 6657 8 Ak 27
- S Ringarum 61041 17 Bg 32
- DK Ringe 5750 27 Ba 35
- DK Ringkøbing 6950 26 Ai 34
- DK Ringsted 4100* 27 Bb 35
- GB Ringwood BH24 40 Si 40
- RUS Rintala 19 Ck 29
- D Rinteln 31737 42 Ak 38
- GR Río 26504 82 Cb 52
- F Riom 63200* 55 Ad 45
- P Rio Maior 2040-092* 68 Sb 51
- F Riom-ès-Montagnes 15400 55 Ac 45
- I Rionero in Vúlture 85028 73 Bf 50
- SRB Ripanj 11232* 59 Ca 46
- UA Ripky 47 Db 39
- E Ripoll 17500 70 Ac 48
- GB Ripon HG4 39 Si 36
- MNE Risan 85 337 74 Bi 48
- S Risbäck 91703 9 Bf 26
- MD Rîșcani 5600 61 Ch 43
- F Riscle 32400 54 Sk 47
- N Risør 4950 16 Ak 32
- N Risøyhamn 8484 2 Bf 22
- N Rissa 7100 8 Ba 27
- S Rissna 83076 9 Bf 27
- EST Risti 90901 18 Ce 32
- FIN Ristiina 50770 19 Ch 29
- FIN Ristijärvi 88401 11 Ci 26
- I Riva del Garda 38066 57 Ba 45
- F Rive-de-Gier 42800 55 Ae 45
- I Rivergaro 29029 57 Ak 46
- F Rivesaltes 66600* 70 Ac 48
- UA Rivne 46 Cg 40
- UA Rivnoe 47 Db 42
- I Rivoli 10098 56 Ah 45
- RKS Rixhevë = Kijevo 24060 74 Ca 48
- TR Rize 53000* 79 Ea 49
- Rizokarpaso 85 De 55
- RUS Rjabinino 23 Fg 30
- RUS Rjabovo 19 Db 31
- RUS Rjabovskij 49 Eb 40
- RUS Rjapusovskij Pogost 12 Di 28
- RUS Rjazan' 32 Dk 36
- RUS Rjazancevo 32 Dk 34
- RUS Rjazanka 49 Ec 38
- RUS Rjazanovka 34 Fd 37
- RUS Rjazanovskij 32 Dk 35
- RUS Rjazanskaja 63 Dk 46
- RUS Rjazap, Iske- 33 Ek 36
- RUS Rjažsk 32 Ea 37
- N Rjukan 3660 16 Ai 31
- E Roa 09300 69 Sg 49
- N Roald 6002 8 Ag 28
- F Roanne 42300* 55 Ae 44
- D Röbel 27 Bc 37
- S Robertsfors 91501 10 Ca 26
- GB Robin Hood's Bay YO22 39 Sk 36
- E Robla, La 24640 68 Se 48
- E Roca de la Sierra, La 06190 68 Sd 51
- GB Rochdale OL11 39 Sh 37
- F Roche-Bernard, la 56130 54 Sh 43
- F Roche-Chalais, la 24490 54 Aa 45
- F Rochechouart 87600 54 Aa 45
- B Rochefort 5580 42 Af 40
- F Rochefort 17300* 54 Sk 45
- F Rochelle, la 17000* 54 Si 44
- F Roche-Posay, la 86270 54 Aa 44
- F Rocheservière 85620 54 Si 44
- GB Rochester ME2 41 Aa 39
- F Roche-sur-Foron, la 74800* 56 Ag 44
- F Roche-sur-Yon, la 85000* 54 Si 44
- D Rochlitz 09306 43 Bc 39
- E Rocío, El 80 Sd 53
- F Rocroi 08230 41 Ae 41


A B C D E F G H I J K L M N O P Q R S T U V W X Y Z

Rocroi 171

(F) Saint-Pourçain-sur-Sioule 03500 55 Ad 44
(F) Saint-Quentin 02100* 41 Ad 41
(F) Saint-Rambert-d'Albon 26140 55 Ae 45
(F) Saint-Raphaël 83700* 56 Ag 47
(F) Saint-Rémy-de-Provence 13210* 55 Ae 47
(F) Saint-Saulge 58330 55 Ad 43
(F) Saint-Saveur-sur-Tinée 56 Ah 46
(F) Saint-Savin 33920 54 Aa 44
(F) Saint-Sever 40500* 54 Sk 47
(F) Saint-Sulpice 81370 55 Ab 47
(F) Saint-Symphorien 33113 54 Sk 46
(B) Saint-Trond = Sint-Truiden 3800 42 Af 40
(F) Saint-Tropez 83990* 56 Ag 47
(F) Saint-Vaast-la-Hougue 50550 40 Si 41
(F) Saint-Valéry-en-Caux 41 Aa 41
(F) Saint-Valery-sur-Somme 80230 41 Ab 40
(F) Saint-Vallier 26240 55 Ae 44
(F) Saint-Vallier 26240 55 Ae 45
(F) Saint-Vaury 23320 55 Ab 44
(F) Saint-Vincent-de-Tyrosse 40230 54 Si 47
(B) Saint-Vith 4780 42 Ag 40
(F) Saint-Vivien-de-Médoc 33590 54 Si 45
(F) Saint-Yrieix-la-Perche 87500 55 Ab 45
(F) Saissac 11310 55 Ac 47
(RUS) Saitbaba 35 Fg 36
(S) Saittarova 3 Cc 23
(RUS) Saja 23 Fh 33
(RUS) Šajduriha 24 Ga 33
(RUS) Šajgino 22 Eg 33
(SRB) Šajince 74 Cc 48
(H) Sajószentpéter 3770 45 Ca 42
(TR) Sakaevi 18800 77 Dd 50
(TR) Sakaltutan 38610 85 Df 52
(TR) Sakarya 46090 76 Da 50
(TR) Sakçagöz 86 Dg 53
(LT) Šakiai 71001 29 Cd 36
(RUS) Šakin 49 Ec 41
(TR) Sakız 57200 76 Ch 49
(RUS) Sakmara 52 Ff 39
(RUS) Sakony 32 Ed 35
(DK) Sakskøbing 4990 27 Bb 36
(UA) Saky 62 Dd 45
(TR) Sakyatan 84 Dc 53
(FIN) Säkylä 27920 18 Cc 29
(S) Sala 73301* 17 Bg 31
(SK) Šal'a 927 01* 44 Bh 42
(LV) Salačgriva 18 Ce 33
(I) Sala Consilina 84036 73 Bf 50
(GR) Sálakos 85106 83 Ch 54
(RUS) Šalakuša 12 Ea 28
(E) Salamanca 37001* 68 Se 50
(RUS) Salamat 35 Gb 37
(GR) Salamína 18900 82 Cd 53
(LT) Salantai 97035 28 Cb 34
(E) Salas 33860 68 Sd 47
(E) Salas de los Infantes 09600 69 Sg 48
(F) Salau 09140 70 Ab 48
(RUS) Salavat 34 Ff 37
(TR) Salbaş 01780 85 Df 53
(F) Salbris 41300 55 Ac 43
(LT) Šalčininkai 17001 29 Cf 36
(E) Saldaña 34100 69 Sf 48
(RUS) Šaldež 33 Ee 34
(LV) Saldus 3801 29 Cc 34
(P) Salema 80 Sb 53
(I) Salemi 91018 72 Bc 53
(S) Sälen 78067 17 Bd 29
(F) Salernes 83690 56 Ag 47
(I) Salerno 84100* 73 Be 50
(RUS) Salgan 33 Ef 35
(H) Salgótarján 3100 44 Bk 42
(RUS) Šalgovaara 11 Dd 27
(HR) Sali 58 Bf 47
(RUS) Šali 33 Ek 35
(F) Salies-de-Béarn 64270 54 Sk 47
(TR) Salihler 17600 75 Cg 51
(TR) Salihler 17600 76 Db 51
(TR) Salihli 83 Ci 52
(BY) Salihorsk 30 Ch 38
(RUS) Salino 31 De 34
(F) Salins-les-Bains 39110 56 Af 44
(TR) Salıpazarı 55530 77 De 49
(GB) Salisbury SP1 40 Si 39
(RO) Săliște 557225 60 Cd 45
(RUS) Šalja 24 Fi 33
(UA) Sal'kove 46 Ck 42
(FIN) Salla 98901 3 Ci 24
(F) Sallanches 74700 56 Ag 45
(E) Sallent 08650 70 Ab 49
(F) Salles 33770 54 Sk 46
(TR) Salmanlı 66910 77 De 51
(RUS) Salmi 19 Db 29
(FIN) Salo 25003 18 Cd 30
(I) Salò 25087 57 Ba 45
(F) Salon-de-Provence 13300 56 Af 47
(RO) Salonta 415500 59 Cb 44
(TR) Şalpazarı 61670 78 Dk 50
(N) Salsbruket 7960 8 Bb 26
(F) Salses 66600 70 Ac 48
(RUS) Sal'sk 64 Eb 44
(RUS) Šal'skij 12 Dg 29
(I) Salsomaggiore Terme 43039 57 Ak 46
(GB) Saltash PL12 40 Sf 40
(GB) Saltburn- by-the-Sea 39 Sk 36
(GB) Saltfleet LN11 39 Aa 37
(S) Saltoluoktafjällstation 2 Bi 23
(S) Saltsjöbaden 13300 17 Bi 31
(AX) Saltvik 22430 18 Ca 30
(RUS) Šalty 34 Fd 36
(RUS) Šalty 34 Fd 37
(RUS) Saltyki 32 Dk 37
(RUS) Saltykovo, Karaja- 49 Ec 38
(TR) Salur 86 Dk 53
(I) Saluzzo 12037 56 Ah 46
(RO) Salva 427255 60 Ce 43
(P) Salvaterra de Magos 2120-051* 68 Sb 51
(E) Salvatierra de los Barros 06175 80 Sd 52
(F) Salviac 46340 55 Ab 46
(RUS) Saly, Sultan- 63 Dk 43
(UA) Šalyhyne 47 De 39
(A) Salzburg 5020* 57 Bd 43
(D) Salzgitter 38226* 43 Ba 38
(D) Salzungen, Bad 36433 43 Ba 40
(D) Salzwedel 29410 27 Bb 38
(E) Sama (Langreo) 68 Se 47
(BY) Samachvalavičy 30 Ch 37
(TR) Samailli 84 Ci 52
(TR) Samandağ 31770 85 Df 54
(TR) Samandere 76 Db 50
(RUS) Samara 34 Fa 37
(RUS) Samarkovo 64 Ed 47
(RUS) Samarskoe 52 Fi 39
(RUS) Samarskoe 63 Dk 44
(RUS) Šamary 24 Fi 33
(F) Samatan 32130 54 Aa 47
(TR) Şambayat 02340 86 Di 53
(UA) Sambir 45 Cd 41
(UA) Sambir 47 Dd 39
(CH) Samedan 7503 57 Ak 44
(GR) Sámi 28080 82 Ca 52
(RUS) Samino 22 Ei 29
(TR) Şamlı 10180 76 Ch 51
(HR) Samobor 58 Bf 45
(RUS) Samoded 12 Ea 27
(RUS) Samofalovka 49 Ee 42
(RUS) Samojlovka 49 Ed 39
(BG) Samokov 2000 75 Cd 48
(SK) Šamorín 931 01 44 Bh 42
(GR) Sámos 83100 83 Cg 53
(GR) Samothráki 68002 75 Cf 50
(RUS) Samovol'no-Ivanovka 51 Fa 38
(I) Sampèyre 12020 56 Ah 46
(RUS) Sampur 49 Eb 38
(TR) Samsun 55000* 78 Dg 49
(I) Samugheo 09086 71 Ai 51
(RUS) Samylovo 21 Ee 32
(E) San Bartolomé de la Torre 21510 80 Sc 53
(I) San Bartolomeo in Galdo 82028 73 Bf 49
(I) San Benedetto del Tronto 63039 72 Bd 48
(I) San Benedetto Po 46027 57 Ba 45
(I) San Bonifácio 37047 57 Bb 45
(TR) Sancak 12300 79 Ea 51
(F) Sancerre 18300 55 Ac 43
(E) Sanchidrián 05290 69 Sf 50
(F) Sancoins 18600 55 Ac 44
(E) Sancti-Spíritus 68 Sd 50
(RUS) Sančursk 33 Eh 34
(N) Sand 4230 16 Ag 31
(N) Sand 4230 16 Bb 30
(N) Sandane 6823 8 Ag 29
(BG) Sandanski 2800 75 Cd 49
(S) Sandared 51820 17 Bc 33
(RUS) Sandata 64 Eb 44
(N) Sandbukta 3 Cb 21
(D) Sande 26452 26 Ai 37
(N) Sande 16 Af 29
(N) Sande 16 Ba 31
(N) Sandefjord 3208* 16 Ba 31
(IS) Sandgerði 245 36 Qh 26
(S) Sandhammaren 27 Be 35
(TR) Sandıklı 03500 84 Da 52
(S) Sandnäset 84040 9 Bg 28
(N) Sandnes 16 Af 32
(N) Sandneshamn 2 Bi 21
(N) Sandnessjøen 8800 2 Bc 24
(PL) Sandomierz 27-600* 45 Cb 40
(I) San Donà di Piave 30027 57 Bc 45
(RUS) Sandovo 20 Dg 32
(UA) Šandrivka 48 Df 42
(S) Sandsjö 91050 17 Be 29
(N) Sandstad 8 Ak 27
(DK) Sandvig 4735 27 Be 35
(S) Sandvik 59010 17 Bg 33
(S) Sandvika 83015 9 Bc 27
(S) Sandviken 81100* 17 Bg 30
(E) San Esteban de Gormaz 42330 69 Sg 49
(I) San Felice Circeo 04017 72 Bd 49
(E) San Felices de los Gallegos 37270 68 Sd 50
(E) San Fernando 37492 80 Sd 54
(RUS) Šanga, Nikola- 22 Ef 32
(D) Sangerhausen 06526 43 Bb 39
(RO) Sângeru 60 Cg 45
(I) San Gimignano 53037 57 Bb 47
(I) San Ginésio 62026 72 Bd 47
(FIN) Sanginkylä 91620 10 Cg 26
(I) San Giórgio Iónico 74027 73 Bh 50
(I) San Giovanni in Fiore 87055 73 Bg 51
(I) San Giovanni in Persiceto 40017 57 Bb 46
(I) San Giovanni Rotondo 71013 73 Bf 49
(S) Sangis 95272 10 Cd 25
(E) San Ildefonso o La Granja 40100 69 Sf 50
(E) San Janvier 81 Sk 53
(E) San José 81 Sh 54
(E) San Juan de Alacant 81 Sk 52
(E) San Juan de Alicante = San Juan de Alacant 81 Sk 52
(TR) Sankok 84 Db 53
(A) Sankt Aegyd am Neuwalde 3193 58 Bf 43
(A) Sankt Anton am Arlberg 8560 57 Ba 43
(CH) Sankt Gallen 9000* 57 Ak 43
(A) Sankt Gilgen 5340 57 Bd 43
(D) Sankt Goar 56329 42 Ah 40
(A) Sankt Johann im Pongau 5600* 57 Bd 43
(D) Sankt Michaelisdonn 25693 26 Ak 37
(CH) Sankt Moritz 7500* 57 Ak 44
(RUS) Sankt-Peterburg 190000* 19 Da 31
(D) Sankt Peter-Ording 25826 26 Ai 36
(A) Sankt Pölten 3100* 44 Bf 42
(A) Sankt Veit an der Glan 9300* 58 Be 44
(B) Sankt-Vith = Saint-Vith 4780 42 Ag 40
(D) Sankt Wendel 66606 42 Ah 41
(E) San Leonardo de Yagüe 42140 69 Sg 49
(TR) Şanlıca 79 Eb 51
(TR) Şanlı Urfa 86 Di 53
(E) San Lorenzo 28200 69 Sf 50
(E) San Lorenzo de Calatrava 13779 81 Sg 52
(E) Sanlúcar de Barrameda 11540 80 Sd 54
(E) Sanlúcar de Guadiana 21595 80 Sc 53
(E) Sanlúcar la Mayor 41800 80 Sd 53
(I) Sanluri 09025 71 Ai 51
(I) San Marcello Pistoiese 51028 57 Ba 46
(RSM) San Marino 47890 57 Bc 47
(E) San Martín de Castañeda 68 Sd 48
(E) San Martín de Montalbán 45165 69 Sf 51
(E) San Martín de Valdeiglesias 28680 69 Sf 50
(I) San Martino di Castrozza 38058 57 Bb 44
(E) San Miguel de Salinas 03193 81 Sk 53
(S) Sänna 17 Be 32
(RO) Sânnicolau Mare 305600 59 Ca 44
(PL) Sanniki 09-540 44 Bk 38
(PL) Sanok 38-500 45 Cc 41
(E) San Pedro del Pinatar 30740 81 Sk 53
(I) Sanremo 18038 56 Ah 47
(E) San Roque 11360 80 Se 54
(E) San Sadurniño = Avenida do Marqués de Figueroa 68 Sb 47
(E) San Sebastián = Donostia 20001 54 Si 47
(E) San Sebastián de los Reyes 28700 69 Sg 50
(I) Sansepolcro 52037 57 Bc 47
(I) San Severino Marche 62027 57 Bd 47
(I) San Severo 71016 73 Bf 49
(RUS) Šanskij Zavod 31 Df 35
(BIH) Sanski Most 58 Bg 46
(I) San Stino di Livenza 57 Bc 45
(E) Santa Amalia 06410 68 Sd 51
(E) Santa Bárbara de Casa 21570 80 Sc 53
(I) Santa Caterina di Pittinuri 09078 71 Ai 50
(I) Santa Cesárea Terme 73020 73 Bi 50
(P) Santa Clara-a-Velha 7665-880* 80 Sb 53
(E) Santa Coloma de Farners 17430 70 Ac 49
(P) Santa Comba Dão 3440-313* 68 Sb 50
(I) Santa Cristina Valgardena = Sankt Christina in Gröden 39047 57 Bb 44
(I) Santa Croce Camerina 97017 72 Be 54
(E) Santa Cruz de Mudela 13730 81 Sg 52
(I) Santa Doménica Taláo 87020 73 Bf 51
(E) Santa Eufemia 14491 81 Sf 52
(E) Santa Eugenia (Ribeira) 68 Sb 48
(P) Santa Eulália 7450-101 68 Sc 51
(E) Santa Eulària del Riu 70 Ab 52
(E) Santa Fé 18320 81 Sg 53
(I) Sant'Ágata di Militelo 72 Be 52
(I) Santa Margherita Lígure 16038 57 Ak 46
(I) Santa Maria Cápua Vetere 81055 73 Be 49
(E) Santa Maria de Arzua 68 Sb 48
(E) Santa Maria del Camí 07320 70 Ac 51
(E) Santa María del Páramo 24240 68 Se 48
(E) Santa Marta 80 Sd 52
(E) Santana 69 Sf 48
(P) Santana da Serra 7670-613 80 Sb 53
(E) Santander 39001* 54 Sg 47
(I) Sant'Ángelo dei Lombardi 83054 73 Bf 50
(I) Sant'Ángelo Lodigiano 26866 57 Ak 45
(I) Sant'Antíoco 09017 71 Ai 51
(E) Sant Antoni 70 Ab 52
(E) Santa Olalla del Cala 21260 80 Sd 53
(E) Santa Pau 17811 70 Ac 48
(E) Santa Pola 03130 81 Sk 52
(I) Sant'Arcángelo 85037 73 Bg 50
(P) Santarém 2000-005* 68 Sb 51
(I) Santa Sofia 47018 57 Bb 47
(I) Santa Teresa di Gallura 07028 71 Ak 49
(E) Sant Carles de la Ràpita 43540 70 Aa 50
(E) Sant Celoni 08470 70 Ac 49
(I) San Teodoro 08020 71 Ak 50
(E) Santesteban 31720 69 Si 47
(I) Sant'Eufémia Lamézia 73 Bg 52
(E) Sant Feliu de Guíxols 17220 70 Ad 49
(E) Sant Francesc de Formentera 07860 70 Ab 52
(E) Santiago de Alcántara 10510 68 Sc 51
(E) Santiago de Compostela 15701* 68 Sb 48
(P) Santiago do Cacém 7540-100* 80 Sb 52
(E) Santibáñez de la Sierra 68 Se 50
(E) Sant Mateu 12170 70 Aa 50
(E) Santo Domingo de la Calzada 26250 69 Sh 48
(GR) Santoméri 82 Cb 53
(E) Santoña 39740 54 Sg 47
(I) Santo Stéfano di Camastra 98077 72 Be 52
(P) Santo Tirso 4640-273* 68 Sb 49
(E) San Vincente de Alcántara 68 Sc 51
(I) San Vincenzo 57027 72 Ba 47
(I) San Vito lo Capo 91010 72 Bc 52
(P) São Bartolomeu de Messines 8375-100* 80 Sb 53
(P) São Brás de Alportel 8150-101 80 Sc 53
(P) São João da Madeira 3700-011 68 Sb 50
(P) São Martinho do Porto 2460-083* 68 Sa 51
(P) São Teotónio 7630-611* 80 Sb 53
(P) São Vicente da Beira 6005-270 68 Sc 50
(TR) Sapanca 17600 76 Da 50
(RUS) Sapërnoe 19 Ck 30
(GR) Sápes 69300 75 Cf 49
(TR) Şaphane 43950 76 Ck 51
(RUS) Šapki 19 Db 31
(RUS) Šapkino 49 Ec 39
(TR) Sapmaz 78 Di 50
(RUS) Šapošnikovo 51 Fb 39
(RUS) Sapožok 32 Ea 37
(NL) Sappemeer, Hoogezand- 9615 26 Ag 37
(I) Sapri 84073 73 Bf 50
(FIN) Sara 39980 10 Cc 28
(RUS) Sara 33 Eg 36
(RUS) Sara 52 Fh 39
(RUS) Sarabikulovo 34 Fb 36
(N) Saraby 3 Cd 20
(RUS) Saraevo 22 Ef 30
(RUS) Saragulka 25 Ge 32
(RUS) Sarai 32 Ea 37
(FIN) Säräisniemi 91760 10 Cg 26
(RO) Saraiu 907255 61 Ci 46
(FIN) Sarajärvi 93250 11 Ch 25
(BIH) Sarajevo 71000* 59 Bi 47
(RUS) Saraj-Gir 34 Fd 37
(GR) Sarakiniko 82 Cd 52
(RUS) Saraktaš 52 Fg 39
(RUS) Šaran 34 Fe 36
(RUS) Sarana 35 Fh 34
(BG) Saranci 2120 75 Cd 48
(AL) Sarandë 74 Ca 51
(RUS) Šaranga 22 Eg 33
(RUS) Saranpaul' 15 Ga 26
(RUS) Saransk 33 Ef 36
(BG) Saransko 8659 75 Cg 48
(RUS) Šarapovo 33 Ee 35
(RUS) Sarapul 34 Fd 34
(RUS) Šarašenskij 49 Ec 40
(RUS) Saraši 34 Ff 34
(BY) Šarašova 45 Ce 38
(UA) Sarata 61 Ck 44
(RO) Sărățel 427301 60 Ce 43
(RUS) Saratov 50 Eg 39
(TR) Saravakpınar = Sırpsındığı 22770 75 Cg 49
(TR) Saray 65830 76 Ch 49
(TR) Saray 65830 77 De 51
(TR) Saray 65830 87 Ee 52
(TR) Saraycık 77 Df 50
(TR) Saraydüzü 77 De 49
(TR) Sarayköy 20300 76 Db 51
(TR) Sarayköy 20300 84 Ci 53
(TR) Sarayönü 42430 84 Dc 52
(RUS) Sarbala 21 Ed 30
(RUS) Šardonem' 13 Ee 27
(CH) Sargans 7320 57 Ak 43
(TR) Sargin 55700 77 Df 49
(UA) Šarhorod 46 Ci 42
(GR) Saria 83 Ch 55
(TR) Sarıbeyler 10590 76 Ch 51
(TR) Sarıbuğday 77 Df 50
(TR) Sarıcakaya 26870 76 Da 50
(TR) Sarıgöl 55810 79 Eb 50
(TR) Sarıgöl 55810 84 Ci 52
(TR) Sarıkamış 36500 79 Ec 50
(TR) Sarıkavak 85 Dd 54
(TR) Sarıkaya 77 Df 51
(TR) Sarıkaya 84 Ci 52
(TR) Sarıkaya 84 Dc 52
(TR) Sarıkonak 87 Eb 52
(TR) Sarıköy 10680 76 Ch 50
(TR) Sarılar 59850 86 Dh 53
(TR) Sarımazı 01956 85 Df 54
(E) Sariñena 22200 70 Sk 49
(TR) Sarıoba 77 Dc 51
(TR) Sarıoğlan 38820* 85 Df 51
(RUS) Šaripovo 34 Ff 36
(TR) Sarısu = Aktepe 79 Ec 51
(TR) Sarıveliler 70800 84 Dc 54
(TR) Sariyar 34886 76 Ck 49
(TR) Sarıyar 57710 76 Db 50
(TR) Sarız 38660* 86 Dg 52
(RUS) Sar'ja 19 Dc 31
(RUS) Šar'ja 22 Ef 32
(H) Sarkad 5720 59 Cb 44
(RUS) Šarkan 23 Fd 33
(BY) Šarkavščyna 30 Ch 35
(TR) Şarkîkaraağaç 84 Db 52
(FIN) Särkisalmi 59310 19 Ck 29
(TR) Şarkışla 58400 78 Dg 51
(BG) Šarkovo 75 Cg 48
(BG) Šarkovo 8753 75 Cg 48
(TR) Şarköy 59800 76 Ch 50
(TR) Şarlakköy 86 Dg 52
(F) Sarlat-la-Canéda 24200 55 Ab 46
(RUS) Šarlyk 34 Fe 38
(RUS) Sarmakovo 64 Ed 47
(RUS) Sarmanaj 34 Fe 37
(RUS) Sarmanovo 34 Fc 35
(RO) Sărmășel Gară 547521 60 Ce 44
(RO) Sarmizegetusa 337415 59 Cc 45
(S) Särna 79090 17 Bd 29
(CH) Sarnen 6060* 56 Ai 44
(BG) Sârnica 6361 75 Cd 49
(BG) Sărnica 4633 75 Ce 49
(S) Särnstugan 76296 17 Bd 29
(RUS) Šarnut 64 Ed 43
(UA) Sarny 46 Cg 39
(I) Saronno 20030 57 Ak 45
(TR) Sarot 76 Db 50
(RUS) Sarova 32 Ed 36
(SK) Šarovce 44 Bi 42
(RUS) Sarpa 65 Ef 43
(N) Sarpsborg, Fredrikstad- 1706* 16 Bb 31
(F) Sarrebourg 57400* 42 Ah 42
(F) Sarreguemines 57200* 42 Ah 41
(F) Sarre-Union 67260 42 Ah 42
(E) Sarria 27600 68 Sc 48
(E) Sarrión 44460 70 Sk 50
(I) Sarroch 09018 71 Ak 51
(I) Sarsina 57 Bc 47
(F) Sartène 20100 71 Ai 49
(GR) Sárti 63078 75 Cd 50
(F) Sartilly 50530 40 Si 42
(TR) Saruhanlı 45800 83 Ch 52
(RUS) Saruj 33 Eh 35
(H) Sárvár 9600 58 Bg 43
(FIN) Sarvela 39960 10 Cc 28
(S) Särvsjön 84035 9 Bd 28
(F) Sarzeau 56370 54 Sh 43
(TR) Sasallı 83 Cg 52
(H) Sásd 7370 59 Bi 44
(TR) Sason 72500 87 Eb 52
(RUS) Sasovo 32 Eb 36
(I) Sàssari 07100 71 Ai 50
(F) Sassenage 38360 56 Af 45
(D) Sassnitz 18546 27 Bd 36
(D) Saßnitz = Sassnitz 18546 27 Bd 36
(I) Sassuolo 41049 57 Ba 46
(RUS) Sasykoli 65 Eh 43
(UA) Sataniv 46 Cg 41
(S) Såtenäs 17 Bc 32
(S) Säter 78301 17 Bf 30
(TR) Satıköy 87 Ea 53
(RUS) Satino 23 Fd 32
(RUS) Satka 35 Fk 35
(RUS) Šatki 33 Ee 35
(H) Sátoraljaújhely 3980 45 Cb 42
(BG) Satovča 2950 75 Cd 49
(RO) Satu Mare 727480 59 Cc 43
(RUS) Šatura 32 Dk 35
(N) Sauda 4200 16 Ag 31
(IS) Sauðárkrókur 551 36 Ql 25
(F) Saugues 43170 55 Ad 46
(F) Saujon 17600 54 Sk 45
(FIN) Saukkola 09430 18 Cd 30
(F) Saulieu 21210 55 Ae 43
(LV) Saulkrasti 2160 18 Ce 33
(F) Sault 84390 56 Af 46
(F) Saumur 49400* 54 Sk 43
(FIN) Saunajärvi 88901 11 Ck 27
(F) Sauveterre-de-Guyenne 33540 54 Sk 46
(FIN) Sauvo 21571 18 Cc 30
(F) Sauzé-Vaussais 79190 54 Aa 44
(F) Sauzon 56360 54 Sg 43
(BY) Sava 30 Da 36
(S) Sävar 91801 10 Ca 27
(RUS) Šavaržakovo 22 Ei 33
(TR) Savaştepe 10580 76 Ch 51
(TR) Savcılı 40410 77 Dd 51
(RUS) Savcyno 20 Dh 33
(F) Savenay 44260 54 Si 43
(RO) Săveni 715300 60 Cg 43
(F) Saverdun 09700 55 Ab 47
(F) Saverne 67700* 42 Ah 42
(I) Savigliano 12038 56 Ah 46
(FIN) Savikylä 75650 11 Ci 27
(RUS) Savinka 50 Eh 40
(RUS) Savino 20 Dg 30



Savino 173

(RUS) Savino 32 Eb 34
(RUS) Savinobor 15 Fg 27
(RUS) Savinskij 12 Ea 28
(FIN) Savitaipale 54801 19 Ch 29
(MNE) Šavnik 81 450 74 Bk 48
(I) Savona 17100 56 Ai 46
(FIN) Savonlinna 57810 11 Ci 29
(FIN) Savonranta 58300 11 Ck 28
(UA) Savran' 47 Da 42
(TR) Şavşat 08700 79 Ec 49
(S) Sävsjö 57601 17 Be 33
(FIN) Savukoski 98800 3 Ci 23
(TR) Savur 47860 87 Ea 53
(UA) Savynci 48 Dh 41
(GB) Saxmundham IP17 41 Ab 38
(S) Saxnäs 9 Bf 26
(FIN) Säyneinen 73770 11 Ci 27
(FIN) Säytsjärvi 99910 3 Ch 21
(RUS) Sazan 52 Fg 39
(TR) Sazılar 77 Dc 51
(RUS) Sažino 35 Fi 34
(RUS) Sazonovo 20 Df 31
(F) Scaër 29390 40 Sg 42
(GB) Scalasaig PA61 38 Sd 34
(GB) Scalby YO12 39 Sk 36
(GB) Scalloway ZE1 38 Si 30
(I) Scansano 58054 72 Bb 48
(RO) Scânteia 927210 61 Ch 46
(GB) Scarborough YO11 39 Sk 36
(GB) Scarinish PA77 38 Sd 34
(IRL) Scarriff = An Scairbh 37 Sb 38
(RUS) Ščekino 31 Dh 36
(RUS) Ščel' 14 Fd 26
(RUS) Ščel'jabož 7 Fg 24
(RUS) Ščeljajur 14 Fd 25
(RUS) Ščelkovo 31 Di 35
(RUS) Ščerbinka 31 Dh 35
(A) Schachendorf 7472* 58 Bg 43
(CH) Schaffhausen 8200* 56 Ai 43
(NL) Schagen 1740 26 Ae 38
(CH) Schanf 7525 57 Ak 44
(A) Schärding 4780 43 Bd 42
(A) Scharnitz 6108 57 Bb 43
(A) Scheibbs 3270* 44 Bf 43
(D) Scherfede 34414 42 Ak 39
(I) Schio 36015 57 Bb 45
(D) Schkeuditz 04435 43 Bc 39
(A) Schladming 8970* 57 Bd 43
(I) Schlanders = Silandro 39028 57 Ba 44
(D) Schleiden 53937 42 Ag 40
(D) Schleiz 07907 43 Bb 40
(D) Schleswig 24837 26 Ak 36
(D) Schleusingen 98553 43 Ba 40
(A) Schlierbach 34599 43 Be 43
(D) Schlotheim 99994 43 Ba 39
(D) Schlüchtern 36381 42 Ak 40
(I) Schluderns = Sluderno 39020 57 Ba 44
(D) Schmalkalden 98574 43 Ba 40
(D) Schmiedeberg, Bad 06905 43 Bc 39
(D) Schnackenburg 29493 27 Bb 37
(D) Schneverdingen 29640 26 Ak 37
(D) Schönberg 16866 27 Ba 37
(D) Schönberg (Holstein) 24217 27 Ba 36
(D) Schönebeck (Elbe) 39218 43 Bb 38
(D) Schongau 86956 57 Ba 43
(D) Schönsee 92539 43 Bc 41
(D) Schopfheim 79650 56 Ah 43
(D) Schramberg 78713 42 Ai 42
(D) Schrobenhausen 86529 43 Bb 42
(A) Schruns 6780 57 Ak 43
(CH) Schuls, Scuols/ 7550 57 Ba 44
(D) Schussenried, Bad 88427 42 Ak 42
(D) Schwaan 18258 27 Bc 37
(D) Schwabach 91126 43 Bb 41
(D) Schwäbisch Gmünd 73525* 42 Ak 42
(D) Schwäbisch Hall 74523 42 Ak 41
(D) Schwabmünchen 86830 43 Ba 42
(D) Schwandorf 92421 43 Bc 41
(D) Schwarmstedt 29690 42 Ak 38
(D) Schwarzenbek 21493 27 Ba 37
(A) Schwaz 6130 57 Bb 43
(A) Schwechat 2320 44 Bg 42
(D) Schwedt/Oder 16303 27 Be 37
(D) Schweinfurt 97421* 43 Ba 40
(D) Schwenningen, Villingen- 78048* 42 Ai 42
(D) Schwerin 19053* 27 Bb 37
(D) Schwetzingen 68723 42 Ai 41
(CH) Schwyz 6430* 56 Ai 43
(I) Sciacca 92019 72 Bd 53
(RUS) Ščigry 48 Dg 39
(I) Scordia 95048 72 Be 53
(RO) Scorniceşti 235600 60 Ce 46
(UA) Ščors 47 Db 39
(RO) Scorţeni 107525 60 Cg 44
(GB) Scourie IV27 38 Se 32
(RUS) Ščuč'e Ozero 35 Fg 34
(BY) Ščučyn 29 Ce 37
(GB) Scunthorpe DN16 39 Sk 37
(CH) Scuol/Schuls 7550 57 Ba 44
(RUS) Ščurovo 20 Di 33
(RUS) Ščutenskie Peski 49 Ea 39
(IRL) Searcóck 37 Sd 37
(GB) Seascale CA20 39 Sg 36
(RUS) Šebekino 48 Dg 40
(TR) Seben 14750 76 Db 50
(RO) Sebeş 515800 60 Cd 45
(RUS) Sebeusad 33 Ei 34
(RUS) Sebež 30 Ci 34
(TR) Şebinkarahisar 28400 78 Di 50
(RO) Sebiş 315700 59 Cc 44
(D) Sebnitz 01855 43 Be 40
(E) Sebta = Ceuta 51000* 80 Se 55
(E) Sebta = Ceuta 51000* 81 Sf 55
(RUS) Sečenovo 33 Ef 35
(F) Secondigny 79130 54 Sk 44
(SK) Sečovce 078 01 45 Cb 42
(RO) Secuieni 617415 61 Ch 44
(LT) Seda 89051 29 Cc 34
(F) Sedan 08200 41 Ae 41
(F) Séderon 26560 56 Af 46
(GB) Sedgefield TS21 39 Si 36
(CZ) Sedlčany 264 01 43 Be 41
(RUS) Šedok 64 Ea 46
(RUS) Sedtydin 14 Fe 29
(LT) Šeduva 82007 29 Cd 35
(PL) Sędziszów Małopolski 39-120 45 Cb 40
(D) Seehausen (Altmark) 39615 27 Bb 38
(D) Seelow 15306 43 Be 38
(F) Sées 61500 41 Aa 42
(D) Seesen 38723 43 Ba 39
(A) Seewiesen 8636 58 Bf 43
(TR) Şefaatli 66800 77 De 51
(TR) Seferihisar 35460 83 Cg 52
(N) Segalstad 2656 16 Ba 29
(RO) Segarcea 205400 60 Cd 46
(RUS) Segeža 12 De 27
(N) Seglvik 9182 3 Cb 20
(RUS) Šegmas 14 Ek 26
(F) Segonzac 19310 54 Sk 45
(E) Segorbe 12400 70 Sk 51
(E) Segovia 40001* 69 Sf 50
(F) Segré 49500* 54 Sk 43
(P) Segura 6060-521 68 Sd 51
(TR) Şehit Nusretbey 86 Di 54
(P) Seia 6270-374* 68 Sc 50
(F) Seiches-sur-le-Loir 49140 54 Sk 43
(F) Seilhac 19700 55 Ab 45
(FIN) Seinäjoki 60100* 10 Cc 28
(RO) Seini 435400 60 Cd 43
(LT) Seirijai 67010 29 Cd 36
(RUS) Šeitovka 65 Ei 44
(PL) Sejny 16-500 29 Cd 36
(RUS) Sejtjakovo 34 Ff 35
(RUS) Sëjva 23 Fd 30
(RUS) Sekači 49 Ed 40
(TR) Şekerli 25530 86 Dk 53
(TR) Seki 48860 84 Ck 54
(TR) Sekili 66930 77 De 51
(TR) Sekizli 85 Dd 53
(BIH) Šekovići 59 Bi 46
(RUS) Šekšema 22 Ef 32
(RUS) Šeksna 20 Di 31
(RO) Şelaru 137425 60 Cf 46
(RUS) Šelaša 13 Ec 29
(D) Selb 95100 43 Bc 40
(N) Selbekken 8 Ak 27
(N) Selbu 7580 8 Bb 27
(GB) Selby YO8 39 Si 37
(RUS) Sel'co 31 De 37
(TR) Selçuk 35920 83 Ch 53
(RUS) Sel'cy 20 Df 33
(RUS) Selehovskaja 12 Di 29
(TR) Selendi 45970 84 Ci 52
(AL) Selenicë 74 Bk 50
(GR) Sélero 67100 75 Ce 49
(F) Sélestat 67600* 42 Ah 42
(SRB) Selevac 11407 59 Ca 46
(IS) Selfoss 801 36 Qi 27
(RUS) Sel'gi 11 Dd 27
(RUS) Selib 14 Ei 27
(D) Seligenstadt 63500 42 Ai 40
(TR) Selim 36900 79 Ec 50
(TR) Selimiye 48230 83 Ch 53
(RUS) Selino 47 De 38
(RUS) Selišči 33 Ef 36
(RUS) Seliše 13 Eg 26
(AL) Selishtë 74 Ca 49
(RUS) Selitrennoe 65 Eh 43
(RUS) Selivanovskaja 49 Eb 42
(RUS) Seližarovo 31 Dd 34
(UA) Seljatyn 60 Cf 43
(N) Selje 6740 8 Af 28
(N) Seljelvnes 2 Bk 21
(N) Seljord 3840 16 Ai 31
(GB) Selkirk TD7 39 Sh 35
(N) Selkopp 3 Ce 20
(F) Selles-sur-Cher 41130 55 Ab 43
(GR) Sellía 82 Ce 55
(RUS) Selo 20 Di 29
(F) Selonnet 04460 56 Ag 46
(S) Selsviken 9 Bf 27
(IS) Seltjarnarnes 170* 36 Qh 26
(RUS) Selty 23 Fc 33
(F) Seltz 67470 42 Ai 42
(UA) Selydove 48 Dh 42
(N) Sem 16 Ba 31
(RUS) Šemaniha 22 Ef 33
(TR) Şemdinli 30800 87 Ee 53
(UA) Semenivka 47 Dc 38
(UA) Semenivka 47 Dd 41
(RUS) Semenov 33 Ee 34
(RUS) Semënovka 49 Ee 41
(RUS) Semenovskoe 21 Dk 32
(RUS) Semenovskoe 31 Df 35
(RUS) Šemetovo 31 Di 36
(RUS) Semibalki 63 Dk 44
(RUS) Semibratovo 21 Dk 33
(RUS) Semibugry 65 Ei 44
(RUS) Semičnyj 64 Ec 43
(RUS) Semigorodnjaja 21 Ea 31
(RUS) Semikarakorsk 64 Ea 43
(RUS) Semiluki 48 Di 39
(CZ) Semily 513 01 44 Bf 40
(BIH) Semizovac 59 Bi 47
(RUS) Semlevo 31 Dd 35
(A) Semmering 2680 58 Bf 43
(RUS) Šemordan 34 Fa 34
(RUS) Šemurša 33 Eh 36
(UA) Semyduby 47 Da 42
(UA) Semypolky 47 Da 40
(RUS) Šemyšejka 33 Ef 38
(RUS) Sëmža 5 Ee 24
(D) Sendenhorst 48324 42 Ah 39
(D) Senftenberg 01968 43 Be 39
(E) Sénia, la 43560 70 Aa 50
(SK) Senica 974 01 44 Bh 42
(I) Senigállia 57 Bd 47
(TR) Senirce 84 Da 53
(TR) Senirkent 32600 84 Da 52
(HR) Senj 58 Be 46
(TR) Şenkaya 25360 79 Ec 50
(UA) Sen'kove 48 Dh 41
(TR) Şenköy 47510 87 Eb 53
(RUS) Šenkursk 13 Ec 28
(F) Senlis 62310 41 Ac 41
(GB) Sennen TR19 40 Se 40
(RUS) Sennoj 49 Ed 40
(RUS) Sennoj 50 Eg 38
(BG) Senokos 2752 61 Ci 47
(I) Senorbì 09040 71 Ak 51
(F) Sens 89100* 41 Ad 42
(SRB) Senta 24400* 59 Ca 45
(RUS) Šentala 34 Fb 36
(TR) Şenyurt 60320 79 Eb 50
(TR) Şenyurt 60320 87 Ea 53
(E) Seoane 68 Sc 48
(TR) Sepetçi 76 Da 51
(UA) Šepetivka 46 Ch 40
(UA) Šepit 60 Cf 43
(PL) Sępólno Krajeńskie 89-400 28 Bh 37
(BG) Septemvri 4490 75 Ce 48
(E) Sepúlveda 40300 69 Sg 49
(RUS) Sepyč 23 Fe 32
(RUS) Serafimovič 49 Ec 41
(RUS) Serafimovskij 34 Fd 36
(B) Seraing 4100 42 Af 40
(RO) Şerbăneşti 237450 60 Ce 46
(RO) Sercaia 507195 60 Cf 45
(RUS) Serdobsk 49 Ee 38
(RUS) Serebrjanka 24 Fk 33
(RUS) Serebrjanskij 19 Ck 32
(RUS) Serebrjanye Prudy 31 Di 36
(SK) Sered' 926 01 44 Bh 42
(RUS) Sereda 31 Df 35
(RUS) Seredka 19 Ci 32
(RUS) Serednikovo 32 Dk 35
(RUS) Seredskaja 21 Ec 30
(UA) Seredyna Buda 47 De 38
(TR) Şerefiye 57400 78 Dh 50
(TR) Şereflikoçhisar 06950 85 Dd 52
(RUS) Seregovo 14 Fa 28
(RUS) Šeremet'evka 34 Fb 35
(GR) Séres 75 Cd 49
(RUS) Serga 23 Fg 33
(RUS) Sergač 33 Ef 35
(RUS) Sergeevsk 34 Fb 37
(RUS) Sergeevskij 23 Fe 30
(TR) Sergen 63700 76 Ch 49
(TR) Sergen 63700 86 Dk 53
(RUS) Sergievka 51 Fb 39
(RUS) Sergievo 12 Dg 28
(RUS) Sergiev Posad 31 Di 34
(RUS) Sergievskoe 64 Ec 46
(UA) Serhijivka 48 Dh 42
(UA) Serhijivka 61 Da 44
(TR) Serik 07500 84 Db 54
(TR) Serinhisar 20430* 84 Ck 53
(TR) Serinkum 13200 87 Ec 52
(TR) Serinyol 31120 85 Dg 54
(RUS) Šer'jag 23 Fe 29
(RUS) Serkova 24 Gc 33
(RUS) Sermenevo 35 Fi 37
(P) Sernancelhe 3640-209* 68 Sc 50
(RUS) Sernovodsk 34 Fb 37
(RUS) Sernur 33 Ek 34
(PL) Serock 05-140 45 Cb 38
(RUS) Seroglazka 65 Eh 44
(E) Serón 81 Sh 53
(RUS) Serov 24 Ga 31
(P) Serpa 7830-320* 80 Sc 53
(RUS) Serpejsk 31 De 36
(RUS) Serpuhov 31 Dh 36
(E) Serra de Outes, A (Outes) 68 Sb 48
(E) Serradilla 10530 68 Sd 51
(I) Serra San Bruno 89822 73 Bg 52
(F) Serres 84200 56 Af 46
(P) Sertã 6100-598* 68 Sb 51
(TR) Servi 12510 87 Ea 52
(GR) Sérvia 50500 74 Cc 50
(P) Sesimbra 2970-041* 80 Sa 52
(S) Seskarö 95394 10 Cd 25
(I) Sessa Aurunca 81037 72 Bd 49
(RUS) Šestakovo 22 Fa 32
(RUS) Šestovoe 25 Gi 33
(I) Sestriere 10058 56 Ag 46
(I) Sestri Levante 16039 57 Ak 46
(RUS) Sestroreck 19 Ck 30
(RUS) Šešurga 22 Eh 33
(GR) Séta 34600 82 Cd 52
(LT) Šėta 58005 29 Ce 35
(F) Sète 34200* 55 Ad 47
(N) Setermoen 2 Bi 22
(RUS) Setraki 49 Ea 41
(I) Séttimo Torinese 10036 56 Ah 45
(GB) Settle BD24 39 Sh 36
(P) Setúbal 2900-001* 80 Sb 52
(E) Seu d'Urgell, la 25700 70 Ab 48
(I) Seui 08037 71 Ak 51
(UA) Sevastopol' 62 Dd 46
(UA) Ševčenkivskyj, Korsun'- 47 Db 41
(UA) Ševčenkovo 48 Dh 41
(RUS) Ševelevskaja 21 Ee 30
(GB) Sevenoaks TN13 41 Aa 39
(RUS) Sever 23 Fd 32
(F) Sévérac-le-Château 12150 55 Ad 46
(RUS) Severka 35 Ga 34
(RUS) Severnoe 34 Fc 36
(RUS) Severnoe 64 Ec 46
(RUS) Severnyj 11 Dc 26
(RUS) Severnyj 7 Gd 23
(RUS) Severnyj 65 Ef 43
(RUS) Severnyj Kolčim 23 Fh 30
(UA) Severodonec'k 48 Di 42
(RUS) Severodvinsk 12 Dk 26
(RUS) Severo-Kospašskij 23 Fh 31
(RUS) Severomorsk 4 Dd 21
(RUS) Severoural'sk 24 Ga 30
(RUS) Severo-Zadonsk 31 Di 36
(FIN) Sevettijärvi 99930 3 Ci 21
(GR) Sevgáraki 82 Cb 52
(E) Sevilla 41001* 80 Se 53
(TR) Sevindikli 41795 76 Ck 50
(TR) Şevketiye 76 Ch 50
(BG) Sevlievo 5400 60 Cf 47
(SLO) Sevnica 8290 58 Bf 44
(RUS) Sevrjukovo 31 Dg 36
(RUS) Sevsk 47 De 38
(BG) Sevštari 7400 60 Cg 47
(TR) Seydim 19110 77 De 50
(TR) Seydişehir 42360* 84 Db 53
(IS) Seyðisfjörður 36 Rf 25
(TR) Seyfeköy 77 De 51
(TR) Şeyhali 77 Dc 51
(TR) Şeyhli 78 Dg 50
(TR) Şeyhmehmet 47510 87 Eb 53
(TR) Seyitgazi 26950 76 Da 51
(TR) Seyitoba 83 Ch 52
(F) Seyne-sur-Mer, la 83500* 56 Af 47
(F) Seyssel 74910 56 Af 45
(SLO) Sežana 6210 57 Bd 45
(F) Sézanne 51120* 41 Ad 42
(I) Sezze 04018 72 Bd 49
(GR) Sfakia 82 Ce 55
(RO) Sfântu Gheorghe 000520* 60 Cf 45
(RO) Sfântu Gheorghe 000520* 61 Ck 46
(GR) Sfinári 73014 82 Cd 55
(NL) 's-Gravenhage = Den Haag 2491* 41 Ae 38
(GB) Shader HS2 38 Sd 32
(GB) Shaftesbury SP7 40 Sh 39
(IRL) Shannon = Sionainn 37 Sb 38
(GB) Sheerness ME12 41 Aa 39
(GB) Sheffield S5 39 Si 37
(GB) Shegra IV27 38 Se 32
(AL) Shëngjin 74 Bk 49
(AL) Shënmëri = Buçimas 74 Ca 49
(GB) Sherborne DT9 40 Sh 40
(GB) Sheringham NR26 39 Ab 38
(NL) 's-Hertogenbosch 5200* 42 Af 39
(AL) Shijak 74 Bk 49
(AL) Shkodër 74 Bk 48
(GB) Shrewsbury SY5 39 Sh 38
(RKS) Shtime = Štimlje 72000 74 Cb 48
(PL) Sianów 76-004 28 Bg 36
(LT) Šiaulėnai 82043 29 Cd 35
(LT) Šiauliai 76001* 29 Cd 35
(RUS) Sibaj 52 Fi 38
(I) Síbari 87070 73 Bg 51
(HR) Šibenik 58 Bf 47
(RO) Sibiu 000550* 60 Ce 45
(RUS) Šičuga 22 Eg 29
(SRB) Šid 22239* 59 Bk 45
(BY) Sidaravičy 30 Da 37
(TR) Side 07330 84 Db 54
(RUS) Sidel'kino 34 Fb 36
(CH) Siders = Sierre 3960 56 Ah 44
(GR) Sidira 82 Cb 52
(GR) Sidirókastro 62300 75 Cd 49
(UA) Sidlyšče 46 Cf 39
(GB) Sidmouth EX10 40 Sg 40
(RUS) Sidorovo 20 Di 33
(RUS) Sidorovo 22 Fa 30
(RUS) Šidrovo 13 Ec 28
(PL) Siedlce 08-100* 45 Cc 38
(D) Siegburg 53721 42 Ah 40
(D) Siegen 57072* 42 Ai 40
(PL) Siemiatycze 17-300 45 Cc 38
(I) Siena 53100 57 Bb 47
(FIN) Sieppijärvi 95800 3 Cd 23
(PL) Sieradz 98-200 44 Bi 39
(PL) Sieraków 42-790 44 Bg 38
(PL) Sierpc 09-200 28 Bk 38
(CH) Sierre 3960 56 Ah 44
(FIN) Sievi 85410 10 Ce 27
(RUS) Sig 12 De 25
(N) Sigdal 16 Ak 30
(F) Sigean 11130 70 Ac 47
(N) Sigerfjord 8400 2 Bf 22
(RO) Sighetu Marmaţiei 435500 60 Cd 43
(RO) Sighişoara 545400 60 Ce 44
(IS) Siglufjörður 36 Rb 24
(D) Sigmaringen 72488 42 Ak 42
(RUS) Šigony 33 Ei 37
(GR) Sígri 81103 75 Cf 51
(S) Sigtuna 19300 17 Bh 31
(LV) Sigulda 2150 18 Ce 33
(RUS) Šihany 50 Eh 38
(RUS) Šihtovo 30 Dc 35
(FIN) Siikainen 29811 10 Cb 29
(FIN) Siilinjärvi 71801 11 Ch 27
(TR) Siirt 56000* 87 Eb 53
(FIN) Siivikko 93350 11 Ch 25
(S) Sikfors 10 Cb 25
(GR) Sikía 75 Cd 50
(GR) Síkinos 84010 83 Cf 54
(H) Siklós 7800 59 Bi 45
(LT) Šilalė 75001 29 Cc 35
(I) Silandro = Schlanders 57 Ba 44
(RUS) Šil'da 52 Fk 39
(TR) Şile 34981* 76 Ck 49
(RUS) Šilega 13 Ee 26
(RUS) Šilekša 21 Ec 33
(TR) Silifke 33940* 85 Dd 54
(RUS) Silikatnyj 33 Ei 37
(I) Silíqua 09010 71 Ai 51
(RO) Siliştea 907290 60 Cf 46
(RO) Silistraru 817177 61 Ch 45
(TR) Silivri 34570* 76 Ci 49
(N) Siljan 3748 16 Ak 31
(DK) Silkeborg 26 Ak 34
(E) Silla 46460 70 Sk 51
(EST) Sillamäe 40231* 19 Ch 31
(TR) Sille 42240 84 Dc 53
(E) Silleda 36540 68 Sb 48
(F) Sillé-le-Guillaume 72140 40 Sk 42
(GR) Silli 75 Ce 49
(A) Sillian 9920 57 Bc 44
(TR) Silopi 73400 87 Ec 53
(RUS) Šilovo 31 Di 37
(RUS) Šilovo 32 Ea 36
(N) Silsand 9303 2 Bh 21
(LT) Šilutė 99001 28 Cb 35
(E) Silván 68 Sd 48
(TR) Silvan 21640* 87 Eb 52
(P) Silves 8300-100* 80 Sb 53
(RUS) Sim 23 Fh 31
(RUS) Sim 35 Fh 35
(RUS) Sima 32 Dk 34
(UA) Simakivka 46 Ci 40
(E) Simancas 47130 69 Sf 49
(RO) Şimand 317335 59 Cb 44
(TR) Simav 43500 76 Ci 51
(RUS) Simbirsk 33 Ei 36
(UA) Simejkyne 48 Dk 42
(RO) Simeria 335900 60 Cd 45
(UA) Simferopol' 62 De 46
(GR) Simi 83 Ch 54
(GR) Sími 85600 83 Ch 54
(BG) Simitli 2730 75 Cd 49
(LT) Simkaičiai 29 Cc 35
(RO) Şimleu Silvaniei 455300 59 Cc 43
(LT) Simnas 64037 29 Cd 36
(FIN) Simo 95201 10 Cf 25
(H) Simontornya 7081 59 Bi 44
(FIN) Simpele = Rautjärvi 56610 19 Ck 29
(S) Simrishamn 27200 27 Be 35
(RUS) Šimsk 19 Da 32
(EST) Simuna 46401 18 Cg 31
(I) Sinalunga 53048 57 Bb 47
(TR) Sinan 87 Ea 53
(TR) Sınanpaşa 03850 84 Da 52
(TR) Sincan 58365 77 Dc 51
(TR) Sincan 58365 78 Dh 51
(TR) Sincik 86 Di 52
(DK) Sindal 9870 16 Ba 33
(D) Sindelfingen 71063* 42 Ai 42
(EST) Sindi 86703* 18 Ce 32
(I) Sindía 08018 71 Ai 50
(TR) Sındırgı 10330 76 Ci 51
(RUS) Sindor 14 Fb 28


4 Savino

A B C D E F G H I J K L M N O P Q R S T U V W X Y Z

(RUS) Verhneural'sk 35 Fk 37
(RUS) Verhnie Kigi 35 Fi 35
(RUS) Verhnie Sergi 35 Fk 34
(RUS) Verhnie Tatyšly 34 Ff 34
(RUS) Verhnie Važiny 20 Dd 29
(RUS) Verhnij Avzjan 35 Fh 37
(RUS) Verhnij Baskunčak 50 Eg 42
(RUS) Verhnij Čegem 79 Ed 47
(RUS) Verhnij Fiagdon 79 Ee 48
(RUS) Verhnij Lomov 32 Ed 37
(RUS) Verhnij Mamon 49 Ea 40
(RUS) Verhnij Tagil 24 Fk 33
(RUS) Verhnij Ufalej 35 Ga 34
(RUS) Verhnij Uslon 33 Ek 35
(RUS) Verhnij Vjalozerskij 4 Df 24
(RUS) Verhnjaja Baksan 64 Ec 47
(RUS) Verhnjaja Balkarija 79 Ed 48
(RUS) Verhnjaja Buzinovka 49 Ed 41
(RUS) Verhnjaja Čegem 79 Ed 47
(RUS) Verhnjaja In"va 23 Fe 32
(RUS) Verhnjaja Jus'va 23 Fe 32
(RUS) Verhnjaja Mara 64 Ec 47
(RUS) Verhnjaja Maza 33 Eh 37
(RUS) Verhnjaja Orljanka 34 Fb 37
(RUS) Verhnjaja Osljanka 24 Fi 33
(RUS) Verhnjaja Palen'ga 13 Ec 26
(RUS) Verhnjaja Peša 6 Eh 24
(RUS) Verhnjaja Pyšma 35 Ga 34
(RUS) Verhnjaja Salda 24 Ga 32
(RUS) Verhnjaja Sanarka 35 Ga 36
(RUS) Verhnjaja Sinjačiha 24 Gb 32
(RUS) Verhnjaja Storona 21 Ea 31
(RUS) Verhnjaja Tojma 13 Ef 28
(RUS) Verhnjaja Tura 24 Fk 32
(RUS) Verhnjaja Vollmanga 22 Eh 31
(RUS) Verhnjaja Zolotica 12 Ea 25
(RUS) Verhokam'e 23 Fd 32
(RUS) Verholuz'e 22 Ei 31
(RUS) Verhoramen'e 22 Ei 31
(RUS) Verhošižem'e 22 Ek 32
(RUS) Verhosun'e 22 Fb 32
(RUS) Verhotur'e 24 Ga 32
(RUS) Verhovaž'e 21 Ec 30
(RUS) Verhov'e 31 Dh 38
(RUS) Verhovino 21 Ee 31
(RUS) Verhovino-D'jakovo 21 Ed 31
(RUS) Verhovskij 12 Ea 27
(RUS) Verhozim 33 Eg 38
(GR) Véria 59100 74 Cc 50
(RUS) Verigino 32 Ea 35
(E) Verín 32600 68 Sc 49
(RUS) Verkola 13 Ef 27
(F) Vermenton 89270 55 Ad 43
(RUS) Vernadovka 32 Ec 37
(F) Vernantes 49390 54 Aa 43
(SK) Vernár 059 17 45 Ca 42
(RO) Verneşti 127675 60 Cg 45
(F) Verneuil-sur-Avre 27130 41 Aa 42
(F) Vernon 27200* 41 Ab 41
(I) Verona 37100* 57 Ba 45
(I) Verrés 56 Ah 45
(F) Versailles 78000* 41 Ac 42
(RUS) Veršiny, Čelno- 34 Fb 36
(D) Versmold 33775 42 Ai 38
(RUS) Vertelim 33 Ee 36
(UA) Vertijievka 47 Db 39
(RUS) Vertjačij 49 Ed 42
(AL) Vërtop 74 Ca 50
(F) Vertou 44120 54 Si 43
(B) Verviers 4800 42 Af 40
(F) Vervins 02140 41 Ad 41
(FIN) Vesanto 72301 10 Cg 28
(RUS) Veščevo 19 Ck 30
(RUS) Ves'egonsk 20 Dh 32
(RUS) Veselaja 32 Ec 37
(RUS) Veselaja 48 Di 40
(UA) Vesele 62 De 43
(CZ) Veselí nad Lužnicí 391 81* 43 Be 41
(SK) Veselí nad Moravou 44 Bh 42
(RUS) Veselovka 35 Fk 35
(RUS) Vesëlyj 64 Ea 43
(UA) Veselynove 62 Db 43
(RUS) Vešenskaja 49 Eb 41
(RUS) Veškajma 33 Eh 36
(RUS) Veškoma 13 Ed 26
(RUS) Vesljana 14 Fa 27
(FIN) Vesmajärvi 99280 3 Cf 23
(F) Vesoul 70000* 56 Ag 43
(GR) Véssa 82102 83 Cg 52
(N) Vestbygd 4550 16 Ag 32
(N) Vesterli 2 Bf 23
(DK) Vesterø Havn 9940 16 Ba 33
(FR) Vestmanhavn = Vestmanna 350 38 Sc 28
(FR) Vestmanna 350 38 Sc 28
(IS) Vestmannaeyjar 900* 36 Qk 27
(N) Vestnes 6390 8 Ah 28
(I) Vestone 25078 57 Ba 45
(N) Vestre Gausdal 16 Ba 29
(N) Vestre Jakobselv 9802 3 Ck 20
(H) Veszprém 8200 58 Bh 43
(H) Veszprémvarsány 8438 58 Bh 43
(H) Vésztő 59 Cb 44
(FIN) Veteli 69701 10 Cd 27
(RUS) Vet'ju 14 Fa 28
(BY) Vetka 47 Db 38
(S) Vetlanda 57400* 17 Bf 33
(RUS) Vetluga 22 Ef 33
(RUS) Vetlužskij 22 Ef 33
(BG) Vetovo 7080 60 Cg 47
(I) Vetralla 01019 72 Bc 48
(BG) Vetrino 9220 61 Ch 47
(BY) Vetryna 30 Ci 35
(FIN) Vetsikko 99981 3 Ch 21
(B) Veurne = Furnes 8630 41 Ac 39
(CH) Vevey 1800* 56 Ag 44
(GR) Vévi 53074 74 Cb 50
(F) Veynes 05400 56 Af 46
(RUS) Veža 21 Ed 29
(RUS) Vezdino 14 Ek 28
(F) Vézelay 89450 55 Ad 43
(TR) Vezirköprü 55900 77 Df 49
(S) Vi 86501 9 Bh 28
(P) Viana do Alentejo 7090-220* 80 Sb 52
(E) Viana do Bolo 32550 68 Sc 48
(P) Viana do Castelo 4900-001* 68 Sb 49
(I) Viaréggio 55049 57 Ba 47
(F) Vias 34450 55 Ad 47
(DK) Viborg 8800 26 Ak 34
(I) Vibo Valéntia 89900 73 Bg 52
(F) Vibraye 72320 41 Aa 42
(E) Vic 08500 70 Ac 49
(F) Vicdessos 09220 70 Ab 48
(BY) Vicebck 30 Da 35
(F) Vic-en-Bigorre 65500* 54 Aa 47
(I) Vicenza 36100 57 Bb 45
(F) Vic-Fezensac 32190 54 Aa 47
(F) Vichy 03200* 55 Ad 44
(F) Vico 20160 71 Ai 48
(RO) Vicovu de Sus 727610 60 Cf 43
(F) Vic-sur-Cère 15800 55 Ac 46
(M) Victoria 72 Be 54
(RO) Victoria 505700 60 Ce 45
(RUS) Vičuga 21 Eb 33
(BY) Vidamlja 45 Cd 38
(FR) Viðareiði 750 38 Sd 28
(DK) Videbæk 6920 26 Ai 34
(RO) Videle 145300 60 Cf 46
(FR) Vidhareidhi = Viðareiði 750 38 Sd 28
(P) Vidigueira 7960-421 80 Sc 52
(BG) Vidin 3700* 59 Cc 47
(RUS) Vidlica 19 Dc 29
(RO) Vidra 627415 60 Cg 45
(RO) Vidra 627415 60 Cg 46
(S) Vidsel 94295 10 Ca 25
(LT) Viduklė 60037 29 Cc 35
(BY) Vidzy 29 Cg 35
(D) Viechtach 94234 43 Bc 41
(P) Vieira de Leiria 2430-592* 68 Sb 51
(LT) Viekšniai 89094 29 Cc 34
(E) Vielha e Mijaran 25530 70 Aa 48
(E) Viella-Mitg Arán = Vielha e Mijaran 25530 70 Aa 48
(D) Vienenburg 38690 43 Ba 39
(F) Vienne 38200 55 Ae 45
(FIN) Vieremä 74200 11 Ch 27
(FIN) Vierumäki 19120 18 Cf 29
(F) Vierzon 18100* 55 Ac 43
(LV) Viesīte 29 Cf 34
(I) Vieste 71019 73 Bg 49
(S) Vietas 2 Bi 23
(LT) Vievis 21058 29 Ce 36
(F) Vif 38450 56 Af 45
(DK) Vig 4560 27 Bb 35
(F) Vigan, le 30120 55 Ad 47
(N) Vigeland 16 Ah 32
(I) Vigévano 27029 56 Ai 45
(F) Vignacourt 80650 41 Ac 40
(I) Vignola 41058 57 Ba 46
(E) Vigo 36201 68 Sb 48
(N) Vigrestad 4362 16 Af 32
(FIN) Vihanti 86401 10 Ce 26
(F) Vihiers 49310 54 Sk 43
(FIN) Vihtari 79940 11 Ci 28
(FIN) Vihti 03401 18 Ce 30
(FIN) Viiala 37831 18 Cd 29
(FIN) Viisanmäki 41661 10 Cg 28
(FIN) Viitasaari 44501 10 Cf 27
(EST) Viitna 45202 18 Cg 31
(EST) Viivikonna 30321* 19 Ch 31
(UA) Vijtivci 46 Cg 41
(IS) Vík 36 Rb 27
(N) Vik 6894 16 Ag 29
(N) Vik 6894 9 Bc 25
(FIN) Vikajärvi 97510 3 Cg 24
(N) Vikanes 5994 16 Af 30
(S) Vikastir 17 Be 30
(N) Vike 6470 16 Af 30
(S) Viksjö 87194 9 Bh 28
(N) Viksøyri 6894 16 Ag 29
(P) Vila de Rei 6100-598 68 Sb 51
(P) Vila do Bispo 8650-405* 80 Sb 53
(P) Vila do Conde 4480-001* 68 Sb 49
(P) Vila Flor 5360-301* 68 Sc 49
(E) Vilafranca del Penedès 08720 70 Ab 49
(P) Vila Franca de Xira 2600-002* 80 Sb 52
(E) Vilagarcía de Arousa 36600 68 Sb 48
(E) Vila Joiosa, la 03570 70 Sk 52
(LV) Viļaka 4583 19 Ch 33
(E) Vilalba 27800 68 Sc 47
(LV) Viļāni 4650 29 Cg 34
(P) Vila Nova de Cerveira 4920-201* 68 Sb 49
(P) Vila Nova de Famalicão 4760-019* 68 Sb 49
(P) Vila Nova de Foz Côa 68 Sc 49
(P) Vila Nova de Gaia 4400-001* 68 Sb 49
(P) Vila Nova de Milfontes 7645-211* 80 Sb 53
(P) Vila Nova de Ourém 2435-019 68 Sb 51
(P) Vila Nova de Paiva 3650-194* 68 Sc 50
(E) Vilanova i la Geltrú 08800 70 Ab 49
(P) Vila Pouca de Aguiar 5450-001* 68 Sc 49
(E) Vila-real 12540 70 Sk 51
(P) Vila Real 5000-047* 68 Sc 49
(P) Vila Real de Santo António 8900-201* 80 Sc 53
(P) Vilar Formoso 6355-201* 68 Sd 50
(P) Vila Velha de Ródão 6030-001* 68 Sc 51
(P) Vila Verde de Ficalho 7830-480* 80 Sc 53
(P) Vila Viçosa 7160-050 80 Sc 52
(E) Vilches 23220 81 Sg 52
(BY) Vilejka 29 Cg 36
(RUS) Vil'gort 23 Fg 30
(S) Vilhelmina 91201 9 Bg 26
(EST) Viljandi 71003* 18 Cf 32
(LT) Vilkaviškis 70001 29 Cd 36
(LT) Vilkija 54015 29 Cd 35
(E) Villablino 24100 68 Sd 48
(E) Villabona 20150 69 Sh 47
(E) Villacañas 45860 69 Sg 51
(E) Villacarriedo 39640 54 Sg 47
(E) Villacarrillo 23300 81 Sg 52
(E) Villacastín 40150 69 Sf 50
(A) Villach 9500* 57 Bd 44
(I) Villacidro 09039 71 Ai 51
(E) Villada 34340 69 Sf 48
(E) Villa del Río 14640 81 Sf 53
(E) Villadiego 09120 69 Sf 48
(E) Villafranca del Bierzo 24500 68 Sd 48
(E) Villafranca del Cid 70 Sk 50
(E) Villafranca de los Barros 06220 80 Sd 52
(E) Villafranca de los Caballeros 45730 69 Sg 51
(E) Villafranca del Panadés = Vilafranca del Penedès 08720 70 Ab 49
(I) Villafranca di Verona 37069 57 Ba 45
(E) Villafruela 09344 69 Sg 49
(E) Villaharta 14210 81 Sf 52
(E) Villahermosa 13332 81 Sh 52
(E) Villahoz 09343 69 Sg 48
(F) Villaines-la-Juhel 53700 40 Sk 42
(E) Villajoyosa = Vila Joiosa, la 81 Sk 52
(E) Villalón de Campos 47600 68 Se 48
(E) Villalpando 49630 68 Se 49
(E) Villamanrique 13343 81 Sg 52
(E) Villamartín 11650 80 Se 54
(E) Villamayor 05380 68 Se 49
(E) Villamayor de Santiago 16415 69 Sh 51
(F) Villandraut 33730 54 Sk 46
(I) Villanova Monteleone 07019 71 Ai 50
(E) Villanubla 47620 69 Sf 49
(E) Villanueva de Córdoba 14440 81 Sf 52
(E) Villanueva de Gállego 50830 70 Sk 49
(E) Villanueva de la Fuente 13330 81 Sh 52
(E) Villanueva de la Serena 06700 68 Se 52
(E) Villanueva de la Sierra 49580 68 Sd 50
(E) Villanueva del Campo 49100 68 Se 49
(E) Villanueva del Fresno 06110 80 Sc 52
(E) Villanueva de los Castillejos 21540 80 Sc 53
(E) Villanueva de los Infantes 47174 81 Sg 52
(E) Villanueva del Rey 14230 80 Se 52
(E) Villanueva del Río y Mina 41350 80 Se 53
(E) Villanueva y Geltrú = Vilanova i la Geltrú 08800 70 Ab 49
(H) Villány 7773 59 Bi 45
(E) Villarcayo 09550 69 Sg 48
(F) Villar-d'Arène 05480 56 Ag 45
(F) Villard-Bonnet 38190 56 Af 45
(F) Villard-de-Lans 38250 56 Af 45
(E) Villardeciervos 49562 68 Sd 49
(E) Villar del Arzobispo 46170 70 Sk 51
(E) Villar del Rey 06192 68 Sd 51
(E) Villarejo de Fuentes 16432 69 Sh 51
(E) Villarejo de Salvanés 28590 69 Sg 50
(E) Villarente 68 Se 48
(E) Villarreal de los Infantes = Vila-real 12540 70 Sk 51
(E) Villarrín de Campos 49137 68 Se 49
(E) Villarrubia de los Ojos 13670 69 Sg 51
(F) Villars 28150 41 Ab 42
(E) Villarta de los Montes 06678 69 Sf 51
(E) Villasana de Mena 09580 69 Sg 47
(I) Villa Santina 33029 57 Bc 44
(I) Villasimíus 09049 71 Ak 51
(E) Villaviciosa 33300 68 Se 47
(E) Villaviciosa de Córdoba 14300 80 Se 52
(F) Villé 67220 42 Ah 42
(F) Villedieu-les-Poêles 50800 40 Si 42
(F) Villefranche-de-Lauragais 31290 55 Ab 47
(F) Villefranche-de-Rouergue 12200* 55 Ac 46
(F) Villefranche-sur-Saône 69400* 55 Ae 45
(E) Villena 03400 81 Sk 52
(F) Villenauxe-la-Grande 10370 41 Ad 42
(F) Villeneuve 33121 55 Ac 46
(F) Villeneuve-de-Marsan 40190 54 Sk 47
(F) Villeneuve-l'Archevêque 89190 41 Ad 42
(F) Villeneuve-lès-Avignon 30400* 55 Ae 47
(F) Villeneuve-sur-Lot 47300* 54 Aa 46
(F) Villeneuve-sur-Yonne 89500 41 Ad 42
(F) Villers-Cotterêts 02600* 41 Ad 41
(F) Villerupt 54190 42 Af 41
(F) Villeurbanne 69100* 55 Ae 45
(D) Villingen-Schwenningen 78048* 42 Ai 42
(N) Vilnes 6985 16 Ae 29
(LT) Vilnius 01001* 29 Cf 36
(UA) Vil'njans'k 62 Df 43
(UA) Vil'nohirs'k 47 De 42
(FIN) Vilppula 35701 10 Ce 28
(UA) Vil'šana 47 Dd 40
(UA) Vil'šanka 47 Da 42
(UA) Vil'šany 48 Df 40
(D) Vilsbiburg 84137 43 Bc 42
(D) Vilshofen 94474 43 Bd 42
(MNE) Vilusi 81 423 73 Bi 48
(RUS) Vil'va 24 Fi 32
(B) Vilvoorde 1800* 41 Ae 40
(E) Vimianzo 15129 68 Sa 47
(P) Vimieiro 7040-010 80 Sc 52
(P) Vimioso 5230-300* 68 Sd 49
(S) Vimmerby 59801 17 Bf 33
(F) Vimoutiers 61120 41 Aa 42
(FIN) Vimpeli 62800 10 Cd 27
(CZ) Vimperk 385 01 43 Bd 41
(E) Vinaròs 12500 70 Aa 50
(E) Viñas, Las 18879 81 Sg 53
(RO) Vinători 707575 59 Cc 46
(I) Vinci 50059 57 Ba 47
(S) Vindeln 92201 10 Bk 26
(DK) Vinderup 7830 26 Ai 34
(RUS) Vindrej 32 Ec 36
(RO) Vinga 317400 59 Cb 44
(S) Vingåker 64301 17 Bf 31
(P) Vinhais 68 Sc 49
(MK) Vinica 2310 74 Cc 49
(N) Vinje 3890 16 Ag 30
(UA) Vin'kivci 46 Ch 41
(HR) Vinkovci 59 Bk 45
(UA) Vinnica = Vinnycja 46 Ci 41
(RUS) Vinnicy 20 De 30
(UA) Vinnycja 46 Ci 41
(RUS) Vinogradnoe 64 Ee 47
(F) Vinon-sur-Verdon 83560 56 Af 47
(S) Vinslöv 28820 27 Bd 34
(N) Vinstra 2640 16 Ak 29
(S) Vintjärn 17 Bg 30
(E) Vinuesa 42150 69 Sh 49
(RUS) Viny 19 Dc 32
(I) Vipiteno = Sterzing 39049 57 Bb 44
(HR) Vira 58 Bg 47
(RUS) Virandozero 12 Dg 26
(TR) Viranşehir 79 Ea 51
(TR) Viranşehir 85 De 54
(TR) Viranşehir 86 Dk 53
(F) Vire 14500 40 Sk 42
(LV) Vireši 4355 18 Cg 33
(RUS) Virga 33 Ee 37
(IRL) Virginia = Achadhan Iúir 37 Sc 37
(RUS) Virma 12 Df 26
(FIN) Virmutjoki 56210 19 Ci 29
(FIN) Virojoki = Virolahti 49900* 19 Ch 30
(FIN) Virolahti 49901 19 Ch 30
(HR) Virovitica 58 Bh 45
(MNE) Virpazar 81 305 74 Bk 48
(FIN) Virrat 34801 10 Cd 28
(S) Virserum 57080 17 Bf 33
(FIN) Virtaniemi 99860 3 Ci 22
(B) Virton 6760 42 Af 41
(EST) Virtsu 90101 18 Cd 32
(FIN) Virttaa 32560 18 Cc 30
(HR) Vis 73 Bg 47
(RUS) Vis 14 Fe 27
(LT) Visaginas 31001 29 Cg 35
(S) Visby 62100* 17 Bi 33
(B) Visé 4600 42 Af 40
(BIH) Višegrad 59 Bk 47
(P) Viseu 3500-001* 68 Sc 50
(RO) Vişeu de Sus 435700 60 Ce 43
(RUS) Visim 24 Fk 33
(RO) Vişina 137515 60 Ce 47
(RO) Vişina 137515 60 Cf 46
(RUS) Visju,ij Bor 19 Dc 33
(S) Viskafors 51520 17 Bc 33
(RUS) Viškil' 22 Ei 32
(S) Vislanda 34030 27 Be 34
(BY) Višneva 29 Cg 36
(RUS) Višnevaja 31 Dh 36
(RUS) Višnevka 50 Eg 41
(RUS) Višnevka 63 Dk 47
(RUS) Višnevoe 49 Ed 38
(RUS) Višnevogorsk 35 Ga 34
(E) Viso, El 14470 81 Sf 52
(E) Viso del Marqués 13770 81 Sg 52
(BIH) Visoko 59 Bi 47
(CH) Visp 3930 56 Ah 44
(S) Vissefjärda 36060 27 Bf 34
(D) Visselhövede 27374 26 Ak 38
(I) Visso 62039 72 Bd 48
(E) Vistabella del Maestrat 70 Sk 50
(S) Vistheden 10 Ca 25
(LT) Vištytis 70037 29 Cc 36
(SRB) Vitanovac 59 Ca 47
(BY) Vitebsk = Vicebck 30 Da 35
(I) Viterbo 01100 72 Bc 48
(BIH) Vitez 58 Bh 46
(AL) Vithkuq 74 Ca 50
(E) Vitigudino 37210 68 Sd 49
(BIH) Vitina 58 Bh 47
(GR) Vitína 22010 82 Cc 53
(SRB) Vitina 61000 74 Cb 48
(MK) Vitolište 7508 74 Cb 49
(E) Vitoria = Gasteiz 69 Sh 48
(F) Vitré 79370 40 Si 42
(F) Vitry-le-François 51300 41 Ae 42
(F) Vitry-sur-Seine 94400 41 Ac 42
(S) Vittangi 98010 3 Cb 23
(F) Vitteaux 21350 55 Ae 43
(F) Vittel 88800* 42 Af 42
(I) Vittória 97019 72 Be 54
(I) Vittorio Vèneto 31029 57 Bc 44
(F) Vivario 20219 71 Ak 48
(E) Viveiro 27850 68 Sc 47
(E) Vivel del Río Martín 70 Sk 50
(F) Viviers 07220 55 Ae 46
(F) Vivonne 86370 54 Aa 44
(RUS) Vižaj 24 Ga 29
(RUS) Vižas 5 Ef 24
(TR) Vize 39400 76 Ch 49
(F) Vizille 38220 56 Af 45
(RUS) Vizim'jary 33 Eg 34
(HR) Vižinada 57 Bd 45
(RUS) Vizinga 22 Fa 29
(RO) Viziru 817215 61 Ch 45
(CZ) Vizovice 763 12 44 Bh 41
(I) Vizzini 95049 72 Be 53
(BY) Vjalikaja Berestavica 29 Ce 37
(BY) Vjalikie Čunaviči 46 Cg 38
(RUS) Vjartsilja 11 Da 28
(RUS) Vjatskie Poljany 34 Fb 34
(RUS) Vjatskoe 21 Ea 33
(RUS) Vjaz'ma 31 De 35
(RUS) Vjazniki 32 Ec 34
(RUS) Vjazovka 33 Ei 38
(RUS) Vjazovka 50 Ef 42
(RUS) Vjazovka 50 Eg 38
(RUS) Vjazovo 32 Dk 37
(RUS) Vjazovoe 48 Dg 39
(RUS) Vjazovoe 51 Fd 39
(NL) Vlaardingen 3130* 41 Ae 39
(AL) Vlad 74 Ca 48
(BG) Vladaja 1641 75 Cd 48
(SRB) Vladičin Han 17510 74 Cc 48
(RUS) Vladikavkaz 79 Ee 48
(RUS) Vladimir 32 Ea 34
(MNE) Vladimir 85 366 74 Bk 48
(BG) Vladimirovo 9379 60 Cd 47
(RUS) Vladimirskoe 31 Dd 35
(RO) Vlad Tepeş 917295 61 Ch 46
(RUS) Vladyčnoe 21 Dk 32
(UA) Vladyslavivka 62 Df 45
(RO) Vlaşca, Drăgăneşti- 147135 60 Cf 46
(SRB) Vlase 17507 74 Cb 48
(BIH) Vlasenica 59 Bi 46
(CZ) Vlašim 258 01 43 Be 41
(RO) Vlaşin 087203 60 Cf 46
(SRB) Vlasotince 16210 74 Cc 48
(NL) Vlissingen 4380* 41 Ad 39
(SK) Vlkolínec 034 03 44 Bk 41
(AL) Vlorë 74 Bk 50
(RUS) Vnukovo 31 Dh 35
(RUS) Voč' 23 Fe 29
(HR) Voćin 58 Bh 45
(A) Vöcklabruck 4840* 43 Bd 43
(HR) Vodice 58 Bf 47
(RUS) Vodla 12 Dh 28
(CZ) Vodňany 389 01 43 Be 41
(HR) Vodnjan 57 Bd 46
(RUS) Vodnyj 14 Fd 27
(GB) Voe ZE2 38 Si 30
(DK) Voerså 9300 16 Ba 33
(IS) Vogar 190 36 Qh 26
(GR) Vogatsikó 52053 74 Cb 50
(I) Voghera 27058 56 Ai 46
(RUS) Vogulka 23 Fg 31
(RUS) Vogulka 24 Fi 33
(RUS) Vogvazdino 14 Fa 28
(D) Vohenstrauß 92648 43 Bc 41
(EST) Võhma 18 Cc 32
(EST) Võhma 70601 18 Cf 32
(RUS) Vohma 22 Eg 32
(RUS) Vohtoga 21 Eb 32
(RUS) Vohtozero 11 Dd 28
(RO) Voineşti 737300 60 Cf 45
(F) Voiron 38500 56 Af 45
(RUS) Voja, Ust'- 15 Fh 26



Voja, Ust'- 181

## W

## X

## Y

Every edition is always revised to take into account the latest data. Nevertheless, despite every effort, errors can still occur. Should you become aware of such an error, we would be very pleased to receive the respective information from you. You can contact us at any time at our postal address: MAIRDUMONT, D-73751 Ostfildern or by e-mail: **korrekturhinweise@mairdumont.com**

Jede Auflage wird stets nach neuesten Unterlagen überarbeitet. Irrtümer können trotzdem nie ganz ausgeschlossen werden. Ihre Informationen nehmen wir jederzeit gern entgegen. Sie erreichen uns über unsere Postanschrift: MAIRDUMONT, D-73751 Ostfildern oder unter der E-Mail-Adresse: **korrekturhinweise@mairdumont.com**

Chaque édition est remaniée suivant les supports les plus récents. Des erreurs ne peuvent malheureusement jamais être exclues. Aussi vos informations sont les bienvenues. Vous pouvez nous écrire à notre adresse postale: MAIRDUMONT, D-73751 Ostfildern ou bien envoyez-nous un courrier électronique à l'adresse suivante: **korrekturhinweise@mairdumont.com**

**Design:** fpm – factor product münchen (Cover) / Stilradar, Stuttgart

→ 2017     © 2012 MAIRDUMONT, D-73751 Ostfildern (6.) Printed in Germany                                01-30-130400